W9-ARZ-227

PSYCHOLOGY OF WORK BEHAVIOR

Psychology of Work Behavior

Frank J. Landy

Professor of Psychology
The Pennsylvania State University

Don A. Trumbo

Late Professor of Psychology
The Pennsylvania State University

 1980 Revised Edition

The Dorsey Press Homewood, Illinois 60430

© THE DORSEY PRESS, 1976 and 1980

All rights reserved. No part of this publication may be
reproduced, stored in a retrieval system, or transmitted,
in any form or by an means, electronic, mechanical,
photocopying, recording, or otherwise, without the prior
written permission of the publisher.

ISBN 0-256-02324-7
Library of Congress Catalog Card No. 79–54416
Printed in the United States of America

4 5 6 7 8 9 0 K 7 6 5 4 3 2

Preface

The history of industrial and organizational psychology is best characterized as the *application* of psychological principles and methods to problems in the work context. It represents one of the most direct attempts to put the principles of behavior to use.

Problems in the work context can be approached from several points of view. We have chosen to identify the individual worker as the unit of analysis. This means that we will always be trying to evaluate the effects of organizational action on the individual. While there is merit in studying these effects on work groups and, perhaps even on the organization itself, we will leave these considerations to the industrial sociologist and the social psychologist.

In the last decade, there has been a rapid expansion in theory and research in almost every phase of industrial/organizational psychology. Human motivation theories have grown up. Personnel selection and criterion development has become much more complex due to both increases in knowledge and increases in pressures from governmental and industrial sources. Advances in areas related to information processing have brought accompanying challenges in the design of the systems in which a worker is likely to be found. In short, a text written even five years ago may have little relationship to today's problems or solutions. We hope that our text will enable the reader to deal with these increasing complexities.

Texts differ in many important respects. One such difference which students often recognize is a "hard-nose"–"soft-nose" distinction. We would like to identify with the "hard-nose" approach. Specifically, we feel that the only way to assure progress in thinking and research is through a dependence on the scientific method for posing and answering questions. Studies without a progression of thought and research and which depend strictly on arm-chair theorizing are processes which ultimately deprive the solution to the problem of any meaning at all. We have tried to provide a good theoretical and empirical background for every topic discussed in the text. In addition, we have tried to point out in each topic the major question of interest and to separate that major question from each of the varied attempts to answer it. We think that the value of such an approach will become obvious in the course of reading the text.

We expect that the text will have most appeal for students taking their first course in industrial and organizational psychology. We expect that the students in such a course would have had at least one previous course in psychology, most likely introductory psychology. The student also would benefit from prior familiarity with basic statistical theory and practice. In addition, we have high hopes that our emphasis on the *individual* as the unit of analysis will provide a unique and valuable approach to many students in the more traditional business school settings.

Recently, the issue of "sexist" treatments of topic areas has assumed major importance. The feeling is that stereotypes are developed and maintained by the way in which information is presented. We have chosen to deal with the problem by alternating the use of personal pronouns throughout the text. For any industrial position, you should be just as likely to encounter females in that position as males. The worker is just as likely to be a "she" as a "he." There is one exception to that treatment. We have chosen to retain the term "man-machine system." In this context, we prefer to think of the term "man" as generic. In addition, there is a large body of information which is likely to appear under that heading rather than under another heading such as "worker-machine system." We think that such continuity of topic headings is important and feel that the reader will accept the spirit in which the term is used.

This revised edition differs in several respects from the first. As you would expect, the field has changed in four years. Consequently, we have updated material in each of the chapters to reflect changes in research, theory, and practice. In addition, we have added several models in an attempt to simplify the presentation of complicated topical areas. These models appear in sections on validation, performance appraisal, satisfaction, and motivation. We have also condensed and rearranged material in the human engineering unit. Finally, we have added new material on sociotechnical systems, validation, alternative work schedules, job satisfaction, accidents, and several other topics.

The text could not have been written without the persistence, encouragement, and active collaboration of many individuals. Janet Barnes, Randy Cheloha, Jan Cleveland, and Marty Epstein aided in the literature updating process. John Hall made useful comments on the motivation chapter. Jim

Farr and Bill Hanton creatively and compulsively examined the entire text with respect to both substance and form; Ann Landy provided useful comments on the human engineering material. Colleagues at Penn State and the University of Stockholm were gracious in the face of the incessant clatter of typewriters, boundless clutter, and unpredictable temperament. Ellen Trumbo was nothing less than magical in transforming scratch and scribble into typed copy.

During the period of time in which the text was being revised, Don Trumbo died. He was a good psychologist and a close friend. Having spent the better part of the last eight years working with Don on manuscript development and preparation, I feel that the revised edition accurately reflects our joint view of current industrial and organizational psychology.

December 1979   FRANK J. LANDY

Contents

xi

SECTION 2
The Social Framework of Industrial and Organizational Psychology

SECTION 3
People, Machines, and the Physical Work Environment

CHAPTER 1
Introduction

In comparison with the physical and biological sciences, psychology has a short history as a scientific discipline. While the disciplines of chemistry and physics and biology have been around for hundreds of years, psychology, as a modern science, has a history of less than 100 years. Industrial psychology, as a special subdiscipline has an even shorter history.

In 1917, it was impossible to receive an advanced degree in industrial psychology—this simply did not exist as an area of specialization in graduate training programs. In 1921, Bruce V. Moore was awarded the first Ph.D. in Industrial Psychology.

In the 59 years that have passed, the area has developed to the extent that there are now specialty areas within industrial psychology—areas such as personnel psychology, social-industrial psychology, and engineering psychology. Employment announcements no longer solicit responses from "industrial psychologists," but specify individuals with backgrounds and interests in work motivation and job satisfaction, criterion development and validation, or systems analysis of man-machine designs. This is evidence of the expanding challenge and scope of industrial and organizational (I/O) psychology. In this introductory chapter, we will try to lay the groundwork for the later discussion of problems addressed by industrial and organizational psychologists.

Despite its youth, industrial and organizational psychology has an interesting and complex history. As is true of most areas within psychology, its roots can be found in experimental psychology, that traditional part of the discipline that seeks general principles or "laws" describing the behavior

1

of its subject matter. In psychology such laws are attempts to describe how *people* (or other animals) respond to certain conditions, or "treatments," systematically manipulated by the experimenter. We emphasize "people," because the goal of experimental psychology has been to describe principles that characterize the behavior of people, *in general.* Such principles are, of course, extremely useful for the understanding of behavior in an industrial setting. They are also useful in predicting how certain conditions of work—or the modification of these conditions—will affect the behavior of the worker.

Many of the studies we will describe in the text differ from classic laboratory studies of learning, perception, motivation, and the like only by virtue of the fact that they deal with the effects of work-related variables on behavior and, in many cases, are conducted in work settings rather than in the laboratory. Because the field conditions of the work setting differ from those of the laboratory, it is often hazardous to generalize from laboratory findings. Principles, or findings, obtained in the laboratory need to be verified (and sometimes modified) in the work setting.

Modern industrial and organizational psychology also has important historical roots in *differential psychology*, the study of individual differences. In the latter part of the 19th century, psychologists became interested in the identification, description, and measurement of the ways in which people differ in abilities, traits, interests, and the like. By combining the methods of scientific observation with the advances that were taking place in psychological measurement and data analysis, these psychologists developed the area known as differential psychology.

It is interesting to note that differential psychologists took as their area of investigation those individual differences in behavior that were (and are) sources of frustration to the experimental psychologist. They were sources of frustration because individual differences often obscure the general principles of behavior the experimentalist seeks. It would be a relatively simple matter to identify behavioral principles if *all* people behaved in one way under one set of experimental conditions and in another way under a second set of conditions. The differential psychologist found these individual differences interesting and challenging and sought to account for them through the measurement and interrelation of abilities, interests, aptitudes, and personality traits.

Industrial and organizational psychology has also been influenced by developments in industrial engineering, including time-and-motion study and the design and arrangements of work and machines.

These three distinct forces—experimental psychology, differential psychology, and industrial engineering—combined to define a new area, which Hugo Munsterberg, another pioneer in the field, called "economic psychology." It now became possible to identify differences as well as similarities among individuals, to take these differences and similarities into account in the design of machines, work stations, and work routines, and to evaluate the relative efficiency of various worker-machine-process combinations. In fact, this was the primary activity of the "economic" psychologist for the first 20 to 30 years of this century.

Work procedures and machines were becoming more standardized and homogeneous by 1930. As a consequence, differences in work behavior could not always be explained in terms of physical differences among individuals or variations in work methods or machines. The psychologists in work settings began to take the "human" characteristics of the worker more seriously. The feelings, the motivations, the social relations among workers—all these topics began to receive attention.

This period was a dramatic one for all areas of psychology. Social psychology was on the verge of dramatic breakthroughs in measuring and understanding attitudes. Clinical psychology was able to expand on the rather rigid propositions of Freudian psychology. Developmental psychology was on the threshold of combining the observations and insights of Piaget with advances in the measurement of individual differences.

The revolution in industrial psychology came in the form of the Hawthorne studies, a series of field experiments that helped to highlight the complexity of work behavior. The Hawthorne studies signaled the beginning of the human-relations movement in industrial psychology. The feelings and internal reactions of workers became important variables. At the same time, the enthusiasm for the industrial use of psychological tests, kindled by the success of intelligence testing for recruit placement in World War I, began to slacken.

At this point, there seem to have been three independent movements in industrial psychology: (1) the testing movement (known as personnel psychology), drawing heavily on the differential-psychology approach; (2) the human-relations movement ("social-industrial" psychology) sparked by the Hawthorne studies; and (3) the experimental/industrial engineering movement, using the methods of experimental psychology and industrial engineering. Each of these three areas appeared to develop relatively independently, each with its own techniques and proponents. In personnel psychology, the development of modern statistical techniques aided in the construction of test batteries and new approaches to the measurement of performance. The human-relations movement discovered the work of Maslow and Rogers and developed theories of work motivation and job satisfaction. Psychologists who were interested in application of experimental methods and principles found new challenges during World War II with the rapid development of new man-machine systems. They also found a new identity in what has come to be known as engineering psychology.

Until recently the overlap of these three distinct but related areas did not receive recognition. The interdependence of the social-organizational structure, machine and system design, and worker characteristics now defines the science of work behavior. In 1973, Division 14 of the American Psychological Association changed its name from "Division of Industrial Psychology" to "Division of Industrial and Organizational Psychology" to underscore this interdependence. While engineering psychology is often treated separately, it should be recognized that it shares the common goal of understanding the relationship of people and work with industrial and organizational psychology.

The recognition of this interdependence has made life both more difficult and more exciting for the student of industrial and organizational psychology: more difficult because the number of variables that must be considered in trying to understand even the simplest reaction of the individual in the work setting has become staggering; more exciting because the understanding of this simplest of behaviors has finally become possible.

The capacity to study industrial behavior in all its complexity is a result of the normal maturation that characterizes the development of any credible science. Industrial psychologists—researcher and practitioner alike—have learned the value of theory. This development is well described by Dunnette (1976) in contrasting the *Handbook of Applied Psychology* published in 1950 (Fryer and Henry) with the *Handbook of Industrial and Organizational Psychology* (Dunnette) published in 1976:

> The 1950 *Handbook* was almost exclusively a handbook of practice, emphasizing techniques and applications and giving little attention to research or research methodology and no attention at all to theories of individual or organizational behavior. In contrast, the current *Handbook* gives heavy emphasis to strategies of research and research methodology, theories of behavior, and very strong emphasis to organizational characteristics and the impact of social psychological forces and influences involving interaction processes between organizations and persons. (pp. 2–8)

The difference between the two *Handbooks* that Dunnette highlights can also be seen in the differing professional activity of the industrial psychologist then and now. As early industrial psychologists became aware of the needs of society, they were able and willing to respond to these needs. World War II and the needs it presented caused industrial and differential psychologists to advance the testing movement which began around World War I. Engineering psychologists also responded magnificently, by producing some of the finest knobs and dials ever to adorn an airplane's instrument panel. Nevertheless, it was not until the late 1950s and early 1960s that psychologists began to work on the *theories* which might explain the various successes and failures of the 1930s and 1940s.

Several excellent histories of the early phases of the field are available. DuBois (1970) traces the development of psychological testing; Fryer and Henry (1950) present an excellent view of both the roots and the status of I/O psychology in 1950; Ferguson (1962) gives a very personal account of the development of the field to 1960; and Dunnette (1976) provides a contemporary overview of I/O psychology. By examining these histories, we can see that Industrial and Organizational Psychology is much more aggressive today than it was 25 years ago. Recently, industrial psychologists have been responsible for introducing and refining concepts such as job enrichment and task design. They have introduced taxonomies to cover physical and mental activities at the work place and have developed elaborate methods of investigation and analysis in validation research. In short, they have adopted an *active* rather than *reactive* mode. We believe that this change is a permanent one and that I/O psychologists will become increasingly active. This is a luxury afforded by a better understanding of the behaviors being studied.

There are several themes that we will follow throughout this book. The first is the importance of individual differences. It is our belief that advances in the understanding of behavior patterns in industry can be made from an analysis of the differences among individuals. We will look at those factors that might account for the fact that one individual succeeds in a particular job while another fails, or the fact that one individual is happy in a particular job while another is miserable. While we will attempt to draw some generalizations from the material we present, these generalizations will be based on observations of such individual differences. This approach is in contrast to theories contending that the behavior of all individuals can be understood on the basis of a single rule or principle. Such approaches seem to follow the human preference to reduce information to its simplest form. While such a strategy may be pleasing, it is usually useless and circular. It is becoming more and more apparent that certain behavior patterns are more influenced by characteristics on which *individuals* differ than by characteristics on which *situations* differ. In each of the chapters of this book, we will try to identify some of these individual differences and the ways in which they affect the understanding and prediction of behavior in industrial settings.

Another theme we stress is that the various topic areas are inextricably bound together and cannot be easily separated. It is impossible to select the best workers for a particular job until we are able to describe success on that job. Further, regardless of which individuals the selection scheme identifies as the most likely prospects for success, the reward system of the organization will have very definite and predictable consequences on whether or not that individual is, in fact, successful on the job. These kinds of interrelationships will emerge as the areas are introduced. We will alert you to some of the more important interrelationships.

A final theme that will be carried through every chapter is the total interdependence of research, theory, and practice. Sterile theories, developed in laboratories and tested only in the mind of the researcher, are useless. Ultimately, theories should be tested in several different settings and "packaged" somehow for local application. Unless the generality of a theory of behavior can be *demonstrated*, the theory is best abandoned. Conversely, dozens of studies on a similar topic are equally useless until and unless someone collects the findings, identifies consistencies in the results, and forms more general principles that might account for these results. In the various chapters, we will identify models and theories that have guided research; where models and theories are not available, we will review available research and identify consistencies. Above all, we will attempt to show how theory complements practice.

There are undoubtedly other themes in this book that will be more evident to you than they are to us. When we present material that is open to speculation, we will identify it as such. This does not mean that we will hide our own preference; it means that the critical evidence or logic is missing from the argument, and we will warn you of this.

The book is separated into four areas. The first appears in Chapters 1 and 2. This material consists primarily of background or contextual information necessary for the interpretation of what will follow. It consists of descriptions aimed at establishing the uniqueness of industrial psychology from other sciences as well as from other areas within psychology. In addition, we describe what industrial psychologists do and where they are likely to do it. Chapter 2 consists of the methodological preparation necessary for working with the raw information (in the form of research results) that appears in the content chapters. Learning this is much like learning a language necessary for the understanding of later chapters. We also present the research methods related to the philosophy of individual differences. Then we show how this philosophy is applied in research related to industrial problems. Finally, we explore some of the favorite tools of the industrial/organizational psychologist; specifically, ways of collecting and analyzing data.

The second major group of chapters deals with what has been traditionally labeled as "personnel psychology." It would probably be more appropriate to call it the "psychology of personnel decisions." It comprises Chapters 3 through 8, predictor-related issues, criterion-related issues, personnel decisions, alternative-selection devices, and two chapters on the theory and application of industrial training. Historically, this area has been the backbone of industrial psychology. Since it deals so heavily with problems of measurement, prediction, and inference, it will undoubtedly continue to be an area of prime importance. Issues such as reliability and validity, raised in the sections on personnel decisions, carry equal importance in the evaluation of motivational programs and of man-machine systems. Criterion development, introduced as a preparation for performance appraisal, is equally crucial in studies of leadership and of skilled operator performance. In short, personnel psychology includes a collection of the techniques that are essential to the psychologist pursuing the understanding of behavior in industrial settings.

The topics in the Personnel Psychology chapters are critically related to personnel administration in any modern organization. Unless the important elements and implications of job analysis, validation, and performance assessment are understood, it is unlikely that the modern personnel department can perform its duties either efficiently or legally. In addition, the complexity and increasing cost of selecting and training employees makes the sections on tests, testing procedures, and training models and devices "must" reading for anyone responsible for personnel decisions. It can be seen that these chapters are relevant both for manager and psychologist equally.

The third area of interest deals with the individual's attempts to adjust to the characteristics of the job, co-workers, superiors, and the organization. It also deals with the modifications the organization makes in an attempt to coexist with the characteristics of its workers. Chapters 9, 10, 11, and 12 deal with work motivation, job satisfaction, leadership, and organizational theory, respectively. These chapters might be thought of as falling on a continuum that begins with the molecular view of the individual's motives and his affective or emotional responses to the work environment (work motivation and job satisfaction), and ends with the molar examination of the effect of the systematic expectancies of the organization on the employee, and the effect of the employee's behavior on those expectancies. Another way of looking at the chapters in this section is that they deal with decisions that the individual makes while at the workplace: decisions about whether or not to expend energy, and whether or not to accept the goals of the leader or the organization. In addition, we will explore the feelings that accompany these decisions and the effect of these feelings on later decisions. This section might be contrasted with the personnel section by stating that it concentrates on the *individual worker* as the decision maker rather than the system or organization (as implied in the notion of a "personnel decision").

As was the case in the personnel section, these chapters are important for the manager as well as the psychologist. The way individuals *feel* about their jobs may ultimately determine how long they *stay*. Job enlargement and enrichment, opportunity to affect decisions, leadership style, and organizational climate may all affect the worker's feelings; for that reason, it is important to be familiar with current thinking on organizational variables. On a more humanistic note, the topics in this section deal with the "quality of work" as perceived by the individual employee.

The last two chapters deal with an area generally referred to as "engineering psychology." Chapters 13 and 14 deal with the worker's environment, the characteristics of that worker in the form of capabilities and limitations, and—consequently—the characteristics of the system formed by combining the worker, the machine, and the physical work environment. This section differs from the two that precede it primarily because it views the human element in the man-machine-environment complex as a component in a system, communicating with machine elements and interacting with physical environmental conditions. It also treats the tasks assigned to the human components and the environmental conditions as potential sources of stress on the individual.

With the increasing complexity of the modern workplace, it is important for the practitioner, whether manager or psychologist, to understand the effects of drugs, alcohol, fatigue, information overload, shift work, and other stressors on industrial performance. In addition, as machine operators are replaced by machine tenders through automation, it is important to recognize that the skills necessary for successful performance change accordingly. The final section will highlight these issues.

INDUSTRIAL AND ORGANIZATIONAL (I/O) PSYCHOLOGY

Before presenting a formal definition of I/O psychology, we will provide a framework to help put it into the proper perspective.

As a Science. To describe a particular activity as "scientific" implies that the activity has certain goals and is carried out in a prescribed manner. The major goals of a scientific endeavor are understanding, prediction, and control. In that respect, I/O psychology is similar to experimental psychology, nuclear physics, and biochemistry. Each of those disciplines has understanding, prediction, and control as a major set of goals. But a scientific endeavor is characterized as much by the *way* in which it is carried out as by the goals it seeks. One of these characteristics is a system of logic that enables a researcher to draw inferences or form hypotheses about the relationships among variables. This system of logic may be inductive (one that proceeds from a broad data base to a principle), or deductive (one that proceeds from a set of *a priori* principles to test those principles in the real world), or both. The logic system, whether inductive or deductive, must be preceded or followed by data (i.e., it must be related to empirical or observable investigation). A third characteristic of scientific activity is that it must be communicable; one must be able to describe procedures and analyses employed, as well as experimental manipulations, to the public at large. If the researchers cannot adequately explain the nature of their activities, then the activity is something less than science. As a matter of fact, this is one of the major distinctions between art and science. Art is something that depends on individual experience and cannot always be communicated to someone else; science, on the other hand, must be communicable if we are ever to add to the body of knowledge, whether that knowledge be related to blood flow, nuclear fission, or work motivation. Given these characteristics, I/O psychology clearly qualifies as a science.

As a Behavioral Science. Psychology, and in particular I/O psychology, is classified as a behavioral science. This separates it from the physical sciences. The behavioral sciences, as their title implies, focus their efforts on the study of behavior of systems and subsystems in which individuals find themselves. A system may be as broad as a culture, as in the case of anthropology, or as narrow as the subjective reality a single individual has created for herself, as in the case of psychology. Some other disciplines which are characterized as behavioral sciences are sociology, political science, and economics. Psychology stands out from the rest of the behavioral sciences primarily because its emphasis is on the understanding, prediction, and control of behavior peculiar to the *individual.* While individuals may form groups and respond to common antecedents, the psychologist continues to be concerned with the behavior of the individual and why the individual may belong to one group rather than another. The study of group process and group behaviors is in the province of the sociologist.

As an Interest Area in Psychology. Industrial/organizational psychology has the industrial situation as its setting. Although work may be done in a laboratory or in a simulated work setting, the industrial psychologist is primarily concerned with the application of psychological principles to the problems workers encounter in the performance of their duties.

We might compare I/O psychology with the other areas of psychology to get an idea of its potential uniqueness. Here are some definitions of various areas from a publication of the American Psychological Association (APA), the primary professional organization for psychologists:

> *Clinical Psychology:* the clinical psychologist specializes in the assessment and therapeutic treatment of persons suffering emotional or adjustment problems.
>
> *School Psychology:* the school psychologists are concerned with increasing the effectiveness of educational institutions to facilitate the intellectual, emotional, and social development of children.
>
> *Industrial Psychology:* the industrial psychologist focuses his scientific research on and applies his professional skills to problems that people encounter at work. (APA, 1970, pp. 6–8)

The other major areas of psychology and the relative distribution of psychologists in each of the interest areas is presented in Figure 1–1. This figure was constructed from data gathered by Boneau (1974).

FIGURE 1–1
Distribution of Psychologists by Interest Area

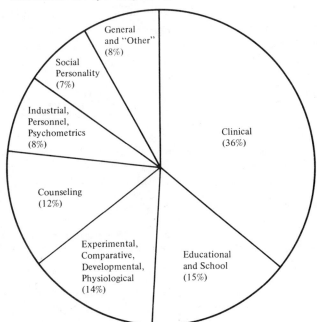

I/O Psychology Compared to Other Areas

When comparing I/O psychology to each of the other areas of psychology, we might make that comparison along three dimensions: (1) the context; that is, where does the research and application go on? (2) the process of the research and application of the particular area; and (3) the content of the area; that is, what are the antecedent and consequent variables that appear most often in research and application in that area of interest?

Context. Traditionally, I/O psychology has been bound to the industrial context, the world of work. This is not true of social psychology or clinical psychology. This is not to say that I/O psychology does not draw from findings in contexts other than the work context in research and application, but rather that it relates those findings to behavior in work settings. In that sense, I/O psychology, like school psychology, is closely allied to a particular setting. While this distinction is becoming more and more blurred, it may be useful for the time being to maintain it.

Process. When we look at the *way* in which I/O psychology approaches research or the application of principles, we find that it is not terribly unique. The I/O psychologist characteristically makes use of the full range of experimental designs and analyses that are employed by other areas in conducting research, but—and it is an important exception—the I/O psychologist applies these findings to industrial settings. In the next chapter, we will see some of the more frequently employed designs and statistical tools of the I/O psychologist.

Content. A final dimension that can be used to characterize I/O psychology is the content of the discipline; that is, the variables under consideration. In this respect, the field is characterized by the three major subareas described above. It considers intraindividual variables such as job satisfaction and work motivation. It also considers prediction and measurement systems as they apply in industry in the form of selection and performance appraisal of employees, and it deals with certain stimulus variables such as information displays, effects of environmental conditions, and strategies for information processing as they relate to man-machine interactions.

The Role of an I/O Psychologist

One of the authors asked his introductory psychology class to gather descriptions of what an I/O psychologist does from friends, relatives, and neighbors. Here are some of the most interesting of those descriptions:

> Industrial psychology is the process of making people do what they don't want to do.
> An industrial psychologist is one who reviews technical inventions to ascertain whether or not the effect of the invention will be beneficial to the society— for example, a nuclear power plant.
> A shrink for machines.
> An industrial psychologist interviews people to see that they are placed in the right positions in factories.

An industrial psychologist is one who investigates the behavior of people at work as opposed to outside of work.

These observations confirm a statement made by a member of a task force commissioned to describe the effective practice of psychology in industry ("Task Force," 1971):

People have the image of psychologists—either you're a numbers man, you're a kind of a nuts-and-bolts guy, or you're a clinical type who comes in to help sick people. But they don't realize that we know a great deal about the normal individual (p. 977).

You can see that many of these definitions come close to the activities we have already described. Unfortunately, at least two of them confuse the I/O psychologist with an industrial engineer and a person who communicates with inanimate objects.

One way of describing the role of I/O psychologists might be to indicate where they are likely to be found and what they are likely to be doing.

Settings. There are four major settings for I/O psychologists—government and industry, consulting firms, academia, and research organizations. While the predominant work setting in which I/O psychologists are found is the industrial setting, this is not exclusive. The activities of the I/O psychologist in this setting might include developing testing programs for the selection of employees, determining equitable pay plans for employees through job analysis and evaluation, developing motivation programs for managers, conducting seminars on leadership for executives, evaluating training programs, or determining the characteristics of a new bank of turret lathes that will fit best with the capabilities and limitations of the organization's employees. While not every I/O psychologist would be concerned with each of the problems mentioned, the problems constitute a reasonable sample of those that confront industrial psychologists. Their activities generally consist of both long-term and short-term projects. The unique challenge of I/O psychologists in industry is that they must not only develop programs for an organization, but must also be accountable for the results of those programs. This may also be the reward of such an activity—being able to develop *and implement* a program.

Generally, consulting firms make use of the skills of the I/O psychologist in much the same way as does industry. In these settings, the I/O psychologist is responsible for the development of a particular action program, such as constructing a performance-appraisal system, developing a recruiting program, or attempting to analyze "human-relations" problems. Unlike the psychologist who works for a single industrial organization, however, the consulting industrial psychologist is not always directly responsible for the implementation of an action program, but may function in an advisory capacity to the management group of the particular organization. Activities are as varied as those of the psychologist in industrial settings.

Thirdly, I/O psychologists are found in academic settings. An example of such a person might be your instructor for this course. Their primary

FIGURE 1–2

Principal Work Settings of I/O Psychologists

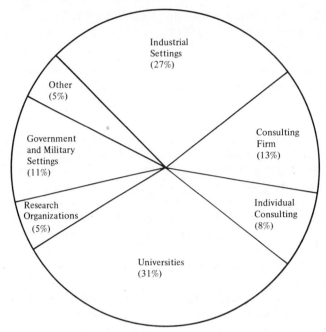

Industrial
Settings
(27%)

Other
(5%)

Government
and Military
Settings
(11%)

Consulting
Firm
(13%)

Research
Organizations
(5%)

Individual
Consulting
(8%)

Universities
(31%)

We are grateful to Neal Schmitt for providing the statistics for Figures 1–2 and 1–3. They are taken from a 1979 survey of members of the Industrial and Organizational Division of the American Psychological Association.

FIGURE 1–3

Principal Work Activities of I/O Psychologists

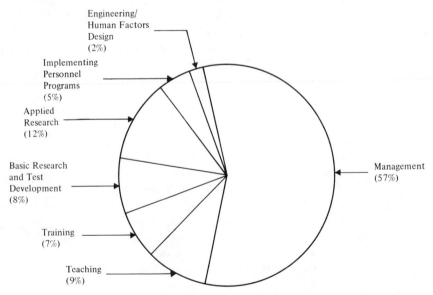

Engineering/
Human Factors
Design
(2%)

Implementing
Personnel
Programs
(5%)

Applied
Research
(12%)

Basic Research
and Test
Development
(8%)

Management
(57%)

Training
(7%)

Teaching
(9%)

responsibilities are teaching and research, but they may also engage in consulting work for government and industry. A typical I/O psychologist in an academic setting might teach three courses during a semester, conduct a research project on a skilled, motor-performance task, such as driving an automobile, and help a local company validate a test battery it has been using for the past decade.

Finally, the I/O psychologist might work for a research organization. Examples of this type of organization are the Educational Testing Service of Princeton, New Jersey, and the American Institutes for Research in Washington, D.C. These organizations concentrate on developing rather broad programs of action in areas germane to I/O psychology, such as selection programs for municipal police departments or training programs for hospital administration. They are usually able to support the kind of long-term basic research necessary to advance the field and to solve the difficult and complex problems of modern society. In these settings, the I/O psychologist's time might be split between research and application and, more often than not, it will involve working with a small group of other psychologists in a team effort.

Of course, there are other settings in which an I/O psychologist might be found, such as government agencies like the United States Civil Service Commission, the Equal Employment Opportunity Commission (EEOC), or the Law Enforcement Assistance Administration of the U.S. Department of Justice, but even so the problems they face will be as varied and challenging as those outlined above.

Boneau (1974) presented figures describing the work settings and activities of I/O psychologists, the data coming from a survey conducted by the National Science Foundation. He found that 8 percent of the psychologists who belonged to the American·Psychological Association classified themselves as industrial or personnel psychologists, while 2 percent classified themselves as engineering psychologists. Figure 1–2 presents the relative distribution of work settings for industrial, personnel, and engineering psychologists lumped together. It can be seen that the majority of these individuals are found in private industry, while the next largest group is found in university settings. The remainder are in private practice or consulting, federal government, or research settings.

Figure 1–3 presents a description of the principal work activity of the I/O psychologists. It can be seen from this figure that management, consulting, and research lead the list of work activities. These percentages describe the locations and work activities of I/O psychologists in 1979 only, and will change as a function of the economy, the nature of the work force, and changes in the field itself.

The Challenge to I/O Psychology

I/O psychology is being challenged constantly by workers, by the government, and by other sciences. For example, Argyris (1972) challenged

I/O psychology to stop ignoring certain crucial problems and variables. He claimed that (1) I/O psychologists construct inconsistent and invalid theories, and (2) because of that, they provide practical contributions that range from incomplete, to misleading, to dangerous, which (3) produce useless knowledge, which, in turn (4) requires society to take over and reorient activities of the industrial psychologist.

Argyris' concerns are borne out in an article by Fincher (1973) on the relationship between personnel testing and public policy formation. Briefly, the problem is that the federal government, through the Equal Employment Opportunity Commission (EEOC), has written a set of guidelines that suggest the practices to be followed by organizations in their hiring practices if they are to avoid unfair discrimination against groups covered in the Civil Rights Act of 1964. Fincher seems to bear out Argyris' fear completely. He recounts the following sequence of events:

1. The social critics such as Baritz *(The Servants of Power)*, Gross *(The Brain Watchers)* and Whyte *(The Organization Man)* decry the abuse of psychological testing.
2. The courts hear a landmark case in which Myart claims that the Motorola company unfairly discriminated against him in a personnel decision.
3. The Civil Rights Act of 1964 is passed, establishing protected subgroups that have been unfairly treated in the past.
4. The Office of Federal Contract Compliance is instituted to withhold federal money from organizations that fail to comply with the Civil Rights Act.
5. The Equal Employment Opportunity Commission is established to provide fair employment and personnel practice guidelines.
6. The Supreme Court of the United States rules that the Duke Power company unfairly discriminated against black workers, even though that discrimination may have been unwitting.
7. The Equal Employment Opportunity Coordinating Council is formed to refine, expand, and explain the earlier employment guidelines of the EEOC.

This sequence perfectly describes what Argyris referred to as "society," through its government, taking over and reorienting the activities of I/O psychologists.

In addition to fair employment there are many other challenges that I/O psychology will be required to meet in the next decade. One of the most dramatic is improving the quality of working life. Currently, a very small portion of the general work force is affected by improvements in task design, enriched jobs, or schemes encouraging joint decision making by supervisors and subordinates. The "average" job is dull and anonymous; it must be made more interesting and personal.

School systems are also challenging industrial psychology. Many students entering the work force today are socially, emotionally, and vocationally ill prepared for the demands of the organization. Consequently, organizations have often redesigned the job to be simpler or have accepted less than adequate performance from the worker—neither response is appropriate. Until the nature of formal education changes, the organization and, ultimately, the industrial psychologist must accept some responsibility for helping the individual adapt to the work environment, while at the same time trying to improve that environment. The issue is not a moral one—it is a practical one!

There are several other issues that will represent challenges for the field of industrial psychology—issues such as rational organizational development and change, the role of the organization and work itself in drug and alcohol abuse, behavioral and cognitive foundations of safe behavior, the effects of shift work, and issues related to the understanding and utilization of older workers.

In the chapters that follow, we will elaborate on the nature of these problems and suggest some solutions.

REFERENCES

American Psychological Association. *A career in psychology.* Washington, D.C.: APA, 1970.

Argyris, C. *The applicability of organizational sociology.* Cambridge, England: Cambridge University Press, 1972.

Boneau, A. An overview of psychology's human resources. *American Psychologist,* 1974, *29,* 821–840.

DuBois, P. *A history of psychological testing.* Boston: Allyn & Bacon, 1970.

Dunnette, M. D. *Handbook of industrial and organizational psychology.* Chicago: Rand McNally and Co., 1976.

Ferguson, L. W. *The heritage of industrial psychology.* Hartford: Finlay Press, 1962.

Fincher, C. Personnel testing and public policy. *American Psychologist,* 1973, *28,* 489–497.

Fryer, D. H., & Henry, E. R. *Handbook of applied psychology* (Vols. I and II). New York: Holt, Rinehart and Winston, 1950.

Task Force on the Practice of Psychology in Industry. *American Psychologist,* 1971, *26,* 974–991.

CHAPTER 2

Methods of Industrial and Organizational Psychology

People are different. That may be the one statement on which we can all agree. We are constantly astounded at *how* different people are. These differences can be a source of joy (particularly when we see how different we are from people we hold in low esteem) or a source of frustration (when we encounter someone whose behavior seems to defy prediction). As a concrete example of an individual difference, think about the wide variation on test scores for your last major examination. After the scores were posted, you and several of your friends tried to determine why there were some of you who received high scores while others received mediocre or even quite low scores. Your first inclination might have been to blame it on the inconsistency of grading policies of the instructor—she gave full credit for an answer on your paper that was awarded only partial credit on your friend's paper (the technical name for such a state of affairs is "unreliability"). You might also explain the differences by claiming that the test really measured knowledge of trivial details of the subject matter and was really only a test of memory (technically, this is a problem of "validity"). Later, when you are alone and basking in the warm glow of your score, which happened to be at the high end of the distribution, you may admit to yourself that the differences in scores were really due to some aspect of "native ability" (an aptitude of some kind), or the amount of time spent studying for the examination (an aspect of motivation).

The example above should give you a feel for the role of individual differences in psychology. Just as you supplied several guesses or hypotheses to account for the fact that the examination scores differed, the psychologist notices or measures differences in the behavior of individuals and sets out to understand and predict such differences.

Each of the major sections in this text presents theories or models that try to account for individual differences. These theories will try to explain such things as why pay satisfies one individual and not another; why individuals with a great amount of mechanical aptitude do better at electrical trouble-shooting than individuals with little mechanical aptitude; or why an increase in the noise level in a particular area of a plant has a negative effect on one worker and a positive effect on another. The answer to each of these questions depends on the measurement of individual differences in behavior. While we have chosen to highlight differences *between* individuals, we can just as easily deal with differences within individuals. These inter- and intraindividual differences are the raw materials for theory building and prediction in psychology.

OBSERVATION

The basic method of science is *observation* of the phenomenon to be investigated. Through observation, the scientist obtains the empirical data that are the foundation of inductive reasoning. What makes the scientist's observations different from those of the person on the street is that the scientist's are systematic. The entire scientific enterprise has contributed to the development of rules, methods, and instruments to increase the systematic properties of scientific observation. These include rules to determine when a set of observations is *adequate* in number and when it is a *representative*, or unbiased, sample of all the observations that might have been made. Systematic observation also implies accurate and precise observation, and scientists have continuously searched for instruments and measuring devices that would increase the precision with which they could describe, or classify, their observations. At a primitive level, the scientist can say that two observations were the same or different—that two insects looked alike or they did not—that two people behaved in the same way or in different ways. In other words, at this level, the observer could only say whether or not two observations differed qualitatively and then could classify these observations into the same or into two *qualitatively* different categories. By contrast, the scientist with an electronic microscope or other precision instrument might well be able to differentiate between two observations that differed by the smallest amount, and to classify these observations into two *quantitatively* different categories. Such power to classify one's observations depends on the precision and accuracy of measurement and on the *level* of measurement one is able to achieve. Different levels of measurement vary not only in the degree of refinement achieved in classifying our observations, but also in the kinds of statements made about the relationships between observations and between categories.

Levels of Measurement

In 1951, Stevens provided a useful scheme for thinking about quantification and measurement. He described the following four levels of measurement:

Nominal Measurement. As the name suggests, nominal measurement is more a matter of naming or classifying observations than of measuring them. Observations are simply placed in two or more qualitatively different categories. Some examples of this level of measurement in industrial psychology are classifying employees as "white-collar" or "blue-collar," male or female, hourly or salaried, minority or nonminority workers, assemblers or machinists. At the nominal level of measurement, we are essentially limited to "same"-"different" relationships; that is, of describing two observations as the same if they fall in the same category and different if they fall in different categories. There is no basis for comparing observations with respect to "less than" or "greater than" because the categories are not ordered along a dimension of magnitude.

Ordinal Measurement. At the ordinal level of measurement, one is able to order the categories or classes of observations along some dimension such as "small-to-large" or "short-to-tall." Thus, we can compare observations in terms of *greater than* or *less than* relationships and the position of the observation in relation to the position of other objects. If three observations can be ordered, A < B < C, then the position of B can be described relative to A and C.

An example of an ordinal scale is the scale of hardness of minerals. We might take ten rocks representing ten different minerals and attempt to scratch each rock with every other rock. If rock A scratched every other rock but could be scratched by no other rock, we could, with some assurance, designate rock A as the "hardest" of the ten and give it a rank of "1." Likewise, we might find that rock D can scratch every rock *except* rock A and can be scratched only by rock A. We would then give rock D a rank of "2," designating it as the second hardest rock. We would continue with this process until we had determined the hardness of each of the rocks and assigned each a rank designating its position on the hardness scale. This would be an ordinal scale. The important property to keep in mind is that we know something about the order of the objects but nothing about *how much* harder one object is than another. Other examples of ordinal scales are rank in graduating class, national rankings for college football teams, and order of finish in a horse race. In each of these instances, we know nothing necessarily about the *distance* between any one object and the object immediately above or below. This is so because we do not have a *unit* of measurement at this level.

In industrial psychology, we find ordinal scales employed often in certain forms of performance appraisal. When employees are ranked on the basis of "overall worth," they are essentially being measured by an ordinal scale of measurement. This often can be a distinct disadvantage if we cannot have the same group of judges rank all the employees. In that case we have no way of knowing if the number "1" person in work group A is "as good as" the number "1" person in group B.

Interval Measurement.   Interval measurement introduces two refinements over ordinal measurement: a *unit* for describing distances along the dimension on which observations are being ordered, and a *zero point* from which to start the counting of the units.

While a ranking of individuals from best to worst on some particular aspect may be useful, it does not carry as much information as knowing the distances *between* those ranks. For example, if we were to examine the class standing of your high-school graduating class, the information would be richer and possibly more useful for prediction if, in addition to ranks, we also had grade point averages. It is possible that in a graduating class, the number "1" senior had 4.00 average, while the number "2" senior had a 2.10 average, and the other 224 seniors were distributed between 2.10 and .00. We can make use of this added information because the average of .00 serves as a zero point on the grading scale. This zero point is missing from the nominal and ordinal scales.

Another example of a zero point would be 0° on the Celsius or on the Fahrenheit temperature scale; with such a zero point, we can then mark off the scale in equal units so that a warning that the "temperature is going to drop 20° in the next hour" has some meaning to us.

Ratio Measurement.   This last example shows the only real limitation of the interval level of measurement. The zero on either temperature scale is an *arbitrarily chosen* zero, or starting point. It does not mean "the point of no temperature," or the absence of temperature; otherwise "20° below zero" would have no meaning. Because the zero point is arbitrary, we cannot talk about the ratio of two temperatures. Thus, for example, it is inaccurate to say that 100° F. is twice as hot as 50° F. or 100 times hotter than 1° F. The properties of an interval level of measurement plus a true zero point define the *ratio level* of measurement. With these properties, one can properly talk about the ratio of one scale value to another. Time is measured on a ratio scale; it is meaningful to think of one activity taking "twice as long" as another activity.

Psychological measures are often assumed to have a true unit of measurement and the properties of an interval scale, but seldom would one argue that zero on a psychological test or scale is anything other than an arbitrary zero point. Therefore, it is inappropriate, for example, to think of a person with an IQ of 100 as "twice as intelligent" as another person with an IQ of 50.

Use of Statistics.   Statistical methods have a prominent place in the behavioral sciences. This is especially true in industrial psychology, where a wide variety of both experimental and measurement statistics are used. Statistics are tools that serve two broad functions: the first is descriptive, the second is inferential.

Descriptive statistics accomplish exactly what the label implies—they *describe* a set of scores. In that sense, descriptive statistics are only concerned with the data you have in hand. Inferential statistics are also well labeled— they help you *infer* something from the set of scores you have. The inference that you draw concerns the likelihood of obtaining a similar distribution of numbers if you were to gather another sample of scores of a similar size. Thus, inferential statistics assume that the scores you have in hand are only a sample of a larger *population* of scores. The question to be answered is "How sure can I be that the entire population of scores looks like this sample of scores?"

The descriptive functions of statistics serve to summarize observations in a quantitative way. When a researcher has made a number of observations, the findings may be communicated in several ways. A tally sheet could be presented with each mark indicating an observation in a given category (a frequency distribution); numbers could replace the marks indicating the frequency of observations in each category or with bars of columns proportional in length to the category frequency (a frequency polygon), or the findings could be summarized with two descriptive statistics. One of these would be a measure of the *central tendency* of the observations; the other would be a measure of their *dispersion*, or *variability* around the point of central tendency. These statistics allow the researcher to communicate the findings in precise quantitative terms rather than as a qualitative picture.

Descriptive statistics also provide a basis for evaluating single observations. Thus, for example, if you learned that on the first quiz you got 25 out of a possible 40 points, that information would be ambiguous. You might ask the instructor, "How did the scores look?" meaning, "What did the distribution look like?" The interpretation of your score of 25 would be different depending on whether the instructor said that the average was 20 or 30, and again different if all scores were close to the average or widely dispersed.

Statistics are also used to describe the relationship or degree of association between two (or more) sets of observations. The researcher who observes and records the production scores and the IQ scores for each of a sample of supervisors can communicate his findings by means of a two-dimensional table, an *X-Y* plot or scattergram, or—more quantitatively—as a *correlation coefficient*. The statistic adds precision to the description of the observations.

The inferential functions of statistics provide an orderly system whereby the scientist can draw conclusions from her observations. These functions are important for hypothesis testing and for generalizing one's results beyond the *sample* of observations. Suppose, for example, a researcher observes and records the scores on a verbal ability test of a sample of 100 first-line supervisors, then calculates the average score of the sample. Suppose further that the average of the sample is five points higher than the average reported for a nationwide sample on which the test was standardized. What can be concluded? Apparently, we could conclude that *for this sample* verbal ability is higher, on the average, than for the standard sample. But what can be said about a larger *population* of supervisors, such as all the supervisors in the company? Through the use of inferential statistics, the researcher can estimate the likelihood, or *probability*, of obtaining the average score from the sample if, indeed, the population of supervisors were not different from the standard sample in verbal ability. The conclusions drawn from the observations can be guided by this probability. If it were highly unlikely that the obtained average would depart from the national average as far as it does, we may conclude that "supervisors in this company have more verbal ability than the average adult." Furthermore, we could state the probability that the conclusion was an accurate one. If, on the other hand, it was likely that the sample average would depart from the national average to the extent that it did, we would conclude that there was no adequate basis for saying that supervisors had more verbal ability than the average adult. In short, the conclusions drawn from a sample of observations can be based upon some estimate of the likelihood that they are true. Statistical tests provide such estimates. They help us to describe the error associated with our sample estimates of population values and the confidence we can have in conclusions drawn from our observations.

STATISTICS AND LEVELS OF MEASUREMENT

Each level of measurement as described requires a different set of descriptive and inferential statistics. This is so because different statistics make different assumptions about the data they describe—assumptions about units of measurement, additivity, the form or shape of the distribution, and the like. The choice of a measure of central tendency, variability, or correlation is, therefore, not a matter of whim, but depends on the nature of the data.

Central Tendency

When our observations can be classified only into qualitatively different categories, that is, when we are using nominal measurement, the central tendency is described by the mode, or the most frequently used category. Thus, if we classify our friends according to their academic majors, we might find that the largest number are in sociology. "Sociology" would then be the *modal category*. If, instead, we could classify our friends into five categories along the dimension from "very happy" to "very sad" ("very happy," "happy," "neither," "sad," "very sad"), then we might use the *median* category, or the category into which the middle individual falls. For example, if our results looked like the following:

Very Happy	Happy	Neither	Sad	Very Sad
15%	50%	20%	10%	5%

then the category of the middle individual is "happy." If we were able to give each person a score on a happiness test, but were unwilling to assume that the differences between adjacent scores were equal (that is, unwilling to assume an interval level of measurement), then we could describe the central tendency of our distribution as the score obtained by the individual in the center of our distribution, or the median score.

With a unit of measurement such as with interval or ratio data, we would use the average, or *arithmetic mean*, to describe central tendency. Thus we might calculate the mean grade point average of our friends, whereas it would be meaningless to speak of their average academic major. However, under some conditions the mean may not be a good representation of the central tendency. For example, the mean financial worth of 5 billionnaires and 4,000 of the rest of us might be one million dollars, a value which describes neither the 5 nor the 4,000 and is not a good indication of the financial well-being of anyone in the distribution. This results when the distribution is asymmetrical ("skewed") with respect to the central tendency. In such a case it would be more appropriate to describe the situation in terms of the financial status of the 2,003rd, or middle, individual.

Dispersion, or Variability

With nominal measurement, we have no precise or standard way of describing the variability of our observations other than in terms of the proportion of cases that fall in the modal category. Obviously, if 98 percent of all observations are in one category, there is little variability. Maximum variability occurs when all categories are used with equal frequency. The same statement holds for ordered categories, or ordinal data. If ten employees are simply rank-ordered, 1 to 10, on job performance, there is nothing to indicate the variability. On the other hand, if out of ten students, two each receive grades of A, B, C, D, F, the variability is greater than when eight receive C and one each B and D grades.

When we have a unit of measurement or are willing to assume that successive scores mark off equal units on the scale dimensions, we can describe (in terms of our unit) how far our observations, *on the average*, depart from the central tendency. Such a description is known as the *average deviation*. It is obtained by taking the absolute difference between each score and the mean, summing up these differences, and dividing by the number of scores. More commonly, with interval data, one computes the *standard deviation* as a measure of variability. It is also obtained by taking the differences between each score and the mean, but in this case each difference, or deviation, is squared and the average of these squared deviation scores is known as the *variance* of the distribution. The standard deviation is the square root of the variance.[1]

---

[1] The equation for average deviation is:

$$A.D. = \frac{\Sigma |X_i - M|}{N}$$

As with the mean, the standard deviation assumes an essentially symmetrical and continuous distribution of scores. When these conditions do not hold, or when one does not wish to assume interval scores, one variability may be described in terms of the interquartile range. This is simply the range of scores between the 25th percentile and the 75th percentile score, or the range of the middle 50 percent of the scores.

The standard deviation is an important statistic for psychologists. The variance, or standard deviation *squared*, is an especially important statistic for the psychology of individual differences. In differential psychology, we are often trying to find a set of measures that helps to explain variability in another set of measures. For example, we might try to account for individual differences on arithmetic test scores on the basis of how "intelligent" the individuals are; in other words, by knowing the "intelligence" of the individuals, we might be able to reduce the variability (unexplained) of the scores. It is the unexplained variance that we are trying to account for, or reduce. In the section on psychological testing, we will see the degree to which knowledge of one attribute helps to reduce unexplained variability on another attribute or the degree to which the second attribute can be *predicted* from the first attribute. For example, if the variation in performance scores for a group of workers can be explained or reduced through knowledge of certain test scores of those individuals, then performance can be "predicted" from the test scores. Consequently, the ability to derive some measure of variability or dispersion from a score distribution is an important goal of measurement in psychology.

MEASURES OF ASSOCIATION

Measures of association—that is, those statistics that indicate the degree to which two variables covary or change together—are also tied to the levels of measurement.

Consider the data in Table 2–1. The column pairs represent three different ways of considering the data. In the far left-hand columns, the actual scores of variables A and B are presented for individuals 1 through 10. In the center columns, the ranks of the 10 individuals for each of the two variables are presented. In the far right-hand columns, individuals have simply been categorized as above the mean (A) or below the mean (B)

---

where X_i is the individual score, M is the mean, N is the number of scores and Σ indicates the sum of all the $X_i - M$ values.

The equation for the variance is:

$$V = S.D.^2 = \frac{\Sigma(X_i - M)^2}{N}$$

and for the standard deviation:

$$S.D. = \sqrt{V} = \sqrt{\frac{\Sigma(X_i - M)^2}{N}}$$

For the data in the left-hand column of Table 2–1, the average deviation for Variable A is 8.8, the variance is 109.24 and the standard deviation is 11.01.

TABLE 2–1

Hypothetical Distribution of Scores on Variables A *and* B

	Raw Scores		Ranks		Scores Categorized as "Above" or "Below"	
Subject	A	B	A	B	A	B
1	26	12	9	7	B	B
2	37	7	5	10	A	B
3	58	24	1	2	A	A
4	46	21	2	3	A	A
5	45	29	3	1	A	A
6	22	11	10	8	B	B
7	33	16	6	5	B	B
8	28	10	8	9	B	B
9	41	18	4	4	A	A
10	30	14	7	6	B	B

on each of the two variables. Start with the data in the far right-hand column, and ask a very simple question: is there a tendency for people who are above the mean on variable *A* to be above the mean on variable *B?* This is another way of asking if variables *A* and *B* are associated. Since we have only two designations for each variable—*above* or *below*—we must use a measure of association that is suited to this gross categorization. In this case, we will use a coefficient known as a chi-square, which will tell us something about the degree of association of variables *A* and *B*. The formula for the chi-square is:

$$\chi^2 = \Sigma \frac{(O - E)^2}{E}$$

The terms O and E correspond to observed frequency and expected frequency, respectively. Any elementary statistics text will describe the computational procedures. A "significant" chi-square value would allow us to conclude that variables *A* and *B* were associated, i.e., if an individual scored above the mean on variable *A*, it would be likely that her score would be above the mean on variable *B*.[2]

The use of chi-square as a measure of association can be very valuable when we have nominal data. Suppose we wanted to look at the relationship between *sex* and *preference for potential rewards for performance*. If we

---

[2] Since chi-square values are unstable when the expected value in any cell is less than 5, we will not calculate a chi-square for the data in Table 2–1.

look at the responses to the question, "Would you like to receive more responsibility as a reward for good performance?" and separate those responses for 50 males and 50 females, the data might look like those in Table 2–2. It is clear from this table that there is some degree of association or relationship between sex of the respondent and the response to the question. More females than males prefer increased responsibility as a reward for good performance.

The chi-square value for these data is 36.00. Once again, this value is "significant" and allows us to conclude that there is some relationship between sex and preference for a specific kind of reward.

When our data are ordinal in nature rather than nominal, there are other techniques available for determining degree of association. Instead of simply looking at the relationship between two variables in a "frequency" sense, we can now make statements about the tendency of high ranks on one variable to go with high ranks on another variable.

Consider the data in the middle column of Table 2–1, the ranks of the individuals on variables A and B. We might now ask the question, "Do high ranks on variable A tend to be associated with high ranks on variable B?" This is a more refined question than the previous one, which dealt only with position above or below the mean. We are permitted to ask this more refined question because our data are more refined—they are ranks instead of simple categories. We can analyze these data using the Spearman Rank-Order Correlation Method. This method yields a coefficient referred to as *rho*, indicating the degree of association between two sets of rank orders. *Rho* coefficients vary from −1.00 to +1.00. In Table 2–3, we have presented the formula for *rho* and computed the value for the data in the middle columns of Table 2–1.

A realistic example of the use of *rho* might help us understand this measure of association. Suppose a police department wanted to look at the relationship between success of officers in the police academy and their actual performance on the street. For the sake of convenience, let's say that we will look at the academy graduating class of 1979 and assume that all of these graduates start out under the command of one particular captain, who follows their progress closely for the first six months following academy graduation. When it comes time to measure the association be-

TABLE 2–2

Frequency Table: Desire for Increased Responsibility

Sex	Increased Responsibility	
	Yes	No
Male	10	40
Female	40	10

TABLE 2–3
Spearman's Rank Order Correlation Coefficient

Persons	Ranks		Differences	
	Variable A	Variable B	D	D²
1	9	7	2	4
2	5	10	−5	25
3	1	2	−1	1
4	2	3	−1	1
5	3	1	2	4
6	10	8	2	4
7	6	5	1	1
8	8	9	−1	1
9	4	4	0	0
10	7	6	1	1
			0	42

$$rho = 1 - \frac{6\Sigma D^2}{N(N^2 - 1)}$$

$$rho = 1 - \frac{(6)(42)}{10(100 - 1)} \quad rho = 1 - \frac{252}{990} \quad rho = 1 - .25 \quad rho = .75$$

tween academy success and on-the-street success, we find that the only data available concerning academy performance are the ranks of the patrol officers in the graduating class. Furthermore, since the department has no readily available form for rating success on the job, the captain ranks these rookie officers from "best" through "worst" on overall performance. We can then compute *rho* for these two sets of ranks to determine the degree of relationship between police academy success and on-the-job success.

In a sense, the nominal relationship we described between sex and reward preference allowed us to predict one class membership from another class membership; that is, females were more likely than males to prefer increased responsibility. With ordinal data we can take one more step in prediction: we can draw conclusions about the tendency for high ranks on one variable to be related to high or low ranks on another variable.

While it certainly may be valuable to know the relationship between class standing and performance rank, there are some problems presented by the nature of the scale of measurement we used. What if we do not want to predict the *rank* or *relative* performance of the officers, but the absolute level of performance in some respect (e.g., number of arrests per month)? This is very often the case. The rank of a particular individual, both in the academy graduating class and in the performance rankings, depends to a great degree on the other people with whom the officer is compared. This means that the true performance levels and the differences between officers are unknown. Without a zero reference point and a unit of measurement, we do not know whether the first-ranked officer in the graduating class of '78 was better or worse than the first-ranked officer in the class of '79. Similarly, while they may each have predicted ranks of "1" in performance on the street, we are not at all sure that their absolute levels of performance (i.e., number of arrests per month) will be equal.

Suppose we had, in addition to the class standing of the recruit, the score on a final examination based on the academy training program. In addition, instead of performance rankings, suppose we had some criterion, or dependent variable, like "number of arrests." With data in that form, we would now be able to estimate the number of arrests related to a given final examination score. In a more technical sense, we would be able to predict performance scores from final exam scores, to the degree that academy success and on-the-job success (arrests) were "correlated." The correlational coefficient, r, is a measure of association for interval measures.

THE CONCEPT OF CORRELATION

Francis Galton, a cousin of Charles Darwin, was interested in the hereditary aspects of height and weight. To get an idea of the relationship between the heights of parents and the heights of offspring, he plotted the respective heights on a graph much like the one displayed in Figure 2–1. To put all the parents and children on a common measuring scale, he transformed the height scores of parents and offspring so that the two groups had identical means. Thus, both sets of data were in standardized, "z-score," form.[3]

Next, Galton computed the means of the heights of those offspring whose parents had a certain height. For example, in Figure 2–1, he would have computed the average heights of all children whose fathers were in the first category (60 inches), then the second category (62 inches), the third, and so on. He found that the means of these columns fell along a straight line represented by the solid line in Figure 2–1.

Examine Figure 2–1 for a moment. You will see that if the line were horizontal instead of tilted up and to the right, we might conclude that fathers' heights were not associated with sons' heights. But Figure 2–1 seems to show that the heights of sons whose fathers are of a *particular* height show less variability than the heights of all sons, regardless of fathers' heights. In our example, the heights of sons whose fathers are 60 inches

---

[3] An obtained, or "raw," score is converted to a standard score by determining its deviation from the mean in standard deviation units, thus:

$$Z_i = \frac{X_i - M}{S.D.}$$

where X_i is a raw score, M is the sample mean and $S.D.$ the sample standard deviation. The result is a new distribution of scores with $M = 0$ and $S.D. = 1.00$.

FIGURE 2–1

A Graphic Plot of the Heights of Fathers and Their Sons

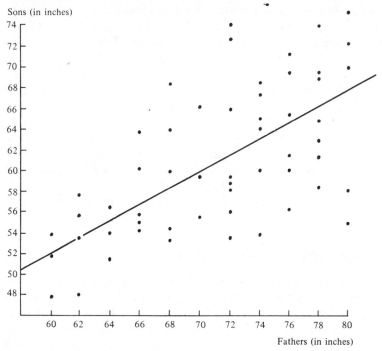

tall vary between 48 and 54 inches, whereas the heights of all sons (regardless of fathers' height) vary from 48 inches to 74 inches. In terms of our earlier discussion, knowledge of fathers' heights reduces the variance or variability of sons' heights. This tendency for scores to cluster around some central point is known as *regression towards the mean*. In Figure 2–1, the data might be examined to see if there is a tendency for sons' heights to cluster around (or regress on) fathers' heights.

While psychologists of today are not that interested in the relationships between the heights of parents and offspring, the nature of Galton's analysis lends itself to many other areas of concern. As an example, look at the data in Figure 2–2. These data represent the scores for a sample of people on two variables: years of formal education *(X)*, and performance on the job *(Y)*. Look at the distribution of the data points for each of the two variables—these distributions appear at the edge of each of the axes of the graph.

If you know the number of years of formal education an individual possesses, you also know something about the range of performance scores that individual is likely to exhibit. In other words, the variation of performance scores is reduced when we know something about the formal education

FIGURE 2–2

Scatterplot of Education and Performance

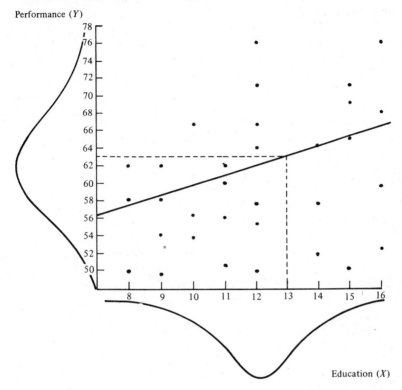

score. This is the essence of using correlational analyses to predict behavior. It doesn't matter whether we are trying to predict performance from job satisfaction, group effectiveness from leadership style, or job success from a test score—the operations are basically the same as those identified and formalized by Galton.

You will notice in Figure 2–2 that no one in the sample had 13 years of formal education. How would we predict a performance score for someone with 13 years of formal education who applied for a job? We would simply interpolate from the available data. We could use the straight line that we plotted through the column means to predict the performance score. We would go up the column representing 13 years of formal education until we reached the line, and then read across for the predicted performance score (63).

While this is a valuable technique for prediction, it would be a little cumbersome to drag out a graph each time we wanted to make a prediction. Fortunately, we can accomplish the same task algebraically.

Since we know that the general equation for a straight line is $Y = aX$

+ b, we can compute a specific equation for our line in Figure 2–2 and use it to obtain a predicted performance score for any individual, once we know his years of education.

A co-worker of Galton, Karl Pearson, was able to show that the strength of the linear relationship between any two variables could be derived from the slope of the regression line. In our formula for the straight line above, the slope is identified as a, since the value of a will vary as a function of the scale of the raw data. When both sets of scores have been standardized, the value of a, the slope of the line, is equivalent to the *correlation coefficient* describing the linear relationship between X and Y. Figure 2–3 presents several different scatterplots of data representing varying correlation coefficients (often designated simply as r).

An inspection of Figure 2–3 reveals something about the correlation coefficient. Specifically, it seems to vary in two important respects—sign and value. The correlation coefficient can assume values from +1.00 to −1.00. The sign (+ or −) tells us about the direction of the relationship. The plus (+) sign indicates a positive relationship between two variables; as one variable increases in value, so does the other. A minus (−) sign indicates an inverse relationship; as the value of one of the variables increases, the value of the other variable decreases. An example of a positive relationship might be height and weight, while an example of a negative relationship might be age and visual acuity. This also indicates that as the value of the correlation coefficient increases, prediction becomes more accurate.

FIGURE 2–3

Scatterplots Representing Varying Degrees of Correlation

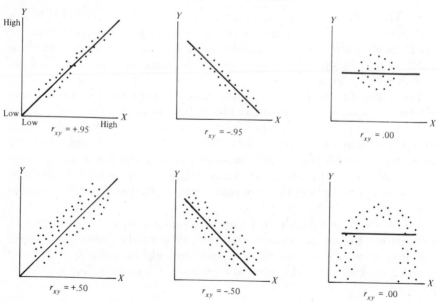

In applied psychology there is an important distinction between a regression formula and a correlation coefficient. A correlation coefficient is an index that tells us something about the strength of the relationship between two variables. However, since we had to change the scales of the two variables so that they had identical means and standard deviations, we cannot make direct predictions of the expected raw score on one variable from the obtained raw score on another variable. We must combine the information about the strength of the relationship with the original means and standard deviations of the two variables to make such a prediction. We can do that by means of a regression equation. The means and the standard deviations of the two variables enable us to calculate the values of a and b in the equation for a straight line presented earlier in this section. With this information, we can predict a value Y for any given value of X. The strength of correlation will determine the accuracy of that prediction.

If we return once again to the data presented in Table 2–1, we can calculate the correlation coefficient for the scores presented in the left-hand column of that table. The raw score formula for calculating r is

$$r = \frac{n\Sigma xy - \Sigma x\Sigma y}{\sqrt{n\Sigma x^2 - (\Sigma x)^2}\sqrt{n\Sigma y^2 - (\Sigma y)^2}}$$

The actual value of r for our data is .75. There is a much simpler computation formula for r based on Z scores (as defined in the footnote on p. 27). This formula is simply

$$r = \frac{\Sigma Z_x Z_y}{N}$$

As a matter of fact, the reason that the raw-score formula looks so complicated is that it first converts raw scores to Z scores before determining the correlation coefficient.

Occasionally, you may run into some forms of the correlation coefficient that are intended for special situations. If one of the variables under consideration is dichotomous (the scores fall in one or the other of two categories) and the other variable is continuous (scores may assume any value), the resulting correlation coefficient may be called a "point-biserial" correlation coefficient; if both variables are dichotomous, the resulting coefficient may be referred to as a "phi coefficient." These may be interpreted in exactly the same manner as the normal correlation coefficient.

Another question related to the association among and between variables is the treatment of multiple variables. What do we do when we have scores from seven different tests and want to predict performance from them? Do we compute the correlation coefficients one at a time, or do we first add the test scores together? As it turns out, we use a procedure known as *multiple regression*. In this procedure, the variables are combined in a way that is most efficient for predicting scores on the dependent variable, performance. What we actually do is to form a new variable that is a linear composite of the test scores, and correlate it with the dependent variable, performance. In effect, then, we are still correlating only two variables, the one that we are attempting to predict and the other derived from the several scores. We will see some specific examples of the use of multiple regression analysis in Chapter 5.

You will remember that we began this chapter with a single problem: how to account for the differences among and within individuals. The correlation coefficient is an attempt to account for variations of behavior on one dimension in terms of variation on a second dimension. So, for example, we attempt to account for and predict variation in job performance in terms of a second variable, perhaps a measure of a particular aptitude. To the degree to which these two variables covary, we have explained the differences among individuals on the performance dimension. In a sense, the larger the correlation coefficient, the more we have reduced the unexplained variability among individuals on some dimension of interest. In terms of *predicting behavior*, this means that we have increased the accuracy with which we can predict performance scores from test, or "predictor," scores.

Multiple regression is another way of approaching the same basic problem. In this case, however, we are hoping to reduce the variability in some dependent or consequent variable by *combining* independent or antecedent variables. In the case of the simple correlation problem, we attempt to account for the variation in one variable by noting the variation in a *second variable*. In the case of multiple correlation or regression, we have attempted to account for the variation in one variable by noting the joint variation in *several other variables*.

Often the problem is one of understanding the variability of many variables at the same time. For example, we might have a set of statements such as those posed in Figure 2–4. The question we might ask of ourselves in analyzing the responses of individuals to these questions is, "While there are 20 questions, are there really 20 *different* categories of information represented?" The answer is probably no. Just from inspection, we would expect the answers to items 1, 5, 7, 15, and 18 to be correlated; they all seem to deal with pay. We would expect that the same would be true for items 2, 3, 11, 14 and 17—each of these items asks the person to indicate satisfaction with supervision. Table 2–4 confirms our suspicions— the intercorrelations are high among the items that describe pay; the same is true of the items that describe supervision. As a result, when contrasting person A's responses with person B's responses, we need not make the comparison on 20 different dimensions—we can reduce those dimensions to a smaller, more basic set. This is one of the major goals of a technique known as *factor analysis*—to take a set of variables and reduce that set to some smaller set on the basis of the intercorrelations of those variables. The logic behind the operation is that there is a *factor* underlying the responses to the items that correlate highly with each other. In the previous

FIGURE 2–4
Job Satisfaction Statements

1. My pay is pretty good.
2. On the whole, my supervisor is pretty fair.
3. I wish my supervisor paid more attention to me.
4. I do not get along with my co-workers particularly well.
5. I make about the amount of money that I am worth.
6. I like to pal around with my co-workers off-the-job.
7. I would like to make more money.
8. My job is quite interesting.
9. The promotional policy at this organization leaves a lot to be desired.
10. There is little challenge in my work.
11. My supervisor is thought of as a fair individual.
12. I prefer to work alone rather than with others.
13. I have no freedom in my work.
14. I can't seem to get the help I need from my supervisor.
15. I would gladly change jobs for the opportunity to make more money.
16. I am happy with the vacation plan.
17. I could do more work if it were not for the interference from my supervisor.
18. An individual's pay should be determined on the basis of the worth of the individual to the company.
19. I occasionally have to do things which go against my conscience in this job.
20. I am in a "dead-end" job.

example, we might propose that there is a "satisfaction with pay" factor accounting for the joint variation of items 1, 5, 7, 15, and 18.

The process is a complicated one mathematically, and we will not go into it here. We will, however, introduce some characteristics of a factor analysis that will prove useful in later discussions. Table 2–5 represents the result of a hypothetical factor analysis of the data in Table 2–4. Through the analysis, we have identified five *factors* in the responses (another way of saying the same thing might be that we have reduced the number of dimensions of difference that must be considered from 20 to 5). The entries in the table are known as *factor loadings*. These factor loadings are the correlations between the individual variables and the underlying factor. In other words, they tell us what the factors are made up of. As correlations, they can assume values between +1.00 and −1.00. The higher the value, the stronger the degree of association between the variable and the factor. Therefore, if we want to know what the nature of any particular factor is, we identify the highest factor loadings (underlined in Table 2–5) and go back to the original variables for the meaning of the particular factor.

Therefore, in Table 2–5, some possible labels for the factors might be "satisfaction with pay" (I), "satisfaction with supervision" (II), "satisfaction with the work itself" (III), and "satisfaction with co-workers" (IV). The fifth factor has no clear interpretation.

TABLE 2–4

Intercorrelations among Responses to 20 Job Satisfaction Statements

Variable

Variable	1	2	3	4	5	6	7	8	9	10	11	12	13	14	15	16	17	18	19	20
1	X	.14	.31	.04	.71	.34	-.63	.41	.21	.07	.19	.19	.21	.23	-.75	.32	.01	.64	.07	.07
2		X	-.64	.07	.04	.22	.22	.32	.10	.13	.64	.17	.14	-.71	.01	.04	-.62	.21	.07	.41
3			X	.43	.17	.09	.11	.01	.13	.40	-.48	.06	.31	.54	.07	.31	.39	.40	.13	.36
4				X	.21	-.75	.26	.07	.22	.23	-.41	.61	.09	.01	.21	.26	.21	.27	.23	.02
5					X	.36	-.60	.14	.27	.22	.19	.27	.17	.04	-.48	.43	.14	.71	.22	.26
6						X	.09	.01	.32	.27	.06	-.49	.14	.31	.10	.14	.17	.21	.06	.31
7							X	.27	.02	.01	.17	.41	-.39	.28	.60	.29	.34	-.85	.14	.02
8								X	.41	-.64	.31	.64	-.75	.21	.06	.06	.07	.26	.27	-.81
9									X	.13	.17	.13	.01	.06	.13	.14	.07	.07	.17	.19
10										X	.02	.19	.61	.14	.05	.74	.29	.22	.19	.58
11											X	.17	.23	-.64	.22	.41	-.81	.48	-.17	.45
12												X	.19	.36	.06	.09	.13	.13	.04	.17
13													X	.19	.27	.41	.07	.21	.31	.68
14														X	.14	.00	.58	.19	.26	.06
15															X	.15	.26	-.64	.04	.07
16																X	.36	.14	.11	.40
17																	X	.28	.04	.32
18																		X	.33	.17
19																			X	.14
20																				X

There is a second characteristic of factor analysis to which we will refer in some of our later discussions of research results. If we assume that our initial problem is to account for all the joint variability in responses to the 20 items, we can determine the *relative importance* of the various factors in reducing or explaining this variability. The term usually used to describe this characteristic of factors is the "percentage of variance accounted for" by the factor. In Table 2–5, this value is indicated in the last entry in each column. From an inspection of these values, you will see that satisfaction with pay accounts for the greatest amount of the variation in responses. In a sense, this means that the psychological aspect of pay seems to pervade (or possibly override) responses to other questions.

All of the analyses described to this point have assumed that the relationships among and between variables were strictly linear. In most cases, that is a good assumption. The linear model of prediction has proved quite valuable in applied areas of psychology. There are, however, instances in which a curvilinear relationship is the best-guess estimate of the way in which two variables are related. The most common example is that of the relationship between intelligence and job success in certain routine

TABLE 2–5

Factor Loadings for Factor Analysis of Responses to Job Satisfaction Statements

Variable	Factor				
	I	*II*	*III*	*IV*	*V*
1	.80	.03	.24	.17	.01
2	.35	.71	.06	.11	.06
3	.21	−.72	.19	.01	.19
4	.06	.05	.19	−.71	.43
5	.64	.43	.27	.06	.22
6	.17	.01	.41	.62	.07
7	−.40	.02	.13	.22	.03
8	.21	.14	.56	.17	.27
9	.02	.07	.07	.14	.17
10	.06	.44	−.54	.08	.24
11	.14	.06	.09	.16	.41
12	.21	.19	.01	−.74	.15
13	.26	.14	−.46	.21	.34
14	.09	−.61	.21	.30	.30
15	.64	.01	.17	.02	.01
16	.14	.07	.29	.16	.32
17	.22	−.53	.31	.17	.07
18	.81	.04	.02	.31	.14
19	.19	.02	.11	.01	−.41
20	.01	.14	−.71	.23	.26
Percent variance accounted for	14%	11%	10%	10%	06%

FIGURE 2–5

*Hypothetical Data Set Describing the Relationship between
Intellectual Ability and Performance*

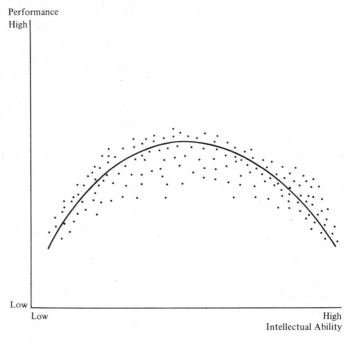

tasks. Figure 2–5 presents such a hypothetical relationship. From this figure, you can see that intermediate scores on the intelligence test are associated with high performance, while either high or low scores are associated with low performance. If we tried to fit a single straight line to these data, our prediction from that line would not be very good. On the other hand, if we fit a curved line to the data and predicted from the curved line instead of the straight line, our prediction would be much better. In addition to making statistical sense, this curvilinear relationship might fit well with our observations that people of subnormal intelligence are unable to master the requirements of the job, while people of above average intelligence are bored by the tasks.

A generally accepted measure of correlation that includes both linear and curvilinear components is known as the *Eta coefficient* or the *correlation ratio* (McNemar, 1969). When the relationship between two variables is truly linear, the correlation ratio and the Pearson product-moment coefficient[4] will be equivalent. As the relationship between the two variables departs from linear and becomes more curvilinear, the Pearson product

---

[4] Correlations are computed by transforming the raw scores to scores that represent deviations from the mean of the respective variables. These deviations are technically known as "moments." Hence the correlation is sometimes referred to as the "product-moment" correlation coefficient.

moment coefficient will decrease, but the value of *Eta* will be affected only by the spread of scores around the (curved) regression line.

Thus, for the hypothetical data presented in Figure 2–5, the Pearson product-moment coefficient might be .03 and the value of *Eta* might be .85. In this example, one would conclude that there is a strong relationship between performance and intellectual ability, but it is not a linear one.

EXPERIMENTAL METHODS

As stated earlier, the basic method of research is the *systematic observation* of the behavior of our subject matter, regardless of whether that subject matter is a chemical compound, a body cell, a society, or some aspect of the behavior of a person doing a task. Science has built up a set of principles and rules of observation that increase the likelihood that the observations will lead the scientist to correct interpretations of the phenomena observed. An experiment is nothing more than a set of procedures for applying these rules so that at least *some* of the alternative interpretations are ruled out while some others (ideally, only one) can be justified.

What is the nature of these rules of observation—or experimental controls? We cannot cover the rules of science in a few sentences, but we can suggest some of the concepts of control. First, the scientist has rules or guiding principles dealing with the adequacy of the sample of observations made. One does not "jump to conclusions" on the basis of a single observation, especially in observing something as complex as human behavior (and as variable as human beings); a sample of observations or different "specimens" of the subject matter is required. Sampling adequacy means more than just the *number* of observations the researcher makes, however. The observations must be "fair," or unbiased; they must fairly sample representatives of the larger population from which the sample was taken and from which the researcher wants to generalize any conclusions. Thus, for example, the researcher who wants to draw conclusions about the effects of music on the productivity of "blue-collar workers" (the population) cannot limit herself to observing only young women assemblers in an electronics plant (the sample). Or, conversely, if she samples a small homogenous group, she must be cautious about generalizing the findings beyond the sample. Adequate sampling will be considered further in Chapter 3 under the headings "Reliability" and "Validity."

In our earlier discussion of levels of measurement, we saw that as one goes from nominal to interval measures, the potential precision of observation increases. Precise measurement means precise observation. Without an interval scale of, say, intelligence, we are perhaps limited to classifying our observations into "very bright," "bright," "about average," "dull," "defective," or the like. What is more, different observers may not agree on the limits of these categories and as a result will classify similar observations in different ways. Thus, lack of precision may also lead to ambiguity and lack of agreement in the classification of observations.

The tasks we set for people to do, the physical environment in which the tasks are carried out, the time of day, the instructions, the incentives, and in some cases, the experimenter, are factors which may affect the behavior being observed. Unless these conditions are standardized so that the only conditions varying are those which the researcher systematically manipulates (the independent variables), then the interpretation of the observations in terms of cause-effect relationships is extremely limited.

The last sentence states the logic of the experiment: variations in A cause variations in B when we can rule out the possibilities that variations in other "extraneous" variables occurred.

A Problem of Control

If an experimental psychologist wanted to study the relationship between mechanical aptitude and job performance, he might go through the following steps:

1. Go out and buy a bottle of mechanical aptitude.
2. Order a litter of human subjects that had been isolated from the potentially contaminating influences of experience with work settings.
3. Inject the subjects with varying amounts of mechanical aptitude and observe their behavior on a carefully controlled experimental version of job performance.

In this case, the control that the experimentalist exerts over the study is rather direct, free from all variables that might affect job performance *except* mechanical aptitude.

Unfortunately (or fortunately, perhaps), we have not quite reached the point where this sequence of operations is possible. In applied settings, we often have to depend on statistical rather than experimental control. This type of statistical control is often referred to as "partialing out" unwanted influences. This is because we are taking out the influence of a variable that might obscure the relationship of interest. In Figure 2–6, we have diagrammed the control problem described above. A, B, and C stand for mechanical aptitude, job performance, and experience, respectively. We are interested in knowing what the relationship is between mechanical aptitude and job performance. As you can see from the figure, since job experience seems to be related to both mechanical aptitude and job performance, to know how strongly mechanical aptitude alone is related to job performance, it becomes necessary to eliminate or partial out the influence of experience. In practice, we do not literally take out the effect of experience; we hold it constant. In our example, we might accomplish this by computing a separate aptitude-performance correlation coefficient for groups of workers with similar degrees of experience. Thus, we might have four correlation coefficients representing the aptitude-performance correlation: for workers with less than one year of experience; one to three years; four to eight years; and nine years or more of experience. If we

FIGURE 2–6
The Problem of "Control"

Mechanical Aptitude   Job Performance

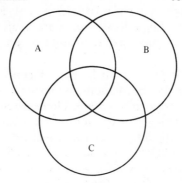

Experience

were then to average those correlation coefficients, we would have effectively eliminated the influence of experience on the aptitude-performance relationship. Fortunately, there are formulas available that make the process of partialing much simpler, computationally.

The design of the data analysis we just described might be useful in another way. Suppose we had reason to believe that the relationship between mechanical aptitude and performance *did* vary as a function of work experience and we were interested in exactly *how* experience influenced the relationship. We might find that the correlation between mechanical aptitude and performance is very high for the "less-than-one-year" group but negligible for the other groups. We might then conclude that after a short period of time on the job, factors other than mechanical aptitude affect performance (factors such as motivation or job satisfaction). If we had not bothered to look at the separate relationships, or had simply partialed out influence of experience, we would have been deprived of some very important and interesting information about the aptitude-performance relationship. In this case, experience would be labelled a *moderator variable.* Moderator variables *affect the degree and kind of relationship between two other variables without necessarily being correlated with either of the other two variables* (Blum and Naylor, 1968). In other words, they are variables that *moderate* a relationship. Probably the most recent example is that of race. In many employment settings, it is proposed that the relationship between test scores and success is not the same for blacks as it is for whites. Another way of stating this is that race is a moderator variable— it moderates the relationship between test success and job success. More will be said of this particular example in Chapter 5. The idea of a moderator variable is not unique to industrial and organizational psychology. In much of the sociological literature, the same technique is known as *stratification,* or the *analysis of data by level.* In an experimental design, such variables might enter into the design as "control variables." It is not uncommon to see separate analyses in experimental studies for male and female subjects. If we were doing an analysis of the relationship of observed test and performance scores, we might also suggest a separate analysis of the correlations for men and women. In this case, sex would be identified as a moderator variable.

The discussion leads us to a final topic of concern, the nature of the research design. It should be obvious by now that control is related to the setting in which the research is done. There are several different settings in which an I/O psychologist may find herself. Four major approaches to gathering data are: (1) the laboratory experiment; (2) the field experiment; (3) the field study; and (4) the simulation. Each of these has its own strengths and weaknesses and will be dealt with individually.

The principal differences among the four major designs for gathering data are in terms of the extent to which (1) the conditions of observation can be systematically controlled by the experimenter, (2) the "treatments" (experimental or independent variables) can be systematically manipulated, and (3) the behavior observations (dependent variables) can be prescribed so as to be representative of some larger population.

A Laboratory Experiment

Many jobs require a person to search a screen for information. As an example, a radar operator is constantly attempting to keep track of one or more objects that may change position, may increase or decrease in number, and may change in their proximity to one another. If that radar operator happens to be an air traffic controller at Chicago's O'Hare airport, the "objects" to which we are referring take on a new meaning.

There are many aspects of this job that would be of interest to the industrial psychologist. For example, how are individuals selected and trained for this job, what types of variables affect their job satisfaction and work motivation, and what kinds of training programs are most efficient for teaching trainees the multitude of tasks that make up this job? Another important aspect of the job would be the nature of the equipment that the controller uses to accomplish task goals. Suppose we are interested in the question of whether the number of objects on the radar screen or "display" affects search time or the speed with which any *one* object can be found and identified.

Carter (1979) has studied exactly that question in the laboratory. He was concerned with the characteristics of the display that affect a subject's search time. He constructed an experimental apparatus that allowed him to vary two characteristics of the display: the number of objects present at any one time, and the relative position of those objects on the screen. There were two levels of density—30 objects or 60 objects. There were three levels of object proximity to the outer edge of the screen. Objects

had either 0, 1, or 2 adjoining "neighbors." The objects could appear in either the top half or the bottom half of the display. In experimental design language, this was a 2 × 3 × 3 × 2 design; the numbers represent the levels of the various factor. Thus, there were many different experimental conditions to which subjects could be assigned. Figure 2–7 presents a few typical displays to which subjects might have been exposed.

The subjects were college students. They were asked to sit in a quiet, darkened room and view a screen like the one depicted in the photograph of the air traffic controller. They were given a number or "target" to search for, and the amount of time it took to find that number was the measure of search speed. Subjects were assigned to conditions randomly and were given training trials prior to test trials. They were also given vision tests prior to the experiment to eliminate any subjects with serious visual deficiencies.

An examination of the results revealed that density had a rather substantial effect on search time. When 30 objects were present, the average search time was 5.5 seconds. But when 60 objects were present, the average search time was 11 seconds! It was also found that targets in the center of the display could be found more quickly than targets toward the outside of the display. Search time was not affected by the number of neighboring

FIGURE 2–7

Experimental Displays

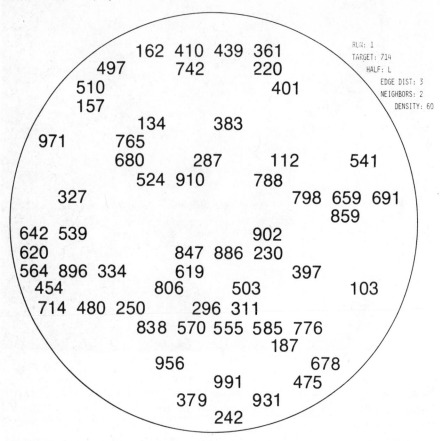

objects. Finally, search time was quicker for targets in the upper half of the display than it was for those in the lower half of the display.

There were a number of advantages to studying this problem in a laboratory experiment. First, operators could be selected and randomly assigned to various experimental conditions. Second, the effect of experience could be controlled through the training trials. Third, it was possible to screen out individuals who might have physical disabilities that might hinder the investigation. Finally, it was possible to make very specific and refined manipulations of the independent variables (display characteristics) and make very exact recordings of the dependent variable (search time).

There were some disadvantages to this approach also, expecially if one were concerned with what people do in real job situations. The results of the experiment were based on observations of subjects who had only brief exposure to the task. Thus, the task was novel, and overall performance might have been quite different from what it would be with actual radar

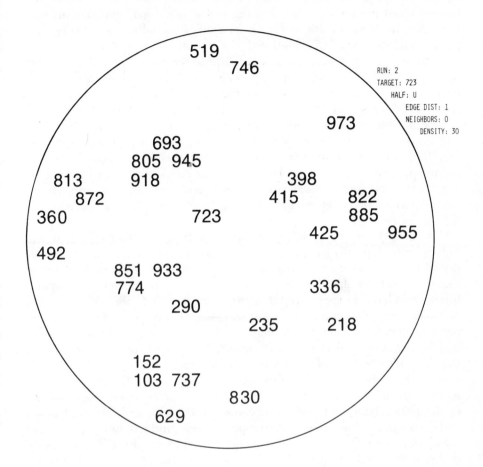

operators on several longer shifts or after several months on the job. Further-more, the more difficult task conditions may have been seen as most chal-lenging by the subjects in the brief period of the experiment, and they may have given more effort to those than to the easier conditions. Finally, the quiet, darkened room might have been very different from actual control tower conditions.

A Field Experiment

Assuming that the task previously described is actually one that radar operators engage in frequently, we might want to carry out a field experiment to test the findings in real settings with a more appropriate subject popula-tion. To carry out a true experiment, we must be able to manipulate the variables (the conditions of the task), much as we did in the laboratory experiment. It is conceivable that several radar screens in an air traffic control center might be modified to allow for the experimental manipulations without prohibitive costs. For our hypothetical field experiment, suppose that there are positions for 12 air traffic controllers in a tower, and three could be modified to present the various combinations of display conditions. To obtain realistic task conditions, we might not tell our twelve operators which three were subjects. We would then ask our operators to find various targets that appear on the screen. We might then record speed and accuracy of target identification for later analysis.

The advantages of the field study lie in its realism and the fact that one need not be concerned with generalizing from the laboratory to the job. This does not mean that the field study is free of problems, artifacts, or ambiguities. As we will see later, a famous series of field experiments— the Hawthorne studies—was plagued with problems, and the appropriate interpretations of those research findings continues to be a controversial topic.

The basis for some of the problems in a field experiment is that the experimenter typically has much less control over the conditions of observation than in a laboratory experiment. In our hypothetical example, suppose that some of the radar units are older models than others, that some operators are much more experienced than others, or that there are work stoppages or radar screen downtime, or a host of other factors that might influence performance, other than the display-speed relationship; furthermore, there may be *negative transfer of training* effects to account for, or to overcome; that is, while one type of display may be inherently better than the others, it may take a good deal of time to overcome, or unlearn, the habits learned on the typical radar displays. It is difficult to do well-controlled experiments in the field setting and there is a certain amount of luck involved when one finds matched or replicate situations, groups, and machines, to provide the appropriate settings for the experimental conditions. Furthermore, there is always the possibility that the experimenter or the experiment as a social happening, will be viewed as more potent variables for behavioral change than the experimental manipulations.

The Field Study. In the field study, the researcher observes, measures, and records what he finds *without* any experimental manipulation. If he finds work groups of different sizes and different levels of morale, he may determine the extent to which these two variables are correlated. However, since he does not manipulate group size as an independent variable or institute other controls such as equal distributions of age, sex, and job tenure among his groups, he is not able to conclude that size of the work group bears a causal relationship to morale. It may be that small work groups tend to be involved in teamwork and it is teamwork that affects morale. It is not likely that morale affects group size, but there are many other correlations in which a B → A causal interpretation is just as defensible as an A → B interpretation.

A field study of the effects of different radar displays like those involved in our laboratory and field experiments would depend upon finding cases of the different machine configurations and then relating these to job proficiency. The likelihood that enough cases could be found of the various configurations or that the cases would be comparable in terms of other variables (age, experience of workers, condition of the machines, similarity of tasks to be performed, and so on) would be very small. However, certain statistical controls might be substituted for experimental controls. Thus, "months of experience" on the job or "age," or "condition of the machine" might be partialed out of the relationship between machine configuration and job performance. As we discussed earlier, partial correlation techniques involve taking into account the relationship of some third variable to the two variables under observation. That is, the relationship between A and B as reflected in a correlation coefficient, is adjusted to take into account the relationship of C to the A–B correlation. It is as though C were made constant and then the A–B relationship examined.

The Simulation Study. The purpose of simulation is to gain some of the control that may be absent in a field experiment, but at the same time to approximate a realistic operating situation so that one can generalize from the research findings to the operational task. The key word here is "realistic," and the critical question for simulation is, "What aspects of the working situation have to be simulated to ensure that the research task is realistic in all those characteristics that may affect the performance of the operators on the task?" This may include simulation of unusual environmental conditions, such as noise, heat, vibration, or even weightlessness. Thus, for example, simulators of the Gemini and Apollo space vehicles included such features as wide-screen projections of the stars and planets, which the astronauts viewed from their cabin, just as they would later in actual space travel. Furthermore, computers were programmed to provide realistic information about the effects of control actions that the astronauts performed; in some cases, they lived in the simulator for several days with realistic "life-support" conditions, including space suits, special food supplies, and oxygen conditions. Some simulators were built to test an individual's endurance and ability to perform under conditions of gravitational forces such as would be experienced in takeoff and reentry.

Returning to our radar problem, we might set our radar screens up in a testing room that simulates as closely as possible actual control-tower conditions. In addition, we might use actual traffic controllers as our subjects. We could then present any "conditions" we wanted and accurately measure the variables of importance.

The major advantages of simulation are realism and control. In addition, as was the case in our radar example, field experiments in which tests are made under actual operations are simply not possible. One cannot risk equipment or lives to answer design or feasibility questions. Simulating the dynamics of the man-machine-environment interactions is usually a very expensive proposition. If something is left out, the researcher or the user of the information may be left with the nagging doubt that the results might have differed in an important way had that aspect been simulated.

The astronaut knows performance in the simulator is not for real, and there is no way to assure that the tensions, anxieties, and emotions of the real situation will not have a profound effect on the individual's behavior and that of the system that she controls.

We will return to some of these issues throughout the book, particularly in the section dealing with engineering psychology and man-machine systems. Meanwhile, each of the four types of research discussed has its place in the search for knowledge in industrial/organizational psychology. Some question may be best approached in the laboratory, while other questions can be assessed only in field experiments, field studies, or simulation research.

SUMMARY

A major task for psychology is to explain the differences among individuals. But before these differences can be explained, they must be adequately measured. They can be measured only with varying degrees of refinement. There are several levels of measurement or refinement that are characteristically used in psychology. Nominal measurement is simply a labeling process. Ordinal measurement enables one to identify the rank or order of a set of measurements. Interval measurement provides information about the distances between ordered objects or measurements. Ratio measurement allows one to speak in absolute terms about the distances between ordered objects or measurements.

The level of measurement used determines the statistics that may be computed on a set of data. Central tendency, dispersion, and degree of association are described in accordance with the level of measurement or refinement used in data collection.

Galton was one of the first to introduce the notions of regression and correlation. The correlation coefficient was constructed as a simple way of describing the relationship between the heights of fathers and sons. Correlation is a procedure for describing the linear relationship between two variables, while regression is a technique for predicting a score on one variable from the score on another variable. Correlation coefficients consist of two distinct characteristics—sign and value. The sign of a correlation coefficient provides information about the direction of the relationship, while the numerical value of the correlation indicates the strength of the relationship. Correlations vary in value between +1.00 and −1.00. There are techniques available for computing correlations between noncontinuous variables as well as between several independent variables and one dependent variable. Factor analysis is a technique for reducing a large set of variables to a smaller set on the basis of intercorrelations.

There are several ways in which data might be gathered in industrial and organizational psychology. Four popular ways are: (1) the laboratory experiment, (2) the field experiment, (3) the field study, and (4) the simulation study. Each of these approaches has its own unique advantages and disadvantages. Two major concerns for any approach to data collection are: (1) realism and (2) the elimination of extraneous variables (control). Our ability to derive useful conclusions from a data set depends on the conditions of realism and control.

REFERENCES

Blum, M., & Naylor, J. *Industrial psychology.* New York: Harper & Row, 1968.

Carter, R. *Visual search and color coding.* Unpublished manuscript. University Park, 1979.

McNemar, Q. *Psychological statistics* (4th ed.). New York: Wiley, 1969.

Stevens, S. S. *Handbook of experimental psychology.* New York: Wiley, 1951.

SECTION **1**
Personnel Psychology

*An organization is a collection of people. Decisions must
be made continually about the effective use of these people.
These decisions include whom to recruit, whom to select,
how to train, and how to place within the organization.
These decisions can be made on the basis of whims or preferences or on the basis of some systematic theme, model, or
theory. This section presents systematic themes, models,
and theories for making personnel decisions. The goal of
personnel psychology is to replace arbitrary and inconsistent
decision strategies with logical and demonstrably efficient
strategies.*

CHAPTER 3
Predictor-Related Issues

The introductory chapter targeted testing and applied prediction as one of the major challenges for I/O psychology in the next decade. The methodology chapter described many of the basic statistical and design tools that have proved useful for prediction. In this chapter, the process of prediction and the nature of tests as individual predictors will be dealt with more fully.

Consider the following definition of a test: *A psychological test is the measurement of some phase of a carefully chosen sample of an individual's behavior.* This definition, provided by Clark Hull in 1928, is broad enough to encompass devices other than the standard paper-and-pencil test. It also includes such diverse things as interviews and actual attempts at performing the duties of a particular job (called *work samples*). A relatively broad definition of the word "test" is accepted. With such a definition in mind, certain other pieces of information must be categorized; answers to questions usually found on application blanks (e.g., "How many brothers and sisters do you have?"), and physical examination data. In Chapter 6, we will deal more thoroughly with the relationship of these items of information to personnel selection.

The distinction between tests and testing will be maintained throughout this chapter. Too often, the failure to make this distinction hides important issues. Personnel *testing* is the systematic application of tests for purposes of making a personnel decision. The decision might be related to such things as hiring, promotion, training or retraining, or job placement. The process used for evaluating a test is very different from the process used to evaluate a testing program. In this chapter, the test itself will be considered. The testing program will be examined in Chapter 5.

Perhaps the first personnel psychologist, at least by inclination if not by action, was Plato. As Hull points out (1928, p. 5), Plato identified an important role for testing in the ideal state, as demonstrated by the following dialogue led by Socrates:

> "Really, it is not improbable; for I recollect, myself, after your answer, that, in the first place, no two persons are born exactly alike, but each differs from each in natural endowments, one being suited for one occupation and another for another. Do you not think so?"
>
> "I do."
>
> ". . . From these considerations, it follows that all things will be produced in superior quantity and quality, and with greater ease when each man works at a single occupation in accordance with his natural gifts. . . ."
>
> "But we cautioned the shoemaker, you know, against attempting to be an agriculturist, or a weaver, or a builder besides, with a view to our shoemaking work being well done; and to every artisan we assigned in like manner one occupation; namely, that for which he was best fitted. . . . Now is it not of the greatest moment that the work of war should be done well? Will it not also require natural endowments suited to this particular occupation?"
>
> "Then, apparently, it will belong to us to choose out, if we can, that special order of natural endowments which qualifies its possessors for the guardianship of the state."
>
> "Certainly it belongs to us."
>
> "Then, I assure you, we have taken upon ourselves no trifling task."

The logic is a simple one. There is a belief that not all individuals are equally well suited for all jobs. A more mechanical way of stating the proposition might be that different individuals have different probabilities of success in different jobs. You have often run across teachers who you felt were remarkably ill-suited for their chosen profession. The same could be said of bus drivers, senators, steel workers, and police officers. Based on that belief, a search is begun for those elements of the particular job on which the well-suited and the ill-suited can be discriminated. For an offensive guard on a football team, this might be the ability to move laterally; for a crane operator, it might be the ability to notice events in the periphery of the visual field (for a textbook writer, it might be knowing when to stop belaboring an obvious point). On the basis of an identification of crucial job elements (a process called *job analysis*), a sample of behavior, or test, can be identified that will help to distinguish well-suited applicants from ill-suited ones *before* they are placed on the job. The great promise of testing for industry and the individual worker has been the possibility of identifying those individuals who will best fit into a particular job opening. Another name for this process is *differential placement*. The implications of such placement are fulfillment for the individual and profitability for the organization.

A further belief is that the test is a sample of the behavior that the individual will display on the job. While perhaps the best strategy would be to allow the individual to perform a particular job for several years and *then* determine whether or not she was suitable for continuing, it would not be fair to either the individual or the organization. Too much would have been invested at that point.

Often an error is made in this sampling logic. It is assumed that *all* of the differences in later job performance are captured by the predictor or test. This, in effect, ignores the roles of motivation, training, leadership, and other factors that affect individual behavior. It is an unwarranted assumption.

The testing process can be directed toward matching individuals with jobs rather than selecting one of *n* people for a particular job opening. If it is, it is known as *placement*. For several reasons, both economic and scientific, the process of differential placement offers greater ultimate benefit than that of simple selection. For convenience, we will approach the discussion of tests, test construction, and test evaluation from the point of view of selection.

On the basis of this brief description of the testing process and the role of tests, you can see that there are many components to the well-developed and administered system. The first component is known as *job analysis* and consists of identifying the elements of the job that are critical to success. Another component is the identification of potential predictors of job success. In addition, there is a component related to the actual measurement of job success so that we can, at some point, actually see if the tests helped us pick the best people for the job. These are the topics we will consider over the next several chapters. In this chapter, we will consider predictors of job success (tests of various types) as well as some technical characteristics of all psychological measures.

TESTING IN PERSPECTIVE

While the logic of testing is well rooted historically, going back considerably farther than Plato, for all practical purposes the modern history of aptitude testing begins with Alfred Binet. In 1904 Binet was charged by the French government with the identification of those children likely to have "difficulties" in the school system. The assumption was that the difficulties were related to the mental capacity of the children. Within a few years, Binet and Theodore Simon (a co-worker) had developed a series of tests aimed at identifying those children who could not benefit from the standard school curriculum. Lewis Terman, a psychologist at Stanford University, adapted the tests for use in the United States. Shortly thereafter, variations on the test were used in industrial settings. In the very first issue of the *Journal of Applied Psychology*, which appeared in 1917, Terman describes a study in which he used a variation of the Stanford-Binet intelligence test to predict the success of police officers and fire fighters in San Jose, California.

While a good deal of research was being done in the area of individual differences in intelligence by Terman and others, there was a growing sentiment toward the use of tests for the *differential placement* of job applicants. This comes through very clearly in the writings of some of the earliest industrial psychologists. One such individual was Hugo Muensterberg (1914) who described not only the basic selection and placement logic, but also the very modern problem of dealing with the relative contributions of ability and motivation to job success.

> The one psychological problem which seems most significant . . . , is the mutual adjustment of mental personality and practical work. *The individual needs the place for which his mental dispositions make him fit, and the work demands the individual whose abilities secure his success.* (p. 415; itals added)

*   *   *   *   *

> A mental analysis of this kind was being carried out at the University of Cincinnati on the feeling of five hundred students in the Engineering Department. They were engaged in practical work in manufacture, construction, and transportation. Their marked characteristics as they appeared at work were classified. It was found that a number of men maintained good grades in all school work but were utter failures at everything which required manual exactitude and vice versa. If a man seeks a place, we ought to know whether his type is that of head efficiency or hand efficiency. Another discrimination referred to the type of men who are settled and the type who are roving. One complains if there is no continuity to the work, and the other if there is not enough variety. (p. 417)

The value of *precision* in testing is demonstrated in this observation:

> . . . A boy may enjoy well the idea of being a type setter in a printing office, and he may show himself industrious in performing the work of the first few months. Yet, after years of training, he may discover that he can never reach the rapidity with which some others set the type, and that he will stay far behind the average in the wage scale. His mental mechanism does not allow him to reach the desirable speed, because his reactions are not quick enough. Then it is too late to change his trade. Exact psychological laboratory measurements in thousandths of a second might have shown his inability before he ever started on the long way, and might have saved years of unsuccessful training. (p. 418)

The first World War provided an excellent opportunity for people interested in applied aptitude testing to try out their new skills. There was a problem, however. How could recruits be efficiently tested by means of individually administered intelligence tests? The answer was that they could not. There were some group tests that were being developed at the time by Otis (see Hull, 1928, for a more detailed description). These tests became known as the Army Alpha and the Army Beta (primarily for illiterates), and served the purposes for which they were intended quite well. In less than 50 minutes, the test could be administered to groups as large as 500. This procedure certainly satisfied what Hull (1928) later described as one of the essential characteristics of an aptitude test: "A method of prognosis which is not at the same time reasonably quick and reasonably inexpensive has no excuse for existence" (p. 2). It is good that Hull is not around today to see the extent and cost of many testing programs in industry.

As Ghiselli pointed out (1966), an implied promise was made to the industrial community by the procedural success of World War I testing. If it could be done so quickly and efficiently for the Army, it could be done equally well for industry. Unfortunately, procedure could not make up for content, and there was a good deal of disappointment among the leaders of industry in the value of testing. There was a brief rekindling of interest during the time of the Depression and an enormous reawakening of interest with the commencement of World War II. Once again, millions of recruits had to be classified, and once again, it was primarily the applied measurement, personnel, and industrial psychologists who developed the programs. After the war, testing became more widespread in industry, with more specific aptitude testing occurring (e.g., tests for "mechanical aptitude," or "eye-hand coordination"). Industry was ready to accept testing as "the answer." Unfortunately, no one had taken the time to ask "the question."

Testing as an activity proceeded rapidly and relatively unchecked at the industrial level until the 1960s. About then, social critics such as Gross (1962) and Whyte (1956) began to question the implications of testing for some traditionally cherished values such as "privacy." Testing also came under fire from psychologists for its overwhelmingly empirical flavor. The implication was that there was no *theory* that related aptitudes and abilities to job success.

The critics demanded both a demonstration of job relatedness (those critics concerned with invasion of privacy) and a theory relating mental measurement to constructs such as job performance (those critics concerned with the single-mindedness of the empirical approach). The critics could never have had the impact they had if the public at large had not also experienced a disenchantment with testing in general. Consequently, it was not too great a leap to include some of these specific objections and general feelings of uneasiness into the Civil Rights Act of 1964 (Title VII). Shortly thereafter, two federal agencies were created to identify abuses of testing as they affected minority groups, and to employ economic sanctions against organizations so identified. The first agency, the Equal Employment Opportunity Commission (EEOC), produced a set of guidelines defining fair employment practices. The heart of these guidelines was the assertion that tests could not be used to unfairly discriminate against minority groups. Guion (1966) has since defined unfair discrimination as "individuals with equal probability of success on the job having unequal opportunities for employment." The second agency, the Office of Federal Contract Compliance (OFCC), was given the power to withhold or recall federal funds from employers who did not comply with the fair employment practices outlined by the EEOC.

As a result of the possible economic sanctions that might be directed against them, many organizations abandoned their testing programs in favor of interviews, background checks, and biographical information that might be obtained on an application blank. This simply postponed the problem; it did not solve it. The most recent version of the guidelines (now known as the "Uniform Guidelines") imposes a much broader definition of a test that includes among other things, interviews, biographical data, and performance ratings (if they are used to make promotion decisions). All of this has led to great activity in the theory and application of testing, activity that was absent for so much of the history of the applied testing movement.

Test constructors and test users must share in the blame equally for the public distrust of testing. For their part, the professionals developing tests did not or would not take the time to consider logical and theoretical relationships among tests and on-the-job behaviors. The test users were equally uninterested in theory—they wanted *results*. The person taking the test was often caught in the middle. The whole testing movement is in the process of correcting past deficiencies in both test development and test use. The rest of this chapter is concerned with the logical, methodological, and theoretical principles that are being currently practiced in the use of personnel tests.

EVALUATION IN PSYCHOLOGICAL MEASUREMENT

It was stated in the opening paragraph of this chapter that "a psychological test is the measurement of a . . . sample of . . . behavior." To equate testing and measurement indicates that tests are used to quantify (measure) observations of behavior. Most tests are designed to achieve at least the ordinal level of measurement, and most test makers prefer to assume that their test scores represent an interval scale of measurement. However, some tests may quite adequately fulfill the purposes for which they were designed just by consistently classifying people into two or more categories. Such tests "measure" at the nominal level and may yield only binary information—that a person has or does not have a certain blood type or disease, for example. Nevertheless, most psychological testing is concerned with assigning a score to an individual that is indicative of his position along some continuum or dimension of individual difference. In this sense, a psychological test is an *operational definition* of a concept—an ability, an aptitude, or an area of achievement—a set of standard procedures or operations for measuring the abstract concept.

Each item of a test may be thought of as an observation of the individual's behavior, the total test of n items constituting a behavior sample of n observations. It is assumed that the sample of stimuli (the test questions) are representative of the population (or "universe") of stimuli that might be presented to elicit behaviors relevant to the concept being considered. Thus, for example, a test of "achievement in arithmetic" presents a sample of stimuli (problems) from the nearly infinite universe of arithmetic problems that might be presented. The responses to these problems constitute a sample of the individual's behavior and, at the same time, a sample of the concept, or attribute, "arithmetic skill."

Because psychological test scores are based on a *sample* of observations, they are subject to error. Just as we know that our confidence in a sample mean depends, in part, on the size of the sample, our confidence in a test score depends on an adequate sample of behavior.

RELIABILITY AND VALIDITY

If we were to ask someone about the characteristics of a good measuring device, they would probably respond with terms like "accuracy," "precision," or "adequacy for the job at hand." The carpenter may find a yardstick graduated to eighths or sixteenths of an inch sufficiently accurate and precise for a job, while the machinist would insist upon calipers accurate to the thousandth or ten-thousandth of an inch. Neither would suggest that a good measuring device ought to measure that dimension or attribute that it was designed to measure; that is, neither would raise the issue of whether the yardstick—or the calipers—measured "length," or the distance between two points. Yet the surveyor might well be concerned that a measuring tape measures length, and that it be relatively uncontaminated by temperature changes that expand and contract the materials from which the tape is made.

In psychological measurement, however, the question of *what* is being measured is at least as important as the questions of accuracy, precision, or consistency of measurement, since the attribute that one attempts to measure is an abstract theoretical concept, such as "intelligence," "clerical aptitude," "authoritarianism," or the like. Of course, it is also true that "length" and "time" are abstractions, but the yardstick and the clock function very well, for most purposes, as operational definitions of these constructs. The psychologist, like the surveyor, but to a greater degree, is plagued by potential and real sources of contamination in attempts to define concepts or theoretical constructs operationally. Furthermore, one person's conceptual definition may differ from that of a colleague's.

The terms "accuracy" or "precision" of measurement may be thought of in both a relative and absolute sense. When we speak of the *tolerance* of a measuring device (e.g., "accurate to ± one-thousandth of an inch"), we are describing the absolute accuracy for assessing the length of the object. On the other hand, if we speak of the confidence we can have of ordering a set of objects on a scale or dimension (i.e., of stating which of each pair of objects is longer or larger), then we are concerned with relative accuracy of measurement.

Two concepts central to the problems of evaluating psychological measurement are *reliability* and *validity*. Reliability refers to the issues in psychological measurement that are like those of precision or accuracy in physical measurement. However, as Guion (1965) points out, the word *accuracy* implies something more than or different from what is meant by either reliability or validity. Accuracy implies the confidence we have in: (1) the reproducibility of an individual measurement (absolute accuracy), (2) the ordering of a set of objects (relative accuracy), and (3) the extent to which the value or score agrees with some absolute standard. Guion offered the example of a thermometer that has slipped in its moorings on a board marked with degree readings. The thermometer may yield dependable measurement both in the sense that it accurately reflects differences among days in warmness and that it yields highly similar readings under identical conditions, but the fact that it reads 20 degrees higher than the local standard makes it inaccurate—though reliable. In other words, accuracy is concerned with both constant and variable error, whereas reliability is concerned with variable errors in measurement.

Validity, as implied by the word, has something to do with the *truth* of a measurement. Thus, validity of a measurement answers the question, "Does this number truly represent what I want it to represent?". This suggests that it is possible to collect the wrong information reliably and precisely! It is possible, and often the case, that we have reliable but not valid measurements. There are separate sets of operations for determining reliability and validity, and we will try to keep them distinct in the following discussion. Nevertheless, bear in mind that reliability and validity are both distinct and related. They are distinct in that they deal with different characteristics of measurements; they are related in that measures must be reliable before they can be shown to be valid.

Reliability

The operational definitions of reliability, which are presented below, reflect the consistency and reproducibility of an observation (score) or set of observations (distribution of scores). If a measuring instrument is to be of any value, it should produce highly reliable measurements. In terms of a correlation coefficient, acceptable reliabilities are of the order .70 and above. Perfect reliability would be represented by a correlation of 1.00 between two sets of measurements on the same sample of people with the same or equivalent measuring devices. Correlation coefficients representing reliability estimates are usually much higher than those representing validity estimates. Validity coefficients in applied settings seldom exceed .50. While the size of the validity coefficients is disturbing (since low values of the correlation coefficient indicate a lack of predictability of one variable from another), it makes sense that the correlation of a variable with itself should be higher than the correlation of a variable with another variable. More will be said about validity later in this chapter. First, we will discuss the procedures for estimating the reliability of a test.

Sources of Unreliability. Suppose that you wished to measure each of several new trees planted in your yard. You would get your measuring device, stand it up beside each tree, and determine as best you could the mark on the scale that corresponded to the highest tip of the tree. You would then record the reading and go on to the next tree. When you were finished, you could order the trees from tallest to shortest (by name or location). Now suppose, for the sake of our example, that you misplaced your recordings and, a week later, went through the whole measuring procedure again—then, as always happens, having done the job over, you would find your first set of observations. Out of curiosity, you might compare the two sets of numbers. If they agreed very well, both with respect to *order* and *magnitude*, then you would conclude that: (1) the trees had not changed appreciably with respect to the attribute (height), (2) you had a good measuring device, and (3) you had done a good job—each time—in using the measuring device. If, on the other hand, the two sets of measures agreed very well in designating the *order*, but not the height, you might conclude that the instrument and the user were accurate, but the trees had changed (i.e., grown by a fixed amount, in the time interval between measures). Finally, if you found that the two sets of measures did not agree either with respect to order or magnitude, then you would be in somewhat of a dilemma, not knowing whether you had: (1) a poor measuring device, subject to a good deal of error or contamination (e.g., it measures differently in the shade and in the sun), (2) a poor user of the device, careless in aligning the object and instrument, in reading the instrument or in recording the values, or (3) an unstable attribute—height— subject to growth spurts and differential rates from one tree to the next, with some trees shrinking, some growing taller, and some remaining unchanged. Frequently, it is difficult to determine whether lack of reliability is the result of the device (yielding an inadequate sample of the attribute), lack of skill on the part of the user, or a lack of stability in the attribute measured.

Estimates of Reliability. In measurement theory, reliability is based on the notion that an obtained measurement (score), X, represents a true score, t, plus some error, e, or $X = t + e$. Actually, as Guion (1965) pointed out, e should refer only to the random unpredictable error, not systematic error, such as the 20 degree constant error in the thermometer. Guion prefers the expression, $X = s + e$, where s is the composite of true score and constant error and e is only the random, unpredictable error of measurement. Reliability is then defined as the freedom of a set of measurements (or observations) from this random variance. As we saw, the instrument, the attribute, and the user can all contribute random variability to the obtained score and, therefore, to the unreliability of the observations.

To the extent that obtained scores *(X)* agree with true scores *(t)*, error variance *(e)* is reduced. Thus, the correlation $r_{x.t}$, is a measure of reliability, since it is the correlation of the obtained score with the true score. Since t values are hypothetical and not accessible to measurement, $r_{x.t}$ cannot be obtained directly. Instead, a number of alternative methods have been devised to estimate reliability. Before describing these, however, it should be pointed out that if one assumes the true score of an individual to be unchanging, then the variable error of measurement could be described in terms of the standard deviation of a sample of repeated measurements of the individual. Thus, for example, with our tree measurements we might measure a given tree 100 times and then obtain the standard deviation of this set of observations as an estimate of variable error. This standard deviation is technically known as the *standard error of measurement.*

Fortunately, there is a statistical method for computing the standard error of measurement that saves us the labor of gathering so many different samples. The formula for the standard error is:

$$SE_{\bar{x}} \text{ or } \sigma_e = \sigma_x\sqrt{1 - r_{xx}}$$

By means of this formula, we can see that the standard error of measurement is related both to the reliability of the measure being considered (represented by the term r_{xx} and the variability in the sample (represented by the term σ_x). The formula states that as the reliability of the measure increases, the standard error decreases, but as the sample variability increases, so does the standard error. We will now consider the various ways of measuring and defining the term r_{xx}, which represents the reliability of a measure.

Operational Definition 1: Test-Retest.   One way to obtain an estimate of reliability is to test and then retest the same set of individuals. Thus, each individual has two scores, X_1, and X_2, each an estimate of the "true" score. The correlation, $r_{x_1x_2}$, between these two sets of scores taken over the sample of individuals, constitutes our estimate. Figure 3–1 illustrates how a high test-retest correlation documents a consistency in the *ordering* of individuals, while Figure 3–2 shows that low reliability means high *uncertainty* as to the relative position of an individual in the distribution. Figure 3–3 demonstrates that a perfect correlation, $r_{x_1x_2} = 1.00$, does *not* necessarily mean that the estimate of the individual's score remains unchanged: if there is a constant change, such as a fixed growth rate, the correlation can be perfect, while the two observations of each individual differ widely (but systematically).

The appropriate time interval between test and retest is difficult to determine exactly. It should be long enough so that the individual cannot remember responses on the first test. It should be short enough so that dramatic changes have not occurred in the individual as a function of some experience (such as training).

Operational Definition 2: Equivalent Forms.   Test and retest scores might differ (either as in Figure 3–2 or Figure 3–3) as a result of the *effects of the initial testing* on retest performance. Thus, the two sets of observations may not be independent.

While guessing is a common test behavior, there is a problem that is introduced by *consistent* guessing behavior. On a multiple-choice test, you may use a common decision rule for all items that you cannot answer. For example, using student folklore, you might always choose alternative *c.* If you use the same decision rule on the retest, the consistency of your

FIGURE 3-1

Score Distributions of Individuals Tested on Two Different Occasions—High Test-Retest Reliability

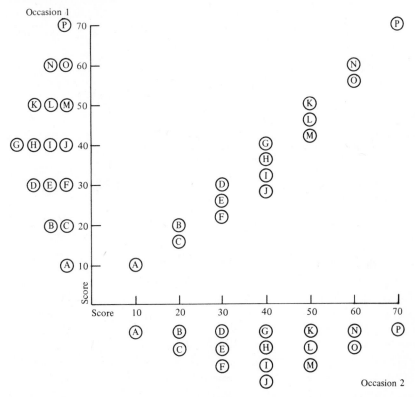

score (and the reliability of the test) will be an artificially inflated estimate of the true score consistency and reliability due to the consistency of your guessing pattern. This would be an example of a systematic error that affects the reliability estimate. For these and other reasons, test developers have often sought to assess reliability by developing and using different forms rather than the identical form at the original and retest sessions. These forms are usually carefully constructed to be equivalent in content, types of questions, difficulty levels, and so on. The analysis of possible outcomes for the test-retest approach is equally true for equivalent forms. To appreciate this, simply substitute "Form A" and "Form B" for "Occasion 1" and "Occasion 2," respectively, in Figures 3-1, 3-2, and 3-3. However, as we shall see, sources of error variance and of systematic variance are not the same in any two estimates of reliability.

Both the test-retest or the equivalent-forms method yields a *coefficient of stability* if some time interval is allowed between first and second measures. Without an appreciable interval between administrations, the correlation between equivalent forms is called a *coefficient of equivalence*. Each

FIGURE 3–2

Score Distributions of Individuals Tested on Two Different Occasions—Low Test-Retest Reliability

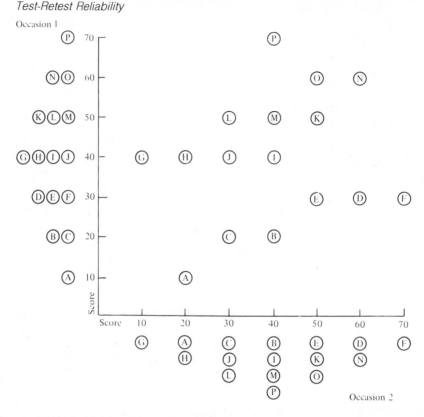

form is presumed to yield a representative sample of the individual's behavior. Low estimates of equivalence, therefore, can be interpreted in terms of inadequate or unrepresentative sampling of the behavioral domain. In terms of a traditional paper-and-pencil test, the domain might consist of all possible test items designed to measure the trait under consideration. The domain of test items for a test on this chapter might consist of 500–600 questions dealing with predictor-related issues. If the coefficient of equivalence for two equivalent 20-question tests of this material were low, we might conclude that the domain had been poorly sampled.

Operational Definition 3: Internal Consistency. A good yardstick should measure equally from both ends, and it should not really matter whether we start at the end or in the middle—the results should be the same. Somewhat analogous to this example is the rationale for internal consistency estimates of reliability. Basically, the approach is to divide a test into two equivalent halves (e.g., odd versus even items), score each half for each individual, then correlate the two sets of scores. A high correlation indicates that the two halves yield consistent information: if one half indicates a high score for individual A, the second half signals the same

FIGURE 3–3

Score Distributions of Individuals Tested on Two Different Occasions—High Test-Retest Reliability

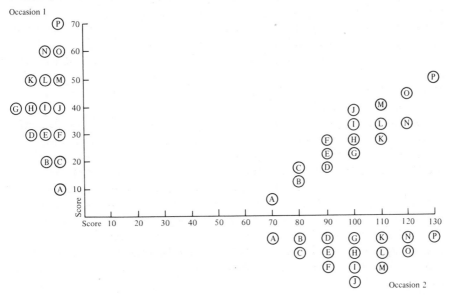

thing. Thus, where two sessions or two forms are not available, they are created (and, it is hoped, are equivalent) from a single administration of a test. Of course, each half test used in the estimation is only half the sample of behavior of the whole test for which the reliability is sought. Small samples are more vulnerable to sampling error, so a split-half reliability estimate is likely to be very conservative. For this reason, it should be corrected using the *Spearman-Brown prophecy formula:*

$$r_{nn} = \frac{nr_{11}}{1 + (n - 1)r_{11}} \quad \text{where}$$

r_{nn} is the reliability of a test n times as long as the one used to obtain the estimate and r_{11} is the obtained estimate of reliability. Thus, if n is two times the length of the half-tests used to estimate reliability, then

$$r_{\text{corrected}} = \frac{2\ r_{\text{obtained}}}{1 + (2 - 1)r_{\text{obtained}}} \quad \text{or, for } r_{\text{obt}} = .60,$$

the corrected estimate would be:

$$r_{\text{corrected}} = \frac{2(.60)}{1 + (1).60} = \frac{1.2}{1.6} = .75.$$

(Note that this formula can be used with whole-test estimates of reliability to predict the effects on reliability of doubling or otherwise increasing the length of a test.)

Other internal consistency estimates of reliability are basically variations of the test-splitting procedure. The best known of these methods are those resulting in the Kuder-Richardson formulas (K-R 20 and K-R 21), which provide an estimate of the reliability coefficient that would be obtained if the test were split into all possible halves, and the individual split-half correlations computed and averaged. The K–R formulas (Richardson and Kuder, 1939) save the researcher the labor of splitting, computing, and averaging. Another similar reliability estimate that is becoming popular is L. J. Cronbach's Alpha coefficient (Cronbach, 1970), which is also a summary reliability statistic.

Factors Affecting Reliability Estimates. It should be clear that the estimate of reliability depends on the particular operational definition (or method) used. Other factors affecting the obtained reliability coefficient are the size of the sample of observations, or the number of items in the test, and the homogeneity of the sample of individuals on which the estimate is based. As in any other context, the size of the sample is inversely related to sampling error. This principle is the basis for the Spearman-Brown prophecy formula presented earlier. Reliability can be increased by increasing the number of items in the test, but it should be clear that the new items must sample the *same universe*, or domain, as the old items if a gain is to be realized.

A sample of people who are relatively homogeneous with respect to the attribute being measured will yield a lower reliability estimate than one with a wide range of ability. If one wants to present evidence for the high reliability of an intelligence test, for example, she should be sure to include both geniuses and morons in the sample. However, if the test is designed to be used to differentiate university graduates, such a sample would be inappropriate: homogeneity of the sample must be judged relative to the population for which the test is constructed.

Most students would object to a test of five true-false items as the sole basis for their grades in a course, recognizing that the sample is too small to provide a reliable estimate of their knowledge of the material. Poorly prepared students, however, might object less than others if they recognized that such a test provided them with a chance for a good grade by luck alone, since there is 1 chance in 32 that they would get a perfect score by flipping a coin on each item ($p = (1/2)^5 = 1/32$). Either a difficult test or a sample of low ability increases the role of chance or "luck," and increases the error variance in the estimate.

Sources of Variance in Test Performance. Thorndike (1949) provided a rather exhaustive list of the factors that may account for variability in test performance. These are summarized in Figure 3–4. Any of these factors could contribute to systematic variance—and thus inflate a reliability estimate—or to error variance—and thus deflate the estimate—*depending on the operational definition of reliability used.* For example, category III, "Temporary But General Characteristics of the Individual," which includes such factors as state of health, tiredness, motivation, emotional stress, and

FIGURE 3–4

Possible Sources of Variance in Performance on a Particular Test

I. Lasting and General Characteristics of the Individual
- A. Level of ability on one or more general traits, which operate in a number of tests.
- B. General skills and techniques of taking tests.
- C. General ability to comprehend instructions.

II. Lasting but Specific Characteristics of the Individual
- A. Specific to the test as a whole (and to parallel forms of it).
  1. Individual level of ability on traits required in this test but not in others.
  2. Knowledges and skills specific to particular form of test items.
- B. Specific to particular test items.
  1. The "chance" element determining whether the individual does or does not know a particular fact. (Sampling variance in a finite number of items.)

III. Temporary but General Characteristics of the Individual
(Factors affecting performance on many or all tests at a particular time.)
- A. Health.
- B. Fatigue.
- C. Motivation.
- D. Emotional strain.
- E. General test-wiseness (partly lasting).
- F. Understanding of mechanics of testing.
- G. External conditions of heat, light, ventilation, etc.

IV. Temporary and Specific Characteristics of the Individual
- A. Specific to a test as a whole.
  1. Comprehension of the specific test task (in so far as this is distinct from I B).
  2. Specific tricks or techniques of dealing with the particular test materials (in so far as this is distinct from II A 2).
  3. Level of practice on the specific skills involved (especially in psychomotor tests).
  4. Momentary "set" for a particular test.
- B. Specific to particular test items.
  1. Fluctuations and idiosyncrasies of human memory.
  2. Unpredictable fluctuations in attention or accuracy, superimposed upon the general level of performance characteristic of the individual.

V. Variance not Otherwise Accounted for (chance)
- A. "Luck" in the selection of answers by "guessing."

Source: Thorndike, R. L. *Personnel selection.* New York: Wiley, 1949, p. 73, copyright © by John Wiley & Sons, Inc. Reprinted by permission of John Wiley & Sons, Inc.

so on, should *reduce* variability of the individual's performance when the two estimates are taken at the same time, as with a split-half estimate, but would more likely increase variability when the estimates are separated in time, as with test-retest with a delay. Differences in such factors as health, tiredness, and motivation are more likely with a delay between tests and, consequently, such factors are more apt to increase variability

TABLE 3-1

Allocation of Variance in Different Estimates of Reliability

Estimate Method	Treatment of Sources of Variance*						
	I	*IIA*	*IIB*	*III*	*IVA*	*IVB*	*V*
Immediate test-retest	S	S	S	S	S	E	E
Delayed test-retest	S	S	S	E	E	E	E
Immediate equivalent forms . . .	S	S	E	S	S	E	E
Delayed equivalent forms	S	S	E	E	E	E	E
Split-half	S	S	E	S	S	S	E

* S = systematic variance; E = error variance; Roman numerals correspond to sources of variance in Table 3–1.
Source: Guion, R. M. *Personnel testing.* New York: McGraw-Hill, 1965, p. 39.

(i.e., contribute to the error variance and reduce reliability) under such conditions. Table 3–1 summarizes the relationship between the different definitions of reliability and the categories of variability in test performance. The conclusion to be drawn is clear: *Different ways of estimating reliability may yield quite different results because they include different sources in the estimate of error variance.*

Validity

At one level of analysis, the question of the validity of a test or other predictor is simply, "How well does the predictor predict that which it was designed or chosen to predict?" In other words, if we know an individual's score on the predictor, how accurately can we predict his score on a criterion? Validity typically is operationally defined as the correlation between the predictor and the criterion scores of a sample of individuals. The result is known as the *validity* coefficient, or simply the predictive validity of the test *for that specific criterion.* It should be clear that while scores on a test may predict, say, quantity of production, they might be unrelated to another criterion—say, turnover. *Validity in this sense is not an inherent property of the test, but is only an empirically demonstrated relationship to a specific criterion.* A test may have as many different validity coefficients as there are different criteria to correlate with it.

For a long time, personnel psychology was concerned almost exclusively with this empirical, nontheoretical definition of validity. It did not matter if the test measured memory capacity, reading skill, or general ability, as long as it yielded scores predictive of some measure of success on the job. More recently, however, industrial psychologists have recognized the limitations of a nontheoretical "shotgun" approach to testing and have begun to ask questions about the logical as well as the empirical validity of their predictors. While empirical validity is concerned with the accuracy with which test scores can predict criterion scores, logical validity is concerned with how well the operational definition (i.e., the test) measures the construct ("construct" validity) or how adequately it samples the domain ("content" validity).

Instead of empirical and logical validities, Guion (1976) refers to criterion-related validities and descriptive validities. Criterion related validities (concurrent and predictive) evaluate inferences about the relationship between test scores and criterion scores. Descriptive validities (content and construct) evaluate the intrinsic meaning of test scores.

As one might expect, the federal agency responsible for enforcing compliance with Equal Employment Opportunity law, the Equal Employment Opportunity Commission (EEOC), presents a more mechanical view of the various ways which might be used to validate a selection procedure.

> In criterion related validity, a selection procedure is justified by a statistical relationship between scores on the test or other selection procedure and measures of job performance. In content validity, a selection procedure is justified by showing that it representatively samples significant parts of the job, such as a typing test for a typist. Construct validity involves identifying the psychological trait (the construct) which underlies successful performance on the job and then devising a selection procedure to measure the presence and degree of that construct. An example would be a test of leadership ability. (p. 38292, Federal Register, 1978)

Predictive, concurrent, content, and construct validity were introduced as terms to describe different experimental designs for validating a selection procedure (APA, 1954). As with most experimental designs, they could be well applied or poorly applied. In practice, this meant that some content validity studies might have led to stronger support for a selection strategy than some criterion related studies that were poorly done. Eventually, psychologists, lawyers, judges, plaintiffs, and defendants fell to arguing about which type of validity was "acceptable" or "permissible." Unfortunately, in the course of these arguments, the essence of the validation *process* was obscured.

Figure 3–5 presents an idealized version of the validation process. We

FIGURE 3–5

An Idealized View of the Validation Process

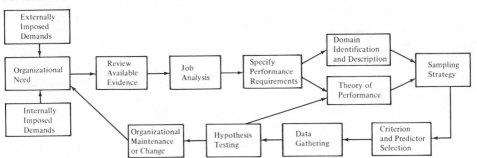

We were aided by Steve Berkley, Randy Cheloha, Gus Colangelo, Steve Kozlowski, Mirian Massenberg, Charles Sproule, and Bob Vance in constructing this model.

will examine each of the components of this process and then use the full model as a means to examine the traditional validity categories.

1. *Organizational Need:* This component implies that there is some reason to be concerned with how people are selected for jobs. This need may arise internally, in the form of poor production, increased waste, or absenteeism. The need may also be suggested externally. For example, there is a law that states that people may not be unfairly discriminated against in employment decisions because of age, sex, race, religion, color, or national origin. To the degree that organizations select a subset of individuals from a large group of applicants, they must be able to demonstrate that their procedures are legal.

2. *Review Available Evidence:* Logically, if one has a problem, the first step in solving it might be to see if others have had a similar problem, and if so, how they have solved it. This might involve reading some text books on the subject of personnel selection and reviewing reports of validation studies in personnel journals.

3. *Job Analysis:* In the past, it was common for a personnel manager to choose a new test for a particular job title by deciding on the test on the basis of how appropriate it seemed. Thus, if she were hiring someone for the job of grinder, she might administer a mechanical reasoning test, since grinding was a "mechanical" activity. She might then look around for a measure of job performance to use to validate that test. This would be a case of the tail wagging the dog; she had the procedures backwards. Until she had identified the level and type of performance she was seeking, it is not likely she could find a test that would predict it—she did not know what to predict. For this reason, the process of job analysis is crucial to any validation strategy. It is important to analyze the job carefully and determine what it requires of the person who will fill it. Once the job is broken down into components, it is much easier to identify a predictor that will distinguish between those who might do well and those who might do poorly on the job. Thus, in our example, once the manager has determined that she will be hiring a grinder, she will either conduct a job analysis of the job or review an existing job analysis before deciding on the hiring strategy. The job analysis would tell her that a grinder must be able to read complicated specifications, use various types of micrometers, lift objects weighing in excess of 100 pounds, and give oral instruction to other machine operators. Given this information, testing procedure will be more than a simple mechanical reasoning test.

    The point we are trying to make with the example is that a job analysis is usually an important step early in any validation study, regardless of the validation design that is being used. The various types of job analysis and examples of completed analyses are presented in the next chapter.

4. *Specify Performance Requirements:* On the basis of the job analysis, we should now have a product that might be called a *job description.* This job description should effectively specify the frequency and importance of various job related activities for the "typical" job with the title being considered.

5. *Theory of Performance:* On the basis of the job description, we should now have some general idea of demands of the particular job as well as individual characteristics that are suited to meeting those demands. At this stage, the "general idea" is a guess or theory. It is a specific theory about the performance of individuals with particular characteristics in a specific job. In that respect, it is more narrow than the psychological theories we are familiar with; nevertheless, it is a theory based on previous data (from the *review available evidence* component) as well as current observation (the *job analysis* component), systematically and representatively gathered.

6. *Domain Identification and Description:* This component determines how broad or narrow our theory will be. It might be a broad-band theory, such as the relationship between mechanical aptitude and accident probability, or it might be a narrow-band theory, such as the relationship between thumb/forefinger dexterity and keypunching speed. The *theory of performance* and the *domain identification* probably occur simultaneously rather than sequentially and are both most likely a result of the job analysis.

7. *Sampling Strategy:* The nature of our theory and width of our domain of interest will affect the variables, procedures, and subjects that we use to test our theory. Thus, if our theory and domain are broad, such as the mechanical aptitude/accident relationship proposed earlier, we would want to sample from a wide variety of tests of mechanical aptitude, job titles, and methods of recording and determining degree of severity of accidents. On the other hand, if our theory is a narrow one, dealing with the relationship between a specific motor skill and a well defined element of performance, a different sampling strategy might be employed.

8. *Criterion and Predictor Selection:* Once we have decided on the conceptual characteristics of the test of our theory of performance, we must still determine how we will operationally define skills, abilities, aptitudes and performance measures. Should we use paper and pencil tests or performance tests, aptitude or ability tests, ratings or objective production measures? The answers to these questions will be found in *theory-of-performance* and *domain-identification* components.

9. *Data Gathering:* The next step in the process is to actually gather the data necessary for testing predictor/criterion relationships.

10. *Hypothesis Testing:* After the appropriate data are gathered, it is necessary to go through the process of testing hypotheses about the predictor/criterion relationships. This hypothesis testing is identical to the verification stage of any scientific endeavor. We made a reasoned

guess—was it correct? The answer to this question has implications for our theory of performance. If our guess was correct, our theory was supported, and we feel confident that we understand the things that go into good job performance. If our hypothesis is rejected, we must modify our theory, sampling strategy, or variable-selection procedure and test it again. This kind of activity is implied by the feedback arrow going from *hypothesis testing* to *theory of performance*.

11. *Organizational Maintenance or Change:* If our hypothesis (and indirectly our theory of performance) is supported, we might want to modify the procedures for selection of new employees to include this new procedure. On the other hand, if we are testing an existing procedure and our hypothesis concerning the predictor/criterion relationship is *not* supported, we would probably suspend the use of this procedure. Regardless of whether or not our hypothesis has been supported, an organizational need has been addressed. This is the need that instigated the theory building and hypothesis testing in the first place.

This idealized view of the validation process with all of its components is intimidating. It describes a very costly and difficult procedure. In fact, the traditional types of validity are represented in various portions of this model. Thus, the *job-analysis, criterion- and predictor-selection, data-gathering* and *hypothesis-testing* components represent the typical criterion-related study. Likewise, the *job-analysis, specify-performance-requirements, theory-of-performance,* and *domain-identification-and-description* components represent content validity. In our opinion, the entire process described in Figure 3–5 comprises construct validity. This means that criterion-related validity and content validity are subsets of the more generalized or idealized validation process, which is represented by the term *construct validity.* This point of view is becoming more and more popular (Guion, 1976; Dunnette and Borman, 1979). If this is a reasonable point of view, then it is likely that the validity of a particular procedure will be determined on the basis of how well the study was designed to test the "theory of performance" rather than on what type of validity it is! Viewed in another way, the model of validity presented in Figure 3–5 is nothing more or less than the scientific method described in Chapter 2. This is as it should be. If personnel psychology is to be thought of as a science rather than an art, its activities must be carefully planned and executed. Validation is one of those activities.

In spite of the fact that Figure 3–5 described the way in which a very elegant validation study might be conducted, seldom do organizations have the time, money, and expertise to carry out such a study. In the next section we will describe the more traditional forms of validation research.

Criterion Related Validity: Concurrent Design. When we are investigating the validity of a selection procedure using a criterion related design, typically, we are looking for a significant correlation between a test (predictor) and job behavior (criterion). The two major forms of criterion related validity differ in terms of the time separating the predictor or test information from the behavior to be predicted, or the criterion information. The *concurrent* approach means that we test *present* employees for whom individual job performance criteria are available. Test scores are then correlated with criterion scores to determine if performance can be predicted from test information. The resulting correlation coefficient (now known as the "validity coefficient") describes the degree of concurrent validity of the test.

There are both advantages and disadvantages to this procedure. The advantage is in the availability of the necessary data. The disadvantage is in the predictive value of the resulting validity coefficient. For example, if there is a high correlation between a test score of mechanical comprehension and production figures, we do not know if the person tested came to the job with that amount of mechanical comprehension or if this was an aptitude developed on the basis of job experience. If the level of mechanical comprehension demonstrated by the test was due to learning on the job, this information will not help us to predict the expected level of production for applicants for that particular job. In addition, the size of the correlation coefficient is affected by having only part of the population of potential workers available. We do not have information about those who are not currently employed by the organization (either because they were not hired or because they quit or were fired).

Criterion Related Validity: Predictive Design.   In the predictive approach to test validation, there is an interval of time that separates the test information from the criterion information. Predictive validation is concerned with the extent to which earlier observations (test scores) are predictive of later behavior (criterion scores). Thus, the predictive validity of IQ scores or reading-readiness measures obtained on preschoolers might be evaluated against performance measures taken after the first year of school.

In an industrial setting, a mechanical comprehension test might be administered to all applicants for the job of machinist, and the scores on that test correlated with production figures after those hired had been on the job for several months. The resulting correlation coefficient would be known as the "predictive validity coefficient" of the test. An important consideration in this approach is that the test scores not be used to make hiring decisions until *after* the validity coefficient has been computed. If the test in question is used to screen applicants, we have the same problem which we encountered in the concurrent approach—we are missing the data from those who are not hired—that is, our sample is inappropriate.

Content Validity.   Content validity is concerned with the extent to which the sample of items in a test (and the sample behavior elicited by these items) is an unbiased representation of the domain (i.e., attribute or trait) being sampled. Keep in mind our earlier definition of a test: *a measurement of some phase of a carefully chosen sample of an individual's* *behavior.* Since this definition included measures other than just paper-and-pencil tests, this also means that test *items* should be broadly defined as well. These *items* can be in a form other than questions on a paper-and-pencil test. They might include questions in an oral interview, questions on an application blank, performance tasks such as tweezer dexterity tasks, or physical strength tests.

For example, if one were attempting to select from among a group of applicants for the job of typist, the test battery might include a typing test. The domain under consideration (typing ability) would have been well represented by the "test item" (i.e., material the individual applicant was asked to type). Similarly, suppose an instructor assigns 100 pages of a text treating one topic and devotes 5 lectures to that topic, but assigns 200 pages and devotes 10 lectures to another topic. Content validity of a test covering these two topics might be demonstrated if approximately one-third of the test items were devoted to the first topic and two-thirds to the second topic. Content validity is determined on the basis of how well the test material samples the job performance domain. This means that content validity is more judgmental than the criterion-related validities. Nevertheless, these judgments can be made empirically. We could ask a number of individuals who are familiar with the job in question to determine how closely test items are related to required job behaviors. We would want these judges to study the job description in question carefully before making their judgments. We could then actually calculate a value for each test item that represented the average judgment of the group concerning how "valid" each item was in this particular situation. Lawshe (1975) has suggested a statistic to be used for content validation; it has been labeled the *Content Validity Ratio* (CVR), and the formula for this statistic is:

$$CVR = \frac{n_e - \frac{N}{2}}{\frac{N}{2}}$$

In this formula, n_e is the number of judges who consider the particular item a good representation of the domain of job behavior, and N is the total number of judges. From this formula it can be seen that negative CVR values mean that fewer than half of the judges consider the item good. If they are equally split—some saying it is good and some saying that it is not good—the CVR value is 0; when all judges consider the item to be a good representation of the domain, the value of CVR would be 1.00. As is the case with any form of validity, a good job analysis must be available that clearly describes the job. By means of that information, it is possible to determine the degree to which items represent job duties. In the past, content validity was characterized as more qualitative and logical rather than empirical. Both the courts and the psychological community now require more objective statements when content validity designs are used in the validation of selection procedures. Statistics like the CVR will help meet this requirement.

Construct Validity. The construct validity of a test of intelligence is essentially an answer to the question, "Does this set of operations [the test] really measure that something [hypothetical construct] we refer to as intelligence?" It is the most theoretical of the definitions of validity, since it is concerned with the abstractions used in referring to psychological structures, functions, or traits, rather than to the prediction of some external criterion. Nevertheless, the evaluation of construct validity may well use predictive validity as evidence that the test measures the construct. For example, the empirical evidence that IQ scores are somewhat predictive of school performance and of success in various occupations and training programs may be cited as evidence of construct validity. Our confidence in *what* it is that a test measures grows with the accumulation of evidence as to its relationship to other measures. As Guion (1965) stated:

> This [construct validity] is not a concept permitting easy operational definition. Only in one limited sense may a specific statement of correlation be considered an operational definition of construct validity. In general, construct validity must be expressed as a judgment, inferred from the weight of research evidence gathered in many independent studies. (p. 128)

Construct validity, while a difficult concept to grasp, may be one of the most important forms of validity for understanding the meaning of a test score. If a test has construct validity, something is known about how it relates to other tests that measure similar but not identical attributes. Making sense of a test score as a piece of information is much like making sense of a particular sentence. The word "match" has a very specific meaning when embedded in the sentence: "In order to receive the federal funds, the university had to promise to match the amount with private funds." The sentence provides the context for the word "match." We know from an examination of the sentence structure that the word "match" is functioning as a verb rather than as an object or subject; we further understand from the word and its context that the university is being requested to provide an amount of money equal to that provided by the federal government. Like a word in a sentence, a test score is embedded in a context, which must be taken into account when interpreting it. More specifically, if we consider a new test to be like the word "match," to understand the meaning of that new test, we must know how it is related to other tests and behaviors. If it is thought to be a test of general intellectual ability, it should have positive correlations with other similar tests, such as the Stanford-Binet or the Wechsler Intelligence Scale. In addition, our new test should correlate with many of the behaviors that the Stanford-Binet and other intelligence tests correlate with—behaviors such as academic performance. In short, to understand the new test score, it is necessary to discover its theoretical context or the domain of behaviors it measures.

There is much less agreement about the meaning of construct validity than about criterion-related or content validity. It is safe to say that construct validity is generally regarded as the most demanding of validity designs by judges, psychologists, and administrators. Since we have defined Figure 3–5 as a model of construct validity, we agree that it will be difficult and costly to apply the construct-validity design to typical validation research. Nevertheless, as is commonly the case in scientific research, the more demanding the design, the stronger the resulting conclusions. If one were to validate a selection procedure using a construct approach, the resulting theory of performance for that particular job would be very well developed. Consequently, the selection procedure would be both more efficient (in terms of actually identifying applicants who are likely to do well on the job) and more defensible (in terms of convincing courts that a particular selection strategy is valid).

Face Validity.   The *face validity* of a measure is not really validity in the technical sense. It refers to a judgment made by those who are being measured, e.g., the individual taking the test. An engineer who is applying for a position may have some doubts about the validity of a vocabulary test that includes words such as "leprechaun," "unicorn," or "veracity," but might judge a test with "stress," "conductance," or "mass" as valid, that is, measuring concepts predictive of success in engineering. Face validity is important to insure a positive attitude toward both the testing and the organization. Face validity is more closely related to the motivation of the person being measured than his ability, and as such, is a critical part of overall test performance. Because they were designed for different purposes to be used in different contexts, many tests used in personnel selection, lack face validity. The effect of this deficiency on attitudes toward testing and toward industrial psychologists can only detract from the value of the obtained scores, and also reduce the acceptance of psychologists in the world of work.

As students of personnel psychology, it is important for you to understand that validity is not a *thing*—it is the statistical result of a *process* called validation. The manner in which the validation might be carried out will vary, just as other experimental designs vary. We should pick the design that best suits our individual situation. The various "types" of validity describe these available designs.

FINDING AND SELECTING TESTS

From what has been said in the previous section, you may have concluded that selection of a test is a straightforward process where you find a reliable and valid test and use it. The fallacy in this is that predictive validity for a situation can be evaluated only after a test has been chosen and a sample of test and criterion data have been obtained. That is not to deny that evidence of test reliability and validity are important information in choosing a test. On the contrary, evidence that a test has been a valid predictor of "success" with a sample of jobs similar to the one being examined is one of the best indicators that the test may be a wise choice. Similarly, in the absence of such empirical validity data, evidence of logical validity and/or of reliability may serve as bases for choosing among tests. It should be evident that these two criteria for evaluation in psychological measure-ment—reliability and validity—are of first-order importance in test selection decisions.

However, there are a number of other factors that must be considered. One does not select a test simply because it is reliable and valid for *some* purpose. A test is selected because it looks as though it may be valid for a *particular* purpose; that it will be a good measure of some attribute that is important for performance on a particular job. The test selection process starts with a hypothesis (or hunch) based on systematic job analysis and worker analysis data regarding those attributes most important for job suc-cess. Then tests are sought to measure one or more of those attributes. At that point, reliability and validity become an important consideration. Other important factors are: (1) the availability of appropriate normative data ("norms") to permit evaluation of obtained scores; (2) standardized administration and scoring procedures, without which test scores may be meaningless; (3) professional training requirements for administration and scoring, and (4) costs and other factors.

This section is concerned with how one goes about finding, evaluating, and selecting a test likely to yield information that will be relevant to personnel decisions.

Remember the last time you took a standardized test? It might have been the College Boards or the Graduate Record Exams. Did you wonder who thought it up or where it came from? If you had to give a test to someone for some purpose, would you know how to go about finding and evaluating a test? Probably not, as most people give little thought to identify-ing an appropriate test and then evaluating its properties. But this may represent a real problem for the personnel manager. What if a new employee has to be hired to run a rather complicated lathe? If the personnel manager wants to explore the possibility of using a test of some kind, how is this gone about?

There are several sources she might use. We will discuss one such source later (*Mental Measurements Yearbook* [Buros, 1978]), but simply because an appropriate test is found does not mean that it can be purchased and incorporated into the employment process. Ideally, the test publisher exer-cises some control over the sale of the test so that society is not abused by the unethical or inappropriate use of tests by those not qualified to administer and interpret them. So, there are really two questions to consider: (1) who may purchase a test? and (2) how may a test be identified and evaluated?

Test Users

In 1953 the American Psychological Association provided a scheme for the classification of tests that helps publishers determine the degree of professional training necessary for the potential user of a particular test.

This helps individuals considering various tests determine which tests they are capable of administering and interpreting. In addition, it helps the publisher determine whether or not an individual should be permitted to purchase a particular test. This classification scheme follows.

Level A Tests. Level A tests are relatively low-level tests requiring little in the way of formal training in administration or interpretation. They can be administered with the help of an instruction manual and can be easily scored and interpreted. These tests are generally of the achievement variety, which check on present proficiency rather than potential achievement (aptitude). An example of a level A test would be a standardized language-proficiency examination used to determine placement of a student in a foreign-language curriculum.

Level B Tests. Level B tests require some degree of training and familiarity with concepts of psychological testing on the part of the purchaser. Unlike the tests of level A, level B tests cannot be mechanically interpreted from a manual. They require some knowledge of concepts such as standardization, norm groups, and errors of measurement. This is primarily due to the inferential nature of the tests. Aptitude tests fall in this category. We are attempting to predict some potential on the part of the individual rather than describe some current level of achievement. This added element of prediction requires specialized training. Such training might be an advanced college course in tests and measurements, with a supporting statistics background.

Level C Tests. Level C tests are the most demanding of the user. In addition to the necessary training described for level B, level C tests require specialized supervision in administration, scoring, and interpretation. An example of such a test would be the Rorschach Inkblot test. Graduate courses are devoted solely to the use of that test (this includes supervised administration as well as classroom instruction).

This classification procedure provides some general form of protection against the abuse of psychological and educational tests. Let us assume that an individual is aware of such restrictions on the purchase of tests and wants to identify some possible tests for use in an industrial setting. How can these tests be found and evaluated? In 1938, Oscar K. Buros published the *First Mental Measurements Yearbook* (MMY—by designation) with the following purposes in mind:

1. To provide information about tests published throughout the English-speaking world.
2. To present frankly critical test reviews written by testing and subject specialists representing various viewpoints.
3. To provide extensive bibliographies of verified references on the construction, use, and validity of specific tests.
4. To make readily available the critical portions of test reviews appearing in professional journals.
5. To provide fairly exhaustive reviews of new and revised books on testing.

FIGURE 3–6

A Typical Entry from the Mental Measurements Yearbook

[675]

Flanagan Aptitude Classification Tests. Grades 9–12, 10–12 and adults; 1951–60; FACT; 2 editions; postage extra; John C. Flanagan; Science Research Associates, Inc. *
a) SEPARATE BOOKLET 16-TEST EDITION. Grades 10–12 and adults; 1951–60; 16 tests; examiner's manual ('53, 27 pages); technical supplement ('54, 16 pages); personnel director's booklet ('53, 27 pages); manual for interpreting scores ('56, 12 pages); $5.10 per 25 self-marking tests; 40¢ per technical supplement; 55¢ per manual for interpreting scores; 80¢ per personnel director's booklet; $6.10 per specimen set; 258(388) minutes in 2 sessions.
1) *FACT 1A, Inspection.* 1953–56; form A ('53, 6 pages); 6(12) minutes.
2) *FACT 2A and 2B, Coding.* 1953–56; forms A ('53, 6 pages), B ('54, 6 pages); 10(30) minutes.
3) *FACT 3A and 3B, Memory.* 1953–56; forms A ('53, 3 pages), B ('54, 3 pages); 4(5) minutes.
4) *FACT 4A, Precision.* 1953–56; form A ('53, 4 pages); 8(15) minutes.
5) *FACT 5A, Assembly.* 1953–56; form A ('53, 6 pages); 12(18) minutes.
6) *FACT 6A, Scales.* 1953–56; form A ('53, 6 pages); 16(28) minutes.
7) *FACT 7A, Coordination.* 1953–56; form A ('53, 8 pages); 2⅔(8) minutes.
8) *FACT 8A, Judgment and Comprehension.* 1953–56; form A ('53, 7 pages); (35–40) minutes.
9) *FACT 9A, Arithmetic.* 1953–56; form A ('53, 6 pages); 10(20) minutes.
10) *FACT 10A, Patterns.* 1953–56; form A ('53, 6 pages); 20(28) minutes.
11) *FACT 11A, Components.* 1953–56; form A ('53, 6 pages); 20(24) minutes.

12) *FACT 12A, Tables.* 1953–56; form A ('53, 6 pages); 10(15) minutes.
13) *FACT 13A and 13B, Mechanics.* 1953–56; forms A ('53, 6 pages), B ('54, 6 pages); 20(25) minutes.
14) *FACT 14A, Expression.* 1953–56; form A ('53, 6 pages); (35–45) minutes.
15) *FACT 15A, Reasoning.* 1957–60; form A ('57, 6 pages); supplementary manual ('60, 6 pages); 40¢ per supplementary manual; 24(30) minutes.
16) *FACT 16A, Ingenuity.* 1957–60; form A ('57, 7 pages); supplementary manual ('60, 6 pages); 40¢ per supplementary manual; 24(30) minutes.
b) IQ-TEST EDITION. Grades 9–12; 1957–60; 10 tests (same as for a plus vocabulary, planning, alertness) in 2 booklets: gray book ('57, 64 pages), blue book ('57, 24 pages); examiner's manual ('58, 70 pages); mimeographed norms ['58, 23 pages]; administrator's manual ('58, 17 pages); technical report ('59, 65 pages); mimeographed manual for planning short batteries ('60, 10 pages); score interpretation booklet for students ('58, 25 pages); separate answer sheets (MRC) must be used with gray book (blue book is scored by students); $3.25 per specimen set; (630) minutes in 3 sessions.
1) *SRA Scored.* Scoring service available only for MRC answer sheets used with gray books.
(a) Complete Rental Plan. Rental and scoring service, $1.60 per student.
(b) Scoring Only Plan. $8.50 per 25 blue books; $25 per 25 gray books; scoring service, $1.36 per student.
2) *School Scored.* $8.50 per 25 blue books; $25 per 25 gray books; $11.25 per 100 MRC answer sheets and 3 examiner's manuals; $2 per set of MRC hand scoring stencils for gray books; $10.75 per 25 score interpretation booklets; $3.25 per set of interpretive materials (administrator's manual, technical report, norms, and manual for planning).

Source: Buros, O. K. *The seventh mental measurements yearbook* (Vol. 2). Highland Park, N.J.: Gryphon Press, 1972, p. 1053.

This was a rather ambitious set of goals, and an index of the success of Buros is the fact that the *Yearbook* has appeared seven more times since then. It is a kind of bible for test users. Figure 3–6 presents a typical entry from the *Seventh Mental Measurements Yearbook* (1972).[1] As you can see from the figure, information such as target populations of subjects, cost, length, time to administer, author, and publisher is included. This information is normally followed by two or more reviews of the test and a bibliography of publications in which information about the test has appeared. The MMY serves the dual purpose of identifying those tests which are poorly constructed and poorly supported with appropriate documentation, and also of highlighting tests with exceptional promise for a particular purpose. (Buros has published another book, *Tests in Print* [1961]. It serves the purpose of an index for the MMY.)

While a source such as Buros' is often useful as a shortcut in the evaluation of a test, potential users should have a framework of their own for determin-

---

[1] The *Eighth Mental Measurements Yearbook* has just been published. While many new tests are reviewed and older reviews brought up to date, structurally the latest edition is identical to the seven earlier editions.

FIGURE 3–7

A Scheme for Test Evaluation

1. Title
2. Author
3. Publisher
4. Forms and groups to which applicable
5. Practical features
6. General type

7. Date of publication
8. Cost, booklet; answer sheet
9. Scoring services available and cost
10. Time required

11. Purpose for which evaluated
12. Description of test, items, scoring
13. Author's purpose and basis for selecting items

14. Adequacy of directions; training required to administer
15. Mental functions or traits represented in each score
16. Comments regarding design of test
17. Validation against criteria: number and type of cases, criterion measure, time interval, result
18. Other empirical evidence indicating what the test measures
19. Comments regarding validity for particular purposes

20. Generalizability (procedure, cases, result)
21. Long-term stability (procedure, time interval, cases, result)
22. Norms (type of scale, selection of sample)
23. Comments regarding adequacy of above for particular purpose

24. Comments of reviewers
25. General evaluation
26. References

Source: Cronbach, L. J. *Essentials of psychological testing* (3rd ed.). New York: Harper, 1970, p. 187, table 6.6, copyright © by Lee J. Cronbach. By permission of Harper & Row, Publishers, Inc.

ing the adequacy of a test. If for no other reason, this is necessary because the MMY is updated on the average of every six years. If a new test comes along, we cannot wait for the new MMY to come out. Cronbach (1970) provides a scheme that is useful for such an evaluation. An examination of this form for evaluation (see Figure 3–7) shows the amount of information necessary before a decision can be made about the use of a test.

Types of Tests

There are many ways in which the thousands of available tests could be categorized. We will use three different schemes. The first consists of the traditional distinctions you are likely to find in a discussion of testing and deals primarily with the administrative aspects of the test. The second was suggested by Cleary and associates (1975) and deals with the behavioral repertory sampled by the test. The third set of categories is the traditional content categories, breaking tests down into areas such as intelligence tests, interest tests, and special aptitude tests.

Traditional Administrative Categories

1. Speed Tests. You have probably taken tests that had rigid and demanding time limits (so demanding that almost everyone who took them was unable to complete them). These were probably speed tests. The score on this type of test is the amount of work done per unit time. In a sense, these might be characterized as tests of maximum rather than average performance. In classroom settings, these tests are often disguised as "open-book" tests. In most cases, the individual must have the information necessary to answer the questions readily at hand; if time is taken to go to the book for the answer, the test cannot be completed. The logic of speed tests is that the individual may be called upon to solve a problem or find an answer in a short period of time and the necessary information must be readily at hand and quickly retrieved. There is some question about how frequent or important this kind of activity is in day-to-day behavior on most jobs. Of course, in many skills such as typing, speed is an important aspect of performance.

2. Power Tests. As opposed to speed tests, power tests have no rigid time limits. The individual is given ample time to complete the test. This might be considered a maximum performance test of another kind (i.e., do your best when time limits are not a factor). While there are some time limits on these tests, the limits are more for the convenience of the person administering the test than anything else. If you ever administer a test to an appreciable number of people, you will discover that some percentage of them will need 5 percent more time than allotted, *regardless of the time allotted.*

The same test can be given under conditions of either "speed" or "power." It is likely that under the two sets of conditions, something quite different is being measured in each.

3. Group Tests. As the name implies, group tests are tests which can be easily administered to groups of people at one time. As mentioned, one of the significant accomplishments of the psychologists attempting to institute a testing program for placement of World War I recruits was the translation of the individual intelligence test of Binet/Terman into a test that could be administered to 500 individuals at one time. Most tests administered in organizations for the purpose of selection or placement are group tests.

4. Individual Tests. Individual tests can be given to only one person at a time. It is clear that the benefit from an individual test must be large enough to outweigh the cost of such a process. For this reason, individual tests are generally administered in special situations. Individual tests are often administered to applicants for high-level managerial positions, for instance. An example of such a test might be one sampling the applicant's ability to solve problems which would normally confront a manager on a day-to-day basis. Since one of the outcomes of the test is intended to be an assessment of the *styles* of problem solving as much as the *products*, a group test is often inappropriate. Other examples of individual tests would be those requiring a certain interpersonal rapport between the person taking and the person administering the test. This characteristic is claimed to be of utmost importance by those involved in using high-level diagnostic tests such as the Rorschach inkblot test.

5. *Paper-and-Pencil Tests.* The paper-and-pencil test is by far the most common in industrial settings (with the exception of the preemployment interview, if that is considered as a test). The important characteristic of this test is that no manipulation of physical objects or equipment is directly related to the score which the individual is given. The facility with a pencil should be unrelated to the score which a person receives on a test (assuming some minimal level of proficiency). These tests range from the more common, general intelligence test which presents items dealing with vocabulary, or numerical operations, to a test such as the Bennett Mechanical Comprehension Test, which requires the individual to visualize some particular mechanical operation and answer a question about it. The common element is that the response is made on paper with a pencil.

6. *Performance Tests.* Performance tests require the individual to make a response by manipulating a particular physical object or piece of equip-·ment. The score which the individual receives on the test is directly related to the quality or quantity of that manipulation. An example might be a test which requires the individual to assemble nuts and bolts. There are many situations in which one might be interested in knowing how well an individual can perform a particular operation rather than simply whether or not the person knows the principles of the operation. An example of this type of test which most of us have encountered is the actual driving part of the driver's examination for certification.

7. *Aptitude Tests.* The claim is often made that aptitude tests measure the *future potential* of an individual for a particular activity. An example of such a test would be the Scholastic Aptitude Test (SAT) or the College Board Entrance Examination (CBEE), both of which are intended to identify the aptitude of the individual for academic curricula of a particular sort.

8. *Achievement Tests.* As opposed to aptitude tests, achievement tests are thought to measure some degree of proficiency which the individual possesses *at the time of testing*. Most examinations related to specific courses, such as your midterm or final examination in Industrial/Organizational psychology, are like that.

Cleary et. al. (1975) suggested another method or set of dimensions for categorizing tests. This method emphasizes the repertory of behavior which is sampled by the test, rather than administrative aspects. They suggest the following four dimensions:

1. *Breadth.* Breadth is the amount of coverage of the test. A test can

vary from a very narrow test of a particular content area (such as knowledge of performance appraisal techniques) to a very broad test of general intellectual ability.

2. Relation of Test to a Particular Training or Educational Program. This is the degree to which a test is independent of a particular curriculum. Police recruits who complete the academy training program are usually given an examination, which will be used as the index of whether or not they successfully completed the training program. The nature of that test is closely tied to the curriculum of the academy, requiring a knowledge of laws and procedures that was provided by the training program. If the academy training program were to change, the test would undoubtedly change with it. On the other hand, many tests, such as general intelligence tests, or tests of eye-hand coordination, are unrelated to the nature of any particular training program and would remain unchanged if the training program were to be modified.

3. Recency of Learning Sampled. Another factor is the passage of time since the individual first displayed the behaviors sampled. As an example of this distinction, Cleary and associates cite the Graduate Records Examination (GRE), which has an arithmetic-operations section based on high-school algebra. On the other hand, the advanced subject area of the GRE might sample information that the individual encountered for the first time only 10 minutes before beginning the examination.

4. Purpose of the Test. How is information to be used? At least two ways in which test information might be used would be (1) to assess the amount of learning which *has occurred* over some specifiable period of time, and (2) to predict how much learning is *likely to occur* in the future. This is another way of making the aptitude/achievement distinction. This distinction makes a little more sense than the traditional aptitude/achievement distinction because it clearly implies that the distinction is not a property of the test, it is a property of the reason for which the test is given. In other words, the same test might be classified as either an aptitude or an achievement test (or both), depending on how the information is used. Thus, your final examination is designed to measure your achievement in industrial and organizational psychology, but it might also be used to indicate your potential (aptitude) for advanced training in this area.

TEST CONTENT

In addition to categorizing tests according to administrative characteristics, it is possible to describe tests in terms of their content area. Buros (1972) has 15 different major headings for tests in the seventh MMY. Many of these tests are irrelevant for our present purposes, for example, courtship and marriage tests. We are primarily interested in categories of tests that have some potential use in organizational settings. For this purpose, we will adopt the classification scheme that Ghiselli has used for reviewing the validity of occupational tests (Ghiselli & Brown, 1955; Ghiselli, 1955, 1966, 1973). We will give examples of the tests represented by the various headings, but we will not attempt to be exhaustive or even representative. If you are particularly interested in a test or test category, you may find adequate information about it in one of the basic reference sources such as Buros (1972) or in one of several good personnel and psychological testing books such as the ones by Guion (1965) and Cronbach (1970). The following headings will be used to categorize tests generally used in industrial settings: *tests of intellectual abilities, tests of spatial and mechanical abilities, perceptual accuracy tests, tests of motor abilities, and personality and interest tests.*

Intellectual Abilities

As we saw in the brief history of industrial aptitude testing, one of the first paper-and-pencil tests to be introduced for industrial use was the general intelligence test. The popularity of this kind of measure continues unabated. The most widely used of these tests is the Wonderlic Personnel Test. The Wonderlic consists of 50 items dealing with verbal, numerical, and spatial facility. These items are mixed together and increase in difficulty from the beginning to the end of the test (this is known as a "spiral omnibus" format). There are several parallel forms for the tests. Guion (1966) has suggested that the Wonderlic is primarily a test of verbal facility, although the test also deals to some degree with deductive logic and numerical facility. Its wide popularity is probably due as much to the ease of administration and scoring as to its psychometric properties (although the norms are quite extensive including minority-group norms). One of the forms takes only 12 minutes to complete and can be given to groups. A single score is derived from the test responses.

There is a strong feeling on the part of many personnel departments that "general intelligence" *must be* related in some way to most of the positions for which hiring and placement are done. However, there are several reasons to question the indiscriminate administration of "general intelligence" tests.

The first and probably most important reservation is that we do not know what "general intelligence" is; a debate of a sort has continued unabated for more than 70 years about the nature of intelligence. Second, there seems to be a good deal of correlation between tests of verbal facility and short spiral omnibus tests of "general intelligence," which raises some concern about how "general" these tests actually are. Third, if intelligence is not a unitary concept, we should at least have some reasoned guesses about how particular aspects of intelligence relate to job-related criteria. Finally, there is no particular reason to think that "general intelligence" is the only, or even most important, dimension for success in many positions.

In support of this last point, Table 3–2, taken from Ghiselli's review (1973), shows the range of relationships between measures of intellectual ability and success for several different occupational categories.

TABLE 3–2
Validity Coefficients for Industrial Occupations

	Machine Tenders	Bench Workers	Inspec- tors	Packers and Wrappers	Gross Manual Workers	All Industrial Workers
Intellectual abilities ..	.21F	.18F	.21D	.18D	.22F	.20F
Intelligence	.21E	.18F	.23D	.17D	.21D	.20F
Immediate memory ..	.17D	.06D	.14B	.24B	—	.15D
Substitution	.19C	.12D	−.01D	.16D	—	.14D
Arithmetic	.21E	.20E	.24D	.16D	.24D	.21F

A = less than 100 cases.
B = 100 to 499 cases.
C = 500 to 999 cases.
D = 1000 to 4999 cases.
E = 5000 to 9999 cases.
F = 10,000 or more cases.
Source: Ghiselli, E. The Validity of Aptitude Tests in Personnel Selection, *Personnel Psychology*, 1970, *26*, 476 (adapted).

While there is probably some value in pursuing and trying to understand the relationship between the construct of intelligence and the construct of industrial proficiency, it probably makes more sense to deal with the two constructs as both distinct and complex; we should examine the relationships between specific aspects of "intelligence" (if we can define the construct adequately), and specific aspects of job performance.

Mechanical and Spatial Abilities

Paper-and-pencil tests of mechanical abilities generally require the individual to identify, recognize, and/or apply a mechanical principle suggested by the test item. Figure 3–8 presents an item from one of the most popular of these tests, the Bennett Mechanical Comprehension Test. This type of test has high face validity for many blue-collar skilled and unskilled positions.

Spatial relations and reasoning would seem to be important for many occupations. A multiple aptitude test battery known as the DAT (Differential Aptitude Test) describes spatial relations as follows:

> The *Spatial Relations* test is a measure of ability to deal with concrete materials through visualization. There are many vocations in which one is required to imagine how a specified object would appear if rotated in a given way. This ability to manipulate things mentally, to create a structure in one's mind from a plan, is what the test is designed to evaluate. It is an ability needed in such fields as drafting, dress designing, architecture, art, die-making, and decoration, or wherever there is a need to visualize objects in three dimensions.

Figure 3–9 is an example of a relatively simple spatial relations test item. The individual is required to visualize some property of the stimulus

FIGURE 3–8

Sample Item from Bennett Mechanical Comprehension Test

Which would be the better shears for cutting metal?

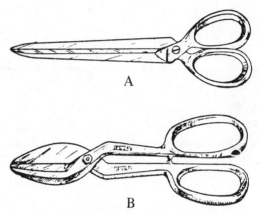

A

B

Source: Bennett Mechanical Comprehension Test, Form BB, Item Y. Reproduced by permission. Copyright 1941, renewed 1969 by The Psychological Corporation, New York, N.Y. All rights reserved.

that is not immediately apparent. This requires some mental manipulation of the stimulus. This is an ability that seems to be modifiable by training.

Perceptual Accuracy

Perceptual accuracy tests are usually straightforward and, like mechanical comprehension tests, have high face validity for many occupations. These tests usually involve some kind of comparison. The individual is presented

FIGURE 3–9

Spatial Relations Test Item

Space Relations. Which one of the figures can be made from the pattern?

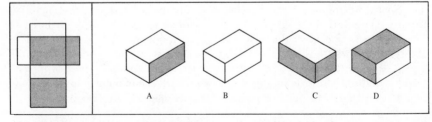

Source: DAT Space Relations Test. Reproduced by permission. Copyright © 1972 by The Psychological Corporation, New York, N.Y. All rights reserved.

FIGURE 3–10

A Perceptual Accuracy Test

A	B	
170—CU—7Z25B43—W47	170—CU—7Z25B43—W47	
248—RT—67F896H—T62	248—RT—76F896H—T62	✓
991—PP—943G56V—55J	991—PP—943G56U—55J	✓
114—NX—621FP5U—7HC	114—NX—621FP5U—7HC	
693—LD—T754DF9—BB6	693—LD—T754DF9—BB6	

with a standard stimulus of some kind and asked to determine if a test stimulus is the same or different. Figure 3–10 presents an example of such a test item. The task of the individual is to compare the two columns of numbers and letters and identify pairs that do not match, such as those checked. For many clerical jobs, this kind of test amounts to a work-sample test, since the job requires exactly the behavior tested. In other cases, it is assumed to measure an aptitude necessary for the development of clerical skills. As Ghiselli points out (1973), these tests do have reasonable validity for many clerical positions. He reports some validity coefficients in the .40s.

Motor Abilities

Tests of motor abilities involve the movement of the limbs in one fashion or another. It may be a complex task in which the individual is required to move arms and legs in coordination, as in the task of flying an airplane or playing an organ; it may be a simple task such as placing pins in slots with the use of tweezers. Motor abilities represent characteristics of the individual which have some potential relationship to job performance not accounted for by tests of intellectual abilities, mechanical and spatial abilities, or tests of perceptual accuracy.

The terms "sensorimotor" and "psychomotor" are often applied to manipulation tests such as those described above. Guion (1965) provides a useful distinction between these two terms. Psychomotor abilities are those primarily requiring muscular movement and control, while sensorimotor tests basically require some initial involvement of sense receptors followed by some muscular movement and control. A tweezer test is an example of a psychomotor test, while driving an automobile on a crowded expressway would be characterized as a sensorimotor test. Both kinds of tests have been useful in selection and placement over the years. One of the disadvantages of motor tests is the time and expense involved. They can seldom be administered to groups and often involve costly equipment. As was true of the perceptual accuracy tests, many of the motor tests amount to work samples for the people taking them: in many jobs, an individual is required in the course of job duties to manipulate nuts and bolts, small pins, etc.

Fleishman and his associates (1966) have been extremely successful in refining our understanding of psychomotor and sensorimotor tests. They were concerned with identifying the factors responsible for variance in human motor performance. Through a program of careful and exhaustive research, they were able to identify 11 factors responsible for differences among individuals in various motor performance tasks. These factors are listed in Figure 3–11. The way in which these factors were identified and their importance in understanding the capabilities and limitations of humans will be discussed more fully in a later chapter. It is relatively easy to think of tests for these various abilities as well as their relationship to tasks that make up certain jobs. For example, crane operators, heavy-equipment operators, and organists are all required to exhibit a high degree of multilimb coordination; watchmakers, surgeons, and bartenders may all be required

FIGURE 3–11

Taxonomy of Abilities

The taxonomy of the more important abilities resulting from this programmatic research as briefly described by Fleishman (1966):

Control precision: This factor is common to tasks which require fine, highly controlled, but not overcontrolled, muscular adjustments, primarily where larger muscle groups are involved. . .

Multilimb coordinations: This is the ability to coordinate the movements of a number of limbs simultaneously. . .

Response orientation: This ability factor . . . appears to involve the ability to *select* the correct movement in relation to the correct stimulus, especially under highly speeded conditions. . .

Reaction time: This represents simply the speed with which an individual is able to respond to a stimulus when it appears. . .

Speed of arm movement: This represents simply the speed with which an individual can make a gross, discrete arm movement where accuracy is not the requirement. . .

Rate control: This ability involves the making of continuous anticipatory motor adjustments relative to changes in speed and direction of a continuously moving target or object. . .

Manual dexterity: This ability involves skillful, well-directed arm-hand movements in manipulating fairly large objects under speed conditions. . .

Finger dexterity: This is the ability to make skill-controlled manipulations of tiny objects involving, primarily, the fingers. . .

Arm-hand steadiness: This is the ability to make precise arm-hand positioning movements where strength and speed are minimized; the critical feature, as the name implies, is the steadiness with which such movements can be made. . .

Wrist, finger speed: This ability has been called "tapping" in many previous studies. . .

Aiming: This ability appears to be measured by printed tests which provide the subject with very small circles . . . The subject typically goes from circle to circle placing one dot in each circle as rapidly as possible. (pp. 152–156)

Source: Fleishman, E. A. Human abilities and the acquisition of skill. In E. A. Bilodeau (Ed.), *Acquisition of skill.* New York: Academic Press, 1966.

to exhibit arm-hand steadiness. Fleishman's taxonomy of motor abilities is very helpful in structuring a rational testing program around a well-done job analysis; it is quite relevant to current models of selection since it encourages considering the complexity of a single operation (such as operating a grinding machine) rather than reducing the ability test to one task that might be a simulation of the job (such as a tweezer dexterity test).

" 'Oops!' has no place in the vocabulary of a surgeon."

Reprinted by permission The Wall Street Journal

Personality and Interest Inventories

It might be more appropriate to label these tests as motivational rather than personality and interest tests. The distinction between motivational and personality variables is becoming less clear. For example, you are likely to see "need for achievement" described as both a personality and motivational variable. However, in keeping with Ghiselli's categorization, we will refer to these tests as personality and interest tests. Two major subcategories of personality tests are *objective* and *projective*. By objective tests we refer to those paper-and-pencil tests that provide a clear stimulus, such as a statement about preferences for various life styles, and a clear set of responses from which to choose. A projective test, on the other hand, presents an ambiguous stimulus to the individual and does not restrict response format. The Rorschach Inkblot test is an example of a projective test.

The logic of personality testing is that knowing the habitual manner in which an individual responds in many different situations should help in determining whether or not the individual will be successful in a particular class of jobs. While this rationale makes sense, it has been hard to demonstrate. Guion and Gottier (1965) reviewed the validity information on personality tests used in industrial settings. Their review covered studies published between 1952 and 1963. Here is their conclusion:

> In brief, it is difficult in the face of this summary to advocate with a clear conscience the use of personality measures in most situations as a basis of making employment decisions about people. It seems clear that the only acceptable reason for using personality measures as instruments of decision is found only after doing considerable research with the measure in the specific situation and for the specific purpose for which it is to be used. Sometimes, unvalidated personality measures are used as instruments of decision because of "clinical insight" or of gullibility or superstition or of evidence accumulated in some other setting. All of these may be equally condemned unless specific situational data can be gathered that the insight, superstition, or borrowed validity is in fact predictive. (p. 160)

The invasion of privacy issue raised by critics in the early 1960s (Gross, 1962) has done much to temper the use of personality tests in industry. This tempering has received an additional boost from current concerns for fair employment. The responsibility for demonstrating that a particular personality test is job-related could be overwhelming in the case of a projective test, such as the Rorschach. A review of the three journals cited as sources by Guion and Gottier for the years following the publication of their article reveals few published reports of attempts to relate personality measures to job performance. This will change, no doubt, in the next several years. A technique known as the "assessment center" is becoming more and more popular, particularly in the identification of managerial talent. We will describe this technique in some detail shortly, but for the present discussion it is useful to know that a significant part of the "assessment" in such centers is the measurement of motivational or personality variables.

The most widely used interest test is probably the Strong Vocational Interest Blank (SVIB). This type of test compares the responses of the individual taking the test to the responses of individuals already successful in particular fields. The implication is that the individual has the greatest likelihood for success (on motivational grounds) in the occupation most closely matching his/her response pattern. Interest tests are used more widely for vocational counseling and guidance than for selection and placement decisions.

Multiple-Aptitude Test Batteries

A final category of tests is defined by structure rather than content. This category includes test batteries which comprise many of the content categories already mentioned. They are generally lengthy tests lasting several hours, and have subsections dealing with items, such as numerical abilities, verbal abilities, and spatial relations. There have been several prominent batteries over the years. One of the first was L. L. Thurstone's Primary Mental Abilities test (PMA), which closely paralleled his theory of intelligence (1938). As opposed to many of the early researchers in the area of intelligence, Thurstone concluded on the basis of factor analyses that intelligence comprised several basic or primary mental abilities. He set about constructing a scale to measure each of these abilities. The scales currently comprising the PMA are as follows: verbal meaning, number facility, reasoning, spatial relations, perceptual speed, memory, and word fluency. These clearly represent a collection of several of the content categories which we have dealt with so far.

There are advantages to having information related to many different abilities. Such information would be particularly valuable for differential job placement purposes. The trade-off, of course, is the cost and time involved in administration. While the PMA represents one of the few attempts to tie tests specifically to a theory of intellectual abilities, there are some complaints that it has not changed appreciably since its introduction (Buros, 1972). Two other more recent batteries in use are the General Aptitude Test Battery (GATB) and the Differential Aptitude Test (DAT).

Assessment Centers

A logical extension of the multiple-aptitude test battery is the *assessment center*. This label derives from the fact that groups of individuals (both those to be assessed and those doing the assessment) are brought together for the purpose of determining the potential of a group of individuals currently employed by an organization. This assessment may imply promotion, placement, or simply career guidance. Finkle (1976) has done a comprehensive review of the development of this technique over the past few decades. In that review, he says that "assessment center . . . refers to a group-oriented, standardized series of activities that provides a basis for judgments or predictions of human behaviors believed or known to be relevant to work performed in an organizational setting" (p. 861). The earliest systematic assessment center approach was by A T & T. An excellent description of the development and logic of the A T & T effort is contained in a book by the psychologists primarily responsible for that program (Bray, Campbell, and Grant, 1974). This program was begun in 1956.

Most assessment centers are similar in several respects (Finkle, 1976):

1. *Assessment is done in groups:* Groups of 12 individuals are usually assessed simultaneously. They may be broken into smaller groups of six or three for particular exercises. Group assessment provides the opportunity for peer evaluation.

2. *Assessment is done by groups:* Evaluators or assessors work in teams to produce and evaluate information. These groups usually consist of managers from the organization who are not personally acquainted with the person being assessed. The team may also include a psychologist.

3. *Multiple methods:* Several different methods are used to gather information about the person being considered. These might include objective testing, projective testing, group and individual interviews, as well as individual and group-based situational exercises. One favorite individual exercise is known as the "in basket." In this exercise, the assessee deals with a series of memos by rerouting them, responding to them in writing, or filing them. A typical group exercise might be a leaderless group discussion. The objective and projective tests might be chosen from the list described earlier in the chapter.

4. *Face validity:* There is almost universal agreement among individuals being assessed and acting as assessors that the process has the appearance of relevance—to a much greater degree than the typical paper-and-pencil test for the selection of managers.

As a result of completing the various tests, exercises, and interviews, the person being assessed has provided the assessment team with a large amount of information. On the basis of this information, the team typically rates each assessee on a series of dimensions. Typical of these dimensions are the following: decision making, human relations skills, administrative ability, persuasiveness, resistance to stress, impact, personal acceptability, flexibility, realism of expectations, motivation, and intellectual ability.

On the basis of these ratings, as well as other notes kept during the assessment period, a rather lengthy narrative report is prepared for each person who was assessed. In Figure 3–12, portions of a typical report are produced.

This report is then condensed, and portions of it are fed back to the person who was assessed by one or more members of the assessment team. The actual activities usually occur over a several-day period, often in a conference center geographically separate from the normal workplace. The members of the assessment team are usually given training in assessment

FIGURE 3–12

". . . there were several indications from his behavior that his strong desire to make a favorable impression promoted above average tenseness in the assessment situation. On several occasions, his behavior was characterized by nervousness and controlled quietness, as though he were reluctant to enter into a situation until he felt absolutely sure of himself."

". . . the picture he created was that of a young man eager to cooperate, comply, and do his best in order to fulfill the expectations others had for him."

"In most respects, the trainee's general abilities compare favorably with the total sample of men in the Management Progress study."

"Most members of the staff anticipated a yery successful career in the Bell System for the trainee . . . There was a mild amount of disagreement concerning the speed with which he is likely to reach the district level of management. Everyone agreed that he presently displays the abilities and potential to perform effectively at the district level."

Source: Bray, D. W., Campbell, R. J., & Grant, D. L. *Formative years in business: A long-term AT&T study of managerial lives.* New York: Wiley, 1974. Copyright © by John Wiley & Sons, Inc. Reprinted by permission of John Wiley & Sons, Inc.

procedures and the particular instruments to be used. This training may last anywhere from three hours to several days.

On the basis of the results of an assessment center, organizations may make many different types of decisions. Among them are the following (Finkle, 1976):

1. An assessee does or does not qualify for a particular job or job level.
2. Assessees may be ranked on a series of variables and placed into different categories of anticipated speed of promotion.
3. Predictions of long-range potential may be made.
4. Development programs for aiding the assessee in personal growth may be provided.
5. Team members may be aided in their role as assessors.

The results of assessment center approaches are encouraging. This approach supports the process of differential placement rather than the more traditional and less useful selection ethic. The strengths and weaknesses of the applicants can be matched with the requirements of various positions in the organization. The early data on predictive validities are promising. In addition, there are several private organizations that now conduct assessment centers for client companies. This provides an opportunity for small organizations with too few employees to do traditional validation projects to take advantage of the cumulative data of the assessment center in drawing inferences about the potential of its people.

In spite of its logical and cosmetic appeal, there have been some misgivings expressed concerning assessment centers. Dunnette and Borman (1979) warn that the "rapid growth of assessment methods may be accompanied by sloppy or improper application of assessment procedures" (p.32). The lack of quality control on assessment procedures could easily lead to indiscriminate and damaging results, similar to those encountered by the random application of "sensitivity training" in the late 60s. The general use of assessment centers (whether they are appropriate or not) is a particularly important issue, due to the cost of this technique. It is extremely expensive, and the benefit should clearly be evaluated in terms of its cost.

Reservations have also been expressed concerning the reliability of the ratings that are made of the assessees (Hinrichs and Haanpera, 1976) as well as the validity of those ratings (Klimoski and Strickland, 1977). There is some concern that instead of predicting future performance, the team members are actually identifying those assessees who fit in the company "mold" most neatly. In effect, they are actually predicting the promotion decisions that will ultimately be made concerning the assessees. This criticism cannot be easily dismissed, since most validation studies of assessment centers have used promotions or salary success as the criterion. The only way to answer this type of criticism is to show that assessment centers are capable of predicting actual behavior of the individual being assessed. Unfortunately, there have been very few studies of this type, and we must remain *cautiously* optimistic of the future of assessment centers.

THE EQUAL EMPLOYMENT OPPORTUNITY COMMISSION (EEOC)

The EEOC has played a rather dramatic role in the development and administration of tests in industry. As the federal government's main administrative agency for the enforcement of the Civil Rights Act in the employment context, it has taken its role seriously. The EEOC has evolved from a weak public advocate status to a strong and active enforcement agency, with broad powers to initiate and negotiate legal and administrative action on behalf of protected minority groups.

As a result of this evolution, accompanied by some sensational court settlements on behalf of minority plaintiffs, employers have become justifiably cautious in the use of tests for employment decisions. As indicated earlier the first reaction of personnel officers was to abandon traditional tests in favor of "nontest" predictors rather than take a chance on accidentally discriminating unfairly against a minority applicant. This was not the best action for several reasons. In the first place, in the view of psychologists and administrative agencies alike (Uniform Guidelines, 1978), the label "test" was not restricted to traditional paper-and-pencil question-and-answer formats exclusively. A test could include a physical examination, an application blank, an interview, a work sample, or even a performance rating (if this rating was used to predict future success in another position). Consequently, employers were often abandoning a standardized measure with some technical documentation for a loosely constructed and poorly documented measure.

This seems almost like rats swimming *toward* a sinking ship instead of away from it! As far as EEOC was concerned, the employer would have to validate the interview, just as it would have been necessary to validate the traditional test.

In addition, regardless of the pressures from EEOC to be fair, there remained the very real need to identify those individuals who would be most likely to help an organization meet its production or service goals. Consequently, employers could not afford to abandon any promising technique for finding such employees, including traditional testing.

It should have been obvious to employers that a more appropriate response would have been to look more carefully at the jobs in question (on the basis of a job analysis) and consider more carefully what kinds of behaviors were required on that job and how these behaviors might be successfully predicted. This is happening to a much greater extent now than it was five years ago and for several reasons. For one thing, the federal guidelines regarding equal employment opportunity have finally stabilized. There had been a good deal of disagreement among federal agencies concerning how strictly and literally the EEOC rules should be interpreted. Recently (Uniform Guidelines, 1978), the EEOC, the Department of Labor, the Department of Justice, and the United States Civil Service Commission agreed on a single interpretation of the guidelines (hence their label—Uniform Guidelines). These uniform guidelines are the result of long and complicated discussions among legal experts, psychologists, employers, and federal administrators. As a result of the agreement among these parties, the employer's responsibility should be clearer now than at any time in the past 15 years. This will undoubtedly help in the formulation of rational and fair testing programs where testing is appropriate.

The Issue of Differential Validation.   In the late 1960s and early 1970s, there were many articles purporting to demonstrate "differential validity," i.e., situations in which a test was valid for one group (usually a majority group) but not for another group (usually a minority group). This was intimidating to employers, particularly those already frightened by the possibility of substantial economic losses through class action suits. Recently, this phenomenon of "differential validity" has come under severe attack. Schmidt and his colleagues (Schmidt, Berner, and Hunter, 1973; Hunter and Schmidt, 1978) have been able to demonstrate that these differences in validity can be just as easily attributed to statistical artifacts as to real differences between majority and minority groups. For example, suppose we had conducted a validity study of the relationship between an ability test and a performance measure for two groups; one of these groups was composed of white males while the other group consisted of black males. If this were the typical organization in the late 1960s, there might have been few black males in the organizational level at which the test was administered. Assume that our two samples consisted of 100 white males

"Can't those Equal Opportunity people leave well enough alone??"

Reprinted by permission The Wall Street Journal

and 25 black males, respectively. Let us further assume that the validity coefficient for the white male sample was .26, while the validity coefficient for the black male sample was .25. In this instance, by looking at the appropriate significance tables, we would conclude that test performance was significantly correlated with job performance for white males but not for black males—a case of "differential validity." The technical explanation for this result is that the "power" to detect significant validity coefficients in the black sample was not as great as the "power" to detect differences in the white sample because the sample size was smaller for black males than white males.

The issue of sample size is only one of the many complications in the controversy surrounding "differential validity." Nevertheless, it is safe to say that substantially different validities for majority and minority samples is probably a lot less common than we thought. A good review of these issues and findings is presented by Linn (1978). As a result of these sophisticated analyses and interpretations, employers may feel a little more secure in introducing experimental test batteries than they had previously. The issue of differential prediction will be considered again in Chapter 5, when we discuss the administration and evaluation of selection programs.

SUMMARY

A psychological test is a device for the measurement of some phase of a carefully chosen sample of an individual's behavior. The process of evaluating a test is different from that of evaluating a testing program. Selection is the process of selecting one of n people for a particular job; placement is the process of matching individuals with jobs.

The psychological testing movement began with Binet's attempt to identify the hard-to-educate in the French school system. His test was transported to the United States and further developed by Terman. A modification of this test was used for the classification of armed forces recruits in World War I. On the basis of the success in test administration during the war, industry adopted testing as a means of classifying job applicants. World War II provided another impetus for the testing process. The use of psychological tests increased until social critics began to examine the theoretical foundation for the testing. Issues such as the invasion of privacy and unfair hiring practices led to a public distrust of testing. The Equal Employment Opportunity Commission was created to monitor the effect of certain personnel practices (including testing) on protected minority groups. The dual pressures from the government and the public have had the effect of encouraging theory building in the area of psychological measurement.

A psychological test yields a measurement of some particular attribute of the person. The degree of trust that can be placed in this measurement depends on several characteristics. Two primary characteristics are reliability and validity. Reliability is concerned with the consistency of the measurement. There are many ways for estimating the consistency or reliability of a measurement. Three popular methods are: test-retest, equivalent forms, and internal consistency. Different ways of estimating reliability may yield different results because they include different sources in the estimate of error variance (i.e., unreliability).

Validity is operationally defined as the relationship between a predictor (e.g., a test score) and a criterion (e.g., a job performance measure). Conceptually, it is the potential of one measure of behavior for predicting another measure of behavior. There are two classes of validity: logical (or descriptive) and empirical (or criterion-related). Logical validity includes content and construct validity. Empirical validity includes concurrent and predictive validity.

Validity is usually measured as a correlation between a predictor and a criterion. As the correlation increases, the ability to predict a person's criterion score from a predictor score improves.

The use of tests is restricted to those qualified to administer, score, and interpret the tests. The American Psychological Association has identified three levels of tests, corresponding to the level of sophistication required of the user.

Types of tests can be considered from several points of view. The first point of view is administrative. Tests can be classified as speed or power, group or individual, paper-and-pencil or performance, and aptitude or achievement.

Tests can also be classified according to the type of behavior sampled. They can require broad or narrow knowledge; they can be closely or loosely tied to a training curriculum; they can sample information that was learned recently or some time ago; the tests can be used as an index of what was learned or what could be learned.

Tests can be categorized according to content. The major content classes are: tests of intellectual ability, tests of spatial and mechanical abilities, perceptual accuracy tests, tests of motor abilities, and personality and interest tests. Multiple-aptitude test batteries are commonly used to gather information for counseling and placement. The assessment center is a promising new approach for gathering both traditional test data and work sample on job applicants.

REFERENCES

American Psychological Association. *Technical recommendation for psychological tests and diagnostic techniques.* Washington, D.C.: APA, 1954.

Bray, D. W., Campbell, R. J. & Grant, D. L. *Formative years in business: a long-term AT & T study of managerial lives.* New York: Wiley, 1974.

Buros, O. K. *The first mental measurements yearbook.* Highland Park, N.J.: Gryphon, 1938.

Buros, O. K. *The seventh mental measurements yearbook.* Highland Park, N.J.: Gryphon, 1972.

Buros, O. K. *The eighth mental measurements yearbook.* Highland Park, N.J.: Gryphon, 1978.

Buros, O. K. *Tests in print.* Highland Park, N.J.: Gryphon, 1961.

Cleary, T. A., Humphreys, L. G., Kendrick, S. A., & Wesman, A. Educational uses of tests with disadvantaged students. *American Psychologist*, 1975, *30*, 15–41.

Cronbach, L. J. *Essentials of psychological testing.* New York: Harper & Row, 1970.

DAT Space Relations Test Manual. Reproduced by permission. Copyright © 1973, 1974 by The Psychological Corporation, New York, N.Y. All rights reserved.

Dunnette, M. & Borman, W. Personnel selection and classification systems. In M. Rosenzweig and L. Porter, *Annual Review of Psychology*, 1979, *30*, 477–526.

Equal Employment Opportunity Commission. Adoption by four agencies of uniform guidelines on employee selection procedures. *Federal Register*, 1978, *43*, 38290–38309.

Equal Employment Opportunity Commission. *Guidelines on employee selection procedures*. Washington, D.C.: U.S. Government Printing Office, 1974.

Finkle, R. B. Managerial assessment centers. In M. D. Dunnette, (Ed.) *Handbook of Industrial and Organizational Psychology*. Chicago: Rand McNally, 1976, 861–888.

Fleishman, E. A. Human abilities and the acquisition of skill. In Bilodeau (Ed.) *Acquisition of skill*. New York: Academic Press, 1966.

Ghiselli, E. E. The measurement of occupational aptitude. *University of California Publications in Psychology*, 8, 1955, 101–216.

Ghiselli, E. E. *The validity of occupational aptitude tests*. New York: Wiley, 1966.

Ghiselli, E. E. The validity of aptitude tests in personnel selection. *Personnel Psychology*, 1973, *26*, 461–477.

Ghiselli, E. E., & Brown, C. W. *Personnel and industrial psychology* (2nd ed.). New York: McGraw-Hill, 1955.

Gross, M. L. *The brain watchers*. New York: Random House, 1962.

Guion, R. M. *Personnel testing*. New York: McGraw-Hill, 1965.

Guion, R. M. Employment tests and discriminatory hiring. *Industrial Relations*, 1966, *5*, 20–37.

Guion, R. M. Recruiting, selection, and job replacement. In M. D. Dunnette (Ed.), *Handbook of Industrial and Organizational Psychology*. Chicago: Rand McNally, 1976, 777–828.

Guion, R. M., & Gottier, R. F. Validity of personality measures in personnel selection. *Personnel Psychology*, 1965, *18*, 135–164.

Hinrichs, J. R. & Haanpera, S. Reliability of measurement in situational exercises: an assessment of assessment center testing. *Personnel Psychology*, 1976, *29*, 31–40.

Hull, C. L. *Aptitude testing*. New York: Harcourt, Brace & World, 1928.

Hunter, J. E. & Schmidt, F. L. Differential and single group validity of employment tests by race; a critical analysis of three recent studies. *Journal of Applied Psychology*, 1978, *63*, 1–11.

Klimoski, R. J. & Strickland, W. J. Assessment centers- valid or merely prescient. *Personnel Psychology*, 1977, *30*, 353–361.

Lawshe, C. H. A quantitative approach to content validity. *Personnel Psychology*, 1975, *28*, 563–575.

Linn, R. L. Single group validity, differential validity, and differential prediction. *Journal of Applied Psychology*, 1978, *63*, 507–512.

Muensterberg, H. *Psychological and industrial efficiency*. Boston: Houghton-Mifflin, 1913.

Richardson, M. W., & Kuder, G. F.   The calculation of test reliability coefficients based on the method of rational equivalence. *Journal of Educational Psychology*, 1939, *30*, 681–687.

Schmidt, F. L., Berner, J. C., & Hunter, J. E.   Racial differences in validity in employment tests: reality or illusion. *Journal of Applied Psychology*, 1973, *58*, 5–9.

Terman, L. M.   A trial of mental and pedagogical tests in a civil service examination for policemen and firemen. *Journal of Applied Psychology*, 1917, *1*, 17–29.

Thorndike, R. L.   *Personnel selection: Test and measurement technique.* New York: Wiley, 1949.

Thurstone, L. L.   *Primary mental abilities.* Chicago: University of Chicago Press, 1938.

Whyte, W. H.   *The organization man.* New York: Simon & Schuster, 1956.

CHAPTER **4**
Criterion-Related Issues

Historically, industrial psychology has been the application of principles of measurement and behavior to personnel decisions—personnel psychology. The field has become much broader than it was originally, and now encompasses such constructs as job satisfaction, work motivation, computer-assisted training programs, and work simulation. Nevertheless, some of the basic issues comprising the traditional area of personnel psychology are indispensable for the extensions of the field as well.

One of the most basic problems in personnel psychology is defining "the criterion." A criterion is a way of describing success. The criterion for measuring student success in this course might be the course grade. A criterion for a football team might be the number of wins versus the number of losses in a season. The criterion for a salesperson might be the dollar volume of his or her sales in a one-month period. In personnel psychology, the criterion usually occupies the role of the variable to be predicted.

The criterion will be approached from a number of vantage points. First, its role in a personnel decision system will be described. Next, some basic issues relating to the development and the use of criteria will be introduced. We will then introduce the technical, statistical aspects of criteria. Finally, methods of criterion development and performance appraisal will be described.

THE CRITERION CONSTRUCT

The increasing importance of the criterion in both research and application of behavioral principles is becoming apparent from several different sources. Employees are becoming increasingly dissatisfied with the way in which their performance is measured. Employment bulletins directed toward behavioral scientists are filled with job offers for individuals who have the technical and practical abilities necessary to "evaluate the success of a drug therapy program," "evaluate the success of a day-care program," or "evaluate the success of a community mental health clinic." Researchers are required to include in their grant applications the way in which they will evaluate the outcomes of their research efforts. Schoolteachers are being trained in the development of "behavioral objectives" for their pupils. Pupils are being trained to interact with the teaching system in terms of "meeting behavioral objectives" and "completing behavioral units." Training programs in industry are no longer being structured solely on the basis of available training equipment in the plant.

All of these developments are variations on the theme of criterion development. They may be responses to earlier excesses and oversights. Employees now realize that performance rating systems that were introduced to eliminate favoritism are so subjective that they actually make favoritism easier. Many social programs that were accepted on face value as being valuable have come off poorly under examination, and consequently checks and balances are being built into the programs. The federal government is becoming much more "product-oriented" in its interaction with researchers. School systems are quickly discovering that it is actually impossible to determine the intended effect of the educational process under existing evaluation procedures; they are redefining the effect in terms of the expected effect of the treatment on the behavior of the pupils.

The previous examples are global descriptions of the role and impact of a criterion in a given situation. You might get a better feel for the importance of the criterion by examining some specific uses of criterion information.

1. *Validation.* Tests suitable for predicting job success cannot be identified until job success has been defined. In addition, after suitable tests have been identified, the validation procedure usually requires some specific measure of job success to compare with test success.

2. *Selection.* After a valid test or predictor has been identified, it is still necessary to provide the personnel office with a decision rule for hiring. This decision rule is usually in the form of a cutoff score on the predictor, e.g., reject individuals with scores lower than 45 on test A and schedule the others for an interview. This cutoff score was determined on the basis of "minimal acceptable *job* performance." Once this level of job performance has been defined, it is possible to work backwards to "minimal acceptable *test* performance."

3. *Compensation.* Since most organizations would prefer to pay workers in proportion to their value, it is necessary to have some measure of that value when making compensation decisions. Performance criteria usually represent that measure of value.

4. *Training.* In many organizations, training is a rather haphazard en-

deavor, influenced more by fad than logic. Training needs can be easily identified on the basis of demonstrated performance weaknesses. This demonstration is made possible by accurate performance measurement.

5. *Motivation and Satisfaction of Employees.* Many organizations have elaborate programs of motivation and satisfaction for their employees. These programs are intended both to increase the satisfaction of the employee and maximize individual performance. Performance measurement is critical for the evaluation of the success of these programs. If they are successful, it should be possible to demonstrate changes in performance levels.

6. *Feedback.* It seems more and more obvious that people seek feedback on the effectiveness of their actions. In the work setting, this means feedback on work performance. This type of feedback requires fair and accurate performance information. The adequacy of performance measurement determines the adequacy of feedback.

Criterion information might also be used for making promotional decisions, evaluating the effectiveness of training programs, providing long-term vocational counseling, and changing organizational structure. The object has not been to overwhelm you with the uses of criterion information, but to point out how important the criterion is in almost every aspect of Industrial/Organizational psychology.

THE COMPLEX NATURE OF CRITERIA

Any single criterion score is an interaction of sampling on three different dimensions simultaneously. The first dimension sampled is a *variables* dimension. The criterion measure that is obtained is only one of several that *might* have been obtained. Instead of collecting data on the number of units produced by a worker, for example, a company might have collected information related to the number of units rejected by the inspection department; or a sales representative for a chemical company might be evaluated on the number of new accounts rather than sales volume. One particular measure of a criterion may yield individual variation unrelated to individual variation on another criterion measure; thus a particular criterion score may contain errors. This possibility suggests care in the selection of criterion measures from the pool of *possible* criterion measures. The most available measure is not always the best.

A second source of variation in criterion data is due to time factors. Any set of criterion scores is a sample of those scores that might have been obtained had the individual been evaluated or observed on several different occasions instead of just one. To the degree that a particular criterion measure yields individual variation due to the *time* at which the measure was obtained, it contains error. An example of such error would be variation in production data from two employees observed on two different days of the week—individual A on Monday morning and individual B on Wednesday morning. If the observations had both been conducted on Wednesday, the production rates of the two individuals might have been identical. This type of variation is often called *state* (rather than *trait*) variation, since it is related to the state of the individual at the time of measurement.

A third sampling dimension that affects the nature of the criterion measure is a "people" dimension. This is a particularly important issue in determining overall worth of the individual to the organization. Employees can contribute in various ways to the success of the organization. You have probably encountered at least two different kinds of teachers in your courses. One teacher has a high degree of expertise in a subject area and provides you with a mountain of technical information. Another teacher plays down technical information and tries to give you a basic understanding of the concepts covered in the course. In their own unique ways, both of these teachers are "good" teachers. Both contribute to the development of the student. Nevertheless, if only one criterion measure was used (a measure of the amount of technical information presented), one of the teachers would be considered as "poor." This is not the same source of error described earlier in this section. In this case, the actual criterion measure chosen is not inappropriate for all people measured, only for some of them.

Finally, there is a less formal but more practical source of error to consider. Often changes in organizational goals or practices require changes in criteria. A company suddenly faced with a new competitor might stress quality of production instead of, as in the company's past, quantity of production.

Criterion measures should always be thought of as tools for gathering *samples* of behavior. As such, the adequacy of the particular sample must be examined if the measures are to be of any use.

Criterion Characteristics

Most texts in industrial psychology contain lengthy lists of requirements for criteria. These texts invariably mention such requirements as freedom from contamination, relevance, and freedom from deficiency. The list also includes such things as freedom from bias, acceptability by management, cost, and predictability. A typical list of characteristics desirable in any criterion (Blum & Naylor, 1968) reads as follows:

1. Reliable	8. Predictable
2. Realistic	9. Inexpensive
3. Representative	10. Understandable
4. Related to other criteria	11. Measurable
5. Acceptable to the job analyst	12. Relevant
6. Acceptable to management	13. Uncontaminated and bias-free
7. Consistent from one situation to another	14. Discriminating

This whole list might be reduced to three requirements: reliability, validity, and practicality. Items 3 and 7 actually define reliability. Items 4, 5, 6,

10, 12, 13, and 14 could be considered as defining *validity.* Items 2, 8, 9, and 11 refer to *practicality.* Conceptually, there is much to be gained from reducing requirements to these three categories. First and foremost, it helps to point out that in spite of its unique position in the personnel system, criterion data must satisfy the same requirements as all other forms of data. If inferences are to be drawn based on criterion data, those data must be reliable and representative. In addition, there must be a practical scheme for gathering the data so that the cost does not greatly exceed the potential benefit.

In the past, the reliability and practicality issues have been the major sources of concern. Validity was a concept most often applied to predictors, not criteria. No doubt one of the reasons for downplaying the validity issue in criterion measures was the lack of any reasonable model for providing such information. However, in the last several years, the notion of construct validity has provided a model for evaluating criterion measures. Two decades ago, Ghiselli and Brown (1955) suggested that instead of talking about a "criterion," we busy ourselves with describing ways of measuring job proficiency. They were not suggesting that there is something intrinsically wrong or evil in the notion of a criterion. They were suggesting that there is something wrong in talking about *the* criterion. Several years later, Dunnette (1963) reinforced this deemphasis of *the* criterion and suggested construct validation studies in place of the ever-popular concurrent and predictive validity studies.

Great advances in the area of criterion measurement and development can be made if three requirements are kept in mind: reliability, validity, and practicality.

JOB ANALYSIS

Unlike published tests, it is virtually unheard of to purchase a criterion instrument. Such instruments are generally developed on a situation-by-situation basis. In this section, we will describe how criterion instruments are constructed.

At the outset, the differences among job analysis, job evaluation, and performance appraisal must be understood. Job analysis and evaluation make statements and inferences about a job, regardless of the person in that job. Job analysis describes important aspects of a job that help to distinguish it from other jobs. Job evaluation attaches a dollar value to a job and derives a logical scheme for relating the dollar value of that job to the value of other jobs. Performance appraisal distinguishes among workers on the basis of their relative performance, independent of the particular job that they are performing. Figure 4–1 presents a graphic description of the functional relationship of job analysis to criterion development.

It might be best to start by describing what job analysis is like rather than describing how it is accomplished. Its purpose is the same as that of a videotape system with stop-action and slow-motion capabilities. Just

FIGURE 4–1

Relationships among Job Analysis, Job Evaluation, Job Description, Criterion Development, and Performance Appraisal

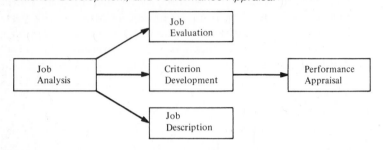

as the videotape system might be used to break down a golf swing into a number of discrete operations for purposes of correction, a job analysis might be completed to break job performance down into a number of discrete elements. Just as we would want to know what the elements of a good golf swing are, we would also want to know what the elements of successful punchpress operation are.

It is the search for these elementary units of performance that best defines job analysis. It is one of the first steps in the process of criterion development. Before we can distinguish behaviorally among individuals with respect to job performance, we must determine the nature of the dimensions on which we will make this distinction.

In the past several years, job analysis has received renewed interest. Little research or concern for job analysis appears in the literature from the early 1940s to the late 1960s. The primary impetus for this renewed interest has been the Federal Government's guidelines on fair employment practices. The government is inclined to be skeptical of claims of valid testing programs unless a job analysis has been done for the position in question. This is an extension of an argument made earlier in the text. Just as it makes little sense to think about the kinds of tests that might be used to predict job success until job success has been defined in behavioral terms, it is wrong to think of the kind of performance appraisal instrument that might be used to measure job success until the elements of the particular job have been identified.

R. M. Guion (1961) contrasts the role of job analysis in a usual criterion development program with the desired role of the job analysis as follows:

1. The psychologist has a hunch (or insight) that a problem exists and that he can help solve it.
2. He reads a vague, ambiguous description of the job.
3. From these faint stimuli he formulates a fuzzy concept of the ultimate criterion.
4. Being a practical psychologist, he may then formulate a combination of several variables that will give him—as nearly as he can guess—a single, composite measure of "satisfactoriness."

5. He judges the relevance of this measure, the extent to which it is neither deficient nor contaminated.
6. He may judge the relative importance of each of the elements in his composite and assign some varying amount of weight to each.
7. He then finds that the data required for his carefully built composite are not available in the company files, nor is there any immediate prospect of having such records reliably kept.
8. Therefore, he will then select "the best available criterion." Typically, this will be a rating and the criterion problem, if not solved, can at least be overlooked for the rest of the research.

In contrast with Guion's description of the way in which criterion development is usually handled, he suggests a different sequence of events in criterion development:

1. Analyze the job and/or organizational needs by new, yet-to-be-developed techniques.
2. Develop measures of actual behavior relative to the behavior expected, as identified in job and need analysis. These measures are to supplement measures of the consequences of work—the so-called objective criteria commonly tried at present.
3. Identify the criterion measures underlying such measures by factor analysis or cluster analysis or pattern analysis.
4. Develop reliable measures, each with high construct validity, of the elements so identified.
5. For each independent variable (predictor), determine its predictive validity for *each one* of the foregoing criterion measures, taking them one at a time.

The role of job analysis in the sequence is much more central in the desired than in the usual sequence. There is no doubt that the care taken in identifying and operationalizing the job elements determines usefulness of the criterion measures.

Job analysis involves a number of very practical issues. The first and most important is how do we identify the job elements. Blum and Naylor (1968)[1] list nine different methods:

1. The questionnaire method—a worker is asked to respond to questions about a job in writing.
2. The checklist method—the worker is given a list of tasks and asked to check off those that are part of the job.
3. The individual interview—a person currently holding the job is interviewed relative to job duties.
4. Observation interview—an individual interview is conducted at the work place.

---

[1] "Job Analysis Methods Headings" (pp. 494–495) from *Industrial Psychology*, Revised Edition by Milton L. Blum & James C. Naylor. Copyright © 1968 by Milton L. Blum & James C. Naylor. Reprinted by permission of Harper & Row, Publishers, Inc.

5. Group interview—a number of workers are interviewed together about their job.
6. Technical conference method—interviews are conducted with "experts," such as those supervising workers on the job of interest.
7. Diary method—workers record their daily activities in a log.
8. Work participation method—the job analyst actually performs the job.
9. Critical incident method—workers and/or supervisors are asked to remember elements of the job that they feel are crucial to success or failure.

These nine methods might be thought of as variations of more general categories. There are really three kinds of data: those data obtained by (1) talking to workers, (2) watching workers, or (3) playing the role of workers. The more sources of information used, the better the description of the job and the job analysis. In most instances, practical considerations determine the method used. Unless the job analyst is a licensed pilot, it is unlikely that data on the job of aircraft pilot can be gathered by the work-participation method. In many jobs requiring little or no formal education of workers, it is difficult to use the questionnaire method because of the heavy dependence on written communication skills.

Being an industrial/organizational psychologist is not without its hazards, and in no area is this more apparent than job analysis and evaluation. In part, this is because the psychologist (conducting a job analysis) is perceived as a threat by the worker. Often the worker believes that the industrial psychologist is trying to change the rate of output (through industrial engineering principles) or is concerned with the proficiency demonstrated by individual workers.

In the process of conducting job analyses and evaluations, the authors have (1) been scared out of their wits by a Boeing 707 while conducting an observation interview with a structural engineer on the main jet landing strip of a major airport; (2) alternately been baked and frozen while doing an observation interview of the job of an electrical troubleshooter in a frozen food factory; (3) been scalded with hot milk after asking a threatening question of a cook in a food plant; and (4) been broiled while interviewing a scarfer in a hot-rolling steel mill.

There are two basic approaches that one might take to job analysis. They are known as the *job-oriented* and the *worker-oriented* approaches. The job-oriented approach tends to emphasize the conditions and/or results of work. McCormick, Jeanneret, and Mecham (1972) describe the approach as dealing with items relating to job content that typically characterize the "technological" aspects of work and reflect what is achieved by the worker. The worker-oriented approach, on the other hand, emphasizes more the behavior of the individual in general form and is often unrelated to the technological aspects of the particular job. Guion (1961) has used the terms "behavior data" and "results-of-behavior data" to connote a similar distinction. If a job analysis is an identification of job elements or building blocks that might be used to describe the particular job, then the distinction in the two approaches revolves around the nature of those building blocks or elements.

Because the worker-oriented elements tend to be more generalized descriptions of human behavior and behavior patterns and less tied to the technological aspects of the particular job, worker-oriented analyses produce data that are more useful in structuring training programs and giving feedback to employees in the form of performance appraisal information. In addition, an organization can generalize from one occupation to another without having to deal with a different set of elements for each job.

An excellent example of a worker-oriented job analysis scheme is provided by the work of McCormick and associates (1972). They have done painstaking research and development over a period of decades to produce an instrument known as the Position Analysis Questionnaire (PAQ). The PAQ consists of 189 worker-oriented job elements comprising six major divisions of worker activity. These divisions and their major subdivisions are as follows:

1. *Information Input*
   Sources of Job Information
   Discrimination and Perceptual Activities
2. *Mediation Processes*
   Decision Making and Reasoning
   Information Processing
   Use of Stored Information
3. *Work Output*
   Use of Physical Devices
   Integrative Manual Activities
   General Body Activities
   Manipulation Coordination Activities
4. *Interpersonal Activities*
   Communications
   Interpersonal Relationships
   Personal Contact
   Supervision and Coordination
5. *Work Situation and Job Context*
   Physical Working Conditions
   Psychological and Sociological Aspects
6. *Miscellaneous Aspects*
   Work Schedule, Method of Pay, and Apparel
   Job Demands
   Responsibility

Arvey and Begalla (1975) have used the PAQ to examine the job of "homemaker." The results of this examination appear in Figures 4–2 and 4–3. Figure 4–2 allows one to determine which activities are most characteristic of the job of homemaker and which are least characteristic. High positive Z scores indicate an activity *very characteristic* of the job, while high negative

FIGURE 4-2

Position Analysis Questionnaire Job Dimension Z Scores and Standard Deviations

Dimension	Average Z score	SD
1. Watching devices/materials for information	.16	.72
2. Interpreting what is heard or seen	.51	.78
3. Using data originating with people	.34	1.06
4. Watching things from a distance	.36	.86
5. Evaluating information from things	1.79	1.03
6. Being aware of environmental conditions	2.30	1.75
7. Being aware of body movement and balance	3.08	1.74
8. Making decisions	.13	.61
9. Processing information	.34	.90
10. Controlling machines processes	−.08	.47
11. Using hands and arms to control/modify	1.36	.83
12. Using feet/hands to operate equipment/vehicles	1.96	1.28
13. Performing activities requiring general body movement	1.89	.91
14. Using hands and arms to move/position things	.41	.67
15. Using fingers vs. general body movement	−.56	.71
16. Performing skilled/technical activities	.96	.89
17. Communicating judgments, decisions, information	.44	.68
18. Exchanging job-related information	1.69	1.27
19. Performing staff/related activities	1.28	.86
20. Contacting supervisor or subordinates	−.38	.94
21. Dealing with the public	1.43	1.63
22. Being in a hazardous/unpleasant environment	1.37	1.08
23. Engaging in personally demanding situations	2.05	.90
24. Engaging in businesslike work situations	.03	.47
25. Being alert to detail/changing conditions	.87	1.11
26. Performing unstructured vs. structured work	−.32	.63
27. Working on a variable vs. regular schedule	−1.48	.89
28. Having decision-making, community, and social responsibility	1.19	.74
29. Performing skilled activities	.49	.63
30. Being physically active/related environmental conditions	2.72	1.01
31. Operating equipment/vehicles	1.50	.99
32. Processing information	1.11	.96

Note: Based on 48 descriptions of homemaker job.

Source: Arvey, R. D., & Begalla, M. E. Analyzing the homemaker job using the PAQ. *Journal of Applied Psychology*, 1975, *60*, 513–517. Copyright © 1975 by the American Psychological Association. Reprinted by permission.

Z scores identify activities *very uncharacteristic* of the job. Thus, we can see that a homemaker must be aware of body movement and balance as well as environmental conditions. The homemaker must be physically active and operate various pieces of equipment with hands and/or feet. We can also see that the homemaker works on a highly variable or irregular schedule and is not likely to engage in activities that require finger movements as opposed to general body movements.

FIGURE 4–3

*Jobs Most Similar to Homemaker Job Based on
Profile Similarity* (D²) *Scores*

Job	D^2
1. Patrolman	6.69
2. Home economist	7.95
3. Airport maintenance chief	9.96
4. Kitchen helper	9.99
5. Fire fighter	10.21
6. Trouble man	10.23
7. Instrument-maker helper	10.67
8. Electrician, foreman	10.91
9. Maintenance foreman, gas plant	11.12
10. Hydroelectric-machinery mechanic	11.17
11. Transmission mechanic	11.55
12. Lineman, repair	12.25
13. Electric-meter repairman	12.36
14. Instructor, vocational training	12.43
15. Gas serviceman	12.75
16. Inspector, motors and generators	12.93
17. Lifeguard	12.84
18. Fire captain	13.05
19. Repairman, switch gear	13.22
20. Home economist, consumer service	13.47

Source: Arvey, R. D., & Begalla, M. E. Analyzing the homemaker job using the PAQ. *Journal of Applied Psychology,* 1975, *60,* 513–517. Copyright © 1975 by the American Psychological Association. Reprinted by permission.

Figure 4–3 tells us which other occupations the homemaker job is most similar to on PAQ dimensions. Most homemakers would not be surprised to find that their job duties are most similar to those of a patrol officer. The PAQ provides an opportunity to learn the essence of a job by virtue of comparing it to other jobs.

Since job analysis plays such an important role in almost every activity of the I/O psychologist, it is surprising that more research has not been done on developing techniques for analyzing jobs. As Prien notes, somewhat bitterly, ". . . the subject (of job analysis) is treated in textbooks in a manner which suggests that any fool can do it and thus is a task which can be delegated to the lowest level technician" (1977, p. 167). In fact, as Prien indicates, most personnel trainees start out in a job-analyst position. While we do not necessarily agree that the lowest-level technician can be equated with "any fool," we do agree that too little attention has been paid to methods and instruments of job analysis. McCormick's careful work should help alleviate some of these problems. If a standard system can be developed for gathering critical information about job duties, the pressures on the individual analyst can be somewhat reduced. Some recent work (Arvey, Passino, and Lounsbury, 1977) has indicated that the PAQ produced job-analysis results that were not affected by the sex of the person performing the job in question; in addition, there were only marginal differences in results as a function of the sex of the job analyst. This is good news for PAQ users, since potential discrimination in all phases of personnel psychology has become such an important concern.

The only negative information to surface concerning the PAQ relates to its readability. Although the technical manual that accompanies the PAQ suggests that an individual with a high-school education can easily comprehend both the instructions and the questions on the form, a study by Ash and Edgell (1975) found that the questions required a college-graduate reading level, and the instructions required a reading level between high-school and college-graduate level. In spite of problems such as readability, which are easily corrected, the PAQ represents one of the few carefully developed, comprehensive, and usable standardized formats for conducting job analyses and should continue to receive much attention, research, and use.

Generalizations of Job Analysis Results. One of the important results of having an instrument like the PAQ available is that it is now possible to compare and contrast various jobs, as was done in Figure 4–3 with the job of "homemaker." This allows one to develop groups or clusters of similar jobs. Once these clusters have been established, it will be possible to develop more focused training programs, to extend or generalize validity findings from a study of one job in a cluster to others in that cluster. This will dramatically reduce the cost of the validation process for large operations with multiple locations and large numbers of job titles. Arvey and Mossholder (1977) have demonstrated how the PAQ might be analyzed with an analysis-of-variance design to determine the significance of the difference among various jobs. Mobley and Ramsay (1973) have also suggested such a procedure based on cluster analysis techniques.

It is becoming clear that unless organizations are allowed to develop techniques such as validity generalization based on carefully done job analyses and pilot validation studies, they will probably opt to abandon testing completely, due to the costliness of validating every test for every job in every location. The development of the PAQ is a major step in combining the strengths of psychometric measurement with the realities of validation and should provide organizations with a defensible tool for generalizing validity findings.

JOB EVALUATION

Job evaluation is the process by which wage rates are applied differentially to jobs. The job evaluator takes a series of factors into account, weighs these factors, and places each job at a point on a continuum. This continuum is then broken into a series of classes, usually corresponding to wage categories. While there *should* be some relationship between job analysis and job evaluation, there seldom is. At best there is some relationship between the job-oriented approach to job analysis and job evaluation. By and large, however, job evaluations consist of factors such as those found in Figure 4–4. The organization determines the relative worth of each of these factors and then breaks down each of the factors into a series of steps. The job to be evaluated is then considered on each of these factors and points assigned depending on the step represented. Figure 4–4 describes a job as seen from the point of view of the job evaluator. This is only one example of a possible evaluation scheme. It relies on the detailed allocation of points in graded steps. There are other methods of assigning dollar values to jobs. Perhaps the simplest is to arrange all jobs to be evaluated on a continuum describing their relative worth to the organization. Money may then be allocated to each of the jobs depending upon its position on the continuum.

Job evaluation schemes often become arbitrary. After a very careful analysis and evaluation is completed, it is not unusual to see the personnel department arbitrarily change the wage rate assigned to the job. There are many reasons for this: the most common reason is that accepting the evaluation would result in lowering the pay for certain jobs, and both organizations and unions often find this totally unacceptable.

Job evaluation is sometimes known as *job classification*, particularly in public sector personnel work, such as federal, state, or city government. The term implies that a job is placed in a class with several other jobs that demand similar levels of effort for the purpose of assigning wage or salary rates. While job evaluations or classifications may be updated every seven years or so in private industry, reclassifications are much more common on a job-by-job basis in public organizations. There is an elaborate mechanism for public employees to request a review of job duties and responsibilities, with an eye toward increasing the monetary value of the particular position. London (1976) studied the perceptions of workers concerning the reclassification process. He noted that pay increases based on reclassification decisions are usually considerably more than increases resulting from either cost-of-living or merit increases. He also noted that requests for reclassification in public-sector organizations were increasing at a rapid rate, an indication that the individual employee sees some value in requesting the review—most likely a monetary one! The study was conducted in a university setting, and the subjects were predominantly female clerical workers. In spite of the fact that reclassification should depend almost exclusively on the nature and conditions of work, the subjects believed that factors such as perseverance and job success (on the part of the person requesting the reclassification) significantly affected the reclassification decision. The subjects were also concerned that the evaluator's accuracy would affect the resulting decision.

London's findings allow for some interesting speculation and extension to the private sector. It seems as if the employees in his study saw classification decisions as potential rewards for good work. The problem with this

FIGURE 4–4

Job Evaluation; Fork Truck Driver

	Points
Experience	
Must learn to operate fork truck and hand truck if he does not have this skill. Two to three weeks on-the-job training	48
Education	
Requires ability to speak, read, and write English and understand simple written instructions. Should have knowledge of simple mathematics in order to complete certain daily reports. Grammar school education desirable	32
Responsibility for Equipment, Tools, Product or Material	
Could damage products if not stacked properly in freezer. Cost would vary from $100 to $500	94
Resourcefulness	
Some variety in the job. Exercises some discretion in keeping freezer in order	52
Responsibility for Work of Others	
None	35
Monotony	
Has a number of tasks to perform, works in several places and moves around	10
Pressure of Work	
Occasionally has problems keeping up with work pace	46
Physical Effort	
On feet most of day when not driving lift truck. Pushes and/or pulls stack of empty pallets with hand truck or moves full pallet with hand truck. Lifting involved in carrying boxes of damaged packages	30
Surroundings	
In freezer (0°) for approximate total of 1½ to 2 hours daily. Occasionally on dock. Noisy in Cartoning Department	38
Hazards	
Operates fork truck—often ice on freezer floor, could skid. When driving fork truck on dock must be cautious, ice and water. Pallets of cases incorrectly stacked in freezer could topple on him	30
Concentration	
Duties require close attention most of the time	75
Total	490

logic is that it puts the decision to give or withhold a reward in the hands of someone who is unfamiliar with the level of performance. In addition, the focus of the evaluator is on the job, not the person. Because of the disparities in monetary results from merit increases versus increases resulting from reclassification, it may not be long before private-sector employees decide to pursue the reclassification route for increasing monetary rewards, rather than the more traditional merit-increase procedure.

PERFORMANCE APPRAISAL

Performance appraisal is the more specific term for criterion measurement for the purpose of describing performance strengths and weaknesses within and between workers. The most general use for performance appraisal is for administrative personnel decisions such as promotions, salary increases, or layoffs. Cummings (1973) has termed this use one of providing structure for a reward/punishment system. He suggests that there are at least three other uses for performance appraisal systems: (1) providing criterion information for the selection process, (2) providing objectives for training programs, and (3) providing elements for supervisory feedback and control.

One logical conclusion of a job analysis is the development of a performance appraisal system. Once the elements of the job are determined, successful performance on that job can be described. There are several kinds of data that can be used to provide such a description. Guion (1965) identified at least three different kinds of measures of job behavior: *objective data* in the form of production information, *personnel data*, and *judgmental data*. The multidimensionality of "job performance" becomes apparent when these categories are considered simultaneously. Is a successful worker one who turns out the greatest numbers of units (objective data), the one who has not been absent for 11 years (personnel data), or the one who is rated high on quality of work and judgment by a supervisor (judgmental data)? Each of these three categories will be examined in turn.

Objective Production Data

After introducing the link between job analysis and performance appraisal, it is somewhat embarrassing to note that seldom is there any explicit relationship between a job analysis and objective indices of performance, such as rate of production. At best, there is a naïve faith that embedded somewhere in the production data are the important job elements as identified by the job analysis. This is a very serious problem, which must be dealt with if any advances are to be made in predicting the results of behavior. We must know how individual behaviors (job elements) combine to yield certain performance profiles, and further, how a particular profile combines with environmental factors to yield an organizational outcome. This lack of attention to the relationship between job analysis and performance appraisal is most apparent in objective production criteria, but exists to a certain degree in the other two categories of criterion information as well. The most widely used variables are in the form of output measurements, or, as Guion (1965) describes the process, "simply a count of the results of work." This count can take many different forms. It might be the number of arrests for a police officer, the number of decisions rendered by a judge in a district court, the number of hamburgers prepared by a grill worker, or the number of swings taken by a professional golfer in completing 18 holes at Augusta.

Unfortunately, there is ample opportunity for variability to be introduced into these measures, which has nothing at all to do with the individual being appraised. The number of arrests made by a police officer may depend heavily on the district or shift to which that officer is assigned. The number of cases heard by a judge may depend heavily on the degree to which the district attorney engages in plea bargaining before the cases reach court. The number of shots required by a professional golfer may depend heavily on the knowledge and judgment of a caddy. Similar objections may be raised to all of the objective criteria mentioned above. There is a seductive appeal to these variables. After all, they define the goals of the organization. While this is true, variance in these measures is often unrelated to the behaviors of the individual. This is the problem of criterion contamination— a situation that will be described later in the chapter.

There are three basic problems with the use of objective production data as criterion measures for individual job success. The first is the simple measurement problem of reliability. Each objective measure probably has an observation period which is not stable. For example, if we were to take the total number of arrests for a patrol officer for a one-week period, the relationship between one week and any other week might be very low. The relationship would increase greatly if we extended the period of observation from one week to one month. A reliable measurement implies a sufficient period of time to observe variations in the target behavior.

The reliability problem is not limited to the period of observation. Rothe and Nye (1959) completed a series of studies designed to assess the stability of output rates for machine operators. They discovered that the *type of pay* can affect the stability of the production data. Greater stability was found for output measures when workers were paid on an incentive system than when they were paid on a day-rate plan. They concluded that performance on the predictors of job performance is often more stable than the performance that is to be predicted. A distinction between accuracy and reliability should be evident from this example. Many objective criteria are accurate in that there is little error in the counting of output as indicated by a counter on the machine or a record of gross sales; yet taken over a short period, this count may not provide a representative estimate of the typical output of the employee.

A second problem which arises with the use of objective data is the changing nature of skilled and semiskilled work. Many former machine *operators* are now machine *tenders*. Manual machines are being replaced

A Machine-Tending Operation

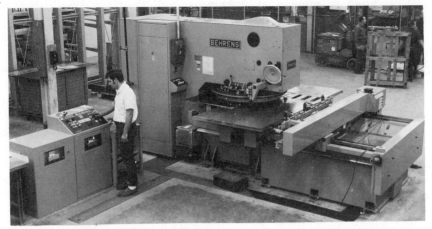

Source: Leeds-Northrup Co.

with automatic and semiautomatic machines. If only objective data are considered no differential performance data on these individuals can be obtained unless a machine malfunctions.

Finally, there are many jobs for which no good objective measures are available. This becomes more troublesome as we go up the occupational ladder. It is very difficult to describe the performance of a middle-level supervisor in objective terms. The problem is one of reducing the supervisory responsibility for the allocation of human resources and delegation of responsibility to units which can be counted.

Personnel Data

The second general class of criterion information is personnel data, those data usually available in the personnel folder of an individual. Some of the more common variables are absences, tardiness, turnover, rate of advancement, type of salary adjustment, and accidents. While there are other potential variables in this category (such as commendations and disciplinary actions), they are usually present in fewer than 5 percent of the cases examined, making them rather useless criteria. Almost all of these measures tend to affect the well-being of the organization, but are rather global in nature. In addition, they also tend to fall prey to the potential confounding effects of other variables (i.e., criterion contamination), and in much the same manner as described for objective production data. Absences might be separated into "excused" and "unexcused." While it may be difficult to predict from psychological test data the number of times an individual will contract a bad head cold each year, it may be easier to predict the number of times a day or more of work will be missed for nonlegitimate reasons. In addition, absences might be recorded as either absolute number of days absent or number of absences regardless of the length of each absence.

Latham and Pursell (1975) suggested that it might make more sense to measure attendance rather than absence. They argued that the typical absence measure is very complex and contains many sources of potential error. For example, they describe situations in which an individual may be listed as absent for a string of 30 days before someone finally decides that the individual has quit. Conversely, it is not that unusual to record a person as having quit after two days of absence and then to have that person report for work on the third day. In both of these examples, the absence measure for that person for the period of time in question would be in error. Latham and Pursell argue that a measure of attendance is much less ambiguous and effectively rules out many traditional sources of error such as those described. In two studies of the reliability of attendance versus absence measures, Latham and Pursell demonstrated dramatically higher reliabilities for attendance indices ($r = .88$) than for absence indices ($r = .32$). Ilgen (1977) took strong exception to some of the mathematical manipulations in the Latham study, and Latham and Pursell (1977) naturally took strong exception to Ilgen's strong exception. While there were some problems with the attendance index, one thing was clear from the dispute— supervisors do a poor job of accurately recording absence and turnover information. Thus, if this type of information is to be used as criterion data, careful procedures should be developed for classifying and recording the information.

Turnover is another difficult variable to deal with. The question is one of classifying turnover as voluntary (quitting) or involuntary (being fired). It is not always that easy to distinguish between them. For example, a professor who knows that his contract is not likely to be renewed the following year looks for a new job before he is fired. Should that be considered voluntary or involuntary turnover?

Rate of advancement might be controlled more by an informal quota system or the expected life span of first-level supervisors than by the behavior of the worker. Type of salary adjustment might reflect more the economic profile of the organization than the behavior of the individual on the job. In short, while there are perfectly acceptable reasons for using personnel data as indices of performance, we often encounter problems in their use.

The arguments that have been raised in relation to the use of objective production data and personnel data do not mean that they are useless as criteria. But if they are to be useful, a careful analysis of the relationship between the elements of the job as identified by job analysis and the elements of behavior as related in the performance appraisal is necessary. Even if this is successfully accomplished there are still many jobs for which performance will have to be described in terms other than those provided by objective and personnel data. This leads to the most pervasive set of performance appraisal data—judgmental data.

Judgmental Data

Due to the fact that objective measures are often impossible to obtain, as well as the fact that they represent results of behavior rather than behavior itself, we must often depend on judgments to estimate the adequacy of performance. These judgments take several forms. They may be a simple comparison of one employee with another on one or more dimensions, they may be a list of statements which are applied to each employee, or they may be some form of rating by which the employee is placed on a continuum, the individual's position determined by the amount or degree of proficiency demonstrated. Occasionally, these judgments have rather dramatic consequences, such as those described in the accompanying article which was taken from a recent edition of the Chronicle of Higher Education (1978).

■ **Administrator Charged in Killing of Colleague**

A University of Michigan administrator has been charged by police with shooting a colleague to death in a dispute over a job-performance evaluation.

Police said Donald Koos's uncomplimentary evaluation of William Aparicio's work apparently motivated Mr. Aparicio to kill the assistant director of the university's Neuro-Psychiatric Institute last week.

University officials said Mr. Koos, 30, and Mr. Aparicio, 46, had worked together for more than a year and seemed to get along well. Mr. Aparicio has been serving as the institute's administrative manager.

Police believe Mr. Aparicio learned recently that he had been turned down in his bid to become the institute's top administrator and that he blamed his rejection on an assessment of his performance by Mr. Koos, also a candidate for the job.

Rating Scales. By far the most widely used judgmental measure is the rating scale. Guion (1965) reports that 81 percent of the validation studies reported in the *Journal of Applied Psychology* between January 1950 and July 1955 relied on some form of rating as the criterion. A review of the literature published since Guion's report shows that while

FIGURE 4–5

Examples of Graphic Rating Scales

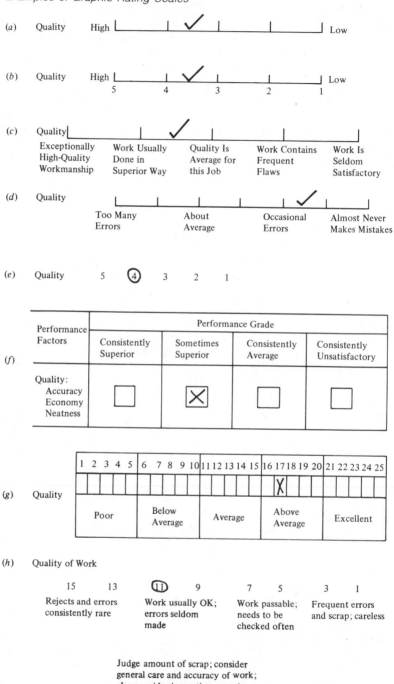

Source: Guion, R. M. *Personnel testing*. New York: McGraw-Hill, 1965.

the percentage of validation studies using ratings as criteria has decreased to 72 percent, performance ratings still play a major part in validation.[2]

Figure 4–5, taken from a book in personnel testing by Guion (1965), presents most of the common forms of rating scales. The scales can be distinguished from one another on three different dimensions: (1) the degree to which the meaning of the response categories is defined, (2) the degree to which the person interpreting the ratings (e.g., personnel manager) can tell what response was intended by the rater, and (3) the degree to which the performance dimension rated is defined for the rater.

The first dimension, the ambiguity of the response categories, is usually handled through the process of "anchoring." Anchors are placed along a rating scale to define each of the response categories. Just as a ruler is marked off in inches or millimeters, the rating scale must be marked off in units of some type that allow the rater to make meaningful statements about the performance of individuals. These anchors are extremely important. Rating scale (a) in Figure 4–5 is an example of the use of "end anchors" without accompanying numerical anchors, while scale (b) has qualitative "end anchors" as well as numerical anchors. These anchors are of little use, since the interpretation of what characterizes high and low quality is left completely up to the rater. Scale (c) specifies more clearly what is meant by each of the categories on the scale; the same is true of scale (h). Consider for yourself the potential ease encountered in using scale (h) as opposed to scale (a).

The second major descriptive characteristic of rating scales is the degree to which the person interpreting the ratings can tell what response was intended. Another name for this characteristic is "response clarity." If your task were to determine what value the rater had in mind, you would probably find that scales (e), (f), and (g) were easier to work with than scales (a), (b), (c), (d), and (i).

The third characteristic is the degree to which the performance dimension rated is defined for the rater. Consider all the possible interpretations which raters might apply to the term "quality of work." This allows for the possibility that a set of ratings on workers might be worthless because they are based on different interpretations by various raters of the dimensions to be considered. Scales (a), (b), (e), and (g) give little or no structure to the rater regarding the performance dimension to be rated. On the other hand, scales (f) and (i), and to a certain degree (c) and (h), give the rater a pretty good idea of what performance dimension is being considered.

Rating Errors

It should be possible to see from the description of the various types of rating scales how ambiguity can lead to errors in ratings that make them useless. These errors can be placed into three major categories: leniency

---

[2] This review was conducted by Frank Saal.

FIGURE 4-6

Graphic Description of Leniency Error on Hypothetical 5-Point Rating Scale: Positive (+) and Negative (−)

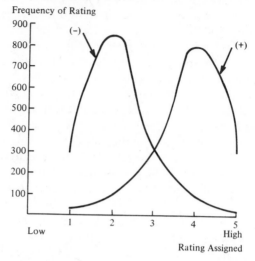

errors, halo errors, and central tendency errors. Figures 4–6 and 4–7 depict leniency and central tendency errors.

Leniency Errors. It is common to encounter raters who would be described as unusually harsh or unusually easy in their ratings. The harsh individual tends to give ratings that are lower than the average level of

FIGURE 4-7

Graphic Description of Central Tendency Error on Hypothetical 5-Point Rating Scale

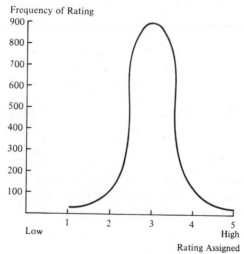

the subordinates on the rated dimension. The easy individual tends to give ratings that are higher than the average level of the subordinates. In other words, if one could accurately measure the amount of a given trait in a group of ratees, the ratings of the harsh rater could be consistently lower than the actual amount of the trait possessed by the ratees, while the ratings of the easy rater would be consistently higher. These kinds of errors usually come about because the rater is applying personal standards to the rating scale. For example, the anchor "excellent" may have completely different meanings to different raters. Two suggestions have been offered to eliminate these errors: (1) a forced distribution in which the rater is required to allocate the ratings so that a given percentage of the ratees fall in the top category, a given percentage in the next category, etc.; and (2) reduce the degree of ambiguity of the scales by improving the definition of the dimension and the nature of the anchors. The second suggestion is somewhat easier to implement than the first. The forced distribution implies some knowledge of what the distribution should look like or how the trait should be distributed in the ratees. This type of knowledge is not easily acquired and raters frequently object to being told that "10 percent of your ratees must be rated poor (or excellent)."

Halo Errors. The term "halo" is meant to imply that there is a general aura surrounding all the individual judgments that are made about a given worker. The rater has a generally favorable or unfavorable impression of the ratee. Ratings are then assigned that are consistent with that impression. Halo errors may also come into play when a rater feels that a particular dimension of performance is extremely important. Ratings are then assigned on the other dimensions that are consistent with the rating on the most important one. Forced distributions of ratings may be of little value, since the rater is still free to distribute ratees on the basis of overall impressions of favorability. One method that has been suggested for the solution of this problem is to rate all of the ratees on one trait, then all of them on another, until all ratees have been rated on all traits or dimensions. The hope is that the rater will be able to distinguish between dimensions if forced to consider all of the ratees on one dimension at a time. It might also be that the problem lies in the definition of the dimensions for the raters. If the dimensions were clearly defined and anchored, the raters would be less likely to depend on overall impressions.

Central Tendency Errors. Central tendency error is characterized by an unwillingness on the part of the rater to assign extreme ratings—either extremely high or extremely low. This error has a potentially serious effect on attempts to establish empirical validity for selection devices. Since the range of variability is restricted on the criterion (see Figure 4–7), the value of the obtained validity coefficient may be drastically reduced. Once again, the forced distribution method has been suggested as a way of eliminating central tendency errors.

Attempts have been made to minimize the effects of halo, leniency, and central tendency errors by using alternative evaluation schemes. Two of the most popular of these alternatives have been the employee comparison methods and the forced-choice checklist.

Employee Comparison Methods

The two most widely used employee comparison methods are the *ranking* procedure and the *pair-comparison* procedure. In the ranking procedure, the rater simply arranges the set of ratees in rank order from high to low on a given dimension of performance. This process can be simplified by using an alternating procedure in which the rater picks out the best and the worst worker, sets them aside, then picks out the best and worst from the remaining set of names until all the ratees are ranked. One of the problems introduced by the use of this method is the nature of the data that result from the ranking. It is of little use to know that an individual is ranked 3rd of 30 on some performance dimension unless you have some notion of whether or not that represents adequate, good, or bad performance. Rankings, because they are ordinal data, do not give you that information. Another criticism of the ranking methods currently in use is that the ranking is usually done on one overall suitability category. When more than one dimension is used, ranking may suffer from halo error to the same degree as rating scales.

Instead of simply ranking the workers on an absolute basis, or using an alternating ranking procedure, each individual may be compared with every other individual in the set to be evaluated. The number of resulting pairs can be calculated from the formula $n(n-1)/2$ where $n =$ the number of people to be evaluated. If there are 10 people to be evaluated, there will be 45 pairs. The task of the evaluator is to choose the better of each pair. Each person's rank is defined as the total number of times that person was chosen as the better of the pair. As in the ranking procedures, in most instances a global dimension of suitability is used as the criterion for making the choice.

The employee comparison methods have the following weaknesses: (1) comparability of evaluations across groups or locations is often lacking; for example, there is no assurance that the top-ranking individual in one group is comparable to the top-ranking individual in another, (2) the use of one global dimension may yield information that is unsuitable for making specific personnel decisions such as job changes, and (3) as the number of individuals in the group becomes larger, the task becomes more tedious. For example, if one were to use a pair-comparison format in a work group with 15 individuals, 105 separate comparisons would be necessary.

Checklist

Another major category of judgmental data is the checklist. In the checklist, a set of statements is presented to the rater. The rater's task is to check those items that best (or sometimes, least) describe the person to be rated. Each of these items has been judged; a numerical value representing the degree of performance represented by that particular statement has been determined. In one treatment of checklist responses, known as summated ratings, the numerical values of each of the statements checked are added to yield a total score for the individual. An example of such a procedure is presented in Figure 4–8.

One variation on this basic theme is the *forced-choice format*. In the general checklist approach as described, the rater is not required to check any of the statements. Consequently, the rater may choose those items to check that have high social desirability but say little about performance. In an effort to avoid such nondiscriminating responses and possibly to identify those raters who were giving socially desirable responses, an effort was made to introduce socially desirable items systematically into the evaluation procedure. The forced-choice format usually presents the rater with a group of statements that have been previously judged for social desirability as well as for their ability to discriminate good from poor performance. The rater is asked to pick two of four statements that best describe the ratee; or the rater might be asked to pick the statements *most* and *least* descriptive of an individual. An example of a set of forced choice statements appears in Figure 4–9. Items *(a)* and *(c)* have been found to distinguish between the good and poor college instructor; items *(b)* and *(d)* do not distinguish the good from the poor instructor but are high and low respectively on social desirability. Since the rater must choose two statements, and it would be logically difficult to choose both the desirable *and* the undesirable items, at least one discriminating item is usually chosen. The forced-choice format was originally introduced in an attempt to reduce or control leniency error and has had some success in accomplishing that end.

FIGURE 4–8

Summated Checklist

	Scale Value*
Statements Checked for Officer Smith	
Goes out of the way to help the public	4.3
Is occasionally sarcastic with juveniles	1.9
Keeps equipment in top shape	3.2
Total for Officer Smith	9.4
Statements Checked for Officer Jones	
Can be counted on to "back up" fellow officer	4.2
Fails to keep gun clean and well oiled	1.4
Takes continuing education courses in law enforcement on own time	4.6
Total for Officer Jones	10.2

* Highest statement value possible = 5.
Lowest statement value possible = 1.

FIGURE 4–9

Example of Forced-Choice Item for Describing Performance of College Teachers

---

a. Is impatient with slow learners
b. Lectures with confidence
c. Acquaints class with objectives for each class in advance
d. Does not tell enough jokes

One of the problems with the forced-choice method is that it is not constructed to give diagnostic information. The rater does not know the scale values of the items chosen—this is an important aspect of the method—therefore, the method cannot provide a basis for appraisal feedback from the rater to the ratee. Instead, the scales are usually directed at providing some index of overall performance. The major stumbling block to developing sets of items for each of several dimensions is the time involved in writing and scaling items that are both matched on desirability and have adequate power of discrimination.

NEW METHODS OF OBTAINING JUDGMENTS

Mixed Standard Rating Scales

A variation on the rating format that has been introduced by Blanz and Ghiselli (1972) is known as the mixed standard scale. In this procedure, items that discriminate good from poor performance are obtained from experts (usually supervisors). Subsequently, three items are chosen to form a scale for a particular performance dimension. One of the items represents good performance, one represents average performance, and one represents poor performance. These items are randomly mixed with items from scales measuring other dimensions. We present an example of a mixed standard scale format used in the measurement of police performance. The letters to the left of the items correspond to the particular performance dimension. Dimension A is *judgment*, dimension B is *job knowledge*, and dimension C is *relation with others*. The instructions and the items given to the rater are as follows:

> Listed below are a number of descriptions of behavior relevant to the job of patrol officer. Your task is to carefully examine each example, and then to determine in your own mind the answer to the following question: Is the patrol officer to be rated "better than this statement," "worse than this statement," or "does this statement fit this patrol officer?"
>
> If you believe that the person you are rating is "better than the statement," put a + in the space to the right of the statement. If you believe that the person is "worse than the statement," put a − in that space. If you believe that the statement "fits" the patrol officer, put a 0 in that space.

Be sure that you write either a +, a −, or a 0 after each of the statements listed below.

			Rating
(B)	1.	The officer could be expected to misinform the public on legal matters through lack of knowledge. (P)	+
(C)	2.	The officer could be expected to take the time to carefully answer a rookie's question. (G)	0
(B)	3.	This patrol officer never has to ask others about points of law. (G)	−
(A)	4.	The officer could be expected to refrain from writing tickets for traffic violations which occur at a particular intersection which is unusually confusing to motorists. (G)	+
(A)	5.	The patrol officer could be expected to call for assistance and clear the area of bystanders before confronting a barricaded, heavily-armed suspect. (A)	+
(C)	6.	The officer could be expected to use racially-toned language in front of minority-group members. (P)	+
(B)	7.	This officer follows correct procedures for evidence preservation at the scene of a crime. (A)	0
(A)	8.	The patrol officer could be expected to continue to write a traffic violation in spite of hearing a report of a nearby robbery in progress. (P)	+
(C)	9.	This officer is considered friendly by the other officers on the shift. (A)	+

The letters G, A, and P immediately following the statements indicate whether the item describes good, average, or poor performance. In practice, the rater is not told which item relates to which scale or the level of performance represented by each item. The scoring scheme for the format is presented in Table 4–1. From this scheme, we derive the following scores for the hypothetical patrol officer rated above. On dimension A, judgment, the officer receives a score of 7; on dimension B, job knowledge, the score is 4; on dimension C, relations with others, the hypothetical patrol officer received a rating of 6. It should be obvious that not all raters will respond as logically as our hypothetical rater. For example, the rater might have said that the ratee was better than the good statement but worse than the average statement. In that case, the scoring scheme presented in Table 4–1 would not apply. Blanz and Ghiselli have extended their scoring scheme to include such rating errors, but empirical evidence supporting that particular scoring scheme for errors of consistency is not yet available.

The logic for the mixed standard format is derived from some early findings indicating that halo errors are smaller when ratings are not made on an obvious scale. The random arrangement of performance statements is thought to make it difficult for the rater to determine what the exact

TABLE 4–1

Mixed Standard Scoring

	Descriptive		
	Statements		
G	*A*	*P*	*Points*
+	+	+	7
0	+	+	6
−	+	+	5
−	0	+	4
−	−	+	3
−	−	0	2
−	−	−	1

+ = The ratee is better than the statement.
0 = The statement fits the ratee.
− = The ratee is worse than the statement.

nature of the performance scale is, that is, what order of merit each of the statements represents. Such a random arrangement is thought to lead to fewer halo and leniency errors.

Aside from the reduction of some traditional rating errors, one of the strengths of the mixed standard format may be that it provides an opportunity to identify those raters who are making logical errors. A rating error implies that the rater is not using the scale as it was intended. If many raters have many errors, it is likely the fault of the scale and the way in which the three statements were derived and arranged. If few raters make few errors, or a few raters are responsible for many errors, the problem is likely to be centered in the rater rather than in the scale for measuring performance. The mixed standard format provides an interesting innovation in performance rating methodology and will probably be tried more often in the future.

Behaviorally Anchored Scales

Another variation in rating scales was introduced in 1963 by Smith and Kendall. In an attempt to develop scales that had unambiguous anchors, they developed a procedure for constructing a performance scale based on Flanagan's (1949) work with "critical incidents." Critical incidents are examples of behavior that appeared *critical* in determining whether performance would be good, average, or poor. The logic of the procedure is that anchors on rating scales should be statements that can discriminate the good from the poor performer. Based on that assumption, groups of judges are asked to provide examples of behavior that characterize the high, the average, and the low performer on some aspect of job behavior.

It might be best in this instance to put the cart before the horse and present examples of the end products or the behaviorally anchored scales, and then describe how they were constructed. Figure 4–10 describes a scale used to measure performance of police officers. If you go back to our earlier discussion of the adequacy of rating scales, you can see that these scales have the potential for satisfying the three criteria. The dimensions are well-defined for the rater, the anchors adequately define the response categories of the scale, and, depending on rating instructions, the response made by the rater is well defined.

The procedure is tedious and occasionally expensive. A brief summary of the steps involved in constructing a behaviorally anchored scale such as the one in Figure 4–10 will shed some light on this practical difficulty.

Constructing a Behaviorally Anchored Scale.   To construct a behaviorally anchored scale, groups of workers and/or supervisors are gathered together for group conferences in which they attempt to identify and define all of the important aspects necessary for successful performance on a particular job. Next, a second group is asked to take the aspects as they have been defined by the first group and provide examples of high, average, and low performance on each of the aspects of performance. Then, a third group is given a list of each of the aspects and a randomized list of the examples provided by the second group. They are asked to place or allocate each example in the category or aspect for which it is written. This is known as "retranslation." It resembles the quality-control check often used to determine whether a translation from one language to another is an adequate one. If examples cannot be allocated to the category for which they are written, they do not represent unambiguous anchors and should not be used.

A fourth group is then asked to consider each of the examples that survived the retranslation and place a scale value on it, indicating the level of performance on a particular aspect that that example represents. The means and standard deviations are then computed, and items are chosen for the final scale that have the following properties: (1) they have mean values which provide anchors for the entire scale, and (2) they have low standard deviations.

If an item has a high standard deviation, it means that judges cannot agree on the level of performance that the example represents, and if they cannot agree, the eventual raters will also probably disagree. The item is then discarded because the level of performance it represents is not clear.

Finally, the resulting scales are administered to a sample of supervisors, who are asked to rate the performance of their subordinates on each of the scales. Each subordinate is rated independently by two supervisors, and the ratings of those supervisors are correlated to provide an estimate of interrater reliability. In addition, the scale scores are intercorrelated to provide an estimate of the degree to which each of the scales is measuring some unique aspect of performance.

This process can take many months and involve large numbers of people. Consequently, it may not be practical for many organizations to undertake

FIGURE 4–10

Behaviorally Anchored Scales: Patrol Officer

Job Knowledge: Awareness of procedures, laws, and court rulings and changes in them.

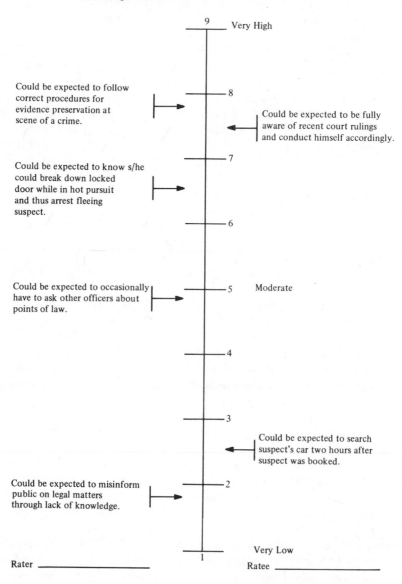

such a project by themselves. On the other hand, as the procedure grows in popularity, it is likely that scales will be developed that will have wide generality and can be used in many different settings.

One of the major advantages of this procedure may have nothing to do with the measurement of performance per se. The degree of involvement of the workers and supervisors in the procedure is very high. In the process of developing the scales, the participants are required to take a long, hard look at performance as it is behaviorally defined. In doing this, they are required to drop many inaccurate stereotypes of the unsuccessful worker. They are no longer permitted simply to label someone as a "loser." They must now describe this individual in terms of what actually qualifies him or her for the "loser" category. While no systematic test of the proposition has been made, it would appear that the procedure provides excellent rater training as well as good rating scales.

Another advantage of the procedure is that it seems to have face validity for both the rater and the person rated. This is due to the fact that the anchors consist of behaviors that subordinates and supervisors have already identified as critical. In addition, these examples are presented in the language of the worker rather than the language of the psychologist or personnel director.

A Comparison of Behaviorally Anchored Scales with other Formats. Because of the time and expense involved in constructing this type of scale, it is reasonable to expect that behaviorally anchored scales would have some advantage over other methods. While the logic on which the system is based is compelling, the results have been disappointing. There have been several extensive reviews of the relative advantages of the behaviorally anchored system, and the conclusion seems to be that they are not much better than carefully constructed graphic scales or summated checklists (Schwab, Heneman, and DeCotiis, 1975; Bernardin, et al., 1976; Bernardin, 1977; Landy and Farr, 1979). There may be a hidden blessing in this finding that supports the use of behaviorally anchored scales. The procedures for scale construction, as described, almost guarantee that the scales will be carefully developed. This is not the case with other formats. It is relatively simple for a manager to develop his own graphic form using sloppy procedures and gather suitably sloppy performance measures. At least the behaviorally anchored scales ensure some quality control in the final product. Thus, it may be that in spite of the fact that well-developed graphic rating scales are as resistant to error as behaviorally anchored scales, it is harder to construct a *good graphic rating scale* than it is to develop a *good behaviorally anchored scale.*

FACTORS AFFECTING RATING

It is not unusual to hear people complain about performance ratings they have received. The most common complaint is that the ratings are "unfair" in some respect. They may feel that either their personality or the personality of the rater has played an inappropriate role in the evaluation of their performance. They may feel that their supervisor has not had sufficient opportunity to really observe their day-to-day performance. They may also feel that the rating process works against them since the supervisor is asked to complete ratings on 15 people in one day, thus limiting the attention paid to any individual.

There has been a good deal of research which supports the feelings of these "complainers" as well as research which is at odds with their assumptions. Even a brief examination of this research demonstrates that the process of performance rating is incredibly complex, with many opportunities for the ratings to be influenced by factors other than the performance of the person rated. Landy and Farr (1979) have reviewed this research and have proposed a model or diagram that they contend describes the rating process. This model is presented in Figure 4–11. Keep in mind that the goal of performance rating is to provide an accurate performance description of the person in question. In the model, this is represented as the box on the right-hand side labeled "Performance Description." All of the other boxes might be thought of as obstacles to accurate performance description and will be described.

Rater Characteristics. The rater possesses certain characteristics that may be related to sets or biases brought to the rating task—for example, dislike for women, or younger employees, or Catholics. These biases may influence the ratings assigned to members of the classes the rater dislikes.

Ratee Characteristics. In addition to the general sets that a rater might have for or against particular groups, ratees "possess" certain characteristics that they carry with them from job to job and setting to setting. The characteristic we are most interested in is their level of performance. Nevertheless, ratees have other accidental characteristics such as sex, age, and race which are their individual properties, not properties of raters.

As the figure indicates, these two boxes meet or interact. It is this *interaction* of rater and ratee characteristics which produces the effect on the performance description rather than either the rater or ratee characteristics alone.

FIGURE 4–11

Process Model of Performance Rating

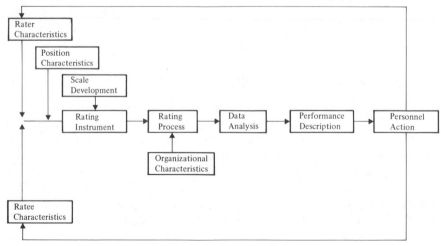

Position Characteristics. In addition to the rater and ratee components, there are characteristics peculiar to the position which the ratee occupies in the organization that may influence the accuracy of the performance description. Some of these characteristics might be line versus staff status, the level in the organization, or the formal reporting relationship of rater to ratee.

Rating Instrument. The particular format used to gather the ratings might influence the performance description. For example, one might choose to use a forced choice scale rather than a simple graphic rating scale or a behaviorally anchored scale rather than one anchored with descriptive adjectives such as "outstanding," "average," or "poor." The nature of the form that is used may distort the performance description.

Scale Development. The manner in which the scale was developed will directly affect the nature of the scale, and thus indirectly affect the accuracy of performance description. For example, there is some question as to whether or not the eventual raters should be directly involved in the development of the rating scales. The procedures for developing behaviorally anchored rating scales imply that this involvement is good both in terms of yielding better scales and in terms of increasing rater motivation.

Rating Process. There are a number of *procedures* that may influence the accuracy of ratings. For example, there may be differences in accuracy depending on whether the ratee gets to see the ratings or they are kept secret. Completing ratings at one time during the year for everyone may produce different results from ratings that are staggered throughout the year. Ratings that require elaborate justification might be significantly different from those that need not be documented.

Organizational Characteristics. The organization in which the ratings are gathered might have certain characteristics that influence the accuracy of ratings. These characteristics are independent of the characteristics of the rater, ratee, or position. Some examples of these characteristics are organization size, union/nonunion status, profitability, turnover levels, full-time/part-time employee ratio.

Data Analysis. Once the ratings are gathered, there are still some decisions to be made regarding data analysis that may affect the accuracy of the performance description. For example, should ratings be averaged or left independent? Should ratings from multiple raters be combined? Should the ratings be factor analyzed? The answers to these and other similar data questions will determine the characteristics of the eventual performance description.

The Performance Description. The combination of all of these elements produces a performance description. On the basis of this performance description, certain personnel actions are taken. Performance information is fed back to employees, salary changes are proposed, layoff lists are established, promotions are made. In many instances, performance descriptions are produced and nothing happens as a result of them; they are "filed." In a sense, this is also a personnel action, although it is an action by default. This type of nonaction has very special meaning to both the ratee and the rater. It tells both of them very clearly that nothing they do makes a difference to the organization.

The arrows from the box labeled "Personnel Action" to the boxes labeled "Rater Characteristics" and "Ratee Characteristics" imply that both action and inaction have an effect on how the rater and ratee approach their jobs. In an ideal setting, performance descriptions allow accurate feedback to the ratee, who subsequently changes his/her behavior to make it more efficient. This increased efficiency is suitably rewarded and the rater feels as if the ratings were a positive force in improving the skills of the subordinate and increasing the efficiency of the organization. Things are not always the way we would like them to be, however. It is also possible that punishments are distributed on the basis of ratings (e.g., layoffs, reprimands). In that case, the supervisor may think twice about being truthful the next time ratings are gathered. As another example, ratees may discover that individuals who always agree with the rater tend to receive the highest ratings, and they may subsequently change their behavior so that they always agree with the supervisor in conversations. These latter two instances are examples of counterproductive effects of the feedback.

While this model does not offer much in the way of explanation concerning *why* these elements may have adverse effects on the accuracy of performance descriptions, it does present a reasonable view of the complexity of the process. A good deal of research has been conducted over the past few decades that addresses the effect of several of these components and it may be useful to review the findings of these studies. A much more complete review of these effects can be found in the Landy and Farr (1979) paper.

1. Rater experience (i.e. training in rating, familiarity with the rating scales) appears to positively affect the quality of the ratings.
2. The relevance of the rater-ratee interaction is more important than the simple frequency of interaction.
3. The sex stereotype of the occupation (i.e. whether a particular job is typically perceived as masculine or feminine) interacts with the sex of the ratee to distort ratings. Thus, males are evaluated more favorably than females in perceived masculine tasks, but females are evaluated more favorably than males in tasks typically characterized as feminine.
4. Experimental studies of the effect of the performance level of the ratee upon performance ratings generally support the validity of the ratings.
5. While people may have preferences for various rating formats (e.g., the "good" portion of the rating scale is on the top or bottom, left or right), these preferences have little or no effect on actual rating behavior.
6. The number of response alternatives available to a rater should not be less than 5 or more than 9.

7. Whether the rating format is behaviorally anchored or forced choice, or even traditional graphic, is less important than whether the anchors were chosen carefully to distinguish between good and poor performance.
8. Ratings for administrative purposes will be more lenient than ratings for research purposes.
9. Rater training is effective in reducing rating errors.

As can be seen from comparing the things we know (as listed above) to the model in Figure 4–11 we have a long way to go. We still know little about the effect of position characteristics, organizational characteristics, rating process variables, data analytic techniques, or past personnel actions on the accuracy of performance ratings. Nevertheless, it is better to identify areas of ignorance than pretend the process of rating is a simple one. We expect knowledge in this area to grow rapidly in the next decade.

THE PERFORMANCE APPRAISAL INTERVIEW

Frequently, performance feedback is dreaded by supervisor and worker alike. One reason for this is the arbitrary nature of the information. The supervisor is given a form by the personnel department and told to evaluate all the workers with that form. The form usually has three dimensions or performance categories on it—quality of work (high, average, or low), quantity of work (high, average, or low), and overall performance (high, average, or low). The supervisor is usually as uncomfortable describing a worker in these terms as the worker is in being described in them. Consequently, supervisors give generally high ratings, since they do not know how to counsel the worker on low ratings. Everyone concerned realizes that the process is little more than ritual, and it loses any value it might have had. Adequate criterion development and measurement are crucial to the continuing development of both subordinates and supervisors.

Regardless of how the information about individual performance is collected—whether a ranking system, a rating system, or a collection of incidents which are critical to job performance—there must be a *formal* feedback system connected to the data collection. We stress the term *formal* because unless one is built into the system, one will develop informally. The most common *informal* feedback system is a result of no *formal* feedback to the subordinate or the rater. In the absence of such feedback, subordinates assume that either they have not been considered or appraised in a long time, or if they had been, it is irrelevant. Time after time, the authors have run into situations in industry where the employee complains that no one has even bothered to look at the quality or quantity of his work for the past two years. In checking into the complaint, we find that the employee's job performance has been rated by a supervisor each six months for the past three years. The supervisor, upon questioning, contends that 30 different people must be rated and that she can hardly "hold each of their hands" while she is doing it. "Besides, no one uses the information anyway."

In this case, the time and money that went into the preparation of the appraisal system is not only wasted but it is counterproductive. For that reason, it is essential that a feedback system be incorporated into the appraisal system from the very beginning. This usually takes the form of a discussion between the supervisor and the subordinate that is related to the behavior of the subordinate. Such a discussion can be quite uncomfortable for all concerned in its initial stages or until each party gets used to the procedure. There is often a tendency for supervisors to avoid uncomfortable issues, and consequently they defeat the purpose of the session. There is also a tendency on the part of the subordinate to explain away deficiencies rather than face up to them. While this situation may be more in the domain of a clinical psychologist rather than an industrial/organizational psychologist, we will mention one research study that makes a point about the dynamics of the feedback session. Kay, Meyer, and French (1965) examined the relationship between critical comments in a feedback session and the number of defensive comments made by the subordinate. Their general finding was that as threats or critical comments increased, defensiveness also increased. Further, they concluded that praise accomplished very little and the reason is fascinating: most supervisors use praise to cushion criticism, forming a "praise/criticism/praise sandwich." A few positive statements begin the feedback session to "put the employee at ease." Then come the negative comments, followed by a few more positive comments so the employee will "leave the session with a positive attitude." In effect, praise becomes a conditioned stimulus announcing the arrival of criticism, exactly as a tone signaled the presentation of food to the dog in Pavlov's classic experiment. In the feedback situation, the individual is put on the alert by positive comments; the positive comments following the criticism merely signal the individual that no more negative comments will come for a while.

Another interesting finding of the Kay et al study was the shape of the relationship between negative comments and defensiveness. The function does not seem to be a linear one, but rather a curvilinear, positively-accelerating one such as described in Figure 4–12. They suggest that an individual has some critical level of criticism that can be absorbed before defensive tendencies begin to appear. Based on this premise, they suggest that such a problem may be solved by having more frequent sessions with the individual so that the absolute number of negative comments in any one session is reduced.

The preceding discussion of the feedback mechanism in the appraisal process suggests several things: (1) it should be a formal part of the system; (2) supervisors should analyze their feedback style to identify such things

FIGURE 4–12
*Hypothetical Relationship between Negative
Comments by Supervisor and Defensive
Responses by Subordinate*

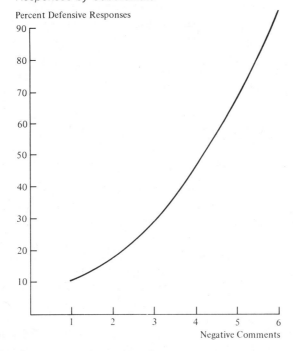

as the praise/criticism/praise sandwich; (3) it should be done frequently enough so that an individual is not overwhelmed by negative comments; and (4) supervisors should be made aware of the relationship between the data they collect on individual performance and the overall personnel decision system.

A recent study (Landy, Barnes, and Murphy, 1978) has added a new dimension to the issue of feedback. Managers were asked to describe the elements that affect their perceptions of fairness and accuracy in performance appraisal. The four predominant elements they mentioned were: (1) frequency of appraisal, (2) plans developed with the supervisor for eliminating weaknesses, (3) supervisor's knowledge of the ratee's job duties, and (4) supervisor's knowledge of ratee's level of performance. Some follow-up studies by the same researchers indicated that satisfaction with the company and with the supervisor were tied closely to satisfaction with the performance appraisal and feedback system (Landy, Barnes, Cleveland, and Murphy, 1978). Thus, it seems as if employees may derive satisfaction or generate dissatisfaction from the performance appraisal and feedback *process*, independent of the results of that process!

Managerial Performance Appraisal

To this point, we have dealt primarily with criterion development, job analysis, and performance appraisal of lower-level line functions, and ignored managerial functions. The general principles that were discussed earlier apply equally to managerial performance. It is likely that greater problems exist in constructing a measure of performance for managers due to the abstract nature of many of their activities, such as resource allocation, planning, and problem solving, but the process should be one similar to the appraisal of a lower-level line worker.

SOME CONTROVERSIES

Multiple versus Composite Criteria

If you have ever come in contact with two or more psychologists on a single occasion, you realize that they cannot discuss any topic for more than two minutes without disagreeing. A favorite topic for disagreement among personnel psychologists is the advisability of combining criterion information to form a single index of performance. Such a combination would produce what is known as a "composite criterion." The best example of a composite criterion might be in terms of an administrative decision. A company finds itself in a slump and decides that it must lay off 20 percent of its workers. Since the company is relatively young, there is little variation in seniority. The company calls in its upper-level managers to determine a way of characterizing each employee in terms of "worth to the company." The managers decide to use a measure of *quality of production*, a measure of *quantity of production*, and a rating of *initiative*. Furthermore, they decide that quantity of production is twice as important as quality of production, which is, in turn, twice as important as initiative. Consequently, they construct an equation like this:

$$4 \times \text{quantity} + 2 \times \text{quality} + 1 \times \text{initiative} = Y$$

They then arrange all of the Y scores from high to low, and they lay off those with scores in the bottom 20 percent. These Y scores would be an example of using a composite criterion for making an administrative decision. A new variable, or index of success, is formed by combining three other variables. The controversy is centered on the question of whether or not the data justify such a combination.

Perhaps another example will strike closer to home. Assume that a student receives a grade report at the end of the term, which states that the student received two As and three Fs. If someone were to take those grades, assign a point value to each of the grades (e.g., A = 4; B = 3; C = 2; D = 1; F = 0), add up the point values, and divide by 5, the student might be described as slightly worse than average. The student would justifiably argue that the averaging process distorted the real state of affairs. This highlights the different purposes that might be served by the same criterion information in *two different forms*. The university is interested primarily in the average of the grades, to determine if the student should be allowed to continue in the academic program. The student and the student's advisor take the information on the grade report and use it to determine what deficiencies must be made up, what general goals might be set for the next term, and how career goals might be changed or modified by the term report. The student's academic dean might argue that any single grade is simply a sample of that student's academic ability and a grade point average derived from several grades is a more stable index of that ability. For that reason, the dean might be unimpressed by the fact that the student received two As. On the other hand, it is of little use to either the student or the advisor to know that the student's grade point average is 1.60. The advisor must have specific pieces of information, the components of that single index called the grade point average, to advise the student efficiently.

Most psychologists who have confronted the problem of multiple versus composite criteria recognize that there is ample justification for either approach. There will always be a need for a single index in making administrative decisions. In addition, there will always be a need for specific performance information of a multidimensional nature for counseling, regardless of how these dimensions might be combined to form a single dimension.

The argument about composite versus multiple criteria is usually presented as if one form of criterion information *excludes* the other, and this is by no means the case. The argument is not about how the information will be gathered, but how it will be used. There are good reasons to consider presenting the information in both forms, since the information often serves two distinct purposes, one administrative and the other diagnostic. The aversion to composite criteria on the part of many researchers may be a result of an overinterpretation of the index. For example, when we combine a series of tests into an equation for the prediction of some criterion, seldom are we charged with implying a *general overall test ability factor*. It is simply accepted that each of the tests explains a different portion of the variance in some potentially complex criterion. Why then should the simple combination of performance information imply the existence of a *general performance factor?* Since it makes sense to use performance information in many different contexts, and since each of those contexts may require the information in a different form, we would suggest that performance information be gathered and recorded in a "multiple" or uncollapsed form. A composite index can always be computed when needed.

Another issue related to the composite/multiple controversy is the compensatory nature of various criteria. For any given job, it may be that there are some areas of performance so critical that an individual cannot make up for deficiencies in that area with an abundance in another area. For example, it may be that a crane operator cannot substitute exceptional interpersonal skills for deficiency in reading work orders. In that case, unless some minimal amount of reading accuracy can be assured, performance will consistently be disasterous. In this case, one would not want to use an equation such as the one on p. 136 to combine performance scores. Interpersonal skills and reading accuracy should remain separate in describing the performance of the crane operator. While most jobs allow for compensatory relationships among performance measures, it is important to recognize that there are instances in which performance scores should not be combined, or at the very least, should not be combined in a strictly linear additive fashion. This point will be discussed again in the next chapter, when we discuss the combination of test scores for prediction purposes.

The Ultimate Criterion

A second consideration that has been a matter of some disagreement is the role of the "ultimate criterion. The ultimate criterion is an idealized version of job performance. It is the criterion that best captures the essence of a particular job activity. The ultimate criterion is usually contrasted with the actual criterion. While measurement of the ultimate criterion is an important goal in personnel research, invariably we must settle for something less. For example, the ultimate criterion of the presidency of the United States might be the judgment of the president's accomplishments by historians 100 years after the completion of term of office. If, however, we are pondering the reelection of a current president, we can hardly wait 100 years for an estimate of success. The ultimate criterion for college teachers might be their total impact on those students with whom they come in contact during their teaching career. But it would be unreasonable to wait until the end of the teaching careers of a group of college teachers to determine whether or not those teachers have been effective.

The examples presented highlight the "temporal" flavor of an ultimate criterion. It could just as easily be called the "long-term measure of success." In that respect, the ultimate criterion seems to satisfy the definitions of reliability and validity. It is reliable in the sense that it is a stable measure and valid in the sense that it perfectly represents a construct which is accepted as defining job performance.

The temporal aspects of the ultimate criterion can be somewhat arbitrary, depending upon the particular problem and investigator. For example, DiStefano and Bass (1959) chose to define the ultimate criterion for a group of lawyers as the opinion of judges before whom these lawyers practiced. The opinion was gathered five years after the lawyer began to practice. While five years was undoubtedly a long enough period of time to get a stable measure of performance, four years might have done as well. This example highlights the temporal aspect of the ultimate criterion. The question of the proper amount of time necessary before criterion measurement can be considered stable is difficult. It is probably better answered with data than with logic. One way of answering the question might be to plot reliabilities as a function of increasing time blocks and define the "proper time" as that point at which the reliability curve levels off. Figure 4–13 presents a hypothetical data set dealing with this relationship.[3] After two months, increases in reliability are negligible. In this case, then, the "proper" amount of time would be two months. In other cases, two years or two decades might be required to achieve a reliable estimate of "ultimate success."

FIGURE 4–13

Reliability of Measurement Plotted as a Function of Length of the Observation Period

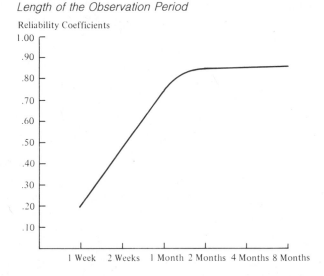

One of the ways in which the ultimate criterion concept has been useful is in the description of the properties and limitations of actual criteria. In other words, it provides a kind of idealized standard for evaluating actual criterion measures. We can describe three properties of the actual criterion: deficiency, relevance, and contamination. Criterion deficiency is defined as the degree to which the actual criterion does not completely measure the ultimate criterion. In our example of the ultimate criterion for the judgment of the president of the United States, if success were measured only in terms of the number of foreign dignitaries entertained during the term of office, the actual criterion would be somewhat deficient.

---

[3] Figure 4–13 describes the reliability of a criterion measure in terms of its test-retest stability. This is an important characteristic for selection research. Nevertheless, there are instances in which test-retest reliability may not be as critical. For example, performance feedback should probably be sensitive enough to highlight inconsistencies in performance as well as consistencies. In that case, a criterion developed to possess maximum test-retest reliability may be so insensitive to current levels of performance as to be useless. Similarly, a criterion measure that is very stable over time may be too insensitive to pick up changes in behavior as a result of training experiences. Thus, in considering issues such as reliability of criteria, it is important to know how the information is to be used. Nevertheless, generally speaking, temporal consistency is an important characteristic of criterion information.

Although entertaining foreign dignitaries is certainly part of the job of the president, there are many more important aspects of the job that have not been included. In other words, criterion deficiency is a measure of the degree to which all of the elements of the ultimate criterion have *not* been measured. Criterion relevance is a measure of the degree to which the actual criterion measures the true or ultimate criterion. Criterion contamination is a measure of the degree to which our actual criterion includes elements unrelated to the ultimate criterion. If we gathered information about the president's eating habits, recreational habits, and color preferences, and included this information as part of our actual criterion, that criterion would be considered contaminated, since it consisted of information unrelated to the ultimate criterion.

There are two major drawbacks to accepting the notion of an ultimate criterion. The first is pointed out by James (1973) in distinguishing between multiple and composite criteria. James has proposed that those who accept the notion of an ultimate criterion must ally themselves with the composite criterion advocates and against the multiple criterion group. Logically, if one can conceive of an ultimate criterion that captures the essence of job success, then it follows that attempts should be made to combine elements to synthesize that ultimate criterion. But it is unnecessary to choose *between* the composite and multiple form of criterion data presentation. In a review of a criterion model presented in a book by Campbell, Dunnette, Lawler, and Weick (1970), James emphasizes the idea of *levels* of criterion measurement. At the lowest and most specific level (individually), we have *job behavior*, or what is actually done by the worker on the job. At a slightly less specific level, we observe *job performance*, which is a collection of value judgments placed on job behaviors. These value judgments (good-bad, effective-ineffective) describe the relationship between individual job behaviors and organizational goals. The third and most global level is that of *organization outcomes*, which are indices of job effectiveness. This approach implies a continuum running from the complexity of multiple criterion information (job behaviors) to the more global composite criterion (organization outcome). The idealized properties of the ultimate criterion prevent us from recognizing that we are really dealing with different *levels* of measurement rather than conceptually different *forms* of measurement.

A second drawback to the notion of the ultimate criterion is that it is not presently, nor was it ever, necessary. We can deal quite adequately with the idea of an "ultimate criterion" by using strategies, designs, terms, and statistics generally associated with reliability and validity.

The ultimate-criterion concept is something from the earlier developmental stages of personnel psychology. It was an attempt to encourage researchers and managers to consider the broader issues of suitability when choosing or developing a criterion measure. Suitability was defined in terms of deficiency, relevance, and contamination. While no new conceptual framework has clearly emerged to take the place of the ultimate criterion approach, it appears that construct validity of criterion measures is a good candidate.

Fortunately, the methods by which construct validity is established are becoming clearer. These methods will eventually replace the concepts of deficiency, relevance, and contamination.

CHALLENGES FOR CRITERION RESEARCH

Criterion related issues have generated a renewed enthusiasm for personnel psychology. This enthusiasm has provided some rather clear challenges to I/O psychologists. The challenges can be thought of as coming from three distinct directions: (1) the government, (2) the workers, and (3) the science of psychology.

The Government

In the past decade, the Equal Employment Opportunity Commission (EEOC) has become a pervading force in personnel psychology. The recently published guidelines for testing, constructed by a loose confederation of federal agencies (Uniform Guidelines, 1978), have clearly placed a major emphasis on criterion development as a means of eliminating unfair hiring practices. In addition, it appears that if performance information is used to make promotional decisions, performance appraisal systems will have to be validated in much the same manner as selection systems. There are major disagreements among government agencies, private industry, and I/O psychologists concerning fair employment issues. Many of the disagreements center around issues such as job analysis and criterion development.

The Workers

Perhaps a bigger challenge to the adequacy of criterion development and performance appraisal systems will be provided by the workers themselves. More and more, their discontent with many traditional personnel practices such as performance appraisal is surfacing. Too often, performance appraisal, as a device, has been used to justify an arbitrary personnel decision. In other instances, the performance information is religiously gathered and just as religiously ignored.

A great credibility gap is developing between what we say we are doing as professionals and the fruits of our work as seen by the worker. It is our feeling that most workers truly desire a fair and rational system of performance appraisal that will help them understand the relationship between their individual efforts and organizational goals. Unfortunately, their patience with such attempts may be wearing thin.

The Science

Still other challenges are constantly being provided by possible interrelationships between and among constructs from related but distinct research avenues. For example, there should be some clear relationships between concepts such as performance appraisal and subordinate goal-setting programs. A system in which a supervisor helps a subordinate set performance goals provides a capsule view of the entire criterion development and performance appraisal system. The individual and the supervisor conduct an individualized job analysis, construct relevant and mutually acceptable criterion dimensions, agree on a way of measuring performance on each of these dimensions, and include a formal, constantly operating feedback loop. The challenge is to describe the relationship between criterion development and goal setting. There are many other such challenges.

SUMMARY

Criterion development and measurement play a central role in all personnel decisions. Some of these decisions are made from a single number that represents an overall score on some criterion measure; other decisions are made on the basis of a profile of scores on various criteria. Consequently, a composite criterion is suitable for some purposes, while multiple criteria are required for other purposes.

The ultimate criterion is an idealized view of measures of work behavior. Actual criteria usually fall short in two respects: (1) actual criteria include variations unrelated to the ultimate criterion (criterion contamination), and (2) actual criteria do not share much variance in common with the ultimate criterion (criterion deficiency). The variance that is shared between the ultimate and actual criterion contributes to valid measurement and is called criterion relevance. The selection of criteria should be based on three criterion characteristics: reliability, validity, and practicality.

Job analysis, job evaluation, job description, and performance appraisal differ in some important respects. Job analysis is a process for identifying critical job elements that are most crucial for job success. Job evaluation is a process for placing a dollar value on those elements and assigning wage rates to jobs according to the number and involvement of the critical elements identified in the job analysis. A job description is a listing of job duties based on the job analysis. Performance appraisal concentrates on describing the job performance of a particular individual, rather than the characteristics of a job.

Performance appraisal data may come in several different forms. Objective data include things that can be counted accurately. Personnel data consist of data found in a personnel folder and relating to peripheral aspects of actual work performance. This would include things like absenteeism, and tardiness. Judgmental data include judgments of a worker's performance by a supervisor or peer. The most common form of judgmental data is the rating form. Other judgmental procedures include ranking and pair-comparison. Halo, leniency, and central tendency are three common forms of rating error. Behaviorally anchored scales and mixed standard scales may help eliminate rating errors.

Employee ratings are affected by rater, ratee, position, and organizational characteristics. In addition, the rating process, nature of the rating scale, and the scale development procedure might also affect the accuracy of performance descriptions. The use to which ratings are put will influence the perceptions of both raters and ratees.

The feedback of rating information should occur frequently. Positive feedback should not be sandwiched between two pieces of negative feedback. If a large number of negative comments are to be given, they should be stretched over several sessions.

The adequacy of criterion development and measurement is being challenged by government and workers. The future of personnel psychology depends on the development of models and techniques for criterion development and measurement.

REFERENCES

Arvey, R. D., & Begalla, M. E. Analyzing the homemaker job using the PAQ. *Journal of Applied Psychology.* 1975, *60,* 513–517.

Arvey, R. D., & Mossholder, K. M. A proposed methodology for determining similarities and differences among jobs. *Personnel Psychology,* 1977, *30,* 363–374.

Arvey, R. D., Passino, E. M., & Lounsbury, J. W. Job analysis results as affected by sex of incumbent and sex of analyst. *Journal of Applied Psychology,* 1977, *62,* 411–416.

Ash, R. A. & Edgell, S. L. A note on the readability of the PAQ. *Journal of Applied Psychology,* 1975, *60,* 765–766.

Bernardin, H. J. Behavioral expectation scales vs. summated ratings: A fairer comparison. *Journal of Applied Psychology,* 1977, *62,* 422–427.

Bernardin, H. J., Alvares, K. M., & Cranny, C. J. A recomparison of behavioral expectation scales to summated scales. *Journal of Applied Psychology,* 1976, *61,* 564–570.

Blanz, F., & Ghiselli, E. E. The mixed standard scale: A new rating system. *Personnel Psychology,* 1972, *25,* 185–200.

Blum, M., & Naylor, J. *Industrial psychology.* New York: Harper & Row, 1968.

Campbell, J., Dunnette, M., Arvey, R., & Hellervik, L. The development and evaluation of behaviorally based rating scales. *Journal of Applied Psychology,* 1973, *57,* 15–22.

Campbell, J. P., Dunnette, M. D., Lawler, E. E., & Weick, K. E. *Managerial behavior, performance, and effectiveness.* New York: McGraw-Hill, 1970.

Cummings, L. L. A field experimental study of the effects of two performance appraisal systems. *Personnel Psychology,* 1973, *26,* 489–502.

Distefano, M. K., & Bass, B. M. Prediction of an ultimate criterion of success as a lawyer. *Journal of Applied Psychology,* 1959, *42,* 40–41.

Dunnette, M. D. A note on the criterion. *Journal of Applied Psychology,* 1963, *47,* 251–254.

Equal Employment Opportunity Commission. *Guidelines on employment testing procedures.* Washington, D.C.: EEOC, 1978.

Flanagan, J. C. The critical incident technique. *Psychological Bulletin,* 1954, *51,* 327–358.

Ghiselli, E. E., & Brown, C. W. *Personnel and industrial psychology.* New York: McGraw-Hill, 1955.

Gilbert, T. F. On the relevance of laboratory investigation of learning to self-instructional programming. In A. A. Lumsdaine & R. Glaser (Eds.), *Teaching machines and programmed instruction.* Washington, D.C.: National Education Association, 1960.

Guion, R. M. Criterion measurement and personnel judgments. *Personnel Psychology,* 1961, *14,* 141–149.

Guion, R. M. *Personnel testing.* New York: McGraw-Hill, 1965.

Ilgen, D. R. Attendance behavior: A re-evaluation of Latham and Pursell's conclusions. *Journal of Applied Psychology,* 1977, *62,* 230–233.

James, L. R. Criterion models and construct validity for criteria. *Psychological Bulletin,* 1973, *80,* 75–83.

Kay, E., Meyer, H., & French, J. R. P. Effects of threat in a performance appraisal interview. *Journal of Applied Psychology,* 1965, *49,* 311–317.

Landy, F. J., Barnes, J. L., Cleveland, J., & Murphy, K. *Attitudes toward performance appraisal (Penn State Report Series).* University Park, Pa., 1978.

Landy, F. J., Barnes, J. L., & Murphy, K. Correlates of perceived fairness and accuracy of performance appraisal. *Journal of Applied Psychology,* 1978, *63.*

Landy, F. J. & Farr, J. L. A process model of performance rating. *Psychological Bulletin.* In Press.

Landy, F. J., & Guion, R. M. Development of scales for the measurement of work motivation. *Organizational Behavior and Human Performance,* 1970, *5,* 93–103.

Latham, G. P., & Pursell, E. D. Measuring absenteeism from the opposite side of the coin. *Journal of Applied Psychology,* 1975, *60,* 369–371.

London, M. Employee perceptions of the job reclassification process. *Personnel Psychology,* 1976, *29,* 67–77.

McCormick, E. J., Jeanneret, P., & Mecham, R. C. A study of job characteristics and job dimensions as based on the position analysis questionnaires. *Journal of Applied Psychology,* 1972, *36,* 347–368. (Monograph)

Mobley, W., & Ramsay, R. Hierarchical clustering on the basis of inter-job similarity as a tool in validity generalization. *Personnel Psychology,* 1973, *26,* 213–226.

Prien, E. P. The function of job analysis in content validation. *Personnel Psychology,* 1977, *30,* 167–174.

Rothe, H. F., & Nye, C. T. Output rates among machine operators: II—Consistency related to methods of pay. *Journal of Applied Psychology,* 1959, *43,* 417–420.

Schwab, D., Heneman, H. G. III, & DeCotiis, T. Behaviorally anchored rating scales: A review of the literature. *Personnel Psychology,* 1975, *28,* 549–562.

Smith, P. C., & Kendall, L. M. Retranslation of expectations: An approach to the construction of unambiguous anchors for rating scales. *Journal of Applied Psychology,* 1963, *47,* 149–155.

Uniform guidelines on employee selection procedures (1978). *Federal Register,* 1978, *43,* No. 166, 38290–38309.

CHAPTER 5
Personnel Decisions

Personnel decisions are decisions about people: about hiring, classifying and placing, transferring and reclassifying, promoting and upgrading, training, and developing people. The objective of these decisions is to maximize the utilization of manpower as evaluated in terms of the growth and profit goals of the company. Personnel decisions are *institutional decisions* designed to maximize payoff in terms of institutional rather than individual goals. By contrast, *individual decisions* involving the selection of career, training, company, job, transfer, or retraining—decisions that are arrived at privately, with friends, or in vocational counseling—reflect the goals and values of the individual. While an institution, such as a medical school, may look at an applicant who, based on her record and test scores, has less than a 50/50 chance of completing medical school training, as a bad risk, the individual might feel that, in spite of any odds, life will be meaningless unless she becomes a doctor. Whereas *probability of success* can govern the institutional decision, it is not the sole consideration in the individual decision.

With the exception of a relatively few institutions with open admissions policies, institutions select people and thereby limit the number of choices available to the individual. For the most part, these two types of decisions are made at very different times and places. Only in the vocational counseling situation are the realities of the two decision processes brought face-to-face. The counselor knows the likelihood on an actuarial basis that the institution will say "yes" to the individual, and he learns something about the values and preferences of the individual. Ideally, he can consider both

145

the potential payoff to the institution and to the individual as a basis for counseling.

In recent years there has been a general increase in the concern for the individual in our society. This is reflected in the civil rights movements, the concerns for invasion of privacy, equality of opportunity, and the like. Guion (1967) describes this trend in U.S. business and industry as an increased concern for the "wholeness and integrity of the applicant." Is such a personal approach inconsistent with the goals of the institution and with efficient personnel decisions? No. By and large, good institutional decisions will be good individual decisions, and bad institutional decisions, based on arbitrary biases, prejudices, and whims rather than on valid information, are bad, not only for the individuals rejected but also quite possibly for the "favored" individual. A good decision is one that results in a good match between individual and job, and decisions based on irrelevant information are often apt to result in mismatches between individuals and jobs. Korman (1971) has suggested that this new concern may lead to something like a placement-counseling approach in the personnel office, where employer and applicant might be seen as

> viewing the selection decision as one where the organization and the individual attempt to see whether the two can be or have the capacity to be mutually beneficial to one another . . . not too different from the general "career choice" process as it takes place in vocational counseling centers and the like (p. 219).

CLASSES OF PERSONNEL DECISIONS

The major classes of personnel decisions with which this chapter is concerned can be grouped into *selection* and *placement decisions*. Basically, selection decisions are all those decisions in which a person is selected *for* or rejected *from* a specific "treatment," that is, a specific job, upgrading, promotion, or training program. Thus, selection involves a single treatment or job (with one or more positions) and with a choice among individuals for that treatment. Whenever there are two or more different jobs under consideration, the simple selection situation no longer exists. Instead, one is faced either with a sequential selection-placement set of decisions or with a pure placement decision (if "reject" is not one of the choices).

The distinction between selection and placement decisions is straightforward. In selection, *applicants* are selected for a job; in placement, a *job* is selected (from among two or more different job openings) for the applicant or new hire. In selection, an applicant is hired because she appears to be qualified for a particular job, while in placement an applicant may be hired on the basis of some general minimum hiring requirements ("high school diploma, social security number, and physical exam"); then a job is selected for him. An example of the latter is given by the Armed Forces in times of a national draft. "New hires" are selected by lottery and on the basis of "general fitness" exams; then, after basic training, decisions have to be made concerning the types of further specialized training or job categories to be selected for the recruits. Selection depends on successful recruiting or a favorable labor market with more applicants than openings, ensuring that one can be selective. Placement, on the other hand, can occur with or without a labor surplus, so long as there are openings in two or more different jobs.

Cronbach and Gleser (1965)[1] presented the following set of questions for classifying personnel decision problems:

1. *(a)* Are the benefits obtained from a decision evaluated in the same way for each person? [institutional decision] or
   (b) Are different values used in deciding about each person? [individual decision]
2. *(a)* Is the decision about each person made independently? [no quota constraints] or
   (b) Are decisions about various persons interrelated? [quota constraints]
3. *(a)* Is each individual assigned to just one of the available treatments? [one "job" per individual] or
   (b) May he be assigned to multiple treatments?
4. *(a)* Is one of the allowable treatments "reject"? [selection] or
   (b) Are all persons retained in the institution? [placement without selection]
5. *(a)* Is the information used in univariate form? [a single "score" for each individual] or
   (b) Is it in multivariate form? [two or more "scores" or items of information]
6. *(a)* Are decisions final? [single-stage testing, final decision] or
   (b) May one decide to obtain further information prior to final decisions? [sequential testing; choices include: reject, accept, test further] (p. 16)

The answer to each of these questions determines the type of decision situation, and there are 64 (2^6) possible types. It is not possible to discuss these in detail, but what has been said and what will be said will reflect on each of these questions.

THE EVALUATION OF TESTING PROGRAMS

Much of Chapter 3 was concerned with the evaluation of tests as measuring devices, and a good deal of emphasis was placed on reliability and validity as criteria of a test's worth. It was emphasized that these and other criteria should be considered in choosing a test for use in a testing program. The present chapter takes up where Chapter 3 left off: having selected a test, or tests, on the basis of the criteria and procedures described, and having incorporated them into a testing program, how then can one determine the utility, or payoff, of the testing program? How and to what

---

[1] L. J. Cronbach & G. C. Gleser, *Psychological Tests and Personnel Decisions* (Urbana: University of Illinois Press, 1965). Copyright © 1965 by The Board of Trustees of the University of Illinois. Reprinted by permission of the University of Illinois Press.

extent is the information in the test scores used? To what extent does it affect the personnel decisions made? Assuming that better decisions are made because of the test, what is the payoff in terms of increased efficiency of the organization, improved proficiency of the worker on the job, reduced turnover, increased satisfaction, or increased profitability?

The best measurement data from the best tests are of little value if they cannot be utilized to guide decisions, if the data cost more than the gains that result from improved decisions, or if they are highly redundant with information that is already available to the decision maker. To illustrate the last point with an example, suppose an organization administered a test to all applicants, even though scores from the same test were available from their schools or on their transcripts. No new information would be made available to the decision maker, and the testing program would be a liability equal to the direct and overhead costs of operating it, not to mention the imposition on the applicant.

Validity and Predictive Efficiency

In Chapter 3, we equated predictor validity with the correlation coefficient, r_{pc}, relating predictor and criterion scores. Generally, this implies the use of the Pearson product-moment correlation, which describes the *linear* relationship between two variables. How is a validity coefficient to be interpreted? Suppose, for example, $r_{pc} = .00$, as illustrated in Figure 5–1. Here the scattergram indicates that at any predictor score, X_i, the mean criterion score, $\bar{Y}_i$, will be the same as the mean, $\bar{Y}$, for the total sample. Furthermore, the variability (σ_{y_i}) of criterion scores at X_i will be comparable to that of the total sample (σ_y). In other words, with r = .00, there is no differential prediction—one predicts the mean criterion score regardless of the predictor score, and the error of prediction is described by σ_{y_i}, which is equal to σ_y for the sample. In contrast, with $r_{pc} = 1.00$, X_i is predictive of Y_i, as shown in Figure 5–2, and $\sigma_{y_i} = 0$; that is, given X_i, there is no error in predicting Y_i. In Figure 5–1, we have no efficiency of prediction; in Figure 5–2, we have maximum efficiency of prediction.

The more important cases involve the interpretation of validity coefficients between .00 and 1.00. Such a case is illustrated in Figure 5–3 with $r_{pc} = .50$. Since we are considering only a linear relationship between the predictor and the criterion, we would use the equation for a straight line to predict individual criterion scores from individual predictor scores. The equation for a straight line is $Y = a + bx$ (where a is equal to the y-intercept or the point where the line cuts the y-axis, and b is equal to the slope of the line; in algebraic terms, the slope is often referred to as "rise over run"). When this equation is used to predict one set of scores from another set of scores, it is referred to as the "regression equation."

In the case of the relationship depicted in Figure 5–3, we can have

FIGURE 5–1

Prediction When r =.00

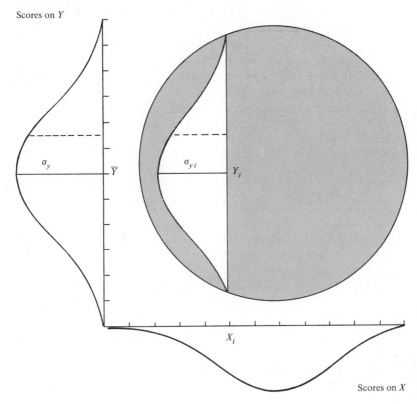

some success in predicting Y scores from X scores. High X scores predict high Y scores, but not without error of prediction. This error is again described by the distribution of Y_i at the given score, X_i. In this case, our predictive efficiency is better than it was when the validity (r_{pc}) was .00, but worse than it was when the validity was 1.00.

The relationship between correlation and predictive efficiency is described by the *coefficient of determination*, r^2, which indicates that portion of the variance in Y accounted for by X. In the case $r = .50$, $r^2 = .25$, or 25 percent of the variance in Y is accounted for by X—better than nothing, but less than 100. You should recognize this concept of "accounting for variance" from Chapter 2. If $r = .50$, it means that if we know the X scores of a group of individuals, we can reduce the variance of their Y scores by 25 percent. This ability to reduce variability in one set of scores from knowledge of another set of scores is the essence of prediction. In the most basic terms, X predicts Y.

Another way of stating the same principle is that differential prediction

FIGURE 5–2

Prediction When r = 1.00

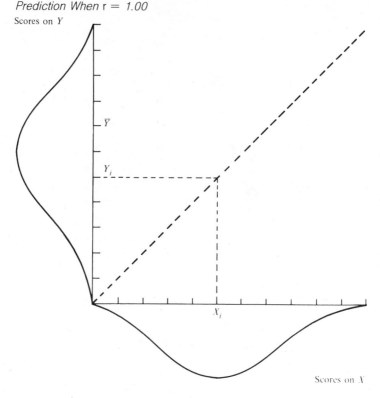

of Y based on knowledge of X reduces the error variance in prediction by 25 percent. The reciprocal value, $1 - r^2$, is known as the coefficient of alienation, which with $r = .50$, would be .75. Therefore, from the point of view of classical measurement theory, a validity coefficient of .50 yields only a modest gain of 25 percent in predictive efficiency. Given the fact that validity coefficients seldom exceed .50 this is a rather disappointing interpretation. But even more disillusioning, perhaps, are the results obtained from applying another formula for evaluating preditive efficiency, the "Index of Forecasting Efficiency," E. Whereas the coefficient of determination describes the reduction in the variance (σ^2) of the error distribution achieved by using predictor scores, E describes the reduction in the standard deviation of the errors in predicting the criterion scores. The index is obtained by the equation:

$$E = 1 - \sqrt{1 - r_{pc}^2}.$$

With an $r_{pc} = .50$, as in our previous example, E is equal to only slightly more than .13, indicating a mere 13-percent improvement in predictive efficiency.

FIGURE 5–3

Prediction When r = .50

Scores on Y

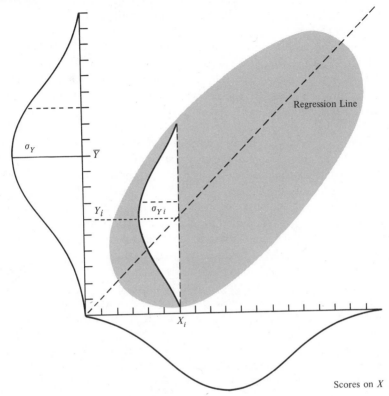

Validity and Personnel Decisions

While good tests (or other sources of information) are not *sufficient* to assure the value of a testing program, they are necessary for its success. In other words, the more valid the data on which decisions are based, the better the decisions and the greater the payoff, *all other things being equal*. In this chapter, we consider what some of these "other things" are that affect the value of a testing program, but first we will have a new look at the concept of empirical validity.

How does one begin to determine the value, for any setting, of tests that have been so carefully selected? The most immediate approach is to conduct a concurrent validity study with present employees. Criterion measures are chosen from available sources, or devices are constructed for the purpose, and the power of the test scores to predict these criteria is described as a correlation (validity) coefficient. This coefficient indicates how well the specific criterion measure can be predicted from the test scores for the present employees. However, such information is of little practical value for personnel decisions—first, because selection and placement decisions have already been made for present employees, and secondly, since criterion scores are already available, predicting them is little more than an academic exercise.

The real value in establishing concurrent validity is that it gives some evidence that the test *may* be useful for the prediction of *future* criterion scores of job applicants and, therefore, potentially useful as a basis for future selection decisions. It should be noted, however, that the size of a concurrent validity coefficient cannot be taken as an accurate estimate of the predictive validity of the test. This is true because, to the extent that prior selection procedures have been valid, the range of criterion scores should be restricted in the sample of current employees. Furthermore, to the extent that the predictor scores are valid, they too should be restricted in range for present employees. *Theoretically*, both of these restrictions should serve to make concurrent validity a conservative estimate of predictive validity, i.e., an estimate *lower* than the true value.

Two procedures have been used for estimating predictive validity with job applicants. Sometimes, having demonstrated some evidence of concurrent validity, the decision maker chooses to use the test as a selection device, together with or in place of established selection methods. Thus, those individuals with the highest predictor scores are selected and those with low scores are rejected. Subsequently, when criterion scores are available, they can be correlated with predictor scores. However, since only applicants with high predictor scores were hired, the validity coefficient is again based on a restricted range.

The alternative procedure is to administer the new predictor to job applicants, but not to include predictor scores in the decision to hire. That is, the existing decision strategy continues to be used, and new predictor scores are simply filed away until criterion data are available. This allows the decision maker to demonstrate what gains would have been made *over the existing strategy* had predictor scores been used in hiring decisions. As an example, suppose that 50 percent of the applicants were hired and, after six months, 50 percent of those were considered successful and 50 percent unsuccessful. Now, an examination of the test scores of these two groups shows that 75 percent of the successes had predictor scores above the median. while only 25 percent of the failures had scores above the median. This would indicate that using the predictor as the basis of hiring decisions would increase the success rate from 50 to 75 percent. (As we will see, the "gain" could also be expressed in terms of a mean difference in proficiency scores between the two strategies.) It should be noted that failure to show a gain over the existing selection method does *not* mean that the predictive validity of the test is zero. Instead, it means that a decision strategy based upon test scores is no more valid (does not lead to a greater percentage of correct decisions) than the existing methods. For example, selecting college students on the basis of standardized entrance exams may yield the same percentage of successes as selecting students on the basis of rank in their high school classes. Yet both may be valid in that each results in a much higher success rate than selecting students by random lottery.

The last statement suggests the third possibility. A predictor may be evaluated using an unselected (except for self-selection) sample, as in an open-admissions college or university. Here, the expectancy would be for a relatively heterogeneous sample and a relatively high failure rate, both of which would increase the likelihood of obtaining a high predictive validity coefficient.

Job Component Validity

Determining the validity of a predictor with any degree of confidence requires a fairly sizable sample. Suppose, for example, a company with 20 machine operators does a concurrent validity study with promising results and then wishes to use the test in selection and determine its predictive validity. However, with a turnover rate of 20 percent and an average growth rate of 10 percent per year, the company hires only about 6 machine operators each year. In this case it would take four or five years to obtain a reasonable sample for a validation study.

Suppose, however, that instead of predicting proficiency in the performance of certain jobs, we attempt to predict certain components that are elements of varying importance in all jobs in the organization. Having obtained criterion measures (probably ratings) on each of these components, one could then determine which of several predictors correlated with each component. A matrix of the results might look like the one in Table 5–1. Predictors could then be chosen for each job that are the most predictive of what are judged to be the two or three most important elements of that job. For example, given a job with elements I and VII (e.g., "salesmanship" and "customer relations"), the best single predictor would be D (it predicts both elements), followed by A and F, which predict elements I and VII, respectively.

Thus, with component validity, one determines how well the tests predict ratings on job components or elements, rather than ratings of overall proficiency on specific jobs. This means that the entire organization can be included in the validation sample. Guion (1965) reported a job component validity study in a small electrical goods company "employing only 48 people from president to stock boy. In no case were there more than three people doing the same kind of work."

The crucial aspect of the component validity approach is the identification and definition of the job elements, since ratings of these elements serve as the criteria against which the predictors are to be evaluated. In his study, Guion identified seven elements—salesmanship, creative judgment, customer relations, leadership, routine judgment, ability to handle detail work, and ability to organize work—that could be rated for all jobs

TABLE 5–1

Relationships between Predictors and Job Elements in Hypothetical Job Component Validity Study

Predictor	Job Element						
	I	II	III	IV	V	VI	VII
A	*			*	*		
B		*		*			
C		*				*	
D	*						*
E			*			*	
F			*		*		*

Predictors *A* and *D* are correlated with ratings of element I (e.g., "customer relations") and could be used to select people for positions where this element is important. Similarly, predictors *B* and *C* could be used where element II is important, and so on.

in the organization. Unless these or similar elements are carefully defined, however, they are not likely to provide either reliable criterion data or consensus as to their importance in specific jobs.

Decision Accuracy versus Prediction Accuracy

Some consideration has been given to the interpretation of a validity coefficient in terms of predictive accuracy or efficiency. The outcome of that discussion was a rather gloomy picture: a high validity coefficient ($r = .50$) was found to account for only one-fourth of the variance in criterion scores ($r^2 = .25$) and to reduce the errors in predicting criterion performance by only about 13 percent ($E = .13$). Thus, from the view of classical measurement theory, a validity coefficient of .50 gains us relatively little in terms of the precision with which we can predict criterion scores.

In contrast to this gloomy picture is the view that the value of a predictor should be measured in terms of improvement in *personnel decisions*, not in the *absolute accuracy* of prediction. Basically, the decision maker is concerned with improving his "batting average" in hiring the "right" people and in rejecting the "wrong" people. He wants to minimize both *false positive* errors (that is, hiring a person who turns out to be a failure) and *false negative* errors (rejecting someone who would have been a success). The situation is illustrated in Figure 5–4. Assume again a validity of .50 and a cutoff score of X_i on the predictor. Assume further that the success rate on the job is 50 percent—half of the *unselected* workers succeed (i.e.,

FIGURE 5–4

Scatterplot of Predictor and Criterion Scores

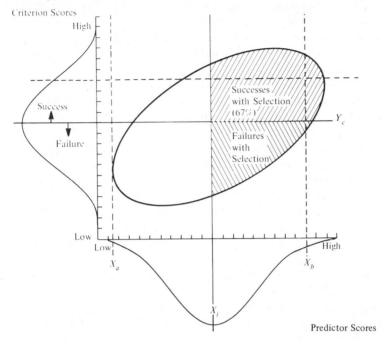

Without the use of the predictor, 50 percent of the employees are successful ($Y > Y_c$). *With a cutoff score of X,* on the predictor scores 67 percent of those selected are successful. The success rate is nearly 100 percent with a very high cutoff score (X_b).

obtain criterion scores greater than Y_c). Decisions to hire, *prior* to use of the test, then, have been half correct and half incorrect; that is, half true positives and half false positives. It is not possible to know the accuracy of the rejection decisions, since no criterion data are available for those not hired. However, given a validity coefficient of .50, and assuming X_i to be a median score so that we would accept the 50 percent of the applicants who score above X_i, we would expect 67 percent of those accepted to be successful (true positives) and 33 percent to be unsuccessful (false positives). In other words, the correct "accept" decisions would be increased from 50 percent to 67 percent (see Taylor-Russell tables, discussed later). It should be noted that the choice of a cutoff score is critical in determining the ratio of "hits" to "misses"; with the cutoff at X_b, there would be few false positives, but a large proportion of the rejections would be false negatives. With the cutoff at X_a, however, there would be no rejections (hence no false negatives), and since no selection would occur, the ratio of true to false positives would remain as it was before the predictor was available.

Validity, Selection Ratio, and Success Rate

The above discussion pointed out that the *predictive validity of a test alone is not sufficient to determine its utility as a selection device*. Unless one can be selective and reject some portion of the applicants with low scores, the predictor score information cannot be used in decisions (there are *no* decisions in this case) and it is of no value. From Figure 5–4 it can be seen that, assuming a relatively fixed distribution of X scores in the applicant population, the setting of a cutoff score defines that proportion of the applicants that will be accepted; that is, the selection ratio. More typically, however, the selection ratio is determined by the supply of applicants relative to the demand created by job vacancies. This information is then used to set the cutoff score.

Figure 5–4 also serves to illustrate the interaction of selection ratio and success rate as it affects decision errors and the utility of selection. If, for example, only 20 percent of the employees were considered successful (Y scores $> Y_b$), then the decision errors would be quite different: false positives would increase and false negatives would decrease nearly to zero using the cutoff X_i in Figure 5–4.

To maximize the proportion of correct decisions (and minimize decision errors), a cutoff score should equate the number of false positives and false negatives. This is illustrated in Figure 5–5. Line X—X' is a cutoff that results in equal errors of the two types. Line W—W' would tend to reduce false positives (proportional to area A), but to produce a greater increase in false negatives (area B). Similarly, a cutoff at Z—Z' increases false positive errors faster than it decreases false negatives.

You might well ask whether or not it is appropriate to value these two types of errors equally. After all, is it not true that in selecting astronauts, for example, the "cost" of a false positive error far outweighs the cost of a false negative error? Why should one be concerned that some of the individuals rejected would have been successful, so long as those accepted are all, or nearly all, successful? Decision theory, the formal theoretical basis for the above interpretation (see Von Neuman and Morganstern, 1947; Wald, 1950), does have provisions for differentially weighting the two types of errors. This would, of course, lead to the identification of different cutoff scores as optimal. Nevertheless, the argument given above is consistent with one view of manpower utilization, which in effect, states that rejecting a person who would have been successful is as much a failure with respect to the utilization of manpower resources as accepting a person who turns out to be unsuccessful.

The Taylor-Russell Tables. Taylor and Russell (1939) provided a set of tables[2] that show the *percentages of new hires who will be successful*

---

[2] To calculate these tables, it was necessary to make certain assumptions about the statistical properties of test scores and criterion scores; therefore, the tables may be somewhat misleading if the actual distributions in question deviate from the "ideal" distributions assumed in the tables. This is true of the Naylor-Shine tables as well.

FIGURE 5–5

Cutoff and Decision Errors

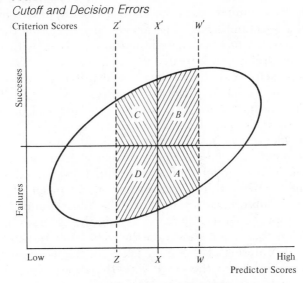

The cutoff, *X—X'*, equates false positive (lower right) and false negative (upper left) errors, resulting in a minimum of decision errors. Raising the cutoff to *W—W'* results in a decrease of false positives *(A)* but an even greater increase in false negatives *(B)*. Similarly, lowering the cutoff to *Z—Z'* yields a decrease in false negatives *(C)* but a larger increase in false positives *(D)*.

as a function of *(a)* predictor validity, *(b)* selection ratio, and *(c)* preselection success rate. These tables summarize what happens to the proportion of true positives to total positives in Figure 5–5 as the predictor cutoff score (X_i) is moved left or right and as the criterion score (Y_c) separating successes from failures is moved up or down. Such an approach is practical: it does not speculate about the likelihood of false negatives (about whom criterion data are not available, except in concurrent validation). However, the approach assumes that it is appropriate and feasible to dichotomize employees into successes and failures, as though all members of the success group had identical job proficiency scores and all failures were equally inept. This is not likely to be the case; performance can be expected to vary continuously as a function of individual differences (although, with either technological limits, such as the assembly line, or "social" limits, as found in restriction of production or in labor-management agreements on work quotas, the assumption may be more realistic: under these conditions a successful employee makes quota, an unsuccessful employee does not).

Thus, there were two limitations to the Taylor-Russell tables: (1) it was necessary to identify a single criterion score separating "success" from failure, and (2) they did not allow for *degrees* of success or failure.

The Naylor-Shine Tables. Naylor and Shine (1965) presented tables that overcame these limitations of the Taylor-Russell approach to evaluating the payoff of a selection device. The tabled values describe the difference in average criterion scores for the selected as compared with the original group. Thus, job proficiency is treated as a continuous variable and, furthermore, this approach avoids the problem of identifying the criterion score separating the successful from the unsuccessful. Instead, as illustrated in Figure 5–6, the means of the two samples (selected and unselected) are subtracted to show the gain from selection.

Percentage Increase in Job Proficiency. The Naylor-Shine tables are only one step removed from describing the payoff from selection in terms of a percentage increase in job proficiency. All that is required is to describe the "gain" in Figure 5–6 as a percentage of the mean of the original sample. Such an approach was summarized by Ghiselli and Brown (1955) in the nomograph shown in Figure 5–7. Here, the criterion of *percentage increase in job proficiency* is shown on the right-hand vertical scales. The graph is read by entering at the lower left with the appropriate selection ratio, moving vertically to the curve with the appropriate validity, then moving horizontally to the appropriate vertical sale. These latter scales introduce a new factor into the evaluation of a selection program: the *variability in job proficiency.* This is described at the top of Figure 5–7 as the ratio of the best to the poorest worker.

It may be noted that at a given selection ratio and validity, the payoff decreases as the ratio of the best to the poorest worker (the "σ of proficiency") decreases. This makes good intuitive sense. If the best worker

FIGURE 5–6

Comparison of Criterion Scores for Unselected and Selected Samples

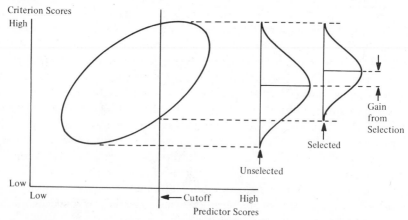

The difference in the means of these two samples represents the gain in job proficiency resulting from the selection program. This gain can be estimated when predictor validity and selection ratio are known (see Naylor and Shine, 1965).

FIGURE 5–7

Percentage Increase in Job Proficiency

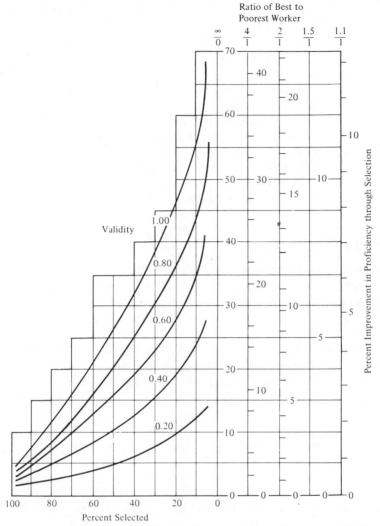

Source: Ghiselli, E. E., & Brown, C. W. *Personnel and industrial psychology,* (2nd ed.). New York: McGraw-Hill, 1955 Fig. 5–4, p. 147.

The relationship between validity, the selection ratio, variability in job proficiency (ratio of the best to the poorest worker), and percent improvement in proficiency.

produces 110 units and the poorest 100 units (ratio 1.1 to 1.0, mean ≅ 105 units), then we would never expect to exceed a 5 percent gain in proficiency, whereas with a ratio of 4 to 1 (e.g., 400 to 100 units with a mean ≅ 250 units) one might expect ideally to get everyone to the level of the best worker. While proficiency will vary from job to job as a result both of true individual differences and of the technical and social restrictions discussed earlier, in only a few cases will the ratio reach or exceed 4 to 1. Hull (1928) summarized productive proficiency data for a number of semiskilled jobs. The ratio varied from 1.4 to 1 to 5.1 to 1, with an average of about 2 to 1. Thus, with a good predictive validity of .50, a reasonable selection ratio at 50 percent and a 2-to-1 ratio of proficiency, one might expect about 5 percent improvement in job proficiency. While this may sound like a small gain, it could mean the difference between profit and loss, or between successful and unsuccessful competition in many enterprises. For the relationships described in this procedure to hold, the scale of measurement for proficiency must be a ratio scale. Since a number of productivity indices can be assumed to be ratio measurements (e.g., number of units produced or time required to complete a task), this technique is quite effective in describing the anticipated gain in productivity from the use of tests for various validity/selection ratio combinations.

Utility and Profitability

Once the payoff resulting from selection is translated into terms of increased proficiency, cost accounting procedures can be used to attach a dollar value to that gain. From that dollar value, one would subtract the cost of the testing to arrive at the final figure representing the net gain from testing.

Unfortunately, there are many jobs in which proficiency cannot be measured objectively, in terms of units produced or time expended. Nevertheless, it should be obvious that a valid selection decision is worth more to an organization than an invalid one! Recently, Hunter and Schmidt (1979) tackled this problem. Instead of looking at the output of the individual in terms of productivity per se, they attempted to *estimate* the worth of the individual to the organization—to put a dollar value on performance, using expert judges.

In one study, they asked the supervisors of computer programmers in the federal government to estimate the value of those programmers in dollar terms. The instructions to the supervisors were as follows:

> Consider the quantity and quality of output typical of the *average programmer* and the value of this output. In placing a dollar value on this output, it may help to consider what the cost would be of having an outside firm provide these products and services.

The question which was used to obtain this information read as follows:

> Based on my experience, I estimate the value to my agency of the average GS 9–11 programmer at _____dollars per year.

In addition, supervisors were also asked to estimate the dollar value of poor (15th-percentile) and outstanding (85th-percentile) programmers. This allowed the researchers to calculate the standard deviation of performance in dollars.

A total of 105 questionnaires were returned from supervisors. None had any difficulty in estimating the dollar value of computer programmers. In addition to this estimate, Hunter and Schmidt had a number of additional pieces of information: (1) a test known as the Programmer Aptitude Test (PAT: McNamara and Hughes, 1961) had an estimated validity of .76 (this estimate was based on published studies); (2) the testing cost was approximately $10 per examinee; (3) there were approximately 4,400 programmers employed by the government at the levels in question; (4) there were approximately 618 new hires a year at these levels; and (5) the average tenure for computer programmers at these levels was 9.69 years.

On the basis of this information, the researchers were able to calculate the expected gain from using the PAT for hiring computer programmers in the federal government. While it might have been reasonable to assume that the previous method had *no* validity, Hunter and Schmidt estimated the gain on the basis of various previous validities ranging from .00 to .50. Remember, the PAT had an estimated true validity of .76. In addition to varying the validity level of the previous selection procedure, Schmidt also varied selection ratios from .05 (1 applicant out of every 20 is hired) to .80 (16 applicants out of every 20 are hired). The results are presented in Table 5–2. The numbers are staggering! The smallest dollar gain was 5.6 *million* dollars. This gain was under the poorest conditions, i.e., a selection ratio (SR) of .80 and a previous procedure with high validity (.50). Under the best conditions (SR = .05; validity of previous procedure = .00), the gain was 97.2 *million* dollars. This would be a rather dramatic payoff for a testing procedure that cost approximately $6,000 per year. Since Hunter and Schmidt had figures available for the number of programmers employed in the private sector, they were able to extrapolate these

TABLE 5–2

Estimated Productivity Increase from One Year's Use of the PAT to Select Computer Programmers in the Federal Government (in millions of dollars)

| SR | True Validity of Previous Procedure | | | | |
	.00	.20	.30	.40	.50
.05	97.2	71.7	58.9	46.1	33.3
.10	82.8	60.1	50.1	39.2	28.3
.20	66.0	48.6	40.0	31.3	22.6
.30	54.7	40.3	33.1	25.9	18.7
.40	45.6	33.4	27.6	21.6	15.6
.50	37.6	27.7	22.8	17.8	12.9
.60	30.4	22.4	18.4	14.4	10.4
.70	23.4	17.2	14.1	11.1	8.0
.80	16.5	12.2	10.0	7.8	5.6

FIGURE 5-8

Estimates of Dollar Gain from Instituting New Selection Procedures

Study	Job Title	Criterion	Dollar Gain*
Lee and Booth (1974)	Clerical workers	Turnover	$250,000
Doppelt and Bennett (1953)	Checkout clerks	Training time	$600/hire
	Adding machine operators	" "	$540/hire
	Produce workers	" "	$348/hire
Rusmore and Toorenaar (1956)	Telephone operators	Training costs	$750,000
Schmidt and Hoffman (1973)	Nurses	Turnover	$233,920
Roche (1961)	Radial drill operators	Productivity	$350,000
van Naersson (1963)	Drivers	Reduction in accidents	No positive utility†
		Failure rate	$ 88,000
		Training time	$185,000
Hunter and Schmidt (1978)	Budget analyst	Productivity	$28,000,000

* The time period for realizing these gains varies from one study to another.
† The selection procedure was estimated to cost more than would be gained in a reduction of accidents.

results to the United States economy as a whole. His analyses showed that under the worst conditions (SR = .80 and validity of previous procedure = .50), the estimated productivity increase as a result of using the PAT for hiring would be approximately 93 million dollars. Under the best of conditions (SR = .05, validity of previous procedure = .00), the gain would be 1.5 *billion* dollars. If a manager were ever tempted to doubt the potential monetary contribution of valid selection procedures to the effectiveness of an organization, these figures would promptly renew her faith.

Using these types of analyses, Hunter & Schmidt (1979) have estimated the "effectiveness gains" in other occupations. These results are summarized in Figure 5–8. Once again, these results help to make the notion of validity more concrete. The conclusion to be drawn from these results is that *valid testing procedures contribute significantly to the cost effectiveness of organizations.* The level of this contribution will depend on: (1) the dollar value of the job being considered, (2) the validity of the previous selection procedure, (3) the selection ratio, (4) the cost of testing, and (5) the validity of the selection procedure being considered. With these types of analyses, it should be somewhat easier to determine the cost benefit characteristics of a particular selection program. While it has not been common to see such utility analyses in the psychological literature, it is likely that they will dramatically increase following the lead of Hunter and Schmidt.

Expectancy Tables. Both the Taylor-Russell and the Naylor-Shine approaches yield data that can be described in expectancy tables—the former in terms of expected percentage successful, the latter in terms of expected

FIGURE 5–9
Expectancy Charts

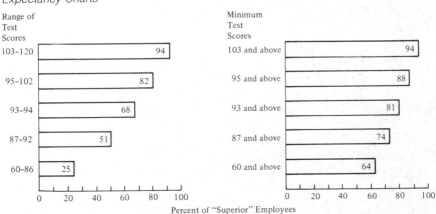

A. Individual Expectancy Chart   B. Institutional Expectancy Chart

Source: McCormick, E. J., & Tiffin, J. *Industrial psychology* (6th ed.). Englewood Cliffs, N.J.: Prentice-Hall, 1974, Fig. 5.8, p. 122.

Illustration of *(a)* an individual expectancy chart, and *(b)* an institutional expectancy chart as a function of scores on the Purdue Mechanical Adaptability Test for the same sample of job incumbents.

mean gain in job proficiency. Expectancy tables may also be developed from empirical data to describe the payoff from selection. Lawshe and Bolda (1958) pointed out that these may take the form of individual or institutional expectancy charts. Both of these are illustrated in Figure 5–9. Individual expectancy charts indicate the likelihood that individuals within each of several score ranges on the predictor will be "successful" (i.e., rated "superior"). Institutional expectancy charts, on the other hand, describe the expected success rate at different selection ratios. Both of the examples in Figure 5–9 assume an existing success rate of 50 percent and a moderately high validity. Expectancy tables are probably the best means for communicating to management the payoff from a selection program. It should be clear, however, that such tables do not speak of payoff in cost accounting terms or even in terms of increase in mean proficiency; rather, like the Taylor-Russell tables, they are concerned only with success rate (or "percent superior" ratings).

LEGAL AND PHILOSOPHICAL EVALUATIONS OF TESTING PROGRAMS

The Equal Employment Opportunity Commission

Title VII of the 1964 Civil Rights Act prohibited discrimination in employment on the basis of race, color, religion, sex, or national origin. The agency charged with administering that law was the Equal Employment Opportunity Commission (EEOC). Over the years, this agency has probably had a greater impact on personnel decision making than any other source. The "rules" for fair employment practices have been published several times and have changed with each publication. These changes have been a result of both increases in knowledge concerning testing and validation and pressure from professional and business communities to implement more workable procedures. There have been significant disagreements even within the government concerning the interpretation and administration of the Civil Rights Act with regard to employment decisions. This disagreement resulted in the publication of two separate sets of rules in 1977. One set, published by EEOC, was very demanding of employers, requiring considerable attention to validation of tests in separate settings, or for each job title; these were considered the "hard-nosed rules." The second set, jointly published by the United States Civil Service Commission, the Department of Labor, and the Department of Justice were entitled the Federal Executive Agency Guidelines (FEA) and were more liberal in interpretation, leaving certain decisions to the discretion of the employer and asking for good-faith effort at fair employment rather than strict adherence to specific prescriptions; these were the "soft-nosed rules." The battle of the rules was awaited with apprehension by psychologist and employer alike. Fortunately for all concerned, the two different groups were able to reach a compromise and in August, 1978, jointly published a set of principles, which are known as the *Uniform Guidelines on Employee Selection Procedures* (Federal Register, 1978).

Adverse Impact. The major mechanism for determining fairness in employment procedures is the consideration of *adverse impact*. In the simplest terms, adverse impact is a measure of the degree to which a particular procedure has a negative effect on the members of a protected minority group. Adverse impact is operationally defined by the "⅘ths" or "80-percent" rule. This rule states that the proportion of minority applicants hired should be no less than ⅘ths or 80 percent of the proportion of majority applicants hired. Thus, if 100 white males apply for employment and 10 are hired, and 100 black males apply for employment at the same company and 6 are hired, the hiring procedure would have had an adverse impact on a racial group, the blacks. Dividing 10 percent into 6 percent, we get a figure of 60 percent; thus, the proportion of black applicants hired was less than 80 percent of the proportion of white applicants hired, a violation of the "⅘ths" or "80-percent" rule. If 8 black applicants had been hired instead of 6, there would have been no problem, since we would then divide 10 percent (the white proportion) into 8 percent (the black proportion) and get a result of 80 percent, exactly what the law requires.

The determination of adverse impact is a critical step in examining the degree to which an employer is using legal selection procedures. As far as the Federal Government is concerned, if there is no adverse impact, the selection procedures are considered nondiscriminatory. This is not necessarily the definition of "fair" as accepted by other interested parties, such as psychologists and applicants. Guion's definition of test fairness is conceptually sounder: "Individuals with equal probabilities of success have equal probabilities of being hired" (Guion, 1966). Similarly, applicants might accept as a "fair" selection procedure one that selects individuals who worked hard to acquire the skills and experience necessary for successful performance on the job in question. Thus, while the Federal Government might accept a random lottery among all applicants as "fair," neither Guion nor the applicants would! Nevertheless, as it now stands, adverse impact is the primary principle defining the fairness of selection procedures in the Uniform Guidelines.

The demonstration of adverse impact is the responsibility of the plaintiffs, those claiming that they have been unfairly treated. While the employer must provide appropriate records, it is the responsibility of the complaining applicant to demonstrate unfairness. The 80-percent rule has the effect of ensuring that plaintiffs can only argue as a member of a *class* of individuals rather than as a single individual. Regardless of how a decision might have been made in a single case, it is necessary to show a pattern of such decisions before adverse impact is upheld.

If adverse impact is demonstrated, it is then the employer's responsibility to demonstrate a "business necessity" that requires the use of the particular selection strategy responsible for the adverse impact. In operational terms, the employer must demonstrate the *validity* of the selection procedure.

Even if the employer is able to demonstrate the validity of the procedure, he may be required to demonstrate that there are no equally valid procedures that would result in less adverse impact. The requirement to demonstrate business necessity and to minimize the adverse impact of otherwise valid procedures has led some employers to address the legality of their selection procedures at the most basic level. They strive to hire in particular proportions regardless of the validity of the procedure. Their logic is that if the 80-percent rule is not violated, they will not have to go through the effort and expense of validation procedures, court fights, and potential damage payments. Rather than being "fair" to all groups, this logic seems more like being uniformly *unfair* to all concerned! At the very least, these employers are abandoning the opportunity to use selection procedures as a means of enhancing organizational effectiveness and profitability, as described earlier in the section on utility.

Affirmative Action. There is considerable confusion surrounding the issue of affirmative action. The terms *Equal Employment Opportunity and Affirmative Action* often appear together in recruiting literature and are often uttered virtually simultaneously by personnel managers and recruiters. Nevertheless, the terms have quite different meanings and mechanisms. Equal employment opportunity is a law. If an employer violates that law, she is subject to penalties as imposed by the judicial branch of government. The law states that today, here and now, members of protected minority groups will have the same opportunity for employment as majority group members. Affirmative action is a social philosophy. The procedures related to it imply that an employer will go beyond the simple condition of equal employment on a day-to-day basis; instead, the employer will set goals for employment decisions over some period of time (e.g., five years) that will guarantee a certain profile of demographic characteristics of employees. The salient demographic characteristics are those pertaining to race, color, religion, sex, and national origin. In practice, the focus has been on blacks and women. The effect of affirmative action programs is to accelerate what would normally come to pass through selection procedures that were equally fair to majority and minority applicants. In addition, affirmative action agreements require the employer actively to seek out or recruit minority applicants who might not otherwise apply for employment. But affirmative action is not a law. It is a voluntary agreement that employers enter into with local, state, and federal government agencies. These agencies can require affirmative-action policies or plans through economic pressures. If an employer does not agree to construct an affirmative-action policy setting specific targets for employment of minority group applicants, the governmental agency may withhold federal funds in the form of grants or contracts from that employer. In addition, the employer must also agree to purchase goods and services from organizations that have affirmative action plans. Thus, if your university refuses to file an affirmative-action plan, they would most likely jeopardize any Health, Education and Welfare (HEW) funds that they currently receive. In addition, faculty members at the university may become ineligible to receive federal research grants until their university complies with the affirmative-action requirements of the federal department from which the funds are requested. A private employer might refuse to file an affirmative-action plan and subsequently be denied access to Department of Defense contracts or Department of Labor training funds. This economic lever is a powerful one, and for all practical purposes has an equal or greater impact than a legal lever. Nevertheless, affirmative action is not a law, and the fiercely independent employer can choose to ignore its implications—at the risk of financial disaster.

Other Pitfalls in the Employment Process

The employment decision process is actually a series of interrelated activities, and testing is only one part of the process. In addition to tests, other components in the system might be a recruiting mechanism, an employment receptionist, an application blank, and one or more interviewers. The American Psychological Association (1969) appointed a task force to consider the potential pitfalls in the entire employment process for members of minority groups. This task force identified the following potential sources of unfair discrimination in hiring:

1. *Recruiting:* An employer might restrict the number of applicants from minority groups by the pattern of contacts or visits to various schools or community organizations; recruiting might also be affected by the type of newspapers and/or magazines in which vacancies are announced.
2. *Initial contact:* Receptionists might exercise some uncalled-for discretion in deciding to whom they shall give application forms. In effect, if an individual is refused an application form, a *reject* decision has been made not by the personnel director, but by the receptionist!
3. *Application forms:* Many biographical items on application blanks have the potential for discriminating against minority applicants. Rejection decisions are often made on the basis of responses to biodata items, in spite of the fact that no relationship has been established between the answers and the probability of success on the job.
4. *Interviews:* Interviewers are prone to error in combining information and making decisions. These tendencies are well documented in the next chapter. These errors are not always random; they are often systematic errors that have adverse effects on minority applicants.

The task force suggested the following remedies for the potential pitfalls of the employment process:

1. Develop a recruiting plan that includes all relevant segments of the local population, regardless of minority or majority status.
2. Inform receptionists daily of jobs available and of the responses that should be made to applicants. Do not allow screening by the receptionist—with the exception of clearly inappropriate applicants (e.g., drunks).

3. Train interviewers to be aware of systematic influences on their judgment processes. Consider having one individual gather information and another combine it to make a decision.
4. Develop weighted application forms that ask only questions having demonstrated relevance for the job in question.

As you can see from the list of ills and cures, the employment process is a minefield for employer and applicant alike. The employer must be aware of potential obstacles to fair employment and take steps to guard against them.

The employer's responsibility under the law for fair employment practices is a substantial one. If an organization has done little to develop accurate predictors of performance, it is unlikely that valid predictor/criterion relationships will be found. Even when an employer has been validly selecting employees on the basis of a particular selection device, it would be difficult to demonstrate that relationship with present employees, since there would be a substantial restriction of range on the predictor variable. In other words, if only individuals with high test scores are hired, there will not be much variation in the predictor variable. The restriction in variability has a depressing effect on the validity coefficient. In a recent article, Landy (1978) facetiously suggests that employers concentrate on hiring a small number of predicted failures (true negatives) to ensure that there is no restriction of range. He further suggests that a side effect might be an increase in the self-esteem of the failures, since they have finally been able to succeed at something—failing. Unfortunately, Landy's proposal is doomed to failure—*it is probably more difficult to predict failures than successes!*

It is unfortunate but true that most employers can no longer successfully plan, implement, and defend a valid selection procedure without the services of an industrial psychologist and a lawyer. This is not likely to change in the near future. As indicated earlier in the chapter, this may have the effect of making "quota hiring" more attractive to employers, a condition that would be unfair to applicant and employer alike.

Summary

This section has dealt with the evaluation of a selection device or selection program. Starting with the view that test scores and other information provide input for personnel decisions, it seems reasonable that the contribution of such information depends upon its fidelity—that is, how consistently the information locates the individual along some attribute dimension (reliability) and how well the information predicts criterion behavior (validity). Beyond these classic measurement criteria, however, the question of the value or worth of the information depends on a host of factors. Information of the highest validity is of little value for selection unless one can be selective; that is, unless there is a choice to be made. Similarly, if the success rate is already high and/or if the ratio of best to poorest worker is low, there is relatively little room for improvement, even from reliable and valid information. Finally, the information gained from testing must be evaluated relative to its costs.

At the same time, information with relatively low predictive validity may have high utility when one can be selective and when the success rate is low or the variability of performance is high. While it is tempting to conclude that the more selective one can be, the greater the payoff, such a position is inaccurate, since testing costs may outrun proficiency gains. Neither very low nor very high selection ratios maximize payoff. As Cronbach and Gleser (1965) have shown "it is always desirable . . . to test at least twice as many men as will be accepted if the test is worth using at all" (p. 41). Whether one should be even more selective depends on the risks involved in the two types of decision errors, on costs of testing, expected gains in proficiency, and other factors.

Finally, as a result of federal legislation as well as basic concepts of social justice, testing must be viewed in human terms, not solely economic ones.

USING MULTIPLE PREDICTOR INFORMATION

Thus far, we have dealt with a simple linear model of the relationship between a predictor and a criterion. In this case, given some predictive validity and some selectivity, the decision-making strategy is rather straight-forward: accept applicants with the highest predictor scores and reject those with low scores. There are two common situations that destroy the simplicity of this model. The first is the availability of two or more relevant (valid) test scores or other predictors; the second is the choice between two or more jobs for the individual. The latter problem, differential placement, will be taken up later.

The availability of two or more pieces of information in personnel decision situations is surely the rule rather than the exception. Even though only a single standardized test is given, the decision maker is likely to have letters of reference, a high school transcript, biographical information, work history, and impressions or ratings from an interview.

The value of multiple sources of information depends on the predictive validities of the separate items and on the uniqueness or independence of the information obtained. If, for example, a standardized test score, high school transcript, and a letter of reference all tell us that an individual is superior in mathematical skills, we have one piece of information from three sources, not three pieces of information. While the consistency of reports may increase our confidence that the information is reliable, it does not increase the amount of information. Similarly, having scores from two standardized tests of mathematical skills yields redundant information to the extent that performances on the two tests are highly correlated. Intuitively, this probably makes sense; more technically speaking, two sources of information that are highly correlated—covary, that is—have common variance. Thus, the variance that two such predictors may account for in the criterion will be largely common variance as well. This is illustrated in Figure 5–10. On the left, two predictors, each with a high validity as shown by its overlap with the criterion variance, account for different portions of the criterion variance. These are independent (uncorrelated) sources of information, as indicated by the fact that they do not overlap each other. On the right the case is quite different: each predictor accounts for approximately the same amount of criterion variance (i.e., has the same high validity), but the variance is essentially the same portion of the criterion because the two predictors measure much the same thing, as indicated by their overlap.

FIGURE 5–10
Correlated and Uncorrelated Predictors

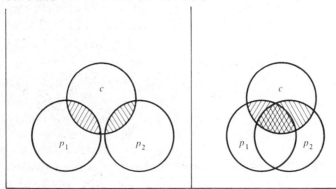

Two predictors, p_1 and p_2, both valid predictors of the criterion, c, as indicated by the overlap of the circles. On the left, p_1 and p_2 account for different portions of the variance in c, since they do not overlap (i.e., are uncorrelated) with each other. However, on the right, p_1 and p_2 are highly correlated and therefore, account for essentially the same portion of variance in c.

Multiple Correlation

The multiple–correlation coefficient, R, indicates the degree of relationship between two or more sets of predictor scores and a set of predicted scores. When the predicted scores are a criterion measure, R is the validity coefficient for the combined predictors. It can be interpreted in the same way as a simple correlation coefficient. For example, if $R = .50$, the coefficient of determination, $R^2 = .25$ and the index of forecasting efficiency, E, is approximately .13. However, R cannot be obtained simply by adding the validity coefficients of the several predictors. Rather, it depends on their intercorrelations as we noted in Figure 5–10.[3]

As with the simple correlation, r, the multiple-correlation coefficient does not tell us what criterion score to predict. For this we need to use the multiple-regression equation discussed below.

Strategies in the Use of Multiple Information. Faced with two or more items of information, the decision maker may explicitly adopt a strategy that relates decisions to the information. Probably most frequently the strategy he uses is not explicit and may vary unpredictably from time to time. Basically, such decision-making strategies are concerned with the way in which the data are combined or used sequentially. A fundamental distinction can be made between *statistical*, or mechanical, strategies and *clinical*, or intuitive, strategies. Statistical strategies are characterized by explicit formulas or rules that dictate decisions. Clinical strategies, on the other hand, require the decision maker to "weigh all the evidence" (usually qualitative impressions as well as quantitative biographical and psychometric data) and then choose among the alternative courses of action. It is possible, of course, to combine statistical and clinical methods. For example, data from several valid predictors might be combined statistically, yielding a predicted criterion score or a statement of expectancy of success, which the decision maker could then combine clinically with less readily quantifiable data, such as letters of reference or impressions gathered from an interview. We shall have more to say about statistical and clinical methods in the next chapter. At this point, we will examine some of the statistical strategies.

Multiple Regression

Multiple correlation describes the relationship between two or more predictors and a criterion measure. Multiple regression, like simple regression, defines the best estimate of the criterion score in terms of optimally-weighted predictor scores, or

---

[3] The equation for the squared multiple-correlation coefficient, R^2, for two predictors, 1 and 2, is:

$$R_{c\cdot12}{}^2 = \frac{r_{1c}{}^2 + r_{2c}{}^2 - 2r_{12}r_{1c}r_{2c}}{1 - r_{12}{}^2}$$

It takes into account the correlation between the two predictors, r_{12}. As r_{12} approaches 1.00, $R_{c\cdot12}{}^2$ approaches the higher of the square of the two single validities as a lower limit. As r_{12} approaches zero, $R_{c\cdot12}{}^2$ increases until, with $r_{12} = 0$,

$$R_{c\cdot12}{}^2 = r_{1c}{}^2 + r_{2c}{}^2,$$

That is, with $r_{12} = 0$, the variance accounted for in the criterion is equal to the sum of variances accounted for by the individual predictors. However, this does not mean that we can simply *add* validity coefficients to obtain R even when $r_{12} = 0$, since

$$R_{c\cdot12}{}^2 = r_{1c}{}^2 + r_{2c}{}^2, \text{ or } R = \sqrt{r_{1c}{}^2 + r_{2c}{}^2}$$

Thus, with $r_{1c} = r_{2c} = .40$, $R = \sqrt{(.40)^2 + (.40)^2} = \sqrt{.32}$ or .57, not the .80 that we would get from adding $r_{1c} + r_{2c}$.

$$\hat{Y} = b_1 X_1 + b_2 X_2 + \cdots b_n X_n$$

where $\hat{Y}$ is the predicted standard[4] criterion score, $X_1, X_2 \cdots X_n$ are the standard scores on the n predictors and $b_1, b_2 \cdots b_n$ are the weights assigned to each of the predictors (these weights essentially reflect the *unique* criterion variance accounted for by each predictor).

Multiple regression is a linear model. It assumes that the predictors are linearly related to the criterion. Furthermore, the fact that $\hat{Y}$ is a function of the *sum* of the weighted predictor scores indicates that scores on the predictors are additive and can compensate for one another. For example, in a two-predictor case with $b_1 = b_2$, persons with the following three combinations of scores would receive the same predicted criterion score: $X_1 = 50, X_2 = 50; X_1 = 100, X_2 = 0; X_1 = 0, X_2 = 100$. Suppose, in a less extreme case, that X_1 and X_2 were "verbal" and "quantitative" scores, respectively. The multiple-regression model would assume that superior verbal ability compensates for inferior quantitative ability. While this system is the most precise and mathematically sophisticated, one may seriously doubt the extent to which the assumption of compensatory traits is tenable.

Multiple Cutoff

Just as in the case of a single predictor, a cutoff score can be set on each of a set of predictors. The decision strategy is to "accept" if the individual's score on each predictor exceeds the cutoff, but to "reject" if any *one* score falls short of the cutoff. In contrast to multiple regression, the multiple-cutoff strategy assumes that traits are not additive or compensatory and that a minimum of each trait is essential to job performance. Thus, for example, a university entrance policy that sets minimum scholastic aptitude test scores, minimum rank in high school class, minimum credits in mathematics, and so on, is using a multiple-cutoff strategy.

The assumption of critical values, or absolute minima, and the lack of any compensation between traits of the multiple cutoff method may be as difficult to accept as the contrasting assumptions of the multiple regression method. If such critical scores exist (or, put another way, if the predictor/criterion relationship is discontinuous), they have seldom been demonstrated, and the setting of cutoff scores is both difficult and arbitrary.

Since neither set of assumptions is intuitively appealing, it is doubtful that the clinical method of combining information ever resembles either the multiple-regression or the multiple-cutoff strategies. Instead, clinical judgment probably allows for some compensation of traits, and, at the same time, recognizes some minimal scores on each predictor. For example,

---

[4] Distributions of scores can be standardized by transforming the raw scores to a distribution having a fixed mean and standard deviation. Thus, "Z scores" have a mean of zero and a standard deviation of 1.00, while "T scores" have a mean of 50 and a standard deviation of 10.

a committee selecting among applicants for a graduate training program might feel that below-average Graduate Record Exam (GRE) scores were compensated for by an excellent grade point average, but that the best possible grade point average could not compensate for extremely low scores on the GRE.

Multiple Hurdles and Sequential Decision Making

In the methods discussed thus far, it was implied that a more or less final decision was made on the basis of all the information available at one point in time. The applicant's folder is completed, including in some cases, the results of an eight-hour battery of tests, then a final decision is made. In simple selection, this decision is dichotomous; the applicant is hired for *the* job or she is rejected. In differential placement, job A is accepted for the new hire and jobs B and C are rejected for her. In practice, it is more likely that final decisions come only after a series of tentative decisions; in other words, information is received and evaluated sequentially over a period of time. Many management development programs employ successive hurdles in that evaluations are made first in accepting people into the program, then periodically after the completion of various phases of testing or training. Cronbach and Gleser (1965) identify three basic strategies of multiple hurdles or sequential selection. These are illustrated in Figure 5–11.

The most general case is illustrated on the left. Here, in contrast to the dichotomous decision of single-stage decision making, three outcomes are recognized. Candidates may be: (1) rejected, (2) accepted, or (3) held for further testing on the basis of the first item of information. This strategy assumes that terminal decisions can be made about some proportion of the applicants on the basis of one item of information. For example, finding that the applicant is a mathematical genius (or moron) may justify a final decision to hire (or reject) without seeking further information, especially when mathematical skills are essential to the job. On the other hand,

FIGURE 5–11
Three Alternative Strategies for Sequential Decision Making

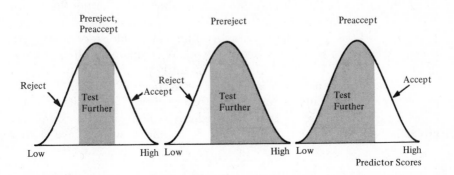

the majority of "fair-to-good" mathematicians are held for further testing, which may include a period of training or observation on the job.

The two variations of sequential testing—prereject and preaccept—shown in Figure 5–11 indicate that only one type of final decision (accept or reject) is permitted on the basis of the first test score or item of information. For all others, the first stage decision is to "test further," that is, to collect additional information.

The greatest disadvantage of multiple hurdles is the amount of time involved in arriving at final decisions. When "time is money," as when the individual is kept on in a management development program, one might wish for an earlier decision. On the other hand, testing costs, both to the institution and to the applicant (in time and convenience) are minimized when decisions are made on some proportion of the applicants after each test. The prospect of making final decisions about even a small percentage of the applicants after a single half hour of testing rather than requiring them to sit through an entire eight-hour battery is, indeed, an appealing one.

Profile Matching

What does the successful person on the job look like? If we have a picture, or profile, of those characteristics relative to other workers, it should be possible to ensure successful workers by selecting applicants whose profiles most closely match an *ideal* profile. This is the rationale of the *job status* approach to validation and, essentially, of profile matching as well. This method assumes that there are traits on which workers in a particular job differ from other workers that are important for success on that job. Thus, for example, finding that lumberjacks are bigger and stronger than other manual laborers leads to the conclusion that strength and size are important for (and, therefore, predictive of) success in this occupation. The assumption may or may not be true. Some traits identified in this way in the "Minnesota Studies" stood up in predictive validity studies and some did not (Dvorak, 1935). Therefore, it would seem risky to assume that the scores that uniquely characterize a group—even a successful subgroup—are predictive of that success. Certainly, to assume that every element in a profile is related to success would be presumptuous. Such an approach seems rational only if one takes the position that it is not so much the *strength* of certain specific traits or abilities but rather the *pattern, configuration,* or *interaction* of these attributes that is predictive of success.

Figure 5–12 is an example of a hypothetical profile, representing the average scores of a group of successful workers compared with appropriate norms (presumably based on other workers in the same and related occupations). The successful group is well above average on traits 3, 5, and 6, about average on traits 2 and 4, and below average on traits 1 and 7. Now, if each of these seven traits has predictive validity and the comparison group is truly appropriate, then traits 3, 5, and 6 would have positive

FIGURE 5–12

Example of Profile Matching

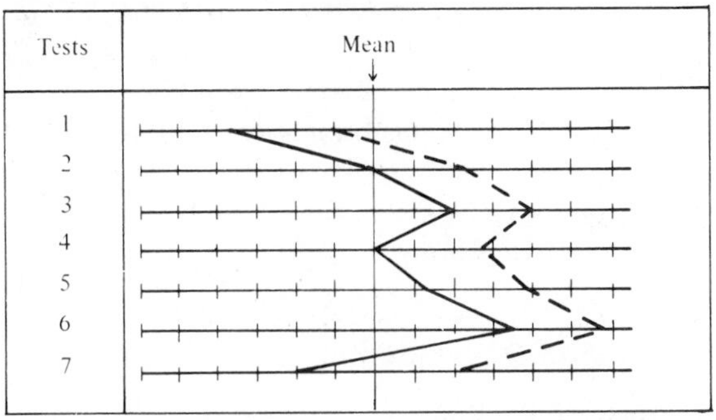

The solid line represents a profile of the incumbents on a hypothetical job as compared to normative distributions for each of seven tests. These workers are below average on tests 1 and 7 and above average on tests 3, 5, and 6. The broken line represents an individual whose profile is similar in pattern, but different in level from the job profile.

validity coefficients (high scores associated with high criterion performance—"success"), traits 1 and 7 negative coefficients (low scores associated with success), and traits 2 and 4 significant curvilinear coefficients (average scores predictive of success, but low and high scores predictive of something less than success). In other words, if we can take the average in Figure 5–12 as characterizing the population from which the "successfuls" are a subsample, then the failures must have values on the opposite side of the mean. However, when the successfuls are average, then they could deviate from the population only if the failures were high and low, but not average, on that trait.

Given this information about the validity of the elements in the profile (usually not presented), it is difficult to understand why profile matching would be preferred to multiple regression. This seems especially true when one considers the problem of "matching" profiles. If, as suggested, one assumes the *pattern* of configuration to be most critical, then the correlation between ideal and obtained scores would be most relevant. The coefficient would reflect the similarity of highs and lows in the two profiles but would be insensitive to whether the obtained profile lay just on, above, or below the standard. By contrast, a concern for the *level* of the obtained scores as compared with the standard can be described in terms of the deviations of individual element scores from the corresponding standard. This index has been defined as:

$$\sum D^2 \;=\; \sum_{1}^{K} (X_0 - X_s)^2$$

where X_0 equals the obtained element score and X_s the standard element score, with these deviation scores squared and summed across the k elements in the profile. This method assumes that a deviation from standard on one element is as significant as that on any other element, and, in this sense, weights all elements as equally significant, or predictive.

Given the conceptual and methodological problems and the dubious nature of some of the assumptions of this method, it is difficult to make a case for its continued use in selection, though it may have some value in differential placement decisions.

Cross-Validation and Reevaluation

A multiple-correlation coefficient describes the relationship between several predictors and the criterion for that specific sample of observations for which the R was computed. Similarly, the multiple-regression equation yields the optimal predictions for that sample. However, the validity coefficient for each of the predictors and the intercorrelations between the predictors, which are used in calculating R and in determining the weights assigned to each predictor in the regression equation, are subject to sampling error. In other words, another sample taken from the same population of workers would, in all likelihood, yield somewhat different correlation coefficients and a different regression equation.

For this reason, the regression equation and the multiple correlation coefficient obtained in one sample need to be validated on a new sample taken from the same population. This is done by using the equation obtained in the first sample to predict the criteria scores in the second sample. This is known as *cross-validation*. Typically, the results are somewhat disappointing. Because the equation has "taken advantage" of all the uniqueness in the first sample, the multiple R and the precision in predicting criterion scores tends to be lower in the new sample.

A simple way of incorporating cross-validation into a validity study is to hold out one-third to one-half of the available sample of subjects from the original validation. The multiple R and regression equation are obtained on the remainder of the sample and then cross-validated with the hold-out sample. Another procedure is to determine the regression equations on each of the two samples, then cross-validate each equation on the other sample. Naturally, the original and hold-out samples should be randomly assigned from the original study sample.

While the foregoing discussion has used multiple R and multiple regression in illustrating cross-validation, it is equally important that any decision-making strategy established on one sample be checked out on a second sample. Nor should the empirical evaluation stop there. Validation should not be considered a one-time operation because jobs change and job applicants change. Therefore, predictor information and a selection strategy for using that information, both appropriate at one point in time, may lead to inappropriate decisions only a few years later.

There are three types of situations in which serious misuse of tests may occur: (1) where tests and a selection strategy have been adopted—perhaps with considerable care—but where no study has been conducted to establish empirically the validity of the procedures; (2) where a testing program and decision strategy were validated 10 or 20 years earlier and the procedures are continued as though the world never changed; and (3) where a serious misuse of tests occurs involving the assumption that cutoff scores or other decision strategies appropriate to a majority group or to a homogeneous sample are therefore equally appropriate to minority groups or identifiable subsamples. This problem will be discussed later under the topic of "moderator variables."

Techniques for Improving Predictive Efficiency

In 1928, Hull pointed out that predictive validities seldom reached as high as .50. Ghiselli (1956, 1966, 1973) in successive summaries of the validity literature has tended to confirm Hull's findings: "Taking all jobs as a whole, then, it can be said that by and large the maximal power of tests to predict success in training is of the order of .50 and to predict success on the job itself is of the order of .35" (Ghiselli, 1966, p. 125). As we have seen, predictors with even modest validities can be useful under favorable conditions of selection ratio, success rate, and variability of performance. Nevertheless, researchers have sought ways to improve prediction in the face of what appears to be a persistent limit of about .50 with standard validation procedures.

Moderator Variables and Subgroup Analysis. Psychologists have discovered that breaking a sample down into smaller subsamples may help improve prediction. The individuals are assigned to subgroups on the basis of some degree of similarity. The logic of the procedure is that the behavior of individuals *within* subgroups might be more predictable than the behavior of all individuals taken as an entire group. Consider the data presented in Figure 5–13. There are two different types of data points in the figure, those represented by *X*s and those represented by *O*s. Taken as a whole, the correlation between variable *A* and variable *B* is low and positive. But if we separate the *X*s from the *O*s, as we have done in Figure 5–14, we discover two quite different and dramatic relationships—one high and positive and one showing no relationship between variables *A* and *B*. If variables *A* and *B* were predictor and criterion variables, respectively, this situation would be labeled "single-group validity," since we were able to demonstrate validity for one group but not the other. If the *X*s represented female applicants and the *O*s represented male applicants, then sex would be considered a *moderator variable*. This would be true because the sex of the applicant moderated or changed the nature of the relationship between variables *A* and *B*.

The example presented in Figure 5–14 is only one of several possibilities in which subgroup analyses may reveal differences. As another example,

FIGURE 5–13

Unmoderated Relationship between A and B

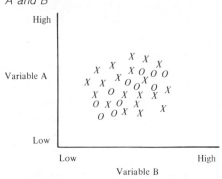

the groups could differ in mean criterion scores (Figure 5–15,A), in mean predictor scores (Figure 5–15,B), or in both (Figure 5–15,C). In most cases such as those illustrated in Figure 5–13, the validity for the total group would be reduced as compared with that of the subgroup for which the predictor is valid, whereas in Figure 5–15,C, total group validity would be inflated. As a matter of fact, a relatively high validity coefficient might be obtained for total group data when the predictor is not valid for either subgroup. This is illustrated in Figure 5–15,D.

Bartlett and O'Leary (1969) have elaborated each of these possibilities and have provided examples from actual research findings. In addition, as they pointed out, the possibilities for inappropriate decisions about subgroup members resulting from heterogeneous total group findings are not limited to cases in which differential validities exist. As shown in Figure 5–16, subgroups with equal validities may have different predictor scores (Figure 5–16,A), different criterion scores (Figure 5–16,B), or both (Figures 5–16,C, and 5–16,D). Figure 5–16,D is a particularly interesting case, since the validity coefficient for the total group would be negative, but the coefficients for the two subgroups would both be positive.

FIGURE 5–14

Moderated Relationship between A and B

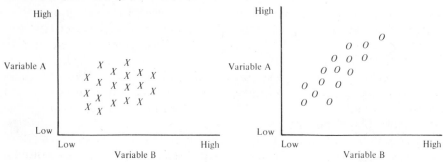

FIGURE 5-15

Differential Validities for Two Subgroups

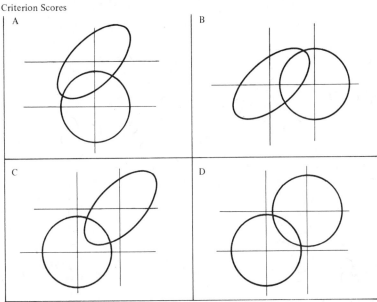

Criterion Scores

Predictor Scores

Source: Adapted from Bartlett, C. J., & O'Leary, B. S. A differential prediction model to moderate the effects of heterogeneous groups in personnel selection and classification. *Personnel Psychology,* 1969, *22,* 1-17.

In A the two subgroups differ only in criterion scores; in B they differ only in predictor scores; in C and D they differ in both criterion and predictor scores. In D the test is not valid for either subgroup, even though the total validity is positive and may be fairly high.

The potential for unfair discrimination resulting from establishing cutoff scores on the predictor based upon total group data is especially apparent in Figures 5–15,B and 5–16,A. In these cases, one subgroup scores systematically lower on the predictor and would have proportionately fewer members receiving scores above the cutoff, but *as a group* they are capable of the same mean performance as the group with higher mean predictor scores. The case is no better in Figures 5–15,A and 5–16,B. Here the member of the high criterion group with a low predictor score is screened out even though his criterion score would in all likelihood be higher than that of a member of the other group who had a high predictor score.

Both of these cases might be considered examples of unfair discrimination. In the first instance, subgroups with unequal likelihood of success have an equal likelihood of being selected; in the second instance, subgroups with an equal likelihood of success have an unequal likelihood of being selected for the job. Often the subgroups involved in the examples cited by Bartlett and O'Leary (1969) differ as to sex or race and the decision

FIGURE 5–16

Identical Validities for Two Subgroups

Criterion Scores

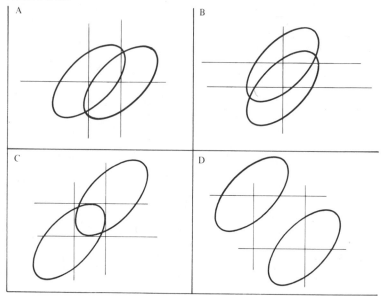

Predictor Scores

Source: Adapted from Bartlett, C. J., & O'Leary, B. S. A differential prediction model to moderate the effects of heterogeneous groups in personnel selection and classification. *Personnel Psychology,* 1969, *22,* 1–17.

Subgroups differ on predictor only (A), on criterion only (B) or on both (C and D). In D, despite a negative total group validity, validity for each of the subgroups is positive.

strategies based on the total group are unfair to one or the other group. Such inequities are in conflict with EEOC guidelines and therefore illegal. Furthermore, the combination of heterogeneous subgroups in the validation sample can mask or distort the true predictive efficiency of the predictor and reduce its apparent usefulness.

Over the years, there have been several ways suggested for the identification of potential moderator variables. One of the first approaches to this procedure was suggested by Ghiselli (1956). He proposed that some people are simply more predictable than others. Examine Figure 5–17. The diagonal line through the scatterplot represents the regression line—it is a graphic representation of the equation that might be used to predict Y from X for the present data. But as we can see, the prediction is far from perfect. We can tell this because for each X score, there is more than one Y score. If prediction were perfect, there would be only one observed Y score associated with each observed X score. Ghiselli suggested that there might be something unique about those individuals who fell farthest from

FIGURE 5–17
Ghiselli's Approach to Moderator Analysis

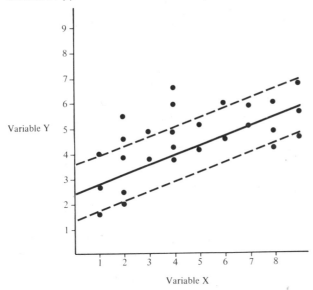

the regression line—the "unpredictables."[5] He reasoned that by separating those who were predictable from those who were not, we might be able to identify a moderator variable that is related to this predictability. Thus, if we were to apply such a procedure to the data in Figure 5–17, we would look for significant differences between individuals falling within the dotted lines paralleling the regression line and those individuals falling outside of the two dotted lines. We might look for differences in experience, socioeconomic status, sex, age, race, or hair color. Unfortunately, we have nothing to guide the search for moderator variables other than our own fertile imagination and the research of others. Nevertheless, if we were able to identify a variable that distinguished the "predictables" from the "unpredictables," we could then subsequently separate individuals on that variable and obtain more accurate prediction for the "predictable" group. But we are left with the problem of predicting performance for the "unpredictable" group. Presumably, we would try a different set of predictors for that group.

Another approach to the problem of identifying the nature and value of moderators is a technique that was developed by Saunders (1956) and

---

[5] This is a slight modification of Ghiselli's procedure. He suggested that we look at the distance from the *ideal* regression line—the one corresponding to $r_{xy} = 1.00$—in determining a person's "predictability"; in our discussion, we deal with the *actual* regression line—the one corresponding to the r_{xy} value in the actual data.

has come to be known as "moderated multiple regression." In this technique, we include potential moderator variables as terms in a multiple-regression equation. We first predict performance from one or more test scores for the entire sample; next we include a moderator variable[6] in the prediction equation (e.g., assign individuals a score for experience if experience is being considered as a moderator) and see if there is a significant increase in the validity of the predictor set. If a significant increase occurred, we would have identified a moderator of the relationship between the predictors and the criterion.

Still another approach to the issue of moderators is known as *quadrant analysis*. In this procedure (Hobert and Dunnette, 1967), individuals are placed in one of four cells: True positive, true negative, false positive, or false negative. These cells were described earlier on p. 154. Since true positives and true negatives were correct predictions, we must devote our attention to the individuals in the false positive and false negative cells since these are the "unpredictables." Our task is to identify variables that help us distinguish false positives from true positives and false negatives from true negatives. If we are able to do that, we have identified a moderator variable.

When the technology of moderator identification became well-known, almost every study either identified or alluded to the presence of potential moderators of predictive relationships. These relationships were not restricted to predictor/criterion relationships. Moderators were claimed for training effects, performance/satisfaction relationships, and leadership effectiveness, to mention just a few areas. Moderators became "popular," a terminal disease for most psychological concepts! Recently, it has become clear that moderators are much less frequent than was originally assumed. This has been demonstrated by the inability of researchers to replicate or cross-validate proposed moderated relationships. Thus for example, in one study the sex of the applicant might have been shown to be a moderator of the predictor/criterion relationship, but a replication of the study failed to support the existence of the moderator.

Moderator Variables and Fair Employment Practices. The identification of moderator variables became quite an important question in fair employment research as affected by the EEOC guidelines. Specifically, when adverse impact was demonstrated, it was the responsibility of the employer to conduct separate validity studies for majority and minority group members. Thus, almost all validity studies required a search for potential moderating effects of race, sex, color, religion, or national origin. There were many claims of moderated validity relationships. The most popular moderator variable was race, and the most popular claim was that certain relationships were valid for whites but invalid for blacks. It has been shown (Humphreys, 1973; Schmidt and Hunter, 1978) that many of these moderator effects

---

[6] The procedure is somewhat more complicated than this; we actually add not only the moderator variable itself, but also certain cross-product terms. The mathematics are unnecessary to the point being made, so they will not be presented.

were actually the result of statistical artifacts. Incorrect analyses were applied to the relationships. Each subgroup validity was examined to see if it was significantly different from .00. Since white subsamples were usually large, small correlations were often significantly different from .00. But the minority samples were commonly very small, requiring much more substantial validities to achieve significance. Thus, it was often concluded that predictors were valid for white subgroups but invalid for black subgroups. The more appropriate test would have been between the two validity coefficients in the black and white subgroups. In most instances, these differences would not have been significant, and the claims for "differential validity" would not have been supported.

The conclusion regarding the potential moderating effects of sex or race in predictor/criterion relationships is similar to the conclusion regarding moderator variables generally: *few studies have been able to demonstrate substantially different predictor/criterion relationships for individuals subgrouped by sex or race.* These results have been very encouraging to those who would like to generalize the findings of validity studies to all employees, regardless of minority or majority status.

Identification of Suppressor Variables. In an earlier section it was shown that two predictors, each of modest validity, will yield the greatest multiple correlation if they are uncorrelated. However, there is one case in which two predictors may be highly effective when taken together, even though they are highly correlated with one another. The case is one in which the first predictor has moderately high validity, but the second has essentially zero validity, as shown in Figure 5–18. Notice that while the second "predictor," P_2, does not account for variance in the criterion scores, it does account for a large part of the variance (since the intercorrelation is high) in P_1, the valid predictor. What is more significant about this three-way relationship is that the variance in P_1 accounted for by P_2 is error variance, not valid in predicting the criterion. Thus, while P_2 does not account for variance in C, it does account for "noise" or error variance in P_1. The "suppressor effect" can be demonstrated statistically from the equation for multiple correlation.[7]

An example of a suppressor variable may help to show how this type

---

[7] Let the validity of P_1 be .40 ($r_{y1} = .40$), the validity of P_2 be .00 ($r_{y2} = .00$), and the intercorrelation of P_1 and $P_2 = .80$ ($r_{12} = .80$), then:

$$R_{y12}^2 = \frac{r_{y1}^2 + r_{y2}^2 - 2r_{y1}\,r_{y2}r_{12}}{1 - r_{12}^2}$$

becomes

$$R_{y12}^2 = \frac{(.40)^2 + (.00)^2 - 2(.40)(.00)(.80)}{1 - (.80)^2} \text{ or } \frac{.16}{.36} \approx .44$$

Then

$$R_{y12} \approx \sqrt{.44} \approx .67$$

thus, while $r_{y1} = .40$, $R = .67$ even though the validity of P_2 is zero.

FIGURE 5–18

Suppressor Effect

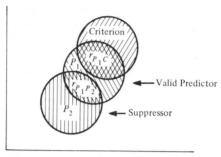

Test P_2 does not correlate with the criterion, but correlates with the valid predictor, P_1. Thus P_2 accounts for some of the variance in P_1 that is "error variance" with respect to predicting the criterion.

of effect is possible. Suppose the valid predictor is designed to measure numerical ability and that this ability is an important component of success on the job in question. However, the test (P_1) has a large number of lengthy "story problems" and long, rather involved instructions to be read by the applicant. In short, the test requires reading skills as well as numerical ability, and test scores confound these two abilities. A second test, P_2, is a relatively pure measure of reading skills and it has no predictive validity, since reading skills, beyond some bare minimum, are not an important component of the job. Nevertheless, knowledge of P_2 scores enables us to, in effect, identify the variance in P_1 scores due to differences in reading skills. Thus, P_2 provides new and relevant information and can be combined with P_1 in a multiple regression equation to yield improved prediction of criterion scores.

MODERN SELECTION MODELS

Cronbach and Gleser's Model

The work of Cronbach and Gleser (1965) provides an important model of personnel decisions in selection and placement based on statistical decision theory. However, the model apparently has had relatively little impact on personnel practices or on research. Guion (1967) suggested that this may be a function of the complexity or the impracticality of the model. Nevertheless, the book *Psychological Tests and Personnel Decisions* probably presents the most definitive statement of the nature of personnel decisions, the identification and evaluation of decision strategies, and the rational basis for evaluation of programs and outcomes that has yet been written.

Among other things, it: (1) presents a taxonomy of decision problems, (2) compares sequential and single-stage selection strategies, (3) demonstrates how testing costs interact with selection ratio to determine the utility of selection and the value of outcomes, and (4) suggests the concept of "adaptive treatment," the modification of the job requirements to fit the ability of the applicant. The impracticality of the model probably results primarily from the difficulty of specifying quantitatively the large number of parameters required to evaluate the outcomes. However, this should not detract from the fact that the model provides a complete rationale that could well serve as the ideal for evaluation of personnel decision making.

Dunnette's Selection Model

At a much more qualitative and conceptual level, Dunnette (1963) has attempted to capture the complexity of the problem of predicting job behavior. His model is illustrated in Figure 5–19. On the left of the model are the predictors *(P);* on the right are the consequences (of job behaviors) as they relate to organizational goals, or in a sense, the evaluation of job behaviors. In between are the individuals with their differences and subgroups that may interact with predictors (e.g., as moderator variables) to determine differential job behaviors. Finally, the relationships between job

FIGURE 5–19
Dunnette's Selection Model

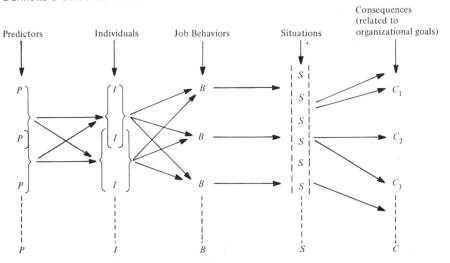

Source: Adapted from Dunnette, M. D. A modified model for selection research. *Journal of Applied Psychology,* 1963, *47,* 317–323.

Modification of Dunnette's selection model, a diagram showing the complexities of any selection system. Every validation is subject to moderating effects of predictors, individuals, and situations.

behaviors and the consequences are seen as mediated by situational factors (what Dunnette called "the situational filter").

The value of Dunnette's model is not that somehow it will improve selection or the evaluation of personnel decisions, but rather that it describes the complexity of the decision process. At the same time, it points out the number of possibilities for improving prediction. Thus, modern selection programs and research are no longer limited to searching for better predictors to improve decisions; they may attempt to improve prediction from the ones they have by identifying suppressor variables; they may seek the "predictables" through moderator variable research; they may concentrate on the prediction of specific job behaviors and worry less about *the* criterion; or they may look to situational factors to improve their understanding of job behavior.

Placement Decisions

Earlier in this chapter consideration was given to classifying personnel decisions. A major distinction was made between selection and placement decisions. Most of the intervening discussion, however, has been concerned with selection rather than placement models and issues. There are several reasons for this, not the least of which is that relatively little in the way of conceptualizing or model building has been done with placement problems. Furthermore, the models that have been developed (see, for example, Cronbach & Gleser, 1965) deal almost entirely with *independent* jobs, even though it is well recognized that a large proportion of jobs involve either successive operations (sequentially-related jobs), such as assembly lines, or simultaneous and dependent operations (coordinate jobs), such as the teamwork involved in placing heavy equipment. Given this state of affairs, we will briefly outline some of the generalizations and models for independent jobs and then hint at some of the complications introduced when jobs are either sequential or coordinated.

Predictor Validity and Placement Decisions. Directly or indirectly, it has been noted throughout this chapter that the higher the validity, the better the predictor, *other things being equal.* That is, given a selection ratio, success rate or spread of job performance, and a cost of testing, the more valid test will lead to more correct decisions and greater gains in job proficiency than the less valid one. In the case of differential placement decisions, however, the magnitude of the overall validity coefficient is less important than *differential validities* for the two or more jobs being considered. As stated earlier, placement decisions involve selecting a job for the new hire. These decisions are aided when *(a)* performance on the two or more jobs is *not* highly correlated, and *(b)* an item of information does *not* have the same predictive validity for the various jobs. Thus, when the individuals who will do well on job *A* will also do well on job *B*, the choice of job assignments is difficult, and, when a high score on predictor *X* is predictive of equally high performance on the two jobs, knowledge of the score does not aid the decision maker in his choice. This situation is illustrated in Figure 5–20,A. Here, in a hypothetical case, the test has the same validity (say, $r = .50$) for performance on both jobs A and B. This is indicated by the parallel regression lines relating the predictor scores to the criterion scores for the two jobs.

Faced with this picture, the decision maker comes up with the same answer regardless of the score: predicted performance level on the two jobs is the same for any given score. In contrast, Figure 5–20,B, illustrates an ideal case for differential placement decisions. The attribute being measured by the predictor (or at least the predictor scores) is positively related to performance on job A but negatively related to performance on job B. Now, with the exception of the point at which the two regression lines intersect, the decision is clear. Scores below this intersection should be given positive weight for assignment to job B, but negative weight for assignment to job A, and the reverse is true for scores above this intersection.

While the situation in Figure 5–20,B, is ideal, differential placement

FIGURE 5–20

Predictor Validity and Differential Placement Strategies

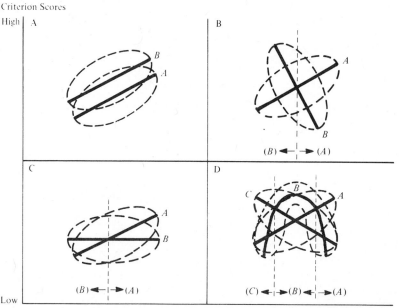

In A, validity coefficients are equal for jobs A and B and provide no basis for placement decisions. In B, validities are opposite in sign and the strategy is clear: place high scorers on job A, low scorers on job B. In C, the predictor is valid for job A, but less so for job B, so high scorers are assigned to A, low scorers to B (since they are predicted to perform poorly on A). In D, two cutoffs are used to assign low scorers to C, middle scorers to B, and high scorers to A.

does not depend on validity coefficients that differ in sign, but only on a difference in magnitude. This is shown in Figure 5–20,C, where the predictor has a high positive correlation with job A and a low, but positive, correlation with job B. Again, the decision strategy is clear. For individuals with scores above the intersection of the regression lines, choose job A; for those below the intersection, choose job B. Finally, Figure 5–20, D, illustrates a case in which there are different optimal levels of the attribute (or score distribution) for three different jobs, A, B, and C. For jobs A and C, the situation is similar to that just described (Figure 5–20,B), with one positive and one negative validity. For job B, however, the relationship illustrated would be curvilinear, with both high and low scores predictive of lower performance than the optimal intermediate scores.

What is important, then, are differential slopes of the functions relating predictor to criterion scores. However, if we relate predictor scores to gains, or *increased utility* from testing, then different slopes may occur as a result of differences in variability of performance on the two jobs, even though the validities are identical. This is illustrated in Figure 5–21. Job A has much greater variability of performance among the incumbents than job B, and even though the two validities are equal, differential placement is possible and quite rational. Assign job A to those with high scores to maximize the gain (since high scorers far outperform the average), but assign

FIGURE 5–21

Variability of Performance with Equal Validities

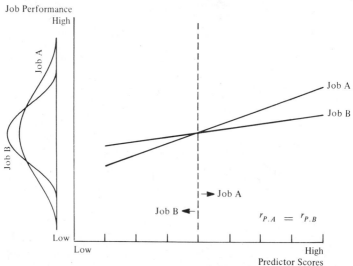

A predictor with equal validities for two jobs that differ in variability of performance. High scorers are assigned to job A to maximize gain, but low scorers are assigned to job B to minimize low performance.

low scorers to job B to minimize the loss (since low scorers are only slightly poorer than the average on job B).

Strategies for Placement.   Implicit in the foregoing discussion is a strategy for placement—namely, use the predictor information to place each person so that the sum of the criterion scores (or the sum of the gains in utility) will be maximized. From the viewpoint of institutional goals, such a strategy would seem ideal. The picture presented by this model may be oversimplified, however. People vary along many dimensions and, while a composite score can always be obtained from a multiple regression equation, it may be that the pattern or profile of attributes is both more analytic and more predictive for placement purposes than any composite score. Such a view was expressed by Guion (1965) when he stated that placement is more concerned with *intra*personal than with *inter*personal differences, reflecting the strengths and weaknesses of the individual *relative to his own average* or norm. The questions then become,

> On what jobs will the individual's strengths be put to best use? On what job will this individual make his best contribution to the employing organization and to himself? (p. 11)

The last sentence reflects a concern for the individual as well as the organization needs. In a way, an emphasis on intrapersonal strengths and weaknesses is consistent both with profile matching and with synthetic or component validity concepts, as discussed earlier. The profile matching notion would use profile similarity (in terms of Σd^2 or r) as a basis for differential placement, with the individual allocated the job for which she has the best match. Similarly, a strategy with the component validity concept (see Table 5–1) would be to identify the individual's two or three relatively high scores, to determine for which job these components were most important, and to allocate that job to the individual.

A somewhat more sophisticated technique for placement based essentially on "similar patterns or profiles to similar jobs" involves *discriminant-function* analysis. This statistical technique is designed to classify people into groups on the basis of multivariate information that is combined in a linear fashion. Placement using discriminant-function analysis assumes that people who are similar in that they are grouped together by this method will work well together. In this sense, it is like profile matching, but unlike it in that a composite *score* is the criterion for group assignment, rather than a composite picture or profile.

Placing Each Person in Accordance with His or Her Highest Potential.   This strategy would look only at the intrapersonal differences. The individual's standard scores on several measures would be compared, and he would be placed on the job for which his highest aptitude score had the greatest predictive validity. This strategy is closely related to that described for component validity. Its greatest limitation is evident in that, while an individual's highest aptitude might be at the 50th percentile, the job might require someone in the upper 25 percent of the population on this attribute. At the same time, the individual's second-highest aptitude might be at the 30th percentile, which might be an adequate level for the job with which that aptitude is associated. Assignment according to highest potential would leave the job inadequately filled, but *assignment to assure that the greatest number of jobs were adequately filled* would place the person on the job for which his aptitude score was at a somewhat lower rank. Equally dubious would be a situation where an individual's highest aptitude is at the 90th percentile, but the only job requiring this aptitude is so easy that a person at the 20th percentile can handle the job. Assignment by highest potential would place the individual in a job for which she was tremendously overqualified, probably resulting in low satisfaction and short job tenure. Thus, either a strategy based on adequately filling the greatest number of jobs or one based on placing people according to their highest ability can lead to glaring mismatches of people and jobs.

None of these strategies considers the possibility that different priorities may exist in filling jobs. It may be much more important to fill a job where a crippling shortage of workers exists than one where present employees can handle the work if given a few hours overtime. Assuming that such priorities exist and the vacancies can be rank ordered according to the urgency for filling them, then a strategy can be used that compares each new hire with the requirements of each job in order of urgency and *places him on the job with the highest priority for which he can qualify.*

Placing Each Person in Accordance with Needs and Abilities. Schoenfeldt (1974) has suggested a placement scheme that he has labeled the *assessment-classification model.* In his approach he first identifies job families or clusters of jobs with similar activities or ability requirements. Next, he subgroups individuals in terms of motivational makeup as derived from past experience or biodata questions. Finally, he matches subgroups of individuals with job families for which their probability of success and satisfaction is greatest. This is a rather sophisticated vocational-guidance approach to placement, one which steps outside of the traditional ability approach to placement. In addition, the suggestion that individuals might be suited for a wide range of jobs with similar characteristics rather than a specific set of job titles provides the employer with considerably greater latitude for the best possible placement. Figure 5–22 presents a schematic representation of Schoenfeldt's approach.

Morrison (1977) tested Schoenfeldt's assessment-classification model with a sample of blue-collar workers in a Canadian manufacturing organization. He was able to identify two homogeneous clusters of jobs or job families. One family consisted of process operators—those involved with the monitoring of ongoing operations such as the extraction of sulfur from substances. A second job family consisted of heavy-equipment operators, such as employees who operated power shovels or cranes. Morrison was able to demonstrate that three characteristics separated the process operators from the heavy-equipment operators. Successful process operators were more

FIGURE 5–22

A Modified Version of Schoenfeldt's Model

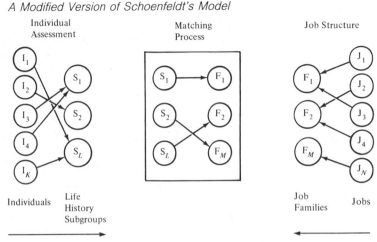

Source: Adapted from Schoenfeldt, L. F. Assessment classification model to match individuals and jobs. *Journal of Applied Psychology*, 1974, *59*, 584. Copyright © 1974 by the American Psychological Association. Reprinted by permission.

likely to have a more favorable self-image, to have been raised in an urban environment, and to prefer standardized work schedules. Since these data were gathered six months after the subjects joined the organization, and since it had been established that dissatisfied and/or unsuccessful employees left the organization prior to this six-month point, it was assumed that those remaining were reasonably capable and satisfied. While neither Schoenfeldt nor Morrison would claim that life experiences are sufficient for the accurate prediction of industrial success, they have demonstrated that life experiences and employee interests might also play a role in differential placement.

Placement in Sequential Jobs. "Sequential jobs" can refer to an assembly team or successive machine operations where each worker's operation depends on the completion of one or more prior operations. "Successive jobs" can also refer to a hierarchy of jobs based upon different levels of the same aptitude or skill. In the latter case, where the placement question may be: "At what labor grade or wage level do we start this individual?" the absolute level of the predictor validity is important. The same aptitude is presumed to be relevant for each job; therefore, the higher the validity, the more accurately the employees can be classified. A prime example of this type of placement is in the allocation of ability-graded training classes to students or employees. In this situation, a highly valid measure more accurately measures the aptitude and/or achievement levels for which the various training programs are designed.

When jobs are sequential in the sense that they represent successive and dependent operations, then the placement strategy may well be to attempt to select people for one line who constitute a homogeneous group with respect to output rate. In such situations it may be reasonable to have "slow, medium, and fast" teams, rather than three teams, or lines, forced to operate at the rate of their slowest worker. Thus, as with hierarchically related jobs or with ability-graded training, the goal is to establish homogeneous work groups with respect to speed of production. Absolute level of validity would be important for choosing the work groups, while differential validities would be important for choosing the jobs within the groups for the individual employee.

Coordinate Jobs. When the relationship between jobs involves coordinate rather than sequential activities, the efficiency of the system may depend on something more than the technical competence of the individuals to perform their individual functions in the group. It may depend on skills of communication, of interpersonal relations, or simply of coordination, not important in independent or even sequential jobs. The concept here is one of a multiman-machine system where systems performance measures, rather than individual performance measures, are particularly relevant. Selection and placement must both be concerned with the relationships among people and between performances of related jobs. Unfortunately, we know relatively little about the selection and placement of people on teams although there is some evidence (Van Zelst, 1952) that teams based on sociometric choices are more efficient and rewarding to the members.

Further Considerations

Should initial selection and placement be concerned primarily with an ideal match of the employee to the present job, or should the strategy be to select and place those applicants with the highest overall potential for growth and advancement within the organization? In filling a position of machinist, should the personnel office be looking for the best available machinist and one who is apt to remain a machinist throughout her career, or should one look for a potential foreman, plant manager, or vice president? In a relatively "tight" labor market, the question may be more academic than real; persons with supervisory or administrative skills and experience are not likely to be candidates for semiskilled or skilled jobs. That is, self-selection of applicants will restrict the extent to which an organization can "overhire" for a job. However, in a period of high unemployment, it may be possible to pursue such a strategy. Engineers may be available for drafting positions, master mechanics as machinists, and supervisors as assemblers. Two problems may arise for the organization that seeks to "take advantage" of the labor market to hire highly-skilled people who are over-qualified for the available jobs. First, these employees may be bored, discontent, and restless in their routine jobs. Second, when there is a change in labor-market conditions, the organization may have a higher turnover rate as these over-qualified employees leave for more appropriate jobs. This is likely to occur unless the present organization is in a position to promote them to more responsible positions.

Another economic situation that tempts an organization to overhire is one in which the government issues defense contracts on a "cost-plus" basis. In such a situation, as during the post World War II Cold War period, hundreds of experimental and applied experimental (engineering) psychologists were hired into defense industries to "human-engineer" new military equipment. Actually, a large percentage of these research-oriented Ph.D. psychologists spent their time thumbing through handbooks or engaging in other relatively low-level tasks. The turnover was astounding as these people moved from company to company and out of industry into academia where they could use their research skills. Whether industry today is more aware of the possible drawbacks of overhiring is not clear. It is reported, however, that many students feel that the Ph.D. degree is a handicap in some hiring situations and it is better to "forget to mention" that achievement.

Obviously, the questions discussed above are related to the organization's policy with respect to "promotion within" versus "hiring from without." If one adheres to a strong promotion-from-within policy, then it is imperative that one select for potential as well as immediate placement. If, on the other hand, the organization espouses a policy of hiring from without for all (or nearly all) management or technical-professional positions, then selection and placement should focus on finding the person to fit *the* job, and—what is more—to seek those persons who will likely be content to remain at the job level at which they are hired and not be especially motivated by advancement or promotion opportunities. The issue is obviously not an either-or case, but it is a complex one for which we do not have any clear answers or even adequate models.

Decisions versus Decision Makers

In describing the way in which information might be combined and utilized in making hiring or placement decisions, we have glossed over a rather substantial assumption—decision makers use information in a rational and accurate manner. Herbert Simon was awarded the Nobel prize in economics for his demonstrations that man's rationality is limited (Simon, 1960). The implications for personnel hiring and placement decisions are that employers (and maybe even psychologists) may use accurate information in an inaccurate manner. The most common example of this type of information misuse is in the employment interview, which we will examine in the next chapter. More generally, several studies have demonstrated the misuse of information in other activities of the personnel decision process. In a study by Roose and Doherty (1976), judges were asked to assume the role of managers with the task of hiring life insurance sales personnel. They were given a test score but were instructed to use it only on a pass/fail or dichotomous basis; i.e., if the individual applicant had achieved a passing score, the judges were instructed to ignore how much higher the particular score was than the cutting or passing score. The judges were unable to treat the data dichotomously when it was presented in continuous raw-score form. The researchers suggested that if the data were to be treated dichotomously by the judges, it should be presented to them dichotomously.

In a second study in which the employment process was simulated (Schaffer, Mays, and Ethridge, 1976), the effect of the Buckley amendment on employment decisions was examined. The Buckley amendment guaranteed to students the right to examine their permanent files if they requested such access. This amendment has led to two types of permanent files— open files and confidential files. Open files, as the name suggests, are open to the individual student's inspection. Presumably, for college students this would include the potential inspection of letters of recommendation. On the other hand, students may choose a closed or "confidential-file" option in which they give up the right to examine their file and accompanying letters of recommendation. The data indicated that judges acting as prospective employers were more favorable toward "confidential-file" applicants than they were toward "open-file" applicants when they made the simulated employment decisions.

As a final example, Peters and Terborg (1975) asked undergraduate students to assume the role of prospective employers and consider the qualifications of fictitious candidates for positions. The results showed that both the order in which information was presented as well as the similarities in attitudes between the prospective employer and the applicant affected the hiring decision. In addition, it was found that if an applicant with attitudes dissimilar to those of the "employer" was hired, the suggested starting salary was lower than that suggested for applicants with attitudes similar to those of the "employer"! In spite of some attempts to eliminate this attitudinal affect in subsequent studies, it remained an important effect on the hiring decision.

All of these studies were simulations. They did not evaluate the behaviors of "real" employers making "actual" decisions about "real" applicants. As such, they are open to criticism. Nevertheless, they do raise disturbing possibilities. For example, a withdraw/pass (WP) grade may mean one thing to a student and quite another to a prospective employer or medical school admissions board. A regular high school diploma and a General Education Development (GED) certificate may be functionally equivalent but may be treated very differently by employment offices. More studies of the decision processes of employers must be carried out in the field. No matter how elaborate and refined our knowledge of test theory and validity of tests, this information is relatively useless unless we know *how* predictor information is used by decision makers.

SUMMARY

Personnel decisions can be classified as to whether they involve choosing among people for a job, training program, promotion, and the like, or choosing among jobs for the person. Finer classification of decisions involves questions of quotas—single versus sequential decision stages, fixed versus adaptive treatments, and single versus multiple predictors.

The quality of the information on which such decisions are made is described in terms of predictor reliability and validity. The more valid the information, the more accurately one can predict decision outcomes. However, even though validity coefficients are low and do not permit accurate predictors of criterion *scores*, predictors may contribute appreciably to the quality of personnel decisions. The extent to which this is true depends upon a number of parameters in the testing program. The *selection ratio*, which describes how much freedom of choice the decision maker has, can determine that a predictor of modest validity can be used effectively, or that a predictor of high validity will be ineffective. The *success rate*, or, alternatively, the *variability of performance*, describes the "room for improvement" in job performance and sets limits for the payoff from a testing program.

The value, or payoff, from a selection program can be described in terms of (1) the expected increase in success rate, (2) the expected increase in the average criterion scores, (3) the expected percentage increase in job proficiency, and potentially (4) the payoff in dollars resulting from the increased proficiency.

The testing process is very sensitive to variables other than those we intend to measure. It is possible for these other variables to contribute to unfair personnel decisions. The Federal Goverment has developed guidelines for the protection of citizens against intentional or unintentional abuses of fair testing practices.

Typically, the decision maker is confronted with two or more relevant pieces of information—that is, two or more valid predictors. These may be combined clinically to arrive at a decision, or they may be combined statistically, using one of several strategies. While *multiple regression* enjoys the greatest mathematical justification, the assumption of complementary and additive traits is difficult to accept. *Multiple cutoffs* pose the problem of the setting of appropriate cutoff scores, while *multiple hurdles* or *sequential decisions* may prolong the decision process. Finally, *profile matching* lacks a clear rationale and accepted scoring method. Some combined strategy involving sequential decisions may prove most economical both in testing costs and the imposition on the applicants.

Current research directed toward improving predictions and, consequently, personnel decisions, is less concerned with finding some optimum combination of predictors that will yield a particularly high validity. Instead, emphasis is on identifying individual and situational variables that tend to limit predictive efficiency. Moderator variables and subgroup analyses often identify "unpredictables" among the original validation sample. Not only do such subgroups lead to a distorted picture of predictor validity, but also they may be unfairly discriminated against by a strategy that treats them in the same way as the "predictables." Prediction may also be improved through the identification of suppressor variables. In effect, this involves the measurement of irrelevant (error) variance in the predictor scores so that they may be corrected as estimates of criterion scores.

While the emphasis in personnel psychology and in the present chapter has been on selection, there are good reasons why more attention should be given to differential placement. First, more than one job may be available at any time; second, while successful selection depends on a labor surplus, placement does not and, in fact, may be more crucial when labor is in short supply.

Placement decisions are fostered more by information that is differentially predictive than by information that is similarly predictive of performance on two or more jobs. Ideally, a predictor with positive validity for one job and negative validity for the others would be most beneficial to placement decisions. However, with the exception of work by Cronbach and Gleser (1965), relatively little attention has been given to models and strategies for differential placement. Such models would have to consider the interrelationships among jobs as well as the effects of placement decisions on the individual.

REFERENCES

American Psychological Association Task Force on Employment Testing of Minority Groups. Job testing and the disadvantaged. *American Psychologist*, 1969, *24*, 637–650.

Bartlett, C. J., & O'Leary, B. S. A differential prediction model to moderate the effects of heterogeneous groups in personnel selection and classification. *Personnel Psychology*, 1969, *22*, 1–17.

Cronbach, L. J., & Gleser, G. C. *Psychological tests and personnel decisions.* Urbana: University of Illinois Press, 1965.

Curtis, C. T. Family Educational Rights and Privacy Act of 1974. U.S. Congress, Senate, *Congressional Record*, 1974, *120*, 19067–19614.

Doppelt, J. E., & Bennett, G. K. Reducing the cost of training satisfactory workers by using tests. *Personnel Psychology*, 1953, *6*, 1–8.

Dunnette, M. D. A modified model for selection research. *Journal of Applied Psychology*, 1963, *47*, 317–323.

Dvorak, B. J. Differential occupational ability patterns (University of Minnesota Bulletin). Minneapolis Employment Stabilization Research Institute, 1935.

Ghiselli, E. E. *The measurement of occupational aptitude.* Berkeley: University of California Press, 1955.

Ghiselli, E. E. Differentiation of individuals in terms of their predictability. *Journal of Applied Psychology*, 1956, *40*, 374–377.

Ghiselli, E. E. *The validity of occupational aptitude tests.* New York: Wiley, 1966.

Ghiselli, E. E. The validity of aptitude tests in personnel selection. *Personnel Psychology*, 1973, *23*, 461–478.

Ghiselli, E. E., & Brown, C. W. *Personnel and industrial psychology.* New York: McGraw-Hill, 1955.

Guion, R. M. *Personnel testing.* New York: McGraw-Hill, 1965.

Guion, R. M. Employment tests and discriminatory hiring. *Industrial Relations,* 1966, *5,* 20–37.

Guion, R. M. Personnel selection. *Annual Review of Psychology,* 1967, *18,* 191–216.

Hobert, R. D., & Dunnette, M. D. Development of moderator variables to enhance the prediction of managerial effectiveness. *Journal of Applied Psychology,* 1967, *51,* 50–64.

Hull, C. L. *Aptitude testing.* New York: Harcourt, Brace & World, 1928.

Humphreys, L. Statistical definitions of test validity for minority groups. *Journal of Applied Psychology,* 1973, *58,* 1–4.

Hunter, J. E., & Schmidt, F. L. Fitting people to jobs. In E. A. Fleishman (Ed.) *Human performance and productivity.* In press.

Korman, A. K. *Industrial and organizational psychology.* Englewood Cliffs, N.J.: Prentice-Hall, 1971.

Landy, F. J. Adventures in implied psychology: The value of true negatives. *American Psychologist,* 1978, *33,* 756–760.

Lawshe, C. H., & Bolda, R. A. Expectancy charts. I. Their use and empirical development. *Personnel Psychology,* 1958, *11,* 545–559.

Lee, R., & Booth, J. M. A utility analysis of a weighted application blank designed to predict turnover for clerical employees. *Journal of Applied Psychology,* 1974, *59,* 516–518.

McCormick, E. J., & Tiffin, J. *Industrial psychology* (6th ed.). Englewood Cliffs, N.J.: Prentice-Hall, 1974.

McNamara, W. J., & Hughes, J. L. A review of research on the selection of computer programmers. *Personnel Psychology,* 1961, *14,* 39–51.

Morrison, R. F. A multivariate model for the occupational placement decision. *Journal of Applied Psychology,* 1977, *62,* 274–277.

Naylor, J. C., & Shine, L. C. A table for determining the increase in mean criterion score obtained by using a selection device. *Journal of Industrial Psychology,* 1965, *3,* 33–42.

Peters, L. H., & Terborg, J. The effects of temporal placement of unfavorable information and of attitude similarity on personnel selection decisions. *Journal of Applied Psychology,* 1975, *13,* 279–293.

Roche, U. F. The Cronbach-Gleser utility function in fixed-treatment employee selection. Unpublished doctoral dissertation. Summarized in Schmidt, F. L., Hunter, J. E., McKenzie, R. C., & Muldrow, T. W. A case study of the impact of a valid selection procedure on worker productivity. Unpublished manuscript.

Roose, J. E., & Doherty, M. E. Judgment theory applied to the selection of life insurance salesmen. *Organizational Behavior and Human Performance,* 1976, *16,* 231–249.

Rusmore, T. T., & Toorenaar, G. J. Reducing training costs by employment testing. *Personnel Psychology,* 1956, *9,* 39–44.

Saunders, D. R. Moderator variables in prediction. *Educational and Psychological Measurement*, 1956, *16*, 209–222.

Schaffer, D. R., Mays, P. V., & Ethridge, K. Who shall be hired: A biasing effect of the Buckley amendment on employment practices. *Journal of Applied Psychology*, 1976, *61*, 571–575.

Schmidt, F. L., & Hoffman, B. Empirical comparison of three methods of assessing the utility of a selection device. *Journal of Industrial and Organizational Psychology*, 1973, *1*, 13–22.

Schmidt, F. L., & Hunter, J. E. Moderator research and the law of small numbers. *Personnel Psychology*, 1978, *31*, 215–231.

Schoenfeldt, L. F. Utilization of manpower: Development and evaluation of an assessment-classification model for matching individuals with jobs. *Journal of Applied Psychology*, 1974, *59*, 583–595.

Simon, H. A. *The new science of management decision.* New York: Harper, 1960.

Taylor, H. C., & Russell, J. T. The relationship of validity coefficients to the practical effectiveness of tests in selection: Discussion and tables. *Journal of Applied Psychology*, 1939, *23*, 565–578.

Uniform Guidelines on Employee Selection Procedures (1978). *Federal Register*, 1978, *43* (No. 166), 38290–38309.

van Naersson, R. F. Selectie van chauffers. As reported in Hunter, J. E., & Schmidt, F. L. (1978). Fitting people to jobs. In E. A. Fleishman (Ed.) *Human performance and productivity.* In press.

Van Zelst, R. H. Sociometrically selected work teams increase production. *Personnel Psychology*, 1952, *5*, 175–185.

Von Neumann, J., & Morgenstern, O. *Theory of games and economic behavior.* Princeton: Princeton University Press, 1947.

Wald, A. *Statistical decision functions.* New York: Wiley, 1950.

CHAPTER **6**

Interviews and Other
Nontest Predictors

In this chapter we will consider some sources of data, other than standardized tests, that are used to gather information and impressions used in personnel decision making. As a matter of fact, data from psychological tests constitute only a small part of the total information used in personnel decisions. Interviews and biographical information blanks (or application blanks) are used almost universally in business and industry. Thus, for example, Scott, Clothier, and Spriegel (1949) found that over 99% of 325 business organizations reported using the interview as a part of the personnel selection process, and Uhrbrock (1948) reported yearly averages of from 5.4 to 20.8 interviews *per person hired* in one company over a seven-year period. Biographical inventories, or application blanks, appear to be used almost as universally.

Somewhat less well-known and less frequently used sources of information are work-sample and situational tests and the ratings of peers who interact with other applicants. Yet these methods show some promise as sources of information that can be used to improve personnel decisions.

THE INTERVIEW

The preemployment or selection interview is part of a decision-making process. Both the interview and the process of which it is a part can be evaluated, but the two should not be confused. The interview (the face-to-face interaction between the interviewer and the applicant) is one component of the total process leading to a decision about the applicant. Frequently, studies purporting to evaluate the interview have instead examined the validity of the interviewer's predictions or decisions. However, these decisions are based on the total information and impressions that the interviewer has gained about the applicant and not solely on the face-to-face interview. Typically, the interviewer has had access to biographical and work-history data, letters of recommendation, telephone conversations with former employers, and psychological test scores, or some subset of these. Each of these sources of information may contribute to the predictions or decision about the applicant, but to assume that the predictive validity of the final rating or recommendations indicates the value of the face-to-face interview or any other source of information is, of course, fallacious. Without some knowledge of an interviewer's strategy, we cannot determine how the information received is used. The face-to-face interview may play a determining role, or it may have a trivial influence on the interviewer's decisions.

The time order in which the interviewer receives the information may be important. If the interview occurs before any other information is received, it may "color" the impression of the individual, and nonconfirming or contrary evidence from other sources may be discounted or overlooked. On the other hand, an interview that comes late in the total information-gathering, impression-forming process may serve only to confirm the impressions of the interviewer, contributing little or nothing to the decision process. We will have more to say later about the order effects of information on overall evaluations. For the present, our only point is that the fact that an interview is included in the total decision process provides no indication of the contribution of that face-to-face interaction to the final impressions and evaluations of the interviewer.

The Role of the Interviewer

The first purpose of the interview is to gather information about the applicant. In the most limited conception, the only role of the interviewer would be to report "factual" information about the applicant obtained by asking questions in the interview. This is the type of interviewing used in survey research, where the interview competes with the questionnaire as a method of data collection. The applicant, like the survey respondent, is presented with standardized questions and a limited choice of responses—responses to open-ended questions are recorded verbatim by the interviewer for later coding. In many surveys the interviewer's role ends with the gathering of information; the coding or interpretation of responses is left to experts in the survey research headquarters.

In contrast, preemployment interviewers seldom function strictly as gatherers of information. Usually, they are required to interpret the information gained from the interview and to draw inferences about certain traits, attributes, attitudes, and potentials that the applicants possess. These frequently take the form of ratings along several dimensions, together with overall ratings (or rankings) of the applicants. The latter often constitute predictions or recommendations by the interviewers. Distinctions as to the role of interviewers can be made again at this point: they may provide ratings as one source of information to a decision maker, with or without overall ratings or recommendations, and these ratings may be based exclusively on the face-to-face interview, or they may be based on the interview and whatever ancillary data are available.

If the interviewer is expected to integrate interview and other data, weighing different sources and resolving conflicting evidence to arrive at an evaluation, the interviewer is being asked to use *clinical skills* and to function as a sort of human computer. If, on the other hand, the interviewer's ratings are integrated with the other items of information by means of a multiple-regression equation, with each variable assigned its own optimum weight, then the predictions are *actuarial*, or statistical, rather than clinical in nature. While the interviewer's ratings are a matter of clinical judgment, the strategy whereby they are combined and used to arrive at predictions or decisions may be either a matter of judgment or of statistical methods.

Clinical versus Actuarial Predictions

The question of clinical versus actuarial, or statistical, predictions has been studied by Meehl (1954). Basically, the issue is whether the data relevant to a decision can be evaluated and combined by a human evaluator in such a way as to yield predictions that are more valid than, or equally as valid as, those obtained by statistical combination of the same data. The model for testing this question is really quite simple, as shown in Figure 6–1, but actual field conditions and even experimental studies seldom

FIGURE 6–1

Basic Design for Comparison of Clinical and Statistical Prediction

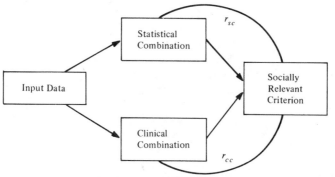

Source: Wiggins, J. S. *Personality and prediction: Principles of personality assessment.* Reading, Mass.: Addison-Wesley, 1973.

present an unbiased test of the issue. As the figure shows, the *same* data are available for clinical combination, on the one hand, and for statistical combination, on the other. Two sets of predictions are tested against an acceptable criterion measure, with three possible outcomes: $r_{sc} = r_{cc}$ (the methods are equally valid); $r_{sc} < r_{cc}$ (clinical methods yield higher validity); or $r_{sc} > r_{cc}$ (statistical methods yield higher validity).

What is the evidence from the relatively fair tests of the model in Figure 6–1? Wiggins (1973), in a thorough review of the research and issues surrounding the clinical-statistical controversy, summarizes the results in terms of the three outcomes listed above. The findings, as reported by Meehl in three earlier reports, are summarized in Table 6–1. It is clear that these results strongly favor the statistical combination of predictor data. In the 51 studies, Meehl (1965) found 33 clearly favored statistical over clinical prediction, 17 failed to establish one method as superior to the other, and only 1 study (Lindzey, 1965) favored clinical over statistical methods. Furthermore, the fairness of the Lindzey study as a test of statistical versus clinical procedures has been seriously questioned by Wiggins (1973). The evidence strongly suggests that the general practice of clinical combination of data must be challenged. This is not to deny the value

TABLE 6–1
Meehl's "Box Scores" of Studies Comparing Clinical with Statistical Prediction

Source	No. of Studies	Prediction Domain	"Box Score"		
			Stat > Clin	Stat = Clin	Stat < Clin
Meehl (1954)	16–20	Success in academic or military training, recidivism and parole violation; recovery from psychosis	11	8	1
Meehl (1957)	27	Success in academic or military training, recidivism and parole violation; recovery from psychosis; personality description; outcome of psychotherapy	17	10	0
Meehl (1965)	51	Success in academic or military training, recidivism and parole violation; recovery from psychosis; personality description; outcome of psychotherapy, response to shock treatment; formal psychiatric nosology; job success and satisfaction; medical (nonpsychiatric) diagnosis	33	17	1

Source: Adapted from Wiggins, J. S. *Personality and prediction: Principles of personality assessment.* Reading, Mass.: Addison-Wesley, 1973.

of interviewing or observational-judgmental methods for gathering data and making inferences about traits or attributes. Rather, it is to bring into question the use of clinical methods for combining the observations and judgments into a composite prediction. In medical terms, the distinction is between observing and recording information about symptoms, on the one hand, and making a diagnosis, on the other. (Incidentally, in that context, Overall & Hollister [1964] have demonstrated the power of statistical models for accurate diagnosis of diseases from observations of symptoms.)

The implications of these findings for decision making in industry and other organizations are far reaching. They go well beyond questions of the role of the interviewer in the decision process, suggesting, first, that a clear distinction be made between data-gathering and decision-making functions, and, second, that statistical techniques be used to a greater extent in combining information into predictions and decisions. This approach has the added advantage of making the decision-making strategy explicit and, consequently, more susceptible to analysis and refinement. Human decision makers are likely to resist the idea of turning over their decision-making responsibilities to a computer. However, they might be less resistant to a compromise strategy in which they would give primary weight to a statistical prediction but reserve a "veto" power in the final decision. Subsequent analysis of the outcomes of those decisions where the decision maker overruled the computer would provide an objective test of his clinical skills.

Evaluation of the Interview

There are literally hundreds of studies that have investigated the selection interview. It is beyond the scope of this text and the endurance of the reader to review each of these studies. Fortunately, there are several systematic literature reviews that enable the interested student to trace the history of interview research as well as to accumulate substantiated research findings about the interview. These reviews, historically sequenced are: Wagner (1949), Mayfield (1964), Ulrich and Trumbo (1965), Wright (1969), and Schmitt (1976). The change in emphasis and approach to the interview is well described in Schmitt's (1976) recent review. He examined the previous reviews and, in addition to contrasting earlier conclusions with his own, he considered recent evidence concerning the influences on decision making in the interview. His findings appear in Figure 6–2. It may be easier to evaluate the conclusions in the right-hand column of the figure by matching them with a hypothetical question representing each "variable" in the left-hand column.

1. *Negative-positive nature of the information:* Does favorable information have the same effect as unfavorable information in the interview?
2. *Temporal placement of information:* Does it make any difference if favorable information comes early or late in the interview?
3. *Interviewer stereotypes:* Do interviewers have an "ideal" applicant in mind when they are interviewing real applicants? If so, does this

FIGURE 6–2

Experimental Studies of Decision Making in the Interview

Variables	Studies	Conclusions
1. Negative-positive nature of information	Springbett (1958) Bolster & Springbett (1961) Hollmann (1972)	All three studies agree that negative and positive information are processed differently. Springbett and Bolster & Springbett (1961) maintain negative information is weighted too heavily; Hollmann concludes negative information is weighted appropriately, but positive information is not weighted heavily enough.
2. Temporal placement of information	Blakeney & MacNaughton (1971) Johns (1975) Peters & Terborg (1975) Farr (1973) Springbett (1958) Anderson (1960) Crowell (1961)	The early studies found primacy effects; Blakeney and MacNaughton reported negligible primacy effects and Farr (1973) reported recency effects. Peters and Terborg (1975) found favorable-unfavorable information sequence resulted in better applicant ratings than an unfavorable-favorable sequence. Solution may be an attention hypothesis which suggests interviewers use the information they are forced to attend to.
3. Interviewer stereotypes	Sydiaha (1959, 1961) Bolster & Springbett (1961) Rowe (1963) Mayfield & Carlson (1966) Hakel, Hollmann & Dunnette (1970) London & Hakel (1974) Hakel (1971)	Interviewers seem to have a common "ideal" applicant against which interviewees are evaluated though this generalized applicant may be the effect of halo (Hakel & Dunnette, 1970). Mayfield & Carlson (1966) also suggest that the "ideal" applicant may be at least partially specific or unique to the interviewer and Hakel, Hollmann & Dunnette (1970) found evidence for two clusters of stereotypes.
4. Job information	Langdale & Weitz (1973) Wiener & Schneiderman (1974)	Job information is utilized by interviewers and serves to decrease the effect of irrelevant information for both experienced and inexperienced interviewers.
5. Individual differences	Dobmeyer (1970) Valenzi & Andrews (1973) Rowe (1963)	There are wide individual differences and little or no configurality in cue utilization by interviewers. In addition, interviewers are unable to give an accurate verbal statement of their cue utilization policies.

FIGURE 6–2 *(continued)*

Variables	Studies	Conclusions
6. Visual cues	Washburn & Hakel (1973)	Visual cues were more important than verbal; their interaction was most responsible for ratings.
7. Attitudinal and racial similarity	Baskett (1973) Rand & Wexley (1975) Ledvinka (1971, 1972, 1973) Sattler (1970) Wexley & Nemeroff (1975) Peters & Terborg (1975) Frank & Hackman (1975)	Baskett (1973) reported that applicants' perceived similarity to the interviewer resulted in higher judgments concerning their competency and recommended salary, but no greater likelihood of recommended employment. Subsequent investigators have confirmed the effect of attitude similarity on interview ratings. Ledvinka reported that black interviewers were more likely to elicit responses of job rejection from black interviewees than were white interviewers in exit interviews.
8. Sex	Cohen & Bunker (1975) Dipboye, Fromkin & Wiback (1975)	Similarity of sex appears to have some minimal effect on job resumé ratings though Cohen and Bunker (1975) suggest sexual discrimination of a type that assigns individuals to sex role congruent jobs.
9. Contrast effects	Carlson (1968, 1970) Hakel, Ohnesorge & Dunnette (1970) Rowe (1967) Wexley, Yukl, Kovacs & Sanders (1972) Wexley, Sanders & Yukl (1973); Landy & Bates (1973) Latham, Wexley & Pursell (1975)	The majority of these studies found that an applicant's rating is at least partially dependent on the other individuals being rated at the same time. Landy & Bates (1973) and Hakel et al. (1970) have found the contrast effect to be minimal and Latham et al. found a workshop successful in the elimination of several rating errors including that of contrast effects.
10. Interviewer experience	Carlson (1967a)	Reliability of interview data was not greater for experienced interviewers, but the stress for quotas impaired the judgments of inexperienced interviewers more than it did the experienced interviewers in the sense that inexperienced interviewers were more likely to accept bad applicants.

FIGURE 6–2 (continued)

Variables	Studies	Conclusions
11. Type of information	Carlson (1967b)	Personal history information had a greater effect on interview judgments than photographs of the interviewee. A photograph had its greatest effect on the final rating when it complemented personal history information.
12. Accuracy of interviewer as measured by number of factual questions he is able to answer	Carlson (1967a)	More accurate raters used a structured guide, were more variable in their ratings, and tended to rate lower.
13. Structure of interview	Schwab & Henneman (1969) Carlson, Schwab & Henneman (1970)	Structured interviews result in greater inter-interviewer reliability than interviews conducted without a guide.

Source: Schmitt, N. Social and situational determinants of interview decisions: Implications for the employment interview. *Personnel Psychology*, 1976, *29*, 79–101.

stereotype come from the nature of the job or from the past history of the interviewer?

4. *Job information:* Does it help to give the interviewer a detailed picture of the job for which the applicant is being considered?

5. *Individual differences:* Do all interviewers use basically the same method of combining information? Can interviewers describe how they combine information?

6. *Visual cues:* Are there nonverbal or postural/facial applicant cues that influence interviewer decisions?

7. *Attitudinal and racial similarity:* Are interviewers more lenient toward applicants of their own race or applicants with similar attitudes?

8. *Sex:* Are interviewers more lenient toward applicants of the same sex?

9. *Contrast effects:* Is an applicant's favorability affected by the favorability of others in the applicant group?

10. *Interviewer experience:* Do experienced interviewers produce more valid and reliable decisions than inexperienced interviewers?

11. *Appearance:* Does the personal appearance of the applicant have an effect on interviewer decisions?

12. *Accuracy of interviewer as measured by number of factual questions she is able to answer:* Do more accurate interviewers actually gather more information?

13. *Structure of interview:* Does a standard interview format for every applicant improve the reliability of the interview?

While Schmitt does not answer each of these questions in detail, he does give us a good idea of the potential influences on the eventual interview decision. On the basis of his review, he constructed a model of these potential influences and their relationships to one another. This model is presented in Figure 6–3. The model makes it clear that the interview is much more complex than the traditional prediction device. A test of mechanical comprehension, intelligence, or hand-eye coordination does not have a socioeconomic status, attitude, motivation, or behavior. An interviewer does! Even though a test has certain idiosyncratic characteristics, these characteristics are usually constant and might be thought to affect all applicants equally. The interview is a much more dynamic, interpersonal event. It can and does change form and substance rapidly. It might change between applicants or within applicants. While there may be an advantage to having a flexible and responsive system of evaluation in a clinical or counseling setting, it is just this flexibility and responsivity that make the interview so difficult to evaluate in a selection context.

One of the problems with evaluating the interview is that we must separate the characteristics of the interview (e.g., the traits rated, the questions asked) from the characteristics of the interviewer (e.g., what follow-up questions does he ask? How does he combine information in making a final decision?). We can conceive of a good interview structure and an incompetent interviewer/decision maker; conversely, we can picture a poorly constructed interview format and a terrific interviewer/decision maker.

FIGURE 6–3

Determinants of Interview Outcome

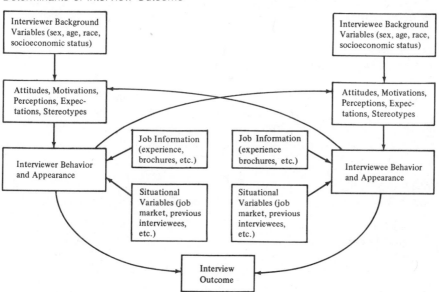

Source: Schmitt, N. Social and situational determinants of interview decisions: Implications for the employment interview. *Personnel Psychology*, 1976, *29*, 79–101.

Since both the interview and the interviewer are components of the predictor, we will examine the validity and reliability of them separately.

Interview versus Interviewer Validity. While it is not often possible to separate the validity of the interview from the validity of the interviewer, three reports that appeared in the early 1950s did just this (Tupes, 1950; Kelly & Fiske, 1950, 1951). The task was to predict the success of graduate students in psychology. Ultimately, more than 500 students from 40 psychology departments were interviewed and given a variety of tests. The design was rather simple. Clinical predictions were made on the basis of credentials alone, credentials plus a one-hour interview, credentials plus test data, and credentials plus test data plus a two-hour interview. In predicting academic performance, the interview did not fare particularly well. Table 6–2 presents the validity coefficients. As you can see, neither the one- nor the two-hour interview added much to a consideration of credentials alone. Unfortunately, since the interview was never used as the *sole* source of information, we still cannot make absolute statements regarding its validity.

Carlson (1972) surveyed 13 studies in which the interview was apparently the sole source of information. Validity coefficients for 9 of these in which some validity was reported ranged from .15 to .25. Meanwhile, Carlson found that interviewers with access to ancillary data made somewhat more valid predictions of job criteria: in 15 of 22 studies, average coefficients were "around .30 to .40." Moreover, "when the judgment or evaluation phase of the interview was either scored or some special ranking or rating method was applied, the average correlation between [such] a 'quantified judgment' and the criterion was around .40 to .60" (Carlson, 1972). Carlson also pointed out that the more recently reported validity coefficients are higher than those reported earlier. He attributes this trend to more sophisticated and realistic research. This last point should be emphasized: researchers too often define unrealistic and impossible tasks for interviewers and then point with scorn at their inadequacies.

It is curious that more often than not we ask interviewers to rate applicants on a number of traits, then validate the ratings against some job performance criteria, and conclude that the resulting low or nonexistent validities reflect the inability of the interviewers to assess the traits. Why is it not just as reasonable to conclude that such findings reflect the lack

TABLE 6–2
Validity Coefficients for Ratings Based on Various Combinations of Information

Basis for Rating Probable Academic Performance	Correlation with Rating of Actual Academic Performance
Credentials alone	.26
Credentials and one-hour interview	.27
Credentials and objective test scores	.36
Credentials, test scores, and two-hour interview	.32

Source: Adapted from Kelly, E. L., & Fiske, D. W. *The prediction of performance in clinical psychology.* Ann Arbor: University of Michigan Press, 1951.

of validity of the traits for predicting job performance? In most cases the traits have been assumed on the basis of job analyses and judgment to be related to success on the job, but these assumptions themselves are seldom tested and may well be questioned.

Reliability of Interviewer Ratings. There are a number of problems with attempts to assess the reliability of interviewer ratings. First, the evaluations of interviewer ratings are not likely to be evaluations of the face-to-face interview. The ratings made by the interviewer are based on whatever information she has gathered about the traits she is rating from whatever sources she has available. This typically includes one or more sources other than the interview. Thus, most reported reliability coefficients are liberal estimates of the interview reliability, since the ratings were not based solely on the interview. Another problem in considering the reliability of interview ratings is that every study seems to deal with a different set of traits to be rated! In an early review of rating reliability, Wagner (1949) reported that the median frequency with which each of 96 traits occurred in the several studies was 1, indicating an almost complete lack of agreement as to the traits that should be rated by the interviewer. In the 30 years that have passed since Wagner's review, there has been little progress on standardizing the dimensions or traits rated by the interviewer.

Ulrich and Trumbo (1965) found few studies that even reported reliabilities. The data they did find are reported in Figure 6–4. The most recent findings tend to be consistent with the Ulrich and Trumbo report. Interviewers tend to be fairly self-consistent, but inter-interviewer reliabilities range from low to high. Regarding the first point, Carlson (1967a, b, 1968) has shown that interviewer self-consistency increases as the judgment task is made easier by (1) providing a relative standard for comparison, (2) increasing the variability among the interviewees, and (3) increasing the consistency of information about each interviewee. In other words, when the "objects" are made more discriminable and less ambiguous, judges are more consistent from initial to repeat evaluations. These findings also suggest that the inter-

FIGURE 6–4

Summary of Results Listed by Ulrich and Trumbo

Study	Results
Strupp & Williams (1960)	"Significant" interrater agreement on nine different traits
Sternberg (1950)	Reliabilities ranged from 0.15 to 0.71
Bonneau (1957)	Interrater reliabilities in 0.80's
Anderson (1954)	Interrater reliabilities in 0.80's
Shaw (1952)	Reliabilities ranging from 0.71 to 0.78
Prien (1962)	Reliabilities of 0.55 and 0.62
Raines and Rohrer (1955)	Reliability of 0.15
Plag (1961)	13 of 15 reliabilities significantly greater than 0
Zaccaria, et al. (1956)	Reliability estimated at 0.72

Source: Blum, M. L. & Naylor, J. C. *Industrial psychology: Its theoretical and social foundations.* New York: Harper, 1968, unnumbered table, p. 153.

viewer's interpretation of the traits to be rated and/or his stereotype of the "ideal" applicant remain quite stable over time.

With respect to inter-interviewer reliability, the more recent research literature also shows the full range of findings. Palacios, Newberry, and Bootzin (1966) report reasonably high reliabilities (from .75 to .91) for 7 different ratings, but Miner (1970) and Stringer and Tyson (1968) report coefficients ranging from the teens to the .80's. Landy (1976), in a study to be presented later, reported values consistently in the .80s.

Since most studies of the reliability of interviews have examined the reliability of the trait ratings made during or after the interview, it should be apparent that these ratings may suffer from the same distortions as other types of ratings. Thus, many of the same factors that influence performance ratings, as described in Chapter 4, are likely to affect interview ratings as well. In general, however, it appears that interviewers have a better chance of agreement in rating some traits than others, probably because (1) they are more likely to possess more common behavioral referents for, say, "intelligence" or "mental ability" than for "submissiveness"; (2) behaviors that are the basis for rating some traits are more consistently displayed by an interviewee from one interview to the next, and/or (3) ancillary data available to the interviewer provide more reliable information for judging some traits than others. It must be remembered that these reliability data do not reflect the reliability of ratings based solely on the face-to-face interview; rather they are estimates of the reliability (agreement) of interviewers who have used interviews and whatever other sources were available and combined the data according to largely unknown and probably idiosyncratic strategies to arrive at their ratings. It is also likely that inter-viewer trait-rating reliability increases with standardization of the interviews, though there is little evidence for this.

Standardization does appear to increase interviewers' agreement on their overall evaluations or predictions, and, as one would expect, more detailed job information also increases agreement. This latter finding is consistent with the notion that agreement depends on the possession of similar stereo-types of the ideal worker; it is also consistent with the notion that the interviewer's ability to predict job performance depends, in part, on knowing *what* job is being performed!

In this connection, the complex relationships among trait ratings, overall ratings or predictions, employment decisions, and job stereotypes deserve a good deal more research. One experimental approach might require inter-viewers to rate applicants on a number of carefully chosen and defined traits with no foreknowledge of the job for which the interviewee was being considered. Following the interview, the interviewer would rate each interviewee for each of several jobs. The relationship between interviewee's trait ratings and overall ratings for the various jobs would provide a descrip-tion of job stereotypes. That is, it would indicate how each of the traits was weighted in the overall evaluation. The recent research by Carlson (1972), cited earlier, is a big step toward understanding the relationship among job information, interviewer information, trait ratings, predictions, decisions, and stereotypes.

Scope of the Interview

The typical selection interview is a jumble of several different types of information. This information ranges from that *given* to the applicant about "the way we do things here" to that *obtained* from the applicant about personal history, preferences, and skills.

Let's concentrate on the interviewer for a moment. What should he look for in the face-to-face interview? There is some evidence that factual information about work history and other biographical items can be obtained with reasonable accuracy in the interview. As you would expect, applicants tend to give socially desirable answers to certain questions (e.g., they might deny they had ever been on welfare when, in fact, they had received welfare payments; Weiss & Dawis, 1960). Other, less threatening information tends to be reported quite reliably in the interview: things such as previous wages, duration of prior employment, age, and education (Keating, Patterson, & Stone, 1950; Vaughn & Reynolds, 1951). But the question remains as to whether the interview is the most efficient means of gathering such information. Most of the items could easily be reported on a preemployment information sheet (application blank). In this form, at least errors of reporting by the interviewer would be eliminated. Furthermore, the released interview time could be used to collect information and/or impressions that cannot be obtained more efficiently and accurately in other ways. It is difficult to see how the preemployment interview can be defended as a means of gathering strictly factual, biographical data.

Given that we will not gather biographical information in the interview, we must still decide whether the goal of the interview should be a broad-band or global assessment of the individual, or a consideration of only a few traits that are presumed to be related to success on the job. As a systematic approach, we might expect personnel management to begin with a list of worker characteristics assumed to be important for the job (on the basis of systematic job analysis), then to decide on the most reliable and economical way to obtain information about each characteristic or attribute. Presumably, the interview would be utilized to assess only those traits that could *not* be evaluated more efficiently by other means. Which traits might then be assigned to the interview?

Using reliability data as a criterion, we might first list "intelligence or mental ability" and "academic grades" on the basis of Wagner's (1949) review. On the other hand, it is not clear that these interviewer assessments were made entirely on the basis of the face-to-face interview. Furthermore, it would seem that both of these items of information might well be obtained more reliably from other, more standardized sources. Factors such as "appearance," "manner," "voice," "conversational abilities," "self-expression" and the like would seem to be prime candidates for the interview, but the reliability data on ratings of these items are not impressive. Perhaps the problem is in defining these traits more adequately and training interviewers to assess the qualities one is looking for. Also, ratings of these traits have seldom been the sole purpose of the interview; perhaps reliability would be enhanced if that were the case.

Wagner (1949) reported reliability coefficients of .72 and .87 for "sociability." One of the studies he reviewed (Rundquist, 1947) had specifically limited the scope of the interview to the assessment of this one trait and obtained a validity coefficient of .37. This compared very well with the (concurrent) validities reported by Wagner, being surpassed only by "intelligence or mental ability" and "academic grades." Rundquist advocated limiting the scope of the interview. Similar views have been expressed by Wilkins (1960) and by Rimland (1960). Wilkins was concerned with what could realistically be expected of the interviewer given limited time and information; Rimland's conclusion followed the analysis of weighted factors used in ROTC admission decisions. He felt the interview should be limited to the assessment of "career motivation." In this connection, factor analytic studies usually indicate that not more than four or five dimensions are reliably distinguished by raters. Woodworth, Barron, and MacKinnon (1957) reported five factors, two of which suggest Rundquist's "sociability" and Rimland's "career motivation" factors.

From these and other results, Ulrich and Trumbo (1965) concluded that:

> The recent literature appears to provide the most information on Wagner's (1949) suggestion that the scope of the interview be limited. The results rather consistently indicate two areas which both contribute heavily to interviewer decisions and show greatest evidence of validity. These two areas of assessment may be described roughly as *personal relations* and *motivation to work*. In other words, perhaps the interviewer should seek information on two questions: "What is the applicant's motivation to work?" and "Will he adjust to the social context of the job?" Such an approach would leave the assessment of abilities, aptitudes, experience, and biographical data to other, and, in all likelihood, more reliable and valid sources. (p. 113, emphasis added)

Some more recent findings tend to support this position, but at least one study indicated that interviewers may be able to collect information of a somewhat broader scope. Thus, Grant and Bray (1969) found that information coded from interviews by others yielded ratings on 18 variables. A number of these were meaningfully related to ratings by an assessment staff who had a good deal more information. Specifically, "career motivation, work motivation, control of feelings, and interpersonal skills" were found to depend heavily on the interview. These items were correlated with salary progress, used as a criterion of managerial success. This study also suggests that the interviewer acting as a gatherer and reporter of information may be more successful than when she acts as a clinician, integrating interview and ancillary data into trait ratings, overall ratings, predictions, or decisions. Such data may be combined by another clinical decision maker, or they may be combined actuarially in a statistical prediction. In fact, the interviewer-as-information-gatherer need not have knowledge about the job (or jobs) for which the applicant may be considered, since she may be asked to collect specific information or rate certain specific traits independent of a specific job consideration. Such information could then be used either clinically or actuarially in considering the applicant for each of a number of positions within the organization, providing that two or more vacancies existed.

Another recent study suggests, contrary to earlier factor-analytic studies, that interviewers may be able to discriminate more than the usual four or five assessment dimensions. Howell and Vincent (1970) identified 10 factors that corresponded nearly 1-to-1 with 12 trait ratings and an overall rating. "Interest in career with the organization and ability to work and get along with others" were among the factors. Others were labeled "judgment, voice and speech, appearance, stability and poise, confidence and alertness, originality and ability to deal with professional problems." Thus, factors related to work motivation and interpersonal relations emerged again as areas of promise for the interview. In summary, it would appear that an interview program might be designed primarily to assess aspects of work motivation and interpersonal relations, leaving the assessment of other traits and abilities to other sources of information.

A Systematic Evaluation of an Interview Program

Rather than continuing to summarize psychometric evidence on the interview, it may be well to look in detail at one research program designed to evaluate and improve the interview for selection (Landy, 1976). In addition to providing an example of research on reliability and validity, this study yields new information on a number of the issues raised earlier as factors affecting reliability.

The problem was the selection of patrol officers for a large metropolitan area. This involved the filling of 200 positions each year. Included in the selection procedure is a broad interview conducted by two regular members and a third member, a patrol officer, who is unique to each interview.

The interviewers are expected to rate the applicants on the nine traits shown in the left column of Table 6–3. These traits are given different potential ranges for numerical ratings, from 0 to 5 for "appearance" to 0 to 12 for "experience" and a number of other traits, including a final overall rating of "suitability."

Reliability and Internal Validity. The first steps in the evaluation of this program included an analysis of the internal relations of the ratings. Ratings on each factor were correlated with ratings of overall "suitability" for each of the "regulars" and the patrol officer. The results, which show the contributions of the specific factors to overall ratings, are shown in Table 6–4. They are surprisingly similar for the three raters:
Not only do they agree perfectly in assigning the least weight to "appear-

TABLE 6–3

Correlations between Factors and "Suitability" Rating for Each of Three Raters

	Officer A	Officer B	Patrolmen
Factor	r	r	r
Appearance (0–5)*	.44	.45	.48
Communication skills (0–10)	.68	.71	.66
Education (0–5).......................	.31	.23	.24
Experience (0–12)	.62	.51	.64
Employment (0–12)	.55	.46	.64
Social sensitivity (0–10)	.56	.68	.71
Apparent emotional stability (0–12)	.72	.75	.77
Responsibility–maturity (0–12)	.72	.70	.76
Sincerity of purpose (0–10)	.73	.66	.76

* Potential range of scores.

ance" and "education" (consistent with the range allowed by the form), but also their suitability ratings indicate that they give the largest weights to "apparent emotional stability," "responsibility—maturity," "sincerity of purpose," and "communication skills" in that order. Further analyses indicate that factors 1, 3, 4, and 5 ("appearance," "education," "experience," "employment") contribute relatively little to the suitability decisions. The multiple correlations between these factors and "suitability" for the three interviewers using all nine factors were .90, .89, and .89, respectively. However, special multiple-regression procedures, known as "stepwise analyses," allow one to determine the extent to which the addition of a variable contributes (or fails to contribute) to the overall predictive power of the regression equation. Table 6–4 shows (left column) the multiple Rs obtained for the three variables with the greatest independent contribution for each interviewer. It will be seen that these coefficients are only very slightly smaller than those based on all nine variables. In other words, the decision strategies, as reflected in the suitability ratings of the interviewers, can be predicted or described as well with the three as with the nine factor ratings.

Internal Cross-Validation. Do these results hold up or are they somewhat

TABLE 6–4

Equations and Cross-Validated Rs for Each of Three Raters

Rater	Original R	Equation*	Cross-validated R†
Officer 1	.89	$.68X_7 + .51X_8 + .71X_9 - 4.73$	.87
Officer 2	.86	$.75X_7 + .47X_8 + .63X_9 - 4.57$	.72
Patrolmen	.87	$+ .55X_8 + .64X_9 - 3.90$	.79

* Comprising the three most important variables as determined by step-up multiple-regression procedures.
† $N = 100$ for the holdout sample.

fortuitous sampling errors? Evidence that the strategies are real and consistent is shown in the right-hand column of Table 6–4. Here the cross-validation results are presented for the three interviewers using a new sample of 100 interviews. Cross-validations of the three-predictor equations are very high, showing only a small amount of shrinkage. These values were obtained by predicting suitability ratings in a new sample using the predictor equations obtained in the original sample.

Convergent and Discriminant Validity. The intercorrelations between raters and traits are shown in Table 6–5. From this matrix one can get a picture of the internal validity of the interview as it is used in this setting. Are the three interviewers rating the applicants in the same way? The answer is seen in the intercorrelations between raters rating the same traits. These coefficients have been circled in Table 6–5 for easy identification. It will be seen that in every case they are positive and above .50. Thus, the answer is yes, the raters do show a fair amount of agreement in rating the traits, although there is some room for improvement. The median

TABLE 6–5
Multitrait, Multirater Matrix

Variable \ Variable	Officer 1				Officer 2				Patrolman			
	6	7	8	9	6	7	8	9	6	7	8	9
Officer 1												
6												
7	54											
8	37	60										
9	37	43	46									
Officer 2												
6	(67)	48	40	36								
7	50	(62)	51	41	67							
8	43	52	(72)	41	45	57						
9	30	40	43	(81)	39	42	40					
Patrolman												
6	(58)	54	40	44	(54)	53	44	37				
7	49	(58)	48	49	52	(56)	52	44	68			
8	39	52	(56)	48	42	50	(60)	44	60	70		
9	31	46	48	(72)	36	45	46	(65)	50	59	63	

correlation between the ratings of the two regular interviewers was .73, whereas the medians for each regular with the ratings of the patrol officers were .60 and .60.

Can the raters discriminate one trait from another? This notion of discriminant validity is evaluated by comparing the correlations of a given trait with the other traits to the interrater agreement on that trait. High correlations among the traits are an indication of *halo* in the ratings, that is, of failure to discriminate one trait from another. Unless there is evidence of higher agreement between raters who rate the *same* trait than there is between different traits rated by the *same* rater, we must be concerned that the raters are not able to distinguish between the traits. Evidence for halo in these data is largely limited to the ratings of the patrolman. The intercorrelations in his trait ratings exceed his agreement with the other two raters in a number of instances. Meanwhile, the two regular interviewers show consistent evidence of discriminant validity. This is not too surprising: the patrolman sees only one interviewee and has no opportunity to establish a frame of reference (or behavioral referents) for each of the traits. These are the conditions where we would expect an overall impression on an outstanding trait to have a strong influence on the ratings of other traits.

External Validity. The final question addressed in this study was that of the external validity of the interviewers' ratings as evaluated against some criteria of actual on-the-job performance. The criterion data consisted of supervisors' ratings of the patrol officers on eight performance dimensions. These dimensions are listed in the left-hand column of Table 6–6. The remaining columns of Table 6–6 show the statistically significant correlations between the ratings on the interview factors by one personnel officer (A) and the "composite" patrol officer (P) and each of the performance dimensions. Each of these is a validity coefficient indicating how the ratings by an interviewer on one factor predict the criterion ratings on one dimension of performance.

There are a number of interesting points in these data. First, they indicate that interviewer ratings can have predictive validity: 43 of the 160 correlations were significantly different from zero. Moreover, the *pattern* of these correlations makes a good deal of sense. Both interviewers' ratings of "appearance" are predictive of the supervisors' ratings of "demeanor-on-the-street," ratings of "communications" are predictive of subsequent ratings on communications in performance of the job, ratings of prior employment predict job knowledge and judgment ratings, and so on. The fact that more of the 160 coefficients were not significant is no indictment of the interviewers; we would be surprised if, for example, ratings of appearance were predictive of job knowledge or judgment. This would suggest a general halo effect in both predictor and criterion ratings. The "overall suitability" ratings of both interviewers are modestly related to ratings on only two dimensions, demeanor and communications, and even these criterion dimensions are predicted better by ratings on some of the specific factors. In

TABLE 6–6

Rater Cue Validities: Significant Correlations between Interview (Factor) Ratings and Supervisory (Criterion) Ratings

Performance Dimension	Appearance A*	Appearance P	Communications A	Communications P	Education A	Education P	Experience A	Experience P	Employment A	Employment P	Social Sensitivity A	Social Sensitivity P	Educational Stability A	Educational Stability P	Responsibility A	Responsibility P	Sincerity A	Sincerity P	Overall Suitability A	Overall Suitability P
Job knowledge				.27			.32		.25	.23	.34							.23		
Judgment							.25		.30	.26	.25									
Initiative				.26			.26				.24									
Dependability							.22		.21											
Demeanor	.24	.26		.25				.25		.24	.34			.27		.27		.36	.24	.33
Attitude							.23		.22											
Relations with others							.26		.28											
Communication			.36	.33			.36	.34	.33	.28	.37		.35	.29		.22		.24	.30	.38

* A is one of the administrative officers; P is the composite patrol officer.

other words, the clinical combination of information (as reflected in the overall suitability ratings) yields validities that are uniformly lower than individual cues (as reflected in specific factor ratings).

The data in Table 6–6 also indicate that the two interviewers have different patterns of cue validities. Interviewer A's ratings of experience and employment record yield his best predictions, whereas the patrolmen predict well from ratings of communication, employment, social sensitivity, and sincerity of purpose. That is, the officer and the patrolmen are picking up valid information from different cues. This suggests that predictions of performance ratings might be improved by using predictors combining different factor ratings of the two interviewers. In fact, Landy found that to be the case: combined predictors yielded validity coefficients ranging from .21 to .54 with a median of .40. Thus, for example, by combining interviewer A's ratings on "appearance" with patrolmen P's ratings on "social sensitivity" and "sincerity of purpose," the performance dimension "demeanor-on-the-street" was predicted with a validity of .46. Meanwhile, the highest single-cue validity for predicting demeanor was .36 (patrolman rating "sincerity") and the highest validity from overall recommendation was .33 (patrolman rating "overall suitability").

These results represent some of the most positive findings for the validity of the interview. They strongly suggest that interviewers' ratings can be used to predict specific dimensions of job performance. They also indicate that different interviewers will see somewhat different cues—will look for different things—perhaps as a function of their positions and responsibilities in the organization. Thus, the personnel representative may look more to experience and past employment as indications of whether the applicant will need special training, be a turnover risk, or the like, while the patrolman is more responsive to cues such as communications and social sensitivity, indicative of how the applicant will behave as a buddy patrolman on the street.

Equal Employment Opportunity and the Interview

Several times we have alluded to the potential for unfair discrimination when the selection interview is used for decision making. This issue is of particular concern in the interview because so many decisions are left up to the discretion of the interviewer: decisions about questions to ask and follow-up questions, decisions as to the length of the interview, the number of questions asked, and often the ultimate decision: whether to employ the applicant or not. Arvey (1979) has reviewed all of the available literature concerning unfair discrimination in the interview. He cites the Washington State Human Relations Commission as an example of a body that has carefully regulated the nature of the preemployment interview. That Commission has stated that it is unfair and illegal to make the following inquiries unless they can be shown to be job related (valid):

1. Information regarding arrests.
2. Information regarding citizenship.

3. Information regarding spouse's salary, children, child-care arrangements, or dependents.
4. Overgeneral information (e.g., "Do you have any handicaps?"), which might highlight health conditions unrelated to job performance.
5. Marital status of the applicant.
6. Military discharge information.
7. Information related to pregnancy.
8. Whether the applicant owns or rents a home.

All of these pieces of information might be used to the disadvantage of one minority group or another. Consequently, unless they are related to job success, the answers to these questions might result in differential hiring rates for minority and majority applicants.

One might expect that the applicant groups suffering the greatest adverse impact are nonwhites, women, and older applicants. Arvey reviewed research dealing with these three variables and came to the following conclusions:

1. The older applicant is often described in less favorable terms than the younger applicant; this suggests that decisions are often less favorable in the case of the older applicant.
2. Women are generally given lower evaluation than men when these candidates have similar or identical qualifications.
3. There seems to be an interaction between sex and type of job being considered that affects evaluations. Female applicants for historically male roles (police officer) receive lower evaluations than male applicants for the same jobs. Arvey calls this the "sex-congruency" hypothesis; we saw similar dynamics operating in the performance evaluation process.
4. Few studies have directly examined applicant race as an influence on interview evaluations. The evidence which was available did not indicate that nonwhite applicants were at a disadvantage in the interview.
5. The qualification of the applicant plays a major role in the eventual applicant evaluation (which is a relief!).
6. Little is known concerning handicapped applicants. Anecdotal evidence suggests that they may be viewed more positively due to higher motivation than the normal applicant (consider the obvious obstacle that they had to overcome in applying for work at all).

In summary, Arvey's review might be taken as an indication that there is a lot to worry about with regard to the fairness of the employment interview. At the very least, employment managers must be aware of these potential pitfalls.

THE APPLICATION BLANK

The application blank is generally recognized as having three purposes. First, it can be used to determine whether an applicant is hireable, that is, whether he meets minimum hiring requirements as set by the organization or by law. For example, the company may require a high school education as a minimum educational requirement, the state may require a chauffeur's license, and the federal government a social security registration or security clearance for a particular job. Usually the issue of hireability can be determined with a small number of questions. Information dealing with other questions need not be included in the initial form: one does not need to know the number of dependents or marital status of the applicant (unless these determine his hireability) for the purposes of withholding tax until it is determined that he is hireable, or, indeed, until he is actually hired. Thus, it might be well to consider a preemployment blank where information essential to the hireability issue is obtained, and a postemployment blank to obtain the information needed for personnel programs and the like.

A second purpose of the application blank has been as a supplement to and preparation for the interview. From this view the application blank provides "leads" to be pursued in the face-to-face interview, or, put another way, the interview may be used to check on first impressions gained from the application blank and other credentials or psychometric data. Thus, McMurray (1945), in his well-known plea for the "patterned" interview, recommended that the interviewer become familiar with the applicant's credentials in preparation for the interview. At any rate, used in this way, information from the application blank is combined with data and impressions from the interview in a clinical evaluation by the interviewer. In this case, its contribution to the impressions, ratings, or predictions of the interviewer are confounded with other sources of information, and therefore not readily determined.

A third purpose of the application blank is to obtain biographical data and work-history information that may be used actuarially to predict some assessable aspect of job proficiency. That is, the application blank can be used to gather items of personal data that are predictive of performance, turnover, absenteeism, or whatever, and that can be combined and weighted into a multiple predictor, with or without other (e.g., psychometric) types of information. In this sense, the information that the applicant has four dependents or has held five different jobs in the past three years is treated in the same way as a score of 78 on a test of some ability—potentially, both items of information may be predictive of some aspect of success.

These three purposes represent criteria for deciding what items should be included in the application blank. Here is a list of specific questions that may be asked of items that are candidates for inclusion on an application blank.[1] If an item cannot be justified on the basis of a positive answer to at least one of the questions, it should be rejected.

1. Is the item necessary for identifying the applicant?
2. Is it necessary for screening out those who are ineligible under the

---

[1] Adapted from Eileen Ahern, *Handbook of personnel forms and records* (New York: American Management Association, 1949), p. 17.

company's basic hiring policies? Specifically, what policy does it pertain to?

3. Does it help to decide whether the candidate is qualified?
4. Is it based on analysis of the job or jobs for which the applicant will be selected?
5. Has it been pretested on the company's employees and found to correlate with success?
6. Will the information be used? How?
7. Is the application form the proper place for it?
8. Will answers provide information not obtained in another step in the selection procedure—for example, through interviews, tests, or medical examinations?
9. Is the information needed for selection at all, or should it be obtained at induction, or even later?
10. Is it probable that applicants' replies will be reliable?
11. Does the question conform to any applicable federal or state legislation?

Evaluating Personal Data Items

It should be apparent that personal data items can be evaluated in the same way as test scores. The validity of the item could be determined as well as its contribution to a multiple prediction equation, or a cutoff value could be set for use in a multiple-cutoff or a multiple-hurdles strategy. While these procedures would be appropriate, they have not been the practice with personal data items. Instead, a relatively simple method has been used in most cases.

The Horizontal Percent Method. Just as with the analysis of items in a test, the items on an application blank can be evaluated in terms of their ability to discriminate among criterion scores or criterion groups. Items that do not discriminate have zero validity for that criterion measure and should not be used; items that have high discriminability should receive greater weights than items that show modest discriminability, that is, low correlations with the criterion. The horizontal percent method (Stead & Shartle, 1940) provides a simple means of assessing the validity of personal data items and a straightforward rationale for weighting each item in a composite score.

The first step, as with any validation procedure, is to choose a criterion measure. Since most of the research on personal data items has used a criterion of job tenure, we will follow the example. Keep in mind, however, that any single or multiple criterion could be used. What items of personal data might be predictive of job tenure (or turnover)? In most personnel offices this question could be answered by identifying two samples of employees, those who remained with the organization more than one year and those who left within the first year. The next step is simply to compare these two criterion groups ("good" and "poor" workers) with respect to personal data items. Table 6–7 provides a hypothetical example, using sex of the applicant as the personal datum. In the sample presented, 40 employees were male, 60 female. Each of these subgroups is tallied under good and poor worker categories, depending on whether they stayed one year or more with the organization. In the sixth column of the figure, the percentage of good workers to the total within each subgroup is calculated. Thus, we see that 20 of the 40 men, or 50 percent, were "successful," while 45 of the 60 women, or 75 percent, were successful. A woman, then, has a higher probability of being successful on this criterion than a man, and women should receive more points. This is reflected in the last column of Figure 6–3, headed "Weight." The category "female" is given a weight equal to the percentage obtained in the previous column (75), while males receive a lower weight (50). The rationale of this scoring procedure may be clearer if we consider an alternative outcome: suppose that of the 65 successful employees 26 were men and 39 women. This would result in percentages of 65 for each category, and the weights would be equal for men and women, reflecting the fact that this item was not differentially predictive. (In this case, it would not make sense to score the item at all, once its lack of validity was determined.)

The validity of other items could be determined and weighted scores assigned in precisely the same way. Of course, the method is not limited to dichotomized variables; age, for example, might be categorized into three or four levels representing approximately equal proportions of the total sample. Likewise, the criterion measure could be represented in three or more levels, such as zero to two, three to five, or six or more absences per quarter. England and Patterson (1960) have described the development of scoring keys for application blanks. Essentially, a stencil or overlay can be prepared for each job, such that only those items that are valid for a given job appear through the windows of the stencil and the appropriate weights to assign to the various response categories are listed beside each window. It should be emphasized that neither the items nor the weights determined to be appropriate to one job or labor grade can be assumed to hold for other jobs. Rather, validation, as with psychological test data, must be determined empirically for each job or labor grade. In fact, validation of personal data items on a large heterogeneous sample and the subsequent use of such data to select job applicants might well prove to be

TABLE 6–7
Evaluation of Personal Data Item by the Horizontal Percentage Method

Personal Data Item	Categories	"Successes" (+1 Year)	"Failures" (−1 Year)	Total	Successes	Weight
Sex	Males	20	20	40	20/40 = 50%	50
	Females	45	15	60	45/60 = 75%	75

discriminatory with respect to a given job classification within the sample. Thus, for example, sex might be predictive of tenure in the general sample, leading to a bias against hiring women, but among the machinists in the sample, sex is unrelated (or even related in the other direction) to tenure. Such procedures are not only discriminatory and therefore contrary to Equal Employment Opportunity Commission (EEOC) guidelines, but they also operate against the interests of the company. Kirchner and Dunnette (1957) validated 15 items against turnover among female office employees, including clerical, stenographic, secretarial, and personal contact. They concluded that the same items and scoring weights could be used in the selection of employees in all of these jobs. However, even though they had a total sample of 268, they did not determine the validity of the weights for each of the specific jobs.

Studies of the Validity of Personal Data. Personal data items may appear in many different forms. Some deal with obvious life-history items such as age, education, number of brothers and sisters, and parents' occupations. Presumably these items are easily verifiable. There are other items, however, that request self-reports from the applicant that are not as easily verified. Examples of these items would be: "Were you viewed positively by most of your high school teachers?" "Were your parents happy with your schoolwork?" "Were you considered a 'joiner' in your circle of friends?" Traditionally, application blanks have been made up of the former type of items—uncomplicated life-history items that require little or no evaluation by the applicant; they simply require a reasonable long-term memory. In the past decade, however, more and more organizations have been looking into the possibility that some of the other type of self-report items are valid for predicting success in various positions. This latter class of items is generally known as "biodata" (short for "biographical data") and often includes information far removed from job activities. In the last chapter, we described a model for placement that was developed by Schoenfeldt (1974). This model placed people in jobs according to interests and life-history information. The Schoenfeldt items would be examples of biodata. The distinction between the more straightforward factual items dealing with life history and the less verifiable and more evaluative type of biodata item may be important. Unfortunately, it is seldom considered in reports of application-blank validation studies. We will return to this point shortly, but it might be useful first to review some of the research on the use of the application blank for selection.

Personal data items have been studied most thoroughly with respect to sales positions and most often using a criterion of job tenure. In what was probably the earliest study, according to Bellows and Estep (1954), *Public Personnel Studies* (1925) described the findings of the Phoenix Mutual Life Insurance Company in the selection of insurance salesmen. Twelve personal data variables were studied with a sample of 500 salesmen. It was found that age, years of previous selling experience, and number of investments were related to success as judged by the company. New hires between 30 and 38 years of age with more than six years of experience and three or more investments had the greatest probability of being successful. The investigators used the "percentage successful" to score each of these variables (and a few more that did not discriminate) to obtain composite scores. Table 6–8 summarizes the results, based on 100 "successes" versus 100 "failures." It can be seen that of those salesmen who obtained scores of 640 or less, none were successful. Thus, had a cutting score of 641 been used to screen applicants, 31 failures would have been rejected and 100 of the remaining 169 would have been successful (a success ratio of 59 percent as compared with 50 percent in the original sample). Similarly, had a cutoff score of 671 been set, 76 of the remaining 103 salesmen would have been successful (74 percent).

Bellows and Estep (1954) also report a study of office equipment salesmen in which age, interviewer's estimate, marital status, and ratings by former employers were predictive of success, defined in terms of short-term or long-term employment with the company. The successful salesman was apt to be over 25 years of age, rated "excellent" by the interviewer, married or engaged, and rated "mostly superior" by his former employer. It will be noted that two of these four variables represent ratings rather than objective biographical data. Nonetheless, they could be combined with age and marital status to yield a modest validity ($r = .27$) for the composite score. The authors acknowledge the modesty of this validity coefficient. However, they point out that it was achieved over and above whatever valid selection procedures were already in use (the company accepted only

TABLE 6–8

The Relationship of Composite Scores Made by 100 Life Insurance Salesmen Who Were Successes and 100 Life Insurance Salesmen Who Were Failures

			SSSSSSSSS SSSSSSSSS SSSSSSSSS SSSSSSSSS
Successes			SSSSSSSSS
		SSSSSSSSS SSSSSSSSS SSSS 24	SSSSSSSSS SSSSSSSSS SSSSS 76
Failures	FFFFFFFFFF FFFFFFFFFF FFFFFFFFFF F 31	FFFFFFFFFF FFFFFFFFFF FFFFFFFFFF FFFFFFFFFF FF 42	FFFFFFFFFF FFFFFFFFFF FFFFFFF 27
	Scores 579–640	*Scores* 641–670	*Scores* 671–732

Source: A method of rating the history and achievements of applicants for positions, *Public Personnel Studies*, 1925, *3*, 209.

"This kind of background is OK if you're a success later but it ain't so hot now."

Reprinted by permission The Wall Street Journal

college graduates in a rather intensive and selective program). At the same time, it was found that the number of accounting courses, which had been used as a basis for selection, was actually *negatively* related to a composite criterion of success.

Another false impression that may have influenced the organization's selection strategy was reported by Marrow and French (1946). A generally accepted stereotype among supervisors in the company was that women over 30 could not keep up with production, had high turnover and absenteeism, and were difficult to teach. The reason for this stereotype is not known, but the researchers showed that it had no basis in reality: the women over 30 had higher production, lower turnover, fewer days lost to illness, and learned new operations more quickly than the younger women. The stereotype that acted against hiring older women had actually been working against the company—if anything, the selection strategy should have been biased to *favor* the older women in a manner consistent with their higher criterion scores.

In another early report, Viteles (1932) used biographical data to predict the average weekly earnings of taxicab drivers. The results indicated that a cutoff score for the valid application-blank items would have rejected 60 percent of the poor drivers but only about 20 percent of the average and best drivers. These results are especially significant since they were obtained after Viteles had failed to find any practically useful validity for either mental ability or accident-proneness tests.

Cascio (1976) reported substantial relationships between life-history items and turnover for clerical employees. The predictors were: age, marital status, children's ages, education, tenure on previous job, previous salary, presence of a friend or relative in the company, location of residence, home ownership, and length of time at the present address. He attempted to use this information to predict those employees who would stay with the organization for longer than one year. He was able to look at the predictor-criterion relationships separately for a sample of minority workers ($N = 80$) and a sample of majority workers ($N = 80$). All subjects were women. The results appear in Table 6–9. As you can see, Cascio was able to predict who would stay and who would leave. The trustworthiness of this prediction scheme is shown by the cross-validated correlation coefficients, which represent the validity of the prediction scheme on an independent sample of subjects.

These data are encouraging for two reasons. Not only do they demonstrate the potential value of application-blank information, but they also indicate that application blanks can be used to make employment decisions in a manner that is fair to both majority and minority applicants.

Cascio's items were fairly traditional and would not be obvious targets for rejected applicants claiming unfair treatment due to minority status. A study by B. Nevo (1976) provides an example of items that might come under substantial attack from rejected applicants. The study looked at the validity of biographical information for identifying individuals who would be successful in the Israeli army. The criterion was rank attained by the time the individual left the army. Data for male and female soldiers were examined separately. Most of the items dealt with characteristics of the subjects' parents. These included father's and mother's age, father's and mother's education, and so on. One item in particular would send chills down the spine of most personnel administrators. It requested information regarding the father's country of origin—i.e., *nationality*. This represents one of the categories of protected applicants under the EEOC guidelines. On the surface, this type of item might represent *prima facie* evidence of intent to discriminate unfairly. Many employers are currently concerned about just this issue. They carefully comb their application blanks for any hints of items that might be interpreted as potentially unfair discriminators. Cascio (1976) points out that employers are permitted to use even the most patently discriminatory items if they can be demonstrated to be job related. Unfortunately, theory and practice would probably clash on this

TABLE 6–9

Correlation of Application Blank Responses with Turnover

	Validity Coefficient	Cross-Validity Coefficient
Majority sample	.77	.56
Minority sample	.79	.58

issue. While Cascio has a reasonable argument based on the guidelines, there is another argument that is equally compelling and could also be made on the basis of the guidelines: employers who are engaging in a personnel practice that has an adverse impact on a particular minority group are required to search for mechanisms for making the decision which are equally valid but have less of an adverse impact. Thus, in this case the employer might have to expend considerable effort and money to show that the application blank is the most valid device available. It is possible that the organization might spend more money in comparison of the application blank to other techniques than it did in the development of the application blank in the first place! The wise employer will avoid the *appearance* as well as the practice of unfair discrimination.

Do Applicants Lie? One of the possibilities that has nagged researchers and personnel managers has been the degree to which the answers to application-blank items are either intentionally or unintentionally distorted. Do people actually report the truth, or do they shade it in a manner that makes them look like better applicants? Cascio (1975) examined the application blanks for 112 applicants to the Dade County, Florida, police department. He examined 17 items and verified the answers to these items for the 112 applicants. He found a very high correlation between fact and self-report. The median correlation between the applicant's answer and the verified truthful answer to the question was .94. Cascio took this as evidence that items that can be easily verified are unlikely to yield distorted responses. This finding may have been a little optimistic, since the applicants were being considered for a position as police officers and were aware that background checks were common in the employment procedure. Nevertheless, it is a comforting finding.

As you might suspect, there is some contradictory evidence as well. Cohen and Lefkowitz (1977) examined the distortion on biodata items and distortions on a standard personality test, the MMPI. They were able to show significant correlations between distortions on the two instruments. As a general principle, it might be wise for the employer to include at least some items that can be easily verified or to verify all responses of a sample of applicants to assess possible distortion.

Cross-Validation and Critical Scores. A study by Fleishman and Berniger (1960) illustrates two methodological refinements with biographical data and raises a question about a third. These researchers studied the application blanks of 120 women office employees at Yale University. The sample was selected so that half were long-tenure (two to four years and still on the job) and half short-tenure (less than two years; 67 percent less than one year) employees. Several items were found to differentiate between these two groups, including local address (reflecting distance from work), age, occupation of husband, number of children, and age of children. Some of these items are shown in Table 6–10. The scoring method represents a simplification of the horizontal percent method: only the numbers from −3 to +3 are assigned to the item categories, depending on the

TABLE 6–10

Comparison of Item Responses by Long- and Short-Tenure Office Employees

Application Blank Items	Percentage of		Weight Assigned to Response
	Short-tenure Group	Long-tenure Group	
Local Address			
Within City	39	62	+2
Outlying Suburbs	50	36	−2
Age			
Under 20	35	8	−3
21–25	38	32	−1
26–30	8	2	−1
31–35	7	10	0
35 and over	11	48	+3
Previous Salary			
Under $2,000	31	30	0
$2,000–3,000	41	38	0
$3,000–4,000	13	12	0
Over $4,000	4	4	0
Age of Children			
Preschool	12	4	−3
Public School	53	33	−3
High School or Older	35	63	+3

Source: Fleishman, E. A., & Berniger, J. One way to reduce office turnover. *Personnel*, 1960, *37*, 63–69. Reprinted by permission of the publisher from *Personnel*, May/June 1960. © 1960 by the American Management Association, Inc.

direction and extent of discrimination between the criterion groups. It should be noted that the highest score (for the items shown) would be obtained by a woman over 35 whose children were of high school age or older and who lived within the city. Actual scores ranged from −17 to 27 and had a validity coefficient of .77 for the tenure criterion.

The cross-validation study consisted of drawing another sample of long- and short-tenure employees, scoring their application blanks for the same items and, with the weights assigned in the original study, then determining the relation of these scores to the criterion. The results were rewarding: most of the same items continued to discriminate in the second study and the validity coefficient shrank only from .77 to .57 in the new sample. Establishing an appropriate cutoff score depends, of course, on supply and demand in the labor market and other practical considerations. Independent of this, however, one can, as the authors did, determine the cutoff point that will provide the *maximum differentiation* between the two groups. This score was located at +4; 68 percent of the high-tenure group had scores of +4 or greater, while 78 percent of the short-tenure group had scores below +4. In other words, with this cutoff three of four hires would have been long tenure, while over two-thirds of those rejected would have been short-tenure employees.

The methodological problem with the simple summated scoring method used in biographical data research can be seen in Table 6–10. Two of the items are *age* and *age of children*. Now, it is quite apparent that responses to these items are apt to be very highly correlated. To the extent that they are related, such items provide redundant information. In the absurd case, *age in years* and *age in months* might both be used in a weighted score, or *age* might be entered twice. In either case, the second item is not contributing to the validity in a way suggested by the weight assigned to it. As we have seen (Chapter 5), the likelihood that the validity of a multiple predictor will be increased by adding a new item of information is inversely related to the correlation of the new item with the old.

Durability of Biographical Item Validities. Changes in the applicant population, job market, and the jobs themselves all suggest that validities are dynamic, not static. This should be as true of biographical data as of test predictors. Periodic revalidation, especially where changes have occurred, is essential if one is to be certain that decision making is based on valid data. In the study cited earlier, Kirchner and Dunnette (1957) found a high degree of agreement between the items that discriminated between short- and long-tenure employees in two successive years, but the predictive validity dropped from .74 to .61. By the next year the validity was down to .38 (Dunnette et al., 1960) and 5 years after the initial study the original items correlated only .07 with the criterion (Wernimont, 1962). A revised scoring key gave a validity of .39 but included only 3 of the original 15 items. On the other hand, Buel (1964) found that, despite an interval of 5 years and a relocation of the office, a validity of .33 was obtained for the items that had originally yielded a coefficient of .49.

Another durability issue concerns whether biographical questionnaires are limited to local use. If a new one must be developed for each circumstance and plant location, the costs begin to approach the benefits of the procedure. Hinrichs, Haanpera, and Sonkin (1976) were able to show some substantial validity for biographical information predictors of sales success in samples from several different countries. The same questionnaire and the same weights were applied to each sample, and substantial validities were found for Swedish, Finnish, Norwegian, and American sales personnel. The authors suggested that the results would have been even more encouraging if they had developed individual weights for each country. Unfortunately, most application blanks used in organizations are not constructed with statistical prediction in mind. Therefore, there is little attention paid to changing, refining, or standardizing the application blank as an instrument. Given the low cost of potentially high gains, organizations might be well advised to pursue the application blank more aggressively as a potential predictor of job success.

Tullar and Barrett (1976) have taken the concept of biographical information one step further. They asked applicants for a sales position to guess what they would be doing in five years; Tullar and Barrett called the responses "Future Autobiographies." The applicants were asked to consider vocation, avocation, jobs, goals, interests, and concerns in their answers. The criteria were rating scales dealing with topics such as industry knowledge, product knowledge, and personal relations. In all, there were 10 criteria of sales success as rated by sales supervisors. The future autobiographies of the applicants were scored on several different categories. One of these categories was labelled "agency" and was defined as the degree to which the individual felt that he had control over the future. The "agency" score was significantly correlated with 7 of the 10 criteria! The researchers concluded that people who describe their future in a positive manner are more likely to be successful in sales positions. There may be some hope for the optimists of the world after all! This approach presents an intriguing alternative to traditional application blanks.

Some Additional Comments on Biographical Data. The utility of biographical data for predicting job tenure and, to a lesser extent, job proficiency, has been adequately demonstrated. Identifying a number of discriminating items leads to a "sketch" of the most promising applicants, and items such as "amount of life insurance," "hobbies," or "leisure-time activities" may lead to inferences about more basic characteristics of the individual.

Lee and Booth (1974) provide a dramatic example of the potential economic advantages of the weighted application blank. They attempted to predict turnover among clerical employees, using an application blank. They were able to estimate the costs of turnover through various cost accounting procedures. These costs included things like recruiting costs, wages to trainees during training, wages to trainers during training, fringe benefits, and so on. Individuals who leave shortly after completing the training program are not able to offset training costs through productive effort. Therefore, it is to the advantage of an organization to reduce turnover. Lee and Booth were able to demonstrate potential savings of $250,000 over a 25-month period through the use of a simple application form. While part of this savings was based on the large number of applicants (1,700 for 400 positions), it is still impressive evidence regarding the potential of the application blank as a selection device.

While the present review has been concerned with the actuarial evaluation of the application blank, others have proposed clinical evaluations. Thus, Lipsitt, Rogers, and Kentner (1964) describe indicators of "energy," "orality," "aggressiveness," and "narcissism" from application-blank responses, while others would interpret the style in filling out the blank or even the handwriting. For the most part, these clinical approaches lack either concurrent or predictive validity evidence as compared with the actuarial, but a sterile empiricism that refuses to ask what it is that the biographical items tell us about the individuals may not realize the full potential of the method.

Biographical information studies typically begin with current (and former) employees who were selected by whatever strategy may have been in use, including the application-blank items. For this reason, studies may be performed on samples that represent a restricted range of the variables under study. It is not possible to know how rejected applicants may have scored on the criterion measure. However, it is possible to compare the biographical data of rejected and accepted applicants. Such comparisons could lead to a description of the strategy of the decision maker, to the identification of certain biases, and/or to the demonstration that selection decisions do not discriminate unfairly against certain groups of applicants.

WORK SAMPLE AND SITUATIONAL TESTS

Work Sample Tests

As the name implies, work sample tests measure job skills by taking a sample of behavior under realistic joblike conditions. Actually, the performance may not be measured at the job station, but instead on a standard test machine and with a standardized task. For example, applicants for the job of sewing-machine operator might be given a standard set of tasks reflecting the various techniques required on the job.

Work sample tests have been used both as predictors of job performance and as criteria for job proficiency. As predictors, they are obviously designed to assess present skill achievement, not aptitude or potential. Therefore, they would be of greatest use in situations in which experienced workers were being recruited. The work sample test is a simple demonstration of proficiency under standardized, controlled conditions, and comparisons can be made with accumulated normative data. As criterion measures, work sample tests provide a means of overcoming machine contamination and factors due to the interdependence of jobs. That is, they provide standardized tasks to be administered under standardized conditions, whereas performance on the job may be biased by a poor machine or inept co-workers. They also provide a solution to the problem of equating performance on jobs involving somewhat different tasks but basically the same skills. Thus, sewing-machine operators sewing pajama tops may be compared with those sewing nightshirts, providing that the same sort of stitching is involved.

The limitation of the work sample test as a criterion measure may be apparent. While the work sample test may provide an accurate assessment of what the employee *can do* (that is her skill level), there is no assurance that her test score reflects what she *will do* on the job. While we may assume that being capable of skillful performance is intrinsically rewarding and should be an incentive to perform, it is also possible that when the skill requirements are low or moderate, even the most skillful worker may become bored and unmotivated. Yet, under the artificial conditions of the work sample test, they may be motivated to "show their stuff." Naturally, the same arguments can be raised against work samples as predictors: they measure the ability but not the motivational determinant of on-the-job performance. It may well be, however, that those who have been motivated to learn a set of skills and who were motivated to perform them in the work sample test are at least more likely to find practicing the skill on the job a satisfying experience. Some indirect evidence of this with respect to job-information tests (rather than job-skill work sample tests) was summarized by Ghiselli and Brown (1948). They found significant validities for supervisors' ratings of proficiency for 6 of 8 jobs with a median of .33. Apparently, proficient workers are knowledgeable about their jobs (or vice versa), and this may be true for skill as well.

A programmatic use of work sample tests has been reported by the Jewish Employment and Vocational Service of Philadelphia (1968). Designed for use with the handicapped and the hard-core unemployed, the testing program is presented in conjunction with a vocational counseling program. The testing setting is realistic; complete with a time clock and workbenches, it resembles a small job shop. The test battery consists of 28 work sample tasks administered over a two-week period. The strategy is one of beginning with the simplest test—the assembling of three sizes of nuts, bolts and washers—and progressing to increasingly more complex tasks. The tests are designed to measure potential skills in 14 general industrial categories, including assembly-disassembly, bindery, clerical, display and printing, electrical, industrial housekeeping, layout design and drafting, mailroom, mechanical, packing, sorting, structural development, textile, tailoring, and metal work. The tests were first developed in the 1930s for testing refugees who could not speak English, later adapted for use with the physically and mentally handicapped, and are now used with clients whose reading ability is below the sixth-grade level.

The work sample tests, as they are used at the evaluation center, also function as situational tests in that, in addition to objective performance measures, the clients are rated on their relationships with co-workers and supervisors, personal habits, work habits, motivation, attention span, and a number of other traits. Thus, the vocational counselor and the potential employer receive a wide variety of data in addition to scores from the work sample battery.

What evidence is there that the work sample evaluation aids the disadvantaged applicants? The staff of the evaluation center report a study that compared the employment records of clients who had only the vocational counseling with those who had counseling and the work sample evaluation. They found that 40 percent of the latter group of 268 were placed on jobs, as compared with only 23 percent of the control (counseling-only) group. "Early returns" on the tenure of these two groups did not show any advantage for either group: after three months approximately 85 percent of both groups remained on the job.

Situational Tests

We have intentionally grouped work sample and situational tests together in this section. In a sense, situational tests are the work samples of the managerial and professional occupations. Although the problems provided in situational tests are not always intended to be realistic samples of problems on the job, there is some evidence that they should share this characteristic with work sample tests. Both work sample and situational tests that do present realistic samples of the job are more easily defended with respect to EEOC guidelines than are standard psychological tests.

Situational tests may be individual problem-solving situations, such as the "in-basket" test (Meyer, 1961), in which the applicant responds to a standardized set of situations such as he might find in the in-basket on his desk, or group problem-solving (or discussion) situations. The best example of the latter is the "Leaderless Group Discussion" (LGD) method developed and investigated by Bass (1954). In this method, observers rate the behavior of each individual in the group, usually in areas of "individual prominence," "group goal facilitation," and "sociability." Both interrater and test-retest reliabilities tend to be high (Bass, 1954; Greenwood & McNamara, 1967; Bray & Grant, 1966). Greenwood & McNamara (1967) found that nonprofessional observer-assessors were as reliable as professionals. However, interrater agreement seems to depend in an important way on the size of the group. Thus, Bass and Norton (1951) found increases in reliability from two-person groups ($r = .72$) to a maximum with six-person groups ($r = .89$), and Carter et al. (1951) reported similar results for four- ($r = .70$) and eight- ($r = .85$) person groups. Test-retest estimates seem to follow the same pattern. Furthermore, the greater the similarity (problem, personnel, etc.) of the retest to the test situation, the higher the reliability estimate, as would be expected (Bass & Norton, 1951).

Bass (1954) reported evidence of validity of LGD for a number of jobs and occupational levels, including shipyard foremen, oil-refinery administrators, administrative trainees, and civil and foreign service administrators. These validities tended to be somewhat lower than for peer nominations. More recently, Bray and Grant (1966) reported that both in-basket and group situational tests proved to be predictive of assessment ratings (internal validity) and of salary progress, taken as one criterion of job proficiency (external validity). In fact, the results with these two techniques yielded consistently higher validities than with a number of standardized ability tests and personality questionnaires, though it was concluded that both sources of information contributed to the assessment ratings that were quite predictive of progress in management. While reliability seems to be relatively independent of the *content* of the group situational test, suggesting—as Carlson (1972) pointed out—that observers can agree on ratings or rankings of "general person quality" probably involving a "valid halo" effect, validity depends somewhat more on content. Thus, Freeburg (1969) found that a relevant task (mathematics problems) not only was better for predicting a math criterion (scores on a math test) than irrelevant content, but also was better for predicting two other criteria (grade point average and general ability scores) for which no specific content was available. Freeburg suggested that the rater's halo "worked"; that she generalized from the specific (math) content to the other two inferred traits on the basis of her "psychological theory" of the relationship among these traits. Factor analyses of the ratings (by both peers and observers) indicated a general factor of "cognitive ability," a secondary factor of "math ability," and four specific factors related to relevant-irrelevant tasks and observer-participant raters.

A Closer Look at Work Sample Tests

Recently, Asher and Sciarrino (1974) reviewed the available research evidence with respect to the validity of work sample tests. They classified work samples as belonging to one of two classes: motor work samples (requiring physical manipulation) and verbal work samples (requiring communication or interpersonal relations skills). Figure 6–5 presents some of the typical content of these two different types of work samples.

FIGURE 6–5

Motor Work Samples	Verbal Work Samples
Carving dexterity test for dental students	A test of common facts of law for law students
Blueprint reading test	Group discussion test for supervisor
Shorthand and stenography test	Judgment and decision-making test for administrators
Rudder control test for pilots	Speech interview for foreign student
Programming test for computer programmers	Test of basic information in chemistry
Map reading test for traffic control officers	Test of ability to follow oral directions

The results of these authors' review were very encouraging. They compared the validity of work sample tests to the estimates of the validity of other common predictors published periodically by Ghiselli (1966). We reported some of Ghiselli's estimates in Chapter 3 in the discussion of IQ tests. Figure 6–6 compares the validities of work sample tests with the validities of other predictors. As you can see, a large percentage of studies using the work sample approach report validities in excess of .50. When you drop the validity coefficient to .30, 78 percent of the motor work sample studies and 60 percent of the verbal work sample studies report significant validities.

Another interesting aspect of this review was a comparison of the results of motor and verbal work sample validation studies. Asher and Sciarrino were able to demonstrate that verbal work samples were better at predicting training success and motor work samples were better at predicting job proficiency. They account for their results by proposing a "point-to-point" validation theory. They contend that the greater the number of common elements in predictor and criteria, the higher the validity of the predictor.

FIGURE 6–6

Proportion of Validity Coefficients .50 or Higher with Job Proficiency as the Criterion

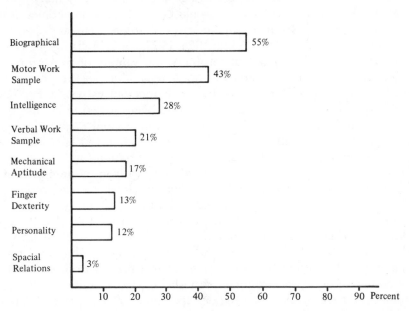

Thus, since most training programs are highly verbally loaded, it makes sense that verbal work samples do a better job of predicting training success.

In a later study, Gordon and Kleiman (1976) suggested that the value of work sample tests had not been adequately assessed, since few studies directly compared the validity of work samples and more traditional predictors by using the same subjects and the same criterion. They made a direct comparison of the value of work samples versus traditional predictors with several classes of police academy recruits. They found that a verbal work sample was a better predictor of academy success (essentially training success) than was an IQ test administered prior to the beginning of the training program. This result also lends support to the Asher and Sciarrino (1974) conclusion that verbal work samples are good predictors of training success. In spite of a general support of the Asher and Sciarrino results, Gordon and Kleiman were not yet ready to accept the "point-to-point" theory. They suggest that an equally plausible explanation for the good showing of work samples is that, since these tests tend to be more realistic than traditional paper-and-pencil tests, the applicant's level of interest and/or motivation may be substantially higher. There is not enough information available to choose between the two competing explanations, but one thing is crystal clear: work samples deserve and will undoubtedly receive a good deal of attention from managers and personnel researchers alike in the coming years. They represent a technique that seems to be both legally and technically defensible.

PEER ASSESSMENT

Early studies of the value of peer ratings largely involved military personnel predicting which of their peers would be most (and, sometimes, least) successful as officers. In an extensive series of studies, Hollander and his colleagues (Hollander, 1954a, 1954b, 1956, 1957, 1965; Hollander & Webb, 1955) have provided evidence of reliability and validity of peer ratings in' the military. Both split-half and test-retest reliabilities in the .90s are reported by Hollander (1957) with the group together as few as five days. These reliabilities held up whether the ratings were staged to be for "real" or for "research" purposes and for different nominations ("future officer," "leadership qualities," and so on). Hollander (1954, 1965) has also shown that peer ratings are moderately valid predictors of training and post-training proficiency ("fitness") ratings. Peer ratings taken early in training correlated .27 with a pass-fail criterion. Adding a final preflight average, ratings by officers, and a standard test succeeded in raising the validity only to .33. In other words, the peer rating was nearly as good alone as with three additional predictors, including grades in the training course. Similar results were reported by Ricciutti (1955), who found that midshipmen (peers) made more valid ratings at an earlier point in time than officers; that is, peer ratings made in the freshman year had modest validities ($r = .25$ to .30) for fitness ratings made on the officers after graduation from the training. Even more impressive were Hollander's (1965) findings that fitness ratings taken after three years as officers were predicted by peer ratings made in the third week of training ($r = .40$). In fact, ratings made later in training were no more valid than those at three weeks ("future officer" ratings). The validity held up rather well even when the effects of academic grades ($r = .28$) and "friendship" ($r = .33$) were statistically taken out of the relationship.

Other studies have examined peer ratings in the industrial setting. Roadman (1964) found that peer ratings taken in the second or third week of a management training program were predictive of subsequent promotion rate among the managers. In fact, 10 of 13 peer-rated traits discriminated between managers who had received two or more promotions and those who had never been promoted. Unfortunately, the author did not report the relationships among ratings on the various traits, either in the form of intercorrelations or factors resulting from a factor analysis. Such information would have provided some indication as to the amount of halo operating in the ratings or the number and character of the independent factors actually being judged by the peers.

These limitations were overcome in a study by Mayfield (1972). His sample was 117 inexperienced life insurance agents attending a three-week training school where they lived together. The sample included 6 classes of the school; each class included about 20 peers. After 18 days in the school, the agents were asked to nominate 3 students in response to each of 12 questions, such as, "With which students would you prefer to discuss

TABLE 6–11

Means, Standard Deviations, Ranges, and Relationship with Criteria for Peer
Nomination Scores and Other Independent Variables

| | | | | Correlation with Criteria | | | |
| | | | | Time Worked | | Production | |
Variable	$\bar{X}$	SD	Range	6 mo.	1 yr.	6 mo.	1 yr.
Peer nomination score . .	51.3	58.8	0–323	.18*	.29†	.29†	.30†
Age	29.4	7.3	21–50	.18*	.24†	.06	.09
Starting monthly pay . . .	602.0	113.2	225–900	.01	.03	.13	.26†
Final course grade	69.0	12.5	36–94	.02	.06	−.02	.02

* $p = .05$ (one-tailed test).
† $p = .01$ (one-tailed test).
Source: Mayfield, E. C. Value of peer nominations in predicting life insurance sales performance. *Journal of Applied Psychology*, 1972, *56*, 319–323.

the handling of a tough case?" "Which students get along best with the other students?" and "Which students do you think would be most likely to cheer you up if you feel low?" In addition, three other predictors were evaluated: age, starting monthly pay, and final course grade.

The peer ratings and the three additional predictors were evaluated against two criteria. The first was job tenure (the number of weeks the agent remained under contract); the second was production (the total amount of insurance sold) expressed as a weekly rate. These two criteria were combined to identify successful and unsuccessful agents with success defined as (1) remaining under contract one year and (2) selling above the median ($500,000).

The results of this study are summarized in Tables 6–11 and 6–12. In Table 6–11 the validity coefficients for "time worked" and "production criteria" are shown for each of the four predictors. Peer ratings had the highest validity coefficients for both criteria and were the only valid pre-

TABLE 6–12

Peer Nomination Score and Success in Terms of a Combined Criterion

Peer Nomination Score	Number Cases in Interval	Number "Successful" Cases	Percent "Successful" Cases
69 and above	23	11	44
43–68	23	9	39
28–42	24	6	25
13–27	25	3	12
0–12	22	0	0

Source: Mayfield, E. C. Value of peer nominations in predicting life insurance sales performance. *Journal of Applied Psychology*, 1972, *56*, 319–323.

dictors of production after six months on the job. Age predicted tenure as well as the peer ratings but did not predict production. Similarly, starting pay predicted production but was not predictive of tenure. Perhaps the biggest surprise was that final course grades were not predictive of either criterion.

Roughly half of the agents survived the first year, and half of these survivors sold $500,000 or more in insurance. Thus, about 25 percent of all agents were successful. Table 6–12 shows how these successful cases were distributed over five score ranges from the peer nominations (these scores are related to the total number of nominations received). The relationship between peer ratings and success is obvious. If such ratings were available for selection and a nomination score cutoff of 28 was set, the success rate would be increased from 25 to 37 percent, approximately a 50 percent improvement. At the same time, false negatives (agents rejected by the cutoff who would have been successful) would be only slightly more than 6% of the sample.

Factors in Peer Ratings

Mayfield did a factor analysis of the data from the 12 nomination items. The outcome was three factors that seem roughly to correspond to the three sample items cited earlier (i.e., "Which student gets along best with other students?"). Mayfield labeled these factors "technical skill," "general sociability," and "ability to form close personal relationships." Scores obtained for each of these factors were checked against the survival and production criteria. Only the third factor was significantly ($r = .19$ and $r = .21$) related to these criterion measures. Mayfield felt this factor was similar to that of "friendship," which—contrary to these results—Hollander (1964) had found to play only a minor role in military ratings by peers. This suggests that peers recognize that different factors make for success in different situations. On the other hand, nominations to one question: "Which student do you think will become the best all-around agent?" were as predictive as any of the others. This is consistent with results reported by Hollander (1965) and others (Waters & Waters, 1970; Weitz, 1958), which indicate that a single nomination item may be sufficient. However, it would be of considerable interest to determine whether peers could predict a number of rather specific performance criteria or job behaviors, such as total sales, customer commendations, complaints, policy cancelations, and so on.

Recently, Kraut (1975) studied the prediction of managerial success from the ratings of both peers and training staff members in a management training institute. In addition, he examined these data separately for 156 middle-level managers and 83 executives, or higher-level managers. The sizes of the groups varied from 12 to 16, and ratings were obtained for several different aspects of performance. These aspects could be reduced to two basic dimensions: *impact* and *tact*. Impact was defined in terms of aggressiveness and originality, while tact was related to cooperation, willingness to compromise, and so on. These ratings were used in an attempt to predict who would be promoted in the future and also the favorability of later performance reviews. For middle-level managers, peer ratings predicted later promotions but not favorability of performance reviews; for the executive sample, peer ratings predicted later performance favorability but not promotional success. Thus, it would be tempting to conclude that peer ratings are "valid" predictors of success. Unfortunately, there are alternative explanations of the relationship between the ratings and the criteria. We might apply the same logic as Klimoski and Strickland (1977) used in describing the apparent validity of assessment center scores: it may be that the middle-level managers are good at predicting who will be promoted, regardless of whether or not the promotion is based on performance. This might account for the fact that peers of the middle-level managers were unable to predict performance level. This explanation would not account for the fact that executive peers *were* able to predict future performance ratings. It may simply be that the dimensions of impact and tact are more closely related to the job demands of the executives than they are to those of the middle-level managers. Thus, middle level peers may be able to predict who will become an executive, and executive peers may be better at predicting who will be a *good* executive!

In summary, then, it appears that peer ratings have much more promise than is suggested by the extent of their use in business and industry. In all likelihood, they may be valid and valuable information for decisions to train, promote, transfer, and the like. It is unfortunate, as Mayfield (1972) lamented, that peer ratings typically are not available prior to hiring so that they could be used in selection decisions. It may be worth considering in some situations combining peer ratings with situational tests or leaderless group exercises using recruits before hiring decisions are made. It appears that such peer evaluations may be more valid even after a brief interaction than the ratings of observers, and the two sources of information may be combined for even better prediction.

Regarding the last point, both Hollander (1965) and Freeburg (1969) reported that participants (peers) made more valid predictions than observers, but Bray and Grant's (1966) results disagreed, with a slight advantage to observer ratings. Also, Lewin, Dubno, and Akula (1971) found no advantage for actual face-to-face contact over ratings made by observers viewing video tapes of the group sessions. The discrepancy in these findings is resolved with a close look at these studies. Hollander's studies and others showing superior ratings by peers often compare ratings by observers who see the group members only in training with ratings by peers who are living with one another 24 hours a day. Similarly, in Freeburg's design participants had full access to verbal as well as visual data about their peers, while observers only saw the overt behavior through one-way vision facilities. Not only were they denied access to the verbal interchanges, but also to the individual and group efforts at desk and chalkboard. Under such a handicap, it is hardly surprising that observers showed lower reliability.

Kaess, Witryol, and Nolan (1961) found such high agreement between observers and participants ($rs \geq .90$) as to suggest that either or both might be used. In addition to the evidence for high interrater reliability, Arbaus and Maree (1951) provide direct support for the notion that one observer (or participant) may provide data as good as that from multiple raters.

The relevant issue is probably not whether the rater is an observer or a participant (peer). In fact, other things equal, one might bet on the observer, since he has only a single task (observation) to perform, while the peer has the task at hand as well as the rating of his peers. The "other things," however, are important. While raters in and out of the group can agree on "general person quality" regardless of task content, the *validity* of the ratings depends on the accuracy of the observer's stereotype and the relevancy of the content of the task. Peers at one occupational level may well be better judges of one another that an observer from another occupational level, because they know what is required. Given content relevant to the job, they will be in a good position to judge. In this respect, Taft (1959) found evidence in the literature that judges with high predictive validities have greater familiarity with the "type" of people involved, indicating that the best assessors, as Carlson (1972) suggests, "are those who are partially contaminated with the experience, standards, and outlook of those who are evaluated in the assessment program and what they should be" (p. 20).

Types of Peer Assessment

Kane and Lawler (1978) have recently reviewed the research in the area of peer assessment. They point out that there are several different forms of peer assessment and that each form might be suited to a specific purpose. The three major types of assessment are peer nomination, peer rating, and peer ranking. Most of the research we have described deals with peer rating. Kane and Lawler contend that ratings are more suitable for feedback than administrative decision making. This is largely due to the fact that rating scales are often subject to distortions that affect their reliability and validity. Nevertheless, they do make it easier to communicate with an individual concerning his or her *unique* strengths and weaknesses.

A second technique of peer assessment is known as *peer nomination*. In this approach, the assessor is asked to nominate members of the group who may fall into an "outstanding" category or a group of people who are extremely high on some characteristic. There has been a good deal of research on this technique, and the conclusion Kane and Lawler draw from this research is that peer nominations seem to be reliable and accurate in distinguishing the best from the worst in a group, but they are relatively useless in providing feedback to the individual nominee. Kaufman and

Johnson (1974) contrasted two types of nominations: nominations of the "best" compared to nominations of the "worst" in a group. They concluded that negative nominations contribute little to the validity of the peer nomination technique. They suggested, as did Gordon (1970) in his consideration of poor performance ratings, that we are not particularly good judges of poor performance, either because we cannot describe it well or because we would rather ignore it than deal with it. In addition, they suggest that positive nominations may be less threatening to peer assessors than negative nominations. Downey (1975) cautions that the use of only positive nominations provides little discrimination among group members not in the "best" category. He suggests that this technique be limited to situations in which little discrimination is necessary, e.g., the presentation of honors or awards.

A third technique that might be used for gathering peer assessments is known as the *peer ranking method*. This approach would require the individual to rank all other individuals in the group from "best" through "worst." This would clearly provide the discrimination lacking in the peer nomination technique, but it makes feedback difficult since the individual being assessed is inevitably encouraged to be "better than person X" rather than to reach some criterion level of performance. There is also the problem of equating positions across groups; is the number one person in group A equal to the number one person in group B? Of the three different peer assessment techniques, the peer ranking method is the biggest question mark. Little research has been done on the technique; nevertheless, from a superficial examination, it seems to offer less than either the nomination or rating approaches.

SUMMARY

In this chapter we have reviewed some nontest methods for collection of information in personnel decision making. As with psychological tests, each of these methods can be evaluated in terms of accuracy, reliability, validity, and—ultimately—in terms of utility and payoff. By the same token, these methods are like psychological tests in that the validity or utility established in one setting provides no guarantee that the method will be useful in another situation. In fact, with nontest predictors one is not even working with a standardized instrument. *The* interview or *the* situational test does not exist in the sense that the Wonderlic Personnel Test does. Therefore, it is even more imperative to emphasize the need for the development, analysis, and evaluation of these methods at the local plant or office level.

The Landy (1976) study provides an example of this type of analysis, evaluation, and potential improvement with the selection interview. It appears that improvement in many settings can come from analysis of the strategies used and the stereotypes that constitute the ideal applicant from the viewpoint of the interviewer. "Valid stereotyping" on the part of interviewers, observers, or peer raters alike depends on the accuracy and completeness of information about job and worker requirements available to the rater. To the extent that the rater looks for irrelevant attributes or gives undue positive or negative weights to some items of information, his predictions will be in error.

There is an old anecdote in industrial psychology about the young personnel manager who was given the responsibility of selecting a middle-level executive for his organization. Armed with the latest theory and measuring devices, he selected a man of obvious ability and impeccable human relations skills. The man was hired, but was fired within six months. The president instructed the personnel manager to try again, and again he selected a man with both technical and human relations skills, and again the man was fired within six months. Desperate and anxious about his own job security, the personnel manager then selected the applicant with highest technical qualifications, but with the lowest score on the human relations test. This man proved to be a whopping success: he won the praise of the president and the personnel manager's job was again secure.

The moral of this story is, of course, that the personnel manager was simply looking for the wrong attributes. Presumably, his stereotype of the ideal middle executive included some notions about human relations skills that were totally incompatible with the social context in this organization. This brings us to the second point of the anecdote: a successful selection and placement decision depends not only on finding a person who has adequate technical skills and job knowledge, but also in identifying an individual whose social attitudes and behavior are compatible with the social context of the job and organization. It has been estimated that nearly 70 percent of terminations are for social-motivational, rather than technical, reasons. Perhaps the training of interviewers and observers should be concentrated on sensitizing them to appreciate the social context that the new hire will enter, and perhaps one of the specific questions they should seek to answer is "Will this individual get along well with the 'gang' in department 13?" At the same time, less emphasis might be placed on training interviewers in "how to interview, how to ask questions, or how to leave a good impression."

Work samples and application blanks show great promise as cost-effective selection devices. They should be considered seriously as part of a selection strategy. The encouraging evidence for the validity of peer ratings may indicate that peers are in a position to sense the reactions of others (as well as their own) to the individual as a social being. Granted, this may lead to nominations based on what Carlson (1972) has called "general person quality" rather than specific qualities, but such a strategy may result in a "valid halo" effect if the rater is sensitive to the appropriate set of social norms. This line of reasoning suggests a selection strategy that has not been studied systematically: place applicants in small groups with a standardized situational problem relevant to the job being considered. Include one or two regular employees from the department in which the job is located. Obtain peer ratings from applicants and employee members of each group as to the motivation to work and the likelihood that they will "get along" in the social context of the job.

REFERENCES

Ahern, E. *Handbook of personnel forms and records.* New York: American Management Association, 1949.

Anderson, C. W. The relation between speaking times and decision in the employment interview. *Journal of Applied Psychology,* 1960, *44,* 267–268.

Arbaus, J. G., & Maree, J. Contributions of two group discussion techniques to a validated test battery. *Occupational Psychology,* 1951, *25,* 73–89.

Arvey, R. Unfair discrimination in the employment interview: Legal and psychological aspects. *Psychological Bulletin,* in press.

Asher, J. J., & Sciarrino, J. A. Realistic work samples: A review. *Personnel Psychology,* 1974, *27,* 519–534.

Baskett, C. D. Interview decisions as determined by competency and attitude similarity. *Journal Of Applied Psychology,* 1973, *57,* 343–345.

Bass, B. M. The leaderless group discussion. *Psychological Bulletin,* 1954, *51,* 465–492.

Bass, B. M., & Norton, F. T. M. Group size and leaderless discussion. *Journal of Applied Psychology,* 1951, *6,* 397–400.

Bellows, R. M., & Estep, M. F. *Employment psychology: The interview.* New York: Rinehart, 1954.

Blakeney, R. N., & MacNaughton, J. F. Effects of temporal placement of unfavorable information on decision making during the selection interview. *Journal of Applied Psychology,* 1971, *55,* 138–142.

Bolster, B. F., & Springbett, B. M. The reaction of interviewers to favorable and unfavorable information. *Journal of Applied Psychology,* 1961, *45,* 97–103.

Bray, D. W., & Grant, D. L. The assessment center in the measurement of potential for business management. *Psychological Monographs: General and Applied,* 1966, *80* (17), p. 53.

Buel, W. D. Voluntary female clerical turnover: The concurrent and predictive validity of a weighted application blank. *Journal of Applied Psychology,* 1964, *48,* 180–182.

Carlson, R. E. Selection interview decisions: The effect of interviewer experience, relative quota situation, and applicant sample on interviewer decisions. *Personnel Psychology,* 1967, *20,* 259–290 (a).

Carlson, R. E. Selection interview decisions: The relative influence of appearance and factual written information on an interviewer's final rating. *Journal of Applied Psychology,* 1967, *51,* 461–468 (b).

Carlson, R. E. Employment decisions: Effect of mode of applicant presentation on some outcome measures. *Personnel Psychology,* 1968, *21,* 193–207.

Carlson, R. E. Selection interview decisions: The relative influence of appearance vs. factual written information on an interviewer's employment decision. *Personnel Psychology,* 1969, *22,* 47–62.

Carlson, R. E. Effects of applicant sample on ratings of valid information in an employment setting. *Journal of Applied Psychology*, 1970, *54*, 217–222.

Carlson, R. E., Schwab, D. P., & Henneman, H. G. Agreement among selection interview styles. *Journal of Applied Psychology*, 1970, *5*, 8–17.

Carlson, R. E. The current status of judgmental techniques in industry. Paper presented at the symposium "Alternatives to paper and pencil personnel testing." University of Pittsburgh, May, 1972.

Carter, L., Haythorn, W., Shriver, B., & Lanzetta, J. The relation of Categorizations and ratings in the observation of group behavior. *Human Relations*, 1951, *4*, 239–253.

Cascio, W. F. Accuracy of verifiable biographical information blank responses. *Journal of Applied Psychology*, 1975, *60*, 767–769.

Cascio, W. F. Turnover, biographical data, and fair employment practice. *Journal of Applied Psychology*, 1976, *61*, 576–580.

Cohen, J., & Lefkowitz, J. Development of a biographical inventory blank to predict faking on personality tests. *Journal of Applied Psychology*, 1974, *59*, 404–405.

Cohen, S. L., & Bunker, K. A. Subtle effects on sex role stereotypes on recruiters' hiring decisions. *Journal of Applied Psychology*, 1975, *60*, 566–572.

Crowell, A. H. *Decision sequences in perception.* Unpublished doctoral dissertation, McGill University, 1961.

Dipboye, R. L., Fromkin, H. L., & Wiback, K. Relative importance of applicant sex, attractiveness, and scholastic standing in evaluation of job applicant resumes. *Journal of Applied Psychology*, 1975, *60*, 39–43.

Dobmeyer, T. W. Modes of information utilization by employment interviewers in suitability ratings of hypothetical job applicants. Paper presented at Midwestern Psychological Convention, Cincinnati, 1970.

Downey, R. G. Note on the Kaufman and Johnson studies of the differential validities of peer nomination techniques. *Journal of Applied Psychology*, 1975, *60*, 245–246.

Dunnette, M. D., Kirchner, W. K., Erickson, J. R., & Banas, P. A. Predicting turnover of female office employees. *Personnel Administration*, 1960, *23*, 45–50.

England, G. W., & Patterson, D. G. Selection and placement: The past ten years. In H. G. Heneman, L. L. Brown, M. K. Chandler, R. Kahn, H. S. Parnes, & G. P. Schultz (Eds.), *Employment relations research.* New York: Harper, 1950, pp. 43–72.

Farr, J. L. Response requirements and primacy-recency effects in a simulated selection interview. *Journal of Applied Psychology*, 1973, *57*, 228–232.

Fleishman, E. A., & Berniger, J. One way to reduce office turnover. *Personnel*, 1960, *37*, 63–69.

Frank, L. L., & Hackman, J. R. Effects of interviewer-interviewee similarity on interviewer objectivity in college admissions interviews. *Journal of Applied Psychology*, 1975, *60*, 356–360.

Freeburg, N. E. Relevance of rater-ratee acquaintance in the validity and reliability of ratings. *Journal of Applied Psychology*, 1969, *53*, 518–524.

Ghiselli, E. E., & Brown, C. W. *Personnel and industrial psychology* (2nd ed.). New York: McGraw-Hill, 1955.

Ghiselli, E. E. *The validity of occupational aptitude tests.* New York: Wiley, 1966.

Gordon, M. The effect of the correctness of behavior observed on the accuracy of ratings. *Organizational Behavior and Human Performance,* 1970, *5,* 366–377.

Gordon, M. E., & Kleiman, L. S. The prediction of trainability using a work sample test and aptitude test: A direct comparison. *Personnel Psychology,* 1976, *29,* 243–253.

Grant, D. L., & Bray, D. W. Contributions of the interview to assessment of management potential. *Journal of Applied Psychology,* 1969, *53,* 24–34.

Greenwood, J. M., & McNamara, W. J. Interrater reliability in situational tests. *Journal of Applied Psychology,* 1967, *51,* 101–106.

Hakel, M. D., Hollman, T. D., & Dunnette, M. D. Accuracy of interviewers, C.P.A.'s, and students in identifying the interests of accountants. *Journal of Applied Psychology,* 1970, *54,* 115–119.

Hakel, M. D., Ohnesorge, J. P., & Dunnette, M. D. Interviewer evaluations of job applicant's resumes as a function of the qualifications of the immediately preceding applicants: An examination of contrast effects. *Journal of Applied Psychology,* 1970, *54,* 27–30.

Hakel, M. D. Similarity of post-interview trait rating intercorrelations as a contributor to interrater agreement in a structured employment interview. *Journal of Applied Psychology,* 1971, *55,* 443–448.

Hinrichs, J., Haanpera, S., & Sonkin, L. Validity of a biographical information blank across national boundaries. *Personnel Psychology,* 1976, *29,* 417–421.

Hollander, E. P. Peer nominations of leadership as a predictor of the pass-fail criterion in Naval Air Training. *Journal of Applied Psychology,* 1954, *38,* 150–153 (a).

Hollander, E. P. Authoritarianism and leadership choice in a military setting. *Journal of Abnormal and Social Psychology,* 1954, *49,* 365–370 (b).

Hollander, E. P. The friendship factor in peer nominations. *Personnel Psychology,* 1956, *9,* 435–447.

Hollander, E. P. The reliability of peer nominations under various conditions of administration. *Journal of Applied Psychology,* 1957, *41,* 85–90.

Hollander, E. P. *Leaders, groups, and influence.* New York: Oxford University Press, 1964.

Hollander, E. P. Validity of peer nominations in predicting a distant, performance criterion. *Journal of Applied Psychology,* 1965, *49,* 434–438.

Hollander, E. P., & Webb, W. B. Leadership, followership, and friendship: An analysis of peer nominations. *Journal of Abnormal and Social Psychology,* 1955, *50,* 163–167.

Hollman, T. D. Employment interviewers' errors in processing positive and negative information. *Journal of Applied Psychology,* 1972, *56,* 130–134.

Howell, M., & Vincent, J. W. Factor analysis of interview data. *Journal of Applied Psychology,* 1970, *54,* 313–315.

Jewish Employment and Vocational Service. *Work samples* (Final Report, Contract 82–4067–46). Washington, D.C.: Manpower Administration, U.S. Department of Labor, 1968.

Johns, G. Effects of informational order and frequency of applicant evaluation upon linear information-processing competence of interviewers. *Journal of Applied Psychology*, 1975, *60*, 427–433.

Kaess, W. A., Witryol, S. L., & Nolan, R. E. Reliability, sex differences, and validity in the leaderless group discussion technique. *Journal of Applied Psychology*, 1961, *45*, 345–350.

Kane, J. S., & Lawler, E. E. Methods of peer assessment. *Psychological Bulletin*, 1978, *85*, 555–586.

Kaufman, G. G., & Johnson, J. C. Scaling peer ratings: An examination of the differential validities of positive and negative nominations. *Journal of Applied Psychology*, 1974, *59*, 302–306.

Keating, E., Patterson, D. G., & Stone, C. H. Validity of work histories obtained by interview. *Journal of Applied Psychology*, 1950, *34*, 6–11.

Kelly, E. L., & Fiske, D. W. The prediction of success in the V.A. training program in clinical psychology. *American Psychologist*, 1950, *5*, 395–406.

Kelly, E. L., & Fiske, D. W. *The prediction of performance in clinical psychology.* Ann Arbor: University of Michigan Press, 1951.

Kirchner, W. K., & Dunnette, M. D. Applying the weighted application blank technique to a variety of office jobs. *Journal of Applied Psychology*, 1957, *41*, 206–208.

Klimoski, R. J., & Strickland, W. J. Assessment centers—valid or merely prescient. *Personnel Psychology*, 1977, *30*, 353–361.

Kraut, A. I. Prediction of managerial success by peer and training staff ratings. *Journal of Applied Psychology*, 1975, *60*, 14–19.

Landy, F. J. The validity of the interview in police officer selection. *Journal of Applied Psychology*, 1976, *61*, 193–198.

Landy, F. J., & Bates, F. Another look at contrast effects in the employment interview. *Journal of Applied Psychology*, 1973, *58*, 141–144.

Langdale, J. A., & Weitz, J. Estimating the influence of job information on interviewer agreement. *Journal of Applied Psychology*, 1973, *57*, 23–27.

Latham, G. P., Wexley, K. N., & Pursell, E. D. Training managers to minimize rating errors in the observation of behavior. *Journal of Applied Psychology*, 1975, *60*, 550–555.

Ledvinka, J. Race of interviewer and the language elaboration of black interviewees. *Journal of Social Issues*, 1971, *27*, 185–197.

Ledvinka, J. The intrusion of race: Black responses to a white observer. *Social Science Quarterly*, 1972, *52*, 907–920.

Ledvinka, J. Race of employment interviewer and reasons given by job seekers for leaving their jobs. *Journal of Applied Psychology*, 1973, *58*, 362–364.

Lee, R., & Booth, J. M. A utility analysis of a weighted application blank designed to predict turnover from clerical employees. *Journal of Applied Psychology*, 1974, *59*, 516–518.

Lewin, A. Y., Dubno, P., & Akula, W. Face-to-face interaction in the peer nomination process. *Journal of Applied Psychology*, 1971, *55*, 495–497.

Lindzey, G. Seer versus sign. *Journal of Experimental Research in Personality*, 1965, *1*, 17–26.

Lipsitt, L., Rogers, F. P., & Kentner, H. M. *Personnel selection and recruitment.* Boston: Allyn & Bacon, 1964.

London, M., Hakel, M. D. Effects of applicant stereotypes, order, and information on interview impressions. *Journal of Applied Psychology*, 1974, *59*, 157–162.

McMurray, R. N. Validating the patterned interview. *Personnel*, 1945, *23*, 263–272.

Marrow, A. J., & French, J. R. P. Changing a stereotype in industry. *Personnel*, 1946, *22*, 305–308.

Mayfield, E. C. The selection interview: A reevaluation of published research. *Personnel Psychology*, 1964, *17*, 239–260.

Mayfield, E. C. Value of peer nominations in predicting life insurance sales performance. *Journal of Applied Psychology*, 1972, *56*, 319–323.

Mayfield, E. C., & Carlson, R. E. Interview decisions: First results from a long-term research project. *Personnel Psychology*, 1966, *19*, 41–55.

Meehl, P. E. *Clinical versus statistical prediction.* Minneapolis: University of Minnesota Press, 1954.

Meehl, P. E. When shall we use our heads instead of a formula? *Journal of Counseling Psychology*, 1957, *4*, 268–273.

Meehl, P. E. Seer over sign: The first good example. *Journal of Experimental Research in Personality*, 1965, *1*, 27–32.

Meyer, H. H. The in-basket as a measure of managerial aptitude. *Behavioral Research Service.* General Electric, 1961, p. 52.

Miner, J. B. Executive and personnel interviews as predictors of consulting success. *Personnel Psychology*, 1970, *23*, 521–538.

Nevo, B. Using biographical information to predict success of men and women in the army. *Journal of Applied Psychology*, 1976, *61*, 106–108.

Overall, J. E., & Hollister, L. E. Computer procedures for psychiatric classification. *Journal of the American Medical Association*, 1964, *187*, 538–588.

Palacios, M. H., Newberry, L. A., & Bootzin, R. R. The predictive validity of the interview. *Journal of Applied Psychology*, 1966, *50*, 67–72.

Peters, L. H., & Terborg, J. R. The effects of temporal placement of unfavorable information and of attitude similarity on personnel selection decisions. *Organizational Behavior and Human Performance*, 1975, *13*, 279–293.

Public Personnel Studies. A method of rating the history and achievement of applicants for positions. *Public Personnel Studies*, 1925, *3*, 202–211.

Rand, T. M., & Wexley, K. N. A demonstration of the Byrne similarity hypothesis in simulated employment interviews. *Psychological Reports*, 1975, *36*, 535–544.

Ricciutti, H. Ratings of leadership potential of the U.S. Naval Academy and subsequent officer performance. *Journal of Applied Psychology*, 1955, *39*, 194–199.

Rimland, B. A follow-up analysis of the new composite system for selecting NROTC regular students. *United States Navy Bureau of Naval Personnel Technical Bulletin*, 1960 (No. 60–8).

Roadman, H. E. An industrial use of peer ratings. *Journal of Applied Psychology*, 1964, *48*, 211–214.

Rowe, P. M. Individual differences in selection decisions. *Journal of Applied Psychology*, 1963, *47*, 304–307.

Rowe, P. M. Order effects in assessment decisions. *Journal of Applied Psychology*, 1967, *51*, 13–22.

Rundquist, E. A. Development of an interview for selection purposes. In G. A. Kelly (Ed.), *New methods in applied psychology*. College Park: University of Maryland Press, 1947, pp. 85–95.

Sattler, J. M. Racial "experimenter effects" in experimentation, testing, interviewing, and psychotherapy. *Psychological Bulletin*, 1970, *73*, 137–160.

Schmitt, N. Social and situational determinants of interview decisions: Implications for the employment interview. *Personnel Psychology*, 1976, *29*, 79–101.

Schoenfeldt, L. F. Utilization of manpower: Development and evaluation of an assessment-classification model for matching individuals with jobs. *Journal of Applied Psychology*, 1974, *59*, 583–595.

Schwab, D. P., & Heneman, H. G. Relationship between interview structure and inter-interviewer reliability in an employment situation. *Journal of Applied Psychology*, 1969, *53*, 214–17.

Scott, W. D., Clothier, R. C., & Spriegel, W. R. *Personnel management: Principles, practices and point of view* (4th ed.). New York: McGraw-Hill, 1949.

Springbett, B. M. Factors affecting the final decision in the employment interview. *Canadian Journal of Psychology*, 1958, *12*, 13–22.

Stead, W. H., & Shartle, C. L. *Occupational counseling techniques*. New York: American Book Company, 1940.

Stringer, P., & Tyson, M. University selection interviewer's ratings related to interviewee self-image. *Occupational Psychology*, 1968, *42*, 49–60.

Sydiaha, D. On the equivalence of clinical and statistical methods. *Journal of Applied Psychology*, 1959, *43*, 395–401.

Sydiaha, D. Bales' interaction process analysis of personnel selection interviews. *Journal of Applied Psychology*, 1961, *45*, 393–401.

Sydiaha, D. Interviewer consistency in the use of empathic models in personnel selection. *Journal of Applied Psychology*, 1962, *46*, 344–349.

Taft, R. Multiple methods of personality assessment. *Psychological Bulletin*, 1959, *56*, 333–352.

Tullar, W. L., & Barrett, G. V. The future autobiography as a predictor of sales success. *Journal of Applied Psychology*, 1976, *61*, 371–373.

Tupes, E. C. An elevation of personality-trait ratings obtained by unstructured assessment interviews. *Psychological Monographs*, 1950, *64* (11, Whole No. 287).

Uhrbrock, R. S. The personnel interview. *Personnel Psychology*, 1948, *1*, 273–302.

Ulrich, L., & Trumbo, D. The selection interview since 1949. *Psychological Bulletin*, 1965, *63*, 100–116.

Valenzi, E., & Andrews, I. R.   Individual differences in the decision process of employment interviewers. *Journal of Applied Psychology*, 1973, *58*, 49–53.

Vaughn, C. L., & Reynolds, W. A.   Reliability of personal interview data. *Journal of Applied Psychology*, 1951, *35*, 61–63.

Viteles, M. S.   *Industrial psychology.* New York: Norton, 1932.

Wagner, R.   The employment interview: A critical review. *Personnel Psychology*, 1949, *2*, 17–46.

Washburn, P. V., & Hakel, M. D.   Visual cues and verbal content as influences on impressions after simulated employment interviews. *Journal of Applied Psychology*, 1973, *58*, 137–140.

Waters, L. V., & Waters, C. W.   Peer nominations as predictors of short-term sales performance. *Journal of Applied Psychology*, 1970, *54*, 42–44.

Weiss, D. J., & Dawis, R. V.   An objective validation of factual interview data. *Journal of Applied Psychology*, 1960, *44*, 381–385.

Weitz, J.   Selecting supervisors with peer ratings. *Personnel Psychology*, 1958, *11*, 25–35.

Wernimont, P. F.   Re-evaluation of a weighted application blank for office personnel. *Journal of Applied Psychology*, 1962, *46*, 417–419.

Wexley, K. N., Sanders, R. E., & Yukl, G. A.   Training interviewers to eliminate contrast effects in employment interviews. *Journal of Applied Psychology*, 1973, *57*, 233–236.

Wexley, K. N., Yukl, G. A., Kovacs, S. Z., & Sanders, R. E.   Importance of contrast effects in employment interviews. *Journal of Applied Psychology*, 1972, *56*, 45–48.

Wexley, K. N., & Nemeroff, W. F.   Effects of racial prejudice, race of applicant, and biographical similarity on interviewer evaluations of job applicants. *Journal of Social and Behavioral Sciences*, 1974, *20*, 66–78.

Wiener, Y., & Schneiderman, M. L.   Use of job information as criterion in employment decisions of interviewers. *Journal of Applied Psychology*, 1974, *59*, 699–704.

Wiggins, J. S.   *Personality and prediction: Principles of personality assessment.* Reading, Mass.: Addison-Wesley, 1973.

Wilkins, W. L.   How good were the GI's—and how poor? *Contemporary Psychology*, 1960, *5*, 243–246.

Woodworth, D. G., Barron, F., & MacKinnon, D. W.   An analysis of life history interviewers' rating for 100 Air Force captains. *United States Air Force Personnel and Training Research Center Technical Note*, 1957 (No. 57–129).

Wright, O. R., Jr.   Summary of research on the selection interview since 1964. *Personnel Psychology*, 1969, *22*, 391–413.

CHAPTER **7**

Personnel Training and Development: Concepts and Models

Individuals differ in their knowledge, technical skills, attitudes, interpersonal skills, and behaviors relevant to the needs of a job and of an organization. These individual differences are the basis for personnel selection, as we have seen. Selection programs exist to reduce the discrepancies between the job and organizational requirements and the attributes of the employees selected. To the extent that selection (and placement) are successful, the people "fit" the various jobs to which they are assigned. To the extent that selection is less than completely successful (or to the extent that "ideal" selection procedures are impractical and uneconomical), new employees do not possess all of the attributes necessary to perform the jobs with acceptable proficiency. Furthermore, job changes resulting from new technology necessitate the development of new skills on the job. Finally, training needs arise as organizations change and grow, leading to new requirements for talent. Thus, personnel psychology has been concerned with two complementary approaches to the matching of people to machines or jobs: "Find (through selection) and fit (through training) the person to the job."

This chapter and the one that follows are concerned with fitting the individual to the job and to the organization by promoting the acquisition of information, skills, attitudes, and patterns of social behavior through training. The present chapter deals with conceptual problems and models

250

of the training process, while the next chapter is concerned with training programs and their evaluation.

To keep a broad perspective of all the possibilities available to matching people and machines, we should remind the reader that there are alternative approaches. One of these, which is dealt with in Chapter 13, is the approach of the engineering psychologist. In brief, the engineering psychologist's answer to the man-machine problem is "Design the machine (or the system) to fit the human operator—to minimize human errors or limitations in the system performance and to maximize the potential contribution of the human components in the system." In other words, this approach would minimize the discrepancy between the job requirements and the operator's abilities by improved engineering of the job.

Closely related to the engineering psychologist's approach is the notion of special *job performance aids*, which may be useless to the experienced operator, but which may be valuable "crutches" to the novice. Thus, checklists, tape-recorded instructions, special labels, or other devices may help the new employee perform the job and learn efficient procedures (and avoid errors) until a point is reached where certain behaviors become essentially automatic. In a sense, such job performance aids may also be thought of as *training aids* where training takes place or is continued on the job.

Finally, there is the "adaptive-treatment" approach. This approach says, in effect, "Modify, or adapt, the standard job to fit with the strengths and weaknesses of the *individual* employee." This approach differs from that of the engineering psychologist in that it begins with the individual, assesses strengths and weaknesses, then searches for ways to modify a job to maximize the use of the individual's potential. As an example, the job of university professor, which normally involves both teaching and research activities, might be modified for the person with a foreign accent or a speech impediment so that she (1) had a reduced teaching load, (2) taught only upper-division or graduate-level classes, or (3) presented material on the chalkboard and through demonstrations, while an assistant "translated" the lecture notes. Similarly, an industrial job that involves some bookkeeping might be modified for the otherwise ingenious person who "just can't work with numbers." Employees often adapt the jobs to fit themselves, as in interdependent teamwork job situations. The adaptive treatment approach acknowledges the fact that individuals differ in their strengths and weaknesses and assumes that, within limits, jobs can be adapted to individuals, as well as individuals to jobs. To date, this approach probably is more evident in educational institutions, in the form of ability-graded classes, than in business or industry.

WHAT IS TRAINING?

Training is the planned activities on the part of an organization to increase the job knowledge and skills or to modify the attitudes and social behavior of its members in ways consistent with the goals of the organization and the requirements of the job. Obviously, only a part of the knowledge, skills, and attitudes acquired by the employees are the result of formal training programs. Even when such programs do not exist, employees learn "to sink or swim" on a job, acquire information (or misinformation) about company rules and policies, pick up skills at pilfering company property, and develop attitudes toward their supervisors, toward production standards, or toward quality workmanship. Even when training programs do exist, their effectiveness may well depend on the context in which they occur. Effective training requires effective learning, retention, and transfer on the part of the trainee. This, in turn, depends upon the trainee's goals and how the training program is perceived with respect to these goals, perhaps even to a greater degree than on learning abilities. Many "well-laid plans" for safety training programs have failed, not because they were inept, but because the trainees learned informally the prevailing attitude that only "sissies" use safety equipment.

Training differs from general education in that the objectives of training are generally narrower, more specific, and more practical. However, with the development of more technical programs in the high schools and universities and, at the same time, increasing concern with broader educational goals, such as "education for leisure" or "education for retirement" on the part of business and industry, the distinction becomes less clear. Furthermore, business and industry often seem to have as much difficulty as educators in defining specific objectives for executive training, management development, or human relations training programs.

DETERMINING TRAINING NEEDS

When it has been concluded that there is room for improvement in the performance of a certain job, it remains to be determined whether such improvement can be realized through recruitment and selection, training, job performance aids, job or machine design, or some combination of these approaches. If it is decided the most feasible route is to improve the training program, then specific training needs must be determined. What is it the employee needs to learn to improve job performance and to increase the contribution to the goals of the organization?

Job and Worker Analysis

The traditional approach to answering this question is to obtain a detailed job description from a job analysis (see Chapter 4). From the job description, a list of the estimated worker characteristics (skills, knowledge, interpersonal behavior, and so on) can be obtained. A system such as the worker-oriented list of job variables described by McCormick and his associates (Cunningham & McCormick 1964a,b; McCormick, Jeanneret, & Mecham, 1972) would provide a definitive checklist for estimating the types of activities and their relative importance for job performance. These data would provide information about the demands of the job. The determination of training needs requires an analysis of the extent to which the current employees, or new hires, possess the requisite attributes, and to what degree. Training needs (or, perhaps, *remedial needs*, which may be overcome by training) are then defined by the discrepancy between the estimated job requirements and the estimated (or measured) attributes of the employees. Figure 7–1 is a diagram of the type of information that could be expected from such an analysis. This figure indicates that in a hypothetical case training needs are greatest in "personal contact," "administrative," and "mental" activities. With this general picture of the areas of training needs, one can proceed to a more specific statement of the objectives of a training program. Thus, for example, Cunningham and McCormick (1964a) list 16 items that load on the factor labeled "personal contact activities." These items are listed in Table 7–1. As a second step in determining training needs, each of these rather specific activities could be reviewed as to its relevance and importance to the particular job. These items could then be rank ordered as a basis for describing the objectives of that portion of the training program designed to improve the employees' "personal contact" skills.

The final training program could be evaluated in terms of *content validity* by comparing the amount of training time devoted to each of the items in Table 7–1 relative to the judged importance of that activity in the overall job performance. The statement of training objectives based upon

FIGURE 7–1

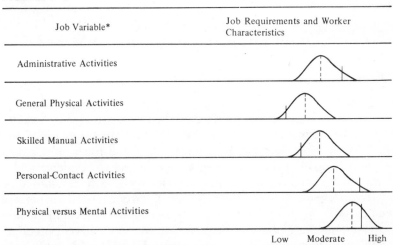

Job Variable*	Job Requirements and Worker Characteristics
Administrative Activities	
General Physical Activities	
Skilled Manual Activities	
Personal-Contact Activities	
Physical versus Mental Activities	

Low   Moderate   High

A schematic representation of the comparison of estimated job requirements with estimated worker attributes in five activity areas. The solid vertical lines represent the estimated needs on each of the variables; the distributions repre-represent the estimated worker attributes for meeting these needs.

Source: Cunningham, J. W., & McCormick, E. J. Factor analyses of "Worker-oriented" job variables, (Contract No. Nonr. 1100 [19], Report No. 4). Washington, D.C.: Office of Naval Research, 1964.

TABLE 7–1

Factor IV: Personal Contact Activities

Item No.	Factor Loading	Name of Item
142	.60	Telephone calls
143	.51	Distractions—people seeking or giving information
109	.47	Persuading
95	.46	Interchange information with customers, clients, patients, etc.
163	.46	Variety of communications
92	.42	Interchange information with clerical workers
93	.42	Interchange information with salesmen
158	.40	Unpleasant or frustrating experiences
119	.38	Dress—tie and jacket
129	.37	Activity domain—people
112	.36	Publicizing
42	.36	Clerical tasks—files
28	.31	Curiosity
97	.30	Interchange information with important persons
58	.30	Walking
27	.29	Intelligence

Source: Cunningham, J. W., & McCormick, E. J. *Factor analysis of "worker-oriented" job variables* (Contract No. Nonr. 1100 [19]. Report No. 4). Washington, D.C.: Office of Naval Research, 1964.

a careful analysis of training needs also provides a basis for identifying criteria whereby the effectiveness of the training can be evaluated.

Critical Incidents

The critical-incidents method offers an alternative—or, perhaps, supplementary—method of assessing training needs. This method seeks to describe those situations in which something "goes wrong" or "goes right" in the performance of a job. As a classic example, Fitts and Jones (1947a,b) used the method to analyze the sources of errors leading to accidents and near accidents among aircraft pilots. Their interviews with several hundred pilots led to the categorization of several types of errors related to perceptual and motor skills in flying, that is, errors in reading information displays and in manipulating aircraft controls. While these data were used largely in formulating recommendations and research on the modification and design of the machine (i.e., human engineering), rather than in designing training programs, the method holds the same promise as a means of discovering training needs. The critical-incidents approach assumes that training needs of present (or new) employees can be estimated from those situations in which the system has failed in some specific way—this failure constitutes an "incident." By the same token, it assumes that particularly effective behaviors can be identified by analyzing incidents in which everything went right.

The critical-incidents approach is appropriate to determining needs for safety training or training for emergencies or breakdowns. In addition, critical-incident methodology has been used to analyze supervisory and executive jobs and is commonly used as a basis for designing exercises for executive training and assessment programs. It may be argued that for many jobs the difference between a successful and an unsuccessful employee is not in the ability to handle the routine of the job, but rather in the handling of the perhaps infrequent, but critical, events. In this respect, Ghiselli and Brown (1955) suggest an example of the operator of a bottling machine in a tomato catsup factory. Almost anyone could handle the routine of this job, which consists largely of watching an automated process (and, perhaps, occasionally providing the machine with a supply of caps and a bit of oil to keep it operating smoothly). However, the critical factor for job performance in this case may be the operator's reactions when the machine is jammed, or when it begins applying too much force to the tops of the bottles, resulting in ground glass in the catsup.

Analytic Employee Appraisals

Systematic employee appraisal programs that attempt to specify, in terms of job activity requirements, the strengths and weaknesses of job incumbents, can serve as a source of information about training needs. Frequently, the outcome of an employee appraisal interview is the recommendation that the employee take part in a certain training program, within or outside the company. Of course, the appraisal of strengths and weaknesses may well include the appraiser's observations of critical incidents in which the employee has been involved, but the emphasis here is on the assessment of individual training needs. At the same time, the recurrence of a particular "weakness" in the appraisals of different individuals might well lead to the identification of a general training need and to the design of a training program.

Further Specification of Training Needs: What Is to Be Learned?

Thus far, we have described the organization's needs for training in terms of task requirements, that is, in terms of the *outcomes* of behavior, rather than in terms of behavior or basic psychological processes. However, before a training program can be designed that makes use of the basic information from experimental psychology, these task requirements should be translated and described in terms of demands on basic psychological processes. Examples of such processes might be signal detection, stimulus discrimination or recognition, short- or long-term memory, response differentiation, response selection and decision making, response execution, or feedback evaluation. Once it is recognized, for example, that an important component of the task is stimulus learning (identification and differentiation

FIGURE 7–2

Analysis and Description of the Procedure of Changing a Tire

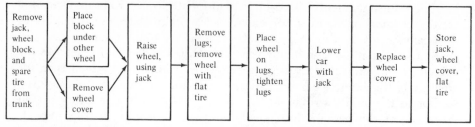

Source: R. Gagne, *The Conditions of Learning*, 3d ed. Copyright © 1965, 1970, and 1977 by Holt, Rinehart and Winston. Reprinted by permission.

of different signals), then, in addition to general principles of learning, one may apply those principles peculiar to stimulus learning as contrasted with response learning, or decision making. Such an analysis also may lead to insights into ways of modifying the job, the machine displays or controls, or suggest such job performance aids as checklists, alerting signals, or the like.

Figures 7–2 and 7–3 present two examples of a very refined task analysis of a commonplace activity. Figure 7–2 is intended to represent the major activities involved in changing an automobile tire, a motor skill (forgive the pun). The second sequence of operations is a cognitive one and is intended to describe how one might balance a checkbook. This second example is interesting because it distinguishes between activities (in rectangles) and decisions (in diagonal boxes). While it may not be necessary to break down every task into such small components, it may be a good way to start, particularly when designing training programs for the elimination of current performance problems.

As Glaser and Resnick (1972) suggest, "When analysis identifies classes of behavior whose properties as learning tasks are known or can be systematically studied, then inferences concerning optimal instructional processes can be formulated and tested" (p. 209).

Determinants of Performance

The specification of training needs often starts with a first-level supervisor. The supervisor notices that the performance of a particular individual may need some form of training. This is often the correct approach, but equally often, it may be incorrect. Before identifying the individual as "the problem," the supervisor should look at the individual's performance a little more closely. Kelley (1967) has suggested that there are three important pieces of information necessary for the complete and accurate definition of a "performance problem": *distinctiveness, consistency,* and *consensus. Distinctiveness* relates to the task specificity of the poor performance: did the poor performance occur on one task but not others? *Consistency* concerns the reliability of the phenomenon. Does the employee *always*

FIGURE 7–3

*Vertically Arranged Flow Chart Showing
Initial Steps in the Process of
Reconciling a Bank Statement
with Checkbook Records*

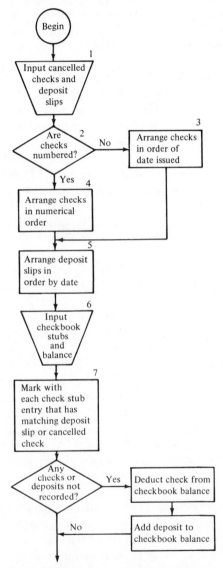

Source; Merrill, P. F. Task analysis: An information
processing approach (Technical Memo No. 27). Talla-
hassee: Florida State University, CAI Center, 1971,
Fig. 2.

In this chart, diagonal boxes indicate
decision points for choice of alternative
steps.

do a poor job on this task (and/or other similar tasks) or was the poor performance a unique occasion? *Consensus* relates to how common poor performance is among the individual's work group members. As you can see from this type analysis, poor performance may be a complicated phenomenon that is affected by combinations of environment and occasions.

If, after examining a poor performance situation, we conclude that the problem is individually based (i.e., it is consistent and is not shared with many other co-workers), it is still necessary to determine whether the individual's problem is a lack of knowledge or skills, or basically a problem in attitudes or motivation. If we accept the time-honored statement that *performance* is a function of *ability* times *motivation* (performance = ability × motivation) then it is clear that poor performance may result from an inadequate level of ability (knowledge or skill), from a low level of motivation, or both. This formulation is complicated by another generally-accepted statement—namely, that performance is related in a curvilinear fashion to motivation, the so-called "inverted-U" hypothesis. This second statement is in general agreement with the first in that it says that performance increases with increased motivation, *but only up to some optimal level*. Beyond this level, which presumably varies with the complexity of the task being performed, performance *decreases* with further increases in motivation.

Several theoretical concepts have been offered to account for this relationship (see Näätänen, 1973), but a thorough review of these is beyond the scope of this discussion. For our purposes, the detrimental effects of excessively high motivation may be thought of in terms of the distraction or disruption that accompanies *overarousal* or *anxiety*, for these are conditions often associated with high motivation.

McClelland (1951) has put forth the qualitative model to account for this relationship shown in Figure 7–4. With low motivation, performance suffers because the individual is engaged in "wishing" rather than performing. Wishing behavior would include fantasy, daydreaming, and other non-productive activities. As motivation increases, wishing gives way to "doing" or "achieving," and performance increases. At the same time, however, wishing is gradually replaced by "defending" behaviors. These activities, both overt and covert, are equally nonproductive and non-task oriented. They are the individual's attempts to alleviate or cope with the negative feelings of anxiety or overarousal. Thus, extremely high motivation increases the task load on the individual: not only does the employee have to perform tasks relevant to the job, but must also "handle" anxiety, fear of failure, the anticipation of punishment or reprimand, and so on. Other chapters in this book deal more thoroughly with the problems of work motivation; the present comment is simply to remind the reader that in training as well as in job performance, motivational factors need to be kept in mind.

To summarize, then, substandard performance may reflect either an environmental need such as improved supervision, co-workers, pay, machine

FIGURE 7–4

A Model to Account for the Curvilinear Relationship between Motivation and Performance

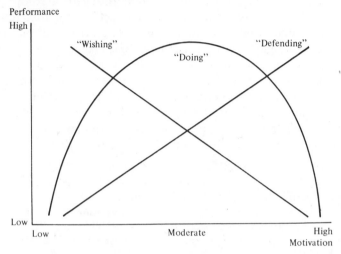

Source: Adapted from McClelland, D. C. *Personality* (New York: Sloane, 1951), by H. C. Smith in *Psychology of industrial behavior*. New York: McGraw-Hill, 1955.

or job design, or a training need. In the latter case, poor performance may result from (1) low ability or skill, (2) low motivation, (3) disruptively high motivation in the form of overarousal or anxiety, or (4) some combination of ability and motivational factors.

Having provided this frame of reference, we may look at a hypothetical case·in which it has been concluded there is a need to improve quality control through training. The scrap rate is too high, and a large percentage of the items produced fail to pass inspection. This substandard performance may, in the light of the previous discussion, result from inadequate knowledge or skill, from a lack of "pride" in the quality of workmanship, or from the disruptive effects of anxiety about one's performance or rate of progress. It may be that the real training needs are *to increase job-related skills,* and a training program may be designed to alleviate this problem. On the other hand, there may be a need to *reduce the anxiety* of the workers about their production or their job security. Yet another possibility may be that the real need is *to change attitudes* toward the importance of quality workmanship. Incidentally, the likelihood that such a program of attitude training will be effective may well depend on the incentives for quality production. Unless there is something to gain (and nothing to lose) from careful workmanship, an exhortation to "take pride in your work" will probably be ineffective. Management must back up its desire for quality production by an incentive system that rewards quality workmanship.

Training for Job Adjustment

Some of the points raised in the previous discussion on the identification of training needs are illustrated rather dramatically in a study at Texas Instruments (Gomersall & Myers, 1966). The setting for the study was a rapidly growing department manufacturing integrated electronic circuits. In addition to rapid growth, the department was characterized by frequent technological and organizational changes in the work. In this context, it was noted that new employees (one-month tenure) were less able to participate constructively in problem-solving activities. At this point, the authors hypothesized that the problem-solving ineffectiveness of the new employees resulted from anxieties arising from the work situation. In the words of the authors, interviews with 405 employees indicated that: .

> Their first days on the job were anxious and disturbing ones.
> "New employee initiation" practices by peers intensified anxiety.
> Anxiety interfered with the training process.
> Turnover of newly hired employees was caused primarily by anxiety.
> The new operators were reluctant to discuss problems with their supervisors [who also felt anxious and inadequate in the unstable work environment] (p. 64).

The net effects of this situation were (1) poor progress in reaching a "competence" level of production, and (2) a relatively high rate of turnover. For example, on one job, new employees required three months to reach the competence level, defined as 85 percent of the industrial engineering standard.

In the light of this evidence, the authors proposed a simple model of the relationship between anxiety and competence on the job. This model is shown in Figure 7–5. The solid lines in the figure describe the status quo as the researchers saw it. Competence increased slowly as anxiety slowly decreased over the three months required to reach the competence level. The broken lines represent the authors' hypothesis: if anxiety could be reduced more rapidly, employees would attain competency more quickly.

A day-long orientation training program was designed in an attempt to reduce the job-related anxiety of the new employees. Specifically, the goals of this training were to reduce fear of failure ("Your opportunity to succeed is very good"), to facilitate the employees' ability to cope with "hazing" practices ("Disregard 'shop talk' "), and to enhance communications and interpersonal relations with supervisors ("Take the initiative in communication" and "Get to know your supervisor"). Following this orientation training, the new employees were introduced to their supervisors and training operators to receive the standard on-the-job training.

The results of this study are summarized in Table 7–2 and Figure 7–6. After one month on the job, the experimental group (which received the one-day orientation training) outdistanced the control group on each of the four criteria listed in Table 7–2. Their production level was three times that of the controls, absenteeism and tardiness were a fraction of

FIGURE 7–5

The Interaction of Competence and Anxiety

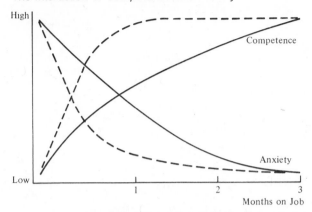

Source: Gomersall, E. R., & Myers, M. S. Breakthrough in on-the-job training. *Harvard Business Review,* 1966, *44,* 62–72.

The hypothesized relationship between job anxiety and job competence proposed by Gomersall and Myers (1966). The solid lines indicate the assumed relationship before the training program; the broken lines indicate the expected effect of the training.

those in the control group, and training hours were reduced by about 40 percent. Replications of this training program on different jobs within the department produced similar results.

Effects on Work Quality.   In the Texas Instrument plant, a "mastery level" of production was defined as 115 percent of standard, or 30 units above the competence level of production. Operators who reached this level were identified as master operators. Employees with the new orientation training reached this level in two or three months, in contrast to the more than five months required by the control group members. Contrary to some expectation, the attainment of mastery was associated with higher- rather than with lower-quality work. In light of our earlier discussion, it

TABLE 7–2

One-Month Performance Levels of Experimental and Control Groups

Performance Index	Experimental Group	Control Group
Units per hour	93	27
Absentee rate	0.5%	2.5%
Times tardy	2	8
Training hours	225	381

Source: Gomersall, E. R., & Myers, M. S. Breakthrough in on-the-job training. *Harvard Business Review,* 1966, *44,* 62–72.

FIGURE 7–6

Results of the Experimental Training Program

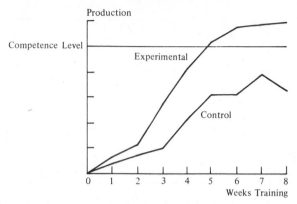

Source: Gomersall, E. R., Myers, M. S. Breakthrough in on-the-job training. *Harvard Business Review*, 1966, *44*, 62–72.

appears that one incentive for quality workmanship at the mastery level was that master operators were privileged in that they no longer had inspection of 100 percent of their output; instead, they could submit whole "lots" for sample inspection, a recognition of their mastery status.

The results of these Texas Instrument studies are exciting and revolutionary. They suggest that we should be at least as concerned with preparing the employee for the social context of the job and for coping with the insecurities and frustrations of a new learning situation as with the development of the technical skills necessary for job performance. Orientation training has frequently been a superficial indoctrination into company philosophy, policy, and rules, sometimes accompanied by the presentation of an employee's handbook and a quick tour of the factory. While these practices may be helpful, the Texas Instrument experience suggests that orientation training directed at the problems of adapting to a position in a specific department may be more valuable.

Despite our enthusiasm, a word of caution is in order regarding the Texas Instrument studies. While the authors phrase the problem and the explanation of their results in terms of a relation between anxiety and performance, their experiments do not test the theoretical model shown in Figure 7–5. At no point in their studies do they show directly that (1) their experimental program does indeed, reduce anxiety, that (2) anxiety is reduced as in Figure 7–5, or that (3) "competence" increases as the level of anxiety decreases. Such conclusions would require the independent measurement of anxiety at several points throughout the experiment, as well as other experimental refinements. Nevertheless, the results are convincing, and the interpretation is certainly not inconsistent with the notion, presented earlier, that extremely high motivation in the form of overarousal or anxiety is related to poor performance and poor problem solving.

EFFICIENT TRAINING PROCEDURES

Efficient training means efficient learning, retention, and transfer on the part of the trainees. Psychologists and educational researchers have been concerned with this problem for some time. Systematic research, theorizing, and model building dates back to the last century. Parallel to the building of a science describing the basic principles of learning has been the accumulative experience and applied research of practitioners who have faced the problems of training in schools, in the military, in industry, and in a host of different training situations.

Learning Principles

Given the amount of effort, ingenuity, and talent represented in these studies over 75 years, one might expect that we would be able to write a detailed section on how to train employees more effectively. The fact that we cannot may reflect at least as much on the complexity of the task as it does on the success of these research endeavors. One problem is that the main thrust of learning theory and research has been to identify those *general principles* of learning that transcend the specific content of the learning task. Thus, for example, it is now generally agreed that "spaced" practice is more efficient than "massed" practice for many (though not all) learning situations. It is recognized that the adverse effects of massed practice (continous practice without interspersed rest periods) may be transient effects on *performance*, rather than real effects on learning per se; but nonetheless, as a generalization, spaced or distributed practice is seen as producing more efficient learning.[1] Having accepted this generalization, the training practitioner is faced with translating it to the training situation. If the plan is to give eight hours of training, the principle suggests, it is probably not efficient to present it all in one eight-hour day. But what *is* the optimal distribution? Should the program be one hour a day for eight consecutive working days? Or one hour a week for eight weeks? Or would two four-hour sessions be better? There is little hint in the research from which the principle was derived. It came from studies of animals running mazes, humans learning lists of nonsense syllables, and other behavioral settings equally remote from the task of, say, learning to troubleshoot a radar system, program a computer, or operate a turret lathe. As Gagne and Rohwer (1969) pointed out in a review of research, findings in much of the basic research on human learning cannot be applied directly to the design of training programs because "(a) the conditions under which the learning is investigated, such as withholding knowledge of learning goals from the subject and the requiring of repetitious responses, are often

---

[1] The important distinction between *performance* and *learning* should be kept in mind. Performance refers to observable, measurable behavior from which learning is *inferred*. However, changes (or lack of changes) in performance do not always accurately reflect the status of learning or the *ability* of the individual to perform.

unrepresentative of conditions under which most human learning occurs; and (b) the tasks set for the learner (e.g., the verbatim reproduction of verbal responses, the guessing of stimulus attributes chosen by the experimenter, among many others) appear to cover a range from the merely peculiar to the downright esoteric" (p. 381).

In the following paragraphs some generally accepted principles of learning will be presented. These principles will be somewhat familiar to the reader and, therefore, rather than attempting to describe each principle in detail, we will summarize some of the problems in applying them to training programs. These summaries come largely from Campbell et al. (1970) and particularly reflect the difficulties of application to management development and executive training programs.

Distributed or Spaced Learning Periods. Distributed practice is concerned with the spacing of the training, the length of training sessions, and the intervals between sessions. Campbell et al. conclude that "as it stands, this principle cannot specify any optimal procedure for any particular kind of management development, but can only point toward an important variable to be considered" (p. 254).

Whole versus Part Learning. Whole versus part learning has traditionally been concerned with whether it is more efficient to practice subtasks or components tasks and then to integrate them into whole task performance, or to practice the whole task from the beginning. "This principle suffers from an inability to define what is a part and what is a whole, and we found no references which tried to relate it empirically to the training of individuals in organizations" (p. 254).

Reinforcement. "One of the difficulties in translating this principle to the management development area is defining before the training starts what will function as a reward. Will praise from the trainer be enough . . . or will some external sort of reward have to be offered . . . ?" And "although certain kinds of responses may be reinforced by the trainers or by the other trainees during the training period, such behavior has little chance of being translated back to the job situation if the trainee's boss does not reward the learning or allow it to be utilized" (p. 254). The problems of identifying rewards or reinforcements may not be as formidable as this quotation suggests, despite individual differences. Furthermore, the second half of the quotation is essentially a recognition by the authors of the importance of reinforcers in modifying and sustaining behavior, a point with which we are certain they would agree.

Knowledge of Results (Feedback). Knowledge of Results (KR) refers in general to those conditions in a performance situation that inform the subject about performance and progress. The information may be qualitative or quantitative, intrinsic to the task or supplied by the trainer, and informative and/or evaluative. Generally, KR (or "feedback") is associated with improved performance." It is not enough to just say that feedback enhances learning. Merely informing a trainee that he was wrong is not as effective as telling him why he was wrong and how he can avoid making similar mistakes in the future. In fact, merely informing an individual of an incorrect response may prove overwhelmingly frustrating for people who want to know 'why' " (p. 255).

Motivation. "This principle says that to learn one must *want* to learn." Many trainers seem to be well aware of this principle and have gone to great lengths to make training interesting. All motivated trainees may not be motivated to learn, however, . . . participants who select themselves for the program often use the training to escape from the stresses of the job and to plan the next phase of their career strategy, rather than for the purpose for which the training was intended" (p. 256). Granted that employers may have many and varied motives for participating in training, we feel certain that Campbell and his associates would agree that motivated trainees are an essential part of effective training.

Transfer of Training. "The question of transfer is perhaps the most important learning consideration that must be faced by the organization that wishes to develop managers. If the goal of development and training is to further the goals of the organization, then training that does not transfer is of no use and may even have considerable negative utility" (p. 257). By "negative utility" the authors apparently meant that the program costs more than it is worth to the organization. Knowledge, skills, and attitudes acquired in training but not utilized on the job cannot contribute to organizational goals.

Practice. "The means for applying this learning principle to management training problems remain a bit fuzzy, although its value for certain kinds of skill learning seems readily apparent" (p. 257–58). Nevertheless, repetition and active involvement in learning, with informative and evaluative feedback, should guide the design of training programs.

Closely related to the principle of practice is that of *overlearning*, which states that practice beyond the point of perfect performance will continue to be beneficial in that it slows down the forgetting process, thus increasing the likelihood that the learning will be remembered. However, the principle is based largely on rote learning and simple skill learning, and the effects are of diminishing returns as overlearning continues. In practice, it is difficult to determine, first, when learning is complete and, second, how much additional training will pay off in overlearning benefits.

Campbell and his associates conclude that while the importance of these principles for management development programs is obvious, the implications for specific recommendations to trainers are quite limited because (to return to Gagne and Rohwer's [1969] phrase) the conditions under which the principles have been formulated are "often unrepresentative of conditions under which most human learning occurs" (p. 381).

These comments regarding the usefulness of learning principles in management training are generally negative—more negative, perhaps, than would be appropriate if all levels and types of training were being considered. At the very least, these principles provide a checklist for the training program developer whereby he may critique his program with such questions as

"Have I adequately provided for knowledge of results?" "Does the training schedule seem to distribute the learning over a 'reasonable' period?" "What reinforcers are available and how are they being utilized?" "How can I increase the likelihood of efficient transfer of training to the job situation?" and so forth.

Learning Capabilities

Gagne (1977) has suggested that the major goal of training (or more generally, learning) is to develop predispositions in individuals such that when they encounter stimulus situations in the work setting similar to those in the training setting, they will be "disposed" to respond in the correct manner. He contends that there are five basic categories of capabilities or predispositions, which cover all the behavior one might attempt to change through training. These capabilities are: intellectual skills, cognitive strategies, verbal information, motor skills, and attitudes. Intellectual skills are further broken down into a series of smaller categories. Figure 7–7 presents examples of each of the capabilities. Gagne's work is extensive and careful. It is our feeling that these five categories are sufficient for describing the content of most training programs. It is likely that Gagne's taxonomy will become widespread in the next few years and will help substantially in the communication of training objectives and programs.

FIGURE 7–7
Five Major Categories of Learned Capabilities, Including Subordinate Types, and Examples of Each

Capability (Learning Outcome)	Examples of Performance Made Possible
Intellectual Skill	Demonstrating symbol use, as in the following:
Discrimination	Distinguishing printed *m*'s and *n*'s
Concrete concept	Identifying the spatial relation "underneath"; identifying a "side" of an object
Defined concept	Classifying a "family," using a definition
Rule	Demonstrating the agreement in number of subject and verb in sentences
Higher-order rule	Generating a rule for predicting the size of an image, given the distance of a light source and the curvature of a lens
Cognitive strategy	Using an efficient method for recalling names; originating a solution for the problem of conserving gasoline
Verbal information	Stating the provisions of the first Amendment to the U.S. Constitution
Motor skill	Printing the letter *R*
	Skating a figure eight
Attitude	Choosing to listen to classical music

Source: Gagne, R. *Conditions of learning* (3rd ed.), New York: Holt, Rinehart, and Winston, 1977, p. 47.

STEPS IN TRAINING

Gagne (1965, 1967) and Gagne and Rohwer (1969) offer what may be considered another checklist for the trainer in terms of a sequence of instructional events, or steps, which the instructor can take. These include:

1. Gaining and maintaining attention.
2. Directing and preparing the learner.
3. Presenting the stimuli.
4. Prompting and learning guidance.
5. Conditions of responding.
6. Feedback.
7. Retention.
8. Transfer.

Each of these represents a major topic, and we can provide only a brief summary of the points raised by Gagne and Rohwer with respect to these instructional events.

Gaining and Maintaining Attention. Gagne and Rohwer see the initial task of the trainer as that of gaining (and then maintaining) the attention of the trainee to the training activities. Their discussion essentially describes factors that affect the "demand characteristics" of stimuli: novelty, animation, relevance to the needs (including curiosity) of the trainee, the use of rewards, and so on. Two views are presented with respect to maintaining attention. Skinner's view that attention is maintained through contingent reinforcement of task-relevant, task-oriented responses is considered, together with Rothkopf's (1967) view that "inspection behavior" (i.e., attention) is facilitated by the insertion of questions in the training text. Certainly, the trainer who has not "captured the attention" of the trainee, or having captured it has failed to maintain it, cannot hope for efficient learning. One of the acclaimed virtues of "programmed instruction" or teaching machines is the systematic presentation of contingent reinforcements, in the form of knowledge of results, following each response. Presumably the effects are not only to reinforce correct responses differentially, but also to maintain the trainee's interest in and attention to the training task.

Directing and Preparing the Learner. The directions given to the trainee as to what the goals of the training are, what should be learned and remembered, and how the material should be organized for efficient learning and retention represent another significant training event. Instructions that (1) help the trainee relate the new material to relevant past learning by stimulating recall of previously learned materials, (2) encourage organizing or categorizing the material to be learned, especially in the trainee's own set of categories, and (3) generally help to "elaborate" the material appear to facilitate learning, especially where a fair amount of "rote" memorization is involved. These "elaborative activities" are reminiscent of the schoolboy schemes for remembering the names of the Presidents of the United States, including "Tyler poked (Polk) Taylor," and "Fillmore pierced (Pierce) Buchanan." Gagne and Rohwer (1969) cite a study by King and Russell (1966) that trainees instructed to "remember the main ideas" actually remembered not only more main ideas, but also more specific words and sentences than trainees instructed to "remember word for word."

It is a sad commentary that we cannot tell our trainees how to learn. While there are a few "principles" taught in effective study courses, we have all too few generalizations to offer the learner such as "Study to remember the main ideas, and the details will be remembered better than if you study for word-by-word memorization." While Gagne and Rohwer do not mention it, we would include goal-setting activities as another part of preparation for learning.

Presenting the Stimuli. Essentially, the question here is how to present the information. Should the material to be learned be presented as words, pictures, or objects? Should it be presented in the visual, auditory (or other sensory) mode? Should the materials be labeled? If so, how should they be labeled? These questions are important for the choice of training media and techniques. In reviewing the relevant research, Gagne and Rohwer concluded there are preferences for pictorial over verbal, concrete over abstract, and grammatically structured over unstructured presentation of materials. Meanwhile, the factors determining the preferred mode of presentation are not clear, but there appear to be individual differences in preference for auditory or visual presentation. Most significant of the factors affecting stimulus presentation were what the reviewers called "presentation context" factors. Chief among these factors is labeling. Meaningful labels of nonverbal stimulus materials facilitate the learning and recognition of these stimuli. However, meaningless or nonsense labels proved to be worse than no labels at all, possibly because the subjects had to learn both the stimuli and the novel responses (Chan & Travers, 1966).

Prompting and Guidance. Gagne and Rohwer define this phase of training as that in which the learner "may be provided with various kinds of extra stimulation having the function of prompting a correct response, and in a more general sense, 'guiding' his performance along lines which avoid extreme errors" (p. 395). This prompting may be "faded out" as the learner becomes more proficient. Thus, in a training situation involving primarily learning to make visual discriminations (e.g., certain inspection or display-monitoring tasks), errors would be minimized by beginning with very easy practice tasks and moving gradually to more difficult discriminations. The technique is not unlike the notion of "successive approximations" or "shaping" in operant conditioning, wherein, as learning progresses, more and more precisely defined responses are required before reinforcements are presented. It is also similar to much of the work in programmed learning, where fewer and fewer "props" or cues are presented as the learning of a label or concept progresses. The authors conclude that "generally these techniques [prompting and learning guidance] appear to make possible the acquisition of behaviors which are intermediate to the criterion behavior desired and thus, through transfer, to facilitate the acquisition of that criterion behavior." However, the authors go on to warn there is evidence that "too much guidance or overprompting may narrow the limits of what is learned beyond what is most desirable for learning transfer" (p. 397).

Conditions of Responding. The main variables considered under this heading were (1) the presence or absence of overt responses to the stimuli and (2) the timing and frequency of such responses. The reviewers conclude that requiring overt responses does not necessarily enhance learning, al-

Photo courtesy of Golf Digest Instruction School

Golf instructors often train students by guiding their hand movements.

though this cannot possibly be true in perceptual-motor skill learning. While prompting and guidance were discussed with respect to stimulus discrimination learning, no evidence was reported on the effects of guiding responses in response differentiation or continuous motor-control tasks. Is it efficient, for example, to "drive" a control (such as the steering wheel of a driving stimulator) with the trainee simply hanging on during some stage in the development of skill? Certainly, in the learning of many skilled control tasks and athletic skills, much of what has to be learned is to discriminate between small differences in response-produced feedback. Whether the acquisition of the "feel" of a correct response can be facilitated in an efficient way by guiding the movements of the trainee through a correct set of movements still appears to be a controversial question.

Providing Feedback. Essentially, feedback is information available to the trainee about the effects of his or her responses on the environment. This information may be *intrinsic to the task*, as when one throws a dart at a target and sees where the dart lands. In this example, the individual also experiences proprioceptive feedback from the muscles, tendons, and joints of the body as the throwing response is executed. The thrower may also receive "augmented" feedback when the trainer calls out his score. One point seems clear: practice without knowledge of results or feedback results in little or no improvement. Thus, the adage "practice makes perfect" is misleading unless there is some way in which the learner can evaluate performance via feedback. At the same time, qualitative feedback may be as effective as highly precise quantitative feedback in some learning situations, especially in the early stages of training.

Gagne and Rohwer concerned themselves largely with the evidence that feedback effects may vary as a function of individual differences. They conclude that "a characteristic of recent research is that it reveals clearly the highly variable nature of feedback effects. Moreover, the research indicates that the sources of this variance are to be found in learner characteristics, type of feedback, timing of feedback, direction of feedback and type of task" (p. 401). This statement applies in particular to extrinsic feedback provided by the experimenter (or the "teaching machine") and does not contradict our earlier statement that some form of feedback is essential to the realization of improvement through practice.

Promoting Retention. The critical question for training is not how much is learned, but rather how much of what is learned can be retained—that is, is available to be recalled and utilized at some later point in time. A fundamental concern with training is the extent to which the behavioral (or attitudinal) changes that occur during the training program *transfer* back to the job situation (see the following section). Materials learned by the trainee but forgotten when a situation arises later on the job in which they might be used are of no value.

One truism that can guide our consideration of effective retention of learning is that those conditions that make for efficient learning also tend to enhance retention. Thus, those factors discussed earlier—distributed practice, elaborative activities, stimulus labeling, organization and meaningfulness of the material, and the like—that appear to facilitate efficient learning also may be expected to promote retention of the training materials. Two other classes of variables that affect retention must be considered in designing a training program. First, the effects of activities, including additional learning, that occur between the training and the recall of the learned material should be examined. These are known as *retroactive effects*. Second, the "context" in which the recall of previously learned material occurs should be considered. Gagne and Rohwer cite some evidence (cf. Adams & Montague, 1967) that *elaborative activities* not only promote more efficient learning but also make such learning more resistant to interference from subsequent learning activities. Regarding the context effects, the general indications are (see Adams, 1967) that recall is enhanced to the extent that the recall situation is similar to the situation in which the original learning occurred. There is some evidence, for example, that students do slightly better on exams measuring the retention of course information when the exam is taken in the classroom where some of the original learning took place, rather than in another room (Adams, 1967). Thus, it would seem that appropriate responses are learned to signals and cues *in a certain context* and to the extent that those context factors are reestablished, recall will be enhanced. This is quite consistent with the notion that transfer from training to utilization on the job is a function of the similarity of the learning and the utilization situations. Since transfer implies that the learning can be retrieved (i.e., has been retained), then it follows that conditions enhancing retention should also foster transfer to the job.

Conditions Affecting Transfer. When training experts speak of transfer of training, they are usually concerned with whether the knowledge, skills, or attitudes learned in the training situation will be available and utilized "back on the job." This is, of course, a critical issue in the evaluation of the utility of a training program. There is little value in training that does not carry over to the job situation. This concept of transfer is somewhat different from the classical notion, which is concerned with the effects of prior learning on subsequent learning. In the training case, concern is with the effects of prior learning on performance in a situation other than that in which the learning occurred. Whereas transfer effects, in the traditional sense, are measured as decreased (or increased) efficiency in the new learning due to the prior learning experience, transfer of training is evaluated as the extent to which the newly acquired knowledge or skill—that is, behavioral change—is evident in the post-training performance. In other words, this concept of transfer looks a good deal like the concept of generalization of learning, or stimulus generalization: to what extent does the learning generalize to other situations?

Gagne (1967) and Gagne and Rohwer (1969) were concerned with yet another aspect of transfer—transfer from one phase of a training program to another phase. This leads to concern with the *optimum sequencing* of training events. If one thinks of the formal educational process, then Gagne's concept of transfer is much like that which has concerned educators for some time: what is the instructional sequence that will provide the maximum positive transfer from one stage of learning to the next? The major difference is that Gagne is concerned with kinds of learning rather than formal content areas such as arithmetic-algebra-trigonometry sequences in the schools.

Sequencing Learning Experiences

By kinds of learning, Gagne refers to the five capabilities listed earlier: intellectual skills, cognitive strategies, verbal information, motor skills, and attitudes. It is his hypothesis that complex skill learning must build on simpler, subordinate skills. This implies there are certain prerequisites for improving the various capabilities. Figure 7–8 gives some examples of prerequisites for the five categories.

The major point is that learning is a sequential process in which complex skills can be built more efficiently if systematic prior training is given on simpler subordinate skills. This suggests that before a training program can be constructed, there should be some consideration of the sequence of learning events. The simpler subordinate skills should be taught first, and the more complex superordinate skills later.

FIGURE 7–8

Prerequisites of Learning for Five Kinds of Learning Outcome, with Examples

Type of Learning Outcome	Example	Prerequisites
Intellectual skill	Finding the hypotenuse of a right triangle	Subordinate intellectual skills: rules for squares and square roots, concepts of right angle, adjacent sides, etc.
Cognitive strategy	Originating a novel set of categories for non-fiction books	Rules for classifying and constructing superordinate categories
Information	Stating "Ontogeny recapitulates phylogeny"	Syntactic rules of Subject-Verb-Object relations, and rules for transforming these relations; previously organized information (knowledge)
Motor skill	Punting a football	Part-skills of holding ball, dropping ball, aiming kick; executive routine for total action
Attitude	Choosing "careful" actions in automobile approach to stop-lights	Rules pertaining to customary stop-light operation; information about traffic situations in which stop-lights occur

Source: Gagne, R. *Conditions of learning* (3rd ed.). New York: Holt, Rinehart, and Winston, 1977, p. 272.

Implications for Training in Business and Industry

The foregoing section may well seem general and abstract to the student looking for guidance in the development of training programs. Students may find it difficult to apply Gagne's hypothesis and the notions of kinds of learning to the specific training situation, like the more traditional "principles of learning." However, the broad implications are straightforward. First, the definition of training needs in terms of behavioral *outcomes* is inadequate. The outcomes ("troubleshooting electronic equipment," "selecting among alternative courses of action," "controlling the overhead crane," etc.) must be translated into terms descriptive of the kinds of learning required; namely, learning verbal associates to signals, rules, precisely controlled motor response, problem-solving skills, and the like. Once the learning requirements are specified as types rather than as outcomes or content, the trainer can analyze the component, or subordinate, learning requirements and plan the sequence of training exercises.

A Case in Point. Gagne (1962) offered three examples of training problems encountered in the military and demonstrated how each might be analyzed with respect to the kinds of learning required for each task. One of these, the troubleshooting of complex equipment, may provide a useful example of the application of this approach to training.

First, the task of troubleshooting is described as one of problem solving. Beginning with the symptoms of malfunction, the troubleshooter makes a series of decisions, each followed by a check at some point in the equipment and each contingent on the outcome of prior checks. What kinds of learning are necessary to solve such a problem? What are the subordinate and component skills required? Gagne suggests the learner "must acquire concepts, principles, rules, or something of that nature which he can arouse within himself at the proper moment and which guide his behavior in diagnosing malfunctions" (p. 84). Troubleshooting is learned, in large part, not by practicing troubleshooting but by learning an "elaborate set of rules" about the functioning of the system. While the classic principles of learning may apply to these rule-learning activities, Gagne concludes that a set of principles of training are relatively more important. These include:

1. Any human task may be analyzed into a set of component tasks which are quite distinct from each other in terms of the experimental operations needed to produce them.
2. These task components are mediators of the final task performance; that is, their presence insures positive transfer to a final performance and their absence reduces such transfer to near zero.
3. The basic principles of training design consist of: (a) identifying the component tasks of a final performance; (b) insuring that each of these component tasks is fully achieved; and (c) arranging the total learning situation in a sequence which will insure optimal mediational effects from one component to another. (Gagne, 1962, p. 88)

Applied to the troubleshooting task, these training principles (or principles for the analysis of training requirements) lead to something like the following: troubleshooting is supported by two general classes of subordinate skills. These are knowledge of the rules of signal flow (i.e., the processes) in the system and the use of test instruments in making the checks. These are illustrated schematically in Figure 7–9, together with such further sub-tasks as selection of test instruments, setting up of test instruments, interpretation of test instrument readings, knowledge of signal flow through a component subsystem, and so on.

FIGURE 7–9

An Analysis of the Requirements for Troubleshooting of Electronic Equipment

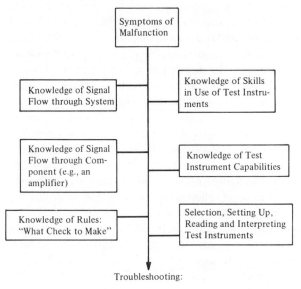

Where do such analyses of the learning requirements come from? According to Gagne they must come from systematic task analyses, which yield statements such as those in Figure 7–7. Thus, in a sense, we are brought back to the earlier section of this chapter in that the determination of efficient training procedures and programs, like the determination of training needs, depends in a very fundamental way on detailed knowledge and systematic analysis of the tasks involved and a description of these in terms of the types of learning required. In Gagne's words,

> If I were faced with the problem of improving training, I should not look for much help from the well-known learning principles like reinforcement, distribution of practice, response familiarity and so on. I should look instead at the technique of task analysis, and at the principles of component task achievement, intratask transfer, and the sequencing of subtask learning to find those ideas of greatest usefulness in the design of effective training. (1962, p. 90)

BEHAVIORAL AND OTHER MODELS FOR TRAINING

Miller's Models

Miller (1961) has suggested that we consider the contrast between the systematic programming of information into a computer, so that it will yield the desired output, and the haphazard way we usually "pour" informa-tion into trainees. This view is quite consistent with Gagne's plea that sequencing of training events is perhaps the most important task in the development of a training program. It is also Miller's view that the training model be made explicit. Thus, returning to the troubleshooting example, Miller suggests two rather contrasting models. Model I would teach troubleshooting by teaching *principles of operation* of the equipment, its construction, and the interaction of the component parts. The model assumes that with this knowledge of the principles of operation, the trainee can deduce the implications of a set of symptoms and work out a logical search strategy for locating the malfunction.

Model II, in contrast, would teach troubleshooting by describing every symptom that might occur and specifying in detail a set of procedures (checks, tests, decisions) for locating and correcting the problem. This second model does not assume it is necessary that troubleshooters understand the principles of operation. Given a set of symptoms, they need know only the prescribed set of procedures. Instead of generating a logical strategy on the basis of knowledge of the system, Model II trainees apply a prescribed strategy.

The contrast between these two models is similar to the arguments regarding the training of practitioners (as contrasted with research scientists) in medicine, for example. Should the general practitioner be trained primarily in the "principles of operation" of the human body—in physiology, anatomy, endocrinology, and organic chemistry—or should he be trained largely in clinical medicine—in recognizing and classifying symptoms, diagnosing malfunctions, and prescribing remedies? As Miller points out, Model I appears to ensure maximum *flexibility* for troubleshooting but may result in *lower reliability* for solving some particular problem. Meanwhile, Model II, which may be characterized as somewhat more of a "cookbook" approach, may well lead to higher reliability for the handling of *anticipated* problems but lower flexibility for the unanticipated, unusual, or bizarre malfunctions.

Model II depends more heavily on *automatized behavior*, or essentially rote-learned associations between stimuli (symptoms) and responses (prescribed tests and checks), or what Miller described as "subroutines" of behavior performed without conscious mediation. Model I, by contrast, is more dependent on *conceptualization behavior*—conceptualization of the cause-and-effect relations between events within the system or of ideas of "process sequence and process relationships." Between these two levels of behavior are the *verbal mediational* processes, whereby the troubleshooter, rather than responding automatically, verbalizes the links between the symptoms observed and the responses made to locate the malfunction.

These three modes of behavior—automatized responses, verbally mediated actions, and strategies built on the conceptualizations of the process linkages in the system—are, in Miller's view, three modes of performing almost any task. Furthermore, he sees them as providing "redundant sets of habits" so that, for example, if the automatized habit fails (e.g., the appropriate response is forgotten or otherwise unavailable), the verbal associations may enable the operator to call up the appropriate responses.

> . . . We can build redundant habit-systems not only for learning but for remembering what responses are required for what task situations. Within each mode we can devise variations and apply them to any task, although probably with diminishing return beyond two or three habit "over-lays" for a given task. In any event, we should see that the diminishing returns curve characteristic in relating practice to learning and recall applies to repetitive practice in the *same mode of behavior;* it need not apply when we superimpose modes of response. By this means we may bring training time for the total job within bounds as well as obtain the gains in reliability of recall that we require. In engineering language, we are duplexing and triplexing the equipment for a function. (p. 102)

In one sense, Models I and II correspond to the learning theory distinction between cognitive and S-R behavior models. Whereas the latter emphasizes the learning of specific responses to specific stimuli, the former is more concerned with perceptual or cognitive learning, the learning of "what leads to what."

The Behavior Modification Model

A third model with a foundation in laboratory studies of learning is behavior modification. This model emphasizes principles of operant conditioning (Skinner, 1969, 1971), chief among which are the principles of contingent reinforcement. The emphasis is on behavioral change (as distinguished from the acquisition of knowledge, skills, or changes in attitudes) through the manipulation of reinforcement contingencies, but recently additional principles from social learning theory have been incorporated into the applications of this model (Meyers, Craighead, & Meyers, 1974). This model is the basis for much of the work in programmed instruction where the "reinforcements" (positive or negative feedback) are in the form of "right" or "wrong" signals following directly after response choices. Skinner (1948, 1953, 1969, 1971) has continued to advocate the use of the principles of operant conditioning to modify behavior in ways consistent with the goals of industrial organizations and even larger societal units.

In the naturalistic setting, Skinnerian techniques have been utilized to modify a number of behavior patterns, including the reduction of littering in a movie theatre (Burgess, Clark, & Hendee, 1971), in a national park (Clark, Burgess, & Hendee, 1972), in an urban park (Kohlenberg & Phillips,

1973), the reduction of pollution behavior (Geller, Farris, & Post, 1973) and the increased use of mass transportation systems (Everett, Haywood, & Meyers, 1974).

In an industrial setting, the time in obtaining customer request information was markedly reduced by having employees self-monitor the time elapsed between the request and the completion of the task (Emery Air Freight Corporation, 1971). In the same setting, a similar technique was used to gain a 100-percent increase in the efficiency in use of containers for air freight shipments. This latter application was estimated to have resulted in savings of $125,000 per month.

Similar results were obtained in a program that utilized behavior modification techniques to increase the punctuality of six chronically tardy workers (Herman, de Montes, Dominquez, Montes, & Hopkins, 1973). Tardiness was reduced from a baseline of 15 percent to 2 percent under the treatment program.

These examples of the application of behavior modification principles are encouraging signs of the potential of these methods for changing specific behavior patterns. They differ from the "teaching-machine" or programmed instruction applications of the same principles in that the latter are concerned with the acquisition of knowledge or specific skills, whereas the former studies were concerned with the reduction or "extinction" of undesired behaviors. Nevertheless, the evidence in both cases indicates that operant conditioning and related methods of "behavior modification" may be effective means for the management of behavior.

The Social Learning Model

Most managers recognize the value of "models" of various types. A new employee is often put under the wing of an older, more experienced employee with the hope that some of this experience will rub off on the new hire. While this technique might be referred to as on-the-job training, the more basic model underlying the anticipated learning is the social learning model (Bandura, 1969). In contrast to the Skinnerian approach described earlier, social learning advocates believe that learning often occurs on the basis of watching others perform and then imitating their performance. In addition, there is often a heavy emphasis on social reinforcement for success in the social learning approach. The social learning model emphasizes the learning principles presented earlier but assumes there is something about watching others perform the target behavior that facilitates learning.

A popular application of social learning theory in the industrial context has been the *behavioral modeling* approach (Goldstein and Sorcher, 1974). Instead of the haphazard pairing of the new and old employee implied by the "rub-off" model, behavioral modeling carefully sequences and controls the nature of the observation done by the trainee. A typical training sequence would involve observing the target behavior portrayed on film or videotape, rehearsing the behavior using a role-playing technique, receiving feedback on the rehearsal, and finally trying the behavior out on the job. Throughout the sequence, there is a strong emphasis on social reinforcement from trainees and eventually supervisors for appropriate behavior.

Kraut (1976) has identified another characteristic that distinguishes behavioral modeling from more traditional approaches. The traditional training model assumes the trainee is first presented with a theory of behavior to change attitudes and values. These changed attitudes and values presumably lead to changes in behavior, which, in turn, lead to superior results. In contrast, behavioral modeling teaches new behavior through observation, role playing, and practice. This new behavior, in turn, leads to superior results. The superior results change attitudes and values and encourage an understanding of the theory that explains the effectiveness of the new behaviors.

The research supporting this approach has been encouraging. Both the General Electric Corporation and IBM have devoted extensive time and resources to the examination of behavioral modeling training for first- and second-level supervisors. General Electric trained 2,700 first-line supervisors to deal with typical employee problems using the behavioral modeling approach, and as a result of the success of the training, developed a similar program for 1200 middle-level managers (Burnaska, 1976). In an evaluation of this training, Burnaska examined differences between 62 managers who had been trained using behavioral modeling and 62 control managers who had received no training. Each group participated in role-playing exercises and were rated on various interpersonal skills by judges who did not know which participants had received training. The role playing was done both one month and four months after training. The analysis of the comparison showed that the trained group was rated higher in interpersonal skills by the judges than the control group. In addition, this difference increased from the one-month observation to the four-month observation, suggesting that the skills acquired in training improve with practice.

Moses and Ritchie (1976) examined the effect of behavior modeling training on first-level supervisors in various telephone companies that were part of American Telephone & Telegraph (AT & T). Two months after supervisors had been trained in interpersonal relations, both trainees and a control group of supervisors who had not experienced training were brought into an assessment center for evaluation. The assessment center was similar to the typical one described in Chapter 3. In this context, supervisors were asked to deal with three problems: absenteeism, discrimination against minority employees, and a theft case. Judges who were unfamiliar with both the training program and the subjects in the study rated supervisors on the way they handled the three situations. There were clear differences in favor of the group that received the behavioral modeling training.

Finally, Latham and Saari (1978) randomly assigned 40 first-line supervisors to either a behavior modeling training group or a control group. The training group received instruction in dealing with typical supervisor/subordinate problem areas such as the orientation of a new employee, the discussion of poor work habits, or the handling of a complaining employee. The training consisted of a film dealing with the particular problem, a group discussion of the behavior of the role model in the film, practice in imitating the behavior of the model, and feedback on the effectiveness of this imitation. There were nine consecutive weekly sessions, each lasting two hours. The initial reaction of the trainees to the modeling training was very positive. If anything, this positive attitude increased over the eight months following training. A comparison of the training and control group supervisors on a test of supervisory skill showed that those supervisors who had had the training received significantly higher scores than the control supervisors. Both trainee and control supervisors were asked to engage in a role-playing exercise related to the problems addressed in the training program several months after the completion of training. Judges rated the trained supervisors significantly higher than the control supervisors on the quality of the solutions. Finally, one year after training, supervisors of the training and control group members rated them on a series of behaviorally anchored scales. Once again, the training group was given significantly higher ratings than the control group.

The evaluations of the behavioral modeling approach seem to provide strong and unequivocal support for the approach. Nevertheless, there are some potential problems that must be recognized. The first relates to the perceptions of the *subordinates* of the supervisors who received training. Burnaska (1976) asked the subordinates of managers who had received training if they could see any change in the manager's behavior following training. He found only a very slight perceived improvement. This is somewhat depressing, since it suggests that even though a supervisor may adopt new behavior patterns, the subordinate has a stereotype of the supervisor that changes at a considerably slower rate. We will discuss this further in the leadership chapter.

A second area for concern is the generalizability of the training approach. The published research on the technique centers on supervisory training, and even more particularly, on interpersonal skills in solving subordinate-centered problems. There is no doubt that supervisors must spend inordinate amounts of time in situations that require these skills. Nevertheless, to be a truly general model of training and learning, it will be necessary to show that behavioral modeling is effective with other groups dealing with other skills as well. It is doubtful that this type of approach would be efficient in the area of psychomotor or cognitive skills.

Finally, there is a rather important issue related to the cost of this type of training. As was true with the assessment center, behavior modeling requires a substantial investment of time and money on the part of the organization. In addition, the personalized attention the trainees receive implies a training department with substantial numbers of trainers. In this respect, behavioral modeling training may follow the route of assessment centers. Large organizations are able to support such an effort, but smaller organizations will find it necessary to subcontract these activities to consulting firms.

The appearance of behavioral modeling is still too recent to warrant any hard and fast judgment about its effectiveness. It has a good deal of promise, based on the available research. If there is any major flaw in the approach, it would be the potential generalizability of the model both in terms of settings and in terms of material to be learned.

Programmed Instruction: "Teaching Machines"

What characterizes programmed instruction is not the use of so-called teaching machines, since many instructional programs do not use machines at all, but instead are in a booklet form. The essence of programmed instruction is self-instruction through the use of tutorial devices without the direct participation of a human instructor. The learning materials are sequenced, together with questions and feedback of correct answers, in a way designed to provide optimum learning. Active involvement of the student in answering questions and systematic feedback at each point are characteristic. Also, the student typically is not allowed to progress beyond a point in the program until he shows evidence of having reached a criterion level of proficiency. Thus, each student may progress at his own rate; the slower learner is not allowed to fall behind, and the faster learner is not held up by a rate of instruction designed for the "average" learner. In Briggs' (1960) terms:

> In summary of the common features of all teaching machine [and other forms of programmed instruction], it may be said that they: (a) require of the student a series of responses to specially prepared materials and stimulus elements; (b) provide knowledge of the correctness or incorrectness of each overt response evoked; and (c) permit the individual student to proceed at his own rate (or at a specially computed rate) in order that each student may master the materials present. (p. 154)

Tutorial Models. Basically two different models of the tutorial instructional process are used in programmed instruction. The first of these has been labeled the *linear* or *compulsive tutor* model by Stolorow (1964). In this model, every trainee gets the same program in the same sequence. The basic assumption is the gradual modification of behavior through the systematic application of reinforcement (defined as the feedback of correct responses), that is, as knowledge of results. This is essentially the model advocated by Skinner (1958), along with the notion of "vanishing" props or guidance cues as the trainee becomes more and more familiar with the concepts.

In contrast to the compulsive tutor model are the *branching* and *idiomorphic* models, which are more adaptive to the progress of the individual trainee. The notion of branching programs (Crowder, 1959) is that the sequencing of materials is made contingent upon the responses of the individual. Thus, depending on progress, the program may repeat a section, skip some material, or progress to the next section. The distinction between this branching method and so-called idiomorphic programming is that the latter uses information other than the trainee's immediately preceding responses to choose among alternative routes and rates of progress through the program. Thus, for example, information about previous training or experience or other diagnostic information might be used within the program itself to tailor the programmed instruction to the individual.

Some of the earliest devices of self-instruction were developed by Pressey (1926, 1950); two examples are shown in Figures 7–10 and 7–11. Pressey's concept of these teaching devices was that they could be used along with conventional textbooks as means of self-testing and self-scoring by the trainee.

Two issues with respect to efficient programming may be mentioned: one has to do with an emphasis on prompting versus confirmation. Prompting provides an abundance of cues that almost assure the trainee will make the correct response, while confirmation allows a higher rate of errors and relies more heavily on feedback following the responses. The second issue has to do with the *pacing* of the trainee. While it has been assumed in most programmed instruction that the trainee should pace herself, there is some evidence that external pacing may be more efficient in some learning situations. However, there is no clear evidence that one method is generally better than another with respect to either of these issues (see Campbell, 1971).

Programmed instruction has usually been linked to the teaching of easily sequenced verbal material. It is a popular technique for language and mathematics training. Recently, there have been some innovative uses of the approach that dramatically expand its scope. Until about 1960, leadership was thought to be a "trait" some individuals had and others did not. As

FIGURE 7–10
Pressey's Teaching-Testing Device, 1925

FIGURE 7–11
Pressey's Punchboard, or "Pocket Tutor" Device

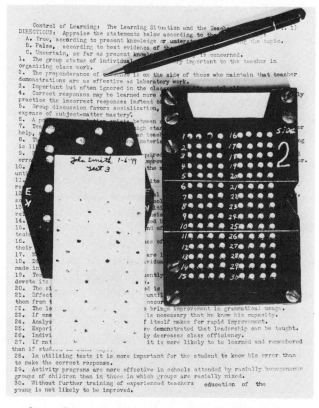

you will see in the chapter on leadership, this view has changed considerably. It is now widely believed that leadership consists largely of what people *do* rather than what they *are*. This new behavioral approach lends itself nicely to training, and leadership training seminars are common in the business world. These seminars usually consist of lectures, role-playing exercises, and feedback. One of the major researchers in the behavioral approach to leadership is Fred Fiedler. He and his colleagues have developed a programmed instruction approach to teaching leader effectiveness (Fiedler, Chemers, and Mahar, 1976). The training program, called Leader Match, consists of a self-paced, programmed manual, which the trainees complete on their own time. The manual takes from four to eight hours to complete, depending on the trainee's reading skill and past exposure to leadership concepts. As Fiedler and Mahar describe the chapters:

> Each chapter consists of a short essay which explains one of the basic concepts of the Contingency (leadership) model and its application. Several short episodes

or probes test whether the trainee has understood the concepts. Trainees select the best answer for the probe and then receive immediate feedback. Each chapter closes with a summary and the book concludes with a self-test and review.

Fiedler has examined the effectiveness of the programmed instruction approach to leadership training (Fiedler and Mahar, In Press), and we will review the results in detail in the next chapter. In general, however, Fiedler concludes that programmed instruction is an extremely effective approach to leadership training. His success suggests that programmed instruction may be more widely applicable than commonly believed.

Attitude-Change Models

In addition to these models, attitude theorists see the problems of training in terms of formation and change of attitudes. There are many theoretical issues with respect to the questions of attitudes, some of which are discussed in Chapter 10. Perhaps the greatest issue for the industrial psychologist is the relationship between attitude change and changes in behavior on the job—or, more directly, the relationship between attitude change as assessed in a training program and changes in the effectiveness, efficiency, or whatever other measures of managerial success we can garner back on the job. The greatest concern with attitudes and attitude change has been in management development and training, a topic treated in the next chapter.

The Goal-Setting Model

Finally, motivational theorists, as suggested earlier, emphasize the importance of having motivated trainees, whatever the content to be learned. This general plea has recently been made more specific by Locke and his associates (Locke, 1968; Locke, Cartledge, & Koeppel, 1968; Locke, Cartledge, & Knerr; 1970) in what has been called goal-setting theory. A basic premise of this theory is that goals take precedence over and determine the relevance of reinforcements or incentives. Explicit and specific goal setting is important not only on the job, but also for efficient training. Thus, Locke sees training in explicit goal setting as leading to greater effort and more efficient learning. Locke's notions are reminiscent of and certainly consonant with such evidence as the Bavelas (1946) study with sewing machine operators, where discussion *plus explicit goal setting* (i.e., the setting of production goals) led to marked changes in production, while group discussion without explicit goal setting was not effective in changing production. These studies tend to emphasize *group* goal setting, or the shift in a group norm and its effect on member behavior, whereas Locke has been more concerned with individual goal-setting behavior. Campbell (1971) has argued that some of the positive effects of goal setting may result from the fact it involves or includes "task-definition activities" that may serve to make clear to the trainee (for the first time) precisely what is expected.

Regardless of the mechanism involved, it does seem that explicit goals jointly agreed upon by trainer and trainee facilitate the training process. Such goal setting and goal definition has been an integral part of the behavioral modeling approach mentioned earlier in the chapter. Trainees are usually told exactly which behaviors to look for in the model. When the behavioral model is depicted on film or videotape, these behavioral objectives are listed prior to and following the scene of interest. It may be that the success of the behavioral modeling approach is due as much to explicit goal setting and definition as it is to either vicarious learning through observation or social reinforcement. We will review the results of the goal-setting model in the next chapter. In addition, we will examine the motivational consequences of goal setting in Chapter 9.

Training Devices: A Warning

All too often, training programs are designed around (or even because of) available training devices. Gilbert (1960) makes the point wryly:

> If you don't have a gadget called a teaching machine, don't get one. Don't buy one, don't borrow one, don't steal one; if you have such a gadget, get rid of it. Don't give it away, for someone else might use it. This is the most practical rule, based on empirical facts from considerable observation. If you begin with a device of any kind, you will try to develop a teaching program to fit that device.

Today a similar concern might be expressed concerning videotape. If a company training department has a video cassette device, it will inevitably be used in training programs dealing with everything from expanded employee benefits through tax accounting procedures. The devices used to support a program of training should be determined *after* training needs, target capabilities, and training models have been selected—not before!

SUMMARY

From a broad systems point of view, personnel training and development are seen as one approach to improving job performance and organizational efficiency. They should be used in combination with selection, placement, human engineering, job design, and adaptive treatment techniques. The identification of poor job performance is a matter of "symptom detection." The cause of poor performance should not automatically be diagnosed as a training deficiency. While a dose of training may reduce the symptoms, prescribing some changes in the engineering or design of the job may also be in order. In order to determine whether the problem is unique to an individual, one must consider the distinctiveness, consistency, and pervasiveness or degree of consensus of the symptom. Even when there is sound evidence that employees need training, it remains to be determined specifically what the job requirments are that are not being met, what knowledge, skills, attitudes, or behaviors need to be acquired, and what types of learning are involved. Job and worker analysis, task analysis, critical incidents techniques, and analytic employee performance appraisals can contribute to the identification of training needs and the specification of the objectives of training programs. These steps, in turn, provide the groundwork for the planning of training exercises and media and for the development of criteria whereby the effectiveness and utility of the training can be evaluated. These latter problems are taken up in the next chapter where we consider training research methods.

In addition to job and task analysis techniques, a systematic approach to the design of training programs should involve a serious attempt to apply the general principles of learning developed largely in experimental psychology laboratories. Bridging the gap between the laboratory and the training program is not easy. There are many unknowns and potential pitfalls, but these provide no excuse for ignoring the guidance these principles offer for the design of training programs.

There are five basic categories of behavior that a training program might attempt to change: intellectual skills, cognitive strategies, verbal information, motor skills, and attitudes. Since these capabilities often require different approaches, the specific categories of behavior to be changed should be specified in advance. The trainer also cannot afford to ignore either the steps in the training process or questions of optimum sequencing of learning exercises as put forth by Gagne and his associates.

The various behavioral, tutorial, attitude-change, and motivational models provide systematic approaches to training, which usually are built on one or more of the general principles of learning. Thus, for example, the behavior modification model is an application of the principles of reinforcement and feedback, as is generally also true of programmed instruction. The behavioral modeling approach emphasizes the observation of correct behavior sequences in role models, role playing, and social reinforcement. The goal-setting model places greater emphasis on the need for a motivated learner.

Which is the best model to guide the designer of training programs? Clearly, there is no answer to this question at this time. While some models may be more appropriate and more readily adapted to some kinds of training programs, they frequently address themselves to different aspects of the training process. Therefore, the trainer may gain insights from an eclectic view in which he seeks the wisdom each model has to offer. The trainer should avoid being seduced into structuring training programs around devices or hardware that are readily available. Training equipment should support rather than determine training objectives.

REFERENCES

Adams, J. A. *Human memory.* New York: McGraw-Hill, 1967.

Adams, J. A., & Montague, W. E. Retroactive inhibition and natural language mediation. *Journal of Verbal Learning and Verbal Behavior,* 1967, 6, 528–535.

Bandura, A. *Principles of behavior modification.* New York: Holt, Rinehart, and Winston, 1969.

Bavelas, A. Group decision in setting production goals. In N. R. F. Maier, *Psychology in industry.* Boston: Houghton Mifflin, 1946.

Briggs, L. J. Teaching machines. In G. Finch (Ed.), *Educational and training media: A symposium.* Washington, D.C.: National Academy of Sciences-National Research Council, 1960.

Burgess, R., Clark, R., & Hendee, J. An experimental analysis of anti-litter procedures. *Journal of Applied Behavioral Analysis,* 1971, *4,* 71–75.

Burnaska, R. F. The effects of behavior modeling training upon managers' behaviors and employees' perceptions. *Personnel Psychology,* 1976, *29,* 329–335.

Campbell, J. P. Personnel training and development. In *Annual review of psychology.* Palo Alto, Calif.: Annual Review, 1971.

Campbell, J. P., Dunnette, M. D., Lawler, E. E., & Weick, K. E. *Managerial behavior, performance and effectiveness.* New York: McGraw-Hill, 1970. Excerpted material copyright © 1970 by McGraw-Hill, Inc.

Chan, A., & Travers, R. M. W. The effect on retention of labeling visual displays. *American Education Research Journal,* 1966, *3,* 55–67.

Clark, R., Burgess, R., & Hendee, J. The development of anti-litter behavior in a forest campground. *Journal of Applied Behavioral Analysis,* 1972, *5,* 1–5.

Crowder, N. A. Automatic tutoring by means of intrinsic programming. In E. H. Galanter (Ed.), *Automatic teaching: The state of the art.* New York: Wiley, 1959, pp. 109–116.

Cunningham, J. W., & McCormick, E. J. Factor analyses of "worker-oriented" job variables, (Contract No. Nonr. 1100 [19], Report No. 4). Washington, D.C.: Office of Naval Research, 1964 (a).

Cunningham, J. W., & McCormick, E. J. *The experimental use of worker-oriented job variables in determining job requirements.* Lafayette, Ind.: Occupational Research Center, Purdue University, 1964 (b).

Emery Air Freight Corporation. *Feedback systems.* Wilton, Conn.: System Performance Division, 1971.

Everett, P., Haywood, S., & Meyers, A. The effects of a token reinforcement procedure on bus ridership. *Journal of Applied Behavioral Analysis,* 1974, *7,* 1–9.

Fiedler, F. E., Chemers, M. M., & Mahar, L. *Improving Leadership Effectiveness: The Leader Match Concept.* New York: Wiley, 1976.

Fiedler, F. E., & Mahar, L. The effectiveness of contingency model training: A review of the validation of leader match. *Personnel Psychology,* in press.

Fitts, P. M., & Jones, R. E. Analysis of factors contributing to 460 "pilot-error" experiences in operating aircraft controls. USAF Material Command Memo, Report TSEAA, 1947a, pp. 694–12.

Fitts, P. M., & Jones, R. E. Psychological aspects of instrument display. I. Analysis of 270 "pilot error" experiences in reading and interpreting aircraft instruments. USAF Material Command Memo, Report TSEAA, 1947b, pp. 694–12.

Gagne, R. M. Military training and principles of learning. *American Psychologist,* 1962, *18,* 83–91.

Gagne, R. M. *The conditions of learning.* New York: Holt, Rinehart & Winston, 1965.

Gagne, R. *Conditions of learning* (3rd ed.). New York: Holt, Rinehart, and Winston, 1977.

Gagne, R. M. *Learning and individual differences.* Columbus, Ohio: Merrill, 1967.

Gagne, R. M. & Rohwer, W. D., Jr. Instructional psychology. In *Annual Review of Psychology.* Palo Alto, Calif.: Annual Review, 1969.

Geller, E. S., Farris, J. C., & Post, D. S. Prompting a consumer behavior for pollution control. *Journal of Applied Behavioral Analysis,* 1973, *6,* 367–376.

Ghiselli, E. E., & Brown, C. W. *Personnel and industrial psychology* (2nd ed.). New York: McGraw-Hill, 1955.

Gilbert, T. F. On the relevance of laboratory investigation of learning to self-instructional programming. In A. A. Lumsdaine & R. Glaser (Eds.), *Teaching machines and programmed instruction.* Washington, D.C.: National Eduction Association, 1967.

Glaser, R., & Resnick, L. Instructional psychology. In *Annual Review of Psychology.* Palo Alto, Calif.: Annual Review, 1972.

Goldstein, I., & Sorcher, M. *Changing supervisory behavior.* New York: Pergamon, 1974.

Gomersall, E. R., & Myers, M. S. Breakthrough in on-the-job training. *Harvard Business Review,* 1966, *44,* 62–72.

Herman, J. A., deMontes, A. I., Dominquez, B., Montes, F., & Hopkins, B. L. Effects of bonuses for punctuality on the tardiness of industrial workers. *Journal of Applied Behavioral Analysis,* 1973, *6,* 563–572.

Kelley, H. Attribution theory in social psychology. In D. Levine (Ed.), *Nebraska symposium on motivation.* Lincoln: University of Nebraska Press, 1967.

King, D. J., & Russell, G. W. A comparison of rote and meaningful learning of connected meaningful material. *Journal of Verbal Learning and Verbal Behavior,* 1966, *5,* 478–83.

Kohlenberg, R., & Phillips, T. Reinforcement and the rate of litter depositing. *Journal of Applied Behavioral Analysis,* 1973, *6,* 391–396.

Kraut, A. I. Developing managerial skills via modeling techniques—some positive research findings: A symposium. *Personnel Psychology,* 1976, *29,* 325–328.

Latham, G. P., & Saari, L. M. *The application of social learning theory to training supervisors through behavioral modeling.* Unpublished manuscript. University of Washington, 1978.

Locke, E. A. Toward a theory of task motivation and incentives. *Organizational Behavior and Human Performance,* 1968, *3,* 157–189.

Locke, E. A., Cartledge, N., & Knerr, C. S. Studies of the relationship between satisfaction, goal setting, and performance. *Organizational Behavior and Human Performance,* 1970, *5,* 135–158.

Locke, E. A., Cartledge, N., & Koeppel, J. Motivational effects of knowledge of results: A goal-setting phenomenon? *Psychological Bulletin,* 1968, *70,* 474–485.

McClelland, D.C. *Personality.* New York: Sloane, 1951.

McCormick, E. J., Jeanneret, P., & Mecham, R. C. A study of job characteristics and job dimensions as based on the position analysis questionnaire. *Journal of Applied Psychology*, 1972, *36*, 347–368. (Monograph)

Meyers, A. W., Craighead, W. E., & Meyers, H. H. A behavioral-preventative approach to community mental health. *American Journal of Community Psychology*, 1974, *2*, 275–285.

Miller, R. B. (Comments). In W. F. Grether (Ed.), *The training of astronauts*. Washington, D.C.: National Academy of Science-National Research Council, 1961.

Moreno, J. L. Psychodramatic production techniques: The technique of role reversal, the mirror technique, the double technique and the dream technique. *Group Psychotherapy*, 1952, *4*, 243–273.

Moses, J. L., and Ritchie, R. J. Supervisory relationships training: A behavioral evaluation of the behavioral modeling program. *Personnel Psychology*, 1976, *29*, 337–343.

Näätänen, R. The inverted-U relationship between activation and performance: A critical review. In S. Kornblum (Ed.), *Attention and performance IV*. New York: Academic Press, 1973.

Pressey, S. L. A simple apparatus which gives tests and scores—and teaches. *School Sociology*, No. 586, 1926, *23*, 323–376.

Pressey, S. L. Development and appraisal of devices providing immediate automatic scoring of objective tests and concomitant self-instruction. *Journal of Psychology*, 1950, *29*, 417–447.

Rothkopf, E. Z., & Bisbicos, E. E. Selective facilitative effects of interspersed questions on learning from written materials. *Journal of Educational Psychology*, 1967, *58*, 56–61.

Skinner, B. F. *Walden two*. New York: Macmillan, 1948.

Skinner, B. F. *Science and human behavior*. New York: Macmillan, 1953.

Skinner, B. F. *Teaching machines. Science*, 1958, *128*, 969–977.

Skinner, B. F. *Contingencies of reinforcement: A theoretical analysis*. New York: Appleton-Century-Crofts, 1969.

Skinner, B. F. *Beyond freedom and dignity*. New York: Bantam, 1971.

Smith, H. C. *Psychology of industrial behavior*. New York: McGraw-Hill, 1955.

Stolorow, L. M. *Some educational problems and prospects of a systems approach to instruction*. Alexandria, Va.: Defense Documentation Center. (Report No. A.D. 435032) (Office of Naval Research Contract Nonr. 3985 (04), 1964, Report #2 [1964].)

CHAPTER **8**

Personnel Training and Development: Methods and Research

In Chapter 7, basic concepts and models of learning and training were presented. The present chapter is devoted to describing some of the methods used in providing an environment in which learning can occur. While little will be said about the relative effectiveness of the various methods, the second section of the chapter considers the problems and procedures for evaluating programs and methods in a training setting. The third section reviews some of the research literature on training, with special emphasis on programs aimed at managers and executives. Finally, in the last section, two special problem areas are considered: training the hard-core unemployed, and the maintenance and updating of skills of older workers.

METHODS OF TRAINING

The training profession has not suffered from a scarcity of methods. New methods, like new laundry detergents, seem to be forthcoming each new season. Some of these methods are based on explicit models of learning and behavior change such as those that were discussed in the prior chapter. In fact, in several cases, model, method, and behavior theory are closely related. Behavior modification and programmed instruction are two examples in which methods have a rational basis in a theory of behavior. Some methods seem to have been the result of trial and error. Others seem to be more the result of technological rather than theoretical developments such as computer-based games or exercises.

It would be a major undertaking to attempt to list and describe all of the specific training methods and innovations that are or have been in use. Instead, we will report the results of a review of methods used in management training and development. Nevertheless, many of the methods described are applicable to training at levels other than management and to other training objectives.

In their extensive review of the literature and their survey of practices in managerial training, Campbell, Dunnette, Lawler, and Weick (1970) identified 22 different methods and techniques that were considered applicable to the training and development of managerial personnel. These techniques were categorized as (1) *information presentation techniques,* including the lecture, the conference or seminar, sensitivity training, laboratory education, systematic observation, closed-circuit television, programmed instruction, training by correspondence, motion pictures, and reading lists; (2) *simulation methods,* including the case method, the incident method, role playing, business games, the task model, and the in-basket technique; (3) *on-the-job training,* including job rotation, committee assignments (or junior executive boards), on-the-job coaching, and performance.

We will not attempt to discuss each of these techniques. Some are well known or little used and need no further elaboration. Others, because they are novel or represent recent innovations in training technology, will be given more attention.

Information Presentation Techniques

Lectures, conference methods, correspondence courses, motion pictures, and reading lists are familiar methods in need of little further description. However, some attention will be given to them when we look at the research directed at evaluating methods.

Systematic Observation. This training method assumes that the trainee can learn managerial techniques and practices by observing a model manager in action. Campbell et al. (1970) thought that the method may be limited because the trainee must judge the relative importance of what he observes. This suggests that the method might well be combined with training in observation, including guidance of the trainee in classifying the situations, the types of problems the manager is solving, and the types of strategies and solutions involved. Observation without a system is seldom systematic, is subject to biases, and is not likely to be an effective or efficient training method.

Closed-Circuit Television. Closed-circuit television, particularly with videotape provisions allowing instant replays, has some unique properties as a training method. It permits trainees to see themselves in action shortly after the action has occurred. This sort of feedback may be valuable for a wide variety of training situations, from learning a golf swing to learning to be sensitive to one's own "stimulus value" in social situations. As an example of the latter, a program of research was conducted by the Air Force on the training of military personnel for interaction with people in cultures very different from their own. This contact interaction program (COIN) made extensive use of self-confrontation through videotape feedback. Trainees engaged in role playing specific social situations that were typical (and perhaps critical) in the foreign culture and then they engaged in evaluative discussions which were centered around the videotape replay of the sessions (eg., Haines, 1964; Haines & Eachus, 1965).

As we described in Chapter 7, behavioral modeling has become a popular training approach. It has been common to present the model via videotape. While there has been considerable research on the modeling aspect of the approach, there has not been much examination of the "delivery system"—videotape. Walter (1975) studied the effects of videotaped modeling and feedback on group problem solving. College students were asked to suggest solutions to some standard problems used for group problem-solving exercises. There were several control conditions involving verbal instructions. The experimental conditions included (1) a presentation of a videotape depicting a group dealing with a similar problem, (2) a presentation of the subjects' first efforts to solve the problem (i.e. feedback), and (3) a combination of feedback and modeling. The modeling condition produced the greatest number of novel and feasible solutions. The modeling-plus-feedback condition was also effective. The "feedback-only" condition was not significantly different from the control conditions. Walter concluded that the study clearly demonstrated the effectiveness of videotaped training inputs. We are inclined to agree, but with one reservation: the study did not provide unequivocal support for the videotape machine. Instead, it suggested that there are certain kinds of information (behavior of models) that can be presented on videotape and can have facilitating effects on trainee behavior. Walter suggests that this facilitating effect is due to the fact that the trainee is not bombarded with verbal and written information. By implication, he is hypothesizing that training often suffers because of information overload induced by instructions. We will see in Chapter 13 that, while the effects of information overload have been examined carefully with respect to skilled performance, little research has been done on the issue with respect to training performance. It is a topic that deserves further examination.

Another more subtle point is contained in the Walter results. One of the more popular activities for trainers is to tape the performance of trainees and play it back to them, pointing out where mistakes were made and how to correct them. The results from the Walter study do not lend support to this technique. Instead, it seems as if it would be better to show the trainees tapes of models performing the action correctly. Unfortunately, this is an instance of the hardware wagging the program, a tendency described in Chapter 7. It is fun to see yourself on TV, even when you are doing something stupid. Trainees are genuinely enthusiastic about having their performance taped. Unfortunately, it does not seem as if they learn much from looking at their mistakes. While it would be ridiculous to dismiss a technique such as videotaped feedback of performance to trainees on the basis of one study, in the absence of careful examinations of the use of videotape in industrial training, we would limit our generalizations of videotaped information presentation to modeling until more information becomes available regarding feedback.

Sensitivity Training: The "T-Group." Like the conference or seminar training method, the "T-group" is a discussion method involving participation by members in a small group. In contrast to the traditional conference, however, the subject matter for the T-group is the behavior of the members. Members are encouraged to reflect on, interpret, and evaluate the actions and reactions of others and of themselves. Members are expected to express freely their reactions to and interpretations of the others' behavior (verbal and other), pointing out evidence of hostility, insecurity, defensive reactions, and other behavior "dynamics." Campbell et al. (1970) have pointed out some of many variations of the original National Training Laboratory groups. These tend to vary with the degree of prominence and other aspects of the role of the group leader or trainer, who may be a passive resource person or an active interpreter of behavior and instigator of conflict. Nevertheless, these authors felt that certain objectives were common to the various sensitivity training techniques:

1. To give the trainee an understanding of how and why he acts toward other people as he does and of the way in which he affects them.
2. To provide some insight into why other people act the way they do.
3. To teach the participants how to "listen," that is, actually hear what the other people are saying rather than concentrating on a reply.
4. To provide insights concerning how groups operate and what sorts of processes groups go through under certain conditions.
5. To foster an increased tolerance and understanding of the behavior of others.
6. To provide a setting in which an individual can try out new ways of interacting with people and receive feedback as to how these new ways affect them. (Campbell et al., 1970, p. 239)

An expansion of T-group training that may involve additional short lectures, role playing, and the like is known as *laboratory education.* Such laboratories are usually held at a live-in training center away from the company. The most well-known laboratory education program is the National Training Lab (NTL), but there are numerous innovators and imitators. (For a detailed description of NTL, see Bradford, Gibb, & Benne, 1964.)

Simulation Methods

Just as training can involve the simulation of a machine control task or of an entire multiple man-machine system, so also can it attempt to simulate certain aspects of the manager's situation. Various simulation methods are designed to provide realistic training in the decision-making or interpersonal-relations aspects of the manager's job.

The Case Method. This method involves the written description of an organizational situation constituting a problem in need of a solution. The problem may be largely technical or logistical, or it may center on interpersonal or intergroup relations. Trainees are encouraged to offer solutions, usually in a conference or seminar setting, where proposals can be evaluated, providing feedback to the trainees. Sometimes the cases are descriptions of real situations where the outcomes of one or more attempted solutions are known. These results may be withheld by the trainer until solutions have been offered and evaluated by the training group and then presented as a basis for further evaluation and perspective on the proposals. Campbell et al. (1970) suggest that the case method may be most effective as a means of illustrating and providing practice in the application of general principles presented through lecture or other more direct methods. A variation of the case method is the *incident method* (Pigors & Pigors, 1955), in which a brief outline of the case is presented and trainees are encouraged to seek additional information by questioning the trainer. After a solution has been reached, the trainer presents the case in full, whereupon the proposed solution is reevaluated. On the face of it, this method offers practice not only in problem solving and decision making based on a static body of information, but also in information-gathering skills necessary for problem solution.

Role Playing. Role playing is similar in many respects to the clinical technique known as *psychodrama.* The basic technique is that of acting out certain prescribed roles in problem situations, usually involving conflicting interests of individuals or of the groups they represent. The basic assumption is that true empathic appreciation of the position of another person is best achieved by "putting yourself in the other person's place." Role playing is thus designed to increase interpersonal sensitivity or human-relations skills. At the same time, the actors are expected to work toward a solution of a problem. This problem constitutes the situation around which the acting takes place. There is no script; the participants are given only a brief description of their role and their position regarding the problem. Maier and his associates (Maier, 1953; Maier & Solem, 1952; Maier & Zerfoss, 1952) have advocated multiple role playing where the larger training group is divided into several role-playing teams and the various problem solutions are presented and discussed. This reduces the high cost and time consumption of a single session. Role playing shares the goals of sensitivity training with the T-groups and of decision making with the case method in a way that would appear to sensitize the decision maker to the participation method and to the impact of decisions on those whose jobs are affected.

Decision making with a different emphasis appears to be the main goal of *business games* as they are used in management training and development. These games usually provide rather detailed information about a business or unit of an organization. This information describes rules and relationships between processes, prices, and departments. Trainees make decisions about prices, inventories, promotional campaigns, and the like. Such games vary from relatively modest cases to complex computer-based programs. Regardless of their complexity, most games operate on a few principles, which, once they are revealed, limit the challenge and the training value. At the same time, they may reinforce the notion that *this* principle is the one to guide all such decision making.

The *in-basket* technique was described in Chapter 6 as a selection assessment device. However, a set of in-basket items such as correspondence, requests or complaints, together with the trainees' report as to how each item would be dealt with, would appear to be a fruitful basis for discussion between trainer and trainees.

On-the-Job Methods

In addition to the unsystematic, often haphazard, "sink-or-swim" policy that is frequently labeled "on-the-job training," there are some identifiable techniques for improving and/or broadening skill on the job. Campbell et al. (1970) identified four types of on-the-job training, some of which are unique to management development and some of which are more broadly applicable.

Job Rotation. Job rotation has very general applications as a training method. It may be used to develop and improve skills from the low-skill levels to top-level management. The goals of job rotation may be to increase the flexibility and adaptability of the work force or, at managerial and administrative levels, to increase the employee's effectiveness on her own job by providing firsthand knowledge of other operations within the organization.

If job rotation is treated as a trial-and-error learning method without some guidance or structuring, it may well be an ineffective and inefficient method, as its critics have suggested. However, as a part of a program that prepares the trainee for the experiences on the rotated job and uses the experiences as the basis for evaluating and coaching, the method may be quite valuable.

Other On-the-Job Methods. Campbell et al. (1970) list *committee assignments*, in which managers-in-training solve real problems in a committee structure, *coaching*, which reminds one of apprenticeship or tutorial training, and *performance appraisal*, which partakes of the notion of coaching, wherein the superior uses the appraisal interview to explore ways of improving the subordinate's performance, as additional on-the-job training techniques for managers.

On-the-job training methods have the advantage that they avoid the problem of transfer of training from a separate training setting to the job setting. They represent the "whole-training" method in the broadest sense of this term. The trainee is expected to develop proficiency at the job tasks and, at the same time, adjust to the physical and social context in which these tasks are performed. On-the-job training also frequently offers opportunities for observing and imitating seasoned operators performing the same job. Obviously, there are many jobs in which at least the initial phases of training cannot be handled on the job. Thus, one cannot train an astronaut on board a space flight or turn loose a novice with a $100,000 airplane. On the other hand, most training programs begun off the job are continued on the job. Seldom is the trainee ready to meet standard production the first day on the job. A major question that apparently has received little attention has to do with providing for continued improvement and development of trainees once they have left the training and are on the job.

The "whole-method" aspect of on-the-job training may produce an overload for the new employee, as suggested by the Texas Instrument study described in the last chapter. Preview of the job and orientation to the physical and social setting, as well as pretraining on the task itself, may facilitate job adjustment.

THE EVALUATION OF TRAINING PROGRAMS AND TECHNIQUES

As the title of this section suggests, it is one thing to evaluate a training program, but it may be quite another matter to evaluate a method or technique. Training programs often involve several methods, media, and specific techniques. When the overall effectiveness of the program is evaluated, little or nothing can be concluded about the component methods. Relative effectiveness of two methods or programs may be assessed by comparing two equivalent groups, each trained using one method or program, on a common criterion measure or measures. Evaluation of the absolute effectiveness of these methods would require the use of an appropriate control group receiving no formal training.

Criteria for Evaluation

As with any personnel program, the evaluation of training programs begins with a consideration of criteria and criterion measures. While the general issues of criterion development and criterion selection were discussed in Chapter 4, there are some special considerations with respect to the choice of criteria for training research.

Internal and External Criteria. Martin (1957) was apparently the first researcher to identify two classes of criteria—internal and external measures. Internal criteria refer to those measures of behavior indicative of performance in the training situation. Thus, grades on a common final examination as a criterion for comparative evaluation of two training programs for psychologists would be an internal criterion, while peer ratings as to professional or scientific productivity made by colleagues five years after graduation would be an external criterion. Generally speaking, external criteria refer to measures of performance on the job for which the training program was designed, rather than performance in training itself. Internal criteria include objective exams, questionnaires reflecting attitude changes by the trainees, and the opinions of trainees, trainers, or others as to the effectiveness of the program. Comparison of training methods or programs may use the number of hours of training required to reach a common training performance level as an internal measure. A similar criterion—hours (days or weeks) to reach standard production on the job *after training*—would be an external criterion. External criteria include measures of quantity or quality of production, time to reach production levels, accident records (for safety training), and other indicators of job behavior or training results. Group performance records are used as criteria for the effectiveness of the training given to the group's supervisor, and employee ratings of their supervisor's leadership, interpersonal or organizational skills may also be appropriate external criteria. The distinction between internal and external criteria is the difference between performance on a test of safety knowledge administered at the end of a safety training program and a measure of safe behavior practices back on the job, or between a score on the "How Supervise?" human relations test obtained from a supervisor at the end of training and ratings by that supervisor's subordinates as to his or her "human-relations" behavior six months later.

Levels of Criteria. Kirkpatrick (1959) identified four "levels" of criteria for the evaluation of training programs: reaction, learning, behavior, and results. The first two levels are what Martin called internal criteria. *Reaction criteria* are measures of the trainees' impressions of the training program— what they thought about it, how valuable it was as a learning experience, and so forth. These are usually assessed by means of questionnaires administered at the end of the training program. *Learning criteria* attempt to determine how much was learned as a result of training and involve the familiar final exams. These measures, whether paper-and-pencil or performance tests, should reflect the objectives of the training program. The more adequately and specifically these objectives have been stated, the easier it will be to identify and evaluate the appropriateness (i.e., the content validity) of criterion measures of learning. Thus, for example, if one objective of a training program for lathe operators is "that the operator shall be able to turn a piece of stock to a specified diameter, plus or minus 10/1000 inches within 5 minutes," then the learning criterion is clear: the examination should include a measure of the trainee's ability to perform the problem stated in the objective within the tolerance and time limits indicated.

Kirkpatrick's last two criterion levels—behavior and results—are levels of external criteria. *Behavioral criteria* refer to measures of performance back on the job. They are designed to answer the question "To what extent are the desired changes in the job behaviors of the trainee realized by the training program?" These may well be the *same* behaviors measured with the learning criteria, as in the case of the lathe operator. However, as was noted in the last chapter, behavioral changes acquired in training and evident in learning criteria do not necessarily *transfer* from the training setting to the job setting. There are numerous reports in which success in training (as measured by learning criteria) was found to be a poor predictor of success on the job or in a chosen career (as measured by behavioral or results criteria).

By *results criteria,* Kirkpatrick refers to measures of the payoff or utility of the training with respect to organizational objectives. Results criteria might measure percentage increases in job proficiency, decreases in accidents, turnover, absenteeism, or improved satisfaction of subordinates with their recently trained supervisor.

The choice of criteria should not be simply a matter of preference or convenience. While careful measurement of internal criteria—reactions and learning—in the context of an adequately designed study can provide valuable information to the trainer, these measurements cannot tell us what impact the training has on job behaviors or organizational goals. Evaluation of the payoff from a training program depends not on what is learned in training, but on how and to what extent job behaviors and effectiveness are changed. Ultimately, the benefits of training should be cost accountable, as Odiorne (1964) insists, but this is a complex evaluation, and there are typically a host of uncontrolled factors (e.g., turnover, market changes) that are confounded with training effects so that accurate measures of gains and costs are not easily obtained.

Furthermore, behavioral criteria are not adequate substitutes for results criteria. While they may indicate that the training program was effective in changing behavior and that the behavioral changes transferred to the job situation, they do not demonstrate that the new behaviors are more effective than the old with respect to organizational objectives. Thus, for example, behavioral criteria might indicate that a training program in decision making for executives had dramatic effects on decision-making behavior on the job, but with the net result that subordinates were excluded from participation in the decision process, which led to low morale and increased grievances and turnover.

While the internal/external distinction is an important one from the scientist's point of view, Goldstein (1978) has proposed a more refined evaluation format. He introduces the format by describing some common complaints that are heard involving the effects of training. The first complaint is from the trainee who claims:

> "There is a conspiracy. I just finished my training program. I even completed a pretest and a post-test. My post-test score was significantly better than the scores of my friends in the on-the-job control group. However, I lost my job because I could not perform the work."

The second complaint comes from the trainer, who objects:

> "There is a conspiracy. Everyone praised our training program. They said it was the best program they ever attended. The trainees even had a chance to laugh a little. Now the trainees tell me that the management will not let them perform their job the way we trained them."

The final complaint comes from an administrative officer in the organization, who says:

> "There is a conspiracy. My competition used the training program and it worked for them. They saved a million. I took it straight from their manuals, and my employees still cannot do the job."

Each of these individuals is claiming that training did not have the intended effect. Goldstein suggests that these and other questions regarding the validity of a training program can be placed in one of four categories:

1. *Training Validity.* Did the trainees match the criteria established for the training program?
2. *Performance Validity.* Did the trainees match the criteria established for success when they were back on the job?
3. *Intraorganizational Validity.* Is the training program equally effective with different groups of trainees within the same company?
4. *Interorganizational Validity.* Is the training program equally effective with different trainees in companies other than the one that developed the training program?

You would expect that a training program that can answer each of those four questions "Yes" would be evaluated very positively. The different kinds of validity might be arranged hierarchically, as is shown in Figure 8–2. This suggests that interorganizational validity is harder to achieve than intraorganizational validity, that performance validity is harder to achieve than training validity, and so on. This is because there are more potential obstacles to training effectiveness as one proceeds up the hierarchy. Figure 8–1 describes some of the "threats" to validity at each of the levels in Figure 8–2. Keep in mind that the threats at one level include all the

FIGURE 8–1

Threats to the Types of Training Validity

Type of Validity	Threat
Interorganizational	Dissimilarity between your organization and the one that developed the training program. This would include, among other variables: dissimilarity of tasks, jobs, needs, climates, products.
Intraorganizational	Unstable training effects, inadequate training evaluation, changes in organization over time, unintended changes in training program over time.
Performance	Inadequate job and/or task analysis, no consideration of transfer mechanism, unspecified organizational goals, organizational conflict.
Training	Availability of "cute" training hardware, lack of clear training objectives, biased assignments of individuals to training and control groups, failure to collect base-rate data.

FIGURE 8–2
Types of Validity in Training Evaluation

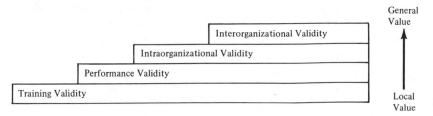

threats at the level below it! This should give you some appreciation for the difficulties in developing a generally applicable training program. More to the point, this suggests that it is important to determine the general purpose of the training prior to designing the evaluation of the training program.

Research Designs

The basic issue in the design of training research, as Campbell (1971) pointed out, is whether we can set up our conditions so as to be able to say that changes in criterion behavior are, indeed, the result of training. Most designs and training studies leave us with an equivocal answer to this question. Since the fundamental purpose of training is to bring about a systematic *change* in behavior (knowledge, skills, attitudes), a simple after-training measure cannot document such training effects. A before-training measure is essential for comparison. However, the demonstration of a change from *before* to *after* measures for a training group does not unequivocally show that the change was due to the training. Since there was a time interval between before-and-after measures, only some portion of which was filled by training, the behavioral changes may have resulted from other experiences or events. Thus, as MacKinney (1957) has argued, a control group is needed that receives the before-and-after measures but not the training. The training and control group should be comparable on the *before* measure; that is, essentially equivalent groups.

Even with before-after measures and a no-training control group, the interpretation of behavior changes is not simple. Suppose, for example, that both groups have *before* scores of 50 and, while the training group has an *after* score of 76, the control group has 63. Is the change in performance of the training group due to the *content* of the training course or to the mere fact that the trainees were selected for training, resulting in a positive effect on work motivation, that is, a "Hawthorne effect"?[1] What

---

[1] The Hawthorne studies are discussed in Chapter 10. The Hawthorne effect refers to evidence noted in these studies that employees may respond to *any* change (or *perceived* change) in their work situation, or simply to the fact that they were chosen for the experiment, by increasing their productivity.

about the change in the control group scores? To what extent are these the result of simply having taken the pretest? From a practical point of view, it could be argued that if *any* "training" program will produce desired changes (via the Hawthorne effect), then by all means find the least expensive program that will satisfy the employee. On the other hand, if the administration of a simple *before* measure can result in half as much gain as an elaborate training program, then it may be reasonable simply to give *before* measures and forget the training. The first of these concerns can be evaluated by adding a "placebo" group. (This term refers to the "sugar-pill" type of control frequently used in drug research.) This group receives *before* and *after* measures, but in place of the training the group members are exposed to, this group receives a "sham" training program of some sort, which presumably can produce the Hawthorne effect. The second concern, that for the effects of the *before* measure, per se, can be evaluated with a fourth group that receives no pretest and no training, but does receive a post-test.

The Complete Design. This brings us to the training research design proposed by Solomon (1949), which is shown in Figure 8–3. This design probably represents the ultimate in experimental elegance and control. Unfortunately, it has some practical limitations. Only one-fourth of the appropriate group can be trained in the evaluation period, and the target group must be large enough to divide into four reasonably large subgroups. The first problem is not so serious: after the value of the training is established using the four groups, the three control groups can then be given the same training.

Quasi-Experimental Designs. Some less complete research designs have been proposed by Campbell and Stanley (1963). They allow for partial control and the elimination of at least some competing explanations of the changes accompanying training without requiring four comparable groups of subjects. The first of these is the "time series experiment," a one-group design that requires a series of before-and-after measures at different points in time. Evidence for a training effect is a *discontinuity* in the series of measures, corresponding to the training program, and greater than point-to-point changes elsewhere in the measures; that is, an atypical change in the data. While this design is an improvement on the simple before-

FIGURE 8–3

The Four-Group Design Proposed by Solomon

Group	Time 1 (before)	Training Period	Time 2 (after)
Experimental	Measure	Train	Measure
Control 1	Measure	Placebo activity	Measure
Control 2	Measure	No training	Measure
Control 3	No	No training	Measure

Source: Based on Solomon, R. L. An extension of control group design. *Psychological Bulletin*, 1949, *46*, 137–150.

after design in that the criterion change corresponding to the training period can be compared with changes that occur at other times without intervening training, it does not rule out other nontraining explanations of the change, including Hawthorne effects.

Another design suggested by Campbell and Stanley seems to offer a reasonable compromise between experimental elegance and practical limitations. In this design, the target group is divided into two comparable groups. Both are given *before* tests followed by training of one group, no training of the other, and *after* measures for both groups. To this point the design does not differ from the simple two-group design. However, following the second measure, the roles of the two groups are reversed: the untrained group is now trained while the trained group stands by for a third test given after the second training period, as illustrated in Figure 8–4.

This design provides additional comparisons and controls not offered by the simple two-group design. Gains made by Group I over the training period can be compared with gains made by Group II over their training period; gains made in training can be compared with gains (or no gains) made in the no-training period, and so on.

For the most part, the various designs described above could be applied to research comparing two or more training programs, methods, or variations, by simply adding one experimental group for each method of training, or by replacing the "sham" training of the placebo condition with a true training alternative. The methodological and logical pitfalls of comparative training research are many, however. The possibilities that certain methods are superior for instructing in specific content areas, or that an outstanding lecture may be more effective than a mediocre programmed learning text, or that the novelty of a T-group experience may produce short-run superiority over an exercise in role playing, suggests only a few of the problems in evaluating training methods.

The evaluation designs just presented are somewhat abstract. We now present two examples of some concrete designs for the evaluation of two industrial training programs. Figure 8–5 describes the evaluation component of the behavior modeling program at American Telephone and Telegraph (AT & T), which was studied by Moses and Ritchie (1976). As can be seen from the figure, there are some deficiencies with respect to the rigorous designs described in Tables 8–2 and 8–3. The most obvious deficiency is the absence of base-line or pretraining measures of performance. Generally,

FIGURE 8–4

A Quasi-Experimental Design Proposed by Campbell and Stanley

Group	Time 1	Time 2	Time 3
I	Measure—Train	Measure—No train	Measure
II	Measure—No train	Measure—Train	Measure

Source: Based on Campbell, D. T., & Stanley, J. C. *Experimental and quasi-experimental designs for research.* Chicago: Rand McNally, 1963.

FIGURE 8-5

An Overview of the Study Design Employed

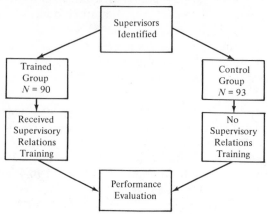

these measures are available in the form of past performance appraisals and can be added to the design to make sure that there were no significant differences between the groups prior to training. Figures 8–6 and 8–7 are slightly more elaborate. They describe the evaluation of a training program for improving employee morale, customer morale, and sales in International Business Machine (IBM) branch locations. Once again, the training approach was one of behavioral modeling (Smith, 1976). In this study, mea-

FIGURE 8-6

Overview of Employee Study Design

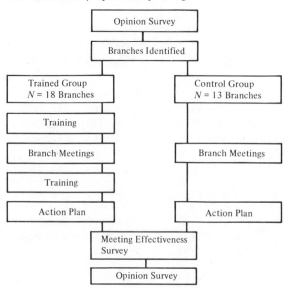

FIGURE 8–7
Overview of Customer Satisfaction Modeling Training Design

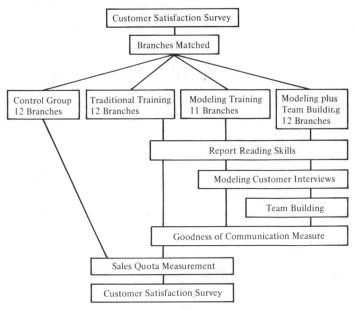

sures of training and control groups were obtained prior to the training program. In Figure 8–6, these premeasures were employee attitudes toward the organization, and in particular toward department meetings. In Figure 8–7, these premeasures consisted of measures of customer satisfaction with each of the branch locations. Branches were then assigned to conditions in such a manner as to ensure matched samples with respect to the variable of interest—customer satisfaction. Subsequently, the effectiveness of three different training conditions were compared to a control condition.

The complete design and the quasi-experimental design as described are idealized views of training evaluation. The designs presented in Figures 8–5, 8–6, and 8–7 are more typical. As you can see, some control is lost in the translation from ideal to real. Accompanying this loss of control is an increase in uncertainty. We are less certain that the training was solely responsible for the change. Nevertheless, there is a point at which the manager must come to an agreement with the scientist. From a practical point of view, it is unlikely that the training manager will be able to include all of the appropriate control groups. But at the very least, there must be premeasures on the variables of interest for the various groups to come to any reasonable conclusion regarding the effectiveness of the training.

Goals of Training Research. There are a number of reasons for conducting training research. The academic psychologist is apt to focus on the need for knowledge about principles of learning, training, and transfer, or about the relative merits of one or the other theories, models, methods, or media. From quite another view, the training practitioner or the vice president for personnel may have a much more pragmatic interest in program evaluation. They may be primarily concerned with determining program effectiveness and with acquiring whatever information may be helpful in modifying the present program to make it more effective. Goldstein (1974), borrowing the terms used by Borg (1963), describes these two types of research as "formal instructional research" and "action research," adding a third category, "casual or 'common sense' research." The last category seems to refer to innovations in educational procedures that are casually and subjectively evaluated, typically by the instructor who initiates the change.

The objectives of action research involve the evaluation and modification of specific local programs. Action research is not concerned with generalization beyond the setting or the sample of subjects to some larger population, nor is it likely to be concerned with the systematic evaluation of independent variable conditions. If a new technique is compared with an old one, interest is primarily in answering the question, "Is the new method better than the old?" and not in attempting to determine why one or the other method is superior.

Both action research and formal research are legitimate approaches to evaluation. The theorist is expected to contribute to the general body of knowledge and principles, while the practitioner is expected to provide the most efficient and effective local programs possible. Unfortunately, as a result, action research seldom contributes to general knowledge and instead becomes the evaluative stage in each training program. Often, with a bit more planning of research design and concern for generalizable knowledge, the action research program could contribute something to the science of instruction.

TRAINING RESEARCH

The literature contains a large number of reports of training research. At least a few studies could be cited involving each of the methods, techniques, and media mentioned in this chapter. A thorough review of this body of research would require another book, however, and might well leave us with little more insight into which methods are best for which training purposes than we had when we began. Relatively few studies have been adequately controlled and even those which were controlled frequently cannot be generalized to the field training situation. Campbell (1971) summarized his impression of the literature on training this way:

> By and large, the training and development literature is voluminous, nonempirical, nontheoretical, poorly written, and dull . . . it is faddish to an extreme. The fads center around the introduction of new techniques and follow a characteristic pattern. A new technique appears on the horizon and develops a large stable of advocates who first describe its "successful" use in a number of situations. A second wave of advocates busy themselves trying out numerous modifica-

tions of the basic technique. A few empirical studies may be carried out to demonstrate that the method "works." Then the inevitable backlash sets in and a few vocal opponents begin to criticize the usefulness of the technique, most often in the absence of data. Such criticism typically has very little effect. What does have an effect is the appearance of another new technique and a repetition of the same cycle.

It is clearly beyond the scope of this chapter to look at all of the research purporting to evaluate each of the methods, techniques, media, and programs of training. Instead, we will review the findings of Campbell et al. (1970), who have presented a systematic description and interpretation of the managerial training literature.

Management Training and Development

One of the most challenging areas of personnel training and utilization is management. It is, at the same time, the area most susceptible to fads, fashion, and fancy in training. With the exception of programmed instruction and behavior modification techniques, most of the many recent techniques have been directed at management development.

At least two aspects of the challenge in this area of training—the specification of training needs and the evaluation of training—stem from the difficulty of writing a job description for "the manager," or for a level of management. Without a clear conception of the necessary behaviors for job proficiency, or of criteria whereby proficiency can be assessed, the problems of specifying what is to be learned and what is to be gained from training loom very large.

Campbell et al. (1970) have pointed out that each of the models and theories which were reviewed in the last chapter provides a different view of management training. Learning theory views the problem as that of learning certain information or responses to relevant situational cues. It emphasizes such principles of efficient learning as reinforcement, distributed practice, and meaningfulness of material. Meanwhile, Gagne's training principles (as described in Chapter 7) emphasize the content and the order in which it should be sequenced; a model with intuitive appeal, but little appeal for management development programs. Behavior modification and programmed learning both emphasize contingent reinforcement and overt behaviors, while attitude and motivation theories emphasize cognitive rather than direct behavioral change.

In organizing the research literature, Campbell et al. (1970) classified the training programs into five content areas: (1) general management or general supervision training, (2) general human relations training, (3) training in problem solving and decision making, (4) laboratory education programs, and (5) specialized programs. They cross-referenced the literature according to the use of internal or external criteria and, finally, they classified each study in terms of whether the design provided "some" or "few" controls ("some" indicated the use of control groups). This classification scheme is presented in Table 8–1, which also shows the number of studies placed in each category.

A few points are worth noting regarding Table 8–1. First, over 70 percent of the studies used internal criterion measures. Of these, nearly 40 percent attempted to evaluate training without benefit of control groups. With respect to type of content, over one-third of the studies dealt with T-group and laboratory education programs.

This area (managerial behavior and attitudes), no doubt represents the most challenging with respect to evaluation because the criteria are often vague, abstract, and difficult to measure. These programs are concerned with "human-relations skills," "interpersonal sensitivity," "problem solving and decision making," and the like, rather than more concrete production criteria, absenteeism, accidents, and similar measures. By the same token, as Campbell et al. (1970) point out, demonstrating a change in these criterion measures as a result of training is *not* equivalent to establishing a change in the *effectiveness* of the manager. This is true even using external criteria (e.g., subordinate, peer, or superior ratings). The relationship between such behaviors and attitudes and effective performance is more theoretical than real at this time. One cannot conclude that because a supervisor is rated more "considerate" by his subordinates after training that he is necessarily more effective as a supervisor. Furthermore, job performance measures that might reflect true changes in job effectiveness as the result of training are all too often ratings made by persons (supervisors, subordinates, or peers) who know not only that the ratee has had the training

TABLE 8–1

Summary of Empirical Studies of Management Training Programs Classified by Campbell et al.

	General Management Programs	General Human Relations	Problem Solving and Decision Making	T-Group and Laboratory Education Programs	Specialty Programs	Total
External Criteria						
Controls						
Some	2	—	—	6	5	13
Few	1	3	1	3	—	8
	3	3	1	9	5	21
Internal Criteria						
Controls						
Some	8	10	3	8	3	32
Few	5	6	—	9	—	20
	13	16	3	17	3	52
Total	16	19	4	26	8	73

Source: Campbell, J. P., Dunnette, M. D., Lawler, E. E., & Weick, K. E. *Managerial behavior, performance, and effectivness.* Chicago: McGraw-Hill, 1970.

but also what the objectives of the training were. Such ratings are suspect because of the possibilities of contamination from knowledge of the purpose of the ratings and the goals of the training program.

Researchers have relied heavily on the Ohio State Leadership research for both internal and external criterion measures. Thus, the "Consideration" and "Initiating Structure" scales have been used in a large proportion of the studies and most frequently as self-reports following training (internal criteria).[2] Alternatively, the "How Supervise?" test (File and Remmers, 1948), which is another-paper-and pencil criterion, has been used. Even when these measures are used as external criteria, however, they do not measure changes in effectiveness of performance, as indicated earlier. What is needed is a greater reliance on direct assessment of individual or subordinate (group) effectiveness and on multiple criteria as measures of the effectiveness of training programs.

Campbell et al. (1970) summarize their systematic review of the management training literature with four major conclusions:

1. General management and general human relations programs do produce results in a wide variety of settings. However, the results are largely with internal criteria (29 of 35 studies), predominantly involving attitudes of "consideration," "employee-centeredness," or "human relations." Much less convincing is the evidence with external criteria; that is, the carry-over of the attitudes to the work situation, particularly in the light of the International Harvester studies (Fleishman, 1953; Fleishman, Harris, & Burtt, 1955; Harris & Fleishman, 1955). These studies failed to show any carry-over from a human-relations training program when external criteria (subordinate ratings) were used. Incidently, these latter studies provide suggestive evidence that human relations attitudes and skills learned in training are likely to be practiced on the job only if the "climate" provided by the supervisor's superiors is conducive to and reinforcing of such behavior. Campbell et al. (1970) conclude that "in general, however, the thrust of these studies reflects an overreliance on one particular class of criterion variables, namely, measures of 'human relations mindedness'."

2. The second conclusion stated that the evidence on T-group and laboratory methods indicates that "back home" changes in behavior are produced. Methodological problems abound, including the facts that, typically, criterion raters know of the training and its goals, that the "changes" are not always specified or predictable, and that criteria have dealt with changes in behavior, not changes in performance efficiency.

3. Evidence on training in problem solving and decision making is sparse and disappointing, according to Campbell et al. (1970). Since the authors did not deal with laboratory studies using nonmanagerial personnel, they failed to report the research of Maier and his associates, which was largely conducted with university students concerned with training participative

---

[2] It may be useful here to turn to Chapter 11 and read the section on the Ohio State Leadership Studies.

group leaders in decision-making skills. Unfortunately, the carryover of such training to the job apparently has not been evaluated (Maier, 1953; Maier & Solem, 1957).

4. Comparative studies are too few to warrant generalizations about the relative effectiveness of the different methods. The issue is complicated by evidence of interactions between methods and individual differences suggesting that the "best" method, like a favorite color, may depend on the individual. These authors also conclude that there is a pressing need for (1) comparative studies; (2) concern with *practical significance* as contrasted with *statistical significance* of research results; (3) research on other than "human relations" techniques; (4) research that systematically isolates elements of training programs, rather than evaluating whole complex programs and then not knowing what the effective elements are; and (5) greater use of external criteria, especially those that reflect effectiveness rather than behavioral change assumed to increase effectiveness.

Sensitivity training remains a controversial issue. Campbell et al. (1970) did not close the door on the technique. They indicated that while there did seem to be training effects that could be attributed to the approach, there was some question of the stability and the relevance of these changes. Recently, Smith (1975) completed a review of controlled studies examining the outcome of sensitivity training. He concluded, as did Campbell et al. that it did produce results. In addition, he encouraged a different approach to future research:

> A variety of effects have now been documented. The more pressing questions have become whether the effects persist, whether the effects can also be created by other training methods, why the effects are detected by some measures and not others, and why these particular effects occur rather than others. (1975, p. 618)

This lament should be familiar to you. It is a concrete example of Goldstein's concern for validity of training, which was presented earlier in the chapter. In terms of research findings currently available regarding sensitivity training, there is some limited support for training validity, although several "threats" to that validity are apparent. There is no systematic support for performance, intraorganizational, or interorganizational validity of sensitivity training. Considering the fact that the approach has been around a sufficient period of time to gather empirical support for all levels of validity as mentioned, we must conclude that sensitivity training has limited value in applied settings.

Leadership Training

Training in interpersonal skills is normally directed toward supervisors rather than subordinates in any given workgroup. Most of the behavioral modeling studies described in Chapter 7 were directed toward improving the interpersonal skills of the supervisor. This implies that interpersonal skills comprise a central component of leadership and supervision. This is probably the case and will be explored carefully in Chapter 11. In spite of this assumed relationship between interpersonal skills and leader effectiveness, few training programs have taken a theory of leadership and based a program of instruction on it. An exception to this rule is the work of Fiedler (Fiedler and Mahar, In Press). In Chapter 7, we described the programmed instruction approach Fiedler has taken in leadership training. To reiterate briefly, trainees are given a self-paced programmed instruction manual and receive immediate feedback on their understanding of critical leadership concepts. Fiedler and Mahar (In Press) have reviewed the results of 12 studies using this leader-training approach, which is called Leader Match. In each of the 12 studies, they found that supervisors who completed the training program performed better than those in "control" groups. Performance was measured from two to six months after training.

As is commonly the case in field studies, there were some rather serious threats to the validity of the findings in each of the 12 studies. In addition, Fiedler and Mahar had two purposes in mind when conducting the review: (1) to determine the effectiveness of the training program, and (2) to support Fiedler's contingency theory of leadership. As a result, we are left with some nagging concerns about both the training effectiveness and the theory. The concerns about the training effectiveness stem from the control problem. Premeasures and postmeasures were not available for all groups, and it was common for trainees to drop out of the training program prior to completion. Also, the number of individuals in treatment and control groups was often substantially different even at the outset of the program, suggesting that subjects were not randomly assigned to treatment and control groups. The implications of these training results for the theory itself will be discussed at length in Chapter 11.

As is the case with a good deal of training research, it is difficult to conclude from the studies of Leader Match that this particular training program is a good one for inducing leader effectiveness. The problems of evaluation were so pervasive that we can only conclude that the evidence is "encouraging." Nevertheless, Fiedler and his associates are virtually alone in their attempts to construct and evaluate theory-based training programs related to leadership. It is our hope that many of the control problems can be eliminated, allowing a fair test of the training program and an unequivocal statement regarding its effectiveness.

Training in Goal Setting

Goal setting theory, described briefly in Chapter 7, has been criticized on the grounds that the experimental tests of predictions from the theory have been conducted almost exclusively in the laboratory with college students (Heneman & Schwab, 1972). However, Latham and his associates (Latham & Ronan, 1970; Latham & Kinne, 1971, 1974; Ronan, Latham, & Kinne, 1973) provide evidence that training in goal setting may have

310 SECTION 1: Industrial and Organizational Psychology

industrial applications. In the first of these studies, a factor analysis revealed that goal setting and "supervision" both loaded on a factor that also included loadings for two measures of production and a negative loading for injuries. In other words, goal setting was related to productivity and safe behavior. These results also seemed to indicate that the effects of goal setting interact with those of supervision. Working within the same industry (pulp wood producers), Latham & Kinne (1971) found evidence that supervisors who set production goals got higher productivity than supervisors who did not set production goals. These researchers interpreted the results as supporting Locke's (1966) view that the establishment of specific production goals is necessary for increased production through supervision. At the same time, supervision is seen as necessary to assure the acceptance of the goals by the workers (Ronan, Latham, & Kinne, 1973).

Since both of the studies cited above were correlational, the causal relation between supervision, goal setting, and production remained unclear. Therefore, these researchers compared performance of work crews for two groups of supervisors. One group received a one-day training session in production goal setting which was based upon technical information. Members of the second (control) group were aware that they were taking part in the study, but were not trained in goal setting. All supervisors kept records of production, turnover, absenteeism, and injuries, which served as dependent variables for the study. The results showed that the production of the experimental crews was significantly higher than that of the control crews. Turnover and injuries were low and not related to training in goal setting, but absenteeism was significantly higher in the control than in the trained group.

Training the "Hard-core Unemployed"

During the 1960s a new vocabulary was born reflecting an intensified concern for the problems of large city ghettos, minority groups, and in general, the disadvantaged segments of our society. Programs were initiated to prepare the hard-core unemployed (HCU) for entry into the work force. The immediate answer to the question "Why are these people chronically unemployed or underemployed?" was in terms of inadequate marketable skills. However, it soon became apparent that the problems of hard-core unemployment were broader than this. They were bound up with the psychology of the ghetto, with expectancies, attitudes, motivational problems, even "language-barrier" problems wherein the words of the trainers had different meanings for the trainees. Triandis, Feldon, Weldon, and Harvey (1975) labelled this syndrome "ecosystem distrust," and characterized it as a basic distrust of people, their motives, and a rejection of authority. This type of distrust forms a formidable obstacle for any social system.

Prerequisite to training the HCU was the need to understand something of their psychology. This has proved to be a complex and frustrating undertaking. As one example, Feldman (1973) found that some workers were less "afraid" of unemployment than others. As a matter of fact, they saw almost as many benefits from not working as from working. Searls, Bravelt, and Miskimins (1973) examined the work values of the chronically unemployed in an attempt to gain some insight into their motivations. In comparing the HCU individual to blue-collar workers, they found that the HCU felt significantly more externally controlled and was less able to delay gratification than the blue-collar worker. The problem, of course, with data like these, is determining whether feelings of external control and an inability to delay gratification are *causes* of chronic unemployment or merely *symptoms*. A person who is unemployed and is used to eating will probably tap into the social welfare system available through local, state, and federal government. In the course of taking advantage of these systems, people often become "institutionalized"—they follow orders, fill out sheets, stand in lines, and would never consider deviating from a set routine. For many families, this has been a life-style for three generations. In cases such as this, it is extremely difficult to label "feelings of external control" as a cause rather than a symptom of unemployment.

Plausible explanations of HCU based on motivational and attitude theories usually failed to gain clear support when put to empirical tests. Thus, for example, Gumpper (1970), working with a number of hypotheses from motivational, personality, and attitude theories, failed to find consistent evidence that trainees who completed the program differed in expectancies, attitudes, or needs from those who dropped out. What he did find was a negative correlation (−.40) between amount of prior unemployment and training completion, indicating ". . . a rather strong tendency for those subjects with greater amounts of prior unemployment to drop out of training before completion of the program" (p. 97). Gumpper suggested that this finding might indicate that trainees with the greatest negative experiences in the labor market were least likely to stay with the program, even though they were told it would lead to steady employment in the future.

One of the most important findings of Gumpper's study was that, while subjects who completed training showed no reliable change in attitudes, those who dropped out or were asked to leave the program showed alarming decrements in their orientation toward work. The possibility that well-intentioned programs designed to aid the disadvantaged can do more harm than good should come, if not as a surprise, at least as a sobering thought. The complexities and subtleties of the problems involved will require more than simple answers or shopworn clichés. As Goldstein (1974) suggests, "programs that include motivational and attitudinal considerations are few; however, research indicates that programs that do not consider such factors are often doomed" (p. 203). Goldstein also pointed out that successful HCU training programs include, in addition to skill training, simulations to acquaint trainees with other aspects of the jobs, practice in job hunting, and interviewing assistance in contacting employers before the end of training, job-placement, counseling, and follow-up programs.

An example of a program that appears to include these components has been developed by the Jewish Employment and Vocational Service (JEVS) of Philadelphia. This program was described briefly in the section on work-sample tests in Chapter 6. Working in collaboration with a local Human Resources Development (HRD) Center of the Pennsylvania State Employment Service, JEVS has developed a program in a simulated industrial setting complete with work stations and time clocks. Trainees are observed and evaluated on work attitude, accuracy of performance, promptness in reporting to work, learning speed, acceptance of authority, expressed job interests, and other work-related behaviors. In this context, 28 work-sample tasks related to available job and training opportunities are administered to each applicant over a two-week period. This testing-work experience phase is preceded and followed by vocational counseling and placement services in the HRD Center.

The work-sample tasks simulate activities that trainees would face on regular jobs and require the use of standard tools and equipment. They range from simple operations like changing an automobile tire to more complex tasks involving reasoning and abstract thinking. Tasks are scheduled to progress from easy to more difficult. Since they are tasks rather than paper-and-pencil tests, they are seen as less threatening to the trainees. The combination of realistic work-setting experiences and vocational counseling and placement services that utilize the data from the work-sample testing and the observations of the trainees appears to provide an effective program for the hard-to-employ. Placement and job-retention rates for the trainees have been relatively high, as indicated by follow-up studies.

The ultimate success of HCU programs—as reflected in placement and job retention records—may well depend on the social climate of the job in which the trainee is placed. Thus, Friedlander and Greenburg (1971) found that work history, biographical data, skills, and personal characteristics had little validity for predicting the trainee's success in holding a job. These researchers found that the only reliable predictor was the amount of supportiveness which the trainee experienced in the new work setting. Trainees typically perceived less supportiveness than reported by their supervisors. They concluded that:

> The HCU's prime method of coping with a work climate that he perceives as highly unsupportive (and his supervisor perceives as highly supportive) is through his own unreliable behavior—being late and/or absent from work. HCUs who are reliable on the job find the situation intolerable after a short period of time and leave the organization. Others cope with the unfavorable climate by being tardy or absent. Furthermore, our findings indicate that the characteristics that supervisors were the most critical of in the HCU was the HCU's lack of reliability . . . tardiness and absence are characteristics frequently ascribed to the black HCU culture, but these can also be viewed as indexes of escape or avoidance behavior from a climate the HCU experiences as intolerable. (p. 293)

Friedlander and Greenburg strongly suggest that adaptation of the social climate of the job situation to the HCUs may be more important than training the HCUs in skill designed to adapt them to the world of work. They suggest a process of mutual adaptation, implying the need for training of managers, supervisors, and fellow employees, as well as the HCU.

DiMarco and Gustafson (1975) compared the attitudes of co-workers and supervisors toward HCU employees. The co-workers held much more positive attitudes than did the supervisors. In addition, the degree to which co-workers and supervisors had been previously exposed to HCU employees was examined. Individuals who had previous contact with HCU employees were more likely to express favorable opinions about them. When the two variables were combined (i.e. co-worker/supervisor and know others/ do not know others), the most negative attitudes were held by supervisors who had not had previous contact with HCU employees. It is reasonable to assume that supervisors with negative attitudes toward the HCU employee will not go out of their way to help them. Thus, as Friedlander and Greenburg suggest, it is somewhat unrealistic to introduce a HCU training program without at least examining the nature of the work group that will receive the trainee.

The view that the major problems with HCU trainees—tardiness and absenteeism—are escape or avoidance reactions suggests also that the HCUs may be faced with a tremendously high level of job anxiety and insecurity. It would be surprising if they were not, given the "culture shock" the first days on the job must bring. From this view, the apparent successes of Texas Instruments (Gomersall & Meyers, 1966), who had an orientation program explicitly designed to reduce the job anxiety of the new worker, may suggest some strategies for HCU programs. Also, the symptoms— absenteeism and tardiness—might well be amenable to a behavior-modification approach, with positive reinforcements made contingent on meeting regular work schedules.

Salipante and Goodman (1976; Goodman and Salipante, 1976) did a large scale evaluation of the impact of federally financed training programs on the HCU problem. They examined 130 training programs in 114 different firms committed to hiring the HCU applicant. The results of this study were somewhat surprising. They found that job-skills training was positively related to the probability that the HCU trainee would continue to work after training but that attitudinal training was *negatively* related to retention if it included role playing! Salipante and Goodman conclude that job-skills training is a very direct indication that a job is waiting, while attitudinal training suggests individual therapy. Additionally, the attitudinal training often includes role-playing components that require interpersonal confrontations—an activity particularly aversive to those with less well-developed interpersonal skills. They did find that personal counseling was positively related to job retention. In the light of these findings, they suggest that the retention rate for HCUs may be increased more effectively through changing organizational practices (such as pay structures and other concrete reward mechanisms) than through training. They further suggest that one of the reasons why training has been such a popular approach to the HCU problem is that the federal government funneled enormous amounts of money into the effort through grants and contracts, creating a new industry and technology.

We would not go as far as Goodman and Salipante (1976) in suggesting that organizational change can have the same effect as training. This approach assumes either that the HCU individual already has the skills and simply needs a particular organizational environment to utilize them or that the skills can be picked up readily on the job. Neither of these assumptions are reasonable. Many HCU individuals are ill-prepared for any gainful employment other than the most meaningless and automatic tasks. In addition, the work of DiMarco and Gustafson suggests that on-the-job experiences may not be ideal for learning required skills. We think that training is an important part of the solution to the HCU problem. Nevertheless, the finding of Goodman and Salipante (1976) with respect to the differential effects of job skills versus attitudinal training requires serious and immediate attention: training programs that concentrate on changing attitudes may be doing more harm than good.

Equal Employment Opportunity Guidelines and Training

On Monday, December 11, 1978, the Supreme Court of the United States agreed to hear arguments regarding the potential adverse impact of training programs. Brian Weber, a Kaiser Aluminum and Chemical Corp. worker, claimed that he was a victim of reverse discrimination since, as a white employee, he was denied access to a company training program because half of all openings in the training program were reserved for blacks. If successful completion of a training program is a prerequisite for promotion within a company, then admission to that training program is, in effect, a type of selection decision. While acceptance in the training program does not necessarily guarantee promotion, nonacceptance does guarantee that an individual will not be promoted. Thus, training programs must be responsive to the EEOC guidelines in a manner similar to testing programs.

Bartlett (1978) has considered the potential sources of discrimination in training programs:

1. *Training as a Job Prerequisite.* The most obvious example of this is the requirement that applicants for positions have certain academic credentials such as a high school or college diploma. As the Supreme Court stated in the *Griggs* v. *Duke Power* case, job relevance of the requirement must be established before it can be used for making selection decisions. To use this prerequisite, it would be necessary to demonstrate that individuals without training perform more poorly than those with training.
2. *Selection for Training.* As was implied in the earlier description of the reverse discrimination suit brought by Weber against Kaiser Alumi-

num, entry into training programs can be a critical issue in personnel decisions. In the past, the court has ruled on several occasions that it is not sufficient to show that devices used for selecting trainees are correlated with training success. It must also be shown that training success is related to job success, i.e., the training program has some job relevance. Thus, the individual responsible for administration of the training program must give some thought to the manner by which individuals are selected for training. This may become a critical issue in training programs of the future.

3. *The Training Process.* The training activities themselves may have adverse impact on particular subgroups. Equipment may be designed for men rather than women, thus requiring strength or reach capabilities that are unrelated to job duties but largely determine training success. The same may be true of vocabulary levels or communication skills that are unrelated to ultimate job success but influence measured training success. For this particular problem, Bartlett suggests that the best way to address it reasonably is to go beyond a simple task analysis and do a "person" analysis, designed to uncover any individual difficulties related to the training process itself. This requires one actually to "look at" the trainee in the training situation—a good idea for lots of reasons.[3]

4. *Retention, Progress, and Graduation.* Occasionally, measures of training success are taken during the training program and are used to determine who will be "washed out" of training prior to completion. This might be thought of as the "football-camp" approach where a certain percentage of the trainees are "cut" at various points in the training sequence. Unless these training measures are validated, there is the potential for unfair discrimination in these retention decisions.

5. *Job Placement Following Training.* At the end of training, trainees are often assigned to jobs based on their success in the training program. Once again, there is the potential for unfair discrimination in these placement decisions unless the training measures have been shown to be job-related.

---

[3] A friend of ours, Irv Goldstein, delights in recalling an incident from his graduate school days as a research assistant. While assisting a professor doing operant conditioning of pigeons, Goldstein noticed that one pigeon was performing at much lower levels than the other subjects. In addition, the particular closed box that served as the experimental apparatus for this pigeon would occasionally shake, and there would be loud thumping noises accompanying the box movement. Goldstein asked the researcher for permission to observe this subject "in action"; the request was denied emphatically and immediately. The operant advocate felt that the pigeon would "shape up" shortly. Nevertheless, Goldstein looked into the box while the researcher was absent and discovered that the poor pigeon had somehow learned the wrong sequence of behaviors for producing the reward. It would go to the back of the box and run full speed to the front of the box, hitting the wall with an alarming impact. The impact was sufficient to trip the dispensing mechanism, thus releasing a reward. As far as the pigeon was concerned, this was the appropriate sequence in the "training" program. Trainers should be aware that it is often useful to "look in the box." In this case, the pigeon was saved, but Goldstein was chewed out.

6. *Promotion, Advancement, and Compensation.* If training is a prerequisite for promotion, advancement, or compensation increases, then the problem is similar to requiring training prior to employment. This was exactly the point of the *Weber* v. *Kaiser* case.

It should be clear from the description above that in addition to evaluating training in terms of its effectiveness and cost, we must also consider whether or not the administration of the training program conforms to existing local, state, and federal regulations regarding employment decisions.

THE MAINTENANCE OF EFFECTIVENESS: RETRAINING AND UPDATING

Much of the emphasis of this chapter has been on the development of skills and knowledge in new employees so that they can reach a competency level of performance on the job for which they are hired. A major exception to this emphasis was found in the section on management development, in which the principal concern was with increasing proficiency on the job and promotability to higher levels of responsibility. In both cases, the emphasis has been on increasing the overall proficiency of employees and, consequently, their value to the organization.

In recent years, an increasing concern has developed for an area of training with a considerably more negative ring. Rather than expressing concern for broadening and increasing skills and adaptability of employees, researchers and theorists in this area have sounded an alarm for the problems of loss of proficiency as learned information and skills become "obsolete," as the applicability of knowledge "erodes," and as the effectiveness of once-valuable employees declines in the face of new knowledge and technology. The alarm may be relatively new, but not the problem. Lukasiewicz (1971) estimated that in 1940 the "half-life" of the knowledge a newly-trained engineer brought to a job was about 12 years. That is, in 12 years one-half of this knowledge would be obsolete or no longer applicable. The basis for the increasing alarm is that the problem has been accentuated by an accelerated growth in knowledge and technology. Lukasiewicz estimated that the half-life of a 1970 graduating engineer was probably five years. Meanwhile, the half-life of the content in a university engineering course ("electronic circuits") was also estimated at about five years (Rosenstein, 1968).

One aspect of the problem of obsolescence is found in rapid changes in knowledge and technology, which, as previously suggested, makes the information and skills that are adequate to accomplish a job at one point in time insufficient, or at best inefficient, only a few years later. That is, obsolescence can come about because an employee's knowledge or skills remain static or change too slowly compared to changes in his field. A second problem, which is related to, yet different from that of technological obsolescence, is that of the loss of effectiveness as a result of the disuse or forgetting of information or skills. Thus, we can conceive of the problem as an increasing discrepancy between job demands and employee skills resulting from (1) changing demands with a relatively static skill level, (2) deteriorating skills such that job demands the employee could have handled earlier cannot now be met, or (3) some combination of these factors. The first situation requires training in new knowledge and techniques—what Dubin (1972a, 1972b) has called the *updating process*. The second situation is concerned with the *maintenance* of previously learned knowledge and skills through refresher training or through continued application on the job.

Electronics engineers may become obsolete because they were trained in a period before solid-state technology or because the job does not give them an opportunity to apply their knowledge of solid-state electronics, and they forget much of what they have learned. Physicians may become obsolete because they learned internal medicine 30 years too soon, or having subsequently specialized in pediatrics, forgotten much knowledge about internal disorders.

Why Does Obsolescence Occur?   You may be thinking that the engineers or the physicians have become obsolete by choice, since in all likelihood they could have maintained skills and learned new ones had they been sufficiently motivated to do so. Others may say that the older workers simply cannot keep up with the new technology because they are older. Yet others may suggest that it is not so much that older employees cannot keep up, but that they are not motivated to do so—they are either "fat, lazy and secure" in the job, or they see nothing in it for them that is worth the effort to learn new techniques. No doubt there are kernels of truth in each of the pat answers, but such simplistic models are inadequate for understanding the problem.

Age and Performance.   In a study of engineers, Dalton and Thompson (1971) explored the relationship between the age of engineers and three measures of effectiveness: performance ratings, job complexity ratings, and salary. The results of this analysis are shown in Figure 8–8. Clearly, ratings of performance and complexity rose and fell together with a steady decline after age 36–40. Meanwhile, salary continued to increase for about 10 years after the ratings peaked and had begun to decline.

At first blush, these data suggest a marked relationship between age and effectiveness as an engineer. However, since both the performance and job complexity criteria are based on subjective ratings, the close relationship between the two suggests some other possibilities. One possibility is that as the performance of engineers declines with age, their supervisors tend to assign them to less and less complex jobs. Another hypothesis is that supervision is biased toward the young "hotshots" who are fresh from university training and are given the more complex jobs, which leaves the less complex jobs for the older engineers. It may also be that, despite efforts to distinguish between ratings of job performance and ratings of job complexity, the supervisors may have had a built-in bias to rate *jobs* when they are supposed to rate *performance* (Levine and Butler, 1952). Thus, we have reason to question the meaning of the performance ratings but, even assuming their validity and freedom from contamination, we may well ask why performance goes down even on increasingly simple jobs at such a precipitous rate. It may well be a "vicious cycle" in which an engineer is given more and more routine assignments, which are less and less challenging and offer fewer opportunities to practice skills. Furthermore, unless the engineer believes that this cycle can be dramatically changed by extra efforts to keep up with new technology, he probably will not make the effort. It should be pointed out, however, that Dalton and Thompson (1971) found a good deal more variability in ratings *within* each age category than between them. The highest ratings for the "over-50" engineers were considerably higher than the average ratings at any age group. Therefore, it is necessary to be cautious when generalizing about *older workers.*

Age, Performance, and Updating. The study by Dalton and Thompson (1971) provides some answers to the question, "How do the 'updating

FIGURE 8–8

*Age and Three Measures of Engineers' Effectiveness;
Performance Ratings, Job-Complexity Ratings, and Salary*

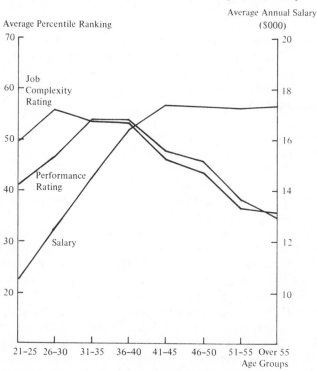

Source: Adapted from Dalton, G. W., & Thompson, P. H. Accelerating obsolescence of older engineers. *Harvard Business Review,* 1971, *49,* 57–67.

activities' of engineers compare at different ages and different performance levels?" The three indicators of updating activity examined were (1) total (reported) hours per week reading professional journals; (2) total number of company courses taken; and (3) total number of college courses taken in the past three years. The first of these showed no systematic relationship

FIGURE 8–9

Engineers' Perceptions of Their Chances for Promotion to Management (lower curve), Chances for Promotion in Engineering (middle) and Maximum Hoped-for Salary (*upper) as Function of Age

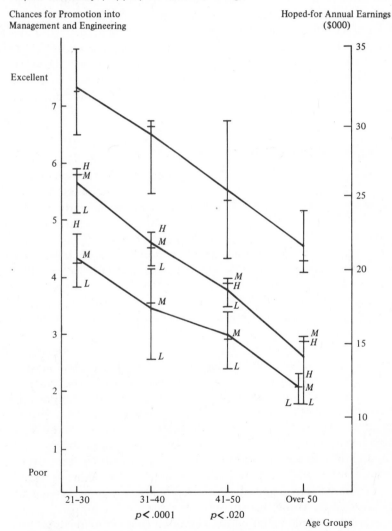

Source: Adapted from exhibits 7, 8, and 9 of Kopelman, R., Thompson, P., & Dalton, G., "Factors contributing to the effectiveness of the older engineer." In Dubin, S. S., Shelton, H., & McConnell. J. *Maintaining professional and technical competence of the older engineer.* Washington, D.C.: American Society of Engineering Education, 1974.

with age or performance ratings, but both company and college course taking declined with age, relatively independently of performance ratings. Thus, in general, participation in activities which might be assumed to counteract obsolescence actually declines with age.

Age and Expectancies.   Some insights as to why engineers do not show evidence of efforts to update themselves (the study also suggests less effort on the job as age increases) may be found in the Dalton and Thompson analyses of age and expectancies with respect to promotion and salaries. The engineers rated their chances for (1) promotion in engineering, (2) promotion into management, and (3) their maximum hoped-for salary. The results for four different age groups are shown in Figure 8–9.

The results are consistent and clear: age is associated with a marked decline in expectancies for advancement either through promotions or salary increases. Certainly these results suggest that two classes of incentives for job performance—(and presumably for the maintenance of skills requisite to job performance), advancement and salary—have lost some of their incentive value for the older engineers.

Combatting Obsolescence

Hall and Mansfield (1975) have suggested that professionals engaged in research and development activities (scientists, engineers) show three distinct stages to their careers. The first stage, called the early career stage (ages 20–34), is characterized by low job involvement, low intrinsic motivation, low needs for security, and high needs for self-actualization. The midcareer stage (ages 35 to 49) is characterized by greater job involvement, more intrinsic motivation, and a general personal stabilization. The late career stage (ages 50 and older) is characterized by high concerns for security and low needs for self-fulfillment and autonomy. In this stage, there is a great concern for holding on to the current job with very little effort devoted to "breaking new ground."

If Hall and Mansfield are correct, it is not difficult to understand why obsolescence is a problem with older workers. In a sense, they have finally learned to do something well and are not excited about the prospects of attempting to develop new skills and to begin making errors all over again. As physicists have been trying to tell us for centuries, bodies at rest tend to stay at rest! Nevertheless, simply labeling workers by stages does not help to alleviate the problem. Kaufman (1975) has examined the problem from a slightly different point of view. He has identified some variables that may help to get the potentially obsolete worker moving again. He found that those in less demanding jobs tended to engage in less demanding updating exercises. While this may be of some small comfort to organizations (i.e., obsolescence seems centered among those individuals who would do the least "damage" to the organization), Kaufman suggests that the organization may reverse this obsolescence trend by enriching the jobs of these workers. This would follow from the fact that those with more challenging jobs tend to treat updating requirements more seriously. While it is inappropriate to draw causal inferences from this type of correlational data, Kaufman's suggestion does at least give the concerned manager a place to start.

In addition to the situation where the job requires new technical information on the part of the incumbent, there are also situations in which the work role systematically changes in some important way. There has been some research done that attempted to identify those individuals who would be most likely to adapt successfully to these role changes. Morrison (1977) found that individuals who had engaged in many management development activities were more likely to adapt successfully to role changes. This is a rather important finding for an organization concerned about the value of nonspecific training, or what has come to be known as generalized management development. Morrison's results suggest that frequent management development activities keep people "loose" and flexible. It is almost as if they were continually learning to learn, a concept that has become popular in some more traditional learning circles (Harlow, 1959).

In summary, it seems as if there is a tendency for workers to become personally and professionally cautious in their work behavior as they get older. This effect is compounded by the diminishing importance of traditional incentives such as pay and promotion. The result is a strong emphasis on the "status quo" with respect to technical knowledge. In rapidly changing fields, to remain constant is to become obsolete. The meager research available suggests that this obsolescence might be reversed through job enrichment and continuing management development activity.

UPDATING AND RETRAINING PROGRAMS

In this section we will describe a few programs in updating and some views of the people who have worked closely with those programs with respect to the reasons for success or failure.

The Technology Utilization Project

Kinn (1973) has reported on some aspects of the Technology Utilization Project (TUP), a study sponsored by the Manpower Administration of the United States Department of Labor and conducted by a number of engineering societies. In the initial program, 150 unemployed professionals were organized into teams in 14 cities with critical unemployment. These teams worked with employers to establish short-range and long-term needs for professionals. The result was the identification of 55,000 jobs that could be filled in the succeeding three years by some of the engineers and scientists laid off as the result of reduced defense and aerospace production. The report of these study teams urged the provision of "short-term supplementary education to prepare professionals for rapid transition to new career fields" (Kinn, 1973, p. 105). A program based on this recommendation was initiated in 8 colleges and universities to retrain 328 engineers. Courses lasted 2 to 12 weeks, and within two months after training 80 percent of the original 328 were placed in new jobs. The average age in this TUP pilot program was 48 and ranged up to 64 years.

While this program appears to have been successful, it was costly and limited to a small portion of those requiring or desiring mid-career changes. Therefore, Kinn recommended that the project concern itself with the collection and dissemination of information about (1) manpower, (2) salary, (3) economic/industrial trends, and (4) personal career data. The latter included the provision of professional career counseling, autoinstructional aids to career changes, and career development articles. In addition, the program sought to provide structured educational programs to develop or sharpen specific engineering skills and to provide placement services.

The Lincoln Training System

The needs for updating and retraining pose special problems for instruction which does not necessarily fit the academic mold of semester-long courses. The needs may be highly specific to the individual and may constitute only a few weeks of a university course. Furthermore, most of those who would be involved in updating (unlike the unemployed engineers in the TUP program) would be working at points sometimes remote from university facilities. Thus, even with full financial support from the employer, it may be a poor use of the employees' time and energy to rely on existing university programs. For these reasons, Butman and Frick (1973) argue for the use of individualized, computer-assisted instruction (CAI) programs. In addition to overcoming temporal and geographic problems, CAI is seen as providing truly self-paced instruction. This means economy of the professional's time and a minimum of time away from work.

The Lincoln Training System (LTS) is a CAI program developed by Lincoln Laboratory. It uses microfiche for storage and transmission of information and instructions. The student interacts with lesson materials by way of a keyboard, and the responses are used by the computer to program subsequent information so that content and rate are optimal to the student's needs and abilities. In its present development, the LTS will be a self-contained instructional terminal, each terminal complete with a small computer for programming the instructional material, rather than dependent on a single, large, centralized computer.

Butman and Frick (1973) report an evaluation study for the LTS conducted at an air force training center. In this study 2 groups of 30 top-level electronics students were carefully matched after 4 weeks of conventional training. For the fifth week, one group was trained on LTS facilities, while the second group used conventional texts, closed-circuit TV, and programmed instruction, which constituted the regular training at the air force facility. Both groups received the same final examination and training time was carefully recorded for each trainee.

FIGURE 8–10

Distribution of Scores and Completion Times for Higher-Level (Self-tutored) Control and LTS Students

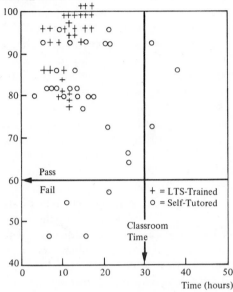

Score (percent)

+ = LTS-Trained
o = Self-Tutored

Classroom Time

Time (hours)

Source: Butman, R. C. & Frick, F. C. Educational technology for training. In S. S. Dubin, H. Shelton, & J. McConnell (Eds.) *Maintaining professional and technical competence of the older engineer.* Washington, D.C.: American Society for Engineering Education, 1973.

The results of this study are summarized in Figure 8–10. They indicate that the trainees receiving the LTS instruction had higher scores on the final exam ($p < .001$) with no failures. Furthermore, learning efficiency was increased with LTS; trainees took significantly less time to complete the material for the fifth week. The final exam and training time data represent internal criteria and do not indicate the extent to which the training improved job effectiveness. Nonetheless, they present a strong case for the CAI system of training.

University versus In-Company Training

In a survey of 4,400 engineers, Kaufman (1973) found that 60 to 65 percent of the respondents checked "to keep from becoming obsolete" and "to prepare for increased responsibility" as important objectives in getting additional education. In contrast, 34 percent checked "to obtain an advanced degree" or "to become an authority in my specialty." Meanwhile, about 45 percent checked "to perform my present assignment better," and 39 percent indicated additional training was important "to remedy deficiencies in my initial training." Thus, these professionals saw training largely in terms of job and career needs and did not see "additional degrees" as particularly relevant.

Factors Related to Course-Taking. Kaufman (1973) reviewed a number of studies that offered some evidence on the characteristics of those who take additional courses. Engineers who leave jobs to enter graduate schools are (1) superior in engineering knowledge and quantitative abilities, (2) more interested in working with ideas, (3) more impulsive, and (4) less tolerant of frustrations (Hemphill, 1963). Graduate course takers also report little autonomy or independence in their jobs and less job satisfaction (Renck, 1969). Kaufman interpreted these findings as suggesting that engineers may seek graduate training ". . . in an attempt to satisfy intellectually-oriented professional goals which are being frustrated at work" (p. 181). In-house course takers also appear to be frustrated, since they have had few promotions and perhaps few intrinsic rewards. Graduate courses were taken almost exclusively in the early part of the career, while in-house course participation continued at least to midcareer. Kaufman (1970) also found that those who participated in graduate courses were those with strongest engineering abilities, whereas those who took in-house courses tended to be weakest in these abilities. However, ability could be used to predict graduate course taking only when "motivation to work with ideas" was also strong (Kaufman, 1973). Kaufman also found evidence of a relationship between continuing education and the challenging nature of work assignments: the more time allocated to challenging work activities, the more graduate courses, but the fewer company courses the engineer is likely to take. These relationships hold even when ability and interest differences are taken into consideration. Kaufman concludes that:

> It seems rather clear that the challenge of the work itself can stimulate continuing graduate education. However, one can speculate that engineers who are frustrated by having only limited amounts of work challenge may attempt to take more in-company courses to make up for a lack of stimulation in their jobs. (p. 183)

Kaufman's findings strongly suggest that continuing education, especially graduate course taking, begins early in one's career and is fostered and perhaps prolonged to the extent that the young professional is given challenging work assignments. As we saw earlier, Dalton and Thompson (1971) found evidence that, indeed, the younger professionals did get the more challenging work (see Fig. 8–8). What this means, of course, is that the older employees whose updating needs may be greater (whose "obsolescence index" may be higher) are getting less challenging work assignments to stimulate them to updating activities.

University-sponsored graduate courses were found to be more effective (as indicated by job performance, publications, and patents) than company courses. As Kaufman (1973) points out, however, this may reflect selective processes among trainees rather than the quality of the course, since:

> Regardless of age, it is likely that the less capable engineers who do not take graduate courses, but who perceive that they are not keeping up-to-date, attempt to reduce their anxiety by participating in the less demanding [non-credit] in-company courses. (p. 184)

With respect to those who take the course, Decker's (1973) findings agree with those just presented. In the case study he reported, videotape recordings were made of the training sessions. Participation rate was increased and the dropout rate greatly reduced by the use of TV tapes. These tapes allowed engineers to keep up or catch up when they had to miss courses by reviewing session tapes; in addition, there was a new management attitude that saw continuing education as a part of one's job rather than as a fringe benefit.

We may summarize this section on the problems of obsolescence, updating, and continuing education by suggesting that an organization that takes the position (1) that continued education is part of the job—not extra curricular night course, catch-as-you-can, but planned programmed training—and (2) that the provision of challenging work assignments commensurate with newly organized skills is an important deterrent to obsolescence, will be likely to maintain a reasonably updated work force, regardless of that force's age. In contrast, the company that preferentially assigns interesting and challenging work to the youngest personnel and views its older workers as "over the hill and fit only to live out their years at the routine drafting board" will experience obsolescence and the motivational as well as efficiency losses which this implies.

SUMMARY

A number of methods and techniques are available for personnel training and development. Some of these methods are primarily useful for specific training purposes such as information presentation, skill development, attitude change, or the modification of interpersonal behavior. Training research usually has been directed toward evaluating training programs, rather than specific techniques, and little evidence exists as to the relative merits of different methods for achieving specific training objectives. The trend in training evaluation research seems to have been to demonstrate that a new technique "works," rather than to show that it is more effective than established techniques for accomplishing the same training objectives. From the point of view of the practitioner, it is perhaps sufficient to show that a program works; that it has positive utility for the organization. From the view of advancing the science of training, however, such action research programs are of little value. What is needed from this view, are systematic studies which test the effects of independent variables including different methods, media, and techniques.

The bulk of training research in business and industry is limited also by the choice of criteria and experimental designs. Predominantly, internal criteria, especially trainee evaluations of the training program, are used with no attempt to determine the impact of the training on job behaviors or organizational outcomes. Research designs frequently lack pretraining measures, seldom employ control groups, and even less frequently provide for systematic follow-up of on-the-job behavior or its consequences.

Broad new challenges for the training profession have resulted from recent technological and social changes. Rapid scientific and technological advances make for technical and professional obsolescence within a few years after formal education is complete. These advances emphasize the need for lifelong education and the updating and retraining of older employees. Greater awareness and concern for the social and economic conditions of the unemployed, underemployed, and underprivileged segments of our society charge the training profession with the responsibility to get these people ready for the job market. These problems are complex: specific skill training is probably only a small part of the solution. Special techniques are needed to facilitate adaptation and assimilation of the HCU into the world of work,—and adaptation may have to come as much from the employer as from the HCU trainee. Society and the behavioral and social sciences will need to spend a good deal of attention and energy if they are to solve these major problems which, by design or by default, have been neglected and have grown large.

REFERENCES

Bartlett, C. J. Equal employment opportunity issues in training. *Human Factors*, 1978, *20*, 179–188.

Borg, W. R. *Educational research*. New York: David McKay, 1963.

Bradford, L. P., Gibb, J. R., & Benne, K. D. *T-group theory and laboratory method*. New York: Wiley, 1964.

Butman, R. N., & Frick, F. C. Educational technology for teaching. In S. S. Dubin, H. Shelton, and J. McConnell (Eds.). *Maintaining professional and technical competence of the older engineer*. Washington, D.C.: American Society for Engineering Education, 1973.

Campbell, D. T., & Stanley, J. C. *Experimental and quasi-experimental designs for research*. Chicago: Rand McNally, 1963.

Campbell, J. P. Personnel training and development. *Annual Review of Psychology*. Palo Alto, Calif: Annual Review, 1971.

Campbell, J. P., Dunnette, M. D., Lawler, E. E., & Weick, K. E. *Managerial behavior, performance, and effectiveness*. New York: McGraw-Hill, 1970.

Dalton, G. W., & Thompson, P. H. Accelerating obsolescence of older engineers, *Harvard Business Review*, 1971, *49*, 57–67.

Decker, W. D. Anatomy of a continuing education program. In S. S. Dubin, H. Shelton, and J. McConnell (Eds.). *Maintaining professional and technical competence.* Washington, D.C.: American Society for Engineering Education, 1973.

Di Marco, N. & Gustafson, D. P. Attitudes of co-workers and management toward hard-core employees. *Personnel Psychology,* 1975, *28,* 65–76.

Dubin, S. S. (Ed.) *Professional obsolescence.* Lexington, Mass.: Health, 1972. (a)

Dubin, S. S. Obsolescence of life-long education: A choice for the professional. *American Psychologist,* 1972, *27,* 486–498. (b)

Feldman, J. M. Race, economic class, perceived outcomes of work, and unemployment. *Journal of Applied Psychology,* 1973, *58,* 16–22.

Fiedler, F. E. & Mahar, L. The effectiveness of contingency model training: a review of the validation of *LEADER MATCH. Personnel Psychology,* in press.

File, Q. Q., & Remmers, H. H. *How supervise?* Manual, 1948 revision. New York: Psychological Corporation, 1948.

Fleishman, E. A. Leadership climate, human relations training, and supervisory behavior. *Personnel Psychology,* 1953, *6,* 205–222.

Fleishman, E. A., Harris, F. F., & Burtt, H. E. *Leadership and supervision in industry.* Columbus, Ohio: Ohio State University, Personnel Research Board, 1955.

Friedlander, F., & Greenburg, S. Effect of job attitudes, training, and organizational climate on performance of the hard core unemployed. *Journal of Applied Psychology,* 1971, *55,* 287–295.

Goldstein, I. L. *Training: Program development and evaluation.* Monterey, Calif.: Brooks/Cole, 1974.

Goldstein, I. L. The pursuit of validity in the evaluation of training programs. *Human Factors,* 1978, *20,* 131–144.

Gomersall, E. R., & Myers, M. S. Breakthrough in on-the-job training. *Harvard Business Review,* 1966, *44,* 62–72.

Goodman, P. & Salipant, P. Organizational rewards and the retention of hard-core unemployed. *Journal of Applied Psychology,* 1976, *61,* 12–21.

Gumpper, D. C. *Training the hard-core unemployed: Implications of economic need, expectancy, and attitudes toward work.* Ph.D. dissertation, The Pennsylvania State University, 1970.

Haines, D. B. *Training for culture-contact and interaction skills.* USAF AMRL-TR no. 64–109 (1964).

Haines, D. B., & Eachus, H. T. *A preliminary study of acquiring cross-cultural interaction skills through self-confrontation.* USAF AMRL-TR no. 65–137 (1965).

Hall, D. T. & Mansfield, R. Relationships of age and seniority with career variables of engineers and scientists. *Journal of Applied Psychology,* 1975, *60,* 201–210.

Harris, E. F., & Fleishman, E. A. Human relations training and the stability of leadership patterns. *Journal of Applied Psychology,* 1955, *39,* 20–25.

Harlow, H. Learning to learn. In S. Koch, *Psychology: a study of a science.* Vol. II. New York: McGraw-Hill, 1959.

Hemphill, J. K. (Ed.). *The engineering study.* Princeton, N.J.: Educational Testing Service, 1963.

Heneman, H. G., III, & Schwab, D. P. Evaluation of research on expectancy theory predictions of employee performance. *Psychological Bulletin,* 1972, *78,* 1–9.

Kaufman, H. G. *Work environment, personal characteristics and obsolescence of engineers.* U.S. Dept. of Labor, Office of Manpower Management Grant no. 91–34–69–23 (1970).

Kaufman, H. G. A comparative analysis of university versus in-company continuing education for engineers. In S. S. Dubin, H. Shelton, & J. McConnell (Eds.). *Maintaining professional and technical competence of the older engineer.* Washington, D.C.: American Society for Engineering Education, 1973.

Kaufman, H. G. Individual differences, early work challenge, and participation in continuing education. *Journal of Applied Psychology,* 1975, *60,* 405–408.

Kinn, J. M. Professional future shock: Can engineers adapt? In S. S. Dubin, H. Shelton, & J. McConnell (Eds.). *Maintaining professional and technical competence of the older engineer.* Washington, D.C.: American Society for Engineering Education, 1973.

Kirkpatrick, D. L. Techniques for evaluating training programs. *Journal of the American Society of Training Directors,* 1959, *13,* 3–9, 21–26; 1960, *14,* 13–18, 28–32.

Latham, G. P., & Kinne, S. B., III. *Goal-setting as a means of increasing the performance of the pulpwood harvester.* Atlanta, Ga.: American Pulpwood Association, Harvesting Research Project, 1971.

Latham, G. P., & Kinne, S. B., III. Improving job performance through training in goal-setting. *Journal of Applied Psychology,* 1974, *59(2),* 187–191.

Latham, G. P., & Ronan, W. W. *The effects of goal-setting and supervision on the motivation of pulpwood workers.* Atlanta, Ga.: American Pulpwood Association, Harvesting Research Project, 1970.

Levine, J., & Butler, J. Lecture vs. group decision in changing behavior. *Journal of Applied Psychology,* 1952, *36,* 29–33.

Locke, E. A. The relationship of intentions to level of performance. *Journal of Applied Psychology,* 1966, *50,* 60–66.

Lukasiewicz, J. The dynamics of science and engineering education. *Engineering Education,* 1971, *61,* 880–882.

MacKinney, A. C. Progressive levels in the evaluation of training programs. *Personnel,* 1957, *34,* 72–77.

Maier, N. R. F. *Principles of human relations: Applications to management.* New York: Wiley, 1952.

Maier, N. R. F., & Solem, A. R. The contribution of a discussion leader to the quality of group thinking: The effective use of minority opinions. *Human Relations,* 1952, *5,* 277–288.

Maier, N. R. F., & Zerfoss, L. F. A technique for training large groups of supervisors and its potential use in social research. *Human Relations,* 1952, *5,* 177–186.

Martin, H. O.   The assessment of training. *Personnel Management*, 1957, *39*, 88–93.

Morrison, R. F.   Career adaptivity: the effective adaptation of managers to changing role demands. *Journal of Applied Psychology*, 1977, *62*, 549–558.

Moses, J. L. & Ritchie, R. J.   Supervisory relationships training: a behavioral evaluation of a behavioral modeling program. *Personnel Psychology*, 1976, *29*, 337–344.

Odiorne, G. S. The need for an economic approach to training. *Journal of the American Society of Training Directors*, 1964, *18(3)*, 3–12.

Pigors, P., & Pigors, F.   *The incident process: Case studies in management development.* Washington, D.C.: Bureau of National Affairs, 1955.

Renck, R.   *Continuing education for R&D careers.* Washington, D.C.: National Science Foundation Report 69–20 (1969).

Ronan, W. W., Latham, G. P., & Kinne, S. B., III.   The effects of goal setting and supervision on worker behavior in an industrial situation. *Journal of Applied Psychology*, 1973, *58*, 302–307.

Rosenstein, A.   *Study of profession and professional education.* Report no. EDP7–68. Los Angeles: University of California Press, 1968.

Salipante, P. & Goodman, P.   Training, counseling and retention of the hardcore unemployed. *Journal of Applied Psychology*, 1976, *61*, 1–11.

Searls, D. J., Bravelt, G. N., & Miskimins, R. W.   Work values of the chronically unemployed. *Journal of Applied Psychology*, 1974, *59*, 93–95.

Smith, P. B.   Controlled studies of the outcome of sensitivity training. *Psychological Bulletin*, 1975, *82*, 597–622.

Smith, P. E.   Management Modeling training to improve morale and customer satisfaction. *Personnel Psychology*, 1976, *29*, 351–360.

Solomon, R. L.   An extension of control group design, *Psychological Bulletin*, 1949, *46*, 137–150.

Triandis, H. C., Feldman, J., Weldon, D. E., & Harvey, W. M.   Ecosystem distrust and the hard to employ. *Journal of Applied Psychology*, 1975, *60*, 44–56.

Walter, G. A.   Effects of videotape training inputs on group performance. *Journal of Applied Psychology*, 1975, *60*, 308–313.

The Social Framework of Industrial and Organizational Psychology

People in organizations have feelings. These feelings are interwoven with the social fabric of the organization. This fabric includes the individual motivations of the worker, the motivations and behavior patterns of supervisors and co-workers, and even the "personality" of the organization itself. This section introduces theories that attempt to explain the reaction of the worker to this fabric. It is structured around the reactions of the worker (motivation and satisfaction), the behavior patterns of the supervisor (leadership), and the nature of the organization. In combination with the decision strategies of the organization, as discussed in Section 1, and the nature of the physical work environment and work systems, discussed in Section 3, these individual worker reactions determine the efficiency of the organization and the well-being of the worker.

CHAPTER 9
The Motivation to Work

Work motivation is currently a "hot" topic. Employers and researchers alike are trying to figure out what forces affect the energy that workers invest in work. What is behind the decision to take one job rather than another? When they have decided on and accepted a job, why do they continue to come to work every day, even when they may not "feel like going to work"? When they arrive at work, why do they work hard to complete the task assigned on a particular day rather than discuss world affairs with co-workers? These are the questions a theory of work motivation must answer. In the past, the answers to these questions were superficial. The most prevalent answer was "Money." But if we simply look at ourselves for data, we know that there are many things we would do even if we were not being paid to do them. In addition, there are an equal number of things we would not do, no matter how much money was offered. These simple data should be sufficient to convince us that we will need an explanation a little more complete than "money."

Most industrial managers subscribe to one of the two points of view shown in Figures 9–1 and 9–2. The cartoon in Figure 9–1 depicts the "trait" approach, hinting that motivation is a physical characteristic that people possess to varying degrees, much like height, weight, or stamina. The cartoon in Figure 9–2, on the other hand, presents the "environmentalist" view; here, motivation is seen as something that is done *to* someone. Interestingly enough, workers and managers do not seem to subscribe to the two approaches equally. Workers usually identify the cartoon in Figure 9–2 as an appropriate motivation theory. They are even more direct in

FIGURE 9–1

The Trait Approach to Motivation

their definition. A common definition of motivation offered by workers is "getting people to do what they don't want to do." Managers choose the cartoon in Figure 9–1 (at least by implication) more often as a theory of motivation that makes more sense to them. Invariably, managers will say the major problem in motivation is dealing with the "lazy" employee. There are kernels of truth in both of the approaches: there are characteristics of individuals (individual differences) that play a part in whether or not energy will be expended on the job. There are also characteristics outside of the individual which affect energy expenditure.

In the late 50s and early 60s, psychologists began to investigate seriously the relationships among job satisfaction, work motivation, and job performance. Soon after this research was begun, it became apparent that a framework for guiding the research—a theory of work behavior—was missing. For several decades, the only statement even coming close to a theory of work behavior was the commonplace belief that "a happy worker is a productive worker." But upon close examination, this "theory" was of little use. Did it mean that if you make a worker happy, she will *then* be productive, or did it mean that productive workers tend to be happier? Even more serious problems were presented by the fact that individuals could be found who were unhappy yet productive (not to mention the slightly larger group of happy and unproductive workers). Recent research has been directed at supplying the missing theoretical framework necessary for a reasonable discussion of the psychological aspects of work behavior.

Work motivation probably does not differ greatly from other kinds of motivation. For that reason, most of the models or theories of work motivation have their roots in the more general field of human motivation. While there are a number of potential definitions of motivation, the following one is most useful for the purposes of this chapter: *motivation concerns the conditions responsible for variations in the intensity, quality, and direction of ongoing behavior* (Vinacke, 1962). This definition makes it clear that work motivation is only one instance of a more general process. While the conditions under which work is performed differ substantially from the conditions under which other behavior patterns occur, new theories are not needed to account for industrial behavior. The work context only requires some different ways of measuring the components of existing motivational models.

In this chapter, broad classes of work motivation theories will be presented. Within each class, variations and modifications will be described. Four general classes will be considered: (1) *need hierarchy* theory, (2) *instrumentality* theory, (3) *reinforcement* theory, and (4) *balance* theory. A section will also be devoted to some incomplete motivational models that do not fit neatly into any of these classes. Next, the various theories will be summarized and their similarities and dissimilarities described. Some topics that are having a great impact on research in work motivation will be introduced. Finally, we will identify what we feel to be the most reasonable view of the relationships between motivation and performance.

FIGURE 9–2
The Environmental Approach to Motivation

"I'D MUCH RATHER LOCK ONE OF
THE LOWEST PERFORMERS OF A WORK
GROUP IN THE BOILER ROOM FOR SEVERAL
WEEKS AS A WARNING TO OTHERS!"

THEORIES OF WORK MOTIVATION

There are several ways in which the theories of work motivation may be presented. A good framework was suggested by Campbell et al. (1970). They classified the theories as either "process" or "content." Process theories have as their objective explaining *how* behavior is initiated, directed, sustained, and stopped. Content theories search for the specific things within individuals that initiate, direct, sustain, and stop behavior. A silly example that might make the distinction clearer is a "theory of 10-speed bicycle riding." A process theory would concentrate on *how* energy is distributed from the rider to various devices, such as the pedals, hand brakes, and shifting levers. A content theory would focus on the nature of the energy source—why is it there to start with? This content/process distinction is a good one to keep in mind while reading the description of the motivational models, and it will be referred to often in the discussion of the four classes of motivation theories that follows.

Some Need Theories

Maslow's Need Hierarchy Theory.   Maslow proposed that all individuals have basic sets of needs that they strive to fulfill. In the context of industrial behavior, an individual strives to fulfill these needs in a work setting. Maslow's theory is, by far, the most popular and well known of the need-hierarchy class. His theory is useful as a place to start because it emphasizes the idea of the "hierarchical" arrangement of needs. In 1943, he proposed that individuals have five basic sets of needs:

1. *Physiological needs:* These are what learning theories generally refer to as basic needs or drives and are satisfied by such things as food, water, and sleep.
2. *Safety needs:* This category refers to the need an individual has to produce a secure environment—one free of threats to continued existence.
3. *Love needs:* These needs are concerned with interpersonal factors. They reflect an individual's desire to be accepted by peers.
4. *Esteem needs:* This describes the need an individual has to occupy a position in time and space as a function of who he is and what he is capable of; this need level transcends the previous level of love needs in that the affection of one's peers is not sufficient.
5. *Self-actualization needs:* This is generally described as the need for self-fulfillment; one strives toward the full realization of unique characteristics and potentials.

The most important characteristic of this need system is that it is arranged in predetermined levels. The arrangement of these needs is described in Figure 9–3.

The most basic unsatisfied need at any given time is considered to be

FIGURE 9–3

Maslow's Hierarchy of Needs

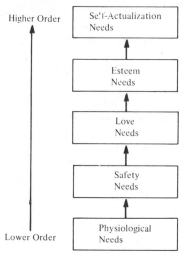

the most important. Individuals will always strive to satisfy basic needs before higher-order needs. Furthermore, individuals will move up the hierarchy in a very systematic manner, satisfying first the physiological needs, then the safety needs, and so on.

This theory has been a popular one in management circles. Most published research on Maslow's model has taken the form of "cross-sectional" research. It has attempted to show differences in the importance of various needs among groups of individuals at various organizational levels. For example, Porter (1961) investigated bottom and middle management and drew conclusions about the importance of the various needs for these two groups. The implication is that various organizational levels have the potential to satisfy various need levels. Porter concluded that the management position within the organization was important in determining the extent of psychological need fulfillment. He also concluded that the greatest differences between bottom- and middle-management positions occurred in the security, esteem, and actualization need categories. In other words, higher levels of the organization appeared to provide greater opportunity for the satisfaction of higher-order needs, while lower levels in the organization provided the opportunity for the satisfaction of only more basic needs.

If our concern is the motivation of employees, this theory tells us that it is essential to know what needs the individual is trying to satisfy. It implies that individuals will instigate, direct, and sustain activity to satisfy certain needs. It further implies that a personnel manager can set up a systematic program of motivation if she knows which needs are most important to an individual at a particular time and provides the environment necessary for the fulfillment of these needs.

What happens when an individual reaches the ultimate level of motivation—the self-actualization level? Is the self-actualized person no longer motivated? If that were the case, there would be good reason for managers to *prevent* workers from satisfying self-actualization needs. The theory takes this into account. It proposes that when an individual reaches the self-actualization level, the process changes—the self-actualization need feeds on itself. The more self-actualized the person becomes, the greater the need for self-actualization.

While a good deal of cross-sectional research has been done on Maslow's model, only recently have longitudinal studies been undertaken. There is an important difference between the two approaches. If Maslow's propositions are to have any value in the explanation of work motivation, they must be supported by data that describe the progress of individuals through the need hierarchy. For example, the theory must be supported with data that show that when an individual's love needs are satisfied, his esteem needs become more important. Most cross-sectional research designs in this area identify individuals at different organizational levels, gather information relating to the need level at which the individuals are operating, and make inferences about what conditions exist in the organizational environment that explain why the individual is operating at this need level. This was the design of the Porter study described earlier. This is a *necessary* but not *sufficient* condition for support of the theory. For the model to receive strong support, these cross-sectional data must be backed up with longitudinal data.

Two studies yield data that contradict the Maslow model. Hall and Nougaim (1968) found that need intensity correlated *positively* with need satisfaction. This means that the more a need is satisfied, the more important it becomes. With the exception of the self-actualization level, this finding is in direct opposition to the need-hierarchy theory of Maslow. The theory would predict that need satisfaction at one level would correlate positively with need importance scores for the *next* level. For example, an individual whose love needs were satisfied should perceive esteem needs as more important than love needs. The Hall and Nougaim data contradict that proposition.

A second study, by Lawler and Suttle (1972), tested three hypotheses related to Maslow's theory:

1. The *satisfaction* of needs in one category should correlate negatively with the *importance* of these same needs and positively with the *importance* of needs in the next higher level of the hierarchy.
2. *Changes in the satisfaction of needs* in one category should correlate negatively with *changes in the importance of needs in the same category,* and positively with *changes in the importance of needs* in the next higher level of the hierarchy.
3. *High satisfaction of the needs* in one category at time 1 should be associated with *low importance of the needs* in the same category at

time 2 and with *high importance of the needs* in the next higher category of the hierarchy at time 2.

From hypotheses 2 and 3 it can be seen that a longitudinal design was used in this study. Since Lawler and Suttle had measurements on the subjects at more than one time, they were able to describe the behavior of individuals as these individuals supposedly moved through the hierarchy. Once again, no support was provided for the Maslow model. On the basis of the data analyses, all three hypotheses were rejected. A recent review of tests of the Maslow need-hierarchy theory (Wahba and Bridwell, 1976) concludes that there is no longitudinal support for the theory and only weak support from cross-sectional studies. Wahba and Bridwell suggest the need-hierarchy theory suffers from both conceptual and operational shortcomings:

> The most problematic aspect of Maslow's theory, however, is that dealing with the concept of need itself. It is not clear what is meant by the concept of need. Does need have a psychological and/or physiological base? Does a need come to existence because of deficiency only or does need always exist even if it is gratified? How can we identify, isolate and measure different needs? There is ample evidence that people seek objects and engage in behavior that are in no way related to the satisfaction of needs. In a discussion of this point, Cofer and Apply (1964) concluded that this is probably also true for animals. Vroom (1964) does not use the concept of needs in his discussion of motivation. Lawler (1971) argued that concept of valence is related to that of need, e.g., objects acquire valence because of their instrumentality for meeting the basic needs of people. Lawler, however, (1971) limits the use of the term to certain stimuli (or outcomes) that can be grouped together because they are sought by people. Even if we accept such a limited view of needs, the remaining question should be, why should needs be structured in a fixed hierarchy? Does this hierarchy vary for different people? What happens to the hierarchy over time? How can we have a fixed hierarchy when behavior is multidetermined? (pp. 234–235)

Criticisms such as these are more than bothersome—they are terminal! Recent research into Maslow's propositions has been sporadic, and has involved the construction of new instruments to test the Maslow propositions (Mitchell & Moudgill, 1976). As a result, we would conclude that Maslow's theory is of more historical than functional value.

Independent of Maslow's theory, there have been some alternative motivational models suggested in which needs play an important role. Recently, there has been some renewed interest in need achievement theory (Atkinson & Feather, 1966). Steers (1975; Steers & Spencer, 1977) has conducted some research suggesting that Need for Achievement (Nach) affects the relationship between performance and satisfaction. In particular, he finds that the correlations between performance and satisfaction are substantial for individuals with high needs for achievement, but do not differ from zero for low need achievers. He interprets this to mean that good performance is a reward *in and of itself* for high need achievers. He further suggests that increasing the scope of the job by making it more autonomous and challenging can have positive effects on the performance of high need achievers. This would suggest that job enrichment might be wasted on low need achievers. In spite of these optimistic conclusions, Steers appropriately points out that these Nach effects on performance may be relatively minor when compared to the effects of reward levels and pressures for production.

ERG Theory. Alderfer (1969, 1972) has proposed a theory called the *ERG theory*. Instead of the five levels of need suggested by Maslow, Alderfer considers the individual to have three basic sets of needs:

1. *Existence needs:* These are material existence needs and are satisfied by environmental factors such as food, water, pay, fringe benefits, and working conditions.
2. *Relatedness needs:* These needs deal with maintaining interpersonal relatedness with significant other people such as co-workers, superiors, subordinates, family, friends, and enemies.
3. *Growth needs:* These needs are manifested in the individual's attempt to seek opportunities for unique personal development. They comprise all needs that involve a person making creative or productive effects on herself and the environment.

While the rearrangement of the various needs from Maslow's hierarchy is interesting, the most unique aspect of Alderfer's theory is the inclusion of a different "process" to explain how people move from one level to another. The "process" of Maslow's model may be expressed as one of "fulfillment-progression," that is, an individual must satisfy one level of need before moving on to the next highest level. In addition to the "fulfillment-progression" component, Alderfer has added a "frustration-regression" component. Alderfer assumes that existence, relatedness, and growth vary on a continuum of concreteness, with existence needs being the most concrete, relatedness needs being moderately concrete, and the growth need being least concrete. He further assumes that when the less concrete needs are not met, more concrete need fulfillment is sought.

This means the rigid ordering of Maslow's hierarchy is no longer appropriate. The difference between Alderfer and Maslow can be described in both *content* and *process* terms. They differ in content terms on the basis of the needs proposed: for Maslow there are five needs; for Alderfer there are three. They also differ in process terms: for Maslow the process is one of fulfillment-progression; for Alderfer, both fulfillment-progression and frustration-regression are important dynamic elements. Figures 9–4 and 9–5 describes the differences between the two models in diagram form.

In a sense, Alderfer's view of motivation is a more hopeful one for managers. It provides them with the possibility of constructively channeling the energy of their subordinates even when the individual's higher-level needs are blocked. This energy can be directed toward lower-level needs. The ERG variation is a very new one. A good deal of research will have

FIGURE 9–4

Dynamic Properties of Maslow's Model (Fulfillment-Progression)

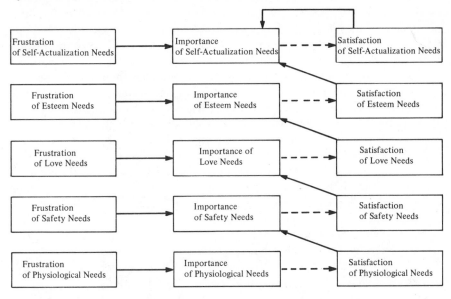

to be done before it can be accepted as a reasonable view of how and why people expend energy in work settings.

In summary, it seems that when Maslow's model is put to the proper test, it leaves much to be desired. Models such as those in the need-hierarchy group tend to be useful in the sense that they provide both process and content statements. As Campbell et al. (1970) point out, good theory must specify *both* content *and* process considerations. It may be that a redefinition of the need levels in Maslow's model as well as the process component

FIGURE 9–5

Dynamic Properties of Alderfer's Model (Fulfillment-Progression; Frustration-Regression)

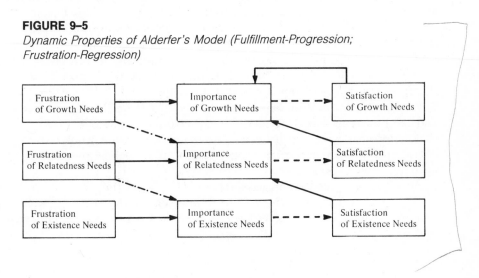

of the model will yield more supportive data. A recent study by Wanous and Zwany (1977) supported the existence of the three categories suggested by Alderfer. Nevertheless, they conclude that need-hierarchy theories may be of little value in day-to-day management practices.

Two-Factor Theory. An extremely popular theory of work motivation over the past 15 years has been Herzberg's *motivator-hygiene* or *two-factor* theory. His theory has the same foundation as all need theories: the assumption that each individual is born with certain needs that must be satisfied. In contrast with the five-factor theory of Maslow, or the three-factor theory of Alderfer, Herzberg (1966) proposes that all individuals have two basic sets of needs, hygiene needs and motivator needs. The hygiene needs are basically maintenance needs. Herzberg likens them to those elements that provide us with a healthy environment. In a work setting these needs would include such things as pay, security, co-workers, general working conditions, and company policies. Motivator needs are higher-order or growth needs. These needs are unique to humans and distinguish them from other animals. These needs seem to be related to some innate characteristic of individuals that requires them to seek challenge, stimulation, and autonomy. These needs are satisfied by things such as responsible work, independence of action, and recognition for the accomplishment of difficult tasks. In short, these needs are satisfied by things that are part of the work itself, rather than the context in which the work gets done.

According to Herzberg, there are two levels of functioning: motivation seeking and hygiene seeking. Motivation-seeking is thought to be clearly preferable since it yields productive activity on the part of the worker and minimal "control" problems for management. In a sense, the theory suggests that if you can move individuals from hygiene-seeking levels to motivation-seeking levels, the individual will be self-motivated and the manager's problems will be over. The motivation seeker is probably best thought of as a person who "loves her work."

Herzberg proposes a rather simple technique for accomplishing this movement from hygiene seeking to motivation seeking—*job enrichment*. He proposes that the only way you can give people an opportunity to satisfy motivator needs is to provide them with interesting work. If the tasks they are currently performing are dull and uninteresting, the tasks must be psychologically "enriched" or made more stimulating. Unlike Maslow's theory or the ERG theory, the motivator-hygiene theory is not arranged hierarchically. There is no hypothesis that motivator needs cannot be satisfied *until* hygiene needs are met. Nevertheless, in practice it would seem that individuals whose hygiene needs are not being met would be more likely to leave the organization, making it impossible to meet their motivator needs.

As with many need theories, Herzberg leaves us in the dark concerning *where* these needs come from. The implication is that these needs are part of the defining characteristics of homo sapiens—those things that distinguish us in the most basic sense from other species and, as a result, do not have to be explained. One of the characteristics of the scientific community in general and psychologists specifically is an unwillingness to take anything as "given." As a result, there has been some reluctance to accept Herzberg's propositions on faith. Since many of the assumptions of the theory are more closely related to the topic of job satisfaction and the meaning of work, a discussion of the research on Herzberg's theory will be postponed until these topics are introduced in the next chapter.

The need theories are appealing. They all include certain elements that we recognize as being part of our own "psychological makeup." No one can deny there is a good feeling that comes from accomplishing a difficult task; nor can one deny that as a result of that feeling the probability is increased that a difficult task will be attempted again. Nevertheless, there are too many elements that are left open to question. Under what conditions will a difficult task be attempted? What will occur if one *fails* at the task? How do individuals differ with respect to their willingness to approach difficult tasks? Why are needs arranged in one hierarchy rather than another? These are a few of the logical questions that arise when need-hierarchy theory is used to explain the behavior of an individual in a work setting. So far the data gathered in support of need theories have not been impressive. For that reason, the search has continued for a way of understanding patterns of work behavior.

Instrumentality Theory

Whether we want to admit it or not, when we are deciding if we should expend some energy, we often ask ourselves the question, "What's in it for me?" We may not be so explicit, and we certainly don't say it out loud, but the principle is an important one. We usually decide to engage in the activity if it will provide us with something that we value. In that sense, the activity is *instrumental* in achieving some valued outcome. This logic is the backbone of a set of theories that will be referred to as *instrumentality* theories. They differ from the need theories in many respects. The most important of these respects is emphasis on cognition. The instrumentality theories stress the process used by an individual to answer the implied question, "Should I expend the energy or not?"

The first work-related version of instrumentality theory was presented by Georgopolous, Mahoney, and Jones (1957) and was labeled "path-goal" theory. They proposed that if a worker sees high productivity as a path leading to the attainment of one or more personal goals, that worker will tend to be a high producer. Conversely, if low productivity is seen as a path to the achievement of goals, low production will result.

There are many examples of this principle: on the positive side, the young worker in a progressive company who sees that productivity is rewarded with rapid advancement and behaves accordingly; on the negative side, the new worker who actively restricts production to match the productivity level of a fellow worker rather than jeopardize a chance to be one of the gang.

In 1964, Vroom formalized many of the instrumentality hypotheses that were in the literature and constructed a theory that has since been labeled VIE theory. The letters stand for Valence, Instrumentality, and Expectancy, respectively. Each of these components plays an important role in the theory. Valence is a component that describes the attracting or repelling capabilities of psychological objects in the environment and has much the same dynamic meaning as the valence of an element in chemistry. Money would have a positive valence for most, while dirty and dangerous working conditions would have a negative valence. The instrumentality component of the theory is based on some earlier work by Peak (1955) and answers the question posed in the beginning of this section, "What's in it for me?" A person evaluates a potential outcome (e.g., a promotion) on the basis of her perception of the relationship between that outcome and other outcomes (e.g., increased money and responsibility) for which she has varying preferences or valences. The relationship between the first outcome, the promotion, and the second outcome, the money, is known as an instrumentality relationship. It answers the question, "Is the promotion *instrumental* in providing me with money—an outcome I value?" This logic can then be extended backward to include the activities necessary to get the promotion.

The expectancy component deals with the odds of receiving a particular outcome. The question a person asks is, "If I expend the energy that is required for a promotion, what is the probability that I will get that promotion?" An expectancy is a probability estimate of a relationship between an action and an outcome.

If these three components are put together (valence, instrumentality, and expectancy), the basic structure of VIE theory emerges. The theory assumes that individuals ask themselves whether or not (1) the action has a high probability of leading to an outcome (expectancy); (2) that outcome will yield other outcomes (instrumentality); and (3) those other outcomes are valued (valence). Since Vroom's formulation of VIE theory, there have been many variations proposed. Rather than present each of these variations, one current and representative treatment of the model will be described.

The Porter-Lawler Model. Most theories of human motivation are based to some degree on drive theory. Drive theory, in its simplest form, states that individuals have basic drives, biological in nature, that must be satisfied. Examples of basic drives are hunger and thirst. As these drives increase in strength, there is an accompanying increase in tension. Tension is aversive to the organism, and anything reducing that tension is viewed positively. In more specific terms, an action that tends to reduce tension is likely to occur again. A more familiar term for describing the reappearance of the action that reduced the tension is *learning*. In the classic case, a hungry animal presented with a food pellet for pressing a bar will be more likely to press the bar again. Human motives, such as the higher-level needs described by Herzberg, Alderfer, and Maslow, are considered to arise primarily from the more basic physiological needs as a function of learning and are labeled *secondary,* or *acquired,* drives.

In a book dealing with managerial attitudes and performance, Porter and Lawler (1968) presented a compelling argument for the choice of an instrumentality model rather than a drive model. They rejected the traditional drive approach because of its emphasis on past response-reward connections. They felt that instrumentality theories more appropriately emphasized the anticipation of future events, an activity much more in keeping with the generally held view of individuals as organisms capable of delaying gratification and dealing with abstract concepts. Such an emphasis provided a cognitive element ignored in most of the drive and need models. They summarized their choice of the instrumentality approach as follows:

1. The terminology and concepts are more applicable to the problems of human motivation; the emphasis on rationality and cognition is appropriate for describing the behavior of managers.
2. Expectancy theory greatly facilitates the incorporation of motives such as status, achievement, and power into a theory of attitudes and performance.

Having chosen the instrumentality approach, Porter and Lawler set out to test an initial model aimed at describing behavior in the industrial setting. This model appears in Figure 9–6. The definitions of the various components in Figure 9–6 are as follows:

1. Value of Reward. This component describes the valence or attractiveness of various outcomes to the individual. Past research in the area of job satisfaction makes it clear that people attach different preference values to outcomes; for example, while one person may value pay more than pleasant co-workers, a second person may value pleasant co-workers more than pay. Although the exact manner by which outcomes acquire preferential value or "valence" is unspecified in the model, at least one way is suggested by the feedback loop from "satisfaction" to "value of reward"—rewards acquire valence as a function of their ability to "satisfy." This would be the position of the drive theorists.

2. Perceived Effort-Reward Probability. This component refers to the subjective estimate of the individual that increased effort will lead to the acquisition of some valued reward. As Porter and Lawler point out, this really comprises two specific subjective estimates or probabilities: (1) the probability that improved performance will lead to the value reward $(P \rightarrow R)$, and (2) the probability that effort will lead to improved performance $(E \rightarrow P)$. These two probabilities are thought to have a multiplicative relationship such that if either one of the values is zero, the perceived effort-reward probability will be zero. An example of this would be the case of a student who values good grades but finds himself in a class being

FIGURE 9–6

Diagram of the Theoretical Model of Porter and Lawler

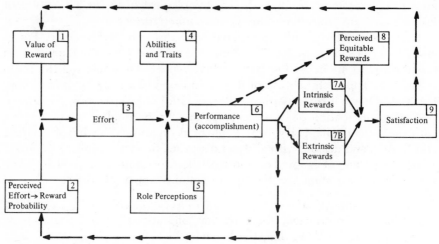

Source: Porter, L. W., & Lawler, E. E. *Managerial attitudes and performance.* Homewood, Ill.: Irwin-Dorsey, 1968.

taught by a professor with a reputation for not giving many As. While the student may see a high relationship between effort and performance, he would probably have a dimmer view of the relationship between performance and valued reward.

3. Effort. This component clarifies the distinction between effort (or expended energy) and performance, a distinction that was rarely clarified in earlier theory or research. This component is intended to supply an explanation of how hard an individual works, rather than how effectively an individual performs. To return to our example of the student striving for good grades, he may very well have expended a great amount of energy in the course but performed poorly on the tests.

4. Abilities and Traits. In the past, models have asked us to accept constant or fixed levels of abilities and traits, generally in the form of the statement "all other things being equal." Porter and Lawler appropriately include this component as an independent source of variation in their model. Abilities and traits refer to relatively stable characteristics of the individual such as intelligence, personality characteristics, and psychomotor skills. These abilities and traits are considered as "boundary conditions" for the individual's performance. They set upper limits for performance.

5. Role Perceptions. The role perception is an individual's definition of successful performance on a particular job. This is a critical factor in determining whether or not effort is transformed into good performance. If the person has an inappropriate definition of success, much of her effort might be wasted. For example, a police officer who defines her role as filling jail cells is likely to make a number of illegal arrests as well as enemies in the community. This would be an inappropriate role perception. Role perceptions might be thought of as the agreement or lack of agreement between a supervisor and a subordinate about the nature of good performance. If they agree, then effort can be transformed into effective performance. If they disagree, it is unlikely that effective performance (at least as defined by the immediate supervisor) will result.

6. *Performance.* Performance refers to the level of accomplishment the individual achieves. Performance has been the overriding concern of industry for decades. While this is understandable, it is important to consider the many components of successful performance as suggested by the model. Performance is the result of the combined effects of effort expenditure, role perceptions, and ability and trait patterns.

7. *Rewards.* While the original model included rewards as a single component, Porter and Lawler decided to distinguish between intrinsic and extrinsic rewards. *Intrinsic rewards* (7A) are rewards that satisfy higher-order needs (in the Maslow sense) and are administered by the individual to himself rather than by some external agent. The wavy-line connection in Figure 9–6 implies that a direct relationship exists between performance and intrinsic rewards only when the job design is such that the worker feels challenged in the completion of job-related activities. *Extrinsic rewards* (7B) are rewards administered by an external agent such as the individual's immediate supervisor. This line is wavy due to the sporadic nature of the relationship between successful performance and extrinsic rewards. External rewards are not always provided when a task is successfully completed; the supervisor may not be aware of the success or may not have the time or inclination to administer the appropriate reward.

8. *Perceived Equitable Rewards.* This component is a description of the level of reward that an individual *feels is appropriate*. It is determined by the individual's perception concerning how well he fits the role requirements of the job, and his perceptions of how well he actually performs on the job.

9. *Satisfaction.* Porter and Lawler refer to satisfaction as a "derivative variable." It is derivative in the sense that its meaning or value is determined by the individual's comparison of what she considers an equitable reward with the amount of the actual reward. To the extent that the perceived equitable reward exceeds the actual reward, the individual is dissatisfied; if the actual reward exceeds the perceived equitable reward, the individual is satisfied. The larger the difference between these two values, the greater the degree of dissatisfaction or satisfaction.

Recent Research on Instrumentality Models. In the past decade, the amount of research being conducted on instrumentality models has grown considerably. This is due, in part, to the general acceptance by managers and researchers alike of the important role cognitive activities play in motivation and performance. An excellent view of this research is provided by Campbell and Pritchard (1976) and Mitchell (1974). The research on the general topic of "instrumentality" has taken several different forms. There are several studies that combine valence, instrumentality, and expectancy in particular ways in an attempt to predict either effort expenditure, performance, or both. Another class of studies deals with basic measurement problems in tests of the models, particularly the way in which each of these three variables is operationally defined or measured. A third class of studies deals with different approaches to testing the basic instrumentality model. Finally, several studies examine characteristics of workers or environments that affect the degree to which instrumentality models can predict worker behavior. We will try to synthesize the results of these studies.

Tests of V-I-E Models. Vroom's basic model (1964) has been expanded several times. The most comprehensive expansion was the Porter and Lawler version (1968) described above. Following that, revisions were also suggested by Graen (1969) and Lawler (1971; 1973). Most of the tests of both the initial model and the later versions have yielded about the same results: effort is predicted more accurately than performance. This makes sense logically. Individuals have effort under their control but not always performance. The environment plays a major role in determining if and how effort will yield high levels of performance.

Another common finding is that valence (or the attractiveness of outcomes) plays a major role in effort expenditure. It is beginning to appear that Valence is not equal to either instrumentality or expectancy in potential impact—its impact is much greater (Feldman, 1974). This possibility was not directly addressed by the early models but is becoming more apparent.

Several studies have concluded that most of the versions of instrumentality theory are unnecessarily complex (Kesselman, Hagen, & Wherry, 1974; Feldman, 1974). This is a constant problem in the behavioral sciences. Theories play a dual role: they are attempts at understanding a behavioral phenomenon but they also represent the thought process of the scientist. No one would ever accuse scientists of being simple-minded (at least not to their faces), so there is no reason to expect their theories to be simple. Thus, models are very often larger and more complex than the behavior they purport to explain. Recent research seems to suggest that this is true for the more complex versions of instrumentality theory.

Another general finding is that even though researchers often conclude that effort and the V, I, and E components are interrelated, this relationship is not particularly strong. Typical correlations between effort and the other components are in the .25 to .40 range. Correlations are occasionally higher, but this is usually when the measure of effort is a self-report. Self-report measures of effort are open to question with respect to tests of the model.

There have been some studies that have tested the predictive power of the instrumentality approach in other cultures. In particular, Matsui and his colleagues (Matsui & Terai, 1975; Matsui & Ikeda, 1976; Matsui, Kasaw, Nagamatsu, & Ohtsuka, 1977) have applied the model in Japan and have found correlations between cognitive components and effort that are similar to American results. While they claim cross-cultural support for the basic propositions, our interpretation would be somewhat more guarded—traditional applications of instrumentality models do no better in other cultures than they do in our own culture.

Finally, it appears that Vroom's proposition—that perceptions are equally if not more important than realities—is a good one. Many studies have demonstrated the advantages of measuring *perceived* instrumentalities and expectancies rather than objective or actual values.

Measurement of V, I, and E Components. Since the instrumentality approach has not been generally successful in predicting efforts or performance, one might be tempted to dismiss it as "wrong." That would be a little too hasty, since its failure might be related more to the way the important variables (valence, instrumentality, and expectancy) are measured than the theoretical propositions themselves. If the values which are used to represent these components are meaningless, the model could hardly be expected to predict motivation or performance. Feldman (1974) tested the possibility that asking subjects how *sure* they were of answers to questions dealing with V, I, and E could be used to improve their answers. He developed a weighting system for using this "certainty" information. The certainty weights did much more harm than good! DeLeo and Pritchard (1974) demonstrated that the typical questionnaire used to measure V, I, and E components did a dreadful job. The resulting measures were unreliable and showed little evidence they were measuring what they intended to. As an example, two different measures of the expectancy component correlated .10. Matsui and Ikeda (1976) suggested that the reasons relationships between effort and cognitive variables were low was that the outcomes were chosen for the subject by the researcher. They allowed subjects to suggest and evaluate their own outcomes. The result was a substantial increase in the correlation between cognitive components and effort.

Liddell and Solomon (1977) identified a critical characteristic of the instrumentality approach: people must be capable of ordering outcomes in terms of their desirability. In other words, we must be sure that the valences *mean* something. As an example, if I report that I prefer chocolate ice cream to strawberry and that I prefer strawberry ice cream to vanilla, then I should report that I prefer chocolate ice cream to vanilla! The technical term for this is *transitivity*. The objects in question can be consistently ordered. In instrumentality theory, we cannot hope to predict an individual's behavior if that individual cannot (or will not) order outcomes consistently. Liddell and Solomon showed that traditional valence questions do seem to produce transitive results.

The Liddell and Solomon results present us with a dilemma. DeLeo and Pritchard said the traditional methods of obtaining valences were poor, yet Liddell and Solomon found traditional methods were suitable. Who was right? There is one important difference between the DeLeo study and the Liddell study. In the DeLeo study, a large number of subjects were asked to express their preferences for outcomes. They were then asked again to express these preferences. The two sets of responses were correlated for reliability estimates. In the Liddell study, subjects were asked to order the preference for outcomes. These orders then were checked for consistency or transitivity. In experimental design terminology, the first study was a between-subjects design while the second study was a within-subjects design. This issue has become a critical one in evaluating the results of research in instrumentality theory. The approach predicts that individuals will be guided by the outcome that is most preferred in a set of outcomes. This means that within-subjects designs are more appropriate tests of the models than between-subjects designs. The data seem to bear this out (Matsui, Kagawa, Nagamatsu, and Ohtsuka, 1977; Parker and Dyer, 1976). Effort is predicted more accurately when an individual's actions are considered in light of his ordering rather than when those actions are viewed in light of his preference for an outcome compared to another individual's preference for that outcome. This also suggests that DeLeo and Pritchard's findings may not be as damaging as they first seemed. The low reliabilities and validities may be due to the method of analysis rather than a flaw in the theory. As the within-subjects design is used more frequently, we expect instrumentality theory to receive more support than it has in the past. In addition, as suggested earlier, some simplifications of the model should also help improve its stature.

Some Thoughts on Instrumentality Theory. As you can tell from the description of the Porter-Lawler model, instrumentality theory is a far cry from "a happy worker is a productive worker." It provides a comprehensive framework for dealing with complex industrial behavior. There is no reason to consider the model complete and final. Modifications are being made continually. Changing the model as new data are gathered in field and laboratory settings is an integral part of theory building. But in spite of its changing nature, the thrust of instrumentality theory is a good one. The cognitive nature of the approach does a good job of capturing the essence of energy expenditure. Very simply put, it says that the force on a person to perform a given action depends on the answers to a series of questions; questions such as "Is a reward being offered that I value?" "If I expend the effort, will my performance improve?" "If I improve my performance, will I actually get the reward?"—questions we ask ourselves day in and day out.

There are some differences between the instrumentality models and the need models. The process components are very different. The need models are based on inferred drives or needs that create tension in the person. To understand why an individual expends energy in a particular situation, we must know something of the history of responses and rewards of that individual. The instrumentality models are based on current estimates by the individual of the chances of obtaining some valued reward. While it might be useful to have some information about the individual's reward history, it is sufficient to measure the individual estimates as cognitive variables rather than historical facts.

Another difference between need models and instrumentality models is in the content portion of the models. Instrumentality models are very unclear about the nature of potential "rewards." The Porter-Lawler model goes so far as to distinguish between intrinsic and extrinsic rewards, but there is no very clear indication about where they come from, how they develop, or the effect of individual differences in personality characteristics on the potential of a reward to modify behavior. In this respect, most of the need theories are much more specific. Although they give little indication of where the needs come from, they are quite specific about the hierarchical or prepotent nature of needs, about the objects in the environment capable of satisfying those needs, and—at least in the case of Maslow's theory—they provide us with a framework for understanding individual differences in the strength of particular needs. In summary, instrumentality theories need some work on the *content* portion of the model, while need theories could be improved with a more reasonable consideration of the *process* of energy expenditure.

In spite of the content flaws of instrumentality theory, it is well accepted by managers. This is probably due to the specific nature of the process described. A manager can understand and apply the principles embodied in each of the components of the model. Instrumentalities make sense. The manager can use this principle to lay out clearly for subordinates the relationships among outcomes—promotions yield salary increases, four unexcused absences yields a suspension of one day, etc. Similarly, the manager can affect effort-reward probabilities by systematically rewarding good performance. As a matter of fact, a useful exercise for managers is to take the Porter-Lawler model and suggest a way in which a manager might directly affect each of the components.

If we consider the ease of application of the need models, they do not compare favorably with the instrumentality models. In particular, Maslow's need hierarchy provides no specific course of action for a manager. There is the vague implication that needs should be measured and satisfied according to the level of functioning of the individual. But how this need satisfaction relates to energy expenditure and performance in an industrial context is not at all clear. Herzberg's two-factor theory is quite clear on how you motivate people—you provide them with an enriched environment. While that would seem to satisfy the objections to need theory, problems remain. As we will see later in the chapter, the concept of job enrichment fits quite nicely in almost all theories of work motivation. Consequently it cannot be used as support for only one of those theories. In addition, there are instances in which enriched jobs have had the opposite effect: the individuals in those jobs were more dissatisfied and less motivated after their jobs were enriched.

We will come back to a discussion of the relative merits of different approaches to the explanation of work motivation at the end of the chapter. We will now consider an approach to motivation in industry that has been receiving increased attention in the last several years—reinforcement theory.

Reinforcement Approaches (Behaviorism)

The reinforcement approach is clearly an example of the "what-you-do-*to* someone" tradition depicted in the cartoon Figure 9–2. Many behaviorists would even go so far as to refuse to use the term "motivation" because it implies a "mentalistic" or hidden process that cannot be directly measured in the individual. Nevertheless, if we consider motivation as just another term for energy expenditure, there is some value in examining the relationship of rewards or reinforcement to levels and directions of energy expenditure.

The major thrust of these approaches is to show that the behavior of an individual in an industrial setting can be accounted for by understanding various STIMULUS—RESPONSE—REWARD associations. Particular attention is paid to the RESPONSE—REWARD association. The term "reward schedule" has come to represent this association. Continuous reward schedules imply that every time a correct response occurs, a reward is presented. Intermittent reward schedules imply that rewards do not always follow correct responses—two or three or seven correct responses may be required before a reward is presented. Punishments may be "scheduled" in the same way as rewards. The reinforcement advocates believe that both the level and the direction of energy expenditure can be changed through manipulations of the reinforcement schedule.

In a typical study using the reinforcement model, the investigator shows either that: (1) individuals rewarded for successful job performance produce more than individuals not rewarded for successful job performance, or (2) individual performance levels can be modified by using reinforcement schedules in various sequences. An example of the first type of study is the research of Yukl and his associates (Yukl & Latham, 1975; Yukl, Latham, and Pursell, 1976). Figure 9–7 is adapted from a study of the effect of contingent reinforcement of unskilled laborers hired to plant tree seedlings. (Yukl & Latham, 1975). As you can see from the figure, those laborers who were paid hourly tended to produce at the lower level.

An example of the second type of study can be seen in the research of Pritchard and his associates (Pritchard, Leonard, VonBergen, & King 1975). Figure 9–8 is adapted from Pritchard's work and describes the effect of changes of reinforcement schedule on the training performance of students learning an electronics task. Since the order of presentation of the various schedules was counterbalanced, it is apparent once again that hourly pay is not conducive to high levels of performance.

These types of studies have suggested to industrial managers that if an organizationally-defined appropriate behavior is followed by a valued reward, that behavior is likely to occur again. Early attempts to apply behaviorist principles to work behavior were little more than "translation" efforts. Pay became a "monetary reinforcement," piece-rate pay became "continuous contingent reinforcement," inconsistent reward structures became "variable reinforcement schedules," and nagging by a supervisor became a "negative reinforcer."

FIGURE 9–7

Effect of Type of Payment on Production

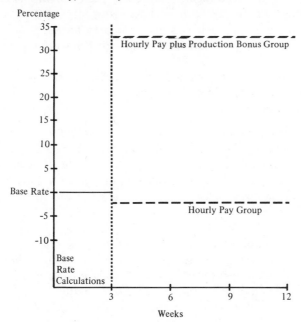

Need theorists argued against the behaviorist approach, contending that it was too mechanical and depersonalizing. The behaviorists countered by translating models of work motivation into the behaviorist framework. In one of the best examples of this type of exercise, Nord (1969) looked at the work of McGregor, Herzberg, and Maslow from a behaviorist perspective. He contended that the theories of Maslow and Herzberg were more popular with managers because:

FIGURE 9–8

Number of Tests Passed under Different Conditions of Reinforcement

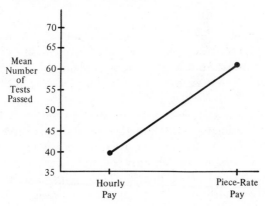

1. Managers would rather conceive of themselves as being "self actualized" (as suggested by need-hierarchy theory) than "manipulated" by their environment (as suggested by behaviorism).
2. The Skinnerian approach was considered to be too simple-minded to take into account the complex social situations offered by the world of work.
3. In the need-hierarchy approach, man was assumed to have an essence or an intrinsic nature that *interacted* with the environment to yield a particular behavior.

After the rhetoric subsided somewhat, a number of studies appeared that were positive to the reinforcement approach. Pedalino and Gamboa (1974) demonstrated that absenteeism could be modified by engaging workers in a game of five-card stud; workers were given a card for each day of work within a given week, and the highest hand at the end of the week was awarded a cash prize. Yukl and Latham (1975) demonstrated that tree planters worked harder for contingent reinforcement than for an hourly wage. Rubenstein, Watzke, Doktor, and Dana (1975) demonstrated that contingent group rewards fostered cooperative behavior while contingent individual rewards were not conducive to cooperative behavior.

Recently, there have been attempts to discriminate among various schedules of reinforcement in terms of their relative efficiency for maintaining high performance levels. In particular, the following schedules have been compared:

1. *Hourly rate:* a non-contingent reinforcement schedule in which the individual is paid at a fixed rate regardless of performance. This is normally considered to be a "control" condition or a base rate for comparison purposes.
2. *Continuous reinforcement schedule:* a contingent reward presented after *each* correct response.
3. *Fixed-ratio schedule:* a contingent schedule in which rewards are presented after a fixed number of correct responses, e.g., after five orders are processed.
4. *Variable-ratio schedule:* a contingent schedule in which the number of correct responses required before a reward occurs varies on some prearranged schedule.
5. *Variable-amount schedule:* contingent rewards vary in amount from one occasion to the next. This is not actually a schedule of reinforcement in the strict sense, but it does represent an experimental condition that has been tested against other traditional schedules.

The one finding that seems to be most common is that hourly pay is not particularly conducive to high-quality or high-quantity work behavior. Yukl and Latham (1975) found that a continuous-reinforcement schedule yielded higher performance than hourly pay, but that variable-ratio schedules were not particularly effective. Pritchard, Leonard, VonBergen, and Kirk (1976) tested the hourly condition against fixed-ratio, variable-ratio, and variable-amount schedules and found that all contingent schedules yielded higher performance than hourly pay, but there were no differences among the various contingent schedules in terms of their performance effects. Chung and Vickery (1976) demonstrated that piece rates, bonuses, and knowledge of results seemed to have additive positive effects on performance levels of college students in a simulated work setting; the hourly-pay condition was again least conducive to high levels of performance. As a result of these and similar other studies, we can question the wisdom of hourly pay rates if productivity is our major criterion.

A second question is related to the effect of different reinforcement schedules on variables other than productivity. It is not uncommon to find that workers in short-cycle monotonous jobs prefer hourly rates to piece rates. They report that piece-rate systems seem to "control" them—they often refer to lucrative piece-rate schedules as "golden handcuffs." Managers occasionally use the threat of piece-rate payment as a technique for controlling the quantity and quality of production for hourly paid workers. Thus, in spite of the fact production is high under continuous-reinforcement schedules, workers may not be particularly happy with the method of payment. As a matter of fact, in Sweden, piece-rate payment schedules have been officially condemned due to the belief that this method of payment induces tension in workers and ultimately damages their mental and physical well-being. While workers' preferences for various schedules are seldom considered in the American studies, Yukl, Latham, and Pursell (1976) did report that workers preferred hourly rates to variable payment schedules (although preferences for continuous contingent schedules were not reported).

Currently, the behaviorist approach to work motivation and performance is not well supported empirically and is somewhat insular in its concern for productivity as the major dependent variable. In addition, some researchers have been able to demonstrate that cognitive variables are capable of explaining some variation in work behavior that cannot be accounted for by reinforcement schedules (Berger, Cummings, and Heneman, 1975). Researchers in this area are on the horns of a dilemma: they must either impose dramatic constraints on the experimental situation (and make it artificial, thus limiting generalizability), or test their models in the field, with all the inevitable disasters that occur in field experiments (see Yukl and Latham, 1975). In general, we agree with Heiman (1975) in his observation that most current extrapolations of behaviorist principles to management practices are too simple-minded to be of much value. While we accept the basic proposition that contingent rewards affect behavior, we are not convinced that the behaviorist model can be usefully applied in any meaningful sense to a wide range of work behavior.

Balance Theories

This class of theories comprises motivational models holding that behavior is initiated, directed, and sustained by the attempts of the individual to maintain some internal balance of psychological tension. Most industrial versions of balance theory are based on Festinger's (1957) theory of cognitive dissonance. The model is deceptively simple, proposing that (1) discrepant cognitions produce psychological tension within the individual; (2) tension is unpleasant for the individual; and (3) individuals will take action to reduce the tension. While this is a rather stripped-down version of the dissonance model, it is sufficient for our purposes. The industrial variation of this model is known as *equity theory.*

Adams' Equity Theory. As suggested in a review of equity theory by Pritchard (1969), Adams' (1965) version of equity theory is perhaps the most extensive and explicit. The general proposition states that individuals form a ratio of their inputs in a given situation to their outcomes in that situation. Inputs are defined as anything the individual feels she personally contributes in a given work setting and may include things such as intellectual abilities, psychomotor skills, personality traits, seniority, or experience. Outcomes are all factors the individual perceives as having some personal value (e.g., money, promotions, or praise). The individual sets up the ratio of inputs to outcomes and compares the value of that ratio to the value of the ratio for "significant others." If the value of the ratio equals the values of the others' ratios, the situation is perceived as equitable and no tension exists; if the values are unequal—that is, the value of the person's ratio is larger or smaller than the value of some significant other's ratio— tension exists, and the individual will be motivated to reduce that tension. The force or intensity of the motivated behavior (amount of energy expended) is thought to be directly proportional to the amount of tension created by the inequality or inequity.

An example of an inequitable situation would be a case in which individual A contributes 5 units of input and receives 4 units of outcome, while individual B contributes 4 units of input and receives 5 units of outcome. The ratios would be 5/4 and 4/5, respectively. Since these values are not equal, inequity exists for both individual A and individual B (assuming of course that individuals A and B perceive each other as a "significant other"). But if individual A contributes 5 units of input and receives 4 units of outcome, while individual B contributes 10 units of input and receives 8 units of outcome, both perceive the situation as equitable. It is important to note that inputs and outcomes are defined as they are *perceived* by the individual.

The bulk of the equity studies have been done in laboratory settings, although there seems to be an increase in the number of studies using field simulations. In a typical equity experiment, subjects are randomly assigned to one of four conditions: (1) hourly rate-overpay condition, (2) hourly rate-underpay condition, (3) piece rate-overpay condition, (4) piece rate-underpay condition. Each of these conditions is considered to be inequitable, two because of underpayment, and two because of overpayment. The dissonance or tension is usually induced through instructions. For example, the overpayment subjects would be told that "more money has become available, and in spite of the fact that we told you your pay would be $1.75 per hour (or .07¢ per piece), we will pay you $2.25 per hour (or .10¢ per piece)." Those in the underpayment condition might be told that "we are sorry but a terrible mistake has been made; we incorrectly advertised this position as paying $1.75 per hour (or .07¢ per piece); since we only have a limited amount of money, we cannot pay you what we advertised but will have to pay you $1.50 per hour (or .04¢ per piece)." Table 9–1 represents the expected results from such an experiment. From the table you can see that the mode of tension reduction depends on the payment condition. In the piece rate-overpayment condition, an increase in input only serves to *increase* the tension, since the individual will be paid more than before. The prediction for this condition would be that the individual will improve the quality of the work while reducing the quantity. A similar logic applies to each of the cells.

The role of the instructions is crucial, and a good deal of research has been done to make sure the instructions have the intended effect. For example, some experiments used the following instructions for the overpayment condition: "I think some kind of mistake has been made. I don't know why they sent you here. I asked for *experienced* workers. The advertised pay rate was for experienced workers, not people who know nothing about the job. Well, it's too late to get somebody else now, so I guess you'll have to do. I'll pay you the advertised rate, but you sure don't deserve it." The problem with an instruction set like this is that the individual may increase the outputs for one of two reasons—either to prove to the "boss" that he is not as inadequate as was originally thought, or to reduce the tension induced by the inequity.

The general findings of the studies testing the equity model have been that equity predictions hold up fairly well in the underpayment conditions but not so well in the overpayment and piece-rate conditions.

Just as in the case of the other motivational theories, there is something quite appealing about equity theory. It describes the way we normally react

TABLE 9–1

The Predicted Effects of Inequitable Payment on the Quantity and Quality of Production

	Quantity of Production		Quality of Production	
Overpayment Condition	Piece Rate ↓	↑ Hourly Rate	↑ Piece Rate	↑ Hourly Rate
Underpayment Condition	↑ Piece Rate	Hourly Rate ↓	Piece Rate ↓	Hourly Rate ↓

to many work-related experiences. Everyone has had the experience at one time or another of feeling "cheated" because of an inappropriate reward. In addition, we all probably moderate our efforts to some degree according to what we consider "a fair day's work." A striking example of just this process can be seen in Figure 9–9, particularly the following passage:

> One service man who was receiving considerably less than his co-workers was asked why he did not insist on equal pay. "I don't want to work that hard" was the obvious answer.

Nevertheless, we cannot let intuitive appeal or common sense substitute for scientific support. Pritchard (1969) and others have raised theoretical questions regarding: (1) the manner in which a comparison person is chosen by an individual; (2) the manner in which a strategy for tension reduction is chosen; and (3) the role of individual differences in equity predictions. These theoretical questions represent some real obstacles for the manager attempting to use equity theory as a day-to-day motivation framework for dealing with subordinates. The most important obstacle is generalizing equity-theory predictions to rewards other than money. A second pitfall is the accurate prediction of the effect of inequity.

A given inequity may lead to quite different attempts to resolve it. These attempts might range from increased inputs to sabotage or quitting. Recent research by Weick (Weick, Bougon, and Maruyama, 1976) suggests there is a tendency to handle any inequity involving low outcomes by requesting higher outcomes for self. If this finding is supported, many of Pritchard's objections will be answered; at the same time, however, it will require a substantial revision of the theory to account for this phenomenon, since there are no elements currently in the theory that would explain the appeal of this strategy over others. Another finding in Weick's research was that increased effort due to overpayment was a lot less common than previously had been believed. This is probably due to the remarkable capacity of individuals to rationalize everything from smoking to war. Nevertheless, this finding also requires a rather substantial rethinking of some of the original propositions of equity theory.

Equity theory places a rather heavy emphasis on the choice of a "referent" for the purpose of evaluating outcomes. In some studies the referent is assumed to be another person with whom the individual works; in other studies the referent is thought to be an idealized or internalized concept— possibly the average of all others with whom the individual ever worked. In any event, there is some confusion about the nature of the referent. Goodman (1974) has done some good research on this topic. In the course of this research, he was able to identify several different potential sources of referents that might be used when an individual evaluates his pay. Figure 9–10 presents these referents and their definitions. Goodman found that people may use more than one referent and that their felt satisfaction with pay was a combination of the appropriate referents. In addition, he found there were individual differences in referent choice. For example,

FIGURE 9–9
A New Approach to Motivation

ARTHUR FRIEDMAN'S OUTRAGE: EMPLOYEES DECIDE THEIR PAY
By Martin Koughan

OAKLAND, Calif.—One thing for sure, Arthur Friedman will never become the chairman of the board at General Motors.

It is not just because the modish, easygoing Oakland appliance dealer does not look the part—Hush Puppies, loud shirts and denim jackets tend to clash with the sober decor of most executive suites. And it certainly is not because he is an incompetent administrator—the Friedman-Jacobs Co. has prospered during the 15 years of his stewardship.

It is mainly because Art Friedman has some pretty strange ideas about how one runs a business.

Five years ago, he had his most outrageous brainstorm. First he tried it out on his wife Merle and his brother Morris.

"Here he goes again," replied Merle with a sigh of resignation, "Another dumb stunt."

"Oh my God," was all that Morris could muster.

His idea was to allow employees to set their own wages, make their own hours and take their vacations whenever they felt like it.

The end result was that it worked.

Friedman first unleashed his proposal at one of the regular staff meetings. Decide what you are worth, he said, and tell the bookkeeper to put it in your envelope next week. No questions asked. Work any time, any day, any hours you want. Having a bad day? Go home. Hate working Saturdays? No problem. Aunt Ethel from Chicago has dropped in unexpectedly? Well, take a few days off, show her the town. Want to go to Reno for a week, need a rest? Go, go, no need to ask. If you need some money for the slot machines, take it out of petty cash. Just come back when you feel ready to work again.

His speech was received in complete silence. No one cheered, no one laughed, no one said a word.

"It was about a month before anyone asked for a raise," recalls Stan Robinson, 55, the payroll clerk, "And when they did, they asked Art first. But he refused to listen and told them to just tell me what they wanted. I kept going back to him to make sure it was all right, but he wouldn't even talk about it. I finally figured out he was serious."

"It was something that I wanted to do," explains Friedman. "I always said that if you give people what they want, you get what you want. You have to be willing to lose, to stick your neck out. I finally decided that the time had come to practice what I preached."

Soon the path to Stan Robinson's desk was heavily travelled. Friedman's wife Merle was one of the first; she figured that her contribution was worth $1 an hour more. Some asked for $50 more a week, some $60. Delivery truck driver Charles Ryan was more ambitious; he demanded a $100 raise.

In most companies, Ryan would have been laughed out of the office. His work had not been particularly distinguished. His truck usually left in the morning and returned at 5 in the afternoon religiously, just in time for him to punch

FIGURE 9–9 *(continued)*

out. He dragged around the shop, complained constantly and was almost always late for work. Things changed.

"He had been resentful about his prior pay," explains Friedman. "The raise made him a fabulous employee. He started showing up early in the morning and would be back by 3, asking what else had to be done."

Instead of the all-out raid on the company coffers that some businessmen might expect, the 15 employees of the Friedman-Jacobs Co. displayed astonishing restraint and maturity. The wages they demanded were just slightly higher than the scale of the Retail Clerks union to which they all belong (at Friedman's insistence). Some did not even take a raise. One service man who was receiving considerably less than his co-workers was asked why he did not insist on equal pay. "I don't want to work that hard," was the obvious answer.

When the union contract comes across Friedman's desk every other year, he signs it without even reading it. "I don't care what it says," he insists. At first, union officials would drop in to see how things were going, but they would usually end up laughing and shaking their heads, muttering something about being put out of a job. They finally stopped coming by. It was enough to convince George Meany to go out to pasture.

The fact is that Friedman's employees have no need for a union; whatever they want, they take and no one questions it. As a result they have developed a strong sense of responsibility and an acute sensitivity to the problems that face the American worker in general that would have been impossible under the traditional system.

George Tegner, 59, an employee for 14 years, has like all his co-workers achieved new insight into the mechanics of the free enterprise system. "You have to use common sense; no one wins if you end up closing the business down. If you want more money, you have to produce more. It can't work any other way. Anyway, wages aren't everything. Doing what you want to is more important."

Roger Ryan, 27, has been with the company for five years. "I know about the big inflation in '74, but I haven't taken a raise since '73. I figure if everybody asks for more, then inflation will just get worse. I'll hold out as long as I can."

Payroll clerk Stan Robinson: "I'm single now. I don't take as much as the others, even though I've been here longer, because I don't need as much. The government usually winds up with the extra money anyway."

Elwood Larsen, 65, has been the company's ace service man for 16 years. When he went into semi-retirement last year, he took a $1.50 cut in pay. Why? Larsen does not think a part-timer is worth as much. "I keep working here because I like it. We all know that if the Friedmans make money, we do. You just can't gouge the owner."

In the past five years, there has been no turnover of employees. Friedman estimates that last year his 15 workers took no more than a total of three sick days. It is rare that anyone is late for work and, even then, there is usually a good reason. Work is done on time and employee pilferage is nonexistent.

"We used to hear a lot of grumbling," says Robinson. "Now, everybody smiles."

FIGURE 9–9 *(concluded)*

As part of the new freedom, more people were given keys to the store and the cash box. If they need groceries, or even some beer money, all they have to do is walk into the office, take what they want out of the cash box and leave a voucher. Every effort is make to ensure that no one looks over their shoulder.

There has been only one discrepancy. "Once the petty cash was $10 over," recalls Friedman. "We never could figure out where it came from."

The policy has effected some changes in the way things are done around the store. It used to open every night and all day Sunday, but no one wanted to work those hours. A problem? Of course not. No more nights and Sundays. ("When I thought about it," confesses Friedman, "I didn't like to work those hours either.")

The store also used to handle TV's and stereos—high-profit items—but they were a hassle for all concerned. The Friedman-Jacobs Co. now deals exclusively in major appliances such as refrigerators, washers and dryers.

Skeptics by now are chuckling to themselves, convinced that if Friedman is not losing money, he is just breaking even. The fact is that net profit has not dropped a cent in the last five years; it has increased. Although volume is considerably less and overhead has increased at what some would consider an unhealthy rate, greater productivity and efficiency have more than made up for it.

Source: *The Washington Post,* February 23, 1975.

FIGURE 9–10
Referent Measures: Conceptual and Operational Definitions

Referent	Conceptual Definition	Operational Example
Other-inside	Refers to others inside the organization to whom a person compares himself	"Well, we only got a 5% raise . . . but the union got 8% and they have much less responsibility
Other-outside	Indicates referents outside the organization	"I get about the same as I would working in a similar job outside"
System-structure	Refers to whether the promised or stated structure of the pay system corresponds to the actual structure. For example if an organization states that it operates on a merit raise system but	"The present raise system does not permit enough graduations to reflect changes in

FIGURE 9–10 (continued)

Referent	Conceptual Definition	Operational Example
	the structure of the pay system does not distinguish between merit and cost of living raises, it is likely that a discrepancy between the expected structure and actual structure will exist and feelings of inequity will follow	cost of living as well as superior performance''
System administration	Indicates referents that arise from the way the pay system is administered. For example if the company policy were to provide an automatic raise at every promotion, then providing a raise at promotion would evoke an equitable referent, nonpayment an inequitable referent. In the case of System-administration referents the issue is not the structure of the system but how the structure of that system is administered	"When I was promoted I never got the 10% raise to bring me up to the lower pay range of that job''
Self-pay history	Refers to whether past or future job input-outcome ratios are used in evaluation of present pay	"I have received good raises in the past and expect the same in the future''
Self-family	Refers to the individual's conception of the level of wages needed to maintain his family's standard of living. In this case the evaluation of present pay is a comparison of present input-outcome ratio with the ideal ratio relevant to meeting one's family role	"I am able to provide for my family . . . we live well''
Self-internal	Refers to the individual's conception of his own worth. In the context of pay this refers to the individual's internal standard of his worth to the company. While clearly shaped by external forces (e.g. parents, educational experiences, friends), the Self-internal referent is entirely internal to the individual and represents a part of his general view of his self-worth	"Given my length of service and education, I feel I am paid well for what I do''

Source: Goodman, P. S. An examination of referents used in the evaluation of pay. *Organizational Behavior and Human Performance*, 1974, *12*, 170–195, Table 1.

college graduates were more likely to choose "other" referents from the outside than the inside. Perhaps this is because they see themselves as more mobile than noncollege graduates. This type of research, directed toward an understanding of the way in which referent sources are chosen and the effect of individual differences on these choices is fascinating and may rekindle some flagging interest in the equity approach.

Another example of this type of research is a study by Middlemist and Peterson (1976). They were also interested in the role of the "other" in equity determination. They were able to demonstrate that individuals *do* pay attention to the efforts and qualifications of other group members; furthermore, they alter their own efforts in accordance with the efforts of co-workers. One finding is of particular interest. The researchers were able to manipulate the level of co-workers so that one group of subjects first worked with a "fast" co-worker and then a slow one; a second group of subjects worked first with a "slow" co-worker and then a fast one. When the co-worker change was from a fast one to a slow one, the referent "other" chosen by the subject for equity purposes seemed to be an internalized "other," similar to the fast co-worker who had left; when the co-worker change was from slow to fast, the referent "other" was the new co-worker. This is important, since equity theory might be interpreted to suggest that the referent "other" is constant, regardless whether that "other" is a real person called "my current co-worker" or an internalized or idealized view of a co-worker.

Weick et al. (1976) have found that the dynamics of equity theory might be different for different cultures. Studies of equity dynamics in the Netherlands yielded very different results from those done in the United States. Dutch subjects placed high values on inputs, regardless of outcomes. Weick suggests this is a result of a Calvinist heritage that stressed hard work as a technique for the expiation of sin. Under such conditions, it would be unlikely that input/outcome ratios would play a major role in work motivation. Kammen (1972) makes the Dutch/American distinction more eloquent:

> The English colonies were established by colonists who believed that in and of himself, man could do little to save his own soul and that gaining the world conferred no profit; yet Americans have behaved ever since as though he who strives shall indeed gain the world, and save his soul in the bargain. (p. 116)

Similar differences should be found between American data and data from social democratic countries that value group solidarity and cohesiveness. In those cultures, the well-being of "Other" should be of much greater concern than the outcomes to "Self." Unfortunately, cross-cultural data is scarce on these issues, and we can only make guesses about the international applicability of motivation models generated by Americans. Cross-cultural studies such as those of Weick et al. can be of enormous benefit in refining and improving work motivation models.

The recent research into equity theory has been creative, appropriately responsive to criticisms of early versions of the theory, and has produced results that can be used to refine and develop the theory further. In the process, many of the original propositions of Adams' version of the theory have been discarded or radically altered. As a result, a theory of social comparison is emerging that is richer and more plausible than the original theory. It is our hope that this development continues.

Korman's Cognitive Consistency Theory. Another variation on the general theme of balance theories is the work of Korman. He emphasizes *self-evaluation* and *self-perception* as well as the more general concept of *self-esteem*. His hypothesis is that "all other things being equal, individuals will engage in and find satisfying those behavioral roles which will maximize their sense of cognitive balance or consistency." He predicts that individuals will be motivated to act in a manner consistent with the self-image that they have when they approach the task. Furthermore, individuals will seek out and be satisfied with those jobs and task roles most consistent with their self-evaluations or self-cognitions. Figure 9–11 represents his model in diagram form.

Korman (1971) provides some evidence in support of the theory, but, as Miner and Dachler (1973) point out, the theory is too general to evaluate its adequacy at the present time. A recent study by Gavin (1973) failed to support Korman's predictions clearly. Gavin concluded that, while there may be some utility to Korman's propositions, it is primarily in the form of suggesting self-evaluation and consistency as a *moderator* of the relationship between expectancy and performance in a Porter-Lawler type model.

Recently, Dipboye (1977a) has questioned the data Korman uses to support his self-consistency theory. Dipboye suggests that one could just as easily conclude from the data that individuals choose alternatives that enhance their self-esteem rather than match their self-image. This is a critical issue, since self-enhancement is a basic mechanism in many of the typical need-hierarchy models (such as Maslow's) and if people were acting in the service of self-enhancement, then Korman's model would have been refuted. Dipboye suggests the critical question to ask is the following: *Will people with low self-esteem choose consistency over enhancement?* If the answer to the question is yes, Korman is supported; if the answer is no, Korman is refuted. As you might have already guessed, Korman did not let that pass without comment (Korman, 1977). He suggested that Dipboye: (1) had not read the most recent version of the theory, (2) did not understand the version he *did* read, (3) was unaware of supportive research on the theory and (4) engaged in too much wishful thinking himself! Seemingly required by law to respond, Dipboye (1977b) claimed that Korman (1) did not understand his own theory, (2) referred to "supportive research" that had not been published, (3) did not understand the manner by which theories are constructed, tested, and dissected, and (4) should keep up the good work. Humor aside, the question is an important one. Self-image undoubtedly plays some role in behavior. The critical ques-

FIGURE 9–11
Korman's Consistency Model of Work Behavior

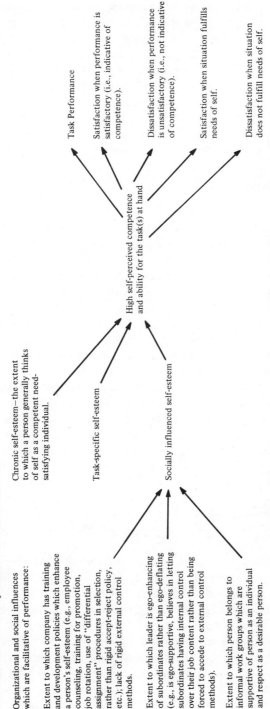

Source: Korman, A. Toward an hypothesis of work behavior. *Journal of Applied Psychology*, 1970, *54*, 32—41.

tion is whether *positive* self-images produce pleasure or *consistent* self-images do. The question remains largely unanswered, and until it is, self-consistency theory cannot develop as a broad-based approach to work motivation.

In summary, the balance theories seem to be making some progress. As is so often the case, this progress is largely a result of articulate critics rather than ardent supporters. Nevertheless, the identification of new variables to examine (in the case of equity theory) and critical questions to answer (in the case of self-consistency theory) suggests that we should soon know whether or not these cognitive balance theories will be of any value in understanding work motivation.

Other "Theories"

It is not completely appropriate to use the label "theory" for this section. The material that will be presented is more tentative than that which has already been presented. In most instances, it does not reach the level of a sophisticated body of interrelated propositions necessary for a theory of work motivation. Instead, either totally new concepts are introduced, or increased emphasis is placed on some constructs that we have seen already.

Activation or Arousal Level. In an article relating task design to activation level, Scott (1966) states that "activation theory offers an explanation for the performance decrements and the dissatisfaction frequently observed in repetitive industrial tasks" (p. 4). Activation is defined as the degree to which stored energy in the organism is released (Duffy, 1962). The energy is considered to be physical and is measured through such things as skin resistance (GSR), brain waves (EEG), and muscle potential (EMG). Arousal level is hypothesized to have an overall "activating" effect on the organism. The arousal continuum is thought to vary from lethargy at the low end to hyperactivity at the high end. It is proposed that each individual has a unique optimal level of arousal and that performance is most efficient when the individual reaches this level. It is further proposed that too much or too little arousal will lead to decrements in performance. This relationship is considered to be a curvilinear one, much like the inverted-U relationship presented in Chapter 7.

The "boredom" and performance decrement that sets in shortly after the initiation of a repetitive activity is thought to be due to a drop in arousal level. If the individual is to be brought up to peak performance in this situation, arousal level must be increased. This might be accomplished through the introduction of stimulus variety in the form of a new task, music, etc. By implication, over- and underarousal are aversive to the individual in a psychological as well as physical sense. Consequently, an individual who is below or above optimal arousal level should be performing less efficiently and should also be less satisfied. Satisfaction and performance would be related only by way of the mechanism of arousal.

Arousal theory implies that individuals should be placed in organizational roles as a function of the arousing capability of the job as well as the optimal arousal level of the individual. There are many other inferences that could be drawn from the arousal propositions. Some of them will be discussed in a later chapter on human performance. At present, it is probably best to think of arousal or activation theory as fulfilling the role of a secondary variable in work motivation. The relationship of the individual's optimal arousal level to the arousing potential of the particular job might be thought of as intervening between the effort and performance components of the Porter-Lawler model. It could possibly be considered a trait. The theory clearly indicates that overstimulation can be bad, a problem seldom dealt with in theories of work motivation.

Goal Setting and Intentional Behavior. Ryan (1970), in his book on human motivation, presents a convincing logical, philosophical, and empirical argument for the role of intention in motivated behavior. He notes that "one of the commonly observed characteristics of intentional behavior is that it tends to keep going until it reaches completion. When we are interrupted before reaching the natural conclusion of the activity, we often experience irritation and resist the interruption" (pp. 95–96). More simply put, once we start something, we will not be happy until we reach a goal we have set for ourselves. Baldamus (1951) called this process one of "traction" (as opposed to distraction) and defined it as "the feeling of being pulled along by the inertia inherent in the particular activity" (p. 42). Ryan reviews a large body of literature suggesting that level of performance is closely related to the goals an individual has set for himself or accepted from someone else.

This emphasis on cognitive processes and the role of intentional behavior is most clearly brought out in the work of Locke (1968, 1970). In a series of carefully controlled and sequenced laboratory experiments, Locke has demonstrated the effect of goal setting on individual performance. His major proposition is that harder goals yield higher performance (if and only if the individual has accepted these goals). He has shown consistently that individuals who set or accept harder goals perform at levels higher than those who set or accept easier goals. This is in direct opposition to theories of achievement motivation. Achievement motivation theories (Atkinson & Feather, 1966) predict that moderately hard goals produce higher performance, while extremely easy or extremely hard goals yield lower performance. The dynamic property of Locke's scheme would be something like "success motivation."

Locke contrasts his approach with those of the need-achievement theorists and the expectancy/instrumentality theorists. Figure 9–12 describes these differences. Need-achievement theory predicts that difficult goals will improve performance up to a point but when goal difficulty exceeds that point, performance will be adversely affected. This relationship is depicted in Figure 9–12,A. Expectancy/instrumentality theory predicts that performance should improve as goals get easier, since the probability of success (and subsequently, the probability of rewards) increases. This relationship

FIGURE 9–12

The Effect of Goal Difficulty in Three Different Theories

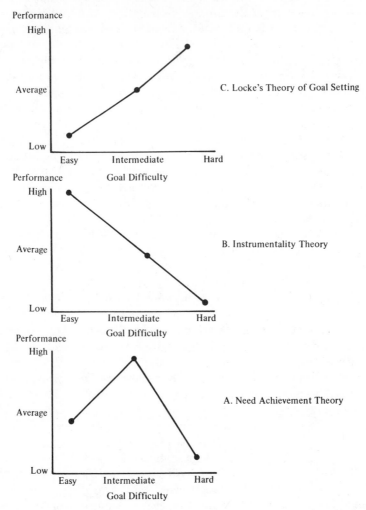

appears in Figure 9–12,B. Locke predicts that performance will increase as goal difficulty increases (assuming of course that the individual accepts the goals in question). This relationship is described in Figure 9–12,C. As you can see, the three approaches make substantially different predictions.

Locke proposes that individuals will invariably set goals for themselves, whether instructed to or not. It is to be hoped these will be the goals of the organization as well. Reaching these goals provides the individual with pleasure, while not reaching these goals is aversive or unpleasant. The implications of this approach for management would be in terms of goal-setting activity. Managers should play an active role in the goal-setting activities of their subordinates. They should also devote time to ensuring that individuals are able to reach their goals. If the goals are set high enough and the individual is able to reach the goals, productivity and satisfaction should result. An extension of this thought might be that individuals will be dissatisfied with aspects of their environment that function as obstacles to goal achievement. For example, an individual might be dissatisfied with co-workers because their constant talking is distracting and interferes with goal achievement.

In addition, it is likely that reinforcers convey information about goal achievement. When an individual completes a difficult task, the absence of reinforcement might act as discordant information. This discordant information might be related to dissatisfaction. For example, an individual who feels she has accomplished a difficult task, yet receives little recognition from her supervisor for that accomplishment, might express dissatisfaction with supervision.

One of the most prolific disciples of Locke's theory is Latham. He and his associates have attempted to test the propositions of Locke's goal-setting theory both in the laboratory and in the field. In addition, they have examined data for educated and uneducated workers, skilled, semiskilled and unskilled workers, union and nonunion workers, and work groups of various racial compositions. Typical of this research is a study done with logging crews (Latham and Baldes, 1975). Specific hard goals were assigned to the drivers of trucks that hauled logs from the logging site to the mill. The subjects were not promised any bonus or incentive for increased production. In addition to the effect of specific hard goals, the effects of knowledge of results and general motivational instructions ("do your best") were also examined. Figure 9–13 presents the results of the study. It is clear that the "do-your-best" condition was ineffective. It is equally clear that specific hard goals had positive effects on productivity. As a matter of fact, the researchers were able to conclude that to bring about a similar increase in productivity, it would have been necessary to add equipment valued at $250,000. This does not include the cost of labor! As can be seen in the figure, a rather sharp drop in productivity occurred at one point. After discussions with the drivers, the researchers discovered this was a "test" by the drivers of the company statement that no punitive actions would be taken if productivity decreased during the experimental period.

As far as the effect of knowledge of results was concerned, the data suggested this type of feedback was useful only to the degree that it was used by the subject to set goals; knowledge of results in the absence of goal setting seemed to have little or no effect on productivity. Several other studies have also examined the effect of knowledge of results on performance. Both Erez (1977) and Kim and Hamner (1976) suggest that goal setting plus feedback is critical for optimal performance.

This approach to motivation is getting a bit complicated. Campbell

FIGURE 9–13

The Effect of Specific Hard Goals on Productivity

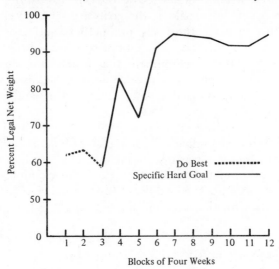

Source: Latham, G. P., & Baldes, J. J. The "practical signifi-cance" of Locke's theory of goal-setting. *Journal of Applied Psychology*, 1975, *60*, 122–124.

Percent legal net weight of 36 logging trucks across blocks as a function of a specific hard goal.

and Ilgen (1976) have made a distinction between task difficulty and goal difficulty. They propose that difficult tasks improve skills, while difficult goals improve motivation. The distinction between tasks and goals is an important one that deserves much more attention. Terborg (1976) looked at the issues of goal difficulty and goal specificity and found that the more difficult the goal, the greater the effort, while goal specificity seemed to have a greater effect on the direction of behavior (or how *focused* the effort was).

In summary, it seems as if the simple goal-setting propositions that Locke introduced in 1968 have become more complex. Instead of considering solely goal difficulty, it seems important to consider, in addition, goal speci-ficity, task difficulty, and knowledge of results, as well as demographic characteristics such as education. Once again, we are forced to accept the possibility that workers *think*, and that the nature of that thought process affects the choices which they make. About the only general conclu-sion we might draw at this point is that hard goals accompanied by knowl-edge of results seem to have a positive effect on productivity, although there is little information available on their effects on worker satisfaction. We will explore the issue of satisfaction in some detail in the next chapter.

The goal-setting research is still a long way from representing a "theory" of motivation. Nevertheless, it does present some findings that are clearly at odds with other existing theories. If and when these diverse findings are placed in a coherent model or theoretical framework general enough to encompass a wide range of industrial behaviors, it may very well take over as the most reasonable approach to work motivation.

SUMMARY OF THE MODELS

While each of the motivational categories has been summarized before, a capsule view of the way each of them treats the two major components of the motivational system—effort expenditure and performance—will prove useful.

Effort Expenditure

The questions related to antecedents and consequences of work motivation in the various models really boil down to a consideration of the "whys" of effort expenditure or "content" questions. Need-hierarchy and balance theories are in agreement that internal tension is the antecedent condition for directed behavior. They differ, however, on the causes of this tension. Balance theories are less rigid in the ordering of needs and more cognitive in dealing with the reduction of tension.

In a sense, neither the instrumentality theorists nor the behaviorists feel compelled to deal with motivation as a psychological construct. The behaviorists feel it is unnecessary to deal with it at all, avoiding, where possible, any reference to internal states of the individual and emphasizing the effects of the environment on behavior. If forced to explain the relationships between rewards and activity more extensively, they would probably consider "work motivation" to be a system of needs acquired through past reinforcements.

The instrumentality theorists prefer to consider motivation in a dual sense. Its first role is that of a simple measure of effort expended. Highly-motivated people would be distinguished from poorly-motivated people by the intensity of directed activity. The second sense in which they would use the concept of motivation is much broader. Their model, by definition, describes motivated behavior. It breaks down the phenomenon of motivated behavior into its functional components, such as perceived probabilities, valued rewards, and equitable reinforcement systems. The goal-setting theories would propose that hard goals lead to greater effort than easy goals.

Job Performance

The explanation of why some people are good performers and others poor performers has provided, and will continue to provide, a major impetus for research on models of work motivation. Need-hierarchy theories are particularly unsuited for making predictions about performance levels. They

"I'm puzzled . . . you seem to be suffering from overwork, but nobody does that anymore."

Reprinted by permission The Wall Street Journal.

are too general and vague and must borrow heavily from other models to make such predictions. For instance, what are the performance implications of the fact that a particular individual is functioning at the security or safety level rather than the esteem level?

Balance theories are less vague in their performance predictions. Their unique shortcoming so far has been an inability to specify *which* strategy an individual will use to reduce tension and *how* that strategy will relate to performance. This set of theories provides the temptation (to which some researchers have yielded) to add a new mode of tension reduction to the pool of strategies already available if none of those currently in the pool fit the data.

The behaviorists see performance as a complex "operant." It is a function of behavior-reward contingencies. They tend to ignore relationships between successful performance and self-esteem (since self-esteem is an intra-individual construct and has no meaning in their theoretical system). They would also disregard the act of goal setting as well as any "sense of accomplishment" resulting from achieving a difficult goal (since goal setting implies cognitive activity, another internal construct). The role of performance in work motivation is probably more sterile and less interesting in this system than in any of the others reviewed.

The instrumentality theorists provide the richest and most explicit description of the role of performance in motivated behavior. Its antecedents are effort expenditure, abilities and traits, and role perceptions. The consequences of performance are both affective and cognitive. They are affective in their effects on satisfaction (through the medium of rewards). They are cognitive in their effects on perceived equitable outcomes and perceived effort-reward probabilities.

A Conclusion

After examining the research that has attempted to test the various theories of work motivation, we see a recurrent finding that has not been given much attention: *the models or theories of work motivation are often more complex than the behavior they attempt to explain.* We saw this particularly in the tests of the various forms of instrumentality theory. Feldman (1974) suggested a simpler model might be more appropriate. One might draw a similar conclusion from the failure of the reinforcement approach to show dramatic differences in behavior when various schedules of reward were introduced. While it is true that clear differences emerged between the contingent (incentive) and noncontingent (hourly) schedules, there have been few studies which have noted reliable differences among the various *contingent* schedules. Once again, the subjects seem less impressed than the researchers with the subtle differences among reinforcement schedules. In equity theory, it seems the subjects are not as "upset" by overpayment as we thought they would be; in addition, when they are underpaid, they commonly attempt to increase their own outcomes rather than try any other of a large number of potential strategies for reducing tension. Finally, Alderfer's reduction of Maslow's need categories from five to three might also be seen as a move toward simplification.

As we suggested earlier, it may be that theories must be complex in order for psychologists to communicate with one another efficiently. The theory, in a sense, tells one psychologist where another psychologist "is coming from" (although, unfortunately, not where she may be "going to").

We would suggest that simpler models of motivation be explored, rather than more complicated ones. Researchers might take current theories and see if there is any difference in predictive efficiency between "full" models and "streamlined" versions.

While we would be the last people in the world to suggest that human motivation is "simple" rather than complicated, we would like to suggest that it may be complicated in a slightly different way than theorists usually propose. The difficulty in understanding human motivation might stem from the fact that the nature of the motivational process within individuals changes over time. The dynamics of motivation for the six-year-old must be different from the six-year-old's mother. The dynamics of motivation for someone in a new job must be different from those of an individual about to retire from a job she has held for 35 years. These differences would not be captured by making any one approach to motivation more complicated, e.g., adding a "certainty" component to VIE theory or another schedule of reinforcement to the operant approach. It may be more valuable to assume that people systematically change the way they make decisions as a reuslt of both maturation and experience.

A SYNTHESIS OF MOTIVATIONAL MODELS

The various motivational approaches are presented as if they were independent of one another, as if we had to choose one and only one of them for understanding behavior. This is the nature of the scientific method. Theories are pitted against one another; the name of the game is to try and *disprove* a hypothesis, to destroy a model. This type of approach is not always the best one. In the case of the different approaches to human motivation, it seems to us there are some compelling arguments and data that can be gathered for each of the four major approaches (reinforcement, need, balance, instrumentality).

An alternative to choosing *the one theory* that best explains motivated behavior for all people might be to propose different theories for different types of people. Thus, some people might expend effort along the lines suggested by equity theory, while others might behave in a manner predicted by reinforcement theory. Unfortunately, if we look at our own behavior, we find that sometimes we behave according to straight reinforcement principles and at others make decisions based on the comparisons of desired rewards to expected rewards. If this is the case, we must somehow develop a scheme for understanding how the motivational theories interact in explaining the behavior of an individual across time. Figure 9–14 is an attempt at developing such a scheme. As you can see, the left-hand side of the figure represents a motivational ladder or hierarchy. It suggests that individuals progress upward in the hierarchy. The hierarchy implies that the most basic motivational approach is the reinforcement approach. As one moves up the hierarchy, motivational principles become more complex and abstract. The right-hand side of the figure describes *why* a particular motiva-

FIGURE 9–14

*Relationships among Motivational Approaches and
Environmental Interactions*

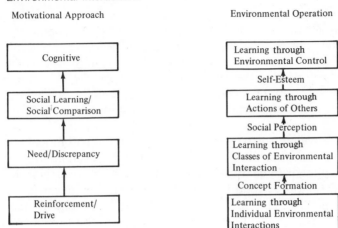

Motivational Approach

Environmental Operation

tional model is a good description of energy expenditure of an individual at any given point in time. The right-hand hierarchy also suggests a series of learning operations that progress from simple observations on the part of the individual to complex attempts to control the immediate environment. In general terms, Figure 9–14 suggests that when we first encounter a new setting or environment (such as our first job), we sit back and try to learn basic associations between our own behaviors and rewards. What makes the boss happy? What makes co-workers angry? What makes me feel good? During this period, it would be most efficient to predict our behavior by looking at the relationship between behavior and environmental rewards and punishments, i.e., schedules of reinforcement.

After some period of time, we collect these associations and give these collections labels. Learning theorists would call this "collecting" and "labeling" activity *concept formation*. Now, we think in terms of categories of rewards rather than in terms of individual associations. This is exactly what Maslow, Herzberg, and other need theorists suggest. There are broad categories of environmental rewards that have the capacity for making people happy or unhappy.

The next stage in the development process is becoming aware of and learning from the actions of co-workers. We watch what happens to them when they do certain things. Presumably we learn from this, and we are better able to obtain rewards and avoid unpleasant situations through this learning. Conversely, we are unhappy when an anticipated reward is denied; this means that our learning was somehow deficient.

Finally, when we think we have the "system" down pat, we start experimenting more directly with methods of obtaining rewards and avoiding unpleasant situations. We begin this experimentation only when we are confident that we have sufficient information about the system to take a chance.

The variables between each of the pairs of boxes on the right-hand side of the figure are meant to suggest the kind of development that must occur in the individual before the next stage of learning can become operational. Thus, concepts covering many different but similar rewards must be formed before need theories are useful in explaining behavior. Similarly, the individual must begin to observe and record the behavior of others before equity theory assumes any explanatory importance. Finally, the individual must develop a certain confidence in his own skills and abilities before he is willing to try to actively control the environment.

This approach suggests that man is a scientist, constantly trying to learn about the immediate environment, and ultimately to control it. Few would argue with the proposition that the longer we are in an environment, the more we know about it and the more efficiently we can interact with it. The model suggested by Figure 9–14 simply states this proposition in more specific terms. The figure also suggests that no one of the traditional motivational approaches is "correct." They are all "correct," but at different times in the development of the individual.

Some might claim that by trying to tie together the different theories of motivation we have made the situation even more complicated. Perhaps we have. Nevertheless, attempts to choose *the* best motivational theory have been frustrating. Under certain conditions, they all seem to predict behavior with some accuracy. Figure 9–14 is an attempt at showing why this is so.

SOME OTHER ISSUES IN WORK MOTIVATION

Job Enrichment

As was mentioned in the section dealing with Herzberg's two-factor theory, job enrichment is considered to be a useful vehicle for increasing work motivation. An enriched job is one that provides a maximum amount of intrinsic satisfaction. This is not to say that extrinsic factors are ignored. Extrinsic factors are considered to be preconditions for motivated behavior, while intrinsic factors are more directly related to motivation. The procedure is one of redesigning the job to provide challenge and a sense of accomplishment to the individual. This is to be distinguished from *job enlargement*, which involves an increase in the variety of tasks the individual performs. Job enlargement does not imply job enrichment.

Job enrichment is generating a lot of interest among managers. There is little doubt that the procedure has proved valuable in many situations. When a particular job is "enriched," the quality and quantity of work usually improve, satisfaction generally increases, and absences and turnover generally decrease. In short, it seems that motivation increases. The real question is "Why do these changes occur?" The two-factor group would contend that enriched jobs satisfy the motivator needs of the individual. They would further contend that enlarged jobs will not necessarily have the same effect. The simple addition of tasks to an individual's organizational role does not necessarily provide challenge.

Porter and Lawler would explain the effect of job enrichment on the basis of the different nature of intrinsic and extrinsic rewards. Their model suggests that intrinsic rewards are more likely to be effective than extrinsic rewards. Since enriched jobs, by definition, provide intrinsic rewards, enriched jobs should have a more direct effect on satisfaction, motivation, and performance than extrinsic reward systems.

Activation theory (Scott, 1966) would propose that stimulus variety or intensity has predictable effects on energy expenditure and performance. Enriched jobs provide exactly that—stimulus variety. Therefore, activation theory would predict that job enrichment will increase activation or arousal level. Activation level would, in turn, affect both job satisfaction and job performance. An interesting implication of this approach is that job enrichment can adversely affect some individuals. A worker who is optimally aroused on his present job would be overstimulated if his job were enriched. In this case, enrichment might actually act as a stressor. Activation theorists would not dismiss job enlargement as easily as the two-factor group. In activation terms, an enlarged job also provides stimulus variety and has the potential for increasing activation level.

The behaviorists would contend that enriched jobs simply bombard the individual with an expanded set of positive rewards. In other words, the opportunity for achieving valued rewards is greatly increased. Since enriched jobs are accompanied by a larger set of potential rewards, the probability of "turning on" or motivating any single individual is increased. In addition, since intrinsic rewards are self administered, the schedule of reinforcement is continuous.

In the same sense, it is possible to derive an explanation from equity theory. An enriched job greatly increases the outcomes in the input/outcome ratio. This would provide the individual with a greater number of strategies for reducing tension.

In practice, most attempts to enrich jobs have also involved changing pay schedules, methods of supervision, planning and decision-making strategies, and work-group interaction patterns. For that reason, it might be better to think of job enrichment as a reorganization of the job or task. In Chapter 12, which deals with the concept of organization in the work setting, we will look more specifically at job enrichment programs.

Intrinsic versus Extrinsic Factors

A great deal of research effort has been spent on the question of the importance of intrinsic and extrinsic factors in work motivation. Herzberg's two-factor theory proposes that these two classes of factors are distinct.

Intrinsic factors (motivators) primarily affect job satisfaction, while extrinsic factors (hygiene) affect job dissatisfaction. Maslow's five levels have been collapsed into lower-level and higher-level needs that parallel the intrinsic-extrinsic distinction. Porter and Lawler distinguish between the power of intrinsic and extrinsic rewards. Behaviorists contend that the difference between the effects of intrinsic and extrinsic rewards is primarily a difference in the schedule of rewards, rather than their unique nature.

It is common for both researchers and managers to think of intrinsic and extrinsic factors as additive. It is assumed that if high levels of pay are combined with interesting work, the result is a greater potential for motivation than if either of these rewards were offered alone. This assumption has been challenged recently. Deci (1972, 1976) contends that when extrinsic rewards are tied to performance, intrinsic motivation suffers. Dynamically, he proposes that external reinforcement makes people feel there are "external" forces controlling their behavior. On the other hand, intrinsic rewards—rewards individuals provide to themselves—strengthen this feeling of control. Thus, Deci suggests that the combination of extrinsic and intrinsic rewards is *subtractive*, not additive; that using both types of reinforcement together yields a lesser potential for motivation than if either were used alone!

The phenomenon that Deci suggests might be easier to understand in an example provided by Zimbardo (1974). He tells a story of a shoemaker, taunted and cursed at by young neighborhood toughs. The shoemaker tried threatening and then cajoling, but nothing seemed to diminish the sadistic activity of the hoodlums. He finally hit upon a scheme. When the boys arrived one day, he paid them each a dollar to scream and curse at him, which they did with gusto. They returned the next day to taunt the shoemaker once again for pay. This time, however, the shoemaker paid them fifty cents instead of a dollar. The following day they showed up and were told by the shoemaker that he could only afford to pay them a dime for their screaming and cursing. The toughs decided their efforts were worth more than ten cents, refused to scream and curse at the shoemaker, and left, never to return. Those doing research on the effect of extrinsic reinforcement on intrinsic motivation propose a similar process in industrial settings. If you pay employees contingently for doing something they already enjoy, they will enjoy it less and be more reluctant to do it in the future.

Deci (1972) performed a laboratory study in which subjects were paid to complete a puzzle they found interesting. They then were provided with an opportunity to continue working on the puzzle for no pay. Deci found that the subjects who had been paid contingently (paid according to number of puzzles solved) spent less time on the puzzles in the nonpay period than those subjects who had been paid hourly to work on the puzzles. From this he concluded that extrinsic reinforcement had diminished intrinsic motivation.

Just as Herzberg's work on satisfaction (1957, 1959) was a radical departure from orthodox thinking of the time, so was Deci's suggestion. Predictably, many people were upset with this formulation, since it challenged some long-standing assumptions. As a result, a significant amount of research has been conducted to test the basic assertion that extrinsic rewards are harmful to intrinsic motivation. In general, the results have not supported Deci. As you might expect, attacks came from many different directions. Dyer and Parker (1975) found that industrial psychologists could not agree on the definitions of "intrinsic" and "extrinsic" rewards. Furthermore, they could not agree as to which of a series of possible rewards were intrinsic and which extrinsic. As a result, they questioned the meaning of Deci's propositions, since it seemed impossible to distinguish the two types of rewards conceptually.

Scott (1976) also attacked the Deci hypothesis conceptually. He argued that the only thing Deci's data demonstrated was that reinforcement is complicated, with multiple contingencies operating. Data damaging to Deci's position have been appearing with some regularity recently (Arnold, 1976; Farr, 1976; Salancik, 1975; Hamner & Foster, 1975). One study even went so far as to reanalyze Deci's original data and show that there never *was* any such relationship between extrinsic and intrinsic motivation (Farr, Vance & McIntyre, 1977). The results of this follow-up research have been useful. It seems fairly clear that the subtractive model suggested by Deci is incorrect. Nevertheless, there is some reason to believe the relationship among various types of rewards is not the simple additive one that has always been assumed. As we will see often in behavioral research, studies directed toward *disproving* a theory or hypothesis often make a greater contribution than the original theory. Nevertheless, without that original theoretical statement, the later studies might never have been conducted.

The research on differential effects of "intrinsic" and "extrinsic" rewards seems to suggest the terms were never necessary in the first place. Since it is impossible to distinguish conceptually between the two types of factors, and the results are equivocal with respect to their interaction, it seems much more reasonable to look at the effect of particular combinations of rewards, such as praise and money, or "the pride of accomplishment" and promotion. Categorizing rewards as intrinsic or extrinsic has added little to the original investigations of the effect of rewards on behavior.

Motivation of Minority Workers

Serious investigation of motivational differences between minority workers and nonminority workers has been notably lacking. A few studies have looked at differences between blacks and whites in the Maslow framework (e.g., Slocum & Strawser, 1972). These studies have been cross sectional rather than longitudinal and have considered group differences rather than individual differences. Greenhaus and Gavin (1972), in an investigation of instrumentality theory, looked at the difference between effort-reward probabilities and job performance for whites and blacks. Watson and Williams (1977) examined the values of 64 black and 64 white managers from a variety of organizations and found the groups similar in orientation: pragmatic and moralistic. These studies suggest that there are no important differences between whites and blacks with respect to work motivation. This is hard to believe. On the basis of the accumulated social history of minority groups, we would expect there to be significant differences, at the very least, in terms of the perceptions of reward systems in industry. For example, the Watson and Williams results may say more about the unique characteristics of those 64 black managers than they do about the similarities and dissimilarities of minority and majority group motivation. Miner (1977) compared three groups of managers on a "motivation-to-manage" scale: white men ($N = 75$), white women ($N = 36$), and black men ($N = 23$). The black men had significantly higher motivation-to-manage scores than either of the other two groups. These results were thought to be revealing in two respects: (1) black men did seek supervisory responsibility, and (2) white women did not avoid assertive roles. Since the opposite results might have been expected on the basis of commonly held beliefs, Miner suggested that the "assumed" motivations of minority employees should not be used as obstacles to upgrading or promotion. Ivancevich & McMahon (1977) examined the goal-setting behavior of white and black technicians in a manufacturing organization and found that goal clarity, feedback, and participation in goal setting were more important for black technicians than for whites.

Research on majority/minority motivation has just barely begun. This research will severely test the strength of existing models of work motivation. We have seen in earlier sections that current models of motivation do not always apply well to workers in other countries. The same may be true of workers who come from substantially different *cultures*, even though they are all from the same country. It is simply impossible, at the present time, to conclude that the models we have discussed in this chapter apply equally well to all subgroups of workers. Nevertheless, this important line of research must be pursued if motivational models are to have any generality.

CONCLUDING COMMENTS

We have covered a lot of ground in this chapter. An attempt has been made to present, as clearly as possible, alternative explanations for motivated behavior in the work setting. A basic understanding of the various approaches is a prerequisite for interpreting research results. Motivational programs such as job enrichment will continue to emerge. If such programs are to be of maximum utility, they must be tied to some theoretical framework.

The sophistication and potential value of research in the area of work motivation has grown tremendously in the past decade. There is every reason to believe that the value will continue to increase.

SUMMARY

Understanding the motivation to work is a matter of understanding why individuals expend energy in one direction rather than another. Viewed in this way, understanding why individuals expend energy in a work setting is no different than understanding why they expend energy in *any* setting.

There are several general classes of theories for explaining human motivation in work settings. Need theories propose an underlying need in the individual that must be satisfied and has the potential for being satisfied in the work setting. Instrumentality theories hold that individuals choose to expend energy in situations that provide an opportunity to achieve some desired reward. Reinforcement approaches view the work setting as simply a variation on free-operant responding, with rewards and punishments as mediated by the organization and the supervisor playing a significant role in shaping behavior. Balance theories propose an individual need for some form of "cognitive harmony." When cognitive disharmony occurs, tensions are created that must be reduced through certain strategies. Both the intensity and the direction of effort expenditure seem to be related to the goals that individuals choose or accept.

Several of the work-motivation theories suggest a more complicated choice process on the part of the individual than current data would support. The complications in motivated behavior may arise from the fact that the motivation *process* changes as a result of maturation and experience.

Job enrichment is a strategy for increasing work motivation. Its value could be explained on the basis of any of the major classes of motivation theory mentioned above. The same is true for management by objectives, a structured goal-setting procedure for subordinates and supervisors.

The distinction between intrinsic and extrinsic rewards is an unnecessary one, since the concepts are ambiguous and the experimental results of the two "types" of rewards ambiguous.

The strength of a particular motivational approach will depend on its ability to handle data from divergent subject groups, such as workers in other countries or workers from minority populations in our country.

REFERENCES

Adams, J. S. Inequity in social exchange. In L. Berkowitz (Ed.), *Advances in Experimental social psychology* (Vol. 2). New York: Academic Press, 1965, pp. 267–299.

Alderfer, C. P. An empirical test of a new theory of human needs. *Organizational Behavior and Human Performance*, 1969, *4*, 142–175.

Alderfer, C. P. *Existence, relatedness, and growth: Human needs in organizational settings.* New York: Free Press, 1972.

Arnold, H. J. Effects of performance feedback and extrinsic reward upon high intrinsic motivation. *Organizational Behavior and Human Performance*, 1976, *17*, 275–288.

Atkinson, J. W., & Feather, N. T. (Eds.) *A theory of achievement motivation.* New York: Wiley, 1966.

Baldamus, W. Type of work and motivation. *British Journal of Sociology*, 1952, *2*, 44–58.

Berger, C. J., Cummings, I. L., and Heneman, H. G. Expectancy theory and operant conditioning predictions of performance under variable ratio and continuous schedules of reinforcement. *Organizational Behavior and Human Performance*, 1975, *14*, 227–243.

Campbell, D. J., & Ilgen, D. R. Additive effects of task difficulty and goal setting on subsequent task performance. *Journal of Applied Psychology*, 1976, *61*, 319–324.

Campbell, J. P., Dunnette, M. D., Lawler, E. E., & Weick, K. E. *Managerial behavior, performance, and effectiveness.* New York: McGraw-Hill, 1970.

Campbell, J. P., & Pritchard, R. D. Motivation theory in industrial and organizational psychology. In M. Dunnette (Ed.), *Handbook of industrial and organizational psychology.* Chicago: Rand McNally, 1976.

Chung, K. H., & Vickery, W. D. Relative effectiveness and joint effects of three selected reinforcements in a repetitive task situation. *Organizational Behavior and Human Performance*, 1976, *16*, 114–142.

Deci, E. L. Notes on the theory and metatheory of intrinsic motivation. *Organizational Behavior and Human Performance*, 1976, *15*, 130–145.

Deci, E. L. The effects of contingent and noncontingent rewards and controls on intrinsic motivation. *Organizational behavior and human performance*, 1972, *8*, 217–229.

DeLeo, P. J., & Pritchard, R. D. An examination of some methodological problems in testing expectancy-valence models with survey techniques. *Organizational behavior and human performance*, 1974, 12, 143–148.

Dipboye, R. L. A critical review of Korman's self-consistency theory of work motivation and occupational choice. *Organizational Behavior and Human Performance*, 1977, 18, 108–126.

Dipboye, R. L. On eliminating the alternative interpretations: A reply to Korman. *Organizational Behavior and Human Performance*, 1977, *18*, 129–130.

Duffy, E. *Activation and behavior.* New York: Wiley, 1962.

Dyer, L. & Parker, D. F. Classifying outcomes in work motivation research: An examination of the intrinsic-extrinsic dichotomy. *Journal of Applied Psychology*, 1975, 60, 455–458.

Erez, M. Feedback: A necessary condition for the goal setting-performance relationship. *Journal of Applied Psychology*, 1977, 62, 624–27.

Farr, J. L. Task characteristics, reward contingency, and intrinsic motivation. *Organizational Behavior and Human Performance*, 1976, *16*, 294–307.

Farr, J. L., Vance, R. J., & McIntyre, R. M. Further examinations of the relationship between reward contingency and intrinsic motivation. *Organizational Behavior and Human Performance*, 1977, *20*, 31–53.

Feldman, J. M. Note on the utility of certainty weights in expectancy theory. *Journal of Applied Psychology*, 1974, *59*, 727–730.

Festinger, L. *A theory of cognitive dissonance.* Evanston, Ill.: Row, Peterson, 1957.

Gavin, J. F. Self-esteem as a moderator of the relationship between expectancies and job performance. *Journal of Applied Psychology*, 1973, *58*, 83–88.

Georgopoulos, B. S., Mahoney, G. M., & Jones, N. W. A path-goal approach to productivity. *Journal of Applied Psychology*, 1957, *41*, 345–353.

Goodman, P. S. An examination of referents used in the evaluation of pay. *Organizational Behavior and Human Performance*, 1974, *12*, 170–195.

Graen, G. Instrumentality theory of work motivation. *Journal of Applied Psychology, Monograph*, 1969, *53* (2, Pt. 2).

Greenhaus, J. H., & Gavin, J. F. The relationship between expectancies and job behavior for white and black employees. *Personnel Psychology*, 1972, *25* (3), 449–456.

Hall, D. T., & Nougaim, K. E. An examination of Maslow's need hierarchy in an organizational setting. Organizational Behavior and Human Performance, 1968, *3*, 12–35.

Hamner, W. C., & Foster, L. W. Are intrinsic and extrinsic rewards additive: A test of Deci's cognitive evaluation theory of task motivation. *Organizational Behavior and Human Performance*, 1975, *14*, 398–415.

Heiman, G. W. A note of "operant conditioning principles extrapolated to the theory of management." *Organizational Behavior and Human Performance*, 1975, *13*, 165–170.

Herzberg, F. *Work and the nature of man*. Cleveland: World Publishing, 1966.

Herzberg, F., Mausner, B., Peterson, R. O., & Capwell, D. F. *Job attitudes: Review of research and opinion*. Pittsburgh: Psychological Service of Pittsburgh, 1957.

Herzberg, F., Mausner, B., & Snyderman, B. *The motivation to work*. New York: Wiley, 1959.

Ivancevich, J. M., & McMahon, J. T. Black-white differences in a goal-setting program. *Organizational Behavior and Human Performance*, 1977, *20*, 287–300.

Kammen, M. *People of paradox*. New York: Knopf, 1972.

Kesselman, G. A., Hagen, E. L., & Wherry, R. J. A factor analytic test of the Porter-Lawler expectancy model of work motivation. *Personnel Psychology*, 1974, *27*, 569–580.

Kim, J. S., & Hamner, W. C. Effect of performance feedback and goal setting on productivity and satisfaction in an organizational setting. *Journal of Applied Psychology*, 1976, *61*, 48–57.

Korman, A. An examination of Dipboye's "A critical review of Korman's self-consistency theory of work motivation and occupational choice." *Organizational Behavior and Human Performance*, 1977, *18*, 127–128.

Korman, A. Toward an hypothesis of work behavior. *Journal of Applied Psychology*, 1970, *54*, 32–41.

Korman, A. Organizational achievement, aggression, and creativity: Some suggestions toward an integrated theory. *Organizational Behavior and Human Performance*, 1971, *6*, 593–613.

Latham, G. P., & Baldes, J. J. The "practical significance" of Locke's theory of goal-setting. *Journal of Applied Psychology*, 1975, *60*, 122–124.

Latham, G. P., & Yukl, G. A. Assigned versus participative goal-setting with educated and uneducated woods workers. *Journal of Applied Psychology*, 1975, *60*, 299–302.

Lawler, E. E. *Pay and organizational effectiveness*. New York: McGraw-Hill, 1971.

Lawler, E. E. *Motivation in work organizations*. Monterey, Calif.: Brooks Cole, 1973.

Lawler, E. E., & Suttle, J. L. A causal correlational test of the need hierarchy concept. *Organizational Behavior and Human Performance*, 1972, *7*, 265–287.

Liddell, W. W., & Solomon, R. J. A total and stochastic test of the transitivity postulate underlying expectancy theory. *Organizational Behavior and Human Performance*, 1977, *19*, 311–324.

Locke, E. A. Toward a theory of task motivation and incentives. *Organizational Behavior and Human Performance*, 1968, *3*, 157–189.

Locke, E. A., Cartledge, N., & Knerr, C. S. Studies of the relationship between satisfaction, goal-setting and performance. *Organizational Behavior and Human Performance*, 1970, *5*, 484–500.

McGregor, D. The human side of enterprise. New York: McGraw-Hill, 1960.

Maslow, A. H. A theory of motivation. *Psychological Review*, 1943, *50*, 370–396.

Matsui, T., and Terai, T. A cross-cultural study of the validity of the expectancy theory of work motivation. *Journal of Applied Psychology*, 1975 *60*, 263–265.

Matsui, T., and Ikeda, H. Effectiveness of self-generation outcomes for improving prediction in expectancy theory research. *Organizational Behavior and Human Performance*, 1976, *17*, 289–298.

Matsui, T., Kagawa, M., Nagamatsu, J., & Ohtsuka, Y. Validity of expectancy theory as a within-person behavioral choice model for sales activities. *Journal of Applied Psychology*, 1977, *62*, 764–767.

Middlemist, R. D., & Peterson, R. B. Test of equity theory by controlling for comparison worker's efforts, *Organizational Behavior and Human Performance*, 1976, *15*, 335–406.

Miner, J. B. Motivational potential for upgrading among minority and female managers, *Journal of Applied Psychology*, 1977, *62*, 691–697.

Miner, J. B., & Dachler, H. P. Personnel attitudes and motivation. In *Annual Review of Psychology*. Palo Alto, Calif.: Annual Review, 1973.

Mitchell, T. R. Expectancy models of job satisfaction, occupational preference and effort: A theoretical, methodological, and empirical approach. *Psychological Bulletin*, 1974, *81*, 1053–1077.

Mitchell, V. F., & Moudgill, P. Measurement of Maslow's need hierarchy. *Organizational Behavior and Human Performance*, 1976, *16*, 334–349.

Nord, W. B. Beyond the teaching machine: The neglected area of operant conditioning in theory and practice of management. *Organizational Behavior and Human Performance*, 1969, *4*, 375–401.

Parker, D. F., & Dyer, L. Expectancy theory as a within-person behavioral choice model: An empirical test of some conceptual and methodological refinements, *Organizational Behavior and Human Performance*, 1976, *17*, 97–117.

Peak, H.   Attitude and motivation. In M. R. Jones (Ed.), *Nebraska Symposium on Motivation*. Lincoln: University of Nebraska Press, 1955, pp. 149–188.

Pedalino, E., & Gamboa, V. U.   Behavior modification and absenteeism. *Journal of Applied Psychology*, 1974, *59*, 694–698.

Porter, L. W.   A study of perceived need satisfactions in bottom and middle management jobs. *Journal of Applied Psychology*, 1961, *45*, 1–10.

Porter, L. W., & Lawler, E. E.   *Managerial attitudes and performance.* Homewood, Ill.: Irwin-Dorsey, 1968.

Pritchard, R. D.   Equity theory: A review and critique. *Organizational Behavior and Human Performance*, 1969, *4*, 176–211.

Pritchard, R. D., Leonard, D. W., VonBergen, C. W., & Kirk, R. J.   The effects of varying schedules of reinforcement on human task performance. *Organizational Behavior and Human Performance*, 1976, *16*, 205–230.

Rubenstein, F. D., Watzke, G., Doktor, R. H., & Dana, J.   The effect of two incentive schemes upon the conversation of shared resource by five-person groups. *Organizational Behavior and Human Performance*, 1975, *13*, 330–338.

Ryan, T. A.   *Intentional behavior.* New York: Ronald Press, 1970.

Salancik, G. R.   Interaction effects of performance and money on self-perception of intrinsic motivation. *Organizational Behavior and Human Performance*, 1975, *13*, 339–351.

Scott, W. E.   Activation theory and task design. *Organizational Behavior and Human Performance*, 1966, *1*, 3–30.

Scott, W. E.   The effects of extrinsic rewards on "intrinsic motivation." *Organizational Behavior and Human Performance*, 1976, *15*, 117–129.

Slocum, J. W., & Strawser, R. H.   Racial differences in job attitudes. *Journal of Applied Psychology*, 1972, *56* (1), 28–32.

Steers, R. M.   Effects of need for achievement on the job performance-job attitude relationship, *Journal of Applied Psychology*, 1975, *60*, 678–682.

Steers, R. M., & Spencer D. G.   The role of achievement motivation in job design. *Journal of Applied Psychology*, 1977, *62*, 472–479.

Terborg, J. R.   The motivational components of goal setting. *Journal of Applied Psychology*, 1976, *61*, 613–621.

Tolman, E. C.   *Purposive behavior in animals and man.* New York: Century, 1932.

Vinacke, E.   Motivation as a complex problem. *Nebraska Symposium on Motivation*, 1962, *10*, 1–45.

Vroom, V. H.   *Work and motivation.* New York: Wiley, 1964.

Wahba, M. A., & Bridwell, L. B.   Maslow reconsidered: A review of research on the need hierarchy theory. *Organizational Behavior and Human Performance*, 1976, *15*, 212–240.

Wanous, J. P., & Zwany, A.   A cross-sectional test of need hierarchy theory. *Organizational Behavior and Human Performance*, 1977, *18*, 78–97.

Watson, J., & Williams, J.   Relationship between managerial values and managerial success of black and white managers. *Journal of Applied Psychology*, 1977, *62*, 203–207.

Weick, E. E., Bougon, M. G., & Maruyama, G.   The equity context. *Organizational Behavior and Human Performance*, 1976, *15*, 32–65.

Yukl, G. A., & Latham, G. P.   Consequences of reinforcement schedules and incentive magnitudes for employee performance: Problems encountered in an industrial setting. *Journal of Applied Psychology*, 1975, *60*, 294–298.

Yukl, G. A., Latham, G. P., and Pursell, E. D.   The effectiveness of performance incentives under continuous and variable ratio schedules of reinforcement. *Personnel Psychology*, 1976, *29*, 221–232.

Zimbardo, P.   Introduction. In Middlebrook, P. N., *Social psychology and modern life*. New York: Knopf, 1974.

CHAPTER 10
Job Satisfaction: The Quality of Work

In the past decade, a phrase that has become popular in describing the relationship between a worker and a job is "the quality of work." This phrase deliberately focuses attention on the *nature* of the activity required of the worker rather than the *amount* of the activity. In addition, it is used to connote the feelings of the worker about the work in the same way as the "quality of life" is used to describe one's reaction to life in general. Another way of describing the quality of work might be the *meaning* work holds for the individual. There is probably no other single activity that consistently demands as much physically, emotionally, and cognitively as work. It occupies most of our waking hours. Consequently, work provides an enormous array of stimulus elements to which we respond in one way or another. In short, work has meaning for us by virtue of the fact that we must respond to work-related stimuli. If we do everything in our power to get to work on time, work hard while there, and talk about our job to friends and family, that represents one set of responses. If we avoid work at every opportunity, do as little as possible while at the job, and religiously engage in activities after work to *forget* our job, that is also a set of work-related responses. Since these responses to work are so intimately tied to other important processes and outcomes such as job performance and work motivation, to get a complete view of the behavior of an individual in a work setting, it is necessary to examine that worker's responses to work elements.

Historically, this set of responses has been labeled "job satisfaction" or "morale." It has been approached primarily as an attitude with potential antecedent conditions leading to it (such as the size or amount of a reward for good performance) and potential consequences (such as absenteeism, high production, increased effort). The topic will be introduced by showing how it fits into each of the major motivational models examined in the last chapter. A brief historical review of the concept will then be presented, followed by a sampling of some current job satisfaction research and theory. Finally, we will look at the relationship among job satisfaction and absenteeism, performance, and the quality of life.

THE ROLE OF SATISFACTION IN THE MOTIVATIONAL MODELS

One common theme that pervades most of the research and application of job satisfaction theory is the emotional character of satisfaction and dissatisfaction. We assume that at any point in time an individual occupies a point on a continuum ranging from extreme happiness through neutrality to extreme unhappiness. One set of variables that is at least partially responsible for the position on the continuum of a person at any particular time is that of job-related stimuli. Thus, it is assumed that an individual's interactions with the work environment affect his emotional state. There are other things that affect the emotional state of the individual in addition to job-related stimuli, but that portion of the variance on the emotional continuum that can be accounted for through work-related stimuli is thought to represent *job satisfaction/dissatisfaction.*

One of the major questions to be posed in job satisfaction research is: *Under what conditions does a positive or negative emotional state arise?* The answer to this question has some rather profound implications for the various theories of work motivation, since most of them are based on a pleasure/pain principle, at least at some level. They imply that individuals will expend energy in maintaining or increasing pleasure or, conversely, in minimizing or decreasing displeasure. Thus, the reaction of an individual to a work-related stimulus (job satisfaction) is thought to represent the potential power that stimulus has for affecting the individual's behavior (i.e., motivating the individual). This potential role of satisfaction in the motivation of workers (and ultimately in the productive efforts of those individuals) has been a major impetus for job satisfaction research. We will briefly outline the role satisfaction has played in each of the four major approaches to motivation described in Chapter 9.

Need Theory

In Maslow's (1943) need hierarchy theory, unfulfilled lower needs (physical, security, and possibly love needs) represent a deficiency in the individual, and this deficiency is experienced as discomfort. Presumably, if individuals were asked questions concerning their relative "happiness" while experiencing this deficiency, they would report some level of dissatisfaction. Need-hierarchy theory (and, in fact, all need theories) proposes that the individual will engage in actions to decrease this discomfort. The same basic operation is implied for upper-level needs (esteem and self-actualization). Once lower-level needs are fulfilled, the degree to which upper-level needs are fulfilled determines the degree of satisfaction that the individual experiences. Once again, the theory implies that individuals will engage in those actions necessary to ensure the fulfillment of those upper-level needs—but now to increase satisfaction rather than decrease dissatisfaction. Thus, in need-hierarchy theory, states of satisfaction and dissatisfaction immediately precede motivated behavior.

Reinforcement Theory

The more radical reinforcement theorists would deny any value to job satisfaction in explaining work behavior such as energy expenditure or performance. They would treat it as simply another behavior, a verbal one. A simple example helps to make their point. A typical job satisfaction questionnaire asks the worker to agree or disagree with the statement, "My pay is pretty good." If the worker agrees, this is taken as evidence of satisfaction with pay. If the worker disagrees, this is taken as evidence of dissatisfaction. A reinforcement theorist would propose that a worker who disagreed with the statement might mean any or all of the following things:

1. I have been deprived of money in the past and I don't like it.
2. The last time I disagreed with that statement I got a raise, and since I would like another raise, I will disagree again.
3. I just read in the newspaper that the company is making record profits and I would like to share in that good fortune.
4. Just as it is traditional for students to complain about dormitory food, it is traditional for workers to complain about pay, so I will, naturally, disagree with the statement.

The rigid reinforcement theorists would view job satisfaction information as rather complicated verbal behavior that can only be made clear through the actions of the worker.

Nevertheless, even for the reinforcement advocates, there would seem to be some value in satisfaction data. If we are attempting to provide rewards to our best workers, the best workers should also be the most satisfied. In that sense, satisfaction data can confirm the fact that a contingent reward plan is working the way we intended it to. Even the most rabid reinforcement proponent would worry if the best producers were the loudest complainers.

A second possible use for satisfaction information in the behaviorist framework is the identification of potential rewards. While it is possible to identify potential reinforcers through simple observation (e.g., make a note of the things an individual does during the lunch hour), it may be more efficient in the long run to *ask* the individual about satisfying and dissatisfying events and objects as a short cut to this identification.

Equity Theory

In equity theory, dissatisfaction is an unpleasant aftereffect of cognitive discrepancies. As such, dissatisfaction represents a source of tension to be reduced, and the person expends energy (is motivated) to reduce this tension. This tension is a result of an individual's comparison of her inputs and outcomes to the inputs and outcomes of some significant other person. In that sense, equity theory emphasizes the role of social stimuli in general emotional states. Nevertheless, the implicit assumption that individuals will engage in activities to reduce tension is similar to the one proposed by Maslow and other need theorists. While the role of dissatisfaction in equity theory is clear, the role of satisfaction is much fuzzier. There has been very little attention devoted to the positive end of the emotional continuum by equity theorists. The most reasonable statement that could be made at present is that satisfaction is considered as the absence of dissatisfaction!

Instrumentality Theory

In Porter and Lawler's (1968) version of instrumentality theory, job satisfaction depends on the match between expected and obtained rewards. Satisfaction, in turn, has a general positive or negative effect on decisions made by the person in the future concerning the value of promised rewards. Since individuals have the capacity to remember pleasant and unpleasant experiences and attach these memories to particular contexts and stimuli, it is assumed that the individual is able to *anticipate* future pleasant and unpleasant outcomes and chooses behavior alternatives (i.e., is motivated) accordingly. As we indicated in the motivation chapter, valence, or the subjective value of the reward, seems to be playing a larger and larger role in explaining the choices individuals make. Furthermore, the research of Liddell and Solomon (1977) demonstrated that individuals do consistently order rewards in terms of their desirability. This would seem to point to an important role for satisfaction in instrumentality approaches to motivation. The essence of the approach is not just that individuals *have* satisfactions and dissatisfactions, but that they *remember* these emotional states.

With the exception of the reinforcement theorists, each of the motivation theories either directly or indirectly places satisfaction/dissatisfaction in the role of an emotional state of some kind. It may have cognitive characteristics as well, but it most clearly is treated as some form of physiological/psychological response system. But viewing satisfaction as it plays a role in theories of motivation is an indirect way of looking at the phenomenon. It might be helpful to look at more direct attempts to account for the feelings we have about our work without confusing these feelings with their potential effects. We will present a short historical view of research in job satisfaction and then some current theories and research in the area.

A SHORT HISTORY OF SATISFACTION RESEARCH

The Hawthorne Studies

As we will see in more detail in the chapter on organizational theory, the approach to understanding work behavior that pervaded the early part of this century was classic organization theory, generally, and scientific management theory, specifically. Taylor proposed scientific management theory in the early 20th century as a way of making the conduct of work-related activities more efficient. The major motivational assumption of the approach was that individual workers valued economic incentives and would be willing to work hard for monetary rewards. It is important to note the rigidity of this assumption. It was assumed that *all* workers valued money more than any other reward. If this were true, it certainly would make the lives of managers easier and the behavior of workers more predictable.

The published psychological literature provides ample evidence that this assumption was accepted in the application of behavior principles to work settings. As a matter of fact, one of the pioneers in industrial psychology, Munsterberg, in a book on general psychology, describes industrial psychology as "economic psychology." Most of the research was conducted on physical working conditions—things such as heating and lighting. Psychologists, economists, and industrial engineers were collaborating in an attempt to identify *the one most efficient system for the production of goods and services.* The worker was considered a potential error in that system and was treated accordingly. As a matter of fact, most training programs of the time were directed at reducing individual differences in behavior. It is impossible to determine if this attempt to homogenize was a symptom or a cause of scientific management programs.

One of the first substantial research efforts that made a break with this restricted view of the worker was conducted at the Hawthorne plant of the Western Electric company in Cicero, Illinois. These studies, which spanned a period of over 12 years, have come to be known as the "Hawthorne studies," and deserve some attention for several reasons.

1. The authors concluded with the radical suggestion that workers have feelings that affect their work behavior.
2. Their approach of field experimentation demonstrated both the strengths and the weaknesses of that particular research design.
3. They suggested that the way in which workers *perceive* objective reality may be more important in understanding behavior than the *facts* of objective reality.

In a sense, these studies represent the beginning of the study of the social aspects of industrial and organizational psychology. While these studies will be briefly described, there are some excellent sources for examining them in their entirety (Roethlisberger and Dixon, 1939).

The studies began with a harmless research question: What is the effect of illumination on productivity? Three departments were involved. Initial performance data were gathered as base-rate information for the evaluation of any changes in performance due to illumination changes. Subsequently, illumination was systematically varied, but the performance data showed no clear effect. The experimenters, suspecting they had not exercised appropriate experimental control, redesigned the experiment with subjects chosen for experience and base-rate production. Experimental and control groups were matched on these two dimensions and physically separated from each other. Lighting was systematically varied for the experimental subjects, while the matched control group worked under constant illumination conditions. This time *both* the experimental *and* control groups increased production to the same degree. This result made it impossible to conclude that performance increases were due to illumination, since the illumination did not change in the control group.

In another series of studies in which experimental control was tightened even more, the experimental group maintained their initial level of performance in spite of the fact that illumination had been reduced by 70 percent. The crowning blow to the simple illumination-productivity hypothesis came when the experimenters only *pretended* to change the illumination level by replacing light bulbs with other light bulbs *of the same intensity*. The workers expressed pleasure with the "increased illumination" and continued to increase their production.

This last result—the fact that a constant level of illumination was perceived as changing—was the first hint that the perception of events may have been as important as the events themselves. Nevertheless, the experimenters chose to refine their experimental procedures and controls even more. In addition, they began to focus on possible confounding variables such as fatigue. The experimental manipulations now included the introduction of work breaks, the shortening of the workday, and the shortening of the workweek. A series of experimental periods were run to determine the effect of these variables on productivity. Table 10–1 gives a description of each of the manipulations. As expected, the introduction of work breaks and shortened work periods had a positive effect on performance. However, something unexpected was found. As the work breaks were removed and the workday and week were lengthened to their original status, production continued to increase, as can be seen in the right-hand column of Table 10–1. On the basis of diaries kept during these studies, it became increasingly obvious that attitudes toward supervision and co-workers were having an effect on the results.

The possibility of the feelings and attitudes of the workers affecting production rate put an entirely new slant on the efforts of the Hawthorne

TABLE 10–1

Hawthorne Studies—Changes in Work Schedules and the Effect of These Changes on Productivity

Period	Length in Weeks	Experimental Conditions of Work	Percent of Standard Output
1	2	Standard	100
2	5	Standard	101
3	8	Standard	105
4	5	Two 5 min. rests	109
5	4	Two 10 min. rests	112
6	4	Six 5 min. rests	113
7	11	15 min. A.M. rest and lunch; 10 min. P.M. rest	116
8	7	Same as 7, but 4:30 stop	123
9	4	Same as 7, but 4:00 stop	125
10	12	Same as 7	124
11	9	Same as 7, but Sat. A.M. off	123
12	12	Standard	122
13	31	Same as 7	131

Source: Adapted from Roethlisberger, F. J., & Dickson, W. J. *Management and the worker.* Cambridge, Mass.: Harvard University Press, 1939, p. 57.

researchers. An interviewing program was introduced to assess the nature of the relationship between methods of supervision and worker attitudes. As a result of these interviews, it became apparent that the effect of wages, working conditions, and other job-related stimuli could not be *legislated* by management. The meaning of these factors was determined by the individual's personal history and work environment.

Later studies showed that group production rates were affected by the guidelines of the informal work group as well as the goals of the organization and the behavior of the immediate supervisor. On the basis of interviews, a counseling program was begun to improve communication in the organization. After the studies and counseling program were completed, the general feeling was that interpersonal relations within the company had improved. This was an incredible leap from the simple illumination-productivity hypothesis that had launched the studies.

The Hawthorne studies do not, by any means, represent the ultimate in field experimentation. They had many problems. Landsberger, in a book titled *Hawthorne Revisited* (1958), points out that two of the most important economic influences of the period were ignored—the Depression and the rise of trade unionism. These two factors must have affected the responses of the workers. Nevertheless, the Hawthorne studies do represent a breakthrough both in understanding the nature of work behavior and the process of field experimentation.

As a function of these studies, interests were shifted from lighting to interpersonal communications, from work curves and boredom to work motivation, from company policy to the perception of this policy by the workers, from variables in the physical environment to variables in the social environment of the employee, and from rigid assumptions about the nature of workers to a consideration of individual differences. In addition, the studies present invaluable information about the process of field experimentation. The substitution of statistical for experimental control is apparent in the designs, particularly in the sampling and matching of subjects for control and experimental groups. The whole logic of covariation and correlation is apparent in the efforts of the experimenters to discover what factor was changing at the same rate and in the same direction as productivity. The Hawthorne studies provide a good historical and methodological foundation for a consideration of the concepts of job satisfaction and the meaning of work.

The Hoppock Study

The Hawthorne studies began a move toward a consideration of both individual and group differences in job satisfaction. In 1935, Hoppock studied the job satisfaction of workers in the community of New Hope, Pennsylvania. The researcher asked two questions: (1) On an absolute level, are workers in New Hope happy? (2) On a relative level, are workers in some occupations happier than others? The answer to the first question seemed to be yes. Only 12 percent of the 309 workers surveyed could be classified as dissatisfied. The basic finding has been replicated time and time again. Workers *reporting* dissatisfaction are usually in the minority.

The answer to the second question can be found in Table 10–2. Again the answer was yes: different levels of satisfaction are related to different occupational levels, with the highest occupational level being accompanied by the highest satisfaction. This is another finding that has been replicated numerous times. We will deal specifically with the relationship between occupational level and satisfaction in a later section.

The data bearing on the effect of occupational level make the data

TABLE 10–2
Job Satisfaction of Various Occupational Levels—Hoppock Study

Occupational Classification	Number of Cases	Range of Indices	Mean Index
1 Unskilled manual	55	100–650	401
2 Semiskilled	74	125–650	483
3 Skilled manual and white-collar	84	125–675	510
4 Subprofessional, business, and minor supervisory	32	250–700	548
5 Professional, managerial, and executive	23	300–700	560

Source: Hoppock, R. *Job satisfaction.* New York: Harper, 1935, p. 255.

relating to the absolute levels of satisfaction somewhat arbitrary. It is clear that not all occupational levels are equally satisfied. There were more unskilled manual workers who reported dissatisfaction than professionals. The 12-percent figure is an average number across all occupational categories.

A final interesting point from these data can be seen in Table 10–2 under the column heading "Range of Indices." A person responding to Hoppock's questionnaire could have received a score ranging from 100 (extreme dissatisfaction) to 700 (extreme satisfaction). The range of values reported for each of the occupational groups show the wide variation of satisfaction even *within* occupations. This is a problem that has plagued satisfaction research from the beginning—individual variation often exceeds group variation. Attempts at understanding this individual variation have not been overwhelmingly successful.

Schaffer's Theory

Hoppock's initial approach to the phenomenon of job satisfaction suggested that certain variables outside of the individual worker affected levels of satisfaction—variables such as occupational group. Schaffer (1953) emphasized variables *within* the individual as contributing to satisfaction and dissatisfaction. He felt there was some psychological "set" or mechanism that operated to make people satisfied or dissatisfied in general. This set was thought to affect satisfaction with work as well. When certain needs the individual had were not fulfilled, tension was created, the amount of tension being directly related to the strength of the unfulfilled need.

This conception was much closer to many of our current theories of satisfaction and motivation than any of the work that preceded it. Schaffer proposed that individuals had 12 basic needs. These needs had the same characteristics as the five need categories in Maslow's hierarchy or the three of Alderfer's model. The set comprised needs such as recognition, affection, mastery, and economic security. Since it was unrealistic to think that the 12 needs were equally important to all individuals, an analysis was done to identify those needs that contributed substantially to overall job satisfaction. This was done by first asking for three pieces of information from each respondent: (1) the importance of each of the 12 needs, (2) the degree to which each of the needs was being satisfied, and (3) an indication of overall job satisfaction. Schaffer was able to determine that the overall job satisfaction of an individual could be predicted from information concerning only the first two most important needs of that individual. In short, if the individual's two most important needs were being satisfied by the job, the individual would report overall job satisfaction; if the two most important needs were not being satisfied, overall dissatisfaction would be reported. The importance of Schaffer's work was not in the identification of the two most important needs of an individual; it was in the demonstration that there are reliable individual differences in the importance of needs. This approach can be seen in the dynamics of current motivation theories (e.g., in Maslow's theory the most important needs would be found at the level in the hierarchy that has not yet been satisfied). In instrumentality theory, these most important needs would be represented by "valences," or in the Porter-Lawler version, the "value of the reward." Even though Schaffer's work was crude by current standards, the results anticipated (or possibly provided the foundation for) some important theories of work motivation.

CURRENT RESEARCH AND THEORY

Schaffer's work was followed closely by the publication of two important reviews of the literature in job satisfaction. The first was conducted by Brayfield and Crockett (1955), and the second by Herzberg, Mausner, Peterson, and Capwell (1957). The Herzberg et al. review provided the basis for the two-factor theory discussed in Chapter 9. These two reviews are often contrasted with each other because they came to different conclusions. Both reviews set out to examine the relationship between job satisfaction and job performance. Brayfield and Crockett concluded that there was no demonstrable relationship between job satisfaction and performance. Herzberg et al. concluded that there was a systematic relationship between job satisfaction and certain work behaviors, as well as between job dissatisfaction and other work behaviors. Katzell (1957) provides reasons for the discrepancies in conclusions from the two reviews:

> [Herzberg] finds that, among studies in which performance was compared with favorability of job attitudes, 54 percent reported a positive relationship, 35 percent no relationship, and 11 percent a negative relationship. Most of the relationships were low. They also conclude that there is more unequivocal evidence of a relationship (negative) between job attitudes and both turnover and absenteeism, with some data also supporting the same trend as regards accidents and psychosomatic illnesses. In general, they conclude with "the belief that positive job attitudes are a tremendous asset to industry is supported by much of the experimental evidence now available."
>
> Brayfield and Crockett, on the contrary, infer in their review that "there is little evidence in the available literature that employee attitudes . . . bear any simple . . . or appreciable relationship to performance on the job." It should be noted that their definition of "performance on the job" excludes absenteeism, accidents, etc. (they do infer that attitudes are related to absenteeism and turnover). This is one source of difference in the tone of the two conclusions. Another reason for the difference is that the two studies do not cover exactly the same literature. Moreover, Herzberg et al. are more receptive to suggestive findings, whereas Brayfield and Crockett slight anything not statistically significant. (Whereas the latter position is more "correct," it also entails the danger of Type II errors regarding the null hypothesis, since most of the studies were based on small N's because the unit measured was more often the group than the individual.) But perhaps the main reason for the disparity is that Brayfield and Crockett state their generalization prior to their consideration of the parameters involved in the relationships between attitudes and

performance, whereas Herzberg et al. more appropriately take such influences into account in arriving at their overall judgment. Both sets of authors make good suggestions on how improved methodology and research design may result in better clarification of these relationships.

In their own ways, both reviews have had a great impact on the field of industrial and organizational psychology. Brayfield and Crockett were much more concerned with methodological considerations in their review. Consequently, the most valuable section of their work relates to the guidelines they proposed for research designs in the area of job satisfaction. Some of these guidelines were:

1. Information must be provided which clearly describes the way individual subjects were selected; for example, randomly from *within* occupational categories, or randomly from the population generally.
2. Criterion measures (those variables to be predicted from job satisfaction responses) should be chosen on the basis of their relevance, reliability, freedom from contamination, and practicality.
3. The way the data were collected must be clearly described. Were the respondents required to identify themselves? Were the data gathered individually or in groups?

These guidelines relate more to the interpretability of results once they are obtained than to job satisfaction itself. The conclusions of the Brayfield and Crockett review that relate to the nature of satisfaction can be summarized as follows:

1. Since people avoid punishing situations and seek out rewarding situations, significant correlations between measures of work approach or

FIGURE 10–1

Relationships among Satisfaction, Performance, Effort or Motivation, and Rewards

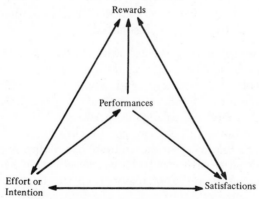

Source: Smith, P. C., & Cranny, C. J. The psychology of men at work. In *Annual Review of Psychology*. Palo Alto, Calif.: Annual Review, 1968.

avoidance (such as absenteeism or tardiness) are to be expected. No such simple relationship holds between satisfaction and performance of job duties.

2. Individual workers differ in motivations to work and perceptions of work-related stimuli.
3. Satisfaction and performance are not causally related; high satisfaction and high performance occur together when high productivity is perceived as a path to certain important goals and when these goals are achieved.

This has been a popular view of the relationship between satisfaction and performance. You will recognize it as the major proposition of the early path-goal theories of motivation (Georgopolous, Mahoney, & Jones, 1957), as well as the underlying theme of most instrumentality theories. Figure 10–1 describes the dynamics of the relationship.

The Two-Factor Theory

In the long run, the conclusions of Herzberg et al. have had a more serious impact on the field. This is probably due to the fact that while the things said by Brayfield and Crockett were more traditional and more frequently heard, the Herzberg review led indirectly to some revolutionary proposals. On the basis of the review, Herzberg concluded that satisfaction and dissatisfaction were two completely different phenomena. They developed from quite different sources and had different initial effects on behavior and different long-term effects on behavior. Subsequently, Herzberg, Mausner, and Snyderman (1959) conducted a study with 203 accountants and engineers from the Pittsburgh area. These individuals were interviewed and asked to describe a time when they felt particularly good or bad about their jobs. The responses were examined for indications of:

1. The situations which led to the feelings.
2. The needs or drives that were activated by these situations.
3. The amount of time the feelings lasted.

The results indicated that the following factors were related to good feelings about a job: achievement and recognition, the nature of the work itself, responsibility, advancement, and salary. Bad feelings about a job seemed to be related to the following factors: company policy and administration, technical supervision, salary, interpersonal relations with supervisors, and working conditions. In addition, good feelings seemed to persist long after the events or situations that caused them had disappeared. This seemed to suggest that negative attitudes had a weaker effect on performance than positive attitudes, if for no other reason than the fact that they did not last as long.

These findings led Herzberg to propose what has come to be known as the *two-factor theory* or the *motivator-hygiene theory.* The basic propositions of the theory are straightforward:

1. Every individual has two sets of needs. One set, labeled *hygiene needs,* relates to the physical and psychological environment in which the work is done. These needs would be met by such persons or things as co-workers, supervisors, working conditions, and company policy. The second set of needs, labeled *motivator needs,* relates to the nature and challenge of the work itself. These needs would be met by such things as the stimulation provided by job duties and responsibility attached to the job.

2. When hygiene needs are not met, the individual is dissatisfied. When the hygiene needs are met, the individual is no longer dissatisfied (but is not satisfied either).

3. When motivator needs are not met, the individual is not satisfied (but not dissatisfied either). When motivator needs are met, the individual is satisfied.

Figure 10–2 graphically depicts this relationship. Increasing amounts of hygiene factors will bring a person from a state of dissatisfaction to a neutral point. Increasing the motivator factors will bring a person from a neutral point to a state of satisfaction.

The Lawler Model of Facet Satisfaction

A recent book on motivation in work organizations by Lawler (1973) proposes a model of job satisfaction that differs from most others. It is really an expansion of the section in the Porter-Lawler model of work motivation dealing with the relationship between actual rewards for perfor-

FIGURE 10–2

The Effects of Motivator and Hygiene Factors on Job Satisfaction

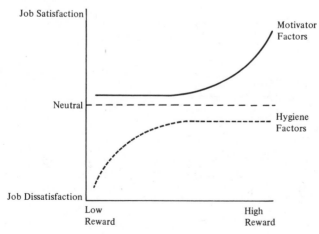

mance and perceived equitable rewards. You will remember that the model predicted that when perceived equitable rewards exceeded actual rewards, dissatisfaction would result. On the other hand, if actual rewards exceeded or equaled perceived equitable rewards, satisfaction resulted. The Lawler model, which appears in Figure 10–3, is a more specific statement of the factors leading to satisfaction and dissatisfaction.

The single most important process implied in the model is *perception*. This process takes the form of *perceived* personal job inputs, *perceived* inputs and outcomes of significant others, *perceived* job characteristics, and *perceived* outcomes (rewards). The importance of the *perception* of reality as opposed to reality itself was first recognized by the Hawthorne researchers and has remained a critical factor since. This model of satisfaction differs in one important respect from the treatment of satisfaction in the motivation model of Porter and Lawler. In the current model, if actual rewards *exceed* perceived equitable rewards, guilt, discomfort, and presumably tension are the result. If perceived equitable rewards exceed actual rewards, dissatisfaction results. In the earlier motivation model of Porter and Lawler, satisfaction was thought to result if actual rewards met or *exceeded* perceived equitable rewards. This change in operation moves the phenomenon of job satisfaction much closer to cognitive dissonance ("equity") theory. It says that some psychological discomfort results from

FIGURE 10–3

Model of the Determinants of Satisfaction

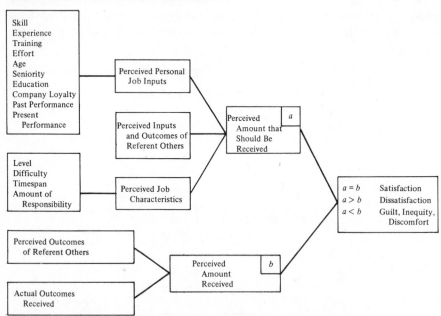

the knowledge that we are receiving more than we deserve. This psychological discomfort is synonymous with physical discomfort (tension), and provides the impetus for actions necessary to relieve this tension.

Although this model describes the satisfaction an individual will experience with any particular aspect or facet of the job (e.g., pay, co-workers, challenge), Lawler feels that the combination of the feelings a worker has about all aspects of the job defines *overall job satisfaction*. He qualifies this somewhat by saying that facets or aspects contribute to overall satisfaction according to their importance to the individual.

Locke's Value Theory

Locke (1976) distinguishes between value and need. He thinks of needs as elements that ensure an individual's survival, much in the sense that we use the term "biological need." He considers needs to be objective, existing regardless of the desires of the individual. Values, on the other hand, are subjective, and represent what a person *desires* at either a conscious or subconscious level. Given this distinction, Locke's theory of job satisfaction might be stated as follows:

> . . . job satisfaction [is] the pleasurable emotional state resulting from the perception of one's job as fulfilling or allowing the fulfillment of one's important job values, providing these values are compatible with one's needs. (p. 1342)

At present, Locke's theory is philosophically rather than empirically based. His argument with the need theorists would seem to be more semantic than ideological. Nevertheless, in the course of presenting his theory, he does suggest an interesting role for the concept of "importance." Intuitively, it is reasonable to expect that job satisfaction is not the simple sum of satisfactions with individual elements of the job; it is more reasonable to expect that the relative *importance* of each of the factors also plays a role in one's overall level of satisfaction. Thus, if pay is extremely important to you and pleasant co-workers are relatively unimportant, pay should play a greater role in determining your overall satisfaction than pleasant co-workers. This would mean that we should get a more accurate prediction of an individual's overall satisfaction if we weigh satisfaction with each specific job element by its importance. In spite of the appeal of this operation, a number of studies have shown that weighting by importance does not improve the prediction of overall job satisfaction (Ewen, 1967; Mikes & Hulin, 1968). Locke suggests that the importance of a particular job aspect affects the *range* of emotional response a given job element can produce, rather than the actual satisfaction with that element. In other words, if something is relatively unimportant to me, I will not be either very satisfied or very dissatisfied with it—I will be indifferent regardless of the amount of that element I receive. On the other hand, if I value a particular job element very highly, then slight variations from optimal amounts of that element will produce wide variations in satisfaction. Figure

FIGURE 10–4

Relationship of Importance to Satisfaction

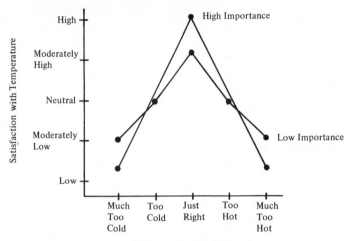

Source: Adapted from Locke, E. A. The nature and causes of job satisfaction. In M. Dunnette (Ed.), *Handbook of industrial and organization psychology.* Chicago: Rand McNally, 1976, p. 1305. Copyright © 1976 by Rand McNally College Publishing Company.

10–4 presents this principle in graphic form. As you can see, when room temperature is unimportant to an individual, wide variation in temperature will produce little variation in satisfaction with temperature; on the other hand, when temperature is of critical importance to an individual, small variations in actual temperature will produce wide variations in expressed satisfaction with temperature. Another way of expressing this mechanism might be with the following equation:

$$OJS = (S_1)^{p1} + (S_2)^{p2} + \ldots (S_j)^{pj},$$

where *OJS* represents overall job satisfaction, *S* represents satisfaction with individual aspects of the job, and *p* represents the importance of each of the elements. It can be seen from this equation that the importance of an element acts as a power function, increasing or decreasing the range of satisfaction with each element (and, subsequently, the range of overall job satisfaction). Mobley and Locke (1970) present data supporting this hypothesis, but more data from a wide variety of settings are necessary before the generality of the finding can be accepted.

Opponent-Process Theory

Landy (1978) has suggested an approach to job satisfaction that departs radically from the more traditional approaches outlined earlier. It is called the *opponent-process theory* and differs from other approaches in proposing that an individual's satisfaction with a particular reward will systematically change over time, even though the reward itself remains constant. As an example, a job tends to be more interesting in the first week than it is after six years on the same job. In the past, this has been dismissed as simply an instance of "boredom," as if labeling the phenomenon somehow explained it. Landy suggests there are some mechanisms within individuals that help maintain some equilibrium in emotional states. Since job satisfaction and dissatisfaction are thought to be, at least in part, emotional phenomena, these mechanisms of emotional balance are thought to play a role in job satisfaction.

As the name implies, opponent-process theory holds that there are opposing processes for dealing with emotional states. For example, whenever we are extremely happy, there is a mechanism that automatically attempts to keep that happiness from getting out of control. Conversely, when we are unhappy, there is a mechanism that opposes that emotional state and attempts to bring the individual back to some neutral level. This "mechanism" sounds somewhat mystical, but in actuality it is thought to be a central nervous system function. The theory assumes that extreme emotional states (either positive or negative) are damaging to the individual and that physiological mechanisms attempt to protect the individual from these extreme states. Landy suggests that this "protection" function is responsible for the fact that individuals differ in job satisfaction. Figure 10–5 represents the way the opponent process works.

There are three components in the figure: *primary emotion, opponent process,* and *stimulus.* The figure suggests that when a stimulus is introduced, it produces an emotion, either positive or negative. Once this primary emotion passes some threshold, an opponent process is automatically acti-

FIGURE 10–5
*Underlying Opponent Processes
after Few Stimulus
Presentations*

Primary Emotion

Emotional
Neutrality

Opponent Process

Stimulus

Onset   Termination

Source: Landy, F. J. An opponent process theory of job satisfaction. *Journal of Applied Psychology*, 1978, *63*, 533–547.

vated to bring this primary emotion under control. When the stimulus disappears, the primary emotion disappears immediately, and the opponent process disappears more gradually. Figure 10–5 is a view of each of the two processes independent of each other. Now look at Figure 10–6. This figure represents the actual changes in the emotional state of an individual during and after stimulus (reward or punishment) presentation. This suggests that shortly after the presentation of a reward, an individual is elated. This elation levels out after a period of time, and when the stimulus that originally elicited the elation disappears, the individual is somewhat depressed or unhappy. This can be seen by the fact that the curve representing the emotional state of the individual dips below the line representing emotional neutrality.

Another proposition of the theory makes it even more intriguing. It is assumed that the opponent process becomes stronger each time it is activated. This means the same stimulus can have different effects on the satisfaction of an individual depending on how often the individual has encountered the stimulus in the past. Figure 10–7 presents a picture of what the primary emotional state and opponent process might look like after many presentations of the same reward or punishment. As you can see, the primary emotion remains exactly the same as it was in Figure 10–5, but the opponent process has grown dramatically in strength. It is both more intense and longer lasting than it was in Figure 10–5. Figure 10–8 represents the changes in emotional state that the individual would be likely to experience during the presence and disappearance of the stimulus (reward or punishment). As you can see, the initial presentation of the stimulus has little observable effect on the individual, but the termination of the stimulus has a rather dramatic effect.

The implications of the opponent-process theory are rather extensive. For one thing, it suggests that studies of job satisfaction should be longitudinal rather than cross sectional in nature. This can be seen by looking at

FIGURE 10–6

*Emotional Response after Few
Stimulus Presentations*

Emotional
Neutrality

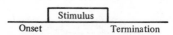

Onset   Stimulus   Termination

Source: Landy, F. J. An opponent process theory of job satisfaction. *Journal of Applied Psychology*, 1978, *63*, 533–547.

FIGURE 10–7

Underlying Opponent Processes after Many Stimulus Presentations

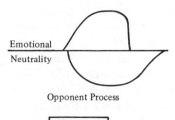

Source: Landy, F. J. An opponent process theory of job satisfaction. *Journal of Applied Psychology*, 1978, *63*, 533–547.

either Figure 10–6 or 10–8. The point at which you ask the question will play a large part in the answer you obtain. If you ask questions with regard to satisfaction shortly after stimulus presentation (e.g., on payday, after the individual has received a reprimand from his supervisor, after a lunch hour card game with co-workers), the response will be different from one you might receive at some other time (midweek, in the evening when the worker is at home, after a worker has been laid off). This means that if I simply wanted to know if individual A was happy or unhappy with his work, I might come to completely opposite conclusions depending on when I measured satisfaction. Most research in the job satisfaction area ignores the possibility of such systematic variation.

Another implication of the opponent-process theory is related to the

FIGURE 10–8

Emotional Response after Many Stimulus Presentations

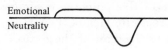

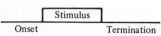

Source: Landy, F. J. An opponent process theory of job satisfaction. *Journal of Applied Psychology*, 1978, *63*, 533–547.

issue of "boredom." Most managers assume the work itself diminishes in "stimulation value," thus resulting in a state of boredom. Opponent-process theory suggests that the stimulus value of the work itself remains unchanged, but the opponent process has become stronger. The most direct test of the two approaches would be to "terminate" the stimulus (tasks that the worker describes as boring) and look at the emotional response to termination. If opponent-process theory is correct, the individual should experience some depression or negative emotion in the absence of the "boring" work. In real life, we normally substitute an interesting task for a boring task and thus eliminate the opponent-process depression by introducing a new positive primary emotion. Nevertheless, anecdotally, we have seen many instances of individuals who have been fired, laid off, or retired who would be very happy to have their old "boring" jobs back, even when the economic issue is not a critical one! The theory suggests that "boredom" has more to do with the scheduling of stimulus presentation than with the tasks themselves. Thus, it is possible to think of individuals becoming "bored" with pay, co-workers, promotional opportunities, supervisory practices, and so on.

Opponent-process theory is too new to characterize as "good" or "bad." This determination can be made only on the basis of research and application. Nevertheless, it is a substantially different approach to the construct of job satisfaction and, as such, probably will receive a good deal of attention.

Tests of the Theories

Two-Factor Theory. The research on two-factor theory has been voluminous and generally discouraging. Two-factor theory came under attack almost immediately on methodological grounds. The major argument was that, since the data were gathered in face-to-face interviews, possibly the respondents were acting defensively when they responded. People might be unwilling to admit to an interviewer that a bad experience was their own fault. Consequently, when relating a dissatisfying time, they would attribute the cause of the dissatisfaction to someone or something other than themselves (e.g., a supervisor, co-worker, or company policy). On the other hand, they would be more likely to take personal responsibility for good events (e.g, accomplishing a difficult task, receiving recognition for meeting a goal). Because of this potential confounding factor, numerous researchers have tried to replicate Herzberg's findings using methods other than face-to-face interviews. In most of these cases, they did not find the same results as Herzberg (Ewen, 1964; Ewen, Smith, Hulin, & Locke, 1966; Hinrichs & Mischkind, 1967; Hulin & Smith, 1965).

In addition to the lack of empirical support, Herzberg has been severely criticized on conceptual grounds. King (1970) identified no less than five distinctly different "theories" suggested by Herzberg at various times. These "versions" are presented in Figure 10–9.

In comparing the versions, it can be seen that version I is the weakest

FIGURE 10–9
Five Versions of the Two-Factor Theory

Version

I. All motivators combined contribute more to job satisfaction than to job dissatisfaction; all hygienes combined contribute more to job dissatisfaction than to job satisfaction.

II. All motivators combined contribute more to job satisfaction than do all the hygienes combined; all hygienes combined contribute more to job dissatisfaction than do all motivators combined.

III. Each motivator contributes more to job satisfaction than to job dissatisfaction; each hygiene contributes more to job dissatisfaction than to job satisfaction.

IV. Theory III holds and, in addition, each principal motivator contributes more to job satisfaction than does any hygiene factor; each principal hygiene contributes more to job dissatisfaction than does any motivator.

V. Only motivators determine job satisfaction, and only hygiene factors determine job dissatisfaction.

Source: King, N. Clarification and evaluation of the two-factor theory of job satisfaction. *Psychological Bulletin*, 1970, *74*, 18–31.

(i.e., would be easiest to support) and version V is the strongest (would be the most demanding to support). In examining the studies that applied to the various versions, King concluded there was little evidence to suggest that any of the theories were supported.

Due to the conceptual and empirical problems in supporting Herzberg's propositions, there has been a substantial decrease in research on the two-factor theory. This might be one way of saying that it has "fallen into disrepute." Nevertheless, Herzberg's theory is probably a reasonable one at the descriptive level. It does a good job of describing what a manager might expect to find—*on the average.* The factors listed as motivators are probably important to a majority of the work force in a particular organization (e.g., the stimulation provided by the job duties). But description is not explanation. Being able to describe the characteristics of a majority of the work force is a long way from understanding the relationships among satisfaction, motivation, and performance. One valuable research line that continues to maintain the interest of investigators is the difference between "intrinsic," or job-content (motivator) and "extrinsic" or job-context (hygiene) factors. Some of these differences will be examined in a later section of this chapter. On the whole, Herzberg has had a positive effect on the research in job satisfaction. As a result of his theory, variables are more clearly understood, the operations involved in measuring important variables are more reasonable, and people are thinking more flexibly about the meaning of job satisfaction than they did before.

Lawler's Facet Satisfaction Theory. There have been few direct tests of Lawler's theory. Wanous and Lawler (1972) present data that purport to show that the discrepancy between a desired amount of a job element and the actual amount received is related to overall job satisfaction. In a reanalysis of those data, Wall and Payne (1973) show that the differences in overall job satisfaction can be accounted for by differences in the amount of the reward received, without any consideration of what was expected. In other words, Wall and Payne conclude that people who received more of the facet were happier than those who received less of that facet. These results are damaging to facet satisfaction theory.

There also seem to be some problems with the theory on a conceptual level. As we indicated in the chapter on motivation, equity theory proposes that overpayment inequity will lead to discomfort. This proposition can also be seen clearly in Lawler's theory of satisfaction. Recent studies have not commonly found this effect in overpayment conditions. Thus, just as equity theory may need some reworking to account for recent experimental findings, other theories that are based on equity, such as Lawler's facet satisfaction theory, will also require some rethinking.

As was the case with many of the motivation theories, it seems to us that Lawler's theory of facet satisfaction is overly elaborate. It is not a particularly realistic view of how workers determine the emotional costs and benefits of their work. Wall and Payne (1973) suggest that instead of all the measures implied by Lawler's model, we simply ask the individual the following questions:

> How much (of a particular job facet) is there now?
>
> How much would you like to have?
>
> And (having considered the above two questions) how satisfied are you? (p. 326)

They suggest that the answer to the third question may do as well or better at predicting overall job satisfaction than the elaborate calculations implied by Lawler. In their words, "it is just possible in the mathematics of affect, seven minus five does not necessarily equal two" (p. 326).

Given the problems outlined, we must conclude that no strong support for Lawler's model has yet been presented.

Value Theory and Opponent-Process Theory. The theories of Locke (value) and Landy (opponent-process) are still too recent to have generated any substantive research. They both show some promise, but for different reasons. Locke's theory has interesting implications for understanding how "importance" affects job satisfaction. Landy's theory has implications for the manner in which satisfaction with various job elements changes over time. Nevertheless, considerable research on these theories will be required before their generality can be accepted.

SOURCES OF JOB SATISFACTION

Up to this point, formal models of job satisfaction have been presented. Another way of studying satisfaction is to examine data that have been gathered on the topic, independent of a particular theoretical orientation. Several reviews have attempted such an examination (Herzberg et al., 1957; Vroom, 1964). But the amount of research is accumulating so rapidly that one must depend on the most ·recent review available for drawing any general conclusions. Locke (1976)'estimates that currently more than 3,300 articles or dissertations have been published on job satisfaction. You will be happy to know that we have decided against presenting the results of each of these studies to you. Instead, we will take advantage of the recent

"I find this work truly fulfilling in many ways—there's the exercise, the sense of accomplishment, and, most important, the opportunity to make lots of noise."

Reprinted by permission The Wall Street Journal

and extensive review that Locke (1976) accomplished and present a synthesis of his conclusions.

Locke has suggested that studies be placed in one of two categories: (1) *events and conditions* or (2) *agents.* While events and conditions are thought to be directly responsible for feelings of happiness or unhappiness, agents are responsible for events and conditions. Thus, the amount of work, the task activity, and compensation are examples of events and conditions; supervisors, co-workers, and customers are examples of agents. Figure 10–10 presents Locke's conclusions with regard to recent research findings.

These conclusions would be very useful were it not for the fact that a number of individual differences must be taken into account before applying them. This seems to be particularly true with the "events or conditions"

FIGURE 10–10
Effects of Various Events, Conditions, and Agents on Job Satisfaction *

Source	Effect
Events or conditions	
Work itself: Challenge	Mentally challenging work that the individual can successfully accomplish is satisfying.
Work itself: Physical demand	Tiring work is dissatisfying.
Work itself: Personal interest	Personally interesting work is satisfying.
Reward structure	Just and informative rewards for performance are satisfying.
Working conditions: Physical	Satisfaction depends on the match between working conditions and physical needs.
Working conditions: Goal attainment	Working conditions that facilitate goal attainment are satisfying.
Agents	
Self	High self-esteem is conducive to job satisfaction.
Supervisors, co-workers, subordinates	Individuals will be satisfied with colleagues who help them attain rewards.
	Individuals will be satisfied with colleagues who see things the same way they do.
Company and management	Individuals will be satisfied with companies that have policies and procedures designed to help the individual attain rewards.
	Individuals will be dissatisfied with conflicting roles and/or ambiguous roles imposed by company and/or management.
Fringe benefits	Benefits do not have a strong influence on job satisfaction for most workers.

* The interested reader is directed to Locke's (1976) review for a more detailed presentation of these conclusions.

category. As an example, before applying the general conclusions about the nature of the work itself listed above, Locke suggests we look at the following individual differences that might modify the effect of the application: urban versus rural workers, Catholic versus Protestant workers, higher-level employees vs. lower–level employees. Other important individual differences might be sex, age, race, and socioeconomic status.

Individual Differences in Job Satisfaction

If these individual differences have such a potentially powerful effect on the relationship between events or agents and job satisfaction, perhaps the individual differences *themselves* are responsible for satisfaction while the events or agents are accidental. This possibility has not escaped the notice of those who study job satisfaction. These studies have usually been accomplished by comparing various demographically defined subgroups of workers on either the *importance* of various job characteristics to their job satisfaction or on the *degree* of satisfaction with particular components of the job (i.e., events/conditions or agents). These two different types of studies (importance versus degree) have come to somewhat different conclusions with regard to the value of studying individual differences in relation to job satisfaction. Studies of women and blacks have concluded that, compared to white men, these two groups tend to concentrate on lower-order needs in deriving satisfaction or dissatisfaction from their jobs (Manhardt, 1972; Herzberg, et al. 1957; Bloom & Barry, 1967; Slocum & Strawser, 1972; Arvey & Mussio, 1974). As a result of these findings, you might expect that, on the whole, blacks and women were less satisfied, in an absolute sense, than white male workers. That does not seem to be the case. The differences among black men, white men, and white women seem to be inconsistent and small. In some studies the women are happier than the men; in others the men are happier. The same reversals are found in groups defined by age and race (Smith, Smith, and Rollo, 1974; Gavin & Ewen, 1974; Glenn, Taylor, & Weaver, 1977; Jones, James, Bruni, & Sells, 1977; Weaver, 1977; Slocum and Strawser, 1972). Regardless of which group turned out to be more satisfied in these studies, the particular characteristic in question (race, sex, age) accounted for very little of the variation in job satisfaction, usually between 2 and 5 percent. Furthermore, it can be shown that when other variables such as education, occupational status, and pay level are held constant, even these small differences disappear (Weaver, 1977).

In the past, these studies were done in single organizations with small samples of unknown composition. Recently, Weaver and his colleagues have undertaken a systematic examination of survey data gathered by the National Opinion Research Center; these data cover a multitude of topics and have the advantage of being gathered from carefully selected and defined samples of respondents (Weaver, 1977; Weaver & Holmes, 1975; Weaver, 1975; Glenn, Taylor, & Weaver, 1977). These studies point rather clearly to the relative unimportance of demographic characteristics in determining overall job satisfaction.

Thus we are left with something of a dilemma. The data suggest that while subgroups differ with respect to *how* they choose to derive satisfaction from their jobs, they do not differ greatly with respect to overall satisfaction on an absolute basis. How can this discrepancy be resolved? The simplest explanation would be that there are really only two classes of workers— the "haves" and the "have-nots." Historically, the "haves" were made up of males, whites, and higher-level occupational positions; the "have-nots" comprised lower-level workers, blacks, and women. The fact that in some of the studies the "have-nots" (e.g., blacks or women) derived satisfaction from the same sources as the "haves" probably meant they worked in an organization that practiced equality of opportunity. In other words, in these studies, the samples consisted of "have-nots" who had reason to believe they had access to the full range of job-related rewards—both content and context factors. Since it seems clear from other studies that content factors are generally rated as more important than context factors, it is not surprising to see a similar result in these studies.

In the studies where the "have-nots" seemed to derive satisfaction from context factors while the "haves" derived satisfaction from the content factors, they were probably responding realistically; that is, it was unlikely they would have jobs that provided them with intrinsic rewards such as responsibility and challenge. This is further supported by the general findings that the "have-nots" were less satisfied than the "haves." It is also interesting to note that in none of the studies did the "haves" derive satisfaction from context factors and the "have-nots" from the content factors.

The general conclusion might be one that is more related to mental health than to anything else. Mentally healthy people seek what is reasonably available to them. The fact that the "have-nots" identify context factors as the predominant sources of job satisfaction may be an indication that they have come to a compromise with their situation and are maintaining a mentally healthy outlook on their environment. It is likely that as opportunities for the full range of job-related rewards are made available to the "have-nots," they will become more similar to the "haves" in sources of job satisfaction, that is, content factors will be uniformly more important than context factors.

THE MEASUREMENT OF JOB SATISFACTION

So far, the history, logic, and theory of job satisfaction have been presented, but nothing has been said about how satisfaction information is gathered—that is, how the variable is measured. Figure 10–11 shows several different ways in which *satisfaction with the work itself* might be measured.

At A in the figure is a format known as the *semantic differential*. The worker is asked to place a mark on the line separating the two bipolar adjectives; this mark indicates how well one or the other of the adjectives

FIGURE 10–11

Ways of Measuring Job Satisfaction

A.   THE WORK ITSELF

Fascinating   — — — — — — —   Boring
Monotonous — — — — — — — —   Challenging
Simple   — — — — — — —   Difficult
Creative   — — — — — — —   Routine
Useless   — — — — — — —   Useful

B.

My work is routine _____
My work is difficult _____
I seem to do many useless things on my job _____
I have the opportunity to be creative in my work _____

C.

1. My work is routine   SA   A   N   D   SD
2. My work is difficult   SA   A   N   D   SD
3. I seem to do many useless things on my job   SD   A   N   D   SD
4. I have the opportunity to be creative in my work   SA   A   N   D   SD

    SA = strongly agree
     A = agree
     N = neither agree nor disagree (neutral)
     D = disagree
    SD = strongly disagree

D.   WORK

Yes	?	No	Fascinating
Yes	?	No	Routine
Yes	?	No	Satisfying
Yes	?	No	Boring
Yes	?	No	Good
Yes	?	No	Creative
Yes	?	No	Respected
Yes	?	No	Hot
Yes	?	No	Pleasant
Yes	?	No	Useful
Yes	?	No	Tiresome
Yes	?	No	Healthful
Yes	?	No	Challenging
Yes	?	No	On your feet
Yes	?	No	Frustrating
Yes	?	No	Simple
Yes	?	No	Endless
Yes	?	No	Gives sense of accomplishment

describes the concept "my work." At B is a checklist format in which the worker is asked to place a check or mark next to those items that best describe the work itself. At C is a format known as a Likert scale. It is named after the person who originally developed the procedure for its use. The worker is asked to read each of the statements and circle one of the alternatives (SA = strongly agree; A = agree; N = neither agree nor disagree—neutral; D = disagree; SD = strongly disagree). At D is a portion of a measuring instrument known as the Job Descriptive Index (Smith, Kendall, and Hulin, 1969). Workers are asked to circle one of the three alternatives: *Yes,?*, or *No* to indicate whether the word describes their jobs. In a sense, this is actually a combination of checklist format and the Likert format. These methods are known collectively as rating scales. In Chapter 4 rating scales were described as aids used to help the supervisor make performance statements about subordinates. In this case, rating scales are aids for workers in making statements about their jobs.

Overall job satisfaction or satisfaction with a specific aspect of the job has generally been measured as an attitude. An attitude might be defined as a feeling, belief, or action tendency toward a psychological object. You might have a feeling about your job—disgust, fear, excitement, apprehension, or enthusiasm. Independent of this feeling, you might have a belief about your job—it is an interesting job, or it is a high-status job. Finally, you might have an action tendency related to your job—you rush to your job, or you tend to talk more to your co-workers than you do to your family. Each of these three components describes an aspect of your attitude toward your job.

Job satisfaction scales usually measure one of the first two components of an attitude—feeling or belief. It is not always clear which of the two components is being considered. This presents a problem for interpretation, since the *feelings* about a job or job aspect are quite different from the *beliefs* about that aspect. For example, we might feel apprehensive every time we get into the car to go to work, yet believe that our job is the best in the world. If beliefs were measured in this instance, it might be concluded that you had a "good attitude" toward your work; if feelings were measured, you might be described as having a "poor attitude" toward your work.

Over the years, an interesting characteristic of satisfaction measurement has been the unwillingness of one researcher to make use of the satisfaction questionnaire developed by another researcher. There has been the tendency to develop a new satisfaction questionnaire for each study. This is the equivalent of every carpenter in the world developing an individual way of measuring lengths. One carpenter might use the standard ruler marked off in inches, while a second uses a ruler marked off in metric units, and a third prefers to measure lengths with a screwdriver (e.g., this page is one screwdriver length long). This preference for varying measuring methods presents no problem until the carpenters try to talk to one another. The same is true of job satisfaction research. Since different ways were used to measure job satisfaction, and even different components of attitudes toward the job were being measured, the literature is very confusing. Fortunately, this is changing. The Job Descriptive Index shown in Figure 10–11 at D is being widely used in satisfaction research. It was very carefully developed and documented, is relatively easy for workers to use and understand, and relates logically and empirically to other measures of job satisfaction. As more and more investigators adopt this instrument for the measurement of satisfaction, differences in results and interpretation due to the nature of the measurement process will disappear and the construct of satisfaction will be better understood.

Attitude scales are the most common measuring instruments in job satisfaction research. The tendency for investigators to develop their own scales has led to the existence of more scales than there is space to describe them. The Institute for Social Research at the University of Michigan has catalogued many of these scales (Robinson, Athanasiou, and Head, 1969), so they will not be described here. In addition, there are a number of good texts available that outline techniques for attitude-scale construction (though we *beg* you not to develop another scale!) (Edwards, 1957); Guilford, 1954; Sherif & Sherif, 1969; Torgerson, 1958).

In addition to attitude scales, Locke (1976) lists the following techniques that might be considered in gathering job satisfaction information:

1. *Overt behavior* (e.g., everyone in attendance on a particular day must be satisfied with his work or he would not be there)
2. *Action tendency scales* (e.g., ask an individual how she *feels like acting*)
3. *Interviews*
4. *Critical incidents* (e.g., ask individuals to remember a time when they were particularly happy or unhappy with their work and describe the circumstances)

Each of these approaches has its own advocates. The behaviorists would favor overt action; Herzberg based his theory on the results of critical incidents; Lawler depends heavily on attitude rating scales. There is no *best* way. But no matter how satisfaction is measured, the technique must be capable of producing reliable and valid data or those data are worthless.

THE CONSEQUENCES OF JOB SATISFACTION AND DISSATISFACTION

Most managers implicitly assume some relationship between job satisfaction and certain organizational outcomes, such as absenteeism, turnover, and productivity. In fact, a large number of studies have explored these possible relationships. We will present the conclusions of these studies.

Satisfaction and Withdrawal from the Workplace

Managers commonly hold that unhappy workers are less likely to come to work than happy workers; similarly, it is commonly believed that one symptom of an unhappy work force is high turnover. Since both turnover and absenteeism are costly to an organization, it would seem logical that one way of reducing these "withdrawal" behaviors would be to increase job satisfaction. Managers who think this way could find support for their position from industrial psychologists. Brayfield and Crockett (1955), Herzberg (1957) and Vroom (1964) all conducted reviews of studies dealing with the satisfaction/withdrawal relationship and concluded that the two variables were substantially related; i.e., unhappy workers were more likely to leave or stay away from the job.

Recently, these time-honored beliefs have been called into question. Several recent reviews have come to quite different conclusions. In the first place, they have questioned the assumption that quitting and absenteeism are similar. In addition, they have been critical of the types of absenteeism studies that are conducted. Finally, they are skeptical of the role of satisfaction in either absenteeism or turnover. We will review these conclusions in some detail.

In 1973, Porter and Steers completed a comprehensive review of absenteeism and turnover research. This was needed, since the last comprehensive review had been that of Vroom (1964), and significant advances had been made in the measurement of satisfaction in the interim. On the basis of the review, Porter and Steers suggested that absenteeism and turnover should not be thought of as similar responses. It is commonly believed that the only difference between absenteeism and turnover is the opportunity to find a new job. Thus, if a worker is dissatisfied with his job but cannot find another one easily, he is more likely to be absent—or so it is commonly believed. Porter and Steers disagreed with this assumption. They felt that absenteeism was much more "spontaneous," while the decision to quit, due to its economic implications, was a much more carefully considered decision. Their review did point to a relationship between satisfaction and turnover, but they were much more cautious about suggesting a satisfaction-absence relationship. They did, however, accept the possibility that under certain extreme conditions, absenteeism might function as a short-term substitute for quitting.

Nicholson, Brown, and Chadwick-Jones (1976) took a much more critical view of the satisfaction—absence relationship. They reviewed 29 studies of the relationship and concluded that most of the results that supported the relationship were artifactual and were due to either a flawed experimental design or an inappropriate analysis. They conducted their own study (1977) of absenteeism in a sample of 1,200 workers from 16 different organizations and concluded that there was no relationship between job satisfaction and absence rate. They then analyzed the absence data from a different perspective, attempting to explain the absence rate on the basis of demographic characteristics such as age and sex. They found that older workers had fewer absences; also, the finding was stronger for men than women in their sample. Nicholson et al. suggested this might be due to a greater "need for regularity" in older workers. In addition, older workers are more likely to have increased levels of economic responsibility for family members, which would seem to require steady attendance. Since the Nicholson et al. study was cross sectional rather than longitudinal, we cannot be sure that individual workers actually *become* more responsible with respect to attendance as they get older; the differences may be due to the fact that the older workers and the younger workers in the sample came from different generations with different values and expectations. Nevertheless, the research of Nicholson and his colleagues is important because it seriously damages the assumed satisfaction—absence relationship.

Steers and Rhodes (1978) have recently suggested that satisfaction is related to absenteeism in a much more indirect way than was suggested by the earlier researchers. After reviewing 104 empirical studies of the satisfaction–absence relationship, they proposed a process model for helping to understand the relationship. This model appears in Figure 10–12. This model suggests that attendance is directly influenced by attendance motivation and the ability to come to work. The motivation to attend work is affected, in turn, by job satisfaction and both internal and external pressures to attend work. This model is a realistic one, since it includes variables

FIGURE 10–12

Major Influences on Employee Attendance

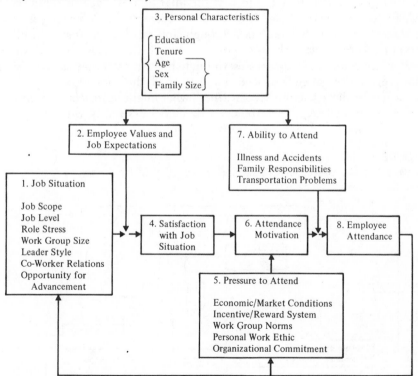

Source: Steers, R. M., & Rhodes, S. R. Major influences on employee attendance: A process model. *Journal of Applied Psychology*, 1978, *63*, 391–407.

such as economic consequences for missing work, problems in the nonwork environment that affect one's ability to attend work, and employee values and expectations. In addition, the model includes a feedback loop suggesting that attendance affects other variables (such as work-group size, leader style, and opportunity for advancement) that have subsequent effects on job satisfaction. Given such a model as this, the original hypothesis that "happy workers are more likely to attend work than unhappy workers" seems somewhat simple-minded. It is now easier to see why the relationship between satisfaction and absenteeism might be low.

Mobley, Horner, and Hollingsworth have pursued the issue of turnover along parallel lines. They suggested that dissatisfaction was not the only, or even the most important, variable contributing to turnover. They proposed a model of the turnover process, which we have presented in Figure 10–13. As you can see, once again job satisfaction is several steps removed from the actual process of quitting. They tested the model in a hospital setting. They collected questionnaire data from 203 hospital employees on all of the variables in the model. They then examined the turnover data 47 weeks later to see who had quit and who had stayed. The results were encouraging for their model. They found that job satisfaction was most closely related to thoughts of quitting and intentions to search for another job; further, they found that the intention to quit was significantly related to actually quitting. Mobley et al. seem to be describing a series of stages that an individual goes through. Job satisfaction seems to play a rather important role early in the process, but this role becomes less important as the individual progresses through the stages. Once again, this is pure conjecture, since we have not examined the individual at each of the stages but have tried to "reconstruct" what might have occurred through correlational analyses. Nevertheless, this model fits nicely with the earlier

FIGURE 10–13

A Simplified Representation of Intermediate Linkages in the Employee Withdrawal Decision Process

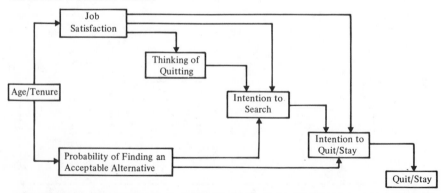

Source: Mobley, W. H., Horner, S. O., & Hollingsworth, A. T. An evaluation of precursors of hospital employee turnover. *Journal of Applied Psychology,* 1978, *63,* 408–414.

conclusion of Porter and Steers that turnover is a less spontaneous process than absenteeism.

Both of the models presented above are tentative: they are the first guesses about the variables responsible for employee withdrawal from the workplace. But they are appealing guesses, since they help us to understand why the observed correlations between satisfaction and withdrawal are low. In addition, they allow for other variables of interest, particularly environmental variables that are not necessarily job related. On the basis of logic, theory, and data, we agree with the tone of these newer approaches: job satisfaction or work-related attitudes contribute in only an indirect way to withdrawal behavior.

Job Satisfaction and Performance

From the earliest days of industrial psychology, the relationship between satisfaction and performance represented a kind of "holy grail." The Hawthorne studies and the subsequent human-relations movement sanctified the search for the relationship. Unfortunately, the search has been a discouraging one. Brayfield and Crockett concluded that "no appreciable relationship" existed. Two decades later, Locke (1976) conducted an extensive review of the satisfaction literature and concluded that "job satisfaction has no direct effect on productivity" (p. 1334).

There is an important difference between the early conceptions of the satisfaction/performance relationship and some more recent considerations of the issue. Historically, researchers attempted to show that satisfaction *caused* productivity. It has been clearly demonstrated that this relationship does not hold. Recently, the opposite relationship has been suggested; i.e., successful performance causes satisfaction (Locke, 1970; Porter and Lawler, 1968). A good deal of Locke's research in goal setting and goal accomplishment seems to support this hypothesis.

The major problem with most studies of the satisfaction/performance relationship is that it is impossible to control other variables that might be influencing one or both of the variables in question. For example, Mirvis and Lawler (1977) have used cost-accounting procedures to show that a modest increase in job satisfaction in a midwestern bank would result in a savings of $17,664 to the organization. They came to this conclusion after examining correlations between various satisfaction measures and employee behaviors (absenteeism, turnover, and productivity). Unfortunately, a significant correlation between satisfaction and behavior does not allow one to conclude that the satisfaction caused the performance. As suggested by Locke, the reverse might have been true—performance might have caused satisfaction. If this were the case, instead of spending time and money on improving the attitudes of employees, it might be better to work directly on performance aids and expanded training programs to increase profits and decrease costs and think of improved job attitudes as a "fringe benefit" of increased productivity.

In summary, we do not know about the relationship between job satisfaction and productive effort. To put it another way, the examination of work behavior has not helped us very much in understanding job satisfaction.

Job Satisfaction and the Quality of Life

It is natural to question the contribution of work to life in general. Some things are obvious; jobs provide economic stability, which allows for nonwork enjoyment and long-range planning unrelated to occupational goals. A less obvious question has to do with whether the very act of working adds to or detracts from the life experience of an individual.

There are examples for both positive and negative contributions of work to the quality of life. For example, in a book detailing the sufferings of the "workaholic" (Oates, 1971), the point is made that work can easily get out of hand, occupying inordinate amounts of time, often to the detriment of those around such individuals and eventually even to the individuals themselves. And yet organizations are constantly trying to "involve" their members, to get them to accept organizational goals as individual ones, in short, to derive life satisfaction from job satisfaction.

On the other hand, there are many studies that demonstrate a relationship between positive mental health and job satisfaction, the implication being that job satisfaction *induces* mental well being (Gechman & Wiener, 1975). Thus the question remains: Does job satisfaction contribute to or detract from the quality of life? Recently London, Crandall, and Seals (1977) analyzed the responses of a sample of 1,297 individuals from various backgrounds and with various demographic characteristics. Their results were surprising. The degree to which an individual was satisfied with a job seemed to have very little impact on general life satisfaction. In addition, for disadvantaged respondents, job satisfaction was *completely unrelated* to life satisfaction. While these results must be viewed with caution, they do suggest that work is less important than we might have suspected once the individual is outside of the work setting. Because we spend so much time at work, it is natural to assume that it has a major impact on our emotional well-being. This does not seem to be true. It may be that work is viewed more as a necessity, much like eating and sleeping. As such, it is unlikely that work would have a major impact on our lives, under normal circumstances. We once conducted a study of absenteeism of deep coal miners. In the course of a conversation with a group of young miners, the question was asked, "Why do you come to work four days a week when your contract calls for five?" One of the miners immediately answered, "Because I can't afford to come to work only three days a week." During the same conversation, another miner was asked, "Do you like your work?" and he answered, "Compared to what?" Such conversations give us the nagging feeling that job satisfaction may be viewed differently by industrial psychologists and managers than by workers.

Job Satisfaction as a Social and Political Phenomenon

Recently, Nord (1977) has suggested that the theory and research in job satisfaction is colored by several assumptions that investigators implicitly accept. These assumptions are:

1. *Job satisfaction is less important than profit.* As a result of this assumption, job satisfaction is always examined in light of productivity, absenteeism, turnover, scrap, and so on. Consequently, we get a distorted view of the emotional consequences of industrial environments on the worker.
2. *Work should be a central life interest.* This assumption lays the groundwork for attempts at increasing job involvement, since workers who are involved in their work must consider it central to their existence.
3. *Interdependence among workers is considered a disadvantage rather than a source of satisfaction.* Since our society is committed to the individual rather than the group, it is difficult to accept the possibility that cooperative effort could, as a process, be a major source of job (and life) satisfaction.
4. *The workplace is treated as an "open system" with respect to valued resources.* Our theories imply that individuals have the choice among alternative rewards. This may be incorrect for two reasons: (1) workers may choose from only those rewards made available to them by managers, and (2) since most resources are fixed, the rewards provided to worker A place a constraint on the rewards available to worker B.
5. *Individual power should increase as individuals progress upward through the organizational structure.* Managers have the power to give rewards and workers have the power to reject those rewards.

We must be careful in dealing with these assumptions. It is tempting to act as a social philosopher rather than a scientist. The social philosopher would point to other cultures, such as Sweden, where job satisfaction is of critical national concern. In Sweden, most research on job satisfaction is directed toward identifying and eliminating sources of stress on the job. This has been accepted as a goal by workers, first-level supervisors, and unions alike. The owners and upper-level managers may have a greater concern for productivity than for worker tranquility, but the distribution of power is such that, as a group, workers have as much and sometimes greater real power than managers and owners. In the role of social philosopher, Locke (1978) has severely criticized Nord for his dim view of the American industrial system. Nevertheless, the Swedes know a good deal more about the effects of working conditions on perceived stress than we do (Frankenhauser, 1974). In addition, they are well ahead of us with respect to the role of job and task design in job satisfaction. Thus, as a scientist, Nord is right: we will learn more about the phenomenon of job satisfaction once we recognize the assumptions that pervade our research and the limiting effect those assumptions have on the research questions we ask. The argument between Nord and Locke with regard to which system is philosophically "better" is one that will not be easily resolved, since it is based on the values of the combatants rather than on empirical evidence.

As was the case with the theories of motivation, we believe our understanding of the phenomenon under consideration will improve in direct proportion to the number of unique settings in which it is studied.

SUMMARY

Job satisfaction plays a role in theories of work motivation. This role is generally one of an emotion or feeling that an individual gets as a result of some job-related characteristic or event.

The Hawthorne studies documented the effect of worker attitudes on worker behavior. Hoppock demonstrated that occupational level affects attitudes toward work. Schaffer found that overall satisfaction with a job was related to the degree to which important needs of the individual were provided for by that job. Brayfield and Crockett concluded there was no appreciable relationship between satisfaction and performance, although there was a relationship between satisfaction and avoidance behaviors such as absenteeism and turnover. Herzberg et al. disagreed with Brayfield and Crockett, contending that satisfaction and dissatisfaction were different phenomena.

Herzberg conducted a study of engineers and accountants and concluded that the factors leading to satisfaction (which he called "motivators") were different than those leading to dissatisfaction (which he called "hygiene factors").

Lawler's facet satisfaction theory is based on equity notions, proposing that individuals compare what they expect with what they get and experience various emotional states as a result of that comparison. Herzberg's theory has been attacked from both methodological and empirical grounds. Lawler's theory has not been extensively tested, but seems to have some flaws. Two new theories, value theory and opponent-process theory, show some promise but are not yet supported by data.

Various factors have been found to influence job satisfaction. These factors can be placed into two categories, events and agents. Demographic characteristics such as sex and race do not seem to account for much of the variation in job attitudes.

Job satisfaction is generally measured as an attitude. While there are many ways to measure attitudes, the most popular way of measuring job satisfaction is with an "attitude scale." Of the existing instruments for measuring job satisfaction, the best-documented and most popular is the Job Descriptive Index.

Job satisfaction is not related to productivity in any direct way. In addition, the assumed relationship between satisfaction and absenteeism has received very little empirical support. More needs to be known about the *process* of withdrawing from work.

The relationship between job satisfaction and the quality of life is unclear, but in our culture, work-related emotions may not have a strong relationship to more general life satisfactions.

REFERENCES

Arvey, R. D., & Mussio, S. J. Job expectations and valences of job rewards for culturally disadvantaged and advantaged clerical employees. *Journal of Applied Psychology*, 1974, *59*, 230–232.

Bloom, R., & Barry, J. R. Determinants of work attitudes among Negroes. *Journal of Applied Psychology*, 1967, *51*, 291–294.

Brayfield, A. H., & Crockett, W. H. Employee attitudes and employee performance. *Psychological Bulletin*, 1955, *52*, 396–424.

Edwards, A. L. *Techniques of attitude scale construction*. New York: Appleton-Century-Crofts, 1957.

Ewen, R. B. Some determinants of job satisfaction: A study of the generality of Herzberg's theory. *Journal of Applied Psychology*, 1964, *48*, 161–163.

Ewen, R. B. Weighting components of job satisfaction. *Journal of Applied Psychology*, 1967, 51, 68–73.

Ewen, R. B., Smith, P. C., Hulin, C. L., & Locke, E. A. An empirical test of the Herzberg 2-factor theory. *Journal of Applied Psychology*, 1966, *50*, 544–550.

Frankenhauser, M. Overstimulation—a threat to the quality of life. In *Man in the communications system of the future*. Stockholm: Swedish Cabinet Office, Secretariat for Future Studies, 1974.

Gavin, J. F., & Ewen, R. B. Racial differences in job attitudes and performance: Some theoretical considerations and empirical findings. *Personnel Psychology*, 1974, *27*, 455–464.

Gechman, A. S., & Wiener, Y. Job involvement and satisfaction as related to mental health and personal time devoted to work. *Journal of Applied Psychology*, 1975, *60*, 521–523.

Georgopolous, B. S., Mahoney, G. M., & Jones, N. W. A path-goal approach to productivity. *Journal of Applied Psychology*, 1957, *41*, 345–353.

Glenn, N. D., Taylor, P. A., & Weaver, C. N. Age and job satisfaction among males and females: A multivariate, multisurvey study. *Journal of Applied Psychology*, 1977, *62*, 189–193.

Guilford, J. P. *Psychometric methods*. New York: McGraw-Hill, 1954.

Herzberg, F., Mausner, B., Peterson, R. O., & Capwell, D. F. *Job attitudes: Review of research and opinion*. Pittsburgh: Pittsburgh Psychological Services, 1957..

Herzberg, F., Mausner, B., & Snyderman, B. B. *The Motivation to Work*. New York: Wiley, 1959.

Hinrichs, J. R., & Mischkind, L. A. Empirical and theoretical limitations of the two-factor hypothesis of job satisfaction. *Journal of Applied Psychology*, 1967, *51*, 191–200.

Hoppock, R. *Job satisfaction.* New York: Harper, 1935.

Hulin, C. L., & Smith, P. C. A linear model of job satisfaction. *Journal of Applied Psychology,* 1965, *49,* 209–216.

Jones, A. P., James, L. R., Bruni, J. R., & Sells, S. B. Black-white differences in work environment perceptions and job satisfaction and its correlates. *Personnel Psychology,* 1977, *30,* 5–16.

Katzell, R. A. Industrial psychology. In *Annual Review of Psychology.* Palo Alto, Calif.: Annual Review, 1957.

King, N. Clarification and evaluation of the two factor theory of job satisfaction. *Psychological Bulletin,* 1970, *74,* 18–31.

Landsberger, H. A. *Hawthorne revisited: Management and the worker, its critics and developments in human relations in industry.* Ithaca, N.Y.: New York State School of Industrial and Labor Relations, 1958.

Landy, F. J. An opponent process theory of job satisfaction. *Journal of Applied Psychology,* 1978, *63,* 533–547.

Lawler, E. E. Job attitudes and employee motivation: Theory, research and practice. *Personnel Psychology,* 1970, *23,* 233–237.

Lawler, E. E. *Motivation in work organizations.* Monterey, Calif.: Brooks/Cole, 1973.

Liddell, W. W., & Solomon, R. J. A total and stochastic test of the transitivity postulate underlying expectancy theory. *Organizational Behavior and Human Performance,* 1977, *19,* 311–324.

Locke, E. A. Job satisfaction and job performance: A theoretical analysis. *Organizational Behavior and Human Performance,* 1970, *5,* 484–500.

Locke, E. A. The nature and causes of job satisfaction. In M. Dunnette (Ed.), *Handbook of industrial and organizational psychology.* Chicago: Rand McNally, 1976.

Locke, E. A. "Job satisfaction reconsidered"—reconsidered. *American Psychologist,* 1978, *33,* 854–855.

London, M., Crandall, R., & Seals, G. W. The contribution of job and leisure satisfaction to the quality of life. *Journal of Applied Psychology.* 1977, *62,* 328–334.

Manhardt, P. J. Job orientation of male and female college graduates in business. *Personnel Psychology,* 1972, *25,* 361–368.

Maslow, A. H. A theory of motivation. *Psychological Review,* 1943, *50,* 370–396.

Mirvis, P. H., & Lawler, E. E. Measuring the financial impact of employee attitudes. *Journal of Applied Psychology,* 1977, *62,* 1–8.

Mobley, W. H., Horner, S. O., & Hollingsworth, A. T. An evaluation of precursors of hospital employee turnover. *Journal of Applied Psychology,* 1978, *63,* 408–414.

Mobley, W. H., & Locke, E. A. The relationship of value importance to satisfaction. *Organizational Behavior and Human Performance,* 1970, *5,* 463–483.

Munsterberg, H. *Psychology, general and applied.* New York: Appleton, 1914.

Mikes, P. S., & Hulin, C. L. Use of importance as a weighting component of job satisfaction. *Journal of Applied Psychology,* 1968, *52,* 394–398.

Nicholson, N., Brown, C. A., & Chadwick-Jones, J. K. Absence from work and job satisfaction. *Journal of Applied Psychology*, 1976, *61*, 728–737.

Nicholson, N., Brown, C. A., & Chadwick-Jones, J. K. Absence from work and personal characteristics. *Journal of Applied Psychology*, 1977, *62*, 319–327.

Nord, W. R. Job satisfaction reconsidered. *American Psychologist*, 1977, *22*, 1026–1035.

Oates, W. E. *Confessions of a workaholic.* Cleveland: World, 1971.

Porter, L. W., & Lawler, E. E. *Managerial attitudes and performance.* Homewood, Ill.: Dorsey, 1968.

Porter, L. W., & Steers, R. M. Organization, work and personal factors in employee turnover and absenteeism. *Psychological Bulletin*, 1973, *80*, 151–176.

Robinson, J. P., Athanasiou, R., & Head, K. *Measures of occupational attitudes and occupational characteristics.* Ann Arbor, Mich.: Survey Research Center, 1969.

Roethlisberger, F. J., & Dixon, W. J. *Management and the worker.* Cambridge, Mass.: Harvard University Press, 1939.

Schaffer, R. H. Job satisfaction as related to need satisfaction in work. *Psychological Monographs*, 1953, *67* (#304).

Sherif, M., & Sherif, C. W. *Social psychology.* New York: Harper, 1969.

Slocum, J. W., & Strawser, R. H. Racial differences in job attitudes. *Journal of Applied Psychology*, 1972, *56*, 28–32.

Smith, P. C., Kendall, L. M., & Hulin, C. L. *The measurement of satisfaction in work and retirement; a strategy for the study of attitudes.* Chicago: Rand McNally, 1969.

Smith, P. C., Smith, O. W., & Rollo, J. Factor structure for blacks and whites of the Job Descriptive Index and its discrimination of job satisfaction. *Journal of Applied Psychology*, 1974, *59*, 99–100.

Steers, R. M., and Rhodes, S. R. Major influences on employee attendance: A process model. *Journal of Applied Psychology*, 1978, *63*, 391–407.

Taylor, F. W. *Principles of scientific management.* New York: Harper, 1947.

Torgerson, W. S. *Theory and methods of scaling.* New York: Wiley, 1958.

Vroom, V. *Work and motivation.* New York: Wiley, 1964.

Wall, T. D., & Payne, R. Are deficiency scores deficient? *Journal of Applied Psychology*, 1973, *58*, 322–326.

Wanous, J., & Lawler, E. E. Measurement and meaning of job satisfaction. *Journal of Applied Psychology*, 1972, *56*, 95–105.

Weaver, C. N. Black-white differences in attitudes toward job characteristics. *Journal of Applied Psychology*, 1975, 60, 438–441.

Weaver, C. N. Relationships among pay, race, sex, occupational prestige, supervision, work autonomy, and job satisfaction in a national sample. *Personnel Psychology*, 1977, *30*, 437–445.

Weaver, C. N., & Holmes, S. L. A comparative study of work satisfaction of females with full-time employment and full-time housekeeping. *Journal of Applied Psychology*, 1975, *60*, 117–118.

CHAPTER **11**
The Supervisor as Leader

The previous chapters on work motivation and job satisfaction considered the relationship between the individual worker and the physical and psychological environment. There are, however, at least two major intervening influences to take into account before we can understand work behavior: the supervisor and the organization. This chapter will deal with the supervisor in the role of "leader," and consequently will consider many of the problems related to the study of leadership. First, a very general historical perspective of leadership research will be presented. Then some organizational influences that interact with leader behavior will be introduced. Managerial and supervisory roles will be compared and contrasted, and the current status of selected models of leadership will be considered.

Of all the subjects treated in the book, the theme of this chapter is perhaps the most elusive. Leadership, as a topic, cuts across many of the formal or traditional areas of psychology. To name but a few, it has roots in social psychology, personality theory, group dynamics, organizational theory, and industrial psychology. We are concerned with leadership as it appears in industrial settings. Therefore, the literature dealing with group dynamics, role theory, and so on, will be mentioned only briefly. This is not meant to imply that these topics are unimportant; they simply do not serve the immediate purposes of the chapter, which is examining the role of the leader in industrial behavior. Before presenting theories and approaches to leadership, some clarifications and definitions are necessary.

SOME BASIC ISSUES IN THE STUDY OF LEADERSHIP

Leader Effectiveness versus Leader Emergence

The effectiveness/emergence distinction has been a source of confusion for a number of years. As a dependent variable, leader emergence is quite different from leader effectiveness. In the former case, we are describing the relationship between the behavior and/or characteristics of an individual and the probability that she will emerge as a leader (either formal or informal) in a demand situation of some kind. In the latter case, that of leader effectiveness, we are describing the relationship between the behavior and or characteristics of an individual in a leadership position (either formal or informal) and some form of outcome that is valued by a group or organization. In addition, both of these variables, emergence and effectiveness, may be affected differently by situational factors such as the nature of the group, stress, or the management philosophy of the organization. Crooked or incompetent political leaders are examples of ineffective leaders who emerge. Studies that have examined leader emergence seem to use a trait approach to the problem. They attempt to find characteristics or traits of individuals that are correlated with the probability that a person will emerge as a leader. On the other hand, studies of leader effectiveness seem to take a quite different approach. Instead of looking at traits of emerging leaders, they examine the *behavior* of leaders for clues to behavioral correlates of effectiveness.

We have used a lot of terms in the preceding paragraph that must be defined before we continue. The first term, of course, would be *leader*. For the purposes of this chapter, Fiedler's (1967) definition is most suitable: a leader is *"the individual in the group given the task of directing and coordinating task-relevant group activities, or who, in the absence of a designated leader, carries the primary responsibility for performing these functions in the group"* (p. 8). Some other definitions are necessary to distinguish among *attempted* leadership, *successful* leadership, and *effective* leadership. Bass (1960) has done a good job of separating these terms:

1. *Attempted leadership:* Person A accepts the goal of changing person B, and, in fact, can be observed attempting to change person B.
2. *Successful leadership:* Person B changes his behavior as a function of person A's effort.
3. *Effective leadership:* As a function of person B's behavior change, person B will be more satisfied, will be better rewarded, or will have attained an important goal.

These will be important distinctions to keep in mind when looking at studies of leadership. The way in which leadership is defined (i.e., attempted, successful, or effective) should have systematic effects on the relationship between leadership behaviors and individual or organizational outcomes. For example, the relationship between group productivity and attempted leadership should be quite different from the relationship between group productivity and effective leadership.

Another distinction has been made by Fiedler (1967). He distinguishes between *leadership behavior* and *leadership style*. Leadership behavior refers to the particular acts of a leader. Leadership style refers to the underlying need structure of the individual leader that motivates various behaviors in leadership situations. Fiedler sees leadership behaviors as differing from one situation to another, while leadership styles remain relatively constant across situations. This implies that the way a need structure will find expression in socially acceptable behaviors in a given situation will vary. Since what is socially acceptable changes from situation to situation, there may appear to be little consistency in individual *behavior* across situations. The more enduring *style* is the key to consistency.

Let us go back for a moment to the effectiveness/emergence distinction. It may be that the trait approach is more suited to the description and understanding of leader emergence. Megargee, Bogart, and Anderson (1966) looked at the effect of the personality dimension of *dominance* on leader emergence. They discovered that dominance may play an important role in who emerges as a leader. When the leadership process *itself* was emphasized, the more dominant individual was more likely to become leader. When the successful completion of the task was emphasized, however, dominance had little or no effect on who emerged as leader; that is, the leader who emerged was just as likely to be low on a dominance measure as high on that measure. It is unlikely that any *one* approach (either the trait *or* the behavioral) will be able to exist without the other. The behavioral approach cannot stand on its own without some notion of enduring characteristics of the individual, as the Megargee et al. study indicates. It is not a very great leap to consider leadership style as similar to what was meant by the word "trait." It might be argued that trait means a consistent way of *behaving*, while a *style* implies an underlying need structure. The important point is that there are probably enduring characteristics of the individual that systematically interact with situational factors to affect behavior in *certain* leadership situations. Thus, for example, the theory of the "authoritarian" personality (Adorno et al., 1950) proposed that the individual high in authoritarian characteristics would behave autocratically in a situation where he had power over others, but behave in a submissive manner when others were accepted as authority figures. Either aggressive or submissive behaviors were predicted depending on the situation.

Content versus Process

Recall the distinction made in Chapter 9 between the content and process aspects of theories of work motivation. This may be a useful distinction to extend to the leadership research. An analog of the process-content distinction in the leadership area might be the trait-behavioral distinction. The trait approach seems more related to content considerations; that is,

FIGURE 11–1

> Bert Lance Resigns
>
> The Shah Leaves Iran
>
> Billy Martin Axed as Manager of the Yankees

what are the characteristics of an individual that contribute to effective leadership? The behavioral approach, on the other hand, seems to emphasize process aspects; that is, how does the individual leader utilize unique characteristics to yield effective leadership behaviors?

Hollander and Julian (1969) carried the argument a little farther. They contended that most studies of leadership concern the *effect* of leadership rather than the leadership *process*. They further proposed that the fatal flaw of most theories of leadership is the emphasis on *parts* of the leadership process rather than the entire process. They concluded that advances will not be made in understanding leader behavior until the entire process is examined. This entire process may include both emergence and acceptance of a leader. Another aspect that may be included is the *decline* of a leader. We know something about how leaders are chosen or appointed; we know something about how leaders behave in varying situations; we know little or nothing about the conditions or behaviors leading to a decline or fall from power. Figure 11–1 reminds us of some recent examples of leadership decline. In short, it will probably be useful to consider something like a "leadership life span" or leadership cycle that would include emergence, performance, and decline. In terms of the content/process distinction, the most acceptable theory of leadership behavior will have to satisfy *both* content and process requirements.

Laboratory Studies versus Field Studies

Leadership studies vary in terms of the settings in which they are carried out. Many are done in the laboratory or some simulated environment and some smaller number in field settings. The advantages and disadvantages of the various designs have been outlined in an earlier chapter. The two approaches are not, nor should they be, mutually exclusive. There is a necessary inductive-deductive sequencing of scientific investigation. One might start from an inductive position and study the situational characteristics and leadership behaviors that can be seen in intact groups in field settings. As an example of this, consider the research supporting Fiedler's leadership theory. Fiedler sampled many diverse groups—basketball teams, bomber crews, the Belgian Navy, and work groups in a steel mill. On the basis of the results of these studies, Fiedler constructed a theory of leadership effectiveness. This theory has been taken into the laboratory to investigate several hypotheses. Other investigators have attempted to test Fiedler's propositions in the more controlled environment of the laboratory. This is an example of an inductive-deductive sequence. Variations emerging from these laboratory studies suggest other studies in the field to identify important variables in the leadership model. This would be an example of the deductive-inductive sequence. In fact, what we have described is more like a spiral sequence than a unilateral sequence. This spiral is depicted in Figure 11–2. Using such an approach, one takes advantage of the strengths of the laboratory and the field in structuring and refining a complex set of interrelationships that may become a theory.

The *results* of a particular study or experiment should be viewed as a dependent variable—not just the "criterion" data gathered, but the *total*

FIGURE 11–2

The Inductive-Hypothetico-Deductive Spiral

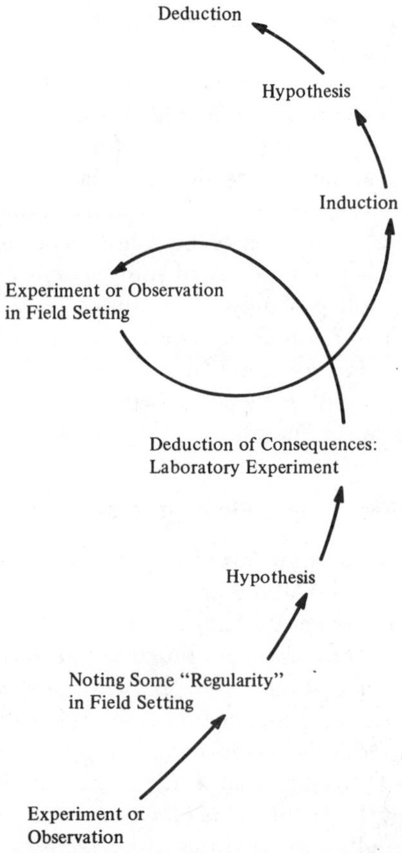

Source: Cattell, R. B. (Ed.) *Handbook of multivariate experimental psychology*, p. 16. Copyright © 1966 by Rand McNally College Publishing Company.

set of results and conclusions. Our concern should be for describing the independent or antecedent variables that led to these results. Lab setting versus field setting might be viewed as an independent variable. The same would be true of male versus female subjects, student versus nonstudent subjects, stressful versus nonstressful conditions, etc. In leadership research, a lab study done with female freshman college students who have known one another for 15 minutes is a "valid" study. It certainly tells us something about the nature of intragroup interactions and leader-member interactions. But this study is only *one* of a number which might have been done. Another study with the same hypotheses might have been done in a steel mill with loading dock work groups who have been together for 15 years. Such a study would also tell us something about the nature of intragroup interactions and leader-member interactions. It is not likely that the results of the two studies will be exactly the same. This does not mean that one of the studies is "good" and the other "bad." They can both help us describe the construct of leadership.

The Supervisory Role

The most obvious symbol of leadership in the industrial setting is the supervisor. It might be useful to take a look at the kinds of activities included in the supervisory role before considering theories of leadership. Descriptions of supervisory responsibilities vary from a one-dimensional description (e.g., the primary responsibility of a supervisor is the motivation of subordinates) to elaborate job descriptions including dozens of major and minor job duties. We will sample some of these treatments of supervisory responsibility.

Mann (1965) implies that the major responsibility of a supervisor is a motivational one:

> One of the basic problems of organizations, then, is how to reconcile, coordinate, or integrate member needs or goals with organizational requirements and objectives. This social-psychological aspect of the role of the supervisor in the complex organization is of key importance; it is here that the supervisor must deal with the motivational problem of relating man and system. (p. 71)

Oldham (1976) has gone even further, suggesting exactly *how* the supervisor goes about motivating the subordinate. He studied the ways in which managers interacted with subordinates and found six basic types of motivational interaction: *rewarding, punishing, setting goals, designing feedback systems, placing personnel,* and *designing job systems.* This is a good description of most of the supervisory activities that directly affect subordinates. As such, it may be a good description of leadership. It is important to distinguish between general management responsibilities, such as budgeting, and leadership responsibilities, such as motivating. This chapter will deal with leadership rather than general management.

Bass, Valenzi, Farrow, and Solomon (1975) looked at the job of leader from a different perspective. While Oldham examined *what* leaders did, Bass et al. were more interested in *how* leaders accomplished their supervisory responsibilities. They were able to describe five distinct *styles* of leadership: direction, negotiation, consultation, participation, and delegation.

French and Raven (1959) proposed a third way of examining the leadership process. They suggested that one should examine the different types of power available to a leader and how that power is typically used. The kinds of power commonly available to a supervisor are as follows:

1. *Reward Power.* The potential of a supervisor to mediate or dispense rewards to a subordinate is reward power. It should be clear from our discussion of work motivation that this is a demonstrable source of power for the supervisor. If rewards valuable to the subordinate can be controlled, the behavior of that subordinate can be influenced.

2. *Coercive Power.* The potential of a supervisor to mediate or dispense punishments to a subordinate is coercive power. Historically, it was the prerogative of the first-line supervisor or foreman to "hire and fire"; the power to "fire" is, of course, an implied threat and a form of coercive power.

3. *Legitimate Power.* The *right* of a supervisor to influence a subordinate and the obligation of a subordinate to accept that influence is legitimate power. McGregor (1967) referred to this as the "right" to govern, or the "consent of the governed."

4. *Referent Power.* The identification of the subordinate with the supervisor is referent power. In this case, the subordinate accepts the supervisor's goals as her own. McGregor refers to this form of power as the "power of example." He further points to this particular form of power as the best example of the nature of the leadership process. The worker perceives the supervisor achieving desired goals; the identification of the worker with the supervisor provides an attractive means for achieving those same desired goals; the worker will continue to identify with the supervisor as long as movement toward those desired goals is perceived. As soon as movement toward those goals stops, identification stops. McGregor uses this paradigm to highlight his belief that leadership is no more a property of the individual "than gravitation is a property of objects" (p. 145). A recent study serves to verify this type of power base. Weiss (1977) studied 130 supervisors and their immediate superiors. He found that the lower-level supervisors tended to imitate the leadership style of their superiors when they viewed their superior as being both competent and successful. Interestingly enough, the probability of supervisors imitating their superiors was *not* related to the number of rewards they received from their superiors. Perhaps the songs are right—love can't be bought!

5. *Expert Power.* The knowledge or expertise that a supervisor has in a special area is expert power.

This has been a popular and useful way of viewing the acquisition and exercise of power. Recently some of the categories have been combined to form a new base of power. Referent power and expert power have been combined to form *incremental power* or *incremental influence.*

Incremental influence is considered to be that degree of control a leader has over subordinates that cannot be explained simply on the basis of prescribed power or reward/punishment power. In the past it has been called *charisma*, or *magnetism*. It is the power that the leader is able to accrue. An important characteristic of incremental influence is that it is the interaction of referent and expert power and considered as a *sixth power base*, not just another name for one of the existing power bases.

A study by Student (1968) might serve to clarify the nature of incremental influence. The study was done in a large manufacturing organization in which 486 hourly employees described the forms of power exercised by their first-line supervisors. Student found that incremental influence was positively related to four of eight production measures, while referent power by itself was related to withdrawal measures (absenteeism, etc.), and expert power was related to accidents. Interestingly enough, legitimate power was *unrelated* to performance measures. The relationship between accidents and expert power makes sense, he suggests, because a good deal of variance in accidents is due to a breakdown in technical knowledge. Therefore, a supervisor who does not have the knowledge base (expertise) necessary to rely on as a source of power will also be less likely to provide the technical knowledge base necessary for the reduction of accidents.

The study by Student poses some interesting questions about the choice of a power base in applied settings. If we are to understand the nature of leadership completely, there are a few things that we will have to know about the use and abuse of power. For example, if a particular leader has more than one power base to work from in a given situation, which one is most appropriate? Do situational and/or personal characteristics modify the decision as to which power base to use? Kipnis and Cosentino (1969) conducted a study aimed at answering some of these questions. They studied the range of social power at the disposal of supervisors for the correction of subordinate behavior. They also investigated the personal and situational factors that could possibly influence the use of those powers. They gathered data from five different manufacturing companies. The participants in the study were 131 blue-collar, hourly-paid supervisors. The supervisors were asked to describe a supervision problem they had recently encountered. They were also asked to describe the corrective action they took. The problems fell into one of four categories:

1. *Attitude:* Lack of interest on the part of the subordinate.
2. *Discipline:* Subordinate disobeyed a company rule.
3. *Work:* Subordinate failed to maintain minimum standards.
4. *Appearance:* Subordinate was inappropriately dressed.

The corrective actions used by the supervisors to deal with these problems fell into one of eight categories:

1. *Verbal:* Diagnostic or corrective talk.
2. *Increased supervision:* Extra instruction, inspection, and so on.
3. *Situational change:* Reassignment, transfer, and so on.

4. *Penalty:* Reprimand, extra work, reduced privileges.
5. *Refer:* Referred to superior or personnel office.
6. *Written warning.*
7. *Termination.*
8. *Example:* Supervisor acted as a model.

Kipnis and Cosentino found that diagnostic talks were used for problems of attitude or discipline, while increased supervision was used for problems of work. Complex problems were likely to be handled by a transfer. Less experienced supervisors were more likely to refer a problem to their superior or the personnel office. Finally, as the size of the work group increased, the use of the official written warnings also increased. The major importance of these findings is that the decision as to which form of power to exercise in the solution of a particular problem seemed to be as much a function of the situation and of the individual as a function of the particular problem. While the categories of power may be slightly better defined than those currently used by first-line supervisors, there are very few supervisors who do not have to make a decision relating to the way in which a subordinate will be "handled" (i.e., coddled or clobbered, persuaded or punished).

In a later study, Goodstadt and Kipnis (1970) suggest that supervisory self-confidence has an effect on the power choice for a problem solution. They found that less confident leaders depended more heavily on formally prescribed powers, while the more confident supervisors used both informal and formal power but more often attempted to persuade subordinates informally. Interestingly enough, Rosen and Jerdee (1974) found that managers tend to respond more to the severity of the *consequences* of a rule violation than the violation itself. This, unfortunately, suggests to the employee that rules may be broken as long as the consequences are not disastrous. The unfortunate part of this principle is that workers have complete control over the act of violation but seldom have any control over the consequences of the violation.

We have presented three approaches to leadership. One is based on the things supervisors do to subordinates (e.g., personal rewards), a second is based on *how* they do it (e.g., negotiation), and a third is based on the *type* of power they use to accomplish their ends (e.g., referent power). There are many other approaches to leadership based on similar taxonomies. Unfortunately, they all *imply* a theory of leadership without ever explicitly stating it. In the next section, we will consider formal attempts to describe leaders, the leadership process, and leader effectiveness.

An Overview of Leadership Research

We often identify someone who is successful at something and ask that person to set forth a package of guidelines that will enable us to be as successful as they. We ask the 100-year-old man how he managed to stay alive so long. He will answer one of two ways. He will either say, "That's a stupid question, ask my doctor," or, "I have been smoking 5 cigars and eating 2 pounds of turnips every day since my 14th birthday." We have a tendency to ask the same questions of "successful" leaders: "What makes successful leaders?" Unfortunately, we usually get answers. The following description of a successful leader is taken from a book written by Field Marshal Montgomery on the topic of leadership.

> . . . the leader must have infectious optimism, and the determination to perse-vere in the face of difficulties. He must also radiate confidence, relying on moral and spiritual principles and resources to work out rightly even when he himself is not too certain of the material outcome. He must have a sound judgment in which others will have confidence, and a good knowledge of human nature. He must be able to see his problems truly and whole. Self-control is a vital component of his make-up. (1961, p. 11)

It might have been just as useful had the Field Marshal described the successful leader as one who smokes five cigars and eats two pounds of turnips every day.

The Montgomery paragraph is specific about the expected qualities of leaders and the nature of leadership effectiveness. If only the phenomenon of leadership were that simple, the chapter could stop here. Unfortunately, as is true with the many areas in psychology, the more closely we examine the problem, the more complex it becomes.

Dubin et al. (1965) have categorized some philosophies that have had a hand in shaping leadership research and practice:

1. *Scientific management:* Work simplification improves productivity; a supervisor who simplifies work is effective.
2. *Welfare capitalism:* Humane treatment of workers improves devotion to the organization; devotion will take the form of higher output; there-fore, the supervisor who practices humane treatment is effective.
3. *Group dynamics:* Participation improves commitment; commitment improves productivity; therefore, a supervisor who increases worker participation in decision making is effective.
4. *Incentive systems:* Worker self-interest in payoffs overrides all other considerations of the worker; payoffs are related (or should be related) to performance; to the degree that the supervisor can focus the attention of the worker on payoffs and ensure that payoffs are related to perfor-mance, the supervisor is effective.

While these descriptions are grossly oversimplified, you will recognize the thrust of each of them in the theories or models of leadership that will be presented shortly. You will note that each of the approaches assumes certain characteristics or capacities in the supervisor. For example, scientific management assumes the supervisor is capable of simplifying the work; welfare capitalism assumes the supervisor is understanding and supportive. Sets of assumptions about the characteristics of good leaders provide the basis for one approach to the study of leadership. This is known as the "trait" approach. This approach assumes that there are certain qualities or traits closely related to leadership effectiveness. Another way of saying the same thing would be that leadership effectiveness is a property of the person with little or no variation from situation to situation; that is, a person who effectively leads in one situation is likely to lead effectively in *all* situations.

Research following the trait tradition has examined both psychological and physical characteristics. A partial list of characteristics studied appears in Figure 11–3. Most of the research takes the same general form. The major hypothesis reads something like this: "Effective leaders will be *XXXXXer* than ineffective leaders." In the space filled with *Xs* you can fill in any of the characteristics appearing in Figure 11–3. In addition,

FIGURE 11–3
Some Characteristics of Leaders That Have Been Studied

Adjustment	Height	Psychoticism
Age	Intelligence	Popularity
Altruism	Introversion	Responsibility
Ambition	Judgment	Scholarship
Authoritarianism	Kindness	Self-confidence
Compatibility	Lability	Sensitivity
Conservatism	Masculinity	Sex
Deference	Maturity	Sociability
Dominance	Motivation	Stature
Empathy	Neuroticism	Supportiveness
Esteem	Originality	Surgency
Extroversion	Perceptiveness	Verbal facility
Fear of failure	Persistence	Vocabulary usage
		Weight

the hypothesis is generally a linear one, though not always stated as such. This means that one can never have too much of *XXXX*; as *X* increases, leadership effectiveness increases. The more the better.

Brown (1954) quotes Tredgold on the topic of leader characteristics: "The longer and more comprehensive the list of qualities, the more obvious it must be that their possession would be of no use as a junior leader in industry, for he would inevitably be in demand elsewhere as a Prime Minister, or maybe as an Archangel" (p. 219). Citing as examples Hitler, Napoleon, and Cromwell, Brown concludes that insanity or injustice, per se, do not prevent an individual from being an effective leader "so long as he is insane in the appropriate direction."

Fiedler (1967) has an interesting insight into the way tests of the trait approach have been carried out. He notes these studies controlled everything *but* leader attributes; therefore, these attributes were the only things that could *possibly* emerge as related to leader effectiveness, since all other variables were held constant. If, in fact, these other variables (such as the nature of the group led or the situation) had been systematically varied, traits might have been less important.

Both logical and empirical investigations of leadership and leader effectiveness from the trait approach have been disappointing. Reviews of the literature by Stogdill (1948) and Mann (1959) have demonstrated little or no relationship between personality factors and leadership effectiveness. More recent reviews have come to the same conclusion (Hollander and Julian, 1969).

Disenchantment with the trait approach gave rise to the "behavioral approach." The essence of this approach is to determine what effective leaders *do*, rather than concentrating on their personal characteristics or traits. Extensive survey and observational studies are conducted to determine the activities of people in leadership positions. These activities are then systematically categorized. The resulting categories are subsequently used to form profiles or descriptions of leaders. The profiles or descriptions are then related to the judged effectiveness of the leaders as well as to other organizational outcomes such as turnover, grievances, or worker morale. As a line of inquiry, the behavioral approach has been considerably more fruitful than the trait approach. It is still generating new lines of research and theory.

Hollander and Julian (1969) suggest that the failure of the trait approach and the relative success of the behavioral approach has been due to the unwillingness or the inability of the trait theorists to distinguish between leadership as a process and the leader as a person. Current theories of leadership emphasize both the dynamics of leadership effectiveness (leadership as a process) and situational factors affecting leader effectiveness. Another distinction between the earlier studies of leadership and current research is the nature of the dependent variable. As Dubin suggested in 1965, there are many possible outcomes related to leadership, and only one of them is productivity. Outcomes such as subordinate satisfaction, subordinate interest in long-time membership in the organization, and the effectiveness of peer cooperation are also affected.

Because of the potential pervasiveness of the effect of supervisors and managers on overall organizational "health," the study of leadership behaviors and effectiveness has assumed great importance in industrial psychology.

THEORIES OF LEADERSHIP

Leadership models are much more tentative and speculative than models of selection or work motivation. This is because of the inherent complexity of the phenomenon of leadership. If we want to consider leadership, we have to consider the abilities of the leader, the motivation of the leader, the organizational context in which the leading is done, the nature of the work group, and so on. It is like having a theory of a plumber or a carpenter. Leadership represents a capsule view of the whole of industrial/

organizational psychology. No wonder it is difficult to come up with a single model that efficiently explains leader behavior. In this section, we will present some of the current approaches to leadership. The presentation is intended to be representative rather than exhaustive. The choice of leadership models is not meant to imply that those chosen are "good" and those not chosen "bad." We have made our choices on the basis of approaches that are: (1) most divergent, (2) representative of a class of studies, and (3) accompanied by data.

The Ohio State Studies

In the early 1950s, researchers at Ohio State University abandoned the trait approach to leadership and adopted the behavioral approach. This approach is well described as follows:

> Focusing on the kinds of behavior engaged in by people in leadership roles, these investigators developed over 1,800 items (for example, "He calls the group together to talk things over"; "He knows about it when something goes wrong") descriptive of what supervisors do in their leadership roles. These items were then classified into ten broad categories of leader behavior (for example, initiation, domination, evaluation, communication). Questionnaires were developed by means of which leader behavior could be described and scored on these ten dimensions. Each supervisor was described in terms of how frequently (for example, always, often, . . . never) he did what each item stated. Repeated use of these questionnaires in a variety of leader-group situations (foreman-worker, executive-subordinate, school principal-teacher, university department head-professor, aircraft commander-crew, submarine officer-crew) showed that these ten categories overlapped with one another and that the items could be grouped into two more basic dimensions of leader behavior. These were labeled *consideration* and *initiating structure*. (Fleishman, 1967, p. 362)

Since the introduction of the Ohio State studies, literally dozens of studies have been done in an attempt to determine how these two dimensions relate to leadership effectiveness, group productivity, group morale, and other relevant dependent variables. Before reviewing this research, we should define the two dimensions in question.

> *Consideration.* Includes behavior indicating mutual trust, respect, and a certain warmth and rapport between the supervisor and his group. This does not mean that this dimension reflects a superficial "pat-on-the-back, first-name calling" kind of human relations behavior. This dimension seems to emphasize a deeper concern for group members' needs, and includes such behavior as allowing subordinates more participation in decision making and encouraging more two-way communication.
>
> *Structure.* Includes behavior in which the supervisor organizes and defines group activities and his relation to the group. Thus, he defines the role he expects each member to assume, assigns tasks, plans ahead, establishes ways of getting things done, and pushes for production. This dimension seems to emphasize overt attempts to achieve organizational goals (Fleishman & Harris, 1962, pp. 43–44)

The similarity between these two terms and other terms can be readily seen. Consideration is very much like "employee-centered supervision," "supportive," "participative," and "human relations-oriented" supervision. Initiating structure, on the other hand, is most similar in meaning to terms like "job-centered," "directive," and "task-oriented" supervision.

Two basic instruments or questionnaires have been used to measure the degree of consideration or initiating structure present in a particular supervisor. The first of these is known as the LOQ (Leadership Opinion Questionnaire) and asks the supervisor questions dealing with ideal methods of supervision. The second instrument is known as the LBDQ (Leader Behavior Description Questionnaire) and is usually completed by a subordinate whose task is to describe how the supervisor behaves in varying situations. Some sample items from the LOQ appear in Figure 11–4.

The general findings of the Ohio State studies have been replicated a number of different times, with different instruments, different theoretical approaches, and different subject populations. Although most of the follow-up studies have proposed additional factors, consideration and initiating structure usually account for approximately 80 percent of the variance in leader behavior. One study (Tscheulin, 1971) attempted to replicate the findings of the Ohio State group after 20 years and in a different culture. When leader behavior was measured in German industry, the factors that emerged were very clearly consideration and initiating structure. There is little doubt that consideration and initiating structure represent reliable phenomena in the measurement of leader behavior.

The independence of the two dimensions is an important practical and theoretical issue. Various studies have shown consideration and initiating structure to be positively correlated, uncorrelated, and negatively correlated. Theoretically, the direction and sign of the relationship could tell us a good deal about the dynamics of leadership. If the two dimensions are positively correlated, this could be taken as evidence for the existence of a "style" as described earlier, a habitual way of responding which pervades most situations. If the two dimensions are negatively correlated, we may be observing sets of behaviors that are mutually exclusive; if this were

FIGURE 11–4

Sample Items from the LOQ

Structure	*Consideration*
1. Put the welfare of your unit above the welfare of any person	1. Give in to your subordinates in your discussions with them
2. Encourage after-duty work by persons of your unit	2. Back up what persons under you do
3. Try out your own new ideas in the unit	3. Get approval of persons under you on important matters before going ahead

Source: Fleishman, E. A. *Leadership opinion questionnaire.* Chicago: Science Research Associates, 1960.

the case, it would be virtually impossible for a leader high on initiating structure to exhibit considerate behavior. If the two dimensions are uncorrelated, the variations in leader behavior are more numerous, and the effects of various combinations of consideration and initiating structure on work group behavior would be much more complex. But what can be concluded from such divergent research findings?

Weissenberg and Kavanaugh (1972) provide a possible solution to the dilemma. After a careful review of all the studies dealing with the relationship between consideration and initiating structure, they discovered that the instrument used to gather information on leader behavior had a lot to do with whether or not the dimensions were independent. The discrepancy seemed to be related to whether the LOQ or the LBDQ was used. In 24 studies using the LOQ, they found 3 significantly positive correlations, 5 significantly negative, and 16 nonsignificant relationships. Of 48 studies using the LBDQ, 34 of the correlations between consideration and initiating structure were significantly positive, 2 were significantly negative, and 12 were nonsignificant. Remember that the LBDQ records the subordinate's description of the supervisor's actual behavior. One interpretation of these data, the one preferred by Weissenberg and Kavanaugh, is that although leaders would prefer to believe that these two dimensions are independent, that is not how they behave in a work setting. An equally plausible explanation might be that even though supervisors can function in such a way that their considerate behaviors are unrelated to their initiating structure behaviors, subordinates cannot perceive the two dimensions as separate. It might be that subordinates have a general perception of supervisors' activities.

This general perception would be much like the "halo" in ratings that we examined in the earlier chapter on criterion development. If the problem is one of perceptions, it is not clear who has the problem, the supervisor or the subordinate. The problem is compounded by the fact that the instructions to the supervisor on the LOQ are to report what *should* be done in various situations, while the subordinate is told in filling out the LBDQ to describe the *typical* behavior of the supervisor.

A review by Korman (1966) considered all the studies in which consideration and initiating structure were treated as independent or antecedent variables. He found little relationship between either of the two dimensions and criterion variables when the LOQ was used. On the other hand, there were many significant relationships between consideration and performance when the LBDQ was used. This seems to point to the supervisor as the one with the discrepant perception of leadership behavior. At the very least, the results point out that different things are being measured by the LOQ and LBDQ. From these results it is impossible to determine if the supervisor actually has a *behavioral style* that pervades all situations, or is just *perceived* as having one.

Even the notion of a general style is not as simple as it first seems. Fleishman and Harris (1962) gathered data in a truck-manufacturing company and looked at the relationship between supervisory behavior and dependent measures such as turnover and grievances. Leader behavior was measured by a variation of the LBDQ. The most interesting relationships they discovered appear in Figures 11–5, 11–6, 11–7, and 11–8. Figure 11–5 depicts the relation between grievance rate and consideration and Figure 11–6 shows the relation between turnover and consideration. There seems to be a clear relationship between consideration and the two dependent variables. High consideration is related to low grievance rate and low turnover. Low consideration is related to high grievance rate and high turnover. Both of the relationships seem to have the same general curvilinear shape such that beyond a certain point increases in consideration cannot further decrease turnover or grievance rate. Figure 11–7 and 11–8 describe the relationship between levels of initiating structure and the two dependent variables. The results seem to be the mirror image of those obtained with consideration. Increased initiation of structure leads to increased grievance rate and increased turnover. Once again, both relationships seem to have the same general curvilinear shape.

These data seem to be clear. They tell us to avoid too much structuring and be considerate of subordinates—or do they? Figure 11–9 really tells the tale. It presents data related to the *interaction* of the two dimensions. Supervisors were separated into three groups, which fell along the consideration continuum: high, medium, and low. The relationship between each of the dependent variables and degree of structure was then examined separately for each of the three groups. As Figure 11–9 clearly shows, the relationship between structuring behavior on the part of the supervisor and grievance rate was very different for each of the groups. For *high-consideration* leaders, structuring behavior could be sharply increased with-

FIGURE 11–5
Relation between Consideration and Grievance Rate

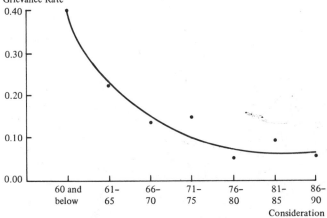

Source: Fleishman, E. A., & Harris, E. F. Patterns of leadership behavior related to employee grievances and turnover. *Personnel Psychology*, 1962, *15*, 43–56.

FIGURE 11–6

Relation between Consideration and Turnover Rate

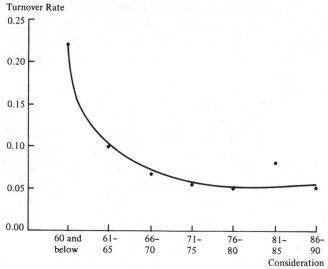

Source: Fleishman, E. A., & Harris, E. F. Patterns of leadership behavior related to employee grievances and turnover. *Personnel Psychology*, 1962, *15*, 43–56.

FIGURE 11–7

Relation between Structure and Grievance Rate

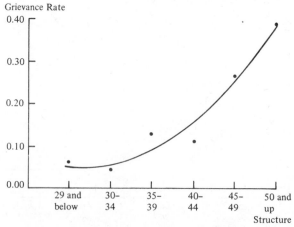

Source: Fleishman, E. A., & Harris, E. F. Patterns of leadership behavior related to employee grievances and turnover. *Personnel Psychology*, 1962, *15*, 43–56.

FIGURE 11–8

Relation between Structure and Turnover Rate

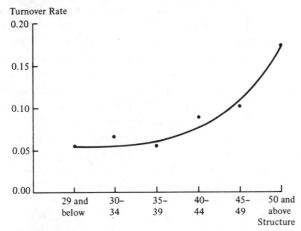

Source: Fleishman, E. A., & Harris, E. F. Patterns of leadership behavior related to employee grievances and turnover. *Personnel Psychology*, 1962, *15*, 43–56.

FIGURE 11–9

Combinations of Consideration and Structure Related to Grievance Rate

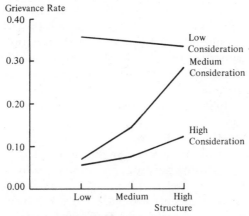

Source: Fleishman, E. A., & Harris, E. F. Patterns of leadership behavior related to employee grievances and turnover. *Personnel Psychology*, 1962, *15*, 43–56.

out any dramatic effect on grievances, so the grievance rate remained minimal. Supervisors designated as *low* on consideration could also increase structuring behavior without affecting grievance rates, so the rate stayed high. The major effect of initiating structure on grievance rate was found in the *medium*-consideration group. For that group there was a very strong positive relationship between structuring behavior and grievance rate. One of the conclusions Fleishman and Harris drew concerning this interaction was that while supervisors can compensate for high structure by increasing consideration, low-consideration supervisors cannot erase the negative effects of lack of concern for subordinates by reducing structure. This finding may mean consideration acts as a threshold or releaser mechanism, a precondition for effective supervision. It may be that the perception of "structuring" behavior changes when a leader is described as considerate; it may be that the structuring behavior is considered to be just another example of consideration by subordinates of highly considerate supervisors. This finding is similar, in some ways, to the results of a study by Crissey and Regan (1951). In that study, interviewers were asked to write qualifying statements about trait ratings they had given. Identical trait ratings were given *positive* qualifying statements by interviewers who had recommended acceptance of the applicant and *negative* qualifying statements by interviewers who had recommended rejection of the candidate. The same traits— and perhaps the same behaviors as well—may be seen as assets when a person is generally approved of, accepted, liked, or recommended, but as liabilities when the person is rejected, disapproved, or disliked. To return to our examination of considerate leaders, if they are viewed as considerate (i.e., liked or approved), then all their behavior may be seen as positive, an asset. On the other hand, if they are not seen as considerate, all behaviors might be viewed in a negative light, a liability.

Recently, House, Filley, and Kerr (1971) conducted a study to look at the relationship between consideration and initiating structure as it related to satisfaction of subordinates. Their hypothesis was that with low consideration, satisfaction would be negatively related to initiating structure. Their data yielded some puzzling results. They found that mean satisfaction scores increased as structure increased when consideration was high, but there was no clear-cut pattern when consideration was low.

Another recent study also suggested some complicated interrelationships among consideration, initiating structure, satisfaction, and performance. Green (1975) used the LBDQ to gather leadership information on 103 first-line managers in three different organizations. He also gathered measures of subordinate performance from peers and job satisfaction information from the subordinates themselves. He gathered data on each of the variables each month for three consecutive months. As a result of this longitudinal design, he was able to identify reciprocal relationships among some of the variables. He found that leader consideration was responsible for subordinate satisfaction, but subordinate performance resulted in changes in leader emphasis on considerate or structuring behavior. For leaders who were high on consideration, an increased emphasis on structure led to higher subordinate performance. As was the case with the Fleishman and Harris (1962) results, we are left with the impression that relationships between leader and subordinate behaviors may be a little more complex than we originally suspected.

An increasing number of studies have begun to question the generality of the assumptions regarding the effects of consideration and initiating structure. Researchers have begun to examine the *conditions under which* consideration is related to satisfaction and structure is related to performance. Another way of saying the same thing is that variables that *moderate* the relationship between leader behaviors and organizational outcomes are being discovered. Kerr, Schriesheim, Murphy, and Stogdill (1974) reviewed research on the Ohio State studies and identified those variables that had been shown to affect the relationship between the independent variables of consideration and initiating structure, and the dependent variables of satisfaction, morale, and performance. These moderator variables were placed in one of three categories; characteristics of subordinates supervised, characteristics of the leader's supervisor, and characteristics of the task(s) being performed. These variables are presented in Figure 11–10.

This table is sobering, since it suggests there is no simple relationship between consideration and satisfaction or structure and performance. The relationship will depend on the level of one or more of the moderator variables.

In addition to the complexity suggested by the Kerr review, there has been some confusion concerning different versions of the actual scales used to measure consideration and initiating structure. Earlier, we described the differences between the LOQ (a self-report measure) and the LBDQ (a subordinate description of leader behavior). In fact, there are several variations of the LBDQ. A number of recent studies have shown these various scales are not equal in terms of reliability and validity. In addition, some scales are more complex (in terms of the number of factors represented by the items) than others. This means it is difficult to compare the results of studies that have used different forms for measuring consideration and initiating structure. To make matters worse, many experimenters made their own modifications to the Ohio State scales. Schriesheim, House, and Kerr (1976) report that 31 percent of recent leadership studies of consider-

FIGURE 11–10

Variables Found to Moderate the Relationship between Leader Behavior and Outcome Variables

Subordinate Characteristics	Supervisor Characteristics	Task Characteristics
Expertise	Upward influence	Time urgency
Experience	Similarity of attitudes	Physical danger
Competence	to those of higher	Permissible error rate
Knowledge of the job	management	External stress
Job level	Similarity of behavior	Autonomy
Expectations concerning	to those of higher	Job scope
the leader	management	Ambiguity
		Importance of work
		Meaningfulness of work

ation and initiating structure used a modified version of the Ohio State scales.

The problems of moderator variables and nonstandard measurement scales have a common foundation. There is no "Ohio State theory" of leadership. There is simply an enormous pile of data and some suggested measuring instruments. Kerr, Schriesheim, Murphy, and Stogdill (1974) observe that any theory of leadership will need some conceptual way of classifying the leader. They propose that the dimensions of consideration and initiating structure remain the best means of leader classification suggested to date. As we will see shortly, not everyone agrees with their proposal.

Fiedler's Contingency Model

One of the most active lines of leadership research is related to Fiedler's contingency model. His theory is generally referred to as an inductive theory because he has been gathering data related to the propositions of the model since 1951 and the model "emerged" from this mass of data. Although the model has changed form significantly over the years, the general thrust has remained the same: *Effective leadership is a joint function of leader characteristics and situational characteristics.*

In some early research, Fiedler (1951) noticed that clinical therapists who were considered to be "good" therapists tended to view their patients as similar to themselves, while therapists considered "bad" saw their patients as quite dissimilar to themselves. Fiedler took this finding and extended it to other settings. Instead of asking respondents to make decisions about the similarity between themselves and others, subjects were asked to describe their most preferred and least preferred co-worker. This co-worker could be real or hypothetical. This was done on a series of bipolar semantic differential scales. From these two descriptions, most and least preferred co-worker, a score was derived. This score was called the *assumed similarity between opposites* score (ASo). The higher the score, the more similar the descriptions of most—and least—preferred coworkers. High ASo scores were thought to indicate warmth, permissiveness, and psychological acceptance. Eventually, only the least preferred co-worker (LPC) scale was used. This description forms the basis of what Fiedler thinks of as leadership style. The score is now called the LPC score. Since the positive end of the semantic differential scales were given high numerical values, and the negative end given low numerical values, it is possible to describe leaders as high LPC leaders or low LPC leaders. The meaning of these terms will be made clear shortly.

While working on the basic element of leadership style, Fiedler also introduced situational variables into his model. He felt that the situational variables moderated the effectiveness of a given leadership style; that is, a high LPC leader might be more effective in one situation than in another. He proposed three major determinants of the leadership situation: leader-member relations, task structure, and position power.

Leader-Member Relations. This particular dimension of the situation is fairly straightforward. It concerns whether or not the members of the group like the leader. If they do, the situation should be favorable for leading; if they do not, the situation should not be favorable for leading. Fiedler suggests that leader-member relations would also include such things as trust of the leader and loyalty to the leader. This seems similar to the concept of incremental influence that was considered earlier in the chapter. Of the three dimensions of the situation, leader-member relations is considered to be, by far, the most important dimension.

Task Structure. The structure or specificity of the task is determined by a taxonomy of task structure developed by Shaw (1963). Four of Shaw's scales have been used in Fiedler's research. These scales are:

1. *Decision verifiability:* The degree to which the correctness of a solution or decision can be verified.
2. *Goal clarity:* The degree to which task requirements are clearly stated and known by group members.
3. *Goal path multiplicity:* The number of different ways that the problem can be solved.
4. *Solution specificity:* The degree to which there is more than one correct solution.

The general idea is that a structured situation is more favorable for a leader than an unstructured situation.

Position Power. The third dimension of the situation that helps determine its favorability is what Fiedler refers to as "fate control," the capacity of the leader for dispensing rewards and punishments. Position power is very close in meaning to the earlier notion of legitimate power. It is the power inherent in a particular organizational role, such as "supervisor." Situations in which the leader has strong position power are thought to be more favorable than those in which the position power is weak.

Simply as a way of progressing with the research, Fiedler dichotomized each of the situational characteristics. Leader-member relations were considered to be either good or bad; task structure was either high or low; position power was either strong or weak. This dichotomization yielded eight distinct kinds of situations. For that reason, they have come to be identified as "octants." Each of the octants represents a particular combination of leader-member relations, task structure, and position power. The nature of each of the octants is described in Figure 11–11. We can see from this figure that octant 1 describes a situation in which leader-member relations are good, task structure high, and position power strong. On the other hand, octant 7 describes a situation in which leader-member relations are poor, task structure is low, and position power strong.

Leadership Style. According to Fiedler, the high LPC leader describes the least preferred co-worker as reasonably nice, intelligent, and so on. High LPC leaders use the positive terms in the bipolar scales (intelligent, cooperative, and so on). Since the LPC score is arrived at by adding the

FIGURE 11–11

Fiedler's View of the LPC/Group Effectiveness Relationship

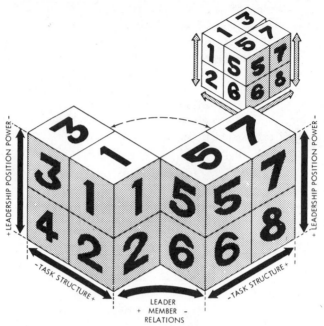

Source: Fiedler, F. E. *Leadership*. Morristown, N.J.: General Learning Press, 1971. © 1971 General Learning Corporation.

values from each of the bipolar scales, the high LPC leader is one who describes the least preferred co-worker in positive terms. On the other hand, the low LPC leader describes the least preferred co-worker in negative terms such as uncooperative and unintelligent. The high LPC leader seems to be able to distinguish between the individual and the work, while the low LPC leader appears unable to do that. The low LPC leader seems to link the performance of the least preferred co-worker to personality characteristics. These two styles, high and low LPC, suggest variations on the theme of consideration and initiating structure. This is further supported by Fiedler's description of the high and low LPC leaders. Both seek esteem, but the high LPC individual seeks esteem through interpersonal relations, while the low LPC leader seeks it through successful task completion. Nevertheless, Fiedler is quick to point out that the interpretation of LPC scores is considerably more complex than just initiating structure and consideration. While the LPC score has also been considered a possible measure of cognitive complexity, the currently favored interpretation is that LPC scores represent a measure of goal hierarchy, with low LPC leaders having significantly different goal structures from those of high LPC leaders. In short, Fiedler is saying that LPC is a motivational measure of some sort. Thus, in terms of the earlier distinction between leadership style and leadership behavior, Fiedler assumes that the LPC score taps the underlying need structure indicative of the more enduring leadership style.

The Contingency Theory. On the basis of the data he has gathered over the years, Fiedler has constructed a model that attempts to predict the effectiveness of certain combinations of leadership style (as identified by LPC scores) and situation favorability. Simply put, he contends that low LPC leaders will be effective in either very favorable or very unfavorable situations, while high LPC leaders will be most effective in situations of moderate favorability. This leads to the major hypothesis of the contingency model: *"The effectiveness of a group is contingent upon the relationship between leadership style and the degree to which the group situation enables the leader to exert influence"* (Fiedler, 1967, p. 15).

Figure 11–12 describes the proposed relationship between leadership style, situation favorability, and group effectiveness. This is a rather complex relationship, but an important one to understand. The graph demonstrates that as the situation moves from high favorability to moderate favorability for the leader (from the extreme left to the center of the horizontal axis), the correlation between LPC scores and group effectiveness changes from negative to positive. In other words, in the extremely favorable situation, the lower the LPC score, the higher the group effectiveness. In the moderately favorable situation, the higher the LPC score, the higher the group effectiveness. The opposite effect occurs when we move from a situation of moderate favorability to a very unfavorable situation (from the center to the extreme right on the horizontal axis). The sign of the correlation

FIGURE 11–12
Fiedler's View of the LPC/Group Effectiveness Relationship

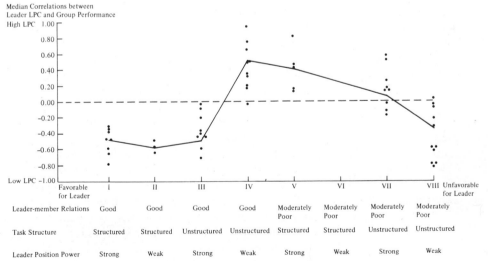

Source: Fiedler, F. E. *Leadership.* Morristown, N.J.: General Learning Press, 1971. © 1971 General Learning Corporation.

coefficients between LPC score and group effectiveness changes from positive to negative. In the very unfavorable situation, the lower the LPC score, the higher the group performance.

The conclusion Fiedler draws from these data is that low LPC is most appropriate in either very favorable or very unfavorable situations. As a function of this conclusion he recommends a program of "organizational engineering." The function of organizational engineering would be to change the nature of the situation to match the style of a particular leader. This suggestion flows from Fiedler's belief that the leadership style is a relatively enduring characteristic of the individual and tied to a motivational system. While we could, of course, opt to change the individual, Fiedler thinks it would be more efficient in the long run to change the situation.

There is more than adequate research support for many of Fiedler's contentions. The graph that appears in Figure 11–12 is, in fact, an accumulation of dozens of studies that have tested the proposed relationship between LPC score and group effectiveness in each of the octants. It might be more accurate to say that the points making up the graph *define* the model rather than support it. This would be more in keeping with the inductive theme and history of contingency theory. The most complete presentation of the studies supporting the theory and its propositions appears in Fiedler's book, *A Theory of Leadership Effectiveness* (1967).

Contingency theory has received mixed support. Fiedler has been quick to criticize studies that have not explicitly adhered to his definitions of the various components of the theory. As a result, a number of researchers have tried to reproduce faithfully the conditions that Fiedler suggested would demonstrate the validity of his theory. One such researcher was Vecchio (1977), who failed to find any support for Fiedler's propositions.

Since it is difficult to control all the situational variables and also get a reasonable spread of high and low LPC leaders, most researchers have been content to examine limited aspects of the theory. The most popular focus for this research is the meaning of LPC. Fiedler and his followers have settled on a cognitive/motivational interpretation of LPC scores. Low LPC leaders are thought to be cognitively simple and somewhat rigid in response patterns. Unfortunately, there is less than unanimous agreement that LPC represents cognitive complexity. Evans and Dermer (1974) agree that the low LPC leaders are cognitively simple, but they found that the high LPC leaders were not necessarily complex. Green and Nebeker (1977) found that high LPC leaders seem to be able to differentiate situational characteristics very well, while low LPC leaders are relatively constant in their response regardless of the situational characteristics. Saskin, Taylor, and Tripathi (1974) found that the nature of LPC changed with the situation. As a result, they concluded that LPC has no meaning independent of the context in which it is measured. Finally, Stinson and Tracy (1974) found that LPC scores were not particularly stable. An individual who is characterized as high LPC today may be characterized differently if the

LPC scales are administered at another time. This is another way of saying that these authors question the reliability of the scale.

The Stinson and Tracy argument is not so difficult to deal with; it is simply necessary to develop a more reliable measure of the LPC construct. This could be done by refining the scale through item analysis, adding more items, or other traditional approaches. But the Sashkin et al. conclusion is much more damaging. It is critical for the theory that the leader characteristics and the situational characteristics be independent of each other. If that were not the case, then Fiedler's whole notion of situational engineering would be circular. If LPC scores are correlated with situational variables, then by changing the situation, you are automatically changing the LPC score, and there can never be an "optimal match."

In addition to the independence of LPC and situational characteristics, Fiedler's contingency theory proposes that each of the situational variables (task structure, leader-member relations, and position power) is independent of the other two variables. But Ilgen and O'Brien (1974) found that leader-member relations were related to task characteristics, particularly the degree of coordination among members required. In addition, member compatibility seemed to affect leader-member relations.

Finally, Justis, Kedia, and Stephens (1978) found that position power had a main effect on the effectiveness of trainers. Trainers who were perceived as high in position power were able to have a greater influence on trainees than trainers with low position power. If Fiedler is correct, one would expect the effect of position power to depend on the trainer's LPC score.

There have been some studies that have supported Fiedler's model, but they have been either limited in scope (Schnier, 1978) or lacking in sufficient control to justify serious consideration. As an example of the latter situation, Fiedler and Mahar (In Press) report the results of 12 studies done in both industrial and military settings. They were testing the effects of a leadership training course in which trainees were taught how to manipulate situational favorability to complement their LPC scores, thus allowing effective coordination of work-group members. In a comparison of 423 trainees and 484 "controls," Fiedler and Mahar concluded that contingency theory was supported because the trainees received higher performance evaluations than the "controls." This might be a reasonable conclusion if individuals were randomly assigned to treatment and control conditions. Unfortunately, this was almost never the case. In one study, for example, the control group consisted of individuals who did not sign up for the training. It is distinctly possible that those who did not sign up for training were poorer performers than those who did elect to go through training. This, then, would account for the performance differences after training! There were other similar problems with almost all of the studies. Thus, while Fiedler's theory may be a valid one, the Fiedler and Mahar (1978) results cannot be used to support it.

Most of the criticism's of Fiedler's model can be placed in one of four categories:

1. The first criticism relates to the nature of the dependent variable in most of the studies. Look again at Figure 11–12. Notice that if we consider situation favorability as the independent variable (or antecedent variable), the *correlation between LPC and group effectiveness becomes the dependent variable, not group effectiveness itself*. If we consider the correlation coefficient to be the dependent variable, we know nothing about the absolute level of performance. It may be of little comfort to know that LPC and group effectiveness are negatively related in octant 1 and positively related in octant 4. Without knowing something about absolute levels of group performance, it is impossible to conceive of "organizational engineering" as proposed by Fiedler. It is distinctly possible that the best match of situation and leader style could yield the lowest levels of performance in an absolute sense.

2. One of the criticisms of the model seems to have as much to do with the nature of inductive reasoning as it does with the specific propositions of contingency theory. There is a general feeling of uneasiness that surrounds the use of the LPC score. It is felt that LPC should have systematic relationships with other logically related variables to qualify as a construct; in other words, construct validity should be demonstrated.

3. A third major criticism has been presented by Graen, Alvares, Orris, and Martella (1970). They criticize the way Fiedler "supports" the theory with data. As far as Fiedler is concerned, the important aspect of the data is the *sign* of the correlation coefficient. The theory predicts positive LPC/group effectiveness correlations in some octants and negative LPC/group effectiveness correlations in other octants. The theory does not necessarily predict that a particular correlation coefficient will be significantly different from zero. This is a point of contention for Graen et al. They claim that this is a completely inappropriate procedure. Their logic is that if you have a nonsignificant correlation, it is not different from zero, and the sign is an accidental characteristic of the particular sample, not an indication of a relationship in the population.

4. One final criticism has to do with the nature of the "situational" determinants of favorability. Critics claim that the characteristics of the *situation* are not independent of the *leader*. In other words, it is possible that some of the LPC score is also represented in the measures of situation favorability, thereby confounding some of the relationships predicted by the model.

It would hardly be fair to the proponents of contingency theory if we did not supply brief rebuttals to these criticisms, as well as our own thoughts on these items.

1. The first criticism, dealing with absolute levels of performance, is a serious one. The practical applications and implications of any leadership theory add or detract from its usefulness. The practical value of the theory will remain questionable until data relating to absolute levels of performance

begin to appear with more regularity. This criticism does not in any sense "destroy" the theory. It simply questions the relevance of the dependent variable. It is silly to contend that the LPC/group effectiveness correlation is *totally* irrelevant; it is not. It provides some useful dynamic information about the *process* of leadership. Unfortunately, the correlation can say little about one class of outcomes of that process, absolute levels of group or individual performance.

2. The fact that LPC does not seem to systematically relate to other variables is not the fault of the contingency researchers. They document numerous attempts to find out what LPC means. Again, this criticism is not sufficient to "destroy" the theory. It would be nice if we knew a little more about the meaning of LPC, but this will not be the first or last time in psychological research that an ambiguous construct has led to advances in one way or another (e.g., "intelligence," "instincts"). Furthermore, data are accumulating that point to LPC as some type of cognitive construct.

3. The criticism addressing the nature of supporting data is a complicated one. Fiedler answers the objection statistically by calculating the probability that a string of correlations would assume a certain consistent value. His argument is that even though a correlation coefficient of $+.20$ is not significant with a given sample size, it can be shown that a number of correlations of the same magnitude and with the same sign have a lower probability of appearing due to chance alone than just one correlation of that value. In other words, one correlation of $-.27$ in octant 8 might not be "significant," but 11 correlations of that value convey some important systematic information. This argument is a complex one and is related more to the theory of statistical sampling than to contingency theory.

4. The fourth criticism concerning the relative independence of leader characteristics and situational characteristics speaks directly to the purpose of leadership research for the past several decades, that is, a description of the interaction between the leader and the situation, a description of the leadership *process.* Available data seem to indicate that leader characteristics and situational characteristics are *not* independent. If Fiedler's contingency theory is to be of any value, this relationship must be better understood.

Contingency theory will generate research for many years to come. The simple fact is that it is still the most interesting and well-described theory available. This is probably why it is so commonly attacked. Nevertheless, available research evidence suggests that there are potentially serious flaws in the theory and these must be corrected. An *interesting* theory may be sufficient for the layman, but empirical support is required by the scientist.

The Vroom-Yetton Contingency Theory

Vroom and Yetton (1975) have proposed a model of leadership that deals with one particular aspect of the leadership process: decision making.

They reviewed past research on leader decision making and found that it was possible to describe a limited number of strategies or styles a manager might use to make decisions or solve problems. These strategies are presented in Figure 11–13.

They also proposed that the effectiveness of decisions could be judged on the following three dimensions: the *quality* or rationality of the decision, the *acceptance* of the decision by subordinates, and the *time* required to make the decision. These dimensions represent the "attributes" of the problem. Thus, as was the case with Fiedler's model, the leader behavior is *contingent* on other variables, in this case problem attributes. As an example, consider the case of a manager who is trying to make a decision about a new pay plan. It may be that her superior wants a recommendation in a matter of days; this would make the problem a *time* problem. On the other hand, the issue might be one of acceptance; for example, it may be that she will lose some key people to other organizations if she

FIGURE 11–13
Decision-Making Strategies

1. Solve the problem yourself, using all information available to *you* at the time.
2. Obtain information from your subordinates, but decide yourself how to solve the problem.
3. Discuss the problem with subordinates individually and ask for their suggestions and ideas; do *not* bring them together as a group.
4. Discuss the problem with your subordinates as a group; you make the decision.
5. Discuss the problem with your subordinates as a group; jointly generate and evaluate alternatives and agree on a solution.

does not get acceptance for the new pay plan. As you can see by examining the decision styles in Figure 11–13 again, some of these strategies are more suited to quick decisions, while others are more suited to high levels of decision acceptance. This is exactly the nature of the theory: it identifies the styles or strategies of decision making that a manager should use in solving problems with specific attributes.

Vroom and Yetton label their theory a *normative* or *prescriptive* theory. This means that they intend to tell managers how they *should* behave in certain situations. The Ohio State approach and Fiedler's model are less obviously normative (but are normative, nonetheless); they *imply* that leaders will be more effective if they adopt some particular consideration/initiating structure balance or modify the situation to match their particular LPC level. Vroom and Yetton specify exactly which strategies to use with problems having particular attributes.

Since the theory is a relatively new one, there has been little substantive research on it. The research that has been done has been of a confirmatory rather than exploratory nature. Jago and Vroom (1978) found that managers who used "acceptable" decision strategies (as determined by the problem attributes) were more likely to report that the decision was an "effective" one than managers who used "unacceptable" strategies. Hill and Schmitt (1977) studied the decision strategies of 33 students asked to play the role of manager. They found that the nature of the problem (i.e., the problem attributes) had a major influence on the strategy the "manager" selected to solve a particular problem. This supports the basic Vroom-Yetton hypothesis that leader behavior is *contingent* on situational variables.

On the basis of the limited research we have described above, we would conclude that there is some support for the Vroom-Yetton theory. On the other hand, in its current form, the model is somewhat limited. It would seem to deal with only one limited aspect of a manager's job: decision making. This may be a reasonable approach to management, since almost everything a manager does (or any worker for that matter) can be translated into a "problem" of one kind or another, requiring a decision. But if it is to occupy a role as a "full-fledged" theory of leadership, the Vroom-Yetton model will have to be modified to deal more specifically with a wider range of problems, including interpersonal relations, rewarding/punishing decisions, and planning/scheduling.

Path-Goal Theory

It should have occurred to you by now that leadership might be thought of as "applied motivation theory." The leader is attempting to get the follower to change or continue a particular behavioral pattern, i.e., attempting to motivate the subordinate. In that respect, the Ohio State studies explore the "personality" of the motivator, while Fiedler examines the interaction between leader personality and environmental conditions. Path-goal theory directly addresses the *process* of subordinate motivation. There are two major propositions to the theory (House & Mitchell, 1974):

1. Leader behaviors will be acceptable and satisfying to subordinates when the subordinates perceive the behavior as an immediate source of satisfaction or instrumental in obtaining future satisfaction.
2. Leader behaviors will increase subordinate effort expenditure when subordinates perceive effective performance as a means to satisfying important needs and when they see the leader as an aid in attaining effective performance.

Based on these propositions, House and Mitchell suggest that good leaders perform the following functions:

1. Recognize subordinate needs and assume control over the outcomes that will satisfy those needs.
2. Individually reward subordinates for work goal attainment.
3. Help subordinates clarify paths to valued goals and expectancies of achieving those goals.
4. Remove obstacles from the paths to important goals.

While most of these functions are implied by instrumentality theories of work motivation (Porter and Lawler, 1968), path-goal theory explicitly directs the supervisor to take certain actions. In addition, as contrasted to the Ohio State and contingency models of leadership, it places a heavy emphasis on the *perceptions* of the subordinate. Thus it is clearly a cognitive approach to leadership.

Both the Ohio State model and the contingency model suggest a somewhat limited range of leader characteristics. Leaders differ, on consideration, initiating structure, or LPC response patterns. House (1971) and House and Dressler (1974) discuss more traditional management "styles" in their presentation of the path-goal hypotheses. House identifies four typical leadership styles:

1. *Directive leadership:* Provides explicit expectations to subordinates. Provides specific work-related guidance to subordinates. Maintains definite standards of performance.
2. *Supportive leadership:* Demonstrates concern for the well-being of subordinates. Treats subordinates as equals.
3. *Participative leadership:* Consults subordinates and asks for suggestions. Considers subordinate suggestions in decision making.
4. *Achievement-oriented leadership:* Sets challenging goals. Stresses performance improvement. Expresses confidence in subordinate's ability to meet the challenging goals.

Instead of looking at considerate leaders vis-à-vis structuring leaders, this approach suggests that the same individual may exhibit very different patterns of leader behavior and, furthermore, that these different patterns will have distinctly different results.

The final component of the path-goal approach is the role of *contingency factors*. These contingency factors operate in a manner similar to the moderator variables of the Ohio State studies (as described in Figure 11–10) and the situational variables of Fiedler's theory (task structure, position power, and leader-member relations). These factors directly affect the relationship between the leader behavior and the effect of that behavior on the subordinate. House suggests that there are two different types of contingency variables: personal characteristics of the subordinates and environmental pressures. An example of a subordinate characteristic would be locus of control or the degree to which the subordinate believes he can have an effect on the environment. An example of an environmental pressure would be the lack of structure of the particular task at hand. Presumably, less task definition would create greater need for leader structuring. Figure 11–14 describes how the combination of leader behaviors and contingency factors results in subordinate perceptions and ultimately subordinate attitudes and behavior. It should be apparent now that instead of being a distinctly different theory of leadership, path-goal theory is more an extension of existing theories of leadership and an application of existing theories of motivation.

FIGURE 11–14
Summary of Path-Goal Relationships

Leader Behavior	and	Contingency Factors	Cause	Subordinate Attitudes and Behavior	

1. Directive		1. Subordinate characteristics
		  authoritarianism
		  locus of control
		  ability
			Influence	Personal
				perceptions
					1. Job satisfaction
					  job ⇒ rewards

2. Supportive					2. Acceptance of leader leader ⇒ rewards

3. Achievement oriented		2. Environmental factors
		  the task
		  formal authority system
		  primary work group
			Influence	Motivational
				stimuli
				Constraints
				Rewards
					3. Motivational behavior
					  effort ⇒ performance
					  performance ⇒ rewards

4. Participative					

Source: House, R. L., & Mitchell, T. Path-goal theory of leadership. *Journal of Contemporary Business*, 1974, 3, 81–97.

A number of tests of path-goal theory have examined the effect of supervisor-imposed structure on employee perceptions. As described, path-goal theory would predict that highly structured leaders would have subordinates who clearly see path-goal relationships. Hammer and Dachler (1975) found that the subordinates of leaders high on initiating structure saw path-goal instrumentalities as *less clear* than subordinates with low initiating-structure supervisors; conversely, subordinates whose leaders were high on consideration saw path-goal instrumentalities quite clearly. This study is extremely damaging to path-goal theory, since it challenges one of the basic propositions of the theory: the proposition that structuring activity on the part of the leader will help illuminate paths to valued goals for subordinates. Hammer and Dachler conclude that the vagueness of the concepts *path, goal, leader consideration,* and *leader initiating structure* are responsible for the negative results. They suggest that the loose notions of paths and goals be replaced with some firmer notions, such as valences, expectancies, and instrumentalities of Vroom's VIE theory of motivation. In addition, they suggest that the concepts of consideration and initiating structure be junked in favor of an explicit set of supervisory behaviors that have been shown to affect subordinate estimates of valence, expectancy, and instrumentality. In short, they suggest we concentrate solely on describing the potential effect of leaders on the motivation of subordinates.

Path-goal theory has the same intuitive appeal as instrumentality theories of work motivation. Nevertheless, it seems to have some of the same problems. Studies such as those by Hammer and Dachler that test fundamental or prerequisite conditions to the validity of the theory have been disappointing. In addition, the number of variables that must be considered in explaining the effect of a leader's behavior on a subordinate's satisfaction and/or performance is depressing. Path-goal theory seems a bit too complicated to be of any descriptive value and too weakly supported to be of any explanatory value. We agree with Hammer and Dachler that much more conceptual work is needed on the meanings of *path, goal, consideration,* and *initiating structure.*

Hammer and Dachler's exhortation that we abandon theories of leadership in favor of motivation theories is revealing. Their point of view is representative of most leadership theorists. Leader behavior is viewed as an *independent variable,* something that affects subordinate behavior. In particular, the effect of leader actions on subordinate satisfaction and performance has been the historical focus of leadership research. This is a narrow view of leadership. Leader behavior may also be thought of as a *dependent variable,* or the *result of* interactions of other variables. Greene's (1975) finding that there were reciprocal relationships between supervisor and subordinate behaviors is particularly salient in this regard. The fact that the balance of initiating structure and consideration depends to some degree on the performance of subordinates says *something* about the phenomenon of leader behavior. It says that leadership patterns are not constants, that they themselves are determined by other variables, that these other variables might include subordinate behaviors, and that we should focus more on leaders than subordinates if we want to understand leadership behavior.

There is one line of research that hints at the potential value of concentrating on the leader rather than the follower. A number of researchers have examined the effect of positive versus punitive behavior on the part of the supervisor. These studies initially set out to document the differential *effects* of positive reinforcements and punishments on subordinate behavior (Sims & Szilagyi, 1975a, 1975b; Keller & Szilyagi, 1978). They were able to document these effects and concluded that positive responses by supervisors were both more common and more effective in changing or maintaining subordinate responses. But other researchers began to examine the use of positive and punitive strategies by supervisors. Hinton and Barrow (1975) found that supervisors often used positive rewards as *incentives* with poorer performers in the hope of inducing better performance. They also found that supervisors who *received* positive economic rewards were much more likely to *give* positive economic rewards to subordinates. In short, they concluded that there was a good deal more discretionary use of rewarding strategies than any existing theories of leadership would suggest. In a later study (1976) these same researchers found that the personality characteristics of supervisors who were prone to positive reward strategies differed from those of puntive supervisors. Finally, Butler and Jaffee (1974) looked at leadership behavior in small discussion groups. They found that when leaders received positive feedback, they were more likely to engage in task-oriented behavior; however, when they received negative feedback, they became tense, antagonistic, and disagreeable (not a surprising finding to children who have the temerity to correct parents or students who dare to criticize teachers).

We find this recent research on variables that influence leader behavior very exciting. It suggests that there is considerable value in examining leader behavior as a dependent variable. While this line of research has been suggested in the past (Nebeker & Mitchell, 1974), it is only recently that it has received substantial theoretical attention. Two theories have been proposed dealing with leader behavior as a dependent variable—Hollander's social exchange theory and the vertical dyad model. We will refer to both of these as "reciprocal" theories, because they both emphasize the reciprocal or exchange relationship between leader and follower.

Reciprocal Theories of Leadership

Several years ago, Lowin and Craig (1968) were able to show that subordinate behavior affected leader behavior. Subjects were recruited for a position advertised in a newspaper as "office manager." Confederates of the experimenters played the role of "subordinate" and were either "high performers" or "low performers." The effect on the subjects (supervisors) was revealing. The high-performing subordinates were treated with high consideration and low initiating structure; the low performers, on the other hand, received little consideration and a lot of structure. These data suggest, at the very least, a reciprocal relationship between leader and follower, each influencing the other. Green's results, described earlier in the chapter, fit nicely into this reciprocal idea. You will remember that the level of performance of the subordinate changed the balance between consideration and initiating structure. Surprisingly, there are only a few theories that give explicit attention to the issue of factors influencing the *leader's* behavior. Indirectly, Vroom and Yetton (1973) suggest the nature of the problem dictates, to some degree, the decision style of the leader. Similarly, Fiedler (1967) suggests that leaders might change the situation to fit their style; this implies that current situation favorability would have an influence on future leader behavior. But these theories do not directly address the dynamic aspects of leader behavior, the spontaneous choices that a leader makes among alternative courses of action. In short, they do not describe how a leader *does* lead, but rather how she *should* lead.

There are two current theories which stress the dynamic and reciprocal aspects of leader behavior. We will describe them briefly.

Hollander's Social Exchange Theory of Leadership. Hollander (1978) suggests that the leadership "problem" is one of coordinating situational variables, leader characteristics and expectations, and follower characteristics and expectations. Figure 11–15 graphically depicts the interrelationships

FIGURE 11–15
Hollander's Social Exchange Theory

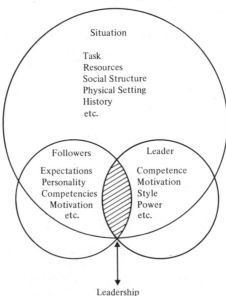

Leadership

Source: *Principles and methods of social psychology,* 3d ed., by Edwin P. Hollander. Copyright © 1976 by Oxford University Press, Inc. Reprinted by permission.

of these variables. It implies that a leader's behavior can be understood only in light of the variables included in the *situation, follower,* and *leader* components. Further, it implies that the critical interaction is between follower expectations and leader behaviors, and that this interaction is imbedded in a particular situation or context. Hollander proposes that leader's change or maintain their behavior to conform to the expectations of the subordinates. This is done because the leader *needs* certain things from the group: loyalty, energy expenditure, praise, and so on. Similarly, the group accepts or rejects the behavior of the leader according to expectations, anticipated rewards, and probability estimates of goal attainment. This process clearly implies an *exchange* between leader and follower. The theory further suggests that this exchange must be seen as an *equitable* one by both leader and follower. Thus, the propositions of Equity theory, as described in Chapter 9, would be important propositions for the social exchange theory of leadership as well. This takes the results of Lowin and Craig (1968) and Greene (1975) one step further by suggesting *why* the leader behavior changed in response to poor subordinate performance: the leader may have felt that the exchange had become an inequitable one, with too much being contributed by the leader and too little by the follower.

At this point, Hollander's propositions are primarily conceptual. The specific hypotheses suggested by the theory have not been tested. As a matter of fact, the theory itself has probably not stopped growing or changing yet. Nevertheless, it is extremely promising because it considers leadership as both a dependent and independent variable.

The Vertical Dyad Model. A second theory that stresses the variables influencing the leader's behavior has been proposed by Dansereau, Graen, and Haga (1974). They suggest that leadership behaviors represent a role that develops over time and is based on the quality of supervisor-subordinate relationships. Any follower and leader form a two-person group called a *dyad;* since the two persons are at different organizational levels, the dyad might be called a *vertical dyad.*

On the basis of a research study conducted in a manufacturing organization, Dansereau et al. proposed that followers fall into two distinct groups: in-group members and out-group members. In-groups are characterized by high latitude for negotiating their own roles, and leaders tend to deal with these groups without resorting to the use of power stemming from formal authority; these types of relationships are thought of as "high-quality" interactions. Out-groups are characterized by low latitude for negotiating their roles and have leaders who commonly attempt to influence them by using formal authority. These two groups of followers are not naturally occurring; i.e., people are not "born" to be in- or out-group members (regardless of what your cousin says). Group membership is a role that develops on the basis of leader/follower interaction.

Their results also suggested that managers typically play two roles simultaneously. They play a supervisory role with out-group members and a leadership role with in-group members. This strongly suggests that follower characteristics have an influence on a manager's behavior. Once again, we are confronted with the reciprocal nature of the leader/follower relationship.

In a recent test of the theory, Graen and Schiemann (1978) demonstrated that in-group members agreed more highly with their supervisors about the nature of work-related situations than did out-group members. This is an unusual finding. It is much more common to find that employees and supervisors agree to only a limited extent about work-related variables. Graen and Schiemann propose that leaders are closer to in-group members, thus are more likely to share common points of view. Studies that do not separate subordinates into in- and out-groups would be unlikely to find high levels of agreement. These results suggest two things: (1) as a classification scheme, the in-group/out-group distinction is a valuable one, and (2) leader behaviors are dynamic and are substantially affected by follower characteristics. As was the case with Hollander's social exchange theory, the vertical dyad model is still too new to have received much empirical investigation. Nevertheless, we expect a good deal of attention to be paid to this theory, and we anticipate major gains in our understanding of the leadership process as a result of this approach.

An Overview of the Theories

Theories of leadership actually fall into two separate categories. One of these categories might be more appropriately called theories of *followership*. This is because these theories consider leadership as an independent variable and are mainly concerned with the effect of leader behaviors on followers. They tend to be prescriptive and suggest the "best" ways of leading. There is, of course, something to be learned from an examination of the effects of leaders' behavior, particularly if the leader strives to improve his effectiveness. Nevertheless, these theories represent the *application* of knowledge regarding leader behavior. They are based solely on a distinction between successful and unsuccessful leaders. The Ohio State Studies, Fiedler's contingency theory, Path-Goal Theory, and, to a certain extent, the Vroom-Yetton model all fall into this group.

Other theories deal with the *dynamics* of leadership. They attempt to understand why leaders behave the way they do. They view leadership as a role or system, capable of being influenced at any time by a number of other variables within the same system. Hollander's social exchange theory and the vertical dyad model fall into this category. Most of the atheoretical studies of management style also fall into this category (e.g., types of power used by leaders). While this second group of theories may also be used prescriptively to improve leader effectiveness, this is not their primary purpose.

Twenty years of research devoted to the first kind of theory have not brought us much closer to an understanding of leader behavior (although they have provided us with a useful vocabulary; e.g., "consideration," "initiating structure"). It may be time to concentrate research efforts on theories like those in the second group.

LEADER INTELLIGENCE

Recently, Fiedler (Fiedler & Leister, 1977) has begun an examination of the role of leader intelligence in leadership effectiveness. In an earlier study, Csoka (1974) had demonstrated that leaders who were experienced but unintelligent were unable to integrate and use their past experience. On the other hand, leaders who were intelligent but inexperienced were unable to understand the task well enough to perform efficiently. Thus, Csoka concluded that experience and intelligence interacted to yield effectiveness. On the basis of these and other findings (Blades, 1976; Chemers, Rice, Sundstrom, & Butler, 1975), Fiedler proposes what he calls a "multiple-screen" model that explains the relationship between leader intelligence and task performance. This model appears in Figure 11–16. You might

FIGURE 11–16
Schematic Representation of Multiple Screen Model

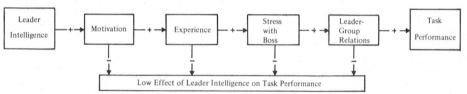

Source: Fiedler, F. E., & Leister, A. F. Leader intelligence and task performance: A test of a multiple screen model. *Organizational Behavior and Human Performance*, 1977, *20*, 1–14.

think of the model as a flow diagram describing how the effect of intelligence is weakened by individual and situational variables. The model proposes that low motivation, inexperience, interpersonal stress with immediate superiors, and poor leader/group relations all act as obstacles to the full use of intellectual capacities by a leader. Conversely, if motivation is high, experience is high, interpersonal stress is low, and leader-group relations are good, then the more intelligent the leader the higher the performance. Fiedler has presented some preliminary data in support of this model (Fiedler & Leister, 1977), and they look promising. While this is not a theory of leadership, it does hold the potential for telling us much about the leadership process.

WOMEN AS LEADERS

One issue occupying a good deal of attention in leadership research is the question of the suitability of women for leadership roles. In Chapter 5, we discussed the Equal Employment Opportunity Commission Guidelines for fair employment. These guidelines have had a substantial impact on the number of women in supervisory roles. While avenues of managerial advancement were often blocked to women in the past by the mindless bias of organizational "tradition," Title VII of the Civil Rights Act of 1964 made this a costly bias. Ten years ago it would have been difficult to study similarities and differences among male and female leaders, due to the small number of women in leadership positions. Recently, these studies have become more common.

There are really two questions that must be addressed. The first concerns the skills and abilities necessary to lead. Are female leaders more or less considerate than male leaders? Do women impose more or less structure? Are women higher or lower on LPC scores than men? The second question is more closely related to subordinates' responses to male and female leaders. It may be that female leaders will not be *permitted* to lead because of stereotypes and biases of followers. We will deal with these two types of questions separately.

There has been very little field research on the first question. Day and Stogdill (1972) examined the LBDQ scores of male and female supervisors and found no differences in the perceived effectiveness of the two groups. Bartol and Wortman (1975) found identical results in a study of male and female supervisors in a civil service setting. Bartol and Wortman also examined the possibility that the sex of the subordinate would interact with the sex of the leader so that female subordinates might describe female leaders differently from male leaders. This was not the case, although the results did suggest that female subordinates respond differently from male subordinates when describing supervisors, but it did not matter whether the supervisor was male or female.

This research is interesting but hardly conclusive. It would be tempting to conclude that there are no behavioral differences between men and women related to leader effectiveness. But the data do not permit such a conclusion. If you will think back to the chapter that dealt with the models of validity, you will recognize this research design as one that might be labeled "concurrent validity." These studies were conducted with women who were currently functioning as managers. There is reason to believe that the industrial world is one dominated by male values, where a premium is placed on aggression, assertiveness, and other characteristics thought to be "typically" male. If that is the case, the females in these two samples may have been required to change their styles to a much greater degree than their male counterparts to function in the organizational setting. The only way to know for sure if that were the case would be to follow a sample of male and female leaders for an extended period of time, from trainee status to long-tenure supervisor. We could then compare and contrast the male and female leaders who were successful with those who were not.

The issue of subordinates' satisfaction with male and female leaders has also received some attention. Petty and Lee (1975) found that female leaders who were high on initiating structure were more likely to have dissatisfied subordinates than male leaders who emphasized structure. This suggests there may be a stereotype of the female that transcends occupational roles: *women are considerate and seldom engage in structuring activities.* Research in the area of person perception predicts that we may be less pleased with those who do not match a stereotype we have in mind for them. To the degree that subordinates think of "management" as a male occupation, female supervisors will meet resistance.

A recent concern surfacing in business circles is the "token" woman manager. The problem is one of antagonism by her subordinates toward the newly appointed female manager due to their belief that she is there solely because she is a woman, and not because she is qualified to do the job. While there have been no good field studies of this situation, Jacobson and Koch (1977) attempted to reproduce the dynamics of this type of situation in a laboratory setting. They formed two-person work groups in which one group member (actually a confederate of the experimenter) was female and the other (the subject) was male. As far as the males in the experiment were concerned, all group members were similar with respect to skills, abilities, and experience. The experimenter explained that each group had to have a leader. The leader was chosen in one of three ways:

1. Merit: *The work group member who performed best on a task would be appointed leader;* in this condition, the woman had been given instruction in the task before the experiment began, and she invariably outperformed her male counterpart.
2. Random: *A coin was flipped to see who was to be the leader;* it was a two-headed coin, and the woman was always given the option of calling the flip. As you might have guessed, she always called "heads."
3. Arbitrary: *The experimenter explained that since women never got to be leaders, they would appoint the woman as the group leader.*

The "task" consisted of reproducing various designs. The female leader manipulated the instructions in such a way that the follower would either succeed or fail. Thus, we have two independent variables in the experiment: the method of leader selection and task success versus failure. The results were fascinating. When the woman was appointed leader on the "arbitrary" basis, she was viewed more negatively than in either of the other two conditions (merit and random). The men did not feel nearly as negative when they felt they had an equal chance to be chosen (random condition) or that they were simply not as good at the task as the women (merit condition). More revealing, however, was the effect of the success-versus-failure manipulation. The degree to which the man was successful or unsuccessful in completing the task was three times more important in his evaluation of his supervisor than the method of initial leader selection. This means that, while women may be the targets of unfair evaluations based on beliefs of subordinates as to how they achieved their supervisor status, in the long run their ability to supervise effectively may easily overcome this penalty.

There is a desperate need for field studies of the leader behavior of individuals from groups currently underrepresented in management circles. The two most obvious groups are blacks and women. Studies of blacks in supervisory roles are even fewer than studies of women. Those that do exist are usually laboratory bound and hopelessly confounded by sampling problems. One of the reasons for the dearth of studies is obviously the fact that there have been so few blacks in supervisory positions in the past. This will change, as will our knowledge of the unique problems facing the black leader.

CLIMATES: ORGANIZATIONAL AND SUBORGANIZATIONAL

The notion of a "climate" within an organization really belongs in the chapter dealing with organizations rather than in the leadership chapter. For that reason, we intend merely to introduce the topic and consider its relationship to leader behaviors. It might be more appropriate to consider the theme of this section to be organizational philosophy rather than climate. We will deal with two of these philosophies: the Theory X/Theory Y approach and the participative-directive approach.

Leadership is not only an independent variable but also a dependent variable. Leader behavior is intricately woven into the fabric of the organization. This fabric includes the organizational philosophy as well as the personal philosophy of the supervisor; it covertly or overtly reinforces and allows certain kinds of behaviors on the part of the leader and disallows and punishes other behaviors. Preferences, expectations, and beliefs on the part of subordinates will also influence the nature of the leader's behavior. In short, the individual leader does not make a choice among alternative action patterns simply on the basis of an individual need structure. The leader also considers the organizational philosophy and the belief systems of the subordinates.

Theory X/Theory Y

Theory X and Theory Y (McGregor, 1960) each embody a set of beliefs about human nature. Theory X assumes that all people are lazy, irresponsible, avoid challenge, and so on, while Theory Y assumes that all people are industrious, responsible, and seek challenge. Organizations could be described on the basis of these two sets of assumptions. We might describe one company as primarily a Theory Y organization, while a second company might fall closer to a Theory X organization.

If we were to know whether the management of a particular company ascribes to Theory X or Theory Y beliefs, we could probably make some initial guesses about what behaviors of a leader would be acceptable and unacceptable in that company. For example, a Theory X company would

FIGURE 11–17
A Stereotyped View of Supervision

"Cancel my appointments, Ms. Jones. I'll be on the fifth floor cracking the whip."

be reluctant to give employees significant amounts of decision-making responsibility. For that reason, we would not be likely to encounter a leader who gives subordinates decision-making responsibility; remember, we are saying this would be unlikely, not impossible. For another example, a Theory Y company would be reluctant to treat workers like children. For that reason, we would not be likely to find a leader who would approach a pilfering problem by searching all subordinates before they left work each day.

We have just implied that a company that has as its historical tradition Theory X beliefs (as seen in a number of "family" companies), is unlikely to develop or tolerate leaders who have different sets of beliefs. There is, however, another aspect to this situation. A company that has a historical tradition of Theory X beliefs will have an employee population with a certain set of *expectations*. This might mean that even if a Theory Y leader were to slip by the company watchdogs, the subordinates might view the leader unfavorably because of the perceived discrepancy between what they expect of a supervisor and how this particular supervisor is behaving. Likert (1958) contends that the reaction to a particular leader behavior will depend to a great degree on what was expected by the subordinate. Too much democratic behavior on the part of a supervisor might be just as aversive to subordinates as too little. Another example might be the instances in which job-enrichment plans have not worked. While there are many possible explanations for the failure of some enrichment programs, one of those explanations would relate to the expected level of participation on the part of the subordinate. It may be that the amount of participation available to subordinates in enriched environments is so far above their expected amount that it is aversive.

A common industrial dilemma might be partially explained by looking at this interaction between supervisor expectations and subordinate expectations. A supervisor comes back from a management workshop excited about the possibility of allowing subordinates to have greater input to decision making at the department level. The first day back, the subordinates are gathered together and their new freedom and responsibility is described to them. The new program is tried out over the next week and proves a dismal failure. Production is down, and the subordinates are grumbling. They are gathered together again and told that in spite of the fact that they were treated as adults, they acted like children. Therefore, they will now be treated as children, a punishment that fits the crime. We might interpret this situation on the basis of expectations. The workers, for their part, are a little scared and very uncomfortable about the new freedom. In Likert's terms, the change was too dramatic, and it exceeded some optimal level, the level expected or acceptable to subordinates. The reaction of the supervisor is also understandable given this kind of explanation. The supervisor expected delight or at least gratitude on the part of the subordinates. This positive reaction was expected to lead to increased production. The expectations were not met. The supervisor is disappointed; like a pendulum, the supervisor swings back to the opposing position and tries to implement it. This is also too extreme for the subordinates, they grumble further, and so on. Each of the parties seems to be making an attempt to balance an unbalanced system without knowledge of the other's attempts. This is a good example of the interdependence of the behavior of the leader and the behavior of those being led.

Directive versus Participative Climates

The preceding discussion implies that any leadership behavior must be viewed in the context of a work system. The system includes subordinate and organizational expectations. Theory X and Theory Y imply a set of thoughts or beliefs. There is another line of literature that relates more closely to action, that of directive versus participative management. The directive leader is one who coordinates the activities of the group, evaluates outcomes for the group, and assumes major responsibilities for all decisions; the participative leader is one who functions primarily as a group member with a particular set of resources for group use. With participative leadership, group members usually have significant input into the decision-making process and collectively evaluate the outcomes of these decisions. It might be best to view directive and participative climates as the concrete applications of Theory X and Theory Y thinking. It is important to see these climates as part of an organizational tradition held by both supervisors and subordinates. For example, a study by Page and McGinnies (1959) indicated that group members classified as low participators were much more favorable to directive leadership than they were to participatory leadership. This could easily be explained on the basis of different sets of expectations held by low and high participators.

These ideas have been presented as nothing more than a fleeting glance at the organization as an organism with a history. Too often we forget that a tradition is built on a history of reinforcement or punishment and is accompanied by certain expectations. It should be clear that the climate or set of expectations that surrounds a supervisory role affects the behavior of the supervisor. In the next chapter, we will take a closer look at the nature of the organization in which supervisors and subordinates interact.

SUMMARY

The supervisor mediates the relationship between the worker and the work environment. Supervision is a form of leadership. A supervisor is the individual designated to direct and coordinate task-relevant work group activities. Research in the area of leadership has distinguished leader emergence from leader effectiveness. A distinction is also made among attempted, successful, and effective leadership.

Supervision can be thought of as a role. One of the characteristics of the supervisory role is the type of power that is used to accomplish change. The different power bases available to a supervisor are: reward power coercive (punishment) power, legitimate power, referent power, and expert power. Studies have found that characteristics of both the leader and the situation determine the type of power that will be used to bring about change in a work-group member.

Early research in leadership is characterized by trait studies concentrating on characteristics of the leader rather than behavior. Trait studies were replaced by behavioral studies that emphasized what the leader actually did that was effective or ineffective. The behavioral approach is best represented by the Ohio State studies, which describe leader behavior on two dimensions—consideration (people-oriented activity) and initiating structure (task-oriented activity). The data gathered relating to these two dimensions indicate that consideration is the more important of the two dimensions. If a leader is described as considerate by subordinates, structure can be added to the situation without any negative effects; if the leader is not described as considerate, increased structure will lead to increased turnover and grievances. There are two instruments used to measure leader behavior: the LOQ (Leadership Opinion Questionnaire), a self-report survey for supervisors, and the LBDQ (Leader Behavior Description Questionnaire) for the description of a supervisor's behavior by subordinates. These two forms seem to measure different aspects of leadership.

Fiedler has introduced a leadership framework that emphasizes both leader characteristics and situational characteristics. The leader characteristics are subsumed under the label LPC, which stands for Least Preferred Co-Worker. This label is thought to represent the cognitive complexity of the leader. The situational variables are position power, leader-member relations, and task structure. These three situational variables are thought to define varying degrees of situational favorability. Certain LPC levels are most suited to certain degrees of situational favorability. This theory has been the object of criticism, both conceptually and empirically. This may be the result of the fact that it is one of the most easily tested theories.

Two other theories that have been receiving attention are Vroom and Yetton's theory of leader decision making, and the path-goal theory. The Vroom-Yetton model is somewhat restricted in its scope, and the path-goal theory is not well defined yet.

Most traditional theories of leadership are concerned primarily with the effects of leader behavior rather than the causes of that behavior. A new class of theories is emerging that deal with leadership as a dependent variable rather than an independent one. Two examples of this new approach are social exchange theory and vertical dyad theory. While there are little data available regarding these theories, they clearly add a new dimension to leadership research.

Under certain conditions, leader intelligence can be shown to be related to leader effectiveness, but the effect of intelligence is suppressed by lack of experience or of motivation on the part of the leader, or interpersonal stress with superiors or subordinates.

The climates in which leaders are asked to lead may make a difference in their effectiveness. This is particularly true of the female leader in a traditional male role.

REFERENCES

Adorno, T. W., Frenkel-Brunswick, E., Levinson, D., & Sanford, R. N. *The authoritarian personality*. New York: Harper, 1950.

Bartol, K. M., & Wortman, M. S. Male vs. female leaders: Effects on perceived leader behavior and satisfaction in a hospital. *Personnel Psychology*, 1975, *28*, 533–548.

Bass, B. M. *Leadership, psychology, and organizational behavior.* New York: Harper, 1960.

Bass, B. M., Valenzi, E. R., Farrow, D. L., & Solomon, R. S. Management styles associated with organizational, task, personal, and interpersonal contingencies. *Journal of Applied Psychology,* 1975, *60,* 720–729.

Blades, J. *The influence of intelligence, task ability, and motivation on group performance.* Unpublished doctoral dissertation, University of Washington, 1976.

Brown, J. A. C. *The social psychology of industry.* Baltimore: Penguin Books, 1954.

Butler, R. P., & Jaffee, C. L. Effects of incentive feedback and manner of presenting the feedback on leader behavior. *Journal of Applied Psychology,* 1974, *59,* 332–336.

Cattell, R. B. (Ed.) *Handbook of multivariate experimental psychology:* Chicago: Rand McNally, 1965.

Chemers, M. M., Rice, R. W., Sundstrom, E., & Butler, W. Leader esteem for the least preferred co-worker score, training, and effectiveness: An experimental situation. *Journal of Personality and Social Psychology,* 1975, *31,* 401–409.

Crissey, W. J. E., & Regan, J. J. Halo in the employment interview. *Journal of Applied Psychology,* 1951, *35,* 338–341.

Csoka, L. S. A relationship between leader intelligence and leader rated effectiveness. *Journal of Applied Psychology,* 1974, *59,* 43–47.

Dansereau, F., Graen, G., & Haga, W. J. *A vertical dyad linkage approach to leadership within the formal organization.* Unpublished report, State University of New York at Buffalo, 1974.

Day, D. R., & Stogdill, R. M. Leader behavior of male and female supervisors: A comparative study. *Personnel Psychology,* 1972, *25*(2), 353–360.

Dubin, R., Homans, G. C., Mann, F. C., & Miller, D. C. *Leadership and productivity.* San Francisco: Chandler, 1965.

Evans, M. G., & Derner, J. What does least preferred co-worker scale really measure? A cognitive interpretation. *Journal of Applied Psychology,* 1974, *59,* 202–206.

Fiedler, F. E. A method of objective quantification of certain countertransference attitudes. *Journal of Clinical Psychology,* 1951, *7,* 101–107.

Fiedler, F. E. *A theory of leadership effectiveness.* New York: McGraw-Hill, 1967.

Fiedler, F. E. *Leadership.* Morristown, N.J.: General Learning Press, 1971.

Fiedler, F. E., & Leister, A. F. Leader intelligence and task performance: A test of a multiple screen model. *Organizational Behavior and Human Performance.* 1977, *20,* 1–14.

Fiedler, F. E., & Mahar, L. The effectiveness of contingency model training: A review of the validation of leader match. *Personnel Psychology,* in press.

Fleishman, E. A. The development of a behavior taxonomy for describing human tasks: A correlational-experimental approach. *Journal of Applied Psychology,* 1967, *51,* 1–10.

Fleishman, E. A., & Harris, E. F.   Patterns of leadership behavior related to employee grievances and turnover. *Personnel Psychology,* 1962, *15,* 43–56.

Fleishman, E. A., Harris, E. F., & Burtt, H. E.   *Leadership and supervision in industry.* Columbus: Bureau of Educational Research, Ohio State University, 1955.

French, J. R. P., & Raven, B. H.   The bases of social power. In D. Cartwright, *Studies in social power.* Ann Arbor: University of Michigan, Institute for Social Research, 1959.

Goodstadt, B. T., & Kipnis, D.   Situational influence on the use of power. *Journal of Applied Psychology,* 1970, *54*(3), 201–207.

Graen, G., Alvares, K. M., Orris, J., & Martella, J.   Contingency model of leadership effectiveness: Antecedent and evidential results. *Psychological Bulletin,* 1970, *74*(4), 285–296.

Graen, G., & Schiemann, W.   Leader member agreement: A vertical dyad linkage approach. *Journal of Applied Psychology,* 1978, *63,* 206–212.

Green, S. G., & Nebeker, D. M.   The effects of situational factors and leadership style on leader behavior. *Organizational Behavior and Human Performance,* 1977, *19,* 368–377.

Greene, C. N.   The reciprocal nature of influence between leader and subordinate. *Journal of Applied Psychology,* 1975, *60,* 187–193.

Hammer, T. H., & Dachler, H. P.   A test of some assumptions underlying path goal model of supervision: Some suggested conceptual modifications. *Organizational Behavior and Human Performance,* 1975, *14,* 60–75.

Hill, T., & Schmitt, N.   Individual differences in leadership decision making. *Organizational Behavior and Human Performance,* 1977, *19,* 353–367.

Hinton, B. L., & Barrow, J. C.   The superior's reinforcing behavior as a function of reinforcements received. *Organizational Behavior and Human Performance,* 1975, *14,* 123–143.

Hinton, B. L., & Barrow, J. C.   Personality correlates of the reinforcement propensities of leaders. *Personnel Psychology,* 1976, *29,* 61–66.

Hollander, E. P.   *Leadership dynamics: A practical guide to effective relationships.* New York: The Free Press, 1978.

Hollander, E. P., & Julian, J. W.   Contemporary trends in the analysis of the leadership process. *Psychological Bulletin,* 1969, *71,* 387–397.

House, R. L.   A path-goal theory of leader-effectiveness. *Administrative Science Quarterly,* 1971, *16,* 321–238.

House, R. L., & Dressler, G.   Path goal theory of leadership: Some post hoc and a priori tests. In J. G. Hunt & L. L. Larson, *Contingency approaches to leadership.* Carbondale: Southern Illinois University Press, 1974.

House, R. L., Filley, A. C., & Kerr, S.   Relation of leader consideration and initiation of structure to R & D subordinates' satisfaction. *Administrative Science Quarterly,* 1971, *16,* 19–30.

House, R. L., & Mitchell, T.   Path-goal theory of leadership. *Journal of Contemporary Business,* 1974, *3,* 81–97.

Ilgen, D. R., & O'Brien, G.   Leader-member relations in small groups. *Organizational Behavior and Human Performance,* 1974, *12,* 335–350.

Jacobson, M. B., & Koch, W. Women as leaders: Performance evaluation as a function of method of leader selection. *Organizational Behavior and Human Performance*, 1977, *20*, 149–157.

Jago, A. G., & Vroom, V. H. A. Hierarchical level and leadership style. *Organizational Behavior and Human Performance*, 1977, *18*, 131–145.

Justis, R. T., Kedia, B. L., & Stephens, D. B. The effect of position power and perceived task competence on trainer effectiveness: A partial utilization of Fiedler's contingency model of leadership. *Personnel Psychology*, 1978, *31*, 83–93.

Keller, R. T., & Szilagyi, A. D. A longitudinal study of leader reward behavior, subordinate expectancies, and satisfaction. *Personnel Psychology*, 1978, *31*, 119–129.

Kerr, S., Schriesheim, C. A., Murphy, C. J., & Stogdill, R. M. Toward a contingency theory of leadership based upon the consideration and initiating structure literature. *Organizational Behavior and Human Performance*, 1974, *12*, 62–82.

Kipnis, D., & Cosentino, J. Use of leadership powers in industry. *Journal of Applied Psychology*, 1969, *53*(6), 460–466.

Korman, A. "Consideration," "initiating structure" and organizational criteria: a review. *Personnel Psychology*, 1966, *19*, 349–361.

Likert, R. Effective supervision: An adaptive and relative process. *Personnel Psychology*, 1958, *11*, 317–332.

Lowin, A., & Craig, J. R. The influence of level of performance on managerial style: An experimental object lesson in the ambiguity of correlational data. *Organizational Behavior and Human Performance*, 1968, *3*, 440–458.

McGregor, D. *The human side of enterprise*. New York: McGraw-Hill, 1960.

McGregor, D. *The professional manager*. New York: McGraw-Hill, 1967.

Mann, F. C. Toward an understanding of the leadership role in formal organization. In R. Dubin, G. C. Homans, & D. C. Miller (Eds.), *Leadership and productivity*. San Francisco: Chandler, 1965.

Mann, R. D. A review of the relationships between personality and performance in small groups. *Psychological Bulletin*, 1959, *56*, 241–270.

Megargee, E., Bogart, P., & Anderson, B. Prediction of leadership in a simulated industrial task. *Journal of Applied Psychology*, 1966, *50*(4), 292–295.

Montgomery of Alamein, Bernard Law Montgomery, 1st viscount. *The path to leadership*. New York: Putnam, 1961.

Nebeker, D. M., & Mitchell, T. R. Leader behavior: An expectancy theory approach. *Organizational Behavior and Human Performance*, 1974, *11*, 355–367.

Oldham, G. R. The motivational strategies used by supervisors: Relationships in effectiveness indicators. *Organizational Behavior and Human Performance*, 1976, *15*, 66–86.

Page, R. H., & McGinnies, E. Comparison of two styles of leadership in small group discussion. *Journal of Applied Psychology*, 1959, *43*, 240–245.

Petty, M. M., & Lee, G. K. Moderating effects of sex of supervisor and subordinate on relationships between supervisory behavior and subordinate satisfaction. *Journal of Applied Psychology*, 1975, *60*, 624–628.

Porter, L. W., & Lawler, E. E. *Managerial attitudes and performance.* Homewood, Ill.: Dorsey, 1968.

Rosen, B., & Jerdee, T. H. Factors influencing disciplinary judgments. *Journal of Applied Psychology,* 1974, *59,* 327–331.

Sashkin, M., Taylor, F. C., & Tripathi, R. C. An analysis of situational moderating effects on relationships between least preferred co-worker and other psychological measures. *Journal of Applied Psychology,* 1974, *59,* 731–740.

Schnier, C. F. The contingency model of leadership: An extension of emergent leadership and leader's sex. *Organizational Behavior and Human Performance,* 1978, *21,* 220–239.

Schriesheim, C. A., House, R. J., & Kerr, S. Leader initiating structure: A reconciliation of discrepant research results and some empirical tests. *Organizational Behavior and Human Performance,* 1976, *15,* 297–321.

Shaw, M. E. *Scaling group tasks: A method for dimensional analysis.* Gainesville: University of Florida, 1963.

Sims, H. P., & Szilagyi, A. D. Leader reward behavior and subordinate satisfaction and performance. *Organizational Behavior and Human Performance,* 1975, *14,* 426–438(a).

Sims, H. P., Jr., & Szilagyi, A. D. Leader structure and subordinate satisfaction for two hospital administrative levels: A path analyses approach. *Journal of Applied Psychology,* 1975, *60,* 194–197(b).

Stinson, J. E., & Tracy, L. Some disturbing characteristics of the LPC score. *Personnel Psychology,* 1974, *27,* 477–486.

Stogdill, R. M. Personal factors associated with leadership. *Journal of Psychology,* 1948, *25,* 35–71.

Student, K. Supervisory influence and work group performance. *Journal of Applied Psychology,* 1968, *52*(3), 188–194.

Tscheulin, D. Leader behavior measurement in German industry. *Journal of Applied Psychology,* 1971, *56*(1), 28–31.

Vecchio, R. P. An empirical examination of the validity of Fiedler's model of leadership effectiveness. *Organizational Behavior and Human Performance,* 1977, *19,* 180–206.

Vroom, V., & Yetton, P. W. *Leadership decision making.* Pittsburgh: University of Pittsburgh Press, 1975.

Weiss, H. M. Subordinate imitation of supervisor behavior: The role of modeling in organizational socialization. *Organizational Behavior and Human Performance,* 1977, *19,* 89–105.

Weissenberg, P., & Kavanaugh, M. The independence of initiating structure and consideration: A review of the evidence. *Personnel Psychology,* 1972, *25*(1), 119–130.

CHAPTER 12

The Role of (the) Organization in Behavior

One of your tasks as a student in this course is understanding the behavior of individuals in work settings. So far, the identification, selection and training of appropriate applicants, theories for understanding why energy is expended at work, and the relationship between the behavior of leaders and the behavior of subordinates have been described. There is another element which must be introduced to fully understand the relationship between a worker and a job; that element is the *organization* which employs the worker. Think about the reaction which you have to someone who says: "I work for the Internal Revenue Service." Now think about your reaction to someone who says: "I work for an international airline." Since you know little about the individuals except their respective employers, your different reactions to these statements must have something to do with the nature of the organization which employs them. Your *views* of the IRS and an international airline are probably very different. The purpose of each of the organizations as well as the way in which that purpose is carried out forms a kind of "personality" for an organization. This personality is transmitted clearly and immediately to the employees of the organization. It may be contained in very obvious sets of rules and regulations, such as, "Show up for work on time," "Take only the allotted time for lunch," etc. It may also be found in much more subtle "traditions" every organization has, such as: "If an employee is divorced, it is unlikely he will ever receive a promotion to upper management," "Middle-level managers are entitled to a full water carafé every morning," or "Newer employees are expected to park in the *back* of the company parking lot." These formal and informal ways of operating, the organizational "personality," have an effect on the choices an individual makes among alternative activities at work. For that reason, the structures and functions of organizations will be examined to determine what effects they have on industrial behavior.

If you have ever been faced with even the simplest of tasks to accomplish, it must be obvious in retrospect that you organized your efforts and/or the efforts of others in a particular way. You no doubt felt that one way of organizing these efforts was more efficient, pleasing, or reasonable than another. You probably organized these efforts systematically so they could be communicated to someone else. If other individuals were involved, you probably expended some effort in clarifying your role in the operation as well as the roles of the various others. This organizing, system building, and clarifying is remarkably similar to activities of even the largest of corporations. In spite of the fact that in large corporations, these activities come under headings such as "company policy," or "organization chart," etc., they imply the same basic operations.

The point can be made even more clearly by looking at the behavior of an individual within a large formal organization such as General Motors or IBM. While there is a formal statement of procedures, rules, and policies, individuals may impose their own set of rules or regulations on their work activity. This has often been seen in informal chains of command, or in informal communication channels. These two different views of organizational behavior or, more specifically, the behavior of an individual in the context of a formal organization, raise an interesting question: *Do individual patterns of behavior create the structure and characteristics of a formal organization, or is there "one best form" of an organization which requires adaptation on the part of the individual?* Another way of phrasing the question is, "Which is the cart and which the horse?" If individual behavior patterns help create organizational personalities, then the title of this chapter should read "The Role of Organization in Behavior." On the other hand, if the organizational personality modifies the behavior of the individual, the chapter title should properly be "The Role of *the* Organization in Behavior." There is some truth to both of these positions. Individuals can radically affect the personality of organizations; Ralph Nader's tactics and accomplishments are ample evidence for this point. Nevertheless, organizations can at the same time carefully control the behavior of its members; the armed forces might be a good example of this position. The rest of the chapter will be devoted to an examination of how individuals and organizations might jointly affect one another.

Classic organization theorists proposed there were a number of "key" variables in an organization (such as size, and number of levels of supervision) that determined the success or efficiency of that organization. These variables were generally considered independently of the individuals in an organization. This approach is reflected in the early works of the sociologist Durkheim, who implied that people could be characterized *as a function of* the structural properties of the society in which they lived. This view has been a pervasive one, and consequently, there is a large body of literature which accompanies it. We will deal in depth with one representation of such an approach: bureaucracy as described by Weber (1947) and those who followed his line of thought.

Modern organizational theorists, on the other hand, seem to begin with the characteristics of the individual organism, the worker, in forming their theory. They propose that it is practically impossible to understand or predict the "behavior" of an organization (if, in fact, an organization can "behave"), without understanding or being able to predict the behavior of the people making up that organization. You are likely to find constructs and concepts in modern theories that are not mentioned in classic theories—processes such as motivation, satisfaction, conflict resolution, and leadership. Implied in these approaches is the idea that the formal organization, as it exists today, is a reflection (although not by any means a perfect one) of the problem-solving, decision-making, and general thought processes of the human organism. This view of the organization is very different from that of the classical theorists. The role of the individual is of maximum importance in modern theories and of questionable value in classic theories. As Argyris has so aptly put it in attacking the peripheral role given the individual in a recent form of classic theory, "the variable human seems to be minimally variable and minimally human" (Argyris, 1972, p. 33).

While all of the variations of the modern-versus-classic argument cannot be discussed here, it will be useful to highlight the distinctions between them. Bennis (1959) classified organizational theorists as either those who studied individuals without organizations (modern) or those who studied organizations without people (classic). March and Simon (1958) charged that while classical theorists dealt with the human organism as an instrument, the modern theorists (in the form of the human relations movement) gave the individual motivations, feelings, and emotions, *without* the capacity to think or reason. Scott (1966) proposed that the distinguishing characteristic of "modern" organization theories was a concern for the relation between organizationally defined properties and the characteristics of the people who populate it. In this chapter, this interaction between organizational characteristics and individual characteristics will be examined. Figure 12–1 provides a framework that highlights the enormity of the task.

Requiring an individual to choose between modern theories and classic theories of the organization is like reliving the experience of the blind men attempting to describe the elephant, one at the trunk and one at the tail. Figure 12–1 gives a sample view of the potential complexity of the organization. First, there is a choice of the level of analysis. It varies from the organization to the individual. In addition, both between and within levels, there are potential interactions between environmental charac-

FIGURE 12–1

A Framework for the Study of Behavior in Organizations

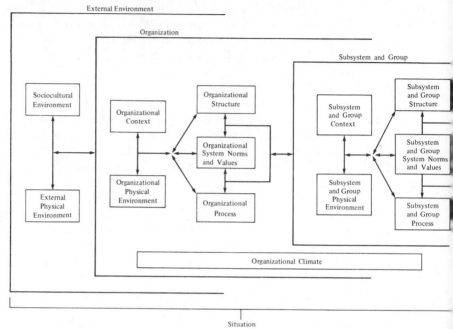

Source: James, L. R., & Jones, A. P. Organizational structure: A review of structural dimensions and their co relationships with individual attitudes and behavior. *Organizational Behavior and Human Performance,* 1976, 97.

teristics, formal and informal structure, and performance. While it is impossible to examine all of the components of the figure, we will look at the interaction among the levels as well as many of the structure and process variables identified.

Figure 12–1 has value in another way. It helps in understanding why so many different disciplines are involved in the study of the organization and its structure. There are topics of interest for historians, political scientists, economists, sociologists, industrial engineers, and psychologists, to mention but a few disciplines. Areas other than psychology will be introduced to the degree that they help in understanding the behavior of an individual in the context of an organization. As a matter of fact, this may be a definition of organizational psychology—a controlled "looting" of other disciplines in the service of understanding the individual in the organization.

Figure 12–2 is a somewhat different figure from Figure 12–1. The latter figure presents an organization in some ideal sense, with an elaborate descrip-

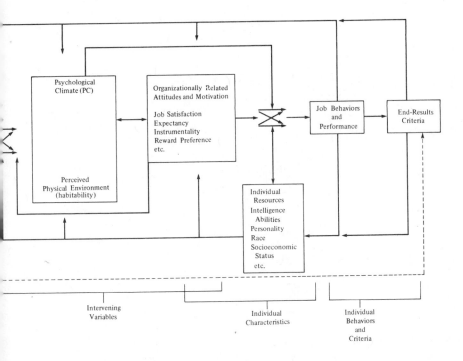

Intervening Variables

Individual Characteristics

Individual Behaviors and Criteria

tion of the variables in the system that may interact. Nevertheless, Figure 12–1 is an abstraction. Figure 12–2, on the other hand, is very real. It is a representation of the "organization" as viewed by the members of that organization. Specifically, it reflects the causal variables that influence the organization of work for individual orchestra members. This is a very different view of organization. While Figure 12–1 represents "the organization," Figure 12–2 represents the organizing process. Throughout the chapter you should keep in mind that both these approaches are important for understanding the individual/organization interaction.

A combination of the classic and modern approaches is the sociotechnical approach to organizations. From this point of view, an organization consists of structural and process characteristics (as emphasized by the classic theorists) as well as social and personal characteristics (as emphasized by the modern theorists). The social and technical characteristics are inextricably bound to form a *system*.

FIGURE 12–2

Cause Relationships Mentioned by a Significant Number of Orchestra Members

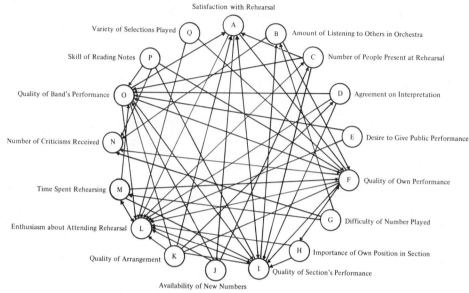

Source: Bougon, M., Weick, K. Y., & Binkhorst, D. Cognition in organizations: An analysis of the Utrecht Jazz Orchestra. *Administrative Science Quarterly*, 1977, *22*, 610.

Now that you have been introduced to the nature of the problem to be explored, the approaches will be presented in some detail. The first approach to be considered will be the classical one.

CLASSIC ORGANIZATION THEORY

It is difficult to distinguish classical organization theory from Weber's bureaucracy. For Weber, the bureaucratic form of organization was a form of social protest against the excesses of the enterpreneurial system as it existed in the early days of the Industrial Revolution. It was an attempt to describe a system that could function free of the injustices of nepotism and favoritism; it was a system that was predictable, allowing the individual worker to make long-range plans; it was also a system that allowed an individual to advance on the basis of merit rather than on the basis of predetermined classes or castes.

Weber proposed that such a system could be characterized or described along a number of dimensions. Those most often mentioned are division of labor, delegation of authority, structure, and span of control. Before dealing with each of these components in turn, let us look in a global sense at the role of these components in solving the basic organizational problem of successfully completing a complex operation. The operation is first broken down into a number of smaller, specifiable components;

FIGURE 12–3

A Representation of Specialization and Delegation Dimensions of a Hypothetical Organization (L = *line;* S = *staff*)

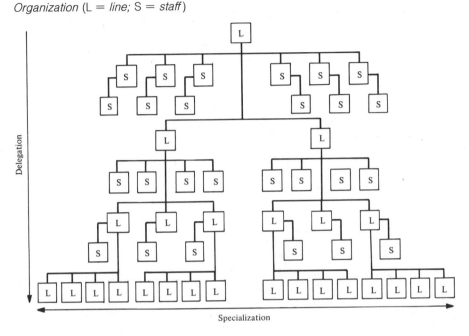

Specialization

this is known as the *division of labor* or *specialization,* and is thought to be necessary for the assignment and discharge of complex responsibilities. This division of labor, in turn, creates a problem of the coordination of these complex responsibilities. Coordination is thought to be best handled through the systematic *delegation of authority.* Figure 12–3 depicts a traditional organizational chart. The vertical dimension of the figure represents the delegation of authority. The horizontal dimension represents division of labor or specialization. It was felt that only through this hierarchical arrangement of authority could supervisors hope to guide the activities of subordinates.

The third and fourth components, *structure* and *span of control,* are interrelated. Structure is basically the height of an organization relative to its width. The structure continuum varies from tall to flat. Span of control, in its simplest form, is the number of subordinates controlled by a single supervisor. Tallness or flatness then is dependent on the number of hierarchical levels of authority and the span of control of each of these levels. Figure 12–4 depicts the relationship between levels of authority, span of control, and organizational structure. Assuming that organizational size remains constant (i.e., a fixed number of employees) the organization becomes flatter as span of control increases and levels of authority decrease. This is shown in Figures 12–4 and 12–5. The bureaucratic model implied

FIGURE 12–4
Small Span of Control Company (size = 1,000)

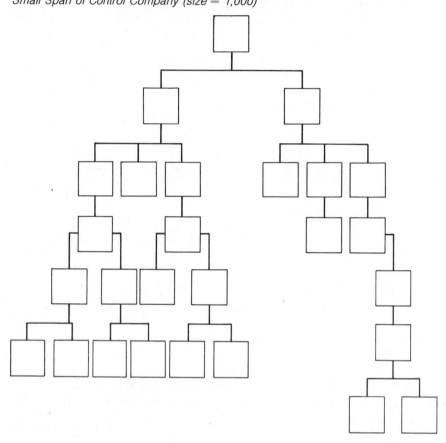

there was one best span of control as well as one best structure. These two variables, structure and span of control, have received most of the attention of researchers, followed by delegation of authority (in the form of models of decision making). Research on the division of labor usually combines this component with the structure component and deals with *line/staff* distinctions, where *line* roles are defined as those having direct responsibility for goods and services, while *staff* roles assume indirect responsibility for such activities. Most of the recent work in the classic tradition has taken the form of a compacting or expansion of these four basic components. Before introducing recent variations in classic theory, the research relevant to the role of the traditional components will be reviewed briefly.

Span of Control

Try to visualize a football coach directing the efforts of all of the individual members of a football team. You would predict it was an impossible task

FIGURE 12–5

Large Span of Control Company (size = 1,000)

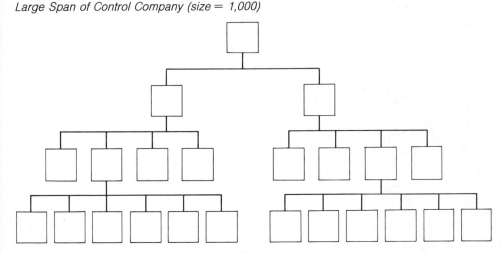

for one individual. The coach needs a staff of specialist coaches (e.g., a backfield coach and a line coach). Without such a system, the performance of the team (or organization) would be unrelated to the wishes and goals of the head coach. But the use of specialist coaches could be carried to an extreme. Suppose there were a coach for every two players, a supervisor for every two coaches, and an administrator for every two supervisors. The control would be so extreme that it would be miraculous if a play ever got from the coach to the team in enough time to run the play. These examples describe the extremes of the span of control.

The search for the most efficient span of control assumed major importance in classic organization theory. Investigations of span of control have taken one of two forms: (1) specifying the "best" number on the basis of the capacities of the individual manager to process information, and (2) specifying the "best" number on the basis of the number and kind of interactions present in the work group. Research on the first approach has looked for support from the work of cognitive psychologists such as Miller. In a now classic work, Miller (1956) proposed that an individual's *span of attention* is limited to seven elements, plus or minus two elements. Organizational theorists have used span of attention as an analog for span of control and proposed that the individual manager can control seven subordinates, plus or minus two. Entwistle (1960) dismissed this analogy as inappropriate due to the fact that Miller was referring to the *momentary consideration of simultaneous stimuli.* Entwistle goes on to support the second approach, relating organizing dynamics to the number and kind of interactions in the work group. He contends that the span of control affects the number of independent subgroups that can form within any particular work group. For example, with a span of control of 4, a supervisor may be required to keep track of as many as fifteen different subgroups.

This would comprise four subgroups of one each, six groups of two each, four groups of three each, and one group of four. This does not even take into account the interactions within and between each of these subgroups. For example, when assigning tasks the manager must take into account the feelings of work group members toward one another as well as toward the supervisor and toward the task. Urwick (1956) pointed out the geometric effect of these complicating factors. In the case of the span of control of 4, 15 sets of interrelationships is a conservative estimate. Taking into account the interactions *within* each group (e.g., since worker A and worker B do not get along well together, the supervisor can never put them together to work on the same task), as well as *between* the groups and the supervisor, the number of potential relationships jumps to 44. With a span of control of 5, the number of relationships increases to 100. A supervisor controlling 7 subordinates is faced with approximately 450 such relationships. It is no wonder supervisors occasionally look out of breath. That is a lot of information to process.

Probably the most reasonable approach to span of control is a combination of the two positions outlined above. The first position, which concentrates on the information-processing characteristics of the organism, might be best viewed as a matter of individual differences. If we accept the assumption that the amount of information individuals can process in a given amount of time varies, a careful monitoring of work-group size is crucial. In this approach, there is no one best span of control; it depends on the processing characteristics of the particular manager.

To complete the logic of this hybrid approach, it is necessary to introduce the work of a British industrial sociologist, Joan Woodward. She was one of the first to point out the importance of technology on the administrative characteristics of the organization. In a series of studies published in 1958, she looked at span of control in three different types of technology:

1. *Small-batch organizations*—those engaged in producing specialty products one at a time.
2. *Large-batch and mass production organizations*—those producing large numbers of discrete units; essentially, assembly line operations.
3. *Continuous process organizations*—those depending on a continuous process for output or product; this would include operations such as chemical operations, distilleries, etc.

Figure 12–6 depicts the relationship between type of technology and span of control. The median span of control for small-batch firms was between 21 and 30, while the median span of control for mass production firms was between 41 and 50, and the median for continuous process firms was between 11 and 20. Dubin (1965) points out that part of the reason for the decreased span of control in continuous process operations is the relative costliness of a mistake. Since the cost of a mistake tends to be higher in continuous process, high-speed operations, more of the responsibilities for inspection and quality control are passed on to first-level management and taken away from the worker. Consequently, the number of supervisory

FIGURE 12–6

Span of Control in First-line Supervision

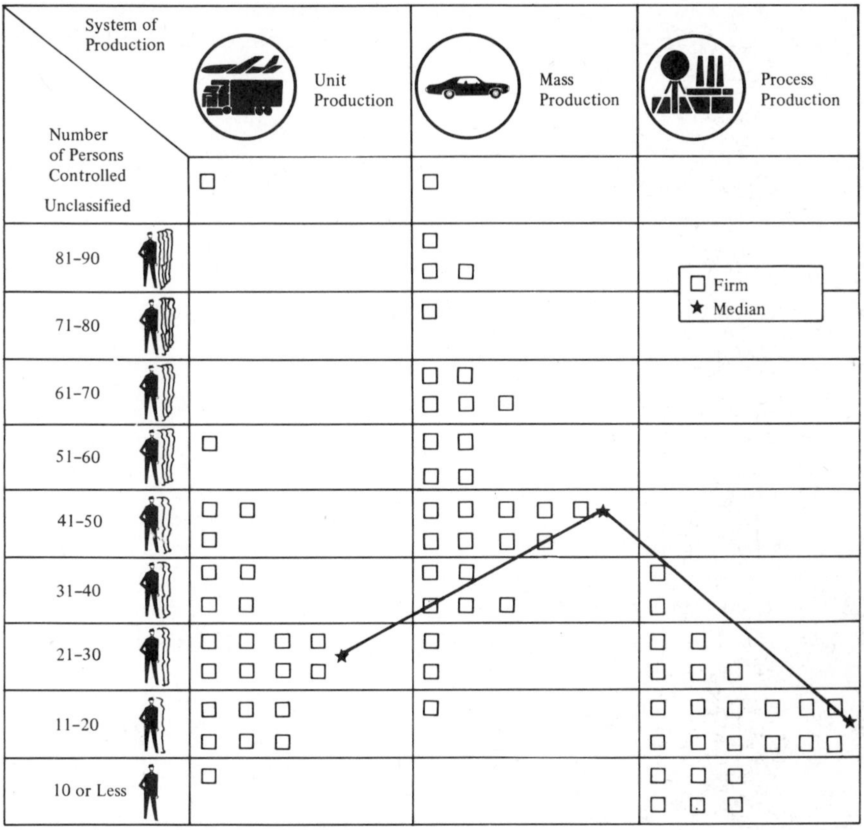

System of Production / Number of Persons Controlled	Unit Production	Mass Production	Process Production
Unclassified	□	□	
81–90		□ / □ □	□ Firm ★ Median
71–80		□	
61–70		□ □ / □ □ □	
51–60	□	□ □ / □ □	
41–50	□ □ / □	□ □ □ □ □★ / □ □ □ □	
31–40	□ □ / □ □	□ □ / □ □ □	□ / □
21–30	□ □ □ □★ / □ □ □ □	□ / □	□ □ / □ □ □
11–20	□ □ □ / □ □ □	□	□ □ □ □ □ / □ □ □ □ □★
10 or Less	□		□ □ □ / □ □ □

Source: Woodward, J. *Management and technology.* London: Her Majesty's Stationery Office, 1958.

personnel tends to increase so that all managerial functions can be attended to as well as the additional responsibilities for inspection and quality control. Woodward's work illustrates the relationship between structural characteristics of an organization and social patterns of its members. While Woodward did not look directly at technological change, it should be apparent if a technology is changed from unit to mass production, there will probably be some accompanying changes in span of control and supervisory processes. If that is the case, careful human resource planning must accompany technological change if the organization is to realize advantages from the technical innovation. Furthermore, these findings suggest there is no *one best* span of control. The best supervisor/subordinate ratio will depend on the nature of the technology. This point will be examined again in much greater detail in a later section dealing with the sociotechnical approach to organizations.

Complicating the issue of the "best" span of control is the fact that there are several different definitions of control span. As an example, Ouchi and Dowling (1974) suggested four different measures of span of control. In examining the supervisor/subordinate reporting relationships in the sales departments of 78 retail department stores, they considered the following measures of span of control:

1. *Raw Span of Control:* The number of sales personnel directly reporting to sales supervisors.
2. *Adjusted Span of Control:* The number of sales personnel directly reporting to sales supervisors, adjusted for the percent of time the supervisor actually supervised them (i.e., taking into account part-time work schedules).
3. *Adjusted Span of Control plus Helpers:* This figure takes into account "buyers" who may also supervise.
4. *Adjusted Span of Control plus Helpers plus Overlapping Supervision:* This figure takes into account the fact a subordinate may be supervised by more than 1 person with the job duties of supervisor (as opposed to buyer).

Table 12–1 presents the span of control figures for each of these definitions. As you can see, the numbers vary substantially, suggesting that careful thought be given to the definition of span of control. Ouchi and Dowling suggest the *Adjusted plus Helper* figure best represents the amount of effort exerted by a supervisor, or in more organizational terms, the closeness of contact between supervisor and subordinate.

TABLE 12–1
Span of Control as Defined by Four Different Measures in 78 Retail Organizations

Variable	Median span	Mean span	Range of span
RAW	8.7	12.9	3–137
Adjusted	14.6	23.3	0–143
Adjusted + Helper	11.8	15.4	3–102
Adjusted + Helper + Overlap	11.4	13.5	2–49

Structure

Organizational structure is a derived variable; that is, it depends on several other variables for its definition. Some of these variables are size, span of control, centralization of decision making, number of levels of supervision, and division of labor. All of these things go together to form a picture of an organization's structure. The most commonly used label for organizational structure is "tall" or "flat." Tall organizations are characterized by small spans of control, many levels of supervision, and centralization of decision making; on the other hand, flat organizations are thought to be characterized by large spans of control, fewer levels of supervision, and decentralized decision making. As you can readily see, the terms *tall* and *flat* are not particularly useful to the organizational psychologist in understanding the interactions of individuals and organizations. The level and type of supervision or the decision-making process might provide a better understanding of motivation, satisfaction, or efficiency. Structure, more than any other concept in organizational psychology, helps to reinforce the idea that an organization is a *system* with a set of interdependent components. This concept will be extended in our later discussion of organizations as sociotechnical systems.

James and Jones (1976) have suggested seven dimensions of structure. These dimensions are total size, centralization of decision making, span of control, pervasiveness of rules, specialization, standardization of process, and interdependence of organizational components.

Some studies have investigated the effect of various aspects of organizational structure on individual and organizational behavior. Evers, Bohlen, and Warren (1976) examined 153 farmer cooperatives and found that less formal structures evolved in smaller firms (less than 10 employees), while the structure became much more formal (with rules, regulations, standardization pressures, and so on) as size increased above 10. This would suggest that size has certain constraining effects on behavior. On the other hand, Moch (1976) examined over 400 hospitals and concluded that increased size led to functional differentiation and decentralization of decision making; these conditions, in turn, led to greater ease in the adoption of innovation. These two studies, in combination, suggest that size, per se, is not the critical variable in organizational functioning. Rather, one must consider the effect size has on other interrelated variables such as specialization and decision making.

In 1950, Worthy suggested that flat organizations were "better" than tall ones. Flat organizations were thought to have characteristics appropriate for both organizational and individual efficiency. They are administratively decentralized and less complex. In addition, satisfaction is thought to be higher in flat organizations, since there would seem to be less punitive control over the individual worker and ample opportunity for increased responsibility and initiative. Ivancevich and Donnelly (1975) questioned 295 sales personnel in three organizations and found that the individuals in flat organizations perceived more satisfaction with self-actualization and autonomy motives, felt they were under less stress, and performed more efficiently than salesmen in either medium or tall organizations. While these data are generally supportive of Worthy, we must remember that the terms "tall" and "flat" cover a multitude of variables whose impact could not have been adequately assessed in only three organizations.

Another example of the fruitfulness of considering some of the formal characteristics of the organization is provided by Ghiselli (1969). He looked at the relationships between the type of advancement system used in a particular organization and the organizational structure (tall versus flat). He defined two different types of advancement systems. The first, the open personnel-procurement system, is characterized by organizations that fill vacancies at all levels of the organization from both inside *and* outside the organization. The second, the closed personnel-procurement system, is characterized by organizations that fill only the lowest-level vacancy from outside the organization and all other vacancies from inside (e.g., military organizations). Ghiselli proposed that the efficiency of these two systems of filling vacancies would vary as a function of the type of advancement policy used and the flatness or tallness of the organization. He proposed that in flat organizations with a closed procurement system, advancement on the basis of *merit* might be a good policy. He reasoned that since the number of individuals in the work group is relatively large, the competition should be stiff. On the other hand, in a tall organization with a closed procurement system, merit may not be the best advancement procedure to use. Instead, something like an aptitude test might provide a more valid basis for the advancement decision. In an open procurement system, these relationships are modified. This concept is similar to the "selection ratio" logic introduced in Chapter 5. If you are making a promotional decision for a work group member in a closed personnel procurement system, the size of that group is analogous to the concept of a selection ratio. This work by Ghiselli suggests important relationships between organizational characteristics and personnel policies.

Criticisms of Classic Theory

Classic organization theory is currently serving at least one function that had never been intended. It is serving as a target for the development of more advanced attempts to understand behavior in organizations. For example, Lowin (1968) showed how participative decision making changes the nature of the traditional hierarchical model of the organization. Specifically, he contended that in the classic model of organization, the individual who makes the decision and the individual who *implements* that decision occupy different positions in the organization chart—decisions are handed down to be implemented. In the traditional model, the decision function and the implementation function are separated. Participative decision making has the effect of giving a single individual both decision and action functions. The segregation of function existing in the traditional model is eliminated. This is related to the discussion in the motivation chapter of the importance of involving individuals in the decision process in order to increase motivation and goal commitment, and represents a clash between the traditional theorist's concern for efficiency and the modern theorist's concern for individual motivation. This clash is the basis for recent criticisms of classic organization theory.

March and Simon (1958) level serious criticisms at the classic approach. They feel that classic organization theory is limited by the facts that:

1. The motivational assumptions are incomplete and inaccurate.
2. The entire process of intraorganization conflict resolution is ignored.
3. There is little appreciation of the limitations on the information-processing capabilities of the individual.
4. There is little appreciation of the role of cognition in decision making or task identification.
5. New activities and new programs are not allowed.

Figure 12–7 is just one example of the problems with classic organization theory. An organizational chart implies (or more formally *demands*) certain interrelationships among and between levels of the organization. As you can see from this figure, reality is often at odds with an ideal. Regardless of what the organization chart *says*, people will develop patterns of behavior to accommodate their own needs and the current organizational environment. For those reasons, classic organization theory should not be considered as a reasonable framework for understanding organizational behavior. In addition, there may even be negative consequences from adopting the classic

FIGURE 12–7

Organizational Chart of a Small Insurance Company Showing Bypassing of a Hierarchical Level

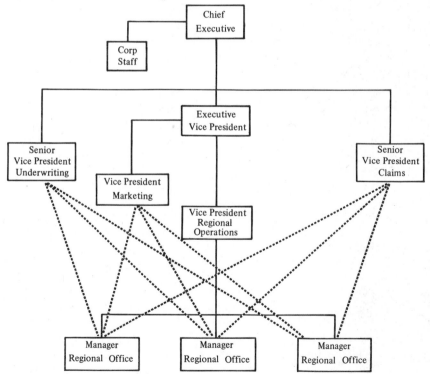

Source: Evans, P. B. Multiple hierarchies and organizational control. *Administrative Science Quarterly,* 1975, *20,* 256.

approach. Korman (1971) presents a pessimistic view of the effect of traditional organizational structure on creative expression. The interdependence of organizational structure and individual motivation is presented in Figure 12–8. This figure does much to highlight the great gap between classic and modern theory. By following the actions and reactions of the organization and the individual, you can see how errors are compounded. You can also see that the emphasis on controlling, so characteristic of classic organization theory, is a counterproductive strategy in many cases.

MODERN ORGANIZATION THEORY

Scott (1961) proposed a scheme for understanding the behavior of individuals in organizations. He contends there are three essential elements that must be examined: (1) the requirements of the organization, (2) the characteristics of the individuals who populate the organization, and (3) the relationship between the organizational requirements and the characteristics of the people in it. Modern organization theory is best described by the third element.

It is often said that the major difference between the classic and modern approaches is the introduction of human feelings and emotions. This is an oversimplification. As early as 1958, March and Simon were advocating not only "allowing" the organism of the capacity to *feel*, but also to *think*. In many of the modern theories, the cognitive functions of the individual play a great part. In addition, this narrow distinction between modern and classic theory—a distinction made solely on the basis of emotions— ignores the effect of environment. Argyris (1972) criticized researchers for placing the environment in a "black box" and acting as if it were trivial or nonexistent. Much of the research described later in this chapter deals with these two characteristics. The cognitive properties of the worker will enter in the form of problem solving, decision making, and conflict resolution. The environmental characteristics will enter the discussion in the form of organizational climate (the organizational "personality").

Before proceeding to descriptions of some modern theories, a different kind of distinction will be made between modern and classic theory. Instead of examining different views of "the organization," the *organizing process* can be considered. On the one hand, the individual interacts with a preexisting structure (the organizational chart or company policy). This structure is really a point on a temporal continuum. It represents the collective organizing process of the company as it exists at that point. It has evolved and will continue to change, though slowly. An individual who comes to work for a particular organization accepts this organizing effort of the company.

On the other hand, the individual has a unique way of organizing thoughts, feelings, and efforts. This individual organizing process may or may not match that of the company. If it does not, we have tension between the individual and the organization. At the intersection of these two organiz-

FIGURE 12–8

A Critical View of Behavior in an Organization Built upon Classic Organization Theory

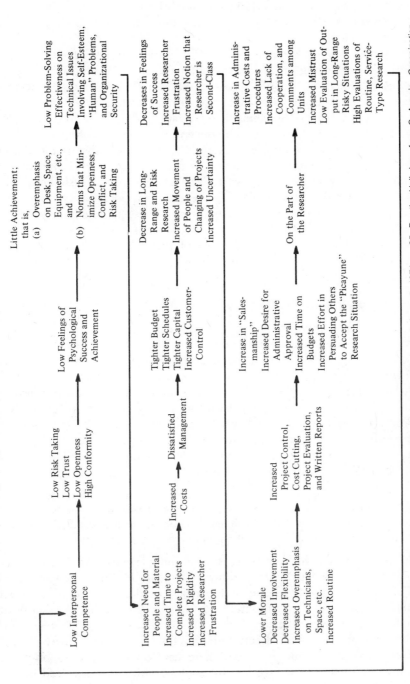

Source: Adapted by Abraham K. Korman, *Industrial and organizational psychology,* © 1971, p. 95, Prentice-Hall, Inc., from C. Argyris, *Organization and innovation* (Homewood, Ill.: Richard D. Irwin, 1965), pp. 236–237. © 1965 by Richard D. Irwin, Inc.

ing processes is the supervisor. The role of the supervisor is to bring the two organizing processes together with a minimum loss to both the company and the individual.

From this point of view, classic organization theory has dealt primarily with the organizing process of the company or "group organizing efforts," while the modern theories have emphasized the organizing processes of the individual. Both approaches are dealing with different facets of the same basic process—the efficient organization of thought and action. Some recent theories and practices are concentrating on the interaction between these two organizing efforts. McGregor has a central dynamic component related to "integration" of the respective goal systems of the individual and the organization; Argyris (1972) deals with the clash between the individual and organizational value sytems and proposes "intervention strategies" and "conflict resolution techniques." These approaches basically support the idea that the organizing *process* is a single phenomenon. We will now present some current views of that process. These are intended to be representative rather than exhaustive.

McGregor's Theory X/Theory Y

As we have seen in earlier chapters, the thoughts of McGregor have had a profound effect on managers. In his book, *The Human Side of Enterprise* (1960), he developed the logical relationships between the beliefs managers held about subordinates and the behavior of those subordinates. In an effort to describe the effect of various belief systems, he developed the two fictional belief systems that he labeled *Theory X and Theory Y.* These terms have been widely used and often misunderstood since they were introduced. McGregor intended the belief systems to be considered as simply *examples* of belief systems which might exist. He states in a work (1967) published after his death:

> It should be apparent that one could find managerial beliefs about the nature of man sufficiently different from X or Y that they might be labeled Theory A or O or S. How many different theories there are would thus become a matter for empirical investigation and classification. (p. 80)

In spite of McGregor's warning, it is commonplace to hear managers discuss organizations, departments, or other individuals in terms of Theory X versus Theory Y as if the two belief systems exhausted the possibilities for beliefs held by managers. Unfortunately, McGregor was not able to describe alternative belief systems clearly before his death in 1964. Therefore, while the generally accepted descriptions of Theory X and Theory Y will be presented, you should not take them as rigid cornerstones of a theory but as examples of managerial philosophies which, in turn, lead to certain managerial strategies.

Theory X managers believe that, in the interest of meeting organizational goals, the behavior of subordinates must be modified, controlled, and directed to meet the needs of the organization. If managers did not engage in these controlling and directing activities, the subordinates would be either apathetic or actively resistant to meeting organizational goals. It is further assumed by Theory X managers that such controlling and directing should be accomplished through persuasions, punishments, and rewards; more generally by controlling mechanisms outside the individual.

Managers holding beliefs labeled Theory Y assume that individual workers are motivated to seek out responsibility and can easily accept responsibility for meeting organizational goals. In addition, this belief system implies that any resistance or apathy encountered in the individual is a function *not* of the basic nature of the individual, but of the individual's experience with the organization. In short, resistance and apathy are learned.

The major component in McGregor's theory of organizational functioning is the integration of the goals of the organization with the goals of the individual. He felt that only through collaborative effort could both sets of goals be met. The task of management and, by extension, the task of the organization and its structure, is to create conditions that facilitate the goal achievement of organization members at all levels. In addition, this goal achievement should result from the direction of individual efforts toward organizational goals. In other words, it is important that the individual see that the goals of the organization and her goals are not mutually exclusive; as a matter of fact, the two goal systems should be viewed as closely related.

It is the component of integration through collaboration that highlights the importance of the two belief systems. The environment or organizational conditions that exist at any given momemt can either help or hinder the process of integration. Theory X belief systems were seen as creating a hindering environment, while Theory Y systems were seen as creating a helping environment.

The description of Theory Y beliefs and practices brings a number of things to mind. The most immediate is the striking similarity between McGregor's description of integration in a Theory Y environment and the earlier path-goal notions of motivation of Georgopolous, Mahoney, & Jones (1957). McGregor's statements imply that if employees see the satisfaction of organizational goals as a path to achieving personal goals, they will expend energy in the direction of satisfying organizational goals. In addition, collaboration as a vehicle for integration suggests management by objectives, a technique described in Chapter 9, in which supervisors and subordinates jointly set goals and explore strategies for achieving those goals.

Chris Argyris' Theory

If you will turn once more to Figure 12–6, which is based on the work of Argyris, you will see that it is quite specific about the possible effect of organizational structure. Argyris makes quite a leap from the demands of the formal system to the probable behavior of people in the system. He makes this leap on the basis of certain assumptions about human nature and, more specifically, about the way the individual progresses from child to adult. In that sense it has been called a developmental theory. He contrasts the way individuals develop with the restrictions put on that development by the formal organization.

Argyris contends that individuals develop:

1. From passive organisms to active organisms.
2. From dependent organisms to independent organisms.
3. From organisms requiring immediate need gratification to organisms able to tolerate delays in gratification.
4. From organisms able to deal only with concrete operations to those able to deal in abstractions.
5. From organisms with few abilities to organisms with many abilities.

If we accept those assumptions (and they seem quite reasonable) then we must also accept the fact that some forms of work and some strategies for technological control (e.g., assembly-line work) are not suited to the level of development of the individual entering the organization. This lack of congruence inevitably leads to tension on the part of the individual, who subsequently engages in certain kinds of activities to relieve this tension. Some of these activities are absenteeism, turnover, unionization, and apathy. The traditional organization, viewing these actions on the part of the worker, comes to the conclusion that more control is needed, institutes such controls, and consequently exaggerates rather than eliminates the maladaptive behavior of the individual.

There are some striking similarities between the thinking of McGregor and that of Argyris. It would not be too difficult to translate Argyris' developmental assumptions into the Theory Y belief system. In addition, the process of matching the goal system of the individual and the demands of the organization plays a crucial role in both approaches.

Lawrence and Lorsch's Theory

While there are many different approaches within the modern school of organizational theory, one that has received a good deal of attention in the last several years is that of Lawrence and Lorsch (1967). They characterize the classical approach as one directed toward finding the best possible organizational structure for coping with all situations. This is fruitless, since an "average" organizational structure is useless in any one situation (although it would be invaluable in the "average" situation). For Lawrence and Lorsch, change is the most important component of an organization. Their goal is to describe the best form of organization for coping with environmental change. In fact, environmental change versus environmental stability is one of the most important components of their approach.

They base their position both on their own data and also on that of

Burns and Stalker (1961). Burns and Stalker found that organizations in stable industries tend to be more "mechanistic." *Mechanistic* is defined as dependent on formal rules and regulations, decisions reached at higher levels of the organization, and smaller spans of control. In contrast, organizations in dynamic, changing industries tended to be more "organic." *Organic* is defined as having larger spans of control, less formalization of procedures, and decisions made at middle levels of the organization. Consequently, they believe that certain environments lead to certain forms of organization.

While these propositions seem straightforward, Lawrence and Lorsch go on to deal with organizational behavior as a function of intraorganizational variables as well as the environment described above. The intraorganizational variables are described in the form of three basic questions, which must be answered to understand organizational behavior:

1. What are the differences among managers with different functional jobs in their orientation toward particular goals?
2. What are the differences in time orientations of different managers in different parts of the organization?
3. What are the differences in interpersonal orientations of managers in different parts of the organization?

The answers to these three questions characterize a single dimension along which organizations differ. This dimension has been labeled *differentiation*, and is defined as the difference in cognitive and emotional orientation of managers in different parts of the organization. This is a very different form of differentiation from that proposed by the classical theorists. For the early traditionalists, differentiation appeared in the form of specialization and division of labor, and was thought to be essential for meeting organizational goals. The inconveniences of coordination of the various special functions were eliminated by the "chain of command" or hierarchical authority levels. Lawrence and Lorsch contend the very act of specialization produces side effects that were not considered by the early theorists. These side effects appear in the new definition of differentiation: inconveniences and inefficiencies caused by different orientations, toward time, goals, and interpersonal relations.

Like McGregor, Lawrence and Lorsch consider collaborative effort to be the best form of activity when unity of organizational movement is demanded by the environment. Their term for collaboration is *integration*, and it is defined as the quality or state of collaboration that exists among departments. Integration cannot be realized until the conflicts between departments—conflicts caused by differentiation—are resolved.

In many ways, this is the most dynamic of the three modern approaches presented. It proposes that a successful organization is one capable of meeting and changing with environmental demands. It further specifies that the point at which the meeting or changing is ultimately done is at the departmental level, not the corporate level. This is remarkably similar to Fiedler's notion of efficient leadership. It seems that Lawrence and Lorsch are describing the equivalent of Fiedler's situation favorability in their environmental change component. As we continue to consider thought and research on organization theory, the relationships between leadership and organization will become harder to ignore.

THE JOB ENRICHMENT APPROACH

The Effect of Technology on Behavior

Earlier in the chapter, we described the work of Woodward with respect to the effect of technology on span of control. This is an indirect way of looking at the effect of technology on behavior of organizational members, and is an extremely important area of concern for the organizational psychologist. As we implied in the beginning of the chapter, the way work is organized may have a substantial effect on behavior.

One problem in looking at the technology/behavior relationship is the need for a good description of technology. The earlier distinctions of batch, continuous, etc. were useful but primitive. Mahoney and Frost (1974) have suggested an approach to technology that is more realistic. It is based on earlier work by Thompson (1967) and consists of three types of technology:

1. *Long-Linked Technology:* Implies knowledge and predictability of cause effect relationships, and high structuring of jobs and work processes; the type of technology described is analagous to the mass-production assembly line.
2. *Mediating Technology:* Involves the choice among a number of alternative processes or programs; jobs are first classified in some way, and then processes appropriate to the classification category are applied. An example of a mediating technology would be an insurance claims unit processing the claims of individuals. In this case, claims must first be grouped and then processed by applying the right set of decision rules.
3. *Intensive Technology:* Considered as highly specialized with a good deal of discretionary performance. The individual receives feedback from the object under consideration, and this feedback determines the nature of the procedure, process, or treatment applied next to the object of interest. Research and development units are representative of intensive technologies. They are constantly involved in evaluating the effects of one treatment and using those results to decide on the next treatment.

They propose that each technology is suited to a particular kind of performance criterion or effectiveness. In addition, they suggest that certain types of variables contribute to these different types of effectiveness. In other words, to a certain extent, the technology determines which effectiveness criteria can be maximized as well as *how* they can be maximized. Figure 12–9 describes the effectiveness criteria and the variables that affect them.

FIGURE 12–9

Proposed Relationships among Types of Technology, Criteria of Effectiveness for Those Technologies, and Variables Contributing to Effectiveness in Those Technologies

Technology	Effectiveness Criteria	Variables Contributing to Effectiveness
Long-linked	Planning Performance Reliability	Supervisory control of work Supervisory emphasis on results Group cohesion
Mediating	Flexibility Planning Performance Supervisory control	Low interchange with other units Limited coordination with other units
Intensive	Performance Cooperation Development Staffing	Minimal delegation Low coordination with other units Emphasis on meeting work commitments to other units

As an example of how this information might be used, we would expect that a mass-production unit should be evaluated in terms of the reliability of the final product, the long- and- short-range planning for future production, and production level. Furthermore, we would expect planning, reliability, and performance to be facilitated by high work group cohesion, an emphasis on turning out high quality and high quantity, and strong initiating structure behavior on the part of the leader.

The work of Mahoney and Frost is just one example of attempts to develop organizational theories which deal simultaneously with organizational characteristics, leader characteristics, and worker behavior. As such, it is presented as an approach rather than as "an answer" or a theory. Nevertheless, it is a substantially different approach from that suggested by the classic organizational theorists.

The Effect of Task and Job Design on Behavior

Within certain limits, technology influences task design. Thus, mass-production jobs do not typically give the person performing the job much discretion in work behavior. Things are to be done in a particular way, and there is little room for variation. On the other hand, intensive technologies commonly involve a good deal of discretion on the part of the employee in the choice of work methods and processes. We have seen in the motivation and satisfaction chapters that individuals can be influenced by a multitude of variables in the environment. The design of the particular job the individual is doing might be one of those variables. Certainly Herzberg suggested that "enriched" jobs had dramatically different effects on individuals than "deprived" jobs.

The effect of task design on employee behavior has been closely examined in the last several years. The most popular model or theory guiding these examinations has been that of Hackman and Oldham (1976). They have proposed a model that has been labelled the "job characteristics model" to explain relationships between technology and worker motivation. This model is reproduced in graphic form in Figure 12–10. The model suggests that certain job characteristics (core job dimensions) produce certain perceptions in individuals (critical psychological states), which in turn lead to certain organizational and individual outcomes (personal and work outcomes). They further suggest that workers who are high in *Growth need strength* will react more positively to jobs with high amounts of the core job dimensions than individuals with low *Growth need strength*. *Growth need strength* is related to the level in the Maslow-type hierarchy that best describes the individual in question. Thus, an individual currently functioning at the self-actualization level is thought to be high on growth need strength, while an individual who considers security needs as most important would be thought to have low growth need strength. The core job dimensions are defined as follows:

Skill Variety: The degree to which the tasks require different skills.
Task Identity: The degree to which the individual completes a "whole" piece of work rather than simply a part.
Task Significance: The degree to which the job has an impact on the lives or work of other people.

FIGURE 12–10
The Job Characteristics Model of Work Motivation

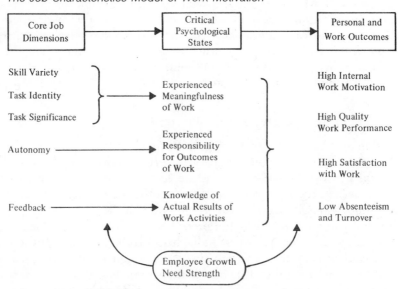

Source: Hackman, J. R., & Oldham, G. R. Motivation through the design of work: Test of a theory. *Organizational Behavior and Human Performance*, 1976, *16*, 256.

Autonomy: Freedom and independence of action.

Feedback: The degree to which the job provides clear and direct information about individual effectiveness.

The theory suggests that these five core dimensions can be combined in a particular way to provide an index of the motivating potential of any job. In other words, each job can receive a score on each of the five dimensions, and these scores can be used to distinguish jobs that have motivating potential from those that do not. This score (called the Motivating Potential Score, or MPS) is a measure of the adequacy of job design. The score is computed by means of the following formula:

$$\text{MPS} = \left[\frac{\text{Skill variety} + \text{Task identity} + \text{Task significance}}{3} \right] \times \text{Autonomy} \times \text{Feedback}$$

The formula suggests that skill variety, task identity, and task significance have additive relationships, and more of one of them can make up for a deficiency in another. This is not the case with autonomy and feedback. If either of these values is zero, the MPS is also zero.

Hackman and Oldham (1975) have produced an instrument that measures the core job dimensions. It is called the Job Diagnostic Survey (JDS) and provides measures of objective job dimensions, individual psychological states resulting from these characteristics, affective reactions to the job characteristics, and measures of growth need strength.

There have been mixed reactions to the theory. As is often the case, researchers first concentrated on the measures of the constructs involved. Brief and Aldag (1975) and Dunham (1976) both expressed reservations about the independence of the five core dimensions. Dunham conducted a factor analysis of responses to the JDS and found a single factor he labeled Job Variety. In addition, Brief and Aldag expressed concern about the proposed mediating influence of growth need strength. This variable did not seem to function in the way suggested by Hackman and Oldham. Finally, Wall, Clegg, Jackson (1978) attempted to test the job characteristics model and concluded that critical psychological states were not produced or affected by the core job dimensions. In addition, they questioned the independence of the core job dimensions as measured by the JDS. On the basis of the research done to date, the job characteristics model has not received much support. This is particularly discouraging for those doing research in job enrichment because the model provided a good theoretical framework for predicting the effects of job enrichment. At a very basic level, the model suggested that for individuals with high growth need strength, an enriched job would result in positive consequences for both the individual and the organization. The results of enriching jobs for individuals with low growth need strength were thought to be much less positive (Oldham, Hackman, and Pearce, 1976). Since the results of job enrichment experiments have not been uniformly positive, this was an appealing explanation. Nevertheless, since the job characteristics model has not received the necessary empirical support, we must look elsewhere for an explanation of the mixed results of job enrichment projects. Below, we will describe some of the job enrichment results.

Job Enrichment

The notion of job enrichment was popularized by Herzberg as a prescriptive addition to his theory of work motivation. He proposed that job enrichment was the vehicle by which individuals could be motivated to do high quality work. In addition, he suggested that job enrichment would lead to increased satisfaction on the part of employees.

In the early days of this research, the guiding principle was somehow to make work "more challenging." Distinctions were made between increasing challenge (job enrichment) and increasing diversity (job enlargement). As is usually the case with new "techniques," there were frequent reports of miraculous successes. Job enrichment seemed to increase satisfaction, decrease absenteeism and turnover, increase motivation, and improve the quantity and quality of production. Unfortunately, most of these successes were being reported on television and in the newspapers. In the scientific journals, the results were somewhat less uniform. Job enrichment did not always have positive results. Locke, Sirota, and Wolfson (1976) briefly reviewed the conditions in which job enrichment failed:

1. When job enrichment destroyed efficient technology (Levitan & Johnson, 1973).
2. When diagnosis, training, and planning were not appropriately carrried out (Sirota & Wolfson, 1972a, 1972b).
3. When non-middle-class, blue-collar workers from urban environments were involved (Hulin, 1971; Locke, 1976).

The broad-band approach to job enrichment, which implied that enriched jobs were the cure for everything from dissatisfaction through summer rashes, has now given way to a more specific consideration of the nature of enrichment. Umstot, Bell, and Mitchell (1976) assigned subjects to coding tasks and contrasted the effects of job enrichment with the effects of goal setting procedures. They were able to demonstrate that job enrichment had an effect on satisfaction but not on productivity. On the other hand, goal-setting activities affected productivity but had much less effect on satisfaction.

Locke, Sirota, and Wolfson (1976) conducted an elaborate field experiment in an attempt to assess the effects of job enrichment. They assigned clerical employees of a large federal agency to various experimental and control groups. The workers were involved in filing, sorting, searching for lost files, and so on. Job enrichment consisted of various manipulations such as forming work teams, deciding on work procedures, and implementing job-rotation schemes. In the course of the study, the researchers measured work attitudes and collected data with respect to absenteeism, turn-over, performance, and grievances. The results are summarized in Table 12–2. As you can see from the table, there were some substantial changes in productivity. The experimental group improved by 23 percent above pre-enrichment base lines. In addition, there was a substantial difference in turnover percentages in favor of the experimental (enriched) groups. Suprisingly, however, there were no changes in the job satisfaction of either the experimental or control subjects. Most attempts at explaining the effect of job enrichment have invoked the notion of changed psychological states (e.g., Herzberg's motivator/hygiene theory or the Hackman and Oldham job characteristics model). Since job satisfaction did not change, Locke and his associates looked more closely at what had actually happened as a result of the job enrichment and came to the conclusion that the productiv-ity changes were a result of more efficient use of manpower, the elimination of unnecessary paper shuffling, better feedback with respect to performance, and the introduction of competition. In short, it was their feeling that most of the effects of job enrichment could be explained in terms of indus-trial engineering principles without any consideration of psychological states represented by terms such as "growth" or "challenge." In addition, since the workers in the experimental groups were making decisions about the nature of work, they most likely eliminated many of the annoying routine tasks that might have led to high absence or turnover rates.

The Locke et al. study is useful from several points of view. First, it demonstrates that the "theory" of job enrichment is on somewhat shaky grounds. This is particularly true in light of the fact attitudes did not change in the experimental group. Additionally, the study amply demon-strates all the confounding issues in job enrichment research. Seldom does the experimenter change only one dimension of the job. Commonly, enrich-ing a job includes one or all of the following changes:

1. Changing the task performed.
2. Changing type and amount of supervision.
3. Changing the method of payment.
4. Changing the level of worker participation in decision making.
5. Changing the social relations of the work group.
6. Changing the overall work technology.

TABLE 12–2
Effects of Job Enrichment

Measure	Experimental Group	Control Group
Productivity	+23%	+2%
Absenteeism	−5%	+7%
Turnover	−6%	+20%
Complaints	No complaints	4 complaints
Attitudes	No change	No Change

There are undoubtedly other changes as well, but you can see the difficulties in determining the factors in the success or failure of job enrichment programs.

At this stage, it is safe to say we still do not know how and when job enrichment will affect attitudes, motivations, and productivity. This leaves the concept out on a limb—a phenomenon without a theory to explain it. This will no doubt change in the near future. But for the present, we might be better off thinking of the global relationship between technology and behavior, as suggested by Mahoney and Frost, rather than a program as specific as job enrichment.

We have dealt with two different theoretical approaches to organizations: the classic and the modern. We have not attempted to list and describe all current examples of these approaches. Instead, we have tried to give you a feel for the differences between the two. Now we will describe an approach that attempts to combine the strengths of the two—the sociotechnical systems approach.

THE SOCIOTECHNICAL SYSTEMS APPROACH TO ORGANIZATIONS

In the chapters dealing with satisfaction, motivation, and leadership, we tended to treat individuals in the workplace as social animals, influenced by attitudes, beliefs, feelings, and aspirations. In the chapters dealing with human engineering and machine design, we will treat individuals as important components in larger man-machine systems. Organizational theory emphasizes the relationship between individuals and *technologies* rather than individuals independent of those technologies or individuals with respect to tasks or machines. One approach to organizational theory has stressed the social implications of technologies for individual behavior. The term *sociotechnical* has been coined to represent this approach. The sociotechnical approach implies an attempt to find the best match between social systems and technical systems rather than exaggerate the importance of one at the expense of the other.

The sociotechnical approach has become almost synonymous with the Tavistock Institute. The Tavistock Institute of Human Relations became involved in examining the social consequences of technological change in the British coal-mining industry in the late 40s. Until then, coal mining had been done by small work groups and primarily by hand. Mass technology was introduced by means of what has become known as the "long-wall" method. Long-wall mining was accomplished by the use of mechanical equipment that carved out substantial amounts of coal from the face or wall and transported it back to a central location for processing. The old days of small autonomous cohesive work groups were gone. Specialization had arrived. New jobs were created. Old social interdependencies were swept away and new ones put in their place.

Trist and Bamforth (1951) examined the results of the change and discovered that all sorts of dysfunctional behavior (rivalry, absenteeism, and so on) could be directly traced to the changes in social patterns demanded by the new technology. On the basis of these observations, Trist and Bamforth suggested that technological change must be accompanied by planned integration for new social relations patterns. Further work in the mining industry demonstrated that particular combinations of social and technical systems yielded high productivity, high satisfaction, low absenteeism, and so on. In these studies, it seemed that the way work groups were formed and the manner in which labor was divided was a critical issue. In some later studies by other Tavistock researchers (Rice, 1958), the sociotechnical principles were again demonstrated in weaving mills in India. The conclusion from these studies was that meaningful tasks, satisfying primary work group relations, and social organization arranged with task accomplishment in mind were critical for productive and satisfied workers.

An Application of the Sociotechnical Systems Approach

The sociotechnical approach is both important and interesting. For that reason, we will present a rather detailed description of a recent sociotechnical experiment. As a result of his interest in the quality of working life, Trist and his colleagues (Trist, Susman, and Brown, 1977) applied the sociotechnical model of the Tavistock Institute to an American coal-mining operation. They were conducting an action research project to see if optimizing the match between social and technical systems could improve the perceived quality of working life.

They were able to interest the United Mine Workers, the United States Commission on Productivity and Work Quality, and a small independent deep coal mine in jointly sponsoring a project designed to assess the effect of autonomous or self-supervised work groups on various individual and organizational outcomes. The experiment was to last for slightly over one year, and the decision to continue with the new sociotechnical system would be made on the basis of the results of the first year.

Prior to the beginning of the experiment, several conditions were agreed to by the management of the mine. These agreements were as follows:

1. In experimental groups, all workers would be paid the same amount rather than the amount typically suggested by the job classification plan; in other words, miners, mechanics, roof bolters, and so on would all be paid the same amount as opposed to the typical differential rate based on job duties.

2. Normal grievance procedures were eliminated for experimental groups, and a joint worker/management council was established for handling grievances.

3. Members of the experimental group would be allowed to try out all of the different mining jobs (e.g., mechanic, helper, or bolter) without

these jobs being posted or made available to other employees of the company.

4. The company relinquished the right to direct experimental crew members at the work site.

These were rather remarkable concessions made on the part of both union and management. From them, you can begin to get a feel for the notion of a sociotechnical system. The typical experiment would change one of those factors but not all. But the essence of the sociotechnical approach is that one deals with a *system*, not a single component.

After management and union representatives agreed to the conditions of the experiment, job openings were posted for three eight-man crews. Volunteers for the experimental groups were chosen on the basis of seniority and qualifications. Those workers chosen for the experiment went through an orientation period which included both on-the-job training and classroom exposure to the principles of autonomous work groups. In addition, the workers were given classroom exercises in group relations and problem solving. A work group consisted of mining machine operators, mechanics, helpers, roof bolters, shuttle car operators, and support men. While each worker bid on only one job, during the orientation period the workers were encouraged to try out as many of the jobs as possible. There was no pressure for production from the management during this orientation period.

The researchers then began a sociotechnical analysis of the work itself. The major source of production is a machine called the continuous miner. This machine consists of a large rotating drum studded with sharp bits. The drum is brought into contact with the wall to be mined. It gouges out coal, scoops the coal underneath the drum toward the rear, and then the coal is transported to a central location for further processing. The continuous miner bites out sections of the wall and creates a "room" 20 feet wide and 18 feet deep. This is done in several different areas until there is a series of adjacent rooms divided by pillars of coal. These pillars are then cut away, allowing for a "controlled collapse" of the mine roof. Theoretically, this is a very efficient way of mining coal. The capacity of the continuous miner is 4,000 tons per shift. In reality, the typical shift produces between 350 and 400 tons of coal. The discrepancy is due to time consumed in moving equipment, waiting time between cars carrying the coal, mechanical breakdowns, poor communications, and unnecessary movements on the part of the work groups. After examining the technical aspects of the work, the researchers identified the following potential problems in the psychosocial environment:

1. The work group members were isolated from one another during the performance of their work.
2. Instead of cooperating with one another, shifts competed.
3. Conditions were very uncertain from one day to the next: there were new geological conditions to be faced every time the next room was started, it was difficult to anticipate equipment breakdowns, and the

distance between actual mining operations and support services was constantly changing.

4. Foremen were in a double bind with concerns for both safety and production.

As a result of this analysis, the researchers introduced the following changes in the operation of the work groups:

1. They attempted to change the view of the mining process from one of production of coal to one of transportation of coal.
2. They fed back performance information in terms of large blocks of time instead of by shift; additionally, they fed back information to entire mine sections rather than to each work group on each shift.
3. They attempted to ensure that group members had several different skills so that uncertainty could be more effectively dealt with.
4. They redistributed responsibilities so group members made day-to-day decisions rather than counting on the foreman for structure.
5. They changed the foreman's role to that of a resource person who provided information rather than directed work.

A number of different strategies were used for accomplishing these changes. In a later section on organizational development, we will describe the specific purpose of each of these techniques. Every six weeks, work-group members and experimenters met to discuss the progress of the last six weeks and the plans for the next six weeks. Researchers visited the actual mine faces twice each week to collect information and provide reinforcement for changed procedures. In addition, there were irregular meetings of the joint worker/management council to handle grievances. Finally, foremen of the experimental work groups met every two weeks to discuss issues with the researchers and general management. As you can see, this was an ambitious undertaking for researchers, workers, and management. Table 12–3 presents some of the results of the experiment. Pre-experiment data were available for both experimental and nonexperimental work groups for 1973. These data were compared with figures for the experimental

TABLE 12–3
Results of the Autonomous Work Group Experiment

Variable	Year	Experimental Group	Comparison Group A	Comparison Group B
Safety violations	1973	18	19	10
	1974	7	37	17
Accidents	1973	6	5	4
	1974	7	14	11
Man hours absent (percent)	1974	2.5	4.4	2.4

year 1974. In addition to these figures, there was a rather substantial decrease in the cost of mining for the experimental groups. The actual production figures were difficult to interpret, but the researchers were able to conclude that production did not *decrease* during the experimental period for the autonomous work group. Finally, the attitudes of the experimental group about the work improved considerably during the experimental period.

A dramatic success such as this should have a happy ending. Unfortunately, that is not the case. The workers were given the opportunity to extend the experiment to the entire mine through their union. The union members voted *not* to expand the experiment by a vote of 79 to 75. The researchers examined the causes for the vote and identified the following possible contributing factors:

1. There were certain wage inequities built into expanding the experiment.
2. Many of the older miners were upset by the fact the experimental groups contained many young workers and apprentices who were receiving higher wages than the more senior miners who were in the nonexperimental groups.
3. There was the fear that the autonomous work groups were subtle attempts to bust the union.
4. The experimental work groups were resented as "elitist."

A recent evaluation of the long-term effects of the experiment was encouraging. Most of the changes seen in 1974 remained, although somewhat diluted. In addition, most of the structural changes in work groups and work process were also intact.

The $5,000,000.00 Misunderstanding

In sharp contrast to the coordinated efforts of the mine workers, mine owners, union officials, and researchers in the work autonomy project described above, Sebring (1977) describes the futile efforts of a state university and a state department of public welfare to work together on solving social problems. The university brought data analysis skills, evaluation skills, and long-range planning skills to bear on the questions; the department of public welfare brought real world experience, a public mandate, and money. By the time the project was terminated, the total price tag was approximately $5,000,000.00!

To make a long story short, the agencies were unable to work with one another. In spite of the fact both parties agreed on the goals of the interaction, each agency existed in a separate and distinct environment. These separate environments were defined by different climates, different pressures, and different "clients." Some of these differences are illuminated in Figure 12–11. As opposed to the coal mining experiment, the sociotechnical problem here was not so much one of adapting the social environment to a new technology; it was more a matter of facilitating a match between two separate sociotechnical systems. This example demonstrates that socio-

FIGURE 12–11

Interface of Environment, Organization, and Interorganizational Relations

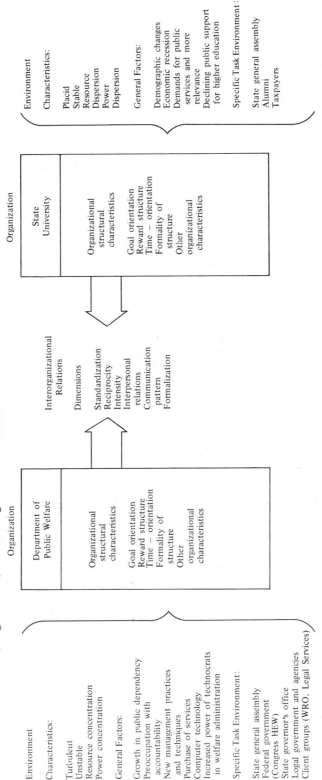

Source: Sebring, R. H. The five million dollar misunderstanding: A perspective on state government—university interorganizational conflict. *Administrative Science Quarterly*, 1977, 22, 520.

technical approaches are just as important in public sector "service" organizations as private sector manufacturing companies.

The descriptions of these two action research projects in sociotechnical engineering should give you a feel for the dramatic differences between the classic approach and the more current sociotechnical approach. The very fact that the sociotechnical approach is a *systems* approach makes it difficult to evaluate its effectiveness in traditional scientific ways. Nevertheless, it is the basis for most modern organization theories, and as such should be understood and appreciated.

ORGANIZATIONAL PROBLEMS: DIAGNOSIS AND THERAPY

The new approaches to understanding organizations and their effects on individuals have emphasized roles, role perceptions, affective reactions, and so on. As a result, new areas of research have emerged to address these changing emphases. We have suggested several times that organizations have "personalities." These personalities can be described, flaws noted, and attempts made to somehow help the organization "adjust"; this process is similar to the one a clinical psychologist might take in dealing with a patient exhibiting adjustment problems. We will describe some organizational parallels to individual diagnosis and adjustment. *Organizational climate* deals with the description of an organizational personality. *Role conflict and ambiguity* deals with some organizational "flaws" (in the sense that organizations can make life difficult for their members), and *organizational development* (OD) represents a form of organizational therapy.

Organizational Climate

The climate of an organization is thought to represent the *perception* of objective characteristics by organization members. As an example, the size of an organization is objective, but a person's feeling about that size is subjective; it is the perception of these objective characteristics that is thought to be represented by the climate of an organization.

Litwin and Stringer (1966) conducted some of the earliest research into the nature of organizational climate. They proposed that climate is made up of six distinct factors: (1) structure, (2) individual responsibility, (3) rewards, (4) risks and risk taking, (5) warmth and support, and (6) tolerance and conflict. Campbell, Dunnette, Lawler, and Weick (1970) have suggested that these factors of climate actually describe the way an organization treats its members. As such, organizational climate might be thought of as the "personality" of the organization. Just as some individuals are aggressive in their dealings with other individuals, some organizations are aggressive in their dealings with members. Of course, organizations do not exist in the same way single individuals do; nevertheless, traditions and styles of organizations do endure over time and seem to have a rather strong influence on managers and upper level executives. Whyte's classic description of the "organization man" is a vivid example of the type of force we are describing (1956).

There has been a good deal of controversy surrounding the construct of organizational climate. There has been a continuing criticism of climate research as unnecessary. Johannesson (1973) claimed that organizational climate was synonymous with job satisfaction. These sentiments were echoed by Guion (1973) who felt the concept of climate was too "fuzzy" to be useful. The argument is not a complicated one. The critics claim that since climate is something that is *perceived* by a worker rather than an objective characteristic, then climate must be the same as satisfaction. Those who accept the value of the climate construct argue that satisfaction is an *evaluative* process: an individual makes a value judgment about the degree to which an organizational characteristic is pleasing or displeasing. Climate is proposed to be a simple descriptive process—individuals perceive an organization as having certain characteristics (such as those identified in the Litwin and Stringer research). These perceived characteristics make up the climate. Individuals may then proceed to evaluate these characteristics as pleasing or displeasing, and it is only at this stage that the concept of satisfaction is introduced. This is a compelling argument. At one time or another, most of us have felt that an organization to which we belonged (scouts, churches, companies) had a "personality." It might have been cold or warm, supportive or demanding, rewarding or punishing. And while all members of the organization could agree on the "personality," they reacted to it differently. As an example, the organization to which you currently belong—a college or university of some type—may have a demanding climate. You may be pleased (satisfied) with such a climate while the person in the seat next to you may be displeased (dissatisfied) with that climate.

There has been a good deal of empirical research on organizational climate. In a study of the success of a training program for the hard-core unemployed, Friedlander and Greenburg (1971) found that the sole correlate of performance was the degree of perceived organizational supportiveness. They suggested that training could be facilitated by paying more attention to climate variables. Using the suggestion of Campbell et al. (1970), they might have concluded the *way* in which the training program was administered was just as important as *what* was taught.

A good deal of recent research has been directed toward identifying the general components of organizational climate. Campbell et al. (1970) reviewed most of the work done to that point and concluded there were four major factors: (1) individual autonomy, (2) degree of structure imposed by the position, (3) reward orientation, and (4) consideration, warmth, and support. Similar factors have been found by Sims and LaFollette (1975) and Muchinsky (1976). There have been many similar studies attempting to identify *the* parameters of organizational climate. Unless researchers are careful, climate research may get sidetracked in the same way as satisfaction research a decade earlier. You will remember from the chapter on job satisfaction that until the Job Descriptive Index (JDI) was published (Smith, Kendall, & Hulin, 1969), there was no way to compare results from study to study, since different measures of satisfaction were used in each study. The same will be true of climate research until a single measure is agreed on. The review of Campbell et al. was well done and the subsequent research reasonably supportive. Thus, it is our feeling that climate is well described by the characteristics of autonomy, structure, reward, and consideration orientations.

A second issue that has received some empirical attention has been the degree to which climate can be shown to be an enduring characteristic of the organization, and one that is perceived similarly by many different organizational members. Schneider and Snyder (1975) were able to demonstrate that subjects agreed more closely about climate than they did about satisfaction with organizational characteristics. This is important support for the contention that climate is a description while satisfaction is an evaluation. Descriptions should be more uniform than the feelings people derive from the characteristics described. Drexler (1977) was able to show a good deal of consistency in the climate descriptions of organizational members within several organizations. Landy (1972) was able to show that individuals from *similar organizations* were in greater agreement concerning their environments than were individuals from *similar occupations*.

All these findings point to the existence of the construct of organizational climate. It also seems as if this construct *is* distinct from job satisfaction. Recent research (Lawler, Hall, & Oldham, 1974; Franklin, 1975), and theory building (Schneider and Snyder, 1975) has begun to focus on the organizational process rather than structural components. Thus, current investigations of climate are more likely to focus on variables such as how performance is appraised or how promotions are made than on organizational size or span of control. It would seem that many of the early arguments regarding climate represented the growing pains of a new concept. Now that many of those pains have subsided, the research can become more focused, and investigations of the impact of climate on individuals can begin. Climate will clearly play a role in most organizational theories of the future. It will represent the organizational members' perceptions of the organization—its personality.

Organizational Flaws: Role Conflict and Ambiguity

As you could see from our earlier discussions, the structural and functional characteristics of organizations are quite complicated. The theories of Argyris and Lawrence and Lorsch suggest that interpersonal conflict may play a major role in the efficiency of a work group or company. Recently, there has been a good deal of interest in a different type of conflict: role conflict. While role conflict may imply interpersonal conflict, it is a broader concept. Miles and Perreault (1976) describe four different types of role conflict:

1. *Person-Role Conflict:* The individual would like to do things in a manner different from that suggested by the job description.
2. *Intrasender Conflict:* The individual receives an assignment without sufficient personnel to complete the assignment successfully.
3. *Intersender Conflict:* The individual is asked to behave in such a manner that one person will be pleased with the result while others will not be.
4. *Role Overload:* The individual is assigned more work than can be effectively handled.

Most of us have been in one or more of the situations described. For example, it is common to perform an action that pleases our parents but annoys our friends (intersender conflict) or to receive assignments from three different instructors which, in combination, might take more than a term or semester to complete (role overload). Those studying the effect of role conflict believe that competing demands such as these produce stress in individuals. This stress, in turn, is thought to produce dissatisfaction and performance problems.

Role conflict is often studied in the context of a second, similar, concept: role ambiguity. Role ambiguity is concerned with the degree to which an individual actually understands what is required on the job. This is different from role conflict in which the individual perfectly understands the competing demands being made. It is common for students completing term papers to feel they do not understand what the instructor expects. Role ambiguity is also thought to produce tension which may negatively affect satisfaction and/or performance.

Rizzo, House, and Lirtzman (1970) suggested that role conflict and ambiguity were related to dissatisfaction and inappropriate organizational behavior. They proposed that conflict and ambiguity resulted in stress, and stress, in turn, resulted in dissatisfaction and poor performance. They developed a questionnaire to measure the degree of conflict and ambiguity individuals experienced in their work, and this questionnaire has been widely used. Schuler, Aldag, and Brief (1977) analyzed responses of individuals from six samples to the Rizzo et al. scales and concluded that the questions did measure the two variables of conflict and ambiguity. Furthermore, these variables did seem to be related to negative states such as dissatisfaction and stress. In a similar study, Keller (1975) found that employees were more satisfied when expectations were clear and non-conflicting.

We are at a very early stage in the understanding of the concepts of role ambiguity and role conflict. If you remember the development of concepts such as leadership and job satisfaction, you can infer that it often takes ten or more years before a new concept's conceptual and operational problems are ironed out. We have not yet reached that stage with the conflict and ambiguity concepts. Nevertheless, they are appealing from both an empirical and theoretical point of view. The implications for theories of work motivation are pretty clear. If we examine the Porter-Lawler cognitive model in light of role conflict propositions, we can easily see that there are instrumentalities, valences, and expectancies canceling one another in situations of conflict. Thus, when high production is expected by a supervisor and moderate production is expected by co-workers, the individual must somehow balance these forces. Similarly, when the job description calls for one behavior while common sense calls for another, there will be some problems in defining good performance (this would be an example of inappropriate role perception in the Porter-Lawler model). Similarly, with respect to role ambiguity, an individual who does not know what is expected probably cannot perform his duties with maximum efficiency. Conflict and ambiguity also have implications for theories of goal setting and a wide range of theories dealing with leadership effectiveness. The notion of work roles and their accompanying demands and pressures is an important one. Research on conflict and ambiguity is likely to increase considerably our understanding of work-related stress, job satisfaction, and leader effectiveness. This type of research is important for another reason as well: it clearly describes some dysfunctional characteristics of organizations: the flaws of organizational personalities.

Organizational Development

Organizational development is a term that frequently appears in discussions of organizational theory. But, unlike other aspects of organizational psychology, organizational development represents a technology rather than a theoretical construct. We will review briefly the history and practical aspects of organizational development in order to show how it relates to other concepts we have dealt with in this and earlier chapters. Beer (1976) has written an excellent chapter in the *Handbook of Industrial and Organizational Psychology* (Dunnette, 1976) describing the history, practical aspects, theory, and research behind organizational development (or OD, as it is most commonly called), and the interested student should read that chapter for a deeper understanding of the concept. What follows is a synopsis of Beer's framework for describing OD.

Historically, industrial psychologists have concentrated on the single individual. Organizational psychology deals with the broader system in which the individual is only one component. Other components include social processes (interpersonal, intragroup, and intergroup), technology, and internal organizational environments (i.e. organizational climates); OD accepts this broader systems approach to understanding human behavior in complex organizations and consists of a series of techniques for modifying or developing social systems in organizations. It is important to keep in mind that OD is a social technology.

As you will remember from our earlier discussions of the Hawthorne studies, the last phase of these experiments was an attempt to introduce a counselling program into the work setting. While these programs were not considered to be particularly effective and were eventually canceled, they are thought to be the earliest examples of organizational development. The first institutionalized approach to OD was through the National Training Laboratories in Bethel, Maine. It was here that many of currently used techniques were first introduced. The best known of these techniques was the unstructured laboratory, more commonly referred to as "sensitivity training," or the formation of T-groups. Sensitivity training was covered in a limited training context in Chapter 7. The unstructured laboratory was based on the notion that individuals will learn much about themselves by examining the way in which they attempt to impose structure on an unstructured environment. Typically, groups of individuals who were unknown to one another would be brought together and provided with no structure or agenda. If there was any task, it was simply the structuring of a situation completely lacking in structure. It was felt the absence of structure or an agenda of some type would create tension in the group members, and this tension would create action of some sort. Group members were asked to observe and comment on the actions taken by others in the group, but to comment in nonevaluative terms rather than critical ones. It was thought this type of feedback might help individuals become aware of their attitudes, values, and behaviors.

The logic of the unstructured laboratory is based on the notion that attitude change is a three-stage process. The first stage is one of *unfreezing*, in which individuals become aware of values and beliefs they hold. The second phase is one of *changing*, in which new beliefs, values, and attitudes are adopted. Finally comes a third stage called *refreezing*, which consists of the stabilization of new attitudes and values. Sensitivity training was thought to facilitate these three stages. Feedback from the group begins the unfreezing process. A supportive environment enables the individual to try out new attitudes and behavior patterns; i.e., the changing process, and the group reinforces the individual for new attitudes (refreezing). It should be kept in mind that sensitivity training or the formation of T-groups is just a conceptual label; there are almost as many variations in the actual process as there are groups.

A different approach to the same process is that of *instrumented laboratory training*. As opposed to the unstructured approach of the sensitivity training group, the instrumented training approach typically involves a group of individuals who are given a particular problem to solve. In the process of solving the problem, the group members are asked to observe the behaviors of others in the group and provide feedback to those individuals with respect to their social behavior. As an example, the group might be given a supervisor/subordinate problem to resolve. In the course of dealing with the problem, their attitudes toward leadership are revealed, these attitudes are made apparent to them by fellow group members, and they are asked to consider alternative attitudes toward supervisor/subordinate relations.

Both the unstructured and the instrumented approaches have a common theme: they both attempt to create a social environment in which the individual can try out or practice new behaviors or attitudes with relative impunity. Nevertheless, these laboratory settings were thought to be somewhat artificial, and the more modern approaches to OD emphasize using local work-related issues to accomplish the unfreezing, changing, and refreezing goals. Since the OD process involves current ongoing organizational issues, the term *intervention* is often used to describe the actual developmental efforts. There are several distinct types of interventions. Two of these are the *diagnostic intervention* and the *process intervention*. The diagnostic intervention involves group members examining the organization and identifying problems related to the social environment. In the process of discussing these problems, values are clarified and changes in attitudes presumably occur. Process intervention differs in so far as it deals more directly with the behavior in question than with attitudes toward the behavior. Typically, a group is asked actually to engage in a social process that is part of their job. Critiques of these activities are then presented to group members, and they are encouraged to try alternative ways of accomplishing their goals. There is a rather dramatic difference between process interventions and other OD techniques. Process interventions assume that the behavior must change before the attitudes; other approaches assume that attitudes change first and, subsequently, behavior changes. Thus, behavioral modeling, described in Chapter 7, is an example of a process intervention.

An enormous amount of artistry is involved in organizational development. For this reason, there has been little evaluative research on the effectiveness of the techniques, as we have already suggested. In many respects, organizational development is like therapy, and the consultant is as much a clinical as organizational psychologist. Like individuals, organizations have personalities, and occasionally these personalities have destructive effects on other individuals in the same environment. At this stage, it is not appropriate to describe OD as anything other than a technology. Some day in the future, it may emerge as a theoretical framework capable of guiding the interactions between individuals and organizations, but it has not yet reached that stage.

CONCLUDING COMMENTS

It should be quite clear to you now that organizations are more complicated than even the most complex organization charts imply. Weick (1976) has suggested that organizations are analogous to a soccer game played on a round, sloped field with several different goals appearing at random locations on the field; players are permitted to enter and leave the field freely and use any number of soccer balls, depending on their preference. The players can arbitrarily "define" a goal whenever they feel like it. This is a very appealing analogy for both organizational members and organizational researchers. It highlights the desperation and frustration implicit in dealing with a complex social system.

In a more serious vein, we began the chapter by asking if organizational psychology was the study of organizations or the organizing process of members of those organizations. There is no doubt that current research and theory are directed toward the organizing process. This is as it must be for psychology. We must not lose sight of the fact that the subject matter for the behavioral sciences is *behavior* of individuals and groups of individuals. Thus, the formal characteristics of organization are of importance only to the degree that they (1) are manifestations of values, beliefs, attitudes, predispositions, or behaviors of the organizational members, or (2) have the capacity to function as "treatments" in the classic experimental sense, helping to explain variance in the behavior of organizational members. Viewed in this light, the evolution of organization theory from classic to modern mirrors the growth of psychology from infant stages in the late 19th century to adulthood 100 years later.

SUMMARY

Individuals and organizations are interactive. There have been several theoretical approaches to describe this interaction. The best-known approach is classic organization theory, which proposes that proper configurations of key elements will lead to organizational efficiency. Some of these elements are span of control, number of levels of administrative hierarchy, division of labor, and structure. Modern organization theory emphasizes the role of the individual to a much greater degree than does the classic approach.

Recently, emphasis has been placed on the interaction between technological aspects of the work organization and individual motivational systems within that organization. This is known as the sociotechnical systems approach. It embeds concepts such as job enrichment in the larger context of technological change and innovation.

Organizational psychology has been characterized by a much greater amount of "action research" than more traditional personnel areas. Action research is aimed at making a change of some kind, often in the process of the organization rather than the substance. This research often begins with a description of the organizational environment. The description is often referred to as the *organizational climate*. This description often uncovers ambiguities and conflicts in work roles. Organizational development (OD) is a process for sensitizing organization members to their attitudes and beliefs. It is felt that sensitization is the first step toward change; OD consists of a variety of techniques for changing attitudes and behaviors.

REFERENCES

Argyris, C. *The applicability of organizational sociology.* Cambridge, England: Cambridge University Press, 1972.

Beer, M. The technology of organizational development. In Dunnette, M. D. (Ed.). *Handbook of industrial and organizational psychology.* Chicago: Rand McNally, 1976.

Bennis, W. G. Leadership theory and administrative behavior: The problem of authority. *Administrative Science Quarterly*, 1959, *4*, 259–301.

Bougon, M., Weick, K. Y., & Binkhorst, D. Cognition in organizations: An analysis of the Utrecht jazz orchestra. *Administrative Science Quarterly*, 1977, *22*, 606–639.

Brief, A. P., & Aldag, R. S. Employee reactions to job characteristics: A constructive replication. *Journal of Applied Psychology*, 1975, *60*, 182–186.

Burns, T., & Stalker, G. M. *The management of innovation.* London: Tavistock Publications Ltd., 1961.

Campbell, J. P., Dunnette, M. D., Lawler, E. E., & Weick, K. E. *Managerial behavior, performance, and effectiveness.* New York: McGraw-Hill, 1970.

Drexler, J. A. Organizational climate: Its homogeneity within organizations. *Journal of Applied Psychology*, 1977, *62*, 38–42.

Dubin, R. Supervision and productivity: Empirical findings and theoretical considerations. In. R. Dubin (Ed.), *Leadership and productivity.* San Francisco: Chandler, 1965.

Dunham, R. B. The measurement and dimensionality of job characteristics. *Journal of Applied Psychology*, 1976, *61*, 404–409.

Entwistle, D.R. Observations on the span of control. *Administrative Science Quarterly*, 1960–61, *5*, 522–533.

Evans, P. B. Multiple hierarchies and organizational control. *Administrative Science Quarterly*, 1975, *20*, 250–59.

Evers, F. T., Bohlen, J. M., & Warren, R. D. The relationships of selected size and structure indicators in economic organizations. *Administrative Science Quarterly*, 1976, *21*, 326–342.

Franklin, J. L. Relations among four social-psychological aspects of organizations. *Administrative Science Quarterly*, 1975, *20*, 422–433.

Friedlander, F., and Greenburg, S. Effect of job attitudes, training, and organization climate on performance of the hard-core unemployed. *Journal of Applied Psychology*, 1971, *55*(4), 287–295.

Georgopolous, B. S., Mahoney, G. M., & Jones, N. W. A path-goal approach to productivity. *Journal of Applied Psychology*, 1957, *41*, 345–353.

Ghiselli, E. The efficacy of advancement on the basis of merit in relation to structural properties of the organization. *Organizational Behavior and Human Performance*, 1969, *4*, 402–413.

Guion, R. M. A note on organizational climate. *Organizational Behavior and Human Performance*, 1973, *9*, 120–125.

Hackman, J. R., & Oldham, G. Development of the job diagnostic survey. *Journal of Applied Psychology*, 1975, *60*, 159–170.

Hackman, J. R., & Oldham, G. R. Motivation through the design of work: Test of a theory. *Organizational Behavior and Human Performance*, 1976, *16*, 250–279.

Hulin, C. L. Individual differences in job enrichment: The case against general treatments. In J. R. Maher (Ed.) *New perspectives in job enrichment.* New York: Van Nostrand Reinhold, 1971.

Ivancevich, J. M., & Donnelly, J. H., Jr. Relation of organizational structure to job satisfaction, anxiety-stress, and performance. *Administrative Science Quarterly*, 1975, *20*, 272–280.

James, L. R., & Jones, A. P.   Organizational structure: A review of structural dimensions and their conceptual relationships with individual attitudes and behavior. *Organizational Behavior and Human Performance*, 1976, *16*, 74–113.

Johannesson, R.   Some problems in the measurement of organizational climate. *Organizational Behavior and Human Performance*, 1973, *10*, 118–144.

Keller, R. T.   Role conflict and ambiguity correlates with job satisfaction and values. *Personnel Psychology*, 1975, *28*, 57–64.

Korman, A. K.   *Industrial and organizational psychology.* Englewood Cliffs, N. J.: Prentice-Hall, 1971.

Landy, F. J.   A procedure for occupational clustering. *Organizational Behavior and Human Performance*, 1972, *8*, 109–117.

Lawler, E. E., Hall, D. T., & Oldham, G. R.   Organizational climate: Relationship to organizational structure, process, and performance. *Organizational Behavior and Human Performance*, 1974, *11*, 139–155.

Lawrence, P. R., & Lorsch, J.   *Organization and environment.* Cambridge, Mass.: Harvard University Press, 1967.

Levitan, A. A., & Johnson, W. B.   *Work is here to stay, alas.* Salt Lake City, Utah: Olympus, 1973.

Litwin, G. H., & Stringer, R.   The influence of organizational climate on human motivation. Paper presented at a conference on organizational climate, Foundation for Research on Human Behavior. Ann Arbor, Mich., March, 1966.

Locke, E. A.   The nature and causes of job satisfaction. In M. D. Dunnette (Ed.) *Handbook of industrial and organizational psychology.* Chicago: Rand McNally, 1976.

Locke, E. A., Sirota, D., & Wolfson, A. D.   An experimental case study of the successes and failures of job enrichment in a government agency. *Journal of Applied Psychology*, 1976, *61*, 701–711.

Lowin, A.   Participative decision making: A model, literature critique, and prescriptions for research. *Organizational Behavior and Human Performance*, 1968, *3*(1), 68–106.

Mahoney, T. A., & Frost, P. J.   The role of technology in models of organizational effectiveness. *Organizational Behavior and Human Performance*, 1974, *11*, 122–138.

March, J. G., & Simon, H. A.   *Organizations.* New York: Wiley, 1958.

McGregor, D.   *The human side of enterprise.* New York: McGraw-Hill, 1960.

McGregor, D.   *The professional manager.* New York: McGraw-Hill, 1967.

Miles, R. H., & Perreault, W. D.   Organizational role conflict: Its antecedents and consequences. *Organizational Behavior and Human Performance*, 1976, *17*, 19–44.

Miller, G. A.   The magical number seven, plus or minus two: Some limits on our capacity for processing information. *Psychological Review*, 1956, *63*, 81–97.

Moch, M. K.   Structure and organizational resource allocation. *Administrative Science Quarterly*, 1976, *21*, 661–674.

Muchinsky, P. M.   An assessment of the Litwin and Stringer organization climate questionnaire: An empirical and theoretical extension of the Sims and LaFollete study. *Personnel Psychology*, 1976, *29*, 371–392.

Oldham, G. R., Hackman, J. R., & Pearce, J. L. Conditions under which employees respond positively to enriched work. *Journal of Applied Psychology,* 1976, *61,* 395–403.

Ouchi, W. G., & Dowling, J. B. Defining the span of control. *Administrative Science Quarterly,* 1974, *19,* 357–365.

Rice, A. K. *Productivity and social organization: The Ahmedabad experiment.* London: Tavistock Publications, 1958.

Rizzo, J., House, R. E., & Lirtzman, J. Role conflict and ambiguity in complex organizations. *Administrative Science Quarterly,* 1970, *15,* 150–163.

Schneider, B. Organizational climates: An essay. *Personnel Psychology,* 1975, *28,* 447–480.

Schneider, B., & Snyder, R. A. Some relationships between job satisfaction and organizational climate. *Journal of Applied Psychology,* 1975, *60,* 318–328.

Schuler, R. S., Aldag, R. J., & Brief, A. P. Role conflict and ambiguity: A scale analysis. *Organizational Behavior and Human Performance,* 1977, *20,* 111–128.

Scott, W. G. Activation theory and task design. *Organizational Behavior and Human Performance,* 1966, *1*(1), 3–30.

Sebring, R. H. The five-million dollar misunderstanding: A perspective on state government-university interorganizational conflicts. *Administrative Science Quarterly,* 1977, *22,* 506–523.

Sims, H. P., & LaFollette, W. An assessment of the Litwin and Stringer organization climate questionnaire. *Personnel Psychology,* 1975, *28,* 19–38.

Sirota, D., & Wolfson, A. Job enrichment: Surmounting the obstacles. *Personnel,* July/August, 1972, 8–19 (a).

Sirota, D., & Wolfson, A. Job enrichment: What are the obstacles? *Personnel,* May/June, 1972, 8–17 (b).

Smith, P. C., Kendall, L. M., & Hulin, C. L. *The measurement of satisfaction in work and retirement.* Chicago: Rand McNally, 1969.

Taylor, F. W. *Principles of scientific management.* New York: Harper, 1947.

Thompson, J. D. *Organizations in action.* New York: McGraw-Hill, 1967.

Trist, E. L., and Bamforth, K. W. Some social and psychological consequences of the long-wall method of coal getting. *Human Relations,* 1951, *4,* 3–38.

Trist, E. L., Susman, G. I., & Brown, G. R. An experiment in autonomous working in an American underground coal mine. *Human Relations,* 1977, *30,* 201–236.

Umstot, D. D., Bell, C. H., & Mitchell, T. R. Effects of job enrichment and task goals on satisfaction and productivity: Implications for job design. *Journal of Applied Psychology,* 1976, *61,* 379–394.

Urwick, L. F. The manager's span of control. *Harvard Business Review,* 1956, *34*(3), 39–47.

Wall, T. D., Clegg, C. W., & Jackson, P. R. An evaluation of the job characteristics model. *Journal of Occupational Psychology,* 1978, *51,* 183–196.

Weber, M. *The theory of social and economic organization.* Translated and edited by A. M. Henderson & Talcott Parsons. New York: Oxford University Press, 1947.

Weick, K. E.   Educational organizations as loosely coupled systems. *Administrative Science Quarterly*, 1976, *21*, 1–19.

Whyte, W. H., Jr.   *The organization man*. Garden City: Doubleday, 1956.

Woodward, J.   *Management and technology*. London: Her Majesty's Stationery Office, 1958.

Worthy, J. C.   Organizational structure and employee morale. *American Sociological Review*, 1950, *15*, 169–179.

People, Machines, and the Physical Work Environment

People and machines make up systems that operate within larger systems or organizations. Efficient man-machine systems depend upon equipment design factors that make full use of human performance capabilities and also recognize human limitations. From an information systems view, human capabilities and limitations are seen in terms of receiving, coding, and transmitting information in communication with machine components of the system. Both the human and machine components are subject to factors in the physical and psychological environment. Human operators, in particular, may be affected by unusual environmental conditions that overstress or understimulate them. These environmental factors interact with physiological states and task demands to determine the total load on the operator.

CHAPTER 13
Designing Work for People

We have seen that from its early beginnings industrial psychology has been concerned with the identification and measurement of individual differences predictive of differential performance on different jobs. This approach to the efficiency of technological systems may be summarized in the phrase, "Find the person to fit the machine (or job)." The machine was accepted largely as a "given"—an unalterable creation of engineers and designers, beyond the domain of psychologists. The industrial psychologist's role was to contribute to productive efficiency through improved selection procedures. To the extent that selection devices and strategies were inadequate to the task, the psychologist sometimes was expected to "fit" the individual to the job through training programs. In a sense, then, the total personnel approach may be described as, "Find the right people (through selection techniques) and fit them (through training programs) to the jobs."

Personnel selection and training continue to be major activities of industrial psychologists. As we have seen in other sections of this book, new and promising devices and models for selection and for the evaluation of selection strategies are being developed. Furthermore, in the areas of management development and personnel training, new theories and techniques as well as empirical findings are being applied, and vigorous attempts are being made to realize the implications for industry of basic research on learning and performance. Taken together with recent developments in industrial-social psychology, which emphasize the role of the social context of work, personnel selection and training continue to be major areas within which psychologists contribute to technological efficiency and to human effectiveness.

In this chapter we will be concerned with yet another approach to studying the interactions of humans and work. The approach is most often called "human engineering" (as well as "biomechanics," "ergonomics," "psychotechnology," or "applied experimental psychology"). In previous chapters we have been concerned with the more subjective characteristics of work—leadership styles, the meaningfulness of the work performed, the worker's view of the potential rewards of work, and so on. Now we would like to examine some of the more objective characteristics of jobs and attempt to understand their influence on workers. We will consider things such as the equipment a worker is required to use and responses that workers are required to make to information provided by that equipment.

As you will see shortly, engineering psychology is the study of systems that vary in complexity and reliability. Perhaps the most complex and unreliable system the psychologist studies is the *human being*. But the human system is embedded in a larger system, which includes the equipment the human uses to accomplish work, the physical environment in which the work is done, and the social-psychological environment of which the worker is a part. We have dealt extensively with the social-psychological environment in the four preceding chapters. In the next two chapters, we will deal with the interactions between workers and physical environments.

Design, both equipment and environmental, can be quite exciting. Our concern in the present chapter will not be with design per se, however. It will be with matching individuals to environments. As we are psychologists, our focus is always on the individual. In this chapter we will consider the individual as a critical part of efficient man-machine systems and, in addition, the broader issue of human engineering research and its place in psychology. In the next chapter, we will deal with the various threats to efficient man-machine systems; once again, these will be threats primarily to the *human* part of the systems, not the machine part.

PREDECESSORS TO HUMAN ENGINEERING

Efforts to fit the job to the operator began largely within engineering and scientific management rather than within psychology. Especially important were those efforts to arrange the work and the workplace optimally. These efforts are embodied in such principles as *work simplification* and *standardization* and utilized the methods of the time and motion analysts. The early work of Taylor (1911) in time analysis, and of the Gilbreths (1919) in motion analysis paved the way for human engineering because these researchers made it apparent that neither the job nor the machine were unalterable but could be analyzed and redesigned for greater efficiency and greater compatibility with the characteristics of the human operator.

Other predecessors of human engineering are to be found in early experimental work on the physical work environment. Thus, as we have seen, the initial phases of the Hawthorne studies were designed to determine the optimum level of illumination at the workplace. While such studies did not investigate the design of the machines or of the job per se, they were concerned with the physical conditions in which men and machines were expected to function. Today, research on the effects of extreme, unusual, even "hostile" environmental conditions on human performance is an important part of human engineering. It should be noted that human performance and, consequently, the performance of any technological system of which people are a part is always evaluated in the context of a particular physical environment. Factors and principles in the design of such systems that hold true for the usual or "normal" working environment may not be appropriate when environmental conditions are changed. Studies seeking principles of human performance and systems design go hand in hand with the investigation of the physical conditions of work. Extreme, unusual, and hostile environmental conditions can often produce unexpected results. We will consider some of these conditions in the next chapter.

AWARENESS OF HUMAN ENGINEERING PROBLEMS

It was not until World War II that the need for the discipline we now call human engineering was fully recognized. Prior to that time, some efforts were made to increase efficiency through job design and improved working conditions, but it took the rapid technological developments spurred on by the wartime emergency to foster the realization that machines effectively outrunning the operator's ability to control them could be designed. In this period, rapid developments in technology drastically changed the work tasks of thousands of people. Pilots, trained on an old generation of aircraft, were familiarized with a second generation but often required to fly a third by the time they reached the war zone. They were faced with new dials, gadgets, previously unheard-of speeds, and fantastic maneuvering capabilities. Submarine crews found themselves with sonar equipment, air traffic controllers with radar and with greatly increased air traffic moving at high speeds. In nearly every such situation tasks were in some respects more complex. It is true that there generally was less physical demand placed on the operator, since muscle power was replaced by motor power, but the number of decisions required and the amount of information to be processed from a variety of sources increased tremendously.

Frequent complaints were received that machines carrying highly respectable engineering specifications for reliable and accurate performance simply were not performing up to standards in field operations. Radar, known to be accurate to within a few yards at, say, 10 miles, showed no such accuracy, it was reported. Similarly, airplanes with the potential for maneuverability and safety of operation fell short on both counts. Thus the evidence piled up that the rapid technological developments fostered by the war had left the human operator far behind. The failures of airplanes, radar, sonar, and other machines were chalked up to "human error," but this was little more than an admission that the performance of technological systems is restricted by the limitations of the humans who must operate them. Failures dismissed as due to "human error" could have been avoided in many cases by better equipment design. Increased efforts to improve selection and training programs, though meeting with some success, were not the complete answer to the problem.

SYSTEMS

An extremely important development in human engineering was the adoption of the notion of *systems*. A system means many different things to different people, and "general systems theory" has developed into a very complex and sophisticated area of study, with applications in many areas of science and engineering. Today, the term *system* is applied to such diverse phenomena as nervous systems, communications systems, and solar systems. While there are a number of issues in the definition of a system, the term generally implies some "communication" or interaction among the component parts of some identifiable entity or aggregate. These issues go beyond the scope and purpose of this chapter, however. Our concern is with man-machine systems. Such systems have component parts, some of which are machines, others of which are people. These components interact to determine the behavior, or performance, of the system. Any system under consideration may, in fact, be a subsystem when viewed in a larger context. Thus, a man and a drill press define a man-machine system, which is at the same time a subsystem of the machine room, which in turn is a subsystem of the factory, and so on.

Man-machine systems are typically designed for some purpose, and the adequacy of the design can be evaluated in terms of how completely and efficiently it achieves this purpose. Among human engineers the purpose of a system is often referred to as its *mission*. Given a certain mission, such as "Place a man on the moon and return him safely to earth," systems designers are able to specify the *systems functions* that must be fulfilled if the mission is to be accomplished. These functions may be grouped into categories such as "systems guidance functions," "personnel (or 'life') support functions," "systems maintenance functions," and the like. Having identified such functions, systems designers must decide on the *allocation of functions* to the human and machine components of the system. In the design of a spaceship, for example, questions arise as to whether certain systems guidance functions should be carried out by humans or by machines, and whether some of the systems maintenance functions should be handled through the use of standby equipment that can be switched on in case of the failure of a subsystem or allocated to human components, who then repair the faulty subsystem or replace it by manually guiding the ship.

A MODEL FOR MAN-MACHINE SYSTEMS

One of the earliest and most influential proponents of the systems approach to human engineering was Franklin V. Taylor. In 1957 he presented the basic model of such a system—a model that has greatly influenced thinking and research in this area. This model is presented in Figure 13–1.

Basically, the model is very simple; it defines a system in terms of human and machine components operating in an interacting environment. The machine component(s) communicate with the human component(s) through the information displays—the dials, gauges, counters, and so forth (and, though not shown in the model, through the sounds, vibrations, sights and smells experienced in the system). These informations sources constitute *potential* sources of input to the human components. The word "potential" is used to indicate that the machine may present information not input by the operator, because her sensing equipment is too limited,

FIGURE 13–1
The Man-Machine System

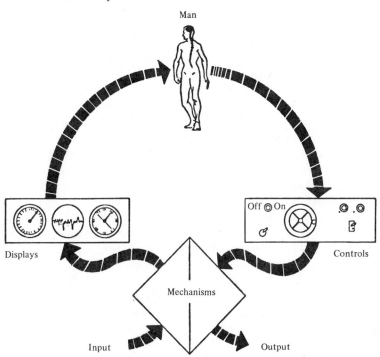

Man

Displays

Controls

Mechanisms

Input

Output

Source: Taylor, F. V. Psychology and the design of machines. *American Psychologist,* 1957, *21,* 249–258.

because her limited attention capacity is occupied with other sources of information, or because she fails to attend at all.

While man and machine do form a system, there are some issues that may be considered from either a human or a machine perspective. You will remember from Chapter 4 that one technique for job analysis (McCormick's PAQ) breaks the job into several components including *input, mediation*, and *output*. We will use these categories to discuss man-machine systems.

Input from the Man-Machine Perspective

The issue of input seems simple enough. The operator receives an instruction from somewhere and carries it out. The heart of the "problem" lies in the concept of an *instruction*. We will substitute the term *information* for *instruction*. This will enable us to take advantage of a large body of research that tells us something about how individuals deal with stimulation received from the external environment.

It is possible to consider input from two different points of view. First we have the mechanism *receiving* that input—the human being. To a certain extent, the human operator is limited by sensory capacities. On the other hand, we might consider the nature of the machinery used to *present* that information or input. In engineering terms, we might study the characteristics of *displays*. We will begin our consideration of input issues with an examination of the capacities of the person receiving the information.

Humans as Sensing Devices.   The operator receives information about the machine and its performance through the senses. Here we run into the first point in the model where human capabilities and limitations must be considered. As every student of introductory psychology should know, human sensory capabilities, sensitivity, and sensory acuity are limited, often much more severely than we realize. The traditional study of sensory psychology and psychophysics has sought to determine what these limitations are, and a good deal of information has been accumulated. However, human engineers have frequently found that this information is limited to the world of the research laboratory and many questions have to be asked again under more realistic performance situations. For example, the absolute thresholds for vision and audition as determined by psychophysicists were obtained in highly-controlled laboratory environments designed to yield optimum estimates of sensitivity under ideal conditions of sensory adaptation. Only rarely have these scientists been concerned with the operator's ability to detect a signal presented against a noisy background or to see a light flash in the peripheral visual field while busily reading instruments directly in the line of sight.

There are several issues that must be considered in trying to understand how the human senses deal with input. First we must consider *ranges* of sensation or the capacity of the individual to detect a stimulus. Next we must consider the efficiency with which an individual *discriminates* among various stimuli, separating the irrelevant from the important. Finally, we must consider the sheer *amount* of input or information that confronts the individual.

Sensory Capacities and Limitations. Humans have limited capacities for taking in information from their environment. They are sensitive to only certain forms of physical energy, to restricted ranges of values on these energy dimensions, and to only finite—and often surprisingly large— changes in the energy or quality of signals. Thus, for example, people are mostly deaf to vibrations of the air below 20 or above 20,000 cycles per second and for all practical purposes are restricted to perhaps less than half of this range. This is clearly a limitation of the operator that requires signals of particular kinds for performance to be efficient.

The same limitations are obvious in each of our senses. We can only see stimuli that exceed certain lower limits of brightness. There are more colors than those we can see—we see only the "visible" spectrum and, compared to the pigeon, we do not do a particularly good job of recognizing different colors! For our eyes to "work" efficiently in the dark, dark adaptation must have occurred. The eye is more than 10,000 times more sensitive when dark adaptation is complete than when it is light adapted. We could describe similar limitations in the other senses, but the examples we have presented should be sufficient to make the point that, as humans, we have some sensory limitations that affect our performance.

Recently there has been some interesting research with respect to the interaction *among* various senses. Freides (1974) reviewed studies relating sensory mechanisms to information processing and concluded that some senses were more refined than others and that organisms might use the "better" senses to help the poorer ones. As an example, he described an experiment in which subjects were required to point to the source of a sound. When the subjects were instructed to "look at" the source of the sound before pointing to it, they were considerably more accurate than when they performed the same task in the dark or were required to keep their heads in a fixed position. Engineering psychologists will have to do much more of this type of research before they completely understand the sensation and perception principles that should guide machine design.

Discriminating among Signals. In many tasks, the detection of the presence of a signal is a necessary but not sufficient condition for making the appropriate response. Signal detection must be followed by signal identification or discrimination. Identification, or recognition, is the process of comparing the present signal with the contents of memory. If the signal is found to "match" something in memory, it is given the label attached to that memorial representation, even though that may be no more articulate than "that same funny sound I heard yesterday."

Basically, the demands for discriminating among signals are of two sorts. In one case, two signals are presented simultaneously, or in quick succession, and the task is to discriminate whether the two signals differ in some respect. This is known as a *comparative* or *relative judgment*. The method is used to determine sensitivity to small differences in signals, or the *difference threshold*. In the other case, a single stimulus is presented and must be classified in an absolute sense—not simply as "different from" or "greater than" a comparison stimulus—and is labeled an *absolute judgment*. The distinction between detecting differences and identifying signals—that is, relative versus absolute judgments—is a very important one, since human capabilities differ markedly in these two skills. Examples of relative judgments might be judging which of two lights was brighter, which of two tones was louder (or higher in pitch), and which of two wines was sweeter. Examples of absolute judgments would be identifying a light as having an "A-level" of brightness, a tone as "loudness B" or "middle C," and a wine as "medium dry." While we can make many more relative than absolute discriminations, we are frequently required to make the latter in man-machine and other everyday situations. In fact, it may be well to mention that many human performance problem situations might be eased by modifying the task so that relative rather than absolute judgments were required.

Findings on Relative Judgments. Sensitivities to differences in stimulation are usually expressed as a ratio, $\Delta I/I$, where I is the intensity of the standard stimulus and ΔI is the increment or change that is just *noticeable*. The reason for this tradition is the evidence that $\Delta I/I$, rather than ΔI, is a constant. This is the well-known Weber Law, $\Delta I/I = K$. In other words, the amount by which a signal must be changed to be just noticeably different is not a constant value but is a constant proportion of the signal with which we start. Thus, if we start with a signal at 100 units and find that we must change it by 10 units (or that a second signal must differ from the first by 10 units) before the difference is reliably detected, then $\Delta I/I = \frac{1}{10}$, and we would predict that a signal of 200 units would have to be changed by 20 units to be equally noticeably different ($\Delta I/I = \frac{1}{10}$; $\Delta I/200 = \frac{1}{10}$, $\Delta I = 20$).

Our abilities to discriminate differences in signals have seldom been described in information terms, but are usually expressed as "Weber ratios," that is, as the ratio of $\Delta I/I$. Such ratios are available for a number of senses and for *frequency* as well as *intensity* differences. Some of the findings are summarized in Table 13–1. This table shows, for example, that we are relatively sensitive to differences in pitch (signal frequency) but quite insensitive to loudness (signal intensity). In fact, two signals would have to differ in intensity by about 10 percent before we could be reasonably confident that the differences in loudness were detectable!

The Amount of Information in Absolute Judgments. In 1956 George A. Miller published an article entitled "The Magical Number Seven, Plus or Minus Two: Some Limits on Our Capacity for Processing Information." This article summarized the results of a number of studies that described, in information-measurement terms, the ability to make absolute judgments. Reference to the "number seven, plus or minus two" implied that roughly

TABLE 13-1
Some Data on Sensitivity

Poor Taste and Good Pitch

The following illustrative Weber fractions* have been taken from the work of various investigators. For each stimulus dimension, the absolute level of stimulus intensity at which the Weber fraction was determined is indicated. These values are *minimal* values, obtained under optimal conditions of judgment.

Pitch (at 2,000 cycles per second) 1/333
Deep pressure (at 400 grams) 1/77
Visual brightness (at 1,000 photons) 1/62
Lifted weights (at 300 grams) 1/53
Loudness (at 100 decibels, 1,000 cycles per second) 1/11
Smell of rubber (at 200 olfacties) 1/10
Skin pressure (at 5 grams per square millimeter) 1/7
Taste, saline (at 3 moles per liter) 1/5

The remarkable range in sensitivities of the various senses is well demonstrated; it is about seventyfold—from pitch, in which a difference of as little as *one third of 1 percent* can be detected, to taste, in which there must be a difference of about 20 percent before it can be detected.

---

* Listed in E. G. Boring, H. S. Langfeld, and H. P. Weld, (Eds.) *Foundations of psychology.* New York: Wiley, 1948.
Source: Kretch, D., Crutchfield, R. S., & Livson, N. *Elements of psychology.* New York: Knopf, 1969 (2nd ed).

seven signals varying along a *single* dimension such as frequency or intensity could be reliably identified. The addition of more signals simply introduced errors at a rate that left the amount of information transmitted unchanged. That is, when more than about seven different signals (seven hues or seven loudnesses, for example) were used, the potential increase in information per signal was counterbalanced by an increase in uncertainty about *which* signal had appeared.

The word "magic" for Miller's "number seven" means that the limit of the capacity to process information was reached with about seven signals in a number of studies involving a variety of sensory channels and dimensions. Some of these findings are summarized as single dimension values in Table 13–2. How should we interpret these results? Briefly, they mean that little will be gained by using more than seven different signals in a situation in which the signals differ along *one dimension only*. Furthermore, where it is highly important to avoid errors, the signal set should be at or below the number indicated in Table 13–2. Thus, for example, if colors (hues) are used to code electrical wires or steam pipes where errors of identification could be very costly, then Table 13–2 indicates that no more than nine hues should be used.

TABLE 13–2

Amount of Information in Absolute Judgments of Various Stimulus Dimensions

Sensory Modality and Stimulus Dimension	No. of Levels that Can Be Discriminated on Absolute Basis
Vision: single dimensions	9
Pointer position on linear scale	
Short exposure	10
Long exposure	15
Visual size	7
Hue	9
Brightness	5
Vision: combination of dimensions	
Size, brightness, and hue*	17
Hue and saturation	11–15
Position of dot in a square	24
Audition: single dimensions	
Pure tones	5
Loudness	5
Audition: combination of dimensions	
Combination of six variables†	150
Odor: single dimension	4
Odor: combination of dimensions	
Kind, intensity, and number	16
Taste	
Saltiness	4
Sweetness	3

* Size, brightness, and hue were varied concomitantly, rather than being combined in the various possible combinations.

† The combination of six auditory variables included frequency, intensity, rate of interruption, on-time fraction, total duration, and spatial location.

Source: Adapted from a table presented by McCormick, E. J. *Human factors engineering.* New York: McGraw-Hill, 1970 (3rd ed.).

In response to the last statement, the reader may say emphatically, "I know that I can identify many more than nine colors without errors." No doubt this is correct, but only if one takes "colors" to mean signals that vary in brightness and/or saturation as well as hue—that is, along more than one dimension. Table 13–2 shows that when signals vary along two or more dimensions, the number of absolutely identifiable signals increases and, along with that, the channel capacity increases. In other words, the upper limit on information transmission depends in an important way on how the information is coded: when signals are coded (differ) along one dimension only, channel capacity is lower than when signals differ along two or more dimensions.

No doubt one reason we are surprised with the results of the studies on absolute judgments is that they do not agree with the thousands of discriminations of which we seem capable outside the laboratory. Again, the answer may be that such discriminations—for example, among faces— are based on a number of dimensions. Thus, Pollack and Ficks (1954) were able to get about 150 discriminable auditory signals by varying signals along six different dimensions.

Nevertheless, the addition of new dimensions is a game of diminishing returns, as Miller (1956) suggested:

> The point seems to be that, as we add more variables to the display, we increase the total capacity, but we decrease the accuracy for any particular variable. In other words, we can make relatively crude judgments of several things simultaneously. (p. 88)

The fact that our ability to make discriminations in relative-judgment situations far exceeds our ability to make absolute discriminations has important implications for the design of a wide variety of jobs. This is especially true of jobs involving quality control inspections, classifications, or grading of products. For example, agriculture-related jobs such as the inspection and grading of meats or grains often require absolute judgments by the inspector. In these and other situations it may be possible to redesign the inspector's task by providing a set of standard stimuli representative of the different grades of the produce against which to compare the sample to be judged. This would convert the task to one involving comparative judgments and should lead to greater speed and accuracy. One of the present authors, in a study (unpublished) of grain grading, demonstrated that untrained university students could grade samples of wheat more quickly and with accuracy comparable to that of experienced inspectors when they had a series of comparison samples immediately in front of them.

Displays. The previous section implies that the "answer" to man-machine problems is to build equipment providing information or input to the operator in a form and at a rate that best matches his sensory capacities. This is the way in which the pure experimental psychologist might approach the situation. A different, perhaps more problem-oriented, approach would be to study the relative efficiency of different ways of providing the same information—the advantages and disadvantages of various *displays*. Look at your watch. It most likely has specific marks that break the face into hours and possibly minutes. This is a display. What if there were no such marks, but only two hands on a round, unmarked face? Which of these two displays do you think would be more efficient in helping you arrive at class on time? A good deal of the human engineering research that was done in the early days of the field was of this type—the identification of efficient displays. This was probably because the engineering psychologist was more often called upon to *redesign* a system that was causing problems than to design a new system. In looking at system failures, engineering psychologists often found evidence that the load of sensory information on the human operator exceeded her capacity to take it in.

A typical problem faced by the engineering psychologist during World War II was the rapid change in the design of fighter aircraft. The pilot was faced with a bewildering array of dials, gauges, and lights. Even control knobs in many instances required visual monitoring, first to be certain that the appropriate control was being manipulated, then to assure that it was moved to the correct setting. Figure 13–2 shows the interior of the cockpit of an aircraft, with its numerous displays, many of them at wide angles to the normal line of sight of the pilot.

One approach to these problems of overloading of the visual system included attempts to present some types of information through other sensory channels, such as the auditory or tactile senses. It is interesting to note in passing that this approach assumed, implicitly at least, that people could process more information, "in parallel," as it were, when the information was addressed to different senses, than when it was presented to a single sensory system. Certainly in the case of vision, involving as it does the fixation and focusing of the eye to different display locations, this assumption may be valid. However, we will explore some models of human information processing, including a "single-channel" model, which suggest that information is only processed serially, not in parallel. At any rate, this approach was valuable because it revealed some human capabilities for processing auditory and tactile information.

Early attempts at auditory signaling systems included variations on Radio Range, a system of interlocking tonal signals whereby pilots can chart their course in "blind" approaches to the runway, and Flybar (flying by auditory reference), a system of signals to indicate the "attitude" of the plane (roll,

FIGURE 13–2
The Cockpit of a Modern Aircraft

Source: United Airlines photo.

bank, and turn). In the latter system various combinations of signal intensities and frequencies were explored to determine man's ability to discriminate and use auditory information to control the attitude of the plane. While such systems have important limitations (see Chapanis, Garner & Morgan, 1949, for an evaluation), these studies provided valuable information about human performance. For example, it was noted that when three different signals were used to indicate the three aspects of the plane's attitude, pilots frequently attended to one signal and lost track of the others. Also, it was discovered that signal systems requiring absolute identification of signal properties (frequency or intensity) were less reliable than those that included a constant reference tone, thus requiring comparative rather than absolute judgments (Chapanis et al., 1949; Forbes, 1946).

Later on, other sensory systems, particularly the sense of touch, were to be investigated as potential channels of information whereby signals from machines could be communicated to the operators.

The second approach to the problem of overloading of the visual channel included attempts to develop more efficient visual displays. Research on the design of visual displays increased rapidly as the result of evidence gathered from interviews with pilots by Fitts and Jones (1947a). These researchers collected reports of 270 errors, which they then classified into nine categories. These errors, summarized in Table 13–3, served to identify many research problems in display design. Much of the subsequent research has been reviewed by Fitts (1951) and by Grether (1968). Fitts (1951) reviewed the problems and the research findings in this area under headings such as "problems involving visibility" (size, brightness contrast, color, discrimination of velocity and acceleration, and so on), "problems related to pattern discrimination" (size of numerals and letters, size of dials, spacing of scale markers, pointer design, and so on) and problems related to the "design of quantitative displays" (interpretation of scales, graphs, and tables, for example). Special attention was given to multiple-pointer instruments, such as the standard three-pointer altitude indicator.

The Arrangement of Displays. In addition to research on the design of specific information displays, investigations were directed toward the arrangement of displays on an instrument panel. Little attention had been paid to the location of displays relative to one another or to the operator. Equally significant were instances where the same information display was to be found in one location in one model and in quite a different place in another model of the same equipment.

The problems of visual displays in complex systems were compounded by the fact that information displays designed by one manufacturer were different from those of another manufacturer, even for the same type of information. The "null" position, or safety region, might be at the 12:00 o'clock position on one dial, but at the 3:00, 6:00, or 9:00 o'clock position on another model. Little wonder that a pilot, swamped with a myriad of decisions to be made within a few seconds, might make an error, especially when he had been transferred suddenly from one type of aircraft to another.

TABLE 13–3

Classification of 270 Errors Made by Aircraft Pilots in Responding to Instruments and Signals

	Relative Frequency
1. *Misinterpreting multirevolution instruments.* Mistakes in comprehending information presented by two or more pointers or by a pointer plus a rotating dial viewed through a "window."	18
2. *Misinterpreting direction of indicator movement (reversal errors).* Improper interpretation of an instrument indication with the result that subsequent actions increase rather than reduce an undesirable condition.	17
3. *Misinterpreting visual and auditory signals.* Failing to respond appropriately to hand signals, warning lights or sounds, or radio range signals.	14
4. *Errors involving poor legibility.* Difficulty in seeing numerals, scale markings, markings, or pointers clearly enough to permit quick and accurate reading.	14
5. *Failing to identify a display.* Mistaking one instrument for another or confusing pointers on a multiple-pointer display.	13
6. *Using an inoperative instrument.* Accepting as valid the indication of an instrument that is inoperative or operating improperly.	9
7. *Misinterpreting scale values.* Difficulty in interpolating between numbered scale graduations or failure to assign the correct value to a numbered graduation.	6
8. *Errors associated with illusions.* Difficulties arising out of a conflict between body sensations and information given by visual displays.	5
9. *Omitting the reading of an instrument.* Failing to refer to an instrument at the proper time.	4
Total	100

Source: Fitts, P. M., & Jones, R. E. Psychological aspects of instrument displays I: Analysis of 270 "pilot-errors." (Table 1, slightly modified.) Aero Medical Laboratory, Air Material Command, Dayton, Ohio: Rept. No. TSEAA-694-12A (1947).

The answer to these problems, the reader may say, is obvious: "Standardize the dial design and arrangement of displays for all models." Certainly, this is a sensible answer and, no doubt, a valid one as far as it goes. Standardization in this sense is quite consistent with the principles of efficient learning and transfer of training. Standardization even of suboptimally designed instruments would almost surely improve human performance and reduce human error, but how much better it would be to standardize with optimally designed displays, arranged in an optimal configuration. Thus, "standardization" as an answer to these problems immediately leads to questions about the optimal way to design certain kinds of information: What kinds of information are to be displayed? What use must be made of the information? Is the interpretation of the information dependent upon information from other sources? If so, how should these sources be arranged relative to one another? Finally, questions are raised as to the optimum design of the individual information display, its size, markings, pointers, and other properties.

All these questions are legitimate starting points for psychological research. They focus attention on the nature of the physical equipment rather than sensory processes of the operator. Nevertheless, both approaches—the sensory approach and the display approach—deal with the information-input part of the man-machine system. In the next section we will consider what happens to this information when it is received by the human operator.

Mediation in Man-Machine Systems

As you could see from our earlier diagram of the man-machine system, the human component mediates or intervenes between two machine components. Information is presented through some mechanical means, and the operator responds through the use of mechanical devices of some type. The mechanical means for input may be as simple as a memo or as complicated as a radar display; similarly, the mechanical devices by which the human responds may be as simple as a telephone or as complicated as the controls in the cab of a multistory crane. Regardless of the sophistication of the physical system, the human being is required to *process* the information before making the appropriate response. It is the information-processing activities of the worker that represent both the strength and the weakness of the *man* part of the man-machine system.

Humans as Processors of Information. The operator is not a simple channel through which the information in a man-machine system flows. Once the information is sensed, it must be coded, or classified and interpreted in some way. In a way, it is as though the operator says, "I see a signal; now what does it mean?" Classifying and interpreting the signal is, in effect, answering the question, "What does it mean?" To classify signals, the operator must compare them with information stored in her long-term memory. Thus, the sound of a buzzer in a particular context means something only when the sound can be matched with the memorial representation of a similar experience with which a certain sound has been associated. The sound may be identified as "the signal that it is lunchtime" or "the signal that the cake is baked" only if, through prior learning, the signal has been coded in such a way.

Even though the signal is coded and its meaning is precisely understood, there is no guarantee that the correct response will be made. Consider the poor fellow watching the needle of a pressure gauge climb steadily into the "danger" zone. He "gets the message," the meaning is unequivocally clear, but instead of closing the shutoff valve, he calls for help or scurries to a safe place. The problem is that while he can *encode* the message, he cannot *decode* it into an appropriate response. Efficient processing of information involves the learning of both stimulus and response codes and the appropriate relationships between them. It may also involve complex transformations of the incoming information, including arithmetic operations, estimates of probabilities, and decisions with respect to the choices among alternative responses. It should be apparent that to predict human performance in a complex man-machine-environment system, a good deal must be known about the ways in which people operate on the information they receive.

An Information-Processing Model. A number of models of varying complexity have been offered by psychologists to describe human information processing. For our purposes, a model that attempts to describe the major steps or stages of processing and some of the principal mechanisms seems appropriate. Such a model was presented by Smith (1968) and is shown in Figure 13–3. It is characterized by four stages. The first stage is the "stimulus-preprocessing" stage, in which physical stimuli are received, registered through the sensory mechanisms, and converted to neural impulses. The second stage is the "stimulus-classification" stage at which the signals are classified or categorized. At this second stage the signal is identi-

FIGURE 13–3
A Simple Model of Stages in the Processing of Information

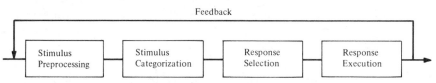

Source: Based on the model suggested by Smith, E. E. Choice reaction time: An analysis of the major theoretical positions, *Psychological Bulletin*, 1968, *69*, 77–110.

fied or "recognized"; that is, it is compared with information stored in memory and can then be labeled as, for example, "a police siren," "a skyrocket," "frying onions," or whatever, including "an unfamiliar signal." This last case implies that the signal does not match anything stored in the person's memory—it is unrecognized.

The third stage of this model, labeled "response selection," refers to the process following stimulus registration and classification in which an "appropriate" response is selected. In the case of a red traffic light, the response might be to press the brake pedal of the car. The choice of responses and the predictability of response selection, of course, depends on memory. However, it may be meaningful to consider this a different type of memory from that referred to in the classification stage. An example may help to make this point clear.

Consider the example just used of the person who saw the pointer on a pressure gauge climbing into the "danger zone. The signal was registered and categorized. The person clearly recognized the meaning of the signal from past experiences stored in memory but did not make the most appropriate response, because that response had not been learned or associated with that signal. In other words, stimulus categorization or recognition depends on what is sometimes called *perceptual memory*, while response selection depends on having associated certain responses with certain signals, or what is often called *associative memory*. Whether we choose to consider these two types of learning as involving different memory processes depends in part on how we choose to treat the recognition process. If we take the position that recognition ("a red traffic light," or "a danger signal") is a response learned to a particular signal—a cognitive response—but not different in kind from the overt response of pressing the brake pedal, then we may find it unnecessary to include two different memory processes in our model of information processing.

The final stage in this simple model is the *execution* of the responses that have been selected. Ability to execute the appropriate response with speed and precision obviously depends, among many other things, on the nature of the response and on how well it has been learned. In a sense, the difference between response selection and response execution is analogous to the difference between theory and practice. People may learn what the appropriate response is; they "know" which response to make and what the desired effects of the response are, but their ability to execute it may be limited by their ability to differentiate a response of one amplitude, force, direction, or duration from another. One can argue at this point that the limitation we are describing is really a limitation of response selection—not of response execution. From this view, response execution is simply the highly automatic "running off" of whatever response was selected, and if it is in error, that is because an inappropriate response—one having the wrong amplitude, force, direction, or duration—was selected. We need not pursue this question at this point, although it obviously is related to the way in which we model the processing of information.

Feedback. One stage in the total process was not made explicit in the model presented by Smith; namely the *feedback* of information about responses and their effects on the environment. Humans are not "open-loop" systems; rather, they receive information about their responses themselves. Without such feedback, or knowledge of results, about the outcomes of one's responses it would be impossible for a person systematically to modify, adapt, and improve performance. When, for example, we push the brake pedal in response to the traffic light, we may feel ourselves thrown forward by the sudden deceleration, and may hear our tires squeal and our passengers complain. We have received feedback about our response that enables us to evaluate its appropriateness. At the same time, we receive information about the response itself—its rate, force, amplitude, direction, pressure, and so on—from the kinesthetic receptors in the muscles, tendons, and joints of our legs and from the touch receptors on the bottom of our feet. The latter information defines "that response" and we know that "that response" was inappropriate, since it did not lead to the desired effect on the environment. This information is stored in memory and serves as a basis for evaluating subsequent responses selected in reaction to similar signals.

If one can assume either that a person can compare the response that has been selected for execution with some *memorial representation* of the "right" response, and/or that such a memorial representation actually governs the response selection process, then it makes sense to conceive of the learning of skilled performance as the *perfecting of the memorial representation of the appropriate response.* This "sharpening" of the criterion for behavior obviously depends on the feedback of information of two sorts: (1) information about the discrepancy of the outcome of the response as compared with some "intended" or "desired" outcome, and (2) information about the characteristics of the response itself.

Central Processing. The model, as presented in Figure 13–3, may raise some additional questions about information processing. For example, it may suggest that there is one "central processor" categorizing signals and selecting responses, with the "raw materials" (the signals) coming in from any or all of the sensory mechanisms. Such a view is a highly acceptable one in current theorizing, though not the only view. If one assumes a *single-channel processor* in which signals get translated into responses, then one can raise a host of questions about how the system works. For example, "What is the *capacity* of this central processor relative to the rate of input from the various senses?" and "If one assumes that the capacity is limited and may well be exceeded by the flow of input, then how is the processor affected? Is there a mechanism for screening out some signals, or channels? Is there provision for *sharing* the capacity of the processor between two or more simultaneous inputs? If so, does the channel process the two signal streams 'in parallel,' that is, by *sharing* the processing capacity, or does it function by *switching* rapidly from one stream to the other, that is, by *serial* processing? What are the limits for processing a single channel of input? What are the limits for processing multiple channels—'for doing two things at once'?" These are only a few of the questions that this and other models have raised about information processing. In most cases the answers are not at all simple, but involve a number of "it depends . . . "—conditions that qualify the answers. Thus, with respect to the questions about whether people can process more than one channel at the same time, it must be said that the answer depends on such factors as the *rate of information* on each channel, whether or not all the information must be processed for effective performance, whether the flow of information is continuous or comes in discrete "bursts," so that switching from one channel to the other could occur, and so on.

It is probably true that with practice and familiarity with a task some of the processing of signals is "short-circuited" or bypassed; that is, the behavior becomes at least partially *automated,* requiring only occasional sampling of the input and of the feedback from the response output. Under such conditions *attention,* or central processing capacity, could be largely diverted to a second, less automated task, with little or no evidence that performance on either task was interfered with by "time-sharing" with the other. Finally, it should be pointed out that the successful processing of truly simultaneous signals from two different sources, which seems to indicate parallel processing, does not eliminate the possibility that signals are processed serially. If one is willing to accept the notion of a short-term "buffer memory" where one of the two signals could be stored while it waits its turn at the central processor, then a serial processing model is quite adequate to account for the processing of simultaneous inputs.

As you can see from even this brief presentation of an information-processing model, the concepts are very complicated. In the past decade, these issues have become the focus of an increasingly important area of psychology known as *cognitive psychology*. We cannot hope to present you with all of the relevant issues with respect to information processing. Nevertheless, by looking at the model we have presented, you can see that there are distinct *operations* that the worker performs on the information prior to executing a response. It should be clear that these operations can be helped or hindered by work design. In particular, it seems as if *feedback* is a critical aspect of the environment that is under the direct control of the organization. One might also consider the possibility of improving the general information-processing capabilities of a work force through selection and training procedures. But even with a select and highly trained work force, the nature of information presentation and environmental feedback can have substantial effects on the efficiency with which the system functions.

Output from the Man-Machine Perspective

In considering the input portion of the man-machine model that we presented, we distinguished between input issues that were primarily human in orientation (e.g., sensory mechanisms) and those that were more related to the machine component (displays). We can make a similar distinction when we consider the *output* of a man-machine system. In our model of information processing, we dealt with a component called *response execution*. The issue of execution is a crucial one in performance. We may be perfectly aware of which response is called for, yet be incapable of making it correctly. This is the point at which the skills and abilities of the worker typically enter the system. While you may *know* what the task of a tennis player is, the fact that you continually miss the ball when you swing at it says something about your capacity to execute the desired response.

Human Performance Abilities. Psychologists have devoted a good deal of effort to the development of selection and training programs designed to ensure that the requisite skills will be attained. However, as Fleishman (1967) pointed out, much of the information regarding predictor tests (and training procedures) that has been gathered in the past proves to be inapplicable as new systems are considered. This is true in part because each new system is somewhat unique, placing new demands or a new combination of demands on the operator. It is also true in part because we do not have an adequate system for classifying the tasks that people perform; that is, a *taxonomy of tasks*. Neither do we have a clear conception of the *structure of human abilities* that underlies performance on different tasks.

Many psychologists have bemoaned this state of affairs and have called for a taxonomy of tasks that will allow more accurate prediction from one set of operations or functions to another.

One approach to this problem used the methodology of correlation and factor analysis, as well as experimentation. An outstanding example of this approach is the work of Fleishman and his associates (e.g., Fleishman, 1966, 1967; Fleishman & Parker, 1962; Fleishman & Rich, 1963). Fleishman made the distinction between *abilities*, which he defines as the more general traits of individuals inferred from intertask correlations, and *skills*, which are defined in terms of performance of specific tasks. Thus, *abilities* are seen as the attributes the individual has inherited or acquired in previous situations and brings to the new task situation. *Skill* is the level of proficiency attained on the task as a function of the level of ability, or abilities, the individual possesses and the particular strategies developed in the task situation. Acquiring a skill, then, refers to developing the sequence of responses or the degree of precision of behavior required on a specific task. By definition, abilities are related to performance on a number of tasks.

Fleishman's approach has been to describe tasks and to identify a taxonomy of basic tasks in terms of the abilities which are required to perform them. Typically, he has given a large battery of performance tests to a large sample of individuals. The scores from the various tasks are then intercorrelated, providing some notion of which tasks "go together"; that is, call upon some of the same abilities. Further information about the abilities common to different tasks is obtained when the intercorrelations are factor analyzed (see Chapter 2 for a description of factor analysis). The outcome of the factor analysis is a set of factors defined in terms of the "loadings" of the different tests on a common factor. These loadings are then examined in an attempt to describe or label the ability common to all of the tests that have significant loadings on the factor. This description, or labeling, of the factors can be thought of as a process of hypothesizing the existence of an underlying ability with certain characteristics.

The hypothesized abilities are tested further by attempts to develop more "pure" performance tests to measure the ability as it has been conceptualized. These *reference tests*, as Fleishman calls them, are then used to predict performance on the tasks that defined the factor. In this way, a set of reference tests are developed and refined, which in turn define a set of abilities. Fleishman has described this procedure for the factor "rate control":

In early studies it was found that this factor was common to compensatory as well as following pursuit tasks. To test its generality, tasks were developed to emphasize rate control, which were not conventional tracking tasks (e.g., controlling a ball rolling through a series of alleyways). The factor was found to extend to such tasks. Later studies attempted to discover if emphasis on this ability is in *judging the rate of the stimulus* as distinguished from *ability to respond at the appropriate rate*. A task was developed involving only button pressing in response to judgments of moving stimuli. Performance on this task did *not* correlate with other rate control tasks. . . . Thus, our definition of this ability was expanded to include measures beyond pursuit tasks, but restricted to tasks requiring the timing of a muscular adjustment to the stimulus change. (Fleishman, 1967, p. 6)

As a result of several years of research involving over 200 different tasks and several thousand subjects, Fleishman and his associates have identified and refined 11 factors that account for a large part of the variance in human motor performance. These factors were listed and described earlier, in Table 3–5. To review briefly, the factors were labeled as follows: control precision, multilimb coordination, response orientation, reaction time, speed of arm movement, rate control, manual dexterity, finger dexterity, arm-hand steadiness, wrist and finger speed, and aiming.

These 11 factors are relatively independent of one another; that is, the possession of a high level of ability on one factor does not necessarily mean a high level of ability on the other factors. This means that the reference test developed to measure one of the abilities should be predictive of performance on tasks or jobs if and only if that particular ability is important in the performance of that task. Fleishman, like Seashore (1951) and others before him, found little evidence to support the notion of a general factor of perceptual motor performance. Therefore, it is probably fallacious to predict that an operator who is highly skilled at assembling very small parts will necessarily be highly skilled at, say, driving a car or steering a ship, assuming that the first task involves *finger dexterity* and the second *control precision*.

Another significant finding from this approach is the consistent evidence that, with practice, performance on a given task is increasingly a function of habits and skills specific to that task. In other words, abilities that were highly related to performance in the early stages of skill development tend to be less important after much practice. It is as though the abilities give the trainee a "head start," but do not necessarily guarantee that a high level of performance will be attained. In addition to the "group" factors that define the abilities, the factor-analytic studies frequently yield evidence for such "task-specific" factors with a high factor loading for a single task. These loadings increase with practice. This means that as skill increases, performance is less dependent on the more general ability factors and more dependent on the strategies developed to cope with the task. This evidence led Seashore (1951) to state what he called the *work-methods hypothesis:*

> . . . that individual differences in any human ability (not just motor skills) are attributed to three groups of factors: (1) the physical constants of the various organs (especially sense organs, nervous system, and musculature) employed, (2) the general qualitative pattern of component actions involved, and (3) the refinement of the component actions with respect to both strength and timing so as to produce an optimal pattern of action, [but that superior performance is usually the result of] . . . hitting upon qualitative patterns of action, or *work methods*, that make the work easier. (p. 1353)

Skilled performance was seen by Seashore as more often limited by inadequate patterning or sequencing of actions than by sensory, nervous-system, or muscular limitations of the operator. On the other hand, a high level of performance was seen by Seashore to be a function of work methods "hit upon rather than carefully thought out or even recognized afterward" (p. 1354). He felt that such work methods or strategies were largely a matter of trial and error and rather impervious to attempts to train the operator. The work-methods hypothesis is consistent with the evidence that task-specific factors increase in importance as practice continues, while the more general abilities tend to decrease or drop out: performance in a given task is increasingly a function of the particular work methods hit upon by the operator and less and less a function of the pattern of abilities that he brings to the task situation.

This point is well illustrated in Figure 13–4, from Fleishman (1966). Here it can·be seen that the factor specific to the task (in this case a reaction time task) accounts for an increasing amount of the total variance in the task performance, while the reference measures of the more general abilities become less and less important.

In one sense, Figure 13–4 presents a discouraging picture. It suggests that while we may be able to develop measures of abilities that rather successfully predict performance and the rate of improvement early in the development of a skill, it may be much more difficult to predict really high levels of performance. Such results also provide an explanation of the fact that early performance on a task is seldom very predictive of later performance: the abilities that give the trainee a "running start" are not necessarily those that ensure the development of a high level of skill. Furthermore, the operator who starts out badly may fortuitously hit upon a strategy at a later time that leads to skillful performance. However, while some abilities (e.g., spatial relations) become less predictive of performance with practice, other abilities (e.g., reaction time and rate of movement) become more predictive as skill develops.

This last point is illustrated in a study by Fleishman and Rich (1963) involving performance on a two-hand coordination task. In this study, 40 subjects were given practice on the task, then divided into two groups on the basis of their scores on a test of spatial ability. Performance on the two-hand coodination task was then compared for these two groups. The results are shown in Figure 13–5. This figure shows that those subjects with high spatial ability had a head start on the task. They performed better during the early stages of practice. However, their advantage was short-lived: after about a half hour of practice, they were no better than the group with low spatial ability scores. When these same subjects were divided into two groups on the basis of their scores on a test of kinesthetic sensitivity, the results were quite different. As Figure 13–6 shows, kinesthetic sensitivity was not related to performance on the coordination task early in training: subjects with high scores on the measure showed an advantage only after the first half of the training session. Thus, the ability (visual-

FIGURE 13–4

Factors Related to Skilled Performance

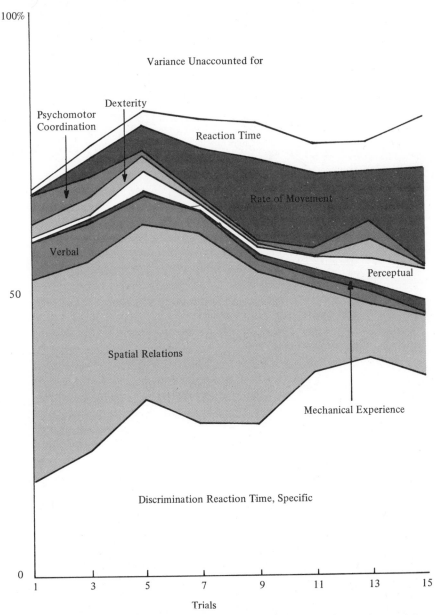

Source: Fleishman. E. A. Human abilities and the acquisition of skill. In E. A. Bilodeau (ed.) *Acquisition of skill.* New York: Academic Press, 1966, p. 160.

Percentage of variance represented by each factor at different stages of practice on the Discrimination Reaction Time Task. Percentage of variance is represented by the area shaded in for each factor.

FIGURE 13–5

Comparison of Two-Hand Coordination Acquisition Curves for Groups High and Low on the Aerial Orientation Test

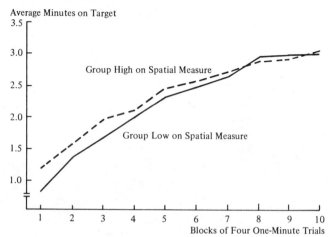

Source: Fleishman, E. A., and Rich, S. Role of kinesthetic and spatial-visual abilities in perceptual motor learning. *Journal of Experimental Psychology*, 1963, *66*, 6–11.

FIGURE 13–6

Comparison of Two-Hand Coordination Acquisition Curves for Groups High and Low on the Kinesthetic Sensitivity Measure

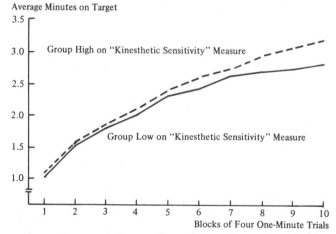

Source: Fleishman, E. A., and Rich, S. Role of kinesthetic and spatial-visual abilities in perceptual motor learning. *Journal of Experimental Psychology*, 1963, *66*, 6–11.

spatial orientation) that was important for performance early in practice was not the same as the ability (kinesthetic sensitivity) related to achievement of a high level of skill on the task. Incidentally, this finding also supports the notion that people rely relatively more on feedback from their environment (via the exteroceptors: vision, audition, etc.) in the early stages of the development of perceptual-motor skills, but come to rely more and more on kinesthetic information as the skill is being perfected.

This emphasis on human performance abilities can be quite useful in developing man-machine systems. One can determine the demands that will be placed on the operator before the fact and develop appropriate training mechanisms to prepare the operator for those demands. But, as was the case with the input to the man-machine system, the psychologist is often consulted after a problem has occurred. This requires one to identify problems with existing control and execution systems rather than to design completely new ones. Thus, a second approach that one might take to system output would be an examination of control devices.

Identifying Problems of Machine Control. Many of the issues raised in the earlier discussion of displays also apply to the control devices by which a worker communicates with and guides the equipment. In many machine systems, the number of controls—knobs, levers, buttons, toggle switches, handwheels, and the like—might increase as rapidly as the number of displays. This is likely to be the case, since most displays imply some control action, at least when some critical level is indicated by the display. Thus, in many systems, such as the aircraft in Figure 13–2, the cockpit space not filled with displays is filled with controls.

One of the early investigations of control problems by psychologists is significant for a number of reasons. In the first place, it demonstrates the first step in any systematic investigation: identify and describe the problem. Second, the study, despite its relative simplicity, gave a good deal of direction to human engineering research in the 1940s and 1950s. The study, conducted by Fitts and Jones (1947b), involved interviews with about 500 pilots and former pilots. Essentially, the researchers applied the critical-incidence technique. Pilots were asked to

> describe in detail an error in the operation of a cockpit control (flight control, engine control, toggle switch, selector switch, trim-tab control, etc.) which was made by yourself or another person whom you were watching at the time.

The researchers analyzed the replies given by the pilots and found that they could be classified into six categories, shown in Figure 13–7. The following examples of some of these types of errors were provided by an experienced pilot.

1. Substitution Errors. In the early days of the retractable landing gear, pilots often attempted to raise the flaps immediately after landing. There were many instances when, through error, the pilot grabbed the landing gear lever and raised the gear instead of the flaps. When the general substitu-

FIGURE 13-7

Classification of 460 Errors Made by Pilots in Operating Aircraft Controls

1. *Substitution errors:* Confusing one control with another or failing to identify a control when it was needed. In general, most of these errors were due to (a) lack of uniformity in the placement of controls, (b) inadequate separation of controls, and (c) lack of a coding system to help the pilot identify controls positively by the sense of touch alone.

2. *Adjustment errors:* Operating a control too slowly or too rapidly, moving a switch to the wrong position, or following the wrong sequence in operating several controls. The most common single kind of error in this category was made by turning the fuel-selector switch so that it was halfway between two tanks and leaving it in a position where fuel could flow from neither tank, or actually turning the switch to the wrong tank.

3. *Forgetting errors:* Failing to check, unlock, or use a control at the proper time.

4. *Reversal errors:* Moving a control in a direction opposite to that necessary to produce the desired result. Many such errors could be traced to the fact that controls sometimes would not move in "expected" directions.

5. *Unintentional activation:* Accidentally operating a control without being aware of it.

6. *Inability to reach:* Difficulty in reaching a control.

Source: Adapted from Fitts, P. M., & Jones, R. E. Analysis of 460 "pilot-error" experiences in operating aircraft controls. Engineering Division, Air Materiel Command, Dayton, Ohio: Rept. No. TSEAA-649-12 (1947).

tion error became obvious, the location of the actuation levers were standardized. The gear lever was placed on the left of the throttles, and the flap lever on the right of the throttles. They have also been coded for touch by making the gear lever handle in the shape of a small tire. The flap lever is shaped like a wing cross section. There are still occasional substitution errors, but they have been greatly reduced.

2. Adjustment Errors. In Cessna aircraft in the mid-sixties, the fuel selector switch was on the floor between the two pilot seats. It had four positions—off at the six o'clock position, left tank at nine, both tanks at twelve, and right tank at three. The selector handle was rotated to point at the desired position. It was required to be in the "both" or twelve o'clock position for landing. In one incident, a student pilot was making his before-landing check as he approached the landing field. When he called, "Fuel selector, both," he put his hand on the selector lever and felt that the instructor pilot had moved it to the three o'clock position. That was a common practice to determine the student's proficiency in performing the checklist items. Without looking at the selector lever, the student pilot turned it so that it was in line with the twelve o'clock/six o'clock position. Approximately 30 seconds later, the engine stopped running as the student had accidentally adjusted the selector to the six o'clock "off" position. Returning the selector to "both" quickly restored engine power, and the student had learned a valuable lesson.

3. Forgetting Errors. The pilot was giving six people a ride to a worksite on a cold winter day in Alaska. He did not use his checklist because he was in a hurry and it was very cold. He forgot to remove an external control lock in his haste. The control lock keeps the ailerons and elevator control surfaces from moving to protect them from damage by the wind when the airplane is on the ground. The rudder controls worked normally and were used to position the aircraft for takeoff. The pilot initiated his takeoff, and as the airplane reached flying speed, it lifted off the ground approximately 10 feet. At that point, the pilot found that he could not control roll and pitch, and the aircraft crashed, killing all aboard, because of the forgotten control lock.[1]

The fruitfulness of Fitts and Jones' critical-incident study should be obvious. Each of the six categories of errors suggests a number of problems in the design of machine controls, some of which may be unique to the task of piloting an airplane, but many of which may be common to the design of a wide range of machines. This analysis led to a host of studies on the design of control devices, on location, size, and shape coding of controls, and on human abilities to perform control operations.

Figure 13–8 shows the device used in one study of control design (Jenkins, 1947). The purpose of this study was to determine the tactile discriminability of various control-knob shapes, so that a set of knobs could be prescribed that would not be confused by the operator. In the experiment, 25 different

FIGURE 13–8
Shape-Coded Controls

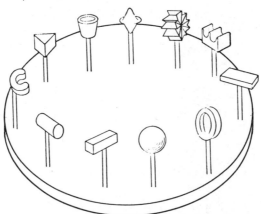

Source: W. O. Jenkins. Tactual discrimination of shapes for coding aircraft-type controls. In P. M. Fitts. *Psychological research on equipment design.* Washington, D.C.: Government Printing Office, 1947.

The apparatus used by Jenkins (1947) to select knobs for shape coding of controls. The 11 knob shapes shown were found to be readily identifiable by touch.

---

[1] The authors are indebted to Ronald T. Talcott for these examples.

knob designs were used. The experimental subject, who was blindfolded, was allowed to grasp one of the knobs for one second. Then the "lazy Susan" on which the knobs were mounted was rotated to a randomly chosen starting position. The subject then felt each knob in turn until he thought he recognized the original knob. In this way, it was possible to determine which shapes were confused with which other shapes. Subjects were tested with and without gloves. As a result of the study, two sets of eight knobs were identified such that the shapes within each set were rarely confused with one another. Thus, the use of either set, together with location coding in a machine system, would allow essentially errorless performance, without the need for visual monitoring.

The Interactions of Controls and Displays. Thus far, we have treated problems of display and control design separately, as though you could determine the optimum design and arrangement of one without considering the other. Up to a point this is probably a safe assumption. We can assess the visibility, legibility, and error rates of dials of different designs, the discriminability of different control shapes, locations, and the precision of control movements in this manner. However, when questions arise as to the optimum design of a display *for a specific control operation*, then both the design of the control and of the display must be considered. In such a situation we are concerned with the extent to which particular display configurations "command" certain control actions rather than others.

Our everyday experiences provide many examples in which information displays command or fail to command appropriate control responses. For example, the selector display on a radio may have a pointer that moves across a fixed horizontal scale of radio wave frequencies. The pointer is controlled by a knob, which may be turned either clockwise or counterclockwise to move the pointer. What should be the linkage between the knob and the pointer? Should a clockwise turn of the knob move the pointer to the left or to the right? Should the linkage be reversed if the pointer is fixed and the scale is moved past the pointer? Suppose the display is placed on the front of the radio but the knob is on the side (as with many small portable models); what should then be the relation between control and pointer movement?

Many questions such as these arise in the design of equipment controls and displays. Figure 13–9 illustrates one problem with which most of us are familiar. Four models of ordinary kitchen stoves are presented, each with a different configuration of controls and burners ("displays"). Now, suppose that your favorite dinner is burning or boiling over on one of the burners. Which configuration will ensure the quickest and most accurate control action? Chapanis and Lindenbaum (1959) conducted an experiment to answer this question.

In their experiment a small light came on near the center of one of the burners on one of the stoves shown in Figure 13–9. The subjects' task was to turn off the light as quickly as possible by turning one of the

FIGURE 13–9
Models of Four Stoves Tested by Chapanis and Lindenbaum

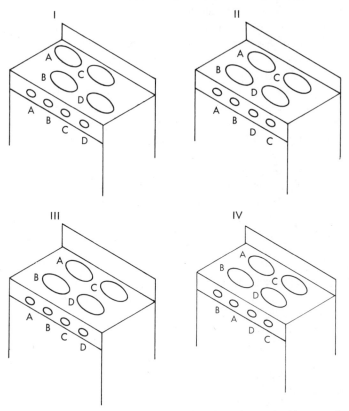

Source: Chapanis, A., & Linderbaum, L. E. A reaction time study of four control-display linkages. *Human Factors*, 1959, *2*, 1–7.

knobs. In all, 1,200 trials were recorded for each stove, 20 trials for each of 60 experimental subjects. The results showed that with stove I there were no errors, while stoves II, III, and IV had 26 percent, 38 percent, and 43 percent errors, respectively. The speed with which responses were made agreed perfectly with the error data: stove I was operated with the shortest average response times, stove IV the longest response times.

A basic method in the study of control-display relationships is to determine the "population stereotype" for responses to information displays. This term refers to the "norm" or typical response of a large sample of people when they are faced with a control-display configuration. A simple example is a situation in which subjects are asked to turn a doorknob to open a door. The experimenter simply records the percentages of people who initially turn the knob clockwise or counterclockwise. The "index of stereotopy" is directly proportional to the percentage of people choosing the preferred response. Thus, in the "doorknob" example, the index of stereotopy would be zero if half of the subjects turned the knob clockwise while the other half turned it counterclockwise.

Data on population stereotypes have been recorded for many display-control configurations. Such information is of obvious value for designing the linkage between controls and displays. The more often a particular control action is chosen in response to a particular display of information, the more *compatible* the display-control arrangement is said to be. The concept, display-control, or stimulus-response (S-R) compatibility refers to the "ease" or naturalness with which a set of responses is linked to a set of signals by the operator. Population stereotypes constitute one of the determinants of S-R compatibility: the higher the index of stereotopy, the more compatible the display-control arrangement.

In a recent study dealing with response stereotypy to auditory information, Simon and his associates (Simon, Mewaldt, Acosta, & Hu, 1976) suggested that population stereotypes might be thought of as examples of performance limitations of the worker. They found that it was more natural for subjects to move a switch up in response to a high tone and down to a low tone than vice versa. In this case, if we designed a system that required the worker to move a switch *up* in response to a *low* tone, we could expect frequent errors. One way of viewing this situation is that the performance of the operator is limited to the degree to which the machine requires a response that is incompatible with a natural tendency. This is not to say that natural tendencies cannot be overcome—most can. But the point is that if we are aware of these tendencies before the fact, we may design the system in such a way that instead of having a performance limitation built into the system, we have a performance strength—a required response that is compatible with a natural tendency.

A Brief Review

In this chapter we have chosen to redefine "work" as an example of a man-machine system. The worker has certain *input* capacities and limitations; these can be seen primarily in the functions of sensory mechanisms. The machine also has capacities and limitations, which interact with those of the worker. The machine may display input information in a variety of ways. Once the worker has received the input, she must do something with it. The process of using input is called *information processing*. This is something that *people* do, and as such is of great interest to the industrial psychologist, since the individual worker mediates between input and output of the system.

The *output* part of the man-machine system has two components as well. The human component defines what responses can be executed by the worker in terms of skills and abilities. The machine contribution to the system at this point is a series of *control* mechanisms by which the worker physically makes a response. The human engineer dissects work in a way that is completely different from that of the personnel or industrial social psychologist. Consequently, these three different types of I/O psychologists should be thought of as complementing one another in attempting to understand the relationship between people and work.

Before leaving the man-machine context, we would like to consider two final issues: (1) the identification of sources of error in systems and (2) automation.

AN ANALYSIS OF SYSTEM ERROR

Chapanis (1951) has described the relationship between component errors in a man-machine system. His discussion of *constant* and *variable* errors is illustrated by Figure 13–10, which represents the performance of two different marksmen. Both marksmen, *on the average*, miss the center of the target. However, marksman A has a larger *variable* error than marksman B. That is, A's shots vary more around his mean than B's. The relative importance of these two types of errors should be evident from this example: Marksman B is extremely consistent in his performance and can achieve a perfect score by a single correction: sighting slightly more to the left. Marksman A has a more serious problem. Correcting his constant error in the same way as B will only slightly improve his score; his major problem is to reduce his variability. Generally speaking, variable errors constitute more serious problems than constant errors.

The above example is probably realistic in a number of ways. First, it is likely that human errors exceed machine errors in many systems. Secondly,

FIGURE 13–10
Constant and Variable Errors

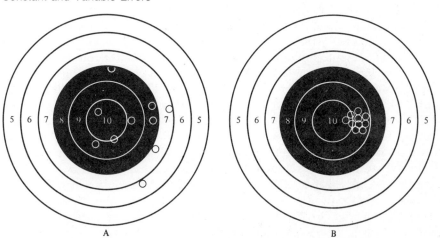

Source: Chapanis, A., Garner, W. R., & Morgan, C. *Applied experimental psychology.* New York: Wiley, 1949, p. 56.

Target patterns for two marksmen with the same *constant* error. Marksman A has a greater *variable* error than Marksman B.

the alternative of reducing human error is realistic in many systems. The tools for accomplishing this have been the subject matter of this and of earlier chapters of this book. They include: better selection and training procedures, better work motivation, and improved human engineering of the machine to fit the human operator.

AUTOMATION AND MAN-MACHINE SYSTEMS

The reader may well ask at this point whether the answer to the problem of systems error might not be, "Get the person out of the system." Since people are very likely to be a major source of error, this would, at first glance, appear to be a reasonable approach. How is it accomplished? The immediate response is, "Automation. Develop automated systems that operate without people." Many examples of automated and partially-automated systems such as oil refineries, spaceships, and engine-block plants can be cited. Yet, while it is obvious that automation has greatly reduced the ratio of men to machine components and drastically changed the remaining jobs, it seldom "gets the person out of the system" completely. Instead, people are kept in the system, fulfilling the functions of monitors and troubleshooters. Rather than performing operations directly on the material with direct sensory feedback about the effects of their actions, they are removed to remote stations where they monitor the system indirectly through symbolic and abstract information displays. The magnitude of the errors that the operator is capable of committing is frequently much greater than in the days of "one worker-one operation" mechanization. The decisions that must be made are often critical to the well-being and successful operation of equipment worth hundreds of thousands of dollars.

A dramatic and sobering example of the critical nature of the interaction between operators and "automatic" equipment is the nuclear accident that occurred at Three Mile Island in Pennsylvania. This accident was the result of compounded man-machine failures. As part of a routine maintenance program, the secondary or backup system for cooling the superheated water from the nuclear reactor was shut down. Through oversight on the part of plant personnel, this secondary system was not turned back on after the maintenance. Two weeks after this backup system was shut down, a pump failed in the *primary* cooling system. Since the secondary system was inoperable, the temperature began to climb in the reactor chamber. Then a valve stuck; an "automatic" emergency system went into operation, exaggerating the negative effect of the stuck valve, and control-room personnel misinterpreted information from faulty instruments. The situation came close to a genuine disaster in which the lives of thousands of people might have been in jeopardy. While it is impossible to "blame" the accident on one thing or one person, it is clear that human decisions played a major role in the accident, in spite of (or possibly *because* of) automated systems or subsystems.

As you would expect, an immediate reaction to this accident was a

"We've decided to rehire you—the machine we bought to replace you won't work either."

Reprinted by permission The Wall Street Journal

demand for improved mechanical, electrical, and chemical systems that would prevent a reoccurrence. But in addition, the role of the man in the man-machine system is once again receiving close attention. For example, as a result of the accident, the Swedish Nuclear Industry has proposed rigid standards for the selection, training, and licensing of control-room personnel in nuclear power plants. Similar suggestions will undoubtedly be considered in all countries with substantial nuclear facilities.

It is true that automation and its forerunner, mechanization, have taken much of the drudgery, inhumanity, and danger out of man's work and for these reasons ought to be vigorously pursued. What the human engineer needs to attend to, however, are the ways in which automation has changed the nature of work, the system's functions that are increasingly allocated to human operators, and those which are likely to be part of man's role in future systems. It is the challenge of human engineering to help people perform these functions to the best of their capabilities, thereby increasing the efficiency and reliability of the system of which they are a part.

SOLVING HUMAN ENGINEERING PROBLEMS

How do human engineers arrive at solutions to the problems of man-machine systems? First, it should be pointed out that human engineering is usually an interdisciplinary effort, involving experts not only from engineering and psychology, but also from anthropometry (the measurement of human physical dimensions), medicine, physiology, and so on. These specialists are frequently identified as a human factors group, or team.

Frequently they are assigned to "human-engineer" a particular system or subsystem that is being designed by the company in which they work. In such cases the goal of the team is to build into the design of that system those features that will maximize human efficiency and that of the system. Their "mission" is, therefore, quite specific to the system. In contrast to the earliest work of human engineers, they are increasingly called upon during the planning and preliminary design phases of system development, where there is more freedom to incorporate human engineering principles.

Even today, however, the experiences of the human engineer are not always happy ones. She is frequently called upon to provide answers to questions that arise suddenly in the process of designing a system. Often answers are required on short notice to avoid costly delays in the design and production schedule. What does the human engineer do in such situations? She acts as an expert consultant. With the aid of handbooks of anthropometry, sensory processes, human-engineering guides, and her own experience, she suggests answers to the problems at hand. Frequently these answers are "best guesses" because the directly relevant information is not available. As human engineering and engineering psychology mature, her chances of finding the appropriate information increase. When design questions are anticipated in advance and handbook answers are not available, the human engineer may seek the answers through experimentation. Then expert opinion may be replaced by experimental results.

Human Engineering Research

Research by human engineers can be classified according to the specificity of the goals and of the results obtained. At one level, the researcher engages in what has been called "quick and dirty" experimentation—"quick" because time pressures preclude more adequate research: "dirty" because such research may not be "elegantly" designed and is lacking in experimental control. Whether quick and dirty or somewhat more elegant, research conducted by human factors groups is frequently addressed to questions unique to the system being designed. Research on such questions as, "Is it better to use a joystick or a handwheel for this control operation?" or, "Which type of illumination is better for this systems control center?" may be used to improve the design of the specific system, but often provides little information to guide the design of other systems.

Problem-versus Principle-Oriented Research. The important distinction to be made is that between *problem-oriented* and *principle-oriented* research. It is, in a loose way, the distinction between science and applied science, or between physics and engineering. Science seeks principles and generalizations about its subject matter. Applied science seeks to solve specific problems by applying scientific facts and, when the facts are missing, by problem-oriented experiments. Human engineers, because of time pressures and practical demands, frequently must conduct research to solve problems, not to seek principles of design or of human performance. This situation—the need for both problem-oriented and principle-oriented re-search—will continue to exist as long as there are gaps in the basic knowledge that is necessary to solve practical problems.

Under the pressures of a wartime emergency, much of the early research in human engineering was system-specific and problem-oriented. However, it soon became apparent to some researchers in the field that with such an approach questions of the same type would continue to arise with each new system. They began to seek principles of design, such as those involved in the design of information displays. This approach led to more systematic research on such variables as size, number of markers, number and shape of pointers, and number coding of displays (see Fitts, 1951; Grether, 1968). It also led to research on principles of human performance and information processing, which we discussed earlier. This research was concerned more with people as processors of information, independent of any particular system. In the next two sections, we will present examples of problem- and principle-oriented research.

An Example of Problem-Oriented Research.   Psychologists often kid one another about the value of their efforts. Sensitivity training is often referred to as "touchy-feely" research; behavior modification advocates are often referred to as the M & M crowd, in honor of their favorite reinforcer; similarly, we often jokingly refer to human engineering as "advanced knobs and dials." There is more than a little truth in this last epithet, since the design of knobs and dials has been a primary concern of much problem-oriented research. Knobs are forms of control and represent the response mechanism for the operator. Consequently, a good deal of research has gone into the design of efficient knobs. Carter (1978) has recently given new status to the study of knobs in an article entitled "Knobology Underwater"! In spite of the possibly humorous overtones of the title, Carter's is an excellent example of problem-oriented research.

Divers are dependent on knobs for the control of life-support systems. It is reasonable to assume that the design of knobs on diving equipment could have important implications for diver safety and efficiency. Carter was working with the Navy divers and discovered that, in spite of the fact that there were suggestions about the best types of knobs to be used on diving equipment, these suggestions were based on research that had not been done in underwater contexts. Since the performance of deep-sea divers in cold water using gloved hands is substantially different from the performance of other workers, Carter felt that it was essential to deter-mine the best knob for use underwater in realistic diving environments. An additional issue in Carter's research was the placement of the knobs on the diving equipment. Since knobs on diving equipment usually appear at one of three places (on the headgear, on the stomach, or on the outside of the leg), he felt that it was important to study the interaction of the knob design and the knob position.

The experiment consisted of examining the speed and accuracy with which divers could adjust each of 15 different knobs in each of three different positions. The knobs varied in size and shape, and the three placement positions were the right side of the headgear, the left side of the abdomen, and the outside of the right leg. Six divers performed speed and accuracy tests in water that varied between 13° and 23° C (55° and 73° F) and at pressures equivalent to those experienced between 100 and 350 feet underwater. The tests lasted for one hour. On the accuracy test, the diver was required to turn the knob to several different specified positions; on the speed test, the diver was required to turn the knobs a specified number of revolutions. In the accuracy test, error was measured as deviation from the specified setting. In the speed test, performance was defined as the amount of time it took to make the appropriate revolutions. The adjustments that the divers made were electrically transmitted to a comfortable dry area (much to Carter's relief) allowing for accurate recording.

Carter's findings were interesting and will undoubtedly influence knob design for underwater diving gear. He discovered that when speed was a critical factor in performance, larger-diameter knobs were better than smaller ones. This seemed to be true independent of the position of the knob (e.g., head versus abdomen). In addition, the largest knob examined also yielded the greatest accuracy of adjustment, regardless of position. The findings were relatively clear: big round knobs were better than alternative designs. Carter was somewhat surprised by these results, since he had to *make the big round knob himself—it was not standard equipment on any existing diving gear.*

The question of *why* large round knobs are more conducive to fast and accurate performance of divers was not determined in Carter's research. He speculated as to possible explanations, but his research was directed toward a specific problem: designing safe and efficient knobs for diving gear. We must conclude that he was successful in his research and that "knobology" is alive and well and living in the ocean.

An Example of Principle-oriented Research. A series of experiments conducted at the Foxboro Company in the late 1940s illustrate the sort of research that can be directed at rather specific questions but, at the same time, yield design principles and theoretical concepts applicable to a wide range of design problems.

The studies, under the direction of Dr. Harry Helson (1949), were concerned with the functional relationships among a number of design variables and performance on a continuous control task. A laboratory apparatus was designed to simulate an antiaircraft fire-control system. A schematic drawing of this apparatus is shown in Figure 13–11. In this system the control is a handwheel, shown at the right, and the display is an indicator with two pointers. The upper pointer is programmed to move "off target," that is, away from the fixed pointer, in a manner controlled by the course generator. The operator's task is to keep the two pointers aligned by turning the handwheel in such a way as to counteract, or compensate for, the deflections of the pointer caused by the course generator.

The reader may have anticipated already some of the design questions

FIGURE 13–11
Schematic Diagram of Apparatus

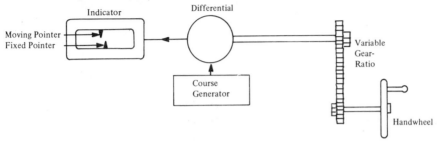

Source: Helson, H. Design of equipment and optimal human operation. *The American Journal of Psychology,* 1949, 62, 473–499.

that the researchers investigated. They began by examining the relationship between speed of handwheel turning and accuracy of performance. To test this relationship, the moving pointer was programmed to move off target at a constant rate, but with different rates for different trials. The slowest rate required only 2 revolutions per minute (rpm) of the handwheel to keep the pointers aligned, while the fastest rate required 200 rpm. Size of the handwheel was also investigated, with a small (radius = 2.25") and a large (radius = 4.50") handwheel being used. Performance accuracy was measured in terms of the total amount of error accumulated in a trial, or "run."

The results of this first study are shown in Figure 13–12. Obviously, speed of turning has a profound effect on handwheel tracking performance. It appears that up to a point, the faster the rate of turning, the better the performance. However, after this point rather large changes in rate have little or no effect on performance. Thus, the differences in performance for speeds between 50 and 200 rpm are very small compared with those between 2 and 50 rpm. The relationship between speed of turning and performance accuracy depends in part on the size of the handwheel: at slower speeds the big wheel is consistently better, but at high speeds the small wheel shows a slight advantage.

Helson and his associates went on to investigate the relationship between speed of turning and the difficulty of the course-to-be-tracked. They found that their first result held up: fast turning was superior to slow turning even for their most difficult course. Also of some interest was evidence that the benefits of fast turning were greater for "green" than for experienced operators. But would fast turning continue to be beneficial with longer periods of continuous control? Perhaps fast turning would lead to fatigue and, in the long run, poorer performance. The results of the next experiment failed to support this possibility: fast turning continued to yield superior performance even after 15 minutes of continuous tracking.

Next the investigators turned to the variables of inertia and friction.

FIGURE 13–12

Tracking-Error as a Function of Speed of Turning

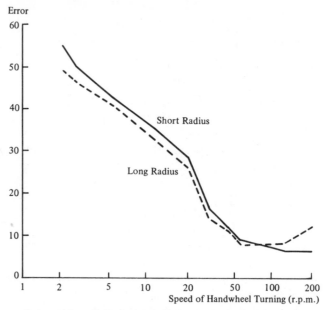

Source: Helson, H. Design of equipment and optimal human operation. *The American Journal of Psychology*, 1949, 62, 473–499.

Inertia was varied by using light (2.5-lb.) and heavy (9-lb.) handwheels and additionally by adding weight to the flywheel. The results were rather convincing. The heavy handwheel was superior to the light handwheel at all speeds of turning and for both small- and large-diameter wheels. Accuracy was increased on the average by 40% with the increase in inertia provided by the heavy handwheel.

Finally, when the relationships of size, speed, inertia and friction to accuracy of performance were investigated, it was concluded that

> friction was found to be deleterious even in small amounts but its effect was greater when other conditions were not optimal, i.e., at slow turning speeds, and with small, light handwheels. Conversely, favorable or optimal values of other variables may be used to offset the bad effects of friction as shown by the lower error scores . . . when the handwheel is heavy and large. (Helson, 1949, p. 487)

A few other design parameters were investigated in the Foxboro studies, but perhaps enough has been said to indicate the significance of this research and the richness of the empirical results.

What can we learn from these studies to warrant the space devoted to them in this chapter? First, with respect to empirical findings, performance data were made available on the design dimensions of size, speed, inertia, friction, and other variables that should prove valuable for anyone faced with the problems of designing a handwheel control system. These data in themselves more than justify the research efforts. In addition, however, the studies show that these design variables interact in important ways in their effects on performance. Figure 13–11 indicates, for example, that optimal size of handwheels may depend on the speed of turning required. Furthermore, the heavy, large handwheel was better up to the point where the operator was unable to handle the heavy load because the target course changed too rapidly. Inertia (the heavy wheel) was also beneficial, but adding flywheel inertia helped only at the slower speeds of turning. Finally, the benefits of fast turning depended on the skill level of the subjects, being greater for inexperienced than for experienced operators.

In addition to these functional relationships and interactions, however, a number of more general principles and theoretical concepts emerge from the Foxboro studies. The first of these concepts is the *U-hypothesis*. This refers to the evidence that performance tends to be optimal over a rather broad range of values of a design variable. That is, the curve relating some design dimension (such as size) to amount of error would tend to be U-shaped, with a range of values yielding near-optimal performance, beyond which error tends to increase. Thus, in Figure 13–11 performance shows little effects of speed of turning between 50 and 200 rpm. At lower values (and, presumably, at higher values), performance deteriorates rather sharply. The implications for designers should be clear: emphasis should be placed on keeping design parameters within the optimal range, not on searching for *the* optimal value. Some variables, like friction, will not conform to the U-hypothesis because their effects are "from bad to worse," never from bad to good to bad. Nevertheless, the second generalization, the *principles of offset and compromise*, covers the problem of friction. These principles are addressed to the practical limitations where friction may exist or where compromise may be necessary. Thus, inertia may be introduced to *offset* the bad effects of friction, and an intermediate speed of turning may serve as a *compromise* when both very slow and very fast targets must be tracked.

Values of design parameters within the optimal range tend to remain optimal, despite changes in other parameters. This notion of *generality of the optimal* needs to be tempered by the evidence of interaction between variables (i.e., the optimal handwheel size at slow rates is not optimal for fast rates) but within limits does appear to describe the "robustness" of some optimal values, for example, speed of turning.

Helson also suggested two generalizations with respect to human performance. The first of these, the *hypothesis of par* or *tolerance*, was based on his observations that operators appear to set definite standards for their performance. When performance falls below this standard or "par" value, they exert greater effort to reduce the error.

Second, Helson observed that subjects' tracking performance showed responses to course changes that were far less than reaction times. Further-more, with a difficult course, subjects seemed to "track through" the com-plexities of the course, aiming for the average course. These two strategies of performance were labeled *anticipation and averaging.* They have been observed repeatedly in tracking studies.

"Comparative" versus "Comprehensive" Research.   Contrast for a mo-ment the difference between two experiments, one designed to determine "whether dial A, B, or C yields better performance in system X," the other to determine "speed and accuracy of dial reading as a function of size, number of markings, and pointer width." In the first study, dials A, B, and C may be prototypes designed by three different engineers. They may differ in size, number of markings, number and dimensions of pointers, scale, and in several other ways. In the experiment, subjects report as quickly and accurately as possible a number of settings on each prototype. Let us suppose that dial B yields the best performance (the fastest average readings and the fewest errors). Thus, given the problem for which it was designed, the research is an obvious success: Dial B is better on both criteria than either dial A or dial C and the problem is solved. But what has been learned about the design of dials? Was performance on dial B superior because it was larger? Had fewer pointers? Or fewer markers, more numbers, or larger numbers? Because the three prototype dials differed qualitatively, or along a number of dimensions, it is impossible to say *why* dial B resulted in better performance. In other words, it is impossible to state a *principle* to guide the future design of dials. Moreover, because the prototypes were not varied systematically along some quantitative dimension, it is impossible to determine what the *functional* relationship is between the performance measures and any dimension of the dial, such as size. Finally, the study, because it began with three prototype designs, is strictly "comparative" research. The outcome says nothing about the myriad of other dials that might be offered by imaginative designers. At best, it may provide only a hint as to the *best* design of a dial for displaying this type of information.

In the second example, an experiment to determine "speed and accuracy of performance as a function of size, number of markings, and pointer width in visual displays," the functions relating each performance measure to each design dimension can be determined. Furthermore, a well-designed study will yield information about the ways in which the design dimensions interact to effect performance. It might be concluded, for example, that "number of markings" interacts with "size"of the dial, so that performance is better for small dials when they have few markers, but with larger dials it is better to have more markers. Such statements of the interaction effects of design dimensions are commonly reported and are obviously important for our understanding of the principles of display and control design. It is the functional relationships between design parameters and performance measures, singly and in interaction, that identify the principles on which design decisions can be made.

Realism in Human Engineering Research. Yet another issue in the design of human engineering research is the question of *realism*. This term refers to the extent to which the experimental situation is similar to, or *simulates*, the real situation of an operator in a man-machine system. It may be apparent to the reader that the question of realism is related to that of problem- versus principle-oriented research. Problem-oriented research, because it seeks answers to specific design problems, must be concerned with realism. If the results of experiments conducted in a laboratory, mock-up, or simulator cannot be generalized to performance in the operating system, they provide, at best, only a tentative answer to the design problem. What could one conclude, for example, about the relative efficiency of dials A, B, and C in a noisy, vibrating aircraft if the experimental results were obtained in a quiet laboratory setting? Can we generalize our findings, or is it conceivable that the "best" dial for laboratory performance is not the best in practice?

As a result of the concern for realism, research in human engineering often involves the use of elaborate simulators. Much discussion has been given to the question of the need for simulation in human engineering and systems research. Clearly, when the experimental situation does not resemble the operating situation in every respect, the research results are open to questions of transfer and generalizability. However, from another point of view it is felt that it is never possible to simulate the *psychological* environment completely, with, for example, the stresses during the countdown in a space vehicle. In a simulator the operator *knows* that he is not in a real system, and that knowledge limits the extent to which the real system can be simulated. Nevertheless, there is some evidence that some degree of simulation does create a realistic psychological environment, especially for operators experienced with the real system environment (see the following section).

Ideally, the most direct solution to the problems of realism and the transfer of research results is to test design parameters in the actual operating situations. The reader will recognize, however, that field studies are often impractical, if not impossible, for a number of reasons. Suppose, for example, that one is concerned with the design of an air traffic control system wherein performance is to be evaluated in terms of the safe and efficient landing of large numbers of aircraft. What would be involved in a field experiment designed to test two or three alternative designs of such a system? First, a number of airplanes would have to be put in the air to test performance under each system configuration. Then, to attain adequate experimental control, the planes would have to perform in very nearly the same way relative to one another and to the control center on each test. Other variables, such as weather conditions, might introduce uncontrolled variance in the systems performance from day to day. Finally, the entire operation could be hazardous to flight crews, civilians, and multimillion-dollar aircraft. In short, such an experiment would be highly impractical. Innovations in such complex systems as air traffic control are better made on the basis of laboratory or simulator research. Unfortunately, evaluation of innovations in systems is often casual and unsystematic, based on subjective impressions of operators that things have improved (or become worse) since the innovation took place.

Research and Common Sense. Psychologists often hear their research findings evaluated by students and laymen with statements such as, "Well, that is interesting, but isn't that just common sense? Wouldn't anyone have predicted your results who had given it a little thought?" It is often true, of course, that research findings seem to agree rather well with what we would "sense" to be the true state of affairs. Surely, we would be rather surprised and perplexed if such were not usually the case. As a matter of fact, researchers are generally pleased when their experiments confirm, or are confirmed, by everyday observation. This gives a sort of "face validity" to their findings.

Nevertheless, it is frequently the case that there is no *common* sense, but that different people looking at the same situation will have different views about what is the "sensible" solution to a problem. In this case, the person with the problem has a dilemma: which "common sense" answer shall he accept? We would advise such a person to seek the views of the "best authority" on the subject, that is, to rely on "expert advice" or the "uncommon sensitivity" that comes with expertise in a field of knowledge. Even then, of course, experts of equal renown may disagree as to the "sensible" answer to this problem. One of the authors of this book has frequently included the following problem as a part of his first lecture in a course on engineering psychology.

One of the instruments included in airplanes for instrument flying is an attitude indicator. This instrument provides information about the tilt, or "roll," of an aircraft in relation to the horizon. In the original design, this instrument contained an "artificial horizon" bar, similar to the solid line through the center of the examples at the top of Figure 13–13. This line remained parallel to the earth's horizon, so that its movement simulated the way the pilot would actually see the horizon move in visual flying. Thus, with a left roll of the ship, the artificial horizon would move clockwise on the instrument. It was thought that this external-reference or "inside-out" display would give the pilot the impression of actually looking at the horizon and therefore be easier to use. At the bottom of Figure 13–13 is an internal-reference or "outside-in" display. Its artificial horizon is fixed on the instrument and therefore always parallel to the wings of the plane, but the line resembling an aircraft moves with the roll of the plane. In this design the pilot sees what someone standing on the ground would see: a rolling aircraft and a fixed horizon; hence the label "outside-in" display.

After a brief description similar to that above, the students are asked what their "common sense" tells them is the better way to display attitude information to the pilot. Voting for the two displays is usually about equally

FIGURE 13–13
Aircraft Displays

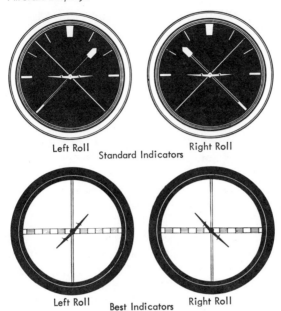

Left Roll   Standard Indicators   Right Roll

Left Roll   Best Indicators   Right Roll

Source: Chapanis, A., Garner, W. R., & Morgan, C. T. *Applied experimental psychology.* New York: Wiley, 1949.

Two kinds of artificial horizon showing a left roll and a right roll. The two top indicators have been standard on aircraft and are examples of inside-out displays. The lower indicators are outside-in displays.

divided. Obviously, common sense is not unanimous in this case and provides no basis for the choice between attitude indicators. Incidentally, the results of research studies on this problem have not always been in agreement, either. While two early studies (Browne, 1945; Loucks, 1947) indicated that novices made fewer errors with the "outside-in" display, subsequent research (Bauerschmidt and Roscoe, 1960) using experienced pilots favored the "inside-out" version.

SOME CONCLUDING COMMENTS

You have been bombarded with a good deal of information in this chapter. Now you know what it feels like to experience information overload. We have dealt with engineering issues as if they were related solely (or primarily) to problems encountered in skilled blue-collar work (such as the job of a tool-and-die maker) or in unique professions (such as pilot or air traffic controller). This is definitely *not* the case. When you read the section describing Miller's hypothesis concerning the "magic number 7 plus or minus 2," did you have the feeling that you had read something like that before? Well, you did! Remember the material describing the research on rating scales for performance appraisal? Most of the research dealing with the number of response categories provided for the rating (i.e., five-point vs. seven-point vs. nine-point scales) indicates that more than nine or less than four categories present problems for the rater. This may very well be another example of the 7 ± 2 hypothesis. The work of researchers described in the chapter on organizational theory also suggests that there may be some optimal number for span of control; as we suggested in that chapter, span of control may simply be a symptom of *span of attention*. Every job has many aspects that might be studied by the engineering psychologist; it does not matter if the job is that of company president or forklift truck driver. As long as individual workers are required to make responses to information received from the environment, then knowledge of human capabilities and limitations will be necessary for work design. Engineering psychology will provide that knowledge.

We have carefully examined the nature of the tasks that confront workers, the "equipment" (cognitive, sensory, and motor) that they bring to the task, and the devices that are provided to them (in the form of displays and controls) for successfully completing their tasks. In addition to these components, there is another major influence on worker behavior: the environment. The physical and psychological environment in which the worker carries out her duties can have the effect of exaggerating strengths and weaknesses, capabilities, and limitations. It is important to be aware of these influences. In the next chapter we will consider the effects of environmental influences on worker effectiveness, satisfaction, and safety.

SUMMARY

Engineering psychology grew out of the experimental and industrial engineering approaches to understanding the relationship of people to machines and to the physical work environment. It is concerned with the design of equipment with which people work, and the objective is more efficient man-machine systems. Because the emphasis is on systems performance rather than human performance per se, there is some doubt as to how much systems research tells us about the principles of human behavior or performance. This depends in part on the design of the research. Thus Helson's studies, which were conducted to answer some questions about the performance of manual control systems, yielded a number of generalizations about human behavior as well.

Work can be redefined in man-machine systems terms. Input components of the system can be studied both in terms of the input capacities of the worker and the input devices of the machine. The worker actively processes the input or information prior to making a response. One model of information processing suggests that environmental feedback is critical for efficient information processing. The output of the man-machine system can be considered both in terms of the skills and abilities that the worker uses to execute the appropriate response and the machine controls used to execute the response physically. These three components—input, mediation, and output—comprise the man-machine system in industry.

A simple model of human information processing describes four general stages: stimulus preprocessing, stimulus categorization, response selection, and response execution. At the first stage, performance is limited by sensory limitations, such as described by absolute and differential sensory thresholds, sensory adaptation processes, and adaptation and contrast effects wherein the same physical signal may be experienced quite differently under different background conditions. An important fact in overcoming some of these limitations is that our ability to make discriminations involving the comparison of two or more signals (comparative judgments) is much greater than our ability to identify signals on an absolute basis (absolute judgments). This fact alone could lead to the improvement of many man-machine systems: whenever possible, tasks allocated to human operators should require comparative, not absolute, judgments. However, when absolute judgments are required, performance will be improved if the different signals are coded along two or more dimensions rather than one.

The concept of display-control (or S-R) compatibility points up the fact that the optimal way to display information depends upon the control requirements, and vice versa. One must be concerned with display-control configurations, rather than with either alone. Compatible configurations often can be predicted on the basis of what the majority of people do naturally; that is, on population stereotypes, and on spatial correspondence between related stimulus and response elements.

One way to consider the output of the man-machine system is to examine the abilities that humans have at their disposal for completing tasks. This approach, exemplified by the work of Fleishman and his associates, has led to the identification of a taxonomy of 11 performance abilities and provided a basis for a taxonomy of tasks. This work also has indicated that, while task performance can be predicted to some degree from ability measures, skill in the performance of a task is often highly specific to that task and apparently dependent upon unique strategies "hit upon" by individual workers.

The systems concept and the view of the operator as a communications link in a system have strongly influenced the way researchers have looked at human engineering problems. Information measures, developed within communications theory, have been useful in describing and quantifying the communications link between the operator and the machine components of the system.

Automation, which might solve the problem of human error by removing the human operator from the system, seldom has this effect. Instead, the operator is removed to a more remote position with respect to system operations, receives information that is more abstract and symbolic (and, therefore, requires more complex transformations), and potentially makes much more serious and costly errors.

In seeking realism, human engineering researchers often develop elaborate and costly simulators. Without realistic simulation, it is often hazardous to generalize from laboratory to operating situations. Furthermore, realistic field experiments are often impractical, impossible, or dangerous to the operators and seldom amenable to adequate experimental control. The question of which aspects of the operating situation need to be simulated is a complex and difficult one.

REFERENCES

Alluisi, E. A., & Morgan, B. Engineering psychology and human performance. *Annual Review of Psychology*, 1976, *27*, 305–330.

Bauerschmidt, D. K., & Roscoe, S. N. A comparative evaluation of a pursuit moving airplane steering display. *IRE transactions on human factors in electronics*, 1960, vol. HFE-1, 62–66.

Boring, E. G., Langfeld, H. S., & Weld, H. P. (Eds.). *Foundations of psychology.* New York: Wiley, 1948.

Browne, R. C. *Comparative trial of two attitude indicators.* British Flying Personnel Res. Comm. Rept. #611, 1945.

Carter, R. Knobology underwater. *Human Factors*, 1978, *20*, 641–647.

Chapanis, A. Theory and methods for analyzing errors in man-machine systems. *Annual, New York Academy of Science*, 1951, *51*, 1179–1203.

Chapanis, A., Garner, W. R., & Morgan, C. T. *Applied experimental psychology: Human factors in engineering design.* New York: Wiley, 1949.

Chapanis, A., & Lindenbaum, L. E. A reaction time study of four control-display linkages. *Human Factors*, 1959, *1*, 1–7.

Fitts, P. M. Engineering psychology and equipment design. In S. S. Stevens (Ed.), *Handbook of experimental psychology.* New York: Wiley, 1951. Pp. 1287–1340.

Fitts, P. M., & Jones, R. E. *Psychological aspects of instrument display. I: Analysis of 270 "pilot-error" experiences in reading and interpreting aircraft instruments.* Aero Medical Laboratory, Air Materiel Command, Dayton, Ohio, Rept. No. TSEAA-694–12A, (1947a).

Fitts, P. M., & Jones, R. E. *Analysis of factors contributing to 460 "pilot-error" experiences in operating aircraft controls.* Engr. Division, Air Materiel Command, Dayton, Ohio, Rept. No. TSEAA-694–12, (1947b).

Fleishman, E. A. Human abilities and the acquisition of skill. In E. A. Bilodeau (Ed.), *Acquisition of skill.* New York: Academic Press, 1966.

Fleishman, E. A., & Parker, J. F. Factors in the retention and relearning of perceptual motor skill. *Journal of Experimental Psychology*, 1962, *64*, 215–226.

Fleishman, E. A., & Rich, S. Role of kinesthetic and spatial-visual abilities in perceptual motor learning. *Journal of Experimental Psychology*, 1963, *66*, 6–11.

Fleishman, E. A. Performance assessment based on an empirically derived task taxonomy. *Human Factors,* 1967, *9,* 349–366.

Forbes, T. W. Auditory signals for instrument flying. *Journal of Aeronautical Science,* 1946, *13,* 255–258.

Freides, D. Human information processing and sensory modality. *Psychological Bulletin,* 1974, *81,* 284–310.

Gilbreth, F. B. *Applied motion study.* New York: Macmillan, 1919.

Grether, W. F. Engineering psychology in the United States. *American Psychologist,* 1968, *23,* 743–751.

Helson, H. Design of equipment and optimal human operation. *American Journal of Psychology,* 1949, *62,* 473–497.

Helson, H. *Adaptation-level theory: An experimental and systematic approach to behavior.* New York: Harper, 1964.

Jenkins, W. C. The tactual discrimination of shapes of coding aircraft-type controls. In P. M. Fitts (Ed.), *Psychological research on equipment design.* Washington, D.C.: U.S. Government Printing Office, 1947.

Loucks, R. B. An experimental evaluation of the interpretability of various types of aircraft attitude indicators. In P. M. Fitts (Ed.), *Psychological research on equipment design,* Washington, D.C.: U.S. Government Printing Office, 1947. Pp. 111–135.

McCormick, E. J. *Human factors engineering.* New York: McGraw-Hill, 1970, 3rd edition.

Miller, G. A. The magical number seven, plus or minus two: Some limits on our capacity for processing information. *Psychological Review,* 1956, *63,* 81–97.

Pollack, I., & Ficks, L. Information of elementary multi-dimensional auditory displays. *Journal of the Acoustical Society of America,* 1954, *26,* 155–158.

Seashore, R. H. Work and motor performance. In S. S. Stevens (Ed.), *Handbook of experimental psychology.* New York: Wiley, 1951.

Simon, J. R., Mewaldt, S. P., Acosta, E., & Hu, J. Processing auditory information. *Journal of Applied Psychology,* 1976, *61,* 354–358.

Smith, E. E. Choice reaction time: An analysis of the major theoretical positions. *Psychological Bulletin,* 1968, *69,* 77–110.

Taylor, F. V. Psychology and the design of machines. *American Psychologist,* 1957, *21,* 120–125.

Taylor, F. W. *The principles of scientific management.* New York: Harper, 1911.

CHAPTER 14
The Work Environment

Typically, people work in a social environment and they work with machines. As we have seen in previous chapters, there are many questions regarding the effects of the social environment and the machine, or "systems environment," on a person's efficiency and well-being that have intrigued psychologists and other scientists. It seems fair to say that the evidence reviewed earlier leaves little doubt as to the importance of both the social context and the machines as factors determining the satisfactoriness of performance and the satisfaction the worker experiences in connection with the job. Many questions remain unanswered, and science is far from ready to specify the details either of ideal social systems or of ideal machine systems. Nevertheless, some progress has been made in formulating more appropriate questions and in designing research and theory that is more likely to provide the answers.

It remains for us to consider what is perhaps the most obvious aspect of the work environment, the conditions under which one works. As indicated earlier, some of the first research in industry was concerned with the physical conditions of work. Thus, for example, the Hawthorne studies began with the question of the effects of illumination on worker productivity. After considerable time and effort, these studies came to naught, at least with respect to establishing the function relating productivity to illumination. These experiences of the Hawthorne researchers should provide fair warning that investigations of the effects of the physical environment are not as simple as they might seem. It should be clear that establishing the relationship between illumination and job performance is far more complex than, say, establishing the relationship of illumination to the growth rate of house plants. No consistent relationships emerged from the Hawthorne studies of illumination: instead, it became apparent that an employee's job performance might well be more affected by her attitudes toward the illumination, the investigators, her supervisors, or her work, than by the physical conditions themselves. To control such factors so as to determine the "true" effects of environmental variables presents a real challenge to researchers.

People are highly adaptable creatures and can work under a fairly wide range of physical conditions if other conditions in their "psychological environment" motivate them to do so. For example, two girls in a minor experiment in the Hawthorne studies worked under a moonlight level of illumination without loss of production and without reporting excessive eyestrain.

This is not to deny the importance of physical environment factors, however. The fact that people *can* adapt to a wide range of conditions does not mean that they always *will* adapt or that they do not pay a price, either physiologically or psychologically, for their adaptation. From both the pragmatic and the humanistic points of view, science has an obligation to identify those conditions that minimize the need for excessive adaptation and the attending costs of such adaptation in manpower resources and human well-being. In connection with the latter point, it may be recalled that in Herzberg's theory of work motivation (see Chapter 10) the *context* of the job, including the physical work conditions, is seen as the primary determinant of negative job attitudes or job dissatisfaction. Furthermore, there is sufficient evidence for adverse physiological effects of extreme environmental conditions to warrant their systematic study either from the standpoint of productive efficiency or of human values.

In the last chapter we presented two models. One was a comprehensive view of man-machine interactions. We examined the input and output capacities of both man and machine. The second model was a much more specific one: it dealt with the way man processes information. As studies of the relationship between work and workers have accumulated, it has become more apparent that the environment in which the work is done can have a major impact on the behavior of the worker. Man-machine systems are like any other kind of system: they break down under great stress. The problem for the psychologist is the identification and understanding of mechanisms in the work environment that place stress on the man-machine system. Furthermore, it is important to understand how these stressors interact. Do they accumulate over time? What are their long-term and short-term effects? Are some stressors "good" for the individual? These are some of the questions we will consider in this chapter.

Our goal should be to determine how different stressors affect specific psychological functions or behavioral mechanisms, such as those involved in sensing, classifying, storing, and retrieving information and in selecting and executing responses. Only when we can describe stressor effects at this level will it be possible to *predict* how performance on certain tasks will be affected by a particular stressor. Different stressors affect performance on different tasks in different, and sometimes contrasting, ways. Furthermore, some stressors may affect one task or one measure of performance but not another. That is, while one stressor may reduce performance rate but not affect error rate, another may increase errors without affecting the rate of performance. Unless some attempt is made to understand such complex and seemingly contradictory results in terms of underlying functions or mechanisms, it is difficult to see how we can arrive at those broader generalizations from which predictions can be made.

DIMENSIONS OF THE PHYSICAL ENVIRONMENT

There are, of course, a large number of dimensions of the physical environment, and it will be impossible to discuss all of them in a single chapter. As humans explore new environments, they face new environmental problems. Aviation and space travel have brought them into contact not only with zero gravity but also with high levels of gravitational forces experienced in rapid acceleration or deceleration of the body, changes in the oxygen level of the air breathed, radiation, changes in air pressure, ionization of the air, and the like. In the past 20 years, science has become increasingly concerned with the effects of extreme, unusual, even "hostile" environmental factors.

We will deal largely with the more commonplace dimensions of our environment, such as heat and noise, because they are relevant to a much larger portion of the world of work. Other aspects of the environment will be mentioned only in so far as they help us to understand the ways in which human behavior is affected by the work environment.

While heat and noise (or their absence) are obvious characteristics of the typical workplace, there are also some less obvious factors that might influence behavior. One of these factors is the work schedule: the particular arrangement of working hours that faces the worker. This would include such diverse considerations as the length of the work day, the work shift, and flexible starting and stopping times. There is a distinct possibility that extreme work schedules may have the same influence on workers as extreme levels of noise or heat. We will consider this possibility.

PHYSIOLOGY AND THE ENVIRONMENT

It should be apparent that physical aspects of the environment act upon the physical organism. Furthermore, the process is one of interaction, since the nature and the amount of environmental effects depend upon the physical state of the organism. These states of the organism are a function of its immediate past history, which determines such processes as light or sound adaptation or temperature regulation of the body. They are also a function of much more gradual processes whereby the organism becomes adjusted to, or acclimated to, its environment. The effects of the physical environment on human behavior cannot be understood except in relation to and in interaction with these physiological conditions and the adaptive processes of the organism.

For this reason, the study of the physical conditions of the work environment goes hand in hand with the study of physiological conditions (and factors affecting such conditions) of the worker. Such a factor, for example, as loss of sleep, while not a condition of the work environment, may be equally important for performance and may determine how the worker is affected by the physical conditions. Loss of a night's sleep may well determine whether one's performance is affected by excessive heat or noise in the workplace. By the same token, alcohol or tranquilizers are not part of the work environment, but their use may affect the worker's tolerance for the physical work conditions. In other words, either excessive heat or loss of sleep might result in a state of physical exhaustion, and it should be clear that a combination of the two would have accumulative effects on behavior. Finally, physiological measures are important because they provide evidence for adaptation, or the lack of it, to environmental conditions, allowing us to assess the degree of stress and the physiological "costs" exacted by the physical conditions or by the adaptation process. In some instances, one can compensate for adverse environmental conditions so that performance is unaffected, and it is only through physiological measures that the cost of increased effort can be measured.

An example of the way in which environmental conditions interact with physical states of the organism to affect performance comes from a study of noise and loss of sleep (R. T. Wilkinson, 1963). In this study, subjects who had gone without sleep during the previous night were compared with subjects who had enjoyed a normal night's sleep. They performed for 30 minutes on a serial reaction task under conditions of quiet and continuous noise. This task requires the subject to press buttons corresponding to each of five lights that come on in rapid succession. Measures of the rate of responding showed no effects of the sleep loss. However, the effects on the number of errors were quite dramatic, as shown in Figure 14–1.

Subjects who had slept made fewer errors overall than subjects who had not slept, especially after the first ten minutes of work on the task, as seen by comparing the solid and the broken lines in Figure 14–1. However, the effects of the noise were completely dependent on whether or not the subjects had slept. With a normal night's sleep, far more errors were made in noise than in the quiet condition, but when there had been a loss of sleep, the noise condition was associated with fewer errors than the quiet condition. One can imagine three different experiments on noise in which the physiological states resulting from sleep loss are ignored. In one, with well-rested subjects, Experimenter One concludes that noise interferes with performance. In the second, where the subjects have worked all night, Experimenter Two concludes that noise actually benefits perfor-

FIGURE 14–1

The Effect of Combinations of Sleep (S) and Sleep Deprivation (SD) with Noise (N) and Quiet (Q) upon Proportional Errors (errors as a percentage of all responses)

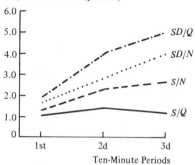

Proportional Errors (percent)

Source: Wilkinson, R. T. Interaction of noise with knowledge of results and sleep deprivation. *Journal of Experimental Psychology*, 1963, *66*, 332–337.

mance. In the third, where half the subjects are rested while the other half come to the experiment from the night shift, Experimenter Three concludes that noise has no effect on performance at all.

STRESSES FROM THE ENVIRONMENT

One way to look at the physical environment factors is to view them as a class of potential "stressors" of the human operator. In this way they may be included with a larger set of conditions that "push" the performance and/or endurance limits under which one can operate. This larger set of stressors includes *task-induced* stresses, those conditions of speed or load demands of the task, or job, itself that test the limits of one's ability to perform. Some of these conditions were presented in Chapter 13 when we considered human performance limitations. Situational and psychological factors resulting from job insecurity, excessive competition, hazardous working conditions, long or unusual working hours, and the like, represent another class of stressors on the worker. Finally, the organism may be stressed by loss of sleep, disease, alcohol, drugs, or other factors that affect the physiological equilibrium of the body.

All stressors pose some degree of threat—physical or psychological—to the operator. In this sense, stressors are somewhat analogous to the stress tests that engineers apply to metals, alloys, structures, or systems to determine the limits of strength, flexibility, or other properties of inanimate objects. While tasks are not created deliberately to test a person to the "breaking point," it is of considerable importance to know the limits within which one can adapt and perform efficiently. Equally important, we need to know the price paid for adaptation to suboptimal conditions, even though the stressors may not appreciably interfere with efficient performance.

In the case of physical environmental stresses, the operator has a certain range of adaptability and tolerance within which he can operate without mobilizing the emergency systems of the organism and with no appreciable effect on his performance. For example, our bodies are continuously making minor adjustments to temperature change through the thermal regulating systems, our eyes accommodate to the distance of the field of view, and our ears adjust to the prevailing noise level. Thus, the question is not whether one can adapt, for one does so continually, but rather the limits and the costs one pays for adaptation to conditions that represent stresses on these adaptive mechanisms. Of course, it is also of interest to know something about the ideal or optimal levels of environmental stimulation for physical and psychological well-being (as well as for performance).

EFFECTS OF SINGLE ENVIRONMENTAL STRESSORS

We can introduce the topic of stressors by looking at research that has been done on the effects of noise on the performance of certain tasks. A low level of noise has been found to increase the percentage of signals detected in vigilance tasks, but more intense noise has a detrimental effect, decreasing signal detections. Therefore, in a task with a low and unpredictable signal rate, noise can be either beneficial or detrimental, depending on its intensity. On the other hand, noise appears to have no effect on the rate of responding in a serial reaction task, where the signal rate is higher than in vigilance tasks, but noise does increase errors in this task. As another example, loss of a night's sleep results in an increase in the number of slow reactions on the serial reaction task, while heat increases errors on the same task.

These effects will be considered in more detail in the following sections. For the time being, they are presented to show that the simple, or "main," effects of environmental stressors are not simple at all. Rather, they depend on the performance task, and even on the measure of task performance that one observes. In other words, there are important *interaction effects* between stressors and tasks and between stressors and measures of performance, as well as between stressors and states of the organism. To complicate the picture further, we will find that the stressors themselves interact, producing accumulative effects in some cases and compensatory, or canceling, effects in other cases. In spite of these problems, we will turn now to a consideration of the single effects of some environmental stressors.

Sound and Noise

At one time or another, most of us have been bothered by noise. Perhaps it was the sound of children playing while we were trying to concentrate on material for a test, or it might have been the sound of traffic outside our window while we were trying to sleep, or maybe even the enraging sound of a dripping spigot in an otherwise quiet environment. The effects that these sounds have on our behavior will depend, at least to some degree, on the nature of the behavior in question. In spite of the traffic noises, we often manage to get back to sleep. On the other hand, disruptive environmental conditions, such as children playing, can have substantial effects on learning and memory; consequently, we might justifiably blame poor test performance on a noisy brother or sister.

These examples are pale reflections of the forces that confront many industrial workers. When an individual first encounters the "environment" of a typical production site of a manufacturing company, the first thing he notices is the noise! Students on field trips to companies often comment that they "couldn't hear themselves think" when they were on the production floor. If those same students had remained on the production floor for several days, they would have marveled at the fact that the noise no longer seemed so aversive. In the material that follows, we will consider the role of noise in industrial performance, adaptation to noise, individual differences in reaction to noise, and the interpretation of noise as a source of physical and psychological stress.

The scientist has no problem defining sound. We can measure its intensity in decibels and its frequency in cycles per second, and, thanks to psychophysical research, we can specify the psychological properties of loudness and pitch. Unfortunately, even though *noise* must be related to *sound,* it is much more difficult to define. Noise is often thought to be an unwanted or an annoying sound, but this means that *noise* must be more *subjective* than *sound.* Parents and children seldom agree about the "annoyance index" of popular music (this difficulty is compounded by the fact that adolescents seem to pass through a period in which intensities of sound less than 100 decibels cannot be perceived).

We will attempt to clarify these problems by using the term *sound* to refer to physical (and/or psychophysical) properties of any auditory stimulus and to define *noise* as irrelevant sounds, that is, any sounds that are unimportant to the task at hand. Using such an approach, any sound may be defined unequivocally as noise in a given situation, independent of its effect on physiological, subjective, or behavioral measures. Most of our interest in this section will be with the effects of noise on people working at some task, either in the real world or in the laboratory.

Noise and Performance.   Unfortunately, there is no simple relationship between noise and task performance. Common sense might suggest that noise always has detrimental effects on performance, but this is not the case. Sometimes it has no effect, and sometimes it even *improves* performance. As an example, think of what you do when you are driving alone on a large empty highway and beginning to get sleepy: you turn on the radio—LOUD! This has the effect of improving your performance in spite of the fact that the sounds from the radio would be viewed as unrelated to the task of getting your car from one point to another. The only way to make sense out of the seemingly contradictory evidence on the noise/performance relationship is to consider specific characteristics of both the noise and the task in question.

Dimensions of Noise. Noises may differ in intensity, frequency, and complexity. Noise sources may produce either continuous or intermittent noise. Each of these dimensions is an important determinant of the effects of noise on performance. For example, when the sound is irrelevant to the task (i.e., "noise"), high frequencies tend to be associated with more errors in performance than low frequencies. On the other hand, when the sound is relevant, as in a task requiring quick reactions to tones, high-frequency tones produce faster reactions than low-frequency tones (Broadbent, 1957). Thus, we can see that in the case of irrelevant sounds, high-frequency tones are distracting; but when the tone is relevant to the task at hand, high-frequency tones actually do a better job of capturing our attention. Similarly, loud noises seem to have adverse effects on performance, while less intense noises often have no effect or even benefit performance. Finally, intermittent or on-off noises generally interfere with performance more than continuous noises. Thus we can see that testing the hypothesis that "noise affects performance" is simple-minded; one must specify which dimension of noise is being considered. This has been one of the primary reasons for contradictory finding in the past—poor descriptions of the dimensions of noise being considered.

Noise and Communication. There is little question that noise may interfere with job performance when the job requires conversation between workers. Noise not only makes communication difficult, resulting in errors; it may also increase the total energy costs of the job. If one has to shout all day long above the roar of an engine, her fatigue level at the end of the day may be as much due to the noise as to the work itself. A good deal of work has been done on determining the conditions under which noise will inhibit communication (this research is reviewed in McCormick [1957] and Poulton [1970]). As a general principle, noise at a particular frequency tends to interfere with speech sounds at the same frequency. This phenomenon is known as "masking." Higher-frequency speech sounds are particularly vulnerable to masking.

Noise and Low-Input Tasks. Often workers are required to look for infrequent, temporally uncertain signals of near-threshold intensity; in addition, they may be required to look for these signals over long periods of time. A perfect example of this type of task would be that of the radar operator responsible for alerting national defense units to the possibility of an enemy attack. This type of task is known as a *vigilance task* and is common in quality-control operations, guarding duties, and even general maintenance operations. You might guess that noise might have particularly damaging effects on this type of task. Research by Broadbent (1954) and by Jerison (1957) indicates that noise may interfere with, improve, or have no effect on vigilance performance, depending on its intensity, continuity, and the length of time the worker is continuously on the job. High-intensity noise (about 95 decibels or higher) does not appear to interfere with the detection of signals in a vigilance task until after an hour or an hour and a half of continuous watch-keeping. Meanwhile, low-intensity noise seems to improve performance, again after considerable time at the task, especially if the noise is intermittent.

Noise and High-Input Tasks. High-input tasks are characterized by frequent signals. While noise does not seem to have a dramatic effect on rate of performance, it does seem to increase errors; furthermore, these errors seem to occur much more quickly than was the case in vigilance or low-input tasks, sometimes occurring as soon as 20 minutes after beginning the task (Wilkinson, 1963). The problem seems to be one of overload. The individual may have to process more information than is reasonable. As we indicated earlier, noise (particularly high-frequency noise) *demands* our attention. Thus, when it is necessary to share our attention between the task at hand and environmental noise, problems arise. A recent study of driver performance (Finkelman, Zeitlin, Filippi, and Friend, 1977) showed that when the driver was required to concentrate on two tasks simultaneously (driving and arithmetic calculations), noise had a negative effect on performance. This suggests that the environment is placing an inappropriate load on the individual. In heavy traffic it is common for drivers to reduce the volume of a car radio or even turn it off completely.

Even though the accumulation of evidence on noise effects is confusing, there are some things we can say. For example, intense noise (95 decibels or higher) does seem to have negative effects on performance, particularly when the noise is intermittent. In contrast, low-intensity noise (less than 95 decibels) has little or no effect on performance.

Changes in Noise Level. Teichner, Arees, and Reilly (1963) suggested that the complex effects of noise on performance might be better understood in the context of *changing* levels of noise rather than *constant* levels. They felt that the evidence on the effects of intermittent versus continuous noise strongly suggested that noise *change* was a source of distraction rather than any absolute characteristic of the noise. In a series of experiments, Teichner and his associates were able to show that more errors were made by groups that experienced a change in noise level (e.g., 81 to 69 decibels or 81 to 93 decibels) than in groups that had a constant noise level. Furthermore, they were able to demonstrate that the loss of proficiency on the task was proportional to the *amount* of change in the noise level, regardless of whether the level was increased or decreased. These results could not be explained by any simple reference to frequency or intensity of noise, such as implied in the earlier sections on noise research. Consequently, Teichner proposed that the results of noise can be understood by considering psychological factors and physiological factors simultaneously. He suggested that physiologically the individual experiences auditory adaptation and arousal; psychologically, the individual experiences distraction and eventually habituation when a new noise level is introduced. Teichner was able to predict under what conditions performance would be adversely affected by changes in noise levels. These studies introduce the concepts of *arousal* and *adaptation*. These processes will be important in understanding the effects of environmental variables on human performance, and we will return to them in a later section.

Noise and Satisfaction. There is one final issue that should be considered with respect to noise. Independent of the effects of noise on performance, people *complain* about noise at the workplace. To some degree, this might be thought of as an indication of dissatisfaction with working conditions. While there has been little research directly addressing the issue of emotional reactions to noise in the work setting, studies in nonwork environments may provide some useful data. Two recent studies suggest that some people may be more vulnerable to noise than others, at least with respect to its annoyance value. Fiedler & Fiedler (1975) considered the noise complaints of residents in an area immediately adjacent to a large airport.[1] Interestingly enough, they found that the complaints of individuals in this high-noise area were roughly the same as complaints from individuals in control low-noise areas. In interviews with residents of the high-noise zone, the residents often said that they adopted a strategy of "not letting the noise bother them." Fiedler and Fiedler concluded that the source, the type, or the intensity of noise might have less to do with its annoyance potential than the individual's "vulnerability" to noise. This suggests that noise vulnerability may be a trait, or at the very least that there are interactions between individual characteristics and situational characteristics and that it is the *interaction* which is responsible for annoyance.

Weinstein (1978) considered the issue of individual differences in sensitivity to noise more directly. As many of you know, college dormitories are noisy places. On the basis of a questionnaire administered to college students prior to their arrival on campus as first-year students, Weinstein was able to distinguish between those students who were bothered by noise and those who were not. He called these groups "sensitive" and "insensitive" subjects, respectively. After the students arrived on campus, Weinstein monitored both their academic progress and their satisfaction/dissatisfaction with dormitory living. The "sensitive" group was significantly more unhappy with the noise level in the dormitories than the "insensitive" students. This dissatisfaction increased over the course of the year. In addition, the academic work of the "sensitive" students seemed to suffer as a result of the noise.

These findings add another dimension to noise research: individual differences. They suggest several things:

1. All individuals are not equally annoyed by the same amount and/or type of noise.
2. It may be possible to use cognitive strategies to reduce the annoyance caused by noise.

---

[1] If puns were criminal offenses, Fiedler and Fiedler would have been given a stiff sentence. The title of their article was "Port Noise Complaints."

3. Rather than adapting, some individuals may in fact become *more* aware of noise.

Historically, the human-engineering approach has tended to deal with the human as constant and the environment as variable. Data such as those presented suggest that it may be critical to examine individual differences when considering the effect of environmental variables on behavior or emotion.

Heat and Cold

As was the case with noise, the effects of heat and cold on performance are not simple. It is clear that extremes of temperature can have dramatic effects on performance. One would not expect a brain surgeon to work well with fingers numbed by cold. But the indirect effects of heat and cold are much greater threats to the efficiency of the typical worker. Consequently, we will consider the role of these indirect effects as environmental stressors.

Like noise, temperature would seem to have simple and obvious characteristics. One need only specify the scale units (i.e., Fahrenheit or centigrade) to talk about high and low temperatures. Unfortunately, the human does not react quite so simply. As you are well aware, a temperature of 100° F on a dry desert may not be as uncomfortable as 85° F in a jungle; our impressions are further modified by the rate of air movement. This has led to the use of the concept of *effective temperature* in place of *objective temperature*. The effective temperature scale combines temperature, humidity, and air movement in computing the comfort index of a particular environment. Some research suggests that humidity may be more important than either of the other two variables in determining relative comfort and efficiency (Pepler, 1958). Unfortunately, most of the research in the use of effective temperature has involved subjects not engaged in actual work, but merely moving back from one room to another, reporting relative comfort. To use the effective temperature concept in industrial settings, it will be necessary to calculate these values in the actual industrial environment. In addition, as we will see shortly, the critical issue may be the combination of temperature extremes and other stressors, rather than temperature by itself.

Complex Effects of Heat. Another approach to studying the effect of heat on performance might be to control body temperature rather than air temperature, humidity, and air flow. In the first experiment to control body temperature systematically, Wilkinson and his associates (Wilkinson, Fox, Goldsmith, Hampton, & Lewis, 1964) demonstrated that different levels of raised body temperature affect performance on two tasks in different and even opposite ways. In their experiment, the subjects were placed in a hot room until their body temperature reached one of three levels—

99.1° F, 100.2° F, or 101.3° F. The desired temperature was then maintained throughout the test session by means of a special heat suit. Testing consisted of measuring performance on a vigilance task (detecting occasional weak tones) and an arithmetic task (performing simple calculations). The results were most interesting: the time taken to respond to the vigilance task signals increased at 99.1°, but then decreased below the level of the control condition at the two higher temperatures, suggesting that a small increase in body temperature interfered with performance, but that larger increases actually improved it. Meanwhile, the ability to detect the signals improved with each increase in the level of body temperature. In contrast, performance on the arithmetic task first improved, then deteriorated with increased body temperature. These complicated results indicate that raised body temperature may either impair or enhance performance, depending on the level to which the temperature is raised and the nature of the task being performed.

Further evidence that heat can improve performance under special circumstances comes from a study by Poulton and Kerslake (1965) in which operators were moved from a room with a normal temperature to a hot room (Effective Temperature = 86° F) while performing two tasks simultaneously. One task was to monitor series of ten letters and to call out any letter that he heard repeated within the series. At the same time, the operator was to monitor five dials and to press a button whenever a signal occurred on one of the dials. The results indicated that a sudden increase in temperature may stimulate a higher level of performance: scores on both tasks showed improvement when the operator was first wheeled into the hot room. This stimulating effect is short lived, however, and may be counteracted as body temperature increases.

Cold. Much of the research on the effects of low temperatures on performance has been of the more obvious type where numbness of fingers or skin temperature of the hands has been related to proficiency on tasks involving manual operations. The purpose of such research is not so much to demonstrate such effects as it is to assess their magnitude, that is, to describe in a quantitative way the losses in performance that can be expected by the direct effects of cold. Research results suggest that manual performance is adversely affected by lowered body temperature, even when hands are kept warm (Lockhart, 1966). This suggests that, in addition to the direct effect of cold on finger and hand dexterity, there is also an indirect effect of lowered body temperature acting as a stressor or detractor. Similar effects have been found for vigilance tasks (Poulton, Hitchings, & Brooke, 1965). Both accuracy and speed of detection of signals dropped as a result of lowered body temperature. Finally, there is some evidence that people may adapt to cold conditions over time (Teichner & Kobrick, 1955), although this is more likely due to increased motivation in stressful conditions or changes in strategies for completing the task than to physiological adaptation.

Stressors and Information Processing

In 1958 Bursill reported the results of three experiments in which he used heat as an environmental stressor. Subjects engaged in two tasks simultaneously: a tracking task (in which the subject was required to follow a moving object) and a visual detection task (in which the subject was required to detect light signals occurring at 20°, 50°, and 80° of visual angle from either side of the tracking display). The most interesting result of these studies was that subjects missed higher proportions of signals at the wider visual angles under heat than under normal temperature conditions. These results suggested that a specific effect of heat stress was to reduce the field of visual attention, either as a direct effect on the visual mechanism or as a more central effect of narrowing or "funneling" of attention. When Bursill made the task easier, subjects no longer made a larger number of errors on wide-angle signals. He took this as evidence that attention, rather than a visual mechanism, was affected by heat stress.

Bursill's experiment was repeated by Hockey (1970a), but with noise rather than heat as a stressor. Similar results were found: noise was related to greater errors at wide visual angles. In a second experiment, Hockey was able to demonstrate *how* attention was affected by stress (1970b). Bursill's results implied that subjects tended to pay attention to those things closest to them (or immediately in front of them). Hockey systematically changed the probability that the lights at various angles would come on and was able to demonstrate that subjects paid more attention to those lights that were more likely to come on, regardless of the central or peripheral position of those lights. It was almost as if the individual "oriented" herself or positioned herself in preparation for responding.

The results of these studies indicate that stressors tend to limit the capacity of subjects to attend to task relevant information—perhaps because the stressor "uses up" some attention capacity. As a result of these data, we might draw the following conclusion about the way in which stress affects information processing:

Under stress, an operator's attention will be directed toward the more probable sources of information and she will be more likely to miss information from less probable sources.

Aftereffects of Stressors

We have seen that some stressors such as heat and noise appear to have significant effects on the performance of certain tasks, the nature of these effects depending on the tasks, the stressors, and possibly individual differences in workers. In other cases, experiments have failed to find any influence of the stressor on the behavioral measures they have recorded. One possible reason for lack of noticeable effect may be that individuals devote more effort to tasks that are performed under stress—i.e., to maintain a given level of efficiency under difficult conditions, they try harder. This possibility has led researchers to look for possible aftereffects of environmental stress. If the worker does maintain performance levels through extra effort, the effects of this increased effort may accumulate over time and appear at some time after the actual presentation of the stressor (minutes later, hours later, or even weeks later). As we will see in a later section, there is good reason to believe that shift work (particularly the night shift) has such cumulative aftereffects.

Glass and Singer (1972) have provided some evidence regarding the aftereffects of noise. They began with the assumption that "while man is adaptable, he pays a price for adaptation," a price more obvious after the stress is over than during the stressful condition.[2] Subjects were exposed to either loud or soft noise. Furthermore, noise was presented either predictably (on/off at regular intervals) or unpredictably (on/off at random intervals). Response measures taken during the experimental conditions indicated that there was a generalized stress response to noise, which decreased with repeated stimulation. This was equally true for predictable and unpredictable noise.

However, Glass and Singer were more interested in the aftereffects of noise than the immediate effects. Consequently, they administered two types of tests to subjects after the experimental sessions. These consisted of a set of insoluble puzzles and a proofreading task. The number of attempts to solve the puzzles was taken as a measure of the subject's tolerance for frustration, while the number of proofreading errors found by the subject was interpreted as a measure of her ability to cope with a task requiring care and attention.

Their results showed that:

1. Subjects who had been exposed to noise made fewer attempts to solve puzzles and missed more proofreading errors than subjects who had previously worked in quiet.
2. Unpredictable noise had a much more negative effect than predictable noise.

As an explanation of why the unpredictable noise condition had a more serious effect than predictable noise, the authors proposed that unpredictability created a feeling of lack of control over the environment, which raised the anxiety of the subjects. As a test of this hypothesis, Glass and Singer simply repeated the experiment but added a "noise control switch" for the subjects. Half of the subjects were told that if the noise became intolerable, they could turn it off by throwing the switch. The other half were told nothing about the switch. All subjects were exposed to the unpredictable noise condition and given the same task and postnoise tests. The results showed that access to the noise switch did not help performance

---

[2] A similar situation was suggested with respect to job satisfaction by Landy's Opponent Process Theory. The same basic mechanism would apply here: while the stimulus is present, the person experiences one state, but when the stimulus disappears, another state takes its place.

during the noise conditions, but the effect of the switch on postnoise tests was dramatic. Subjects who had access to the switch made many more attempts at the puzzles and missed fewer proofreading errors than the subjects who were told nothing about the switch. The results supported the experimenters' predictions, and they concluded:

> . . . that unpredictable noise produced adverse after-effects because it is more aversive than predictable noise, its greater aversiveness being a function of the same helplessness induced in an individual who is able to control and/or predict its onset or offset. (p. 462)

The results of the work by Glass and Singer suggest that it may not be appropriate to examine the effects of stressors only during the stress situation. In spite of the fact that adaptation seems to occur, the fact is that the negative effects are simply being postponed rather than being eliminated. The degree to which these stresses accumulate over time and the effects of these accumulations on worker behavior both in and outside of the work settings is unknown. But there is good reason to believe that the effects of stressors must be examined over long periods of time if we are to understand their impact fully.

THE INTERACTIONS OF TWO OR MORE STRESSORS

Thus far we have attempted to look at the effects of single stressors as they influence the performance of human operators. In doing so, we have often found it difficult to avoid complicating the story with references to the ways in which environmental stressors interact with other stressors of various kinds. No doubt it has become apparent already that to speak of the effects of stress on performance one must specify the conditions under which the stress is experienced. As Wilkinson (1969) has pointed out, stress effects are dependent on (1) the duration of work on the task, (2) the familiarity of the operator with the stress and with the work he has to do under stress, (3) the level of incentive of the operator, (4) the kind of work he has to do, (5) the aspect of performance (i.e., speed or accuracy) that is most important, and (6) the presence of other stresses in the working situation, as well as the nature and level of the stressor itself.

We have seen some evidence that the stress, the task, time on the task, acclimatization to the stress, familiarity with the task, and the measures of task performance all interact with one another to determine the nature and the magnitude of stress effects. The present section is devoted largely to examining how stressors may interact with one another or with the incentive conditions of the task.

A Model of Multiple-Stressor Effects

Before looking at such interactions, however, it may be well to have a conceptual model of what we might expect to find. Such a model has been suggested by Broadbent (1971) in an attempt to determine whether two or more stressors were acting independently on performance. To illustrate how the model works, let us assume that when two different stressors are applied singly in a given task situation, each results in a 10 percent decrement in performance. Now the question is: What would be the expected result if the effects of the two stressors acting together are *strictly additive?* At first glance, one may conclude that the answer is 20 percent, arrived at simply by adding the two percentages obtained for each stressor acting alone. That is, if the two stressors were combined and the net effect was a 20 percent decrement in performance, it would be tempting to conclude that the effects of one stressor were simply added to the other.

Suppose, on the other hand, that one reasons, as Broadbent did, that human performance in the normal unstressed condition leaves a small reserve, or a *margin of safety*, whereby one can compensate for or "absorb" a moderate degree of stress before the performance is affected. From this view, the initial effect of a stressor is to overcome or "use up" this margin of safety, and this effect is not apparent in the performance measures. Now, assume for the moment that this safety margin is equal to five percent of the operator's normal performance level; that is, the operator works at 95 percent of his "true" capacity. This notion is illustrated in Figure 14–2 by the region labeled "the safety margin." It will then be seen that the effect of each stressor alone should be described as the sum of the 10 percent decrement in performance *plus* the 5 percent used up in overcoming the margin of safety. As indicated in the figure, when either stressor is presented alone, part of its effect is absorbed, but when the two stressors are combined, it is reasonable to assume that one of the two overcomes the safety margin, so that the total effect of the second would be seen in reduced performance. Therefore, in our example, simple additive effects of the two stressors would be to reduce performance by 25 percent, rather that the 20 percent suggested by adding the independent values, even though this appears to be a case of "superadditivity."

The first question to be raised about the model in Figure 14–2 is whether there is any evidence that such apparently superadditive effects occur when two or more stressors are combined. The answer to this question is a rather convincing "yes," as shown in Figure 14–3.

This figure summarizes the results of a study by Colquhoun (1962) in which alcohol and two drugs, meclozine and hyoscine, were administered separately and in combination. Performance was evaluated on a vigilance task. As shown in the figure, neither alcohol nor meclozine had much effect on the percentage of signals detected as compared with the control ("placebo") condition. However, when alcohol was given the day after the subjects had taken meclozine ("alcohol plus meclozine residue"), the effect was at least as great as the original effect of the meclozine plus the effect of alcohol alone. When alcohol and either of the drugs were administered on the same day, the results were much more convincing, as shown on the right in Figure 14–3. The combined effects of alcohol

FIGURE 14-2

A Model to Illustrate the "Superadditive" Effects of Stressors

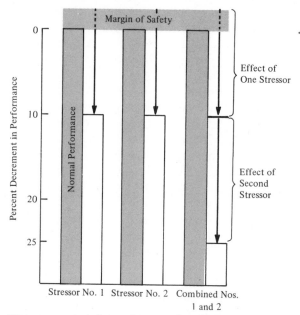

When presented alone, stressors 1 and 2 first overcome the "margin of safety," then decrease performance by 10 percent. When presented together, however, one stressor uses up the margin of safety allowing the second stressor to have full effect on performance.

and meclozine are more than twice as great as one would expect by adding their separate effects, and this outcome is repeated, somewhat less dramatically, for alcohol and hyoscine.

But, the reader may ask, why all this concern for the question of the additivity of the combined effects of different stressors? First, Colquhoun's results with drugs suggest that stressors may have much greater effects in combination than would be expected from their simple effects. In other words, a hot, noisy work environment may degrade performance to a greater extent than one would predict from the results of studies of noise or heat tested separately. This in itself argues for the need to study stressors in combination. It also argues for the model that includes the concept of a safety margin in performance. Furthermore, there is a theoretical significance to Colquhoun's findings that ultimately has some important implications for our understanding of the process by which stressors affect behavior.

To illustrate the last point, let us consider a case in which the combined effects of two stressors are strictly additive and another case in which the combined effects of two other stressors are superadditive, as in Colquhoun's

FIGURE 14–3

Performance under Single and Combined Stressors (Alcohol, Meclozine, and Hyoscine), Showing the Superadditive Effects of Pairs of Stressors

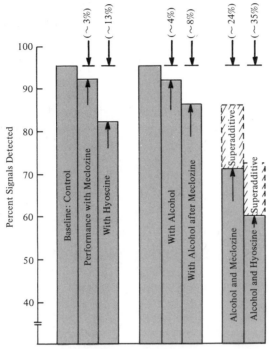

Source: Colquhoun, W. P. Effects of hyoscine and meclozine on vigilance and short-term memory. *British Journal of Industrial Medicine*, 1962, *19*, 287–296.

study. Now, if we assume further that the margin of safety is specific to some behavioral mechanism or to some stage in the processing of information (e.g., short-term memory, stimulus classification, or response selection), then it appears that the stressors with superadditive effects act upon the *same* mechanism or process, while stressors with additive effects act upon *different* mechanisms or processes (that is, each stressor "uses up" a different margin of safety involving a different mechanism). It would also follow that two stressors that individually interfere with performance but in combination produce *less* than the sum of their separate effects are, in some way, compensatory. This suggests that such stressors may act in opposite or antagonistic ways on the same mechanism or process.

Noise and Sleep Loss

With respect to the last point it is again appropriate to ask whether there is any evidence that one stressor may act to cancel or reduce the effects of another. An affirmative answer to this question was provided by Wilkinson (1963) in the study of the effects of sleep deprivation and noise on performance in the serial reaction task. As shown in Figure 14–1, both noise and loss of sleep resulted in increases in errors on the task. However, when the subjects had lost a night's sleep, performance under noise was better than performance in the quiet condition. Thus, the two stressors, noise and loss of sleep, each of which interfered with performance when presented separately, tended to cancel each other when presented together.

Knowledge of Results and Sleep Loss

Another example of the compensatory effects of two stressors presented in combination comes from a second study by Wilkinson (1963). In this study, subjects who had slept and were given knowledge of results (KR) about their performance on the task performed much better than subjects who had slept but were given no KR. Such positive effects of KR are, of course, not surprising. However, when subjects were deprived of a night's sleep before the test, their performance suffered only when no KR was given. In other words, KR compensates for the effects of sleep loss, and this effect is much greater than the positive effect of KR when there has been no loss of sleep.

From these two examples it appears that knowledge of results operates very much as noise does when it is combined with loss of sleep; that is, both factors tend to compensate for the negative effects of sleep loss. Does this mean that KR should be considered as a stressor in the same sense as noise or other environmental conditions? Given our earlier definition of stressors as conditions that "press" the individual to greater effort or a higher level of performance, it may not be unreasonable to consider KR and other incentives or inducements to performance as a class of stressors. In this connection, Poulton (1970) has defined KR as a "mild threat" to the operator, presumably because it increases his awareness of and anxiety about poor performance.

Knowledge of Results and Other Stressors

When KR is combined with noise, the results are not at all what one would predict from the separate effects of the two stressors. By itself, loud noise interferes generally with performance, while KR, almost without exception, enhances performance. Taken together, one might expect that KR would tend to reduce the negative effects of noise, or, vice versa, that noise might reduce the positive effects of KR. However, when Wilkinson (1963) combined these two stressors for subjects working on the serial reaction task, he found that accuracy was poorer under noise with KR than without, whereas in the quiet condition KR markedly reduced the error rate.

A Summary of Combined Effects

While an exhaustive review of the research on stressors would yield additional examples of interaction effects, perhaps enough evidence has been presented to illustrate how complex these interactions are. It appears that there is good evidence that different stressors presented together may act upon the same underlying mechanism, either in the same way, resulting in "superadditive" effects, or in a compensatory manner wherein either (1) two stressors, which by themselves impair performance, cancel each other (e.g., noise and sleep loss) or (2) the negative effect of one stressor is actually reduced when combined with the negative condition of the other (e.g., performance without KR is better in noise than in quiet). The studies combining sleep loss and heat suggest, at least tentatively, additive and independent effects with the two stressors conceivably acting on two different mechanisms or processes.

With the possible exception of the results with heat and sleep loss, none of the evidence reviewed thus far rules out the possibility that all stressor effects can be accounted for in terms of a single underlying mechanism. Thus, it is conceivable, as we have tried to show, that the superadditive effects are not superadditive at all, but additive effects of two stressors acting on the same mechanism. Similarly, when two stressors appear to cancel each other, it could be because they act on one mechanism in opposite ways. Even the interactions of single stressors with time on task, acclimatization to the stress, familarity with the task, the task itself, and the measures of performance could conceivably be accounted for by a single mechanism.

STRESS AND THE CONCEPT OF AROUSAL

In this chapter we have emphasized the importance of relating stressor effects to underlying processes or mechanisms that govern performance or activity in general. In seeking to describe a general mechanism or process to account for the stressor effects, it seems reasonable to assume that all the stresses acting on the operator, from the physical environment, social environment, work, and physical condition as affected by illness, drugs, or loss of sleep, summate in some way to determine a general level of stress. However, as we have seen, the summing of stressors is not a matter of simple addition. Some effects seem to add, but others seem to cancel one another, as with loss of sleep and noise. Furthermore, some stressors appear to have one effect at one level of intensity and a different effect at another level. Thus, for example, a low level of noise may aid performance in a vigilance task. However, when the noise is loud enough or the task itself is sufficiently stimulating, the combination of task and environmental stressors interferes with performance. In the first case, noise seems to provide needed stimulation. In the second, it appears to overstimulate the operator.

The concept of *arousal* has been suggested to account for these stressor effects. Arousal is variously defined by different theorists, but broadly speaking, it refers to the dimension of general alertness, or activation, ranging from sound sleep at one extreme to a state of rage or shock at the other. Arousal has been defined in terms of various physiological measures, such as heart rate, electroencephalogram, galvanic skin response, or other measures of autonomic nervous system activity. Stress is assumed to govern the arousal level of the individual. Furthermore, it is assumed that there is a level, or range, of arousal that is optimal for performing certain activities. Above or below this optimal level, performance suffers because man is "under- or overaroused." This is the notion of the "inverted-U" relation between arousal level and performance. This relationship is illustrated by the curve in Figure 14–4.

If the job has a low rate of input, or the operator has lost a night's sleep, or there is little incentive to produce, the operator's arousal level will be low and his performance will be impaired. If, on the other hand, the task is demanding, the noise level is high, and incentives are strong, he may be too highly aroused to produce well on the same task.

Figure 14–4A also shows how the effects of noise on performance in a vigilance task can be described in terms of arousal. First, it is assumed that the arousal level in quiet ("Q") is not very high, because the low-input vigilance task itself is not very stimulating. The addition of noise ("N") increases the arousal level of the operator, and performance improves. However, if the noise is too loud ("LN"), it increases arousal beyond the optimal level and performance falls off.

FIGURE 14–4
Arousal and Performance

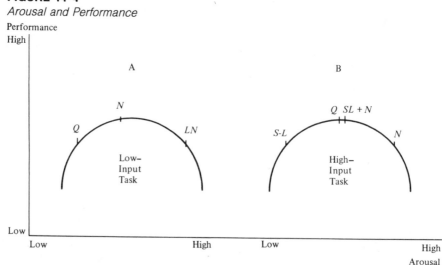

Model of the relation of arousal to performance on a low input task (A) and on a high input task (B). "Q" = quiet, "N" = noise, "LN" = loud noise, "S-L" = sleep loss.

A hypothetical example of a task with a higher input rate (e.g., the choice-reaction task, or a tracking task) is shown in Figure 14–4B. Here, performance in quiet ("Q") is high because the task is sufficiently demanding, or stimulating, to keep the operator aroused. The addition of noise ("N") to this task increases arousal beyond the optimal level, and performance suffers. This example also shows a decrease in performance from sleep loss ("SL"). Notice, however, that while sleep loss and noise are both shown as degrading performance to about the same extent, they are seen to operate in opposite directions on arousal. Loss of sleep reduces the arousal level below the optimal, but noise increases arousal above the optimal level in this example. The effect of combining these two stressors ("SL plus N") is to leave the arousal level somewhere near the optimum for performance. Thus the tendency toward sleep ("underarousal") resulting from sleep loss is counteracted by the noise and, in turn, the tendency toward overarousal by the noise is counteracted by the sleep loss.

A final example of the way in which the "inverted-U" hypothesis may be used to account for stress effects is shown in Figure 14–5.

In this illustration the two factors are noise and knowledge of results (KR). It will be recalled that, while KR nearly always improves performance, the effects of noise are less predictable. They depend, in part, on the task and the intensity of the noise. The example in Figure 14–5 is taken from Wilkinson (1963), who found little effect of noise by itself, but a large positive effect of KR. Noise without KR tended to improve perfor-

FIGURE 14–5
Noise, Knowledge of Results, and
Performance

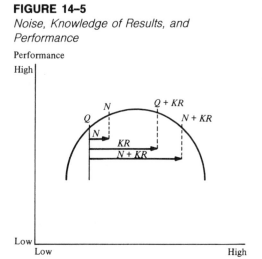

Low performance under quiet (Q) corresponds to low arousal. Noise (N) increases arousal and performance, as does knowledge of results (KR). However, both noise and KR produce overarousal and performance declines.

mance over the quiet condition. However, noise added to KR tended to produce more errors than KR alone. Apparently, noise plus KR resulted in overarousal of the operators, interfering with performance. -

It is tempting to conclude that the concept of arousal provides a complete explanation of the effects of stressors on performance. It is true that many of the complex relationships and interactions seem to be "explained" in a satisfying way when we apply the notion of the inverted-U relationship. In fact, one of the difficulties with the arousal explanation may be that it can too readily "account for" nearly any combination of results! However, Broadbent (1971), for one, has pointed out some evidence from the research on stress that is difficult to handle with the inverted-U curve. We cannot develop Broadbent's arguments here. However, an example of the difficulties he finds is the fact that the effects of noise and sleep loss both show up late in the work session, even though their effects on arousal are presumably in opposite directions. Another difficulty for arousal theory is found in the results on heat. The fact that small and large increases of body temperature have different effects on performance, and these effects appear to be *opposite* for different tasks, is not easily explained in terms of a single mechanism of arousal. In addition, as we have seen, the effects of heat and KR seem to be independent and strictly additive, suggesting that they affect two different mechanisms rather than one. Finally, the very notion of the inverted-U relationship between arousal and performance has been challenged recently by R. Näätänen, a Finnish psychologist. In Part, Näätänen (1973) argues that the decrease in task performance attributed to "overarousal" may reflect instead that the operator is sharing his attention and his responding between the task and the stressor introduced to raise his arousal level. In other words, the stressor is seen as a secondary task, demanding some coping responses by the operator that may compete with task-relevant responses. This is similar to the explanation of noise effects offered by Teichner et al. (1963), presented earlier in this chapter. At any rate, Näätänen argued that one's true performance efficiency at any level of arousal should be assessed in terms of some measure of how well one handles both the task *and* the stressor, not just the task alone.

The arousal concepts that we have just discussed suggest that stress is not a figment of someone's imagination. Extreme intensities of various stimuli may have the effect of pushing the man-machine system past reasonable limits. The arousal model proposes that interactions of various environmental stressors should also be considered, not just the effects of single stressors.

There is one common work condition that is often mentioned by workers in discussions of stress and fatigue: the scheduling of work hours. Most of us feel less than efficient when we are required to put in overtime on an arduous task. A good example of this that might be found in student life is the "all-nighter"—the attempt to read 10 weeks of class assignments in 15 hours. In addition to efficiency losses, we often feel emotionally drained after such an experience. In the next section, we will consider the issue of the work schedule as a potential stressor in the work environment.

THE SCHEDULING OF WORK

Shift Work

In most of our discussion so far, we have assumed that the individuals in question arrive at work at 9:00 A.M. and leave at 4:30 or 5:00 P.M., having enjoyed a leisurely lunch with co-workers. But in many work settings, this is little more than a fantasy. In continuous-process operations, such as the steel industry, it has been common to keep the work activities going around the clock. In part, this is a function of the fact that it would be quite expensive (and in some cases impossible) to restart furnaces each day at 8:00 A.M. Shift work is common in many other settings that require constant monitoring (e.g., police and fire departments). These types of work settings require special systems of manpower allocation. The need has been met by devising various work schedules that allow for the "shifting" of job duties from one group of workers to another group. This type of scheduling has come to be known as "shift work" and seems to be a symptom of industrialized societies. In Europe, "odd" working hours represent about 20% of total working hours; the figure is probably similar in the United States.

Shift work is a complicated concept to deal with, due to the almost infinite number of variations available. For example, consider three shifts: *day* (7:00 A.M. to 3:00 P.M.), *swing or afternoon* (3:00 P.M. to 11:00 P.M.), and *night* (11:00 P.M. to 7:00 A.M.). When you add the variable of *days off*, you might have any one of the following possible shift patterns:

> 5 day-2 off-5 day-2 off
> 2 day-2 swing-2 off-3 night-2 off-2 day
> 6 night-4 off-6 night-4 off
> 5 night-2 off-5 day-2 off-5 swing-2 off

Since there are so many possibilities for scheduling shifts, psychologists have become interested in whether some shift schedules might be more satisfying, healthy, safe, or productive than others. We will review some research that deals with this issue.

The Michigan Study. In spite of the long history of shift work in American industry, there has been little serious consideration of its effects on workers until relatively recently. In 1965 a group of researchers at the University of Michigan (Mott, Mann, McLoughlin, & Warwick) published the results of their investigations of the effect of shift schedules on workers. The investigators gathered information from workers and their wives with respect to the social, psychological, and physiological effects of shift work.

The subjects were blue-collar workers from several continuous-process plants in the eastern United States. Several hundred questionnaires were distributed and interviews conducted with workers and their wives. The response rate was 87%, an extremely high figure, possibly indicating the importance of the topic to shift workers and their families.

In considering the results of this study, remember that they represent the verbal report of the workers rather than "hard" measures of the variables in question; as such, they are open to question. Nevertheless, they are interesting.

Sleep-related problems seemed to be at the heart of shift-work difficulties. Loss of sleep seemed to have negative effects on both physical and social patterns. This suggested that there might be some natural rhythms that are disturbed by unusual shifts. It is generally accepted that human beings are characterized by rhythms of approximately 24 hours in duration (called *circadian* rhythms). The results of the study seemed to point to a mismatch between work requirements and circadian rhythms. Night-shift and rotating-shift workers complained of constant fatigue, poor appetites, constipation, and a variety of other disorders. In addition, these workers reported that they were less interested in the typical social activities that characterized the leisure-time pursuits of their day-shift colleagues.

A more detailed examination of the various shifts showed that steady day shift seemed to have the greatest advantage for the individual worker. Steady afternoon (swing) shift had the greatest negative impact on social patterns both inside and outside the family (the father was often asleep while the children were preparing for school, and by the time the father returned from work, the children were in bed). Steady night-shift work was not as disruptive to social relations as the swing shift, but it did seem to have negative effects on self-reported health. By far the worst schedule seemed to be a weekly rotating shift system in which the worker was on day shift for five days with two days off, followed by the swing shift with 2 days off and then the night shift with two days off. This not only prevented physical adaptation; it also isolated the worker from normal social patterns for two of every three weeks.

The Michigan study was not carefully controlled; in addition, it was not widely representative of either shifts or work settings. Nevertheless, it did point to shift work as a potential stressor in the work environment. In some respects it was a unique stressor, however, since it had rather immediate effects on family and friends. As the Michigan researchers noted, when you ask a worker to adapt to a shift other than a typical day shift, you are asking the worker's family to adapt as well.

The British Steel Corporation Study. From 1970 to 1972, Alexander Wedderburn, a Scottish I/O psychologist, conducted a series of studies of the effect of shift work on British steel workers. The 315 workers came from three different locations and were on one of the following shifts:

1. 6 on, 2 off: A rotating system in which the workers changed shifts about every week.
2. $2 \times 2 \times 3$ rotating: A rapidly rotating shift system in which the individual spent 2 days on one shift (e.g., day), 2 days on another

shift (e.g., swing), and 3 days on the last shift (e.g., night); days off were wedged between various shift changes.

3. 5 × 4 rotating: 5 days on one shift (e.g., day), followed by several days off and 4 days on another shift (e.g., night).

As was the case with the Michigan research, Wedderburn found that sleeping problems and distorted social relations were frequent sources of dissatisfaction for shift workers. In addition, he found that there were definite shift types, i.e., some workers preferred the night shift while others preferred afternoon or day. These preferences were unrelated to age, marital status, number of children in the family, or experience on shift work. Also, he found that 18 percent of the workers said that they liked shift work, while only 8 percent disliked it. When the various types of shift were compared, the 6 on-2 off workers were most negative and the 2 × 2 × 3 workers the most positive.

Workers on various shifts (day, swing, night) were asked to describe the relative advantages and disadvantages of each shift. The day shift was valued for the social flexibility it provided; in contrast, the afternoon shift seemed to restrict social life, yet was thought to be the least tiring of the three shifts and the shift most likely to provide sufficient sleep opportunity. The night shift was described as tiring, socially restrictive, poor for family life, and physiologically disruptive. In spite of these disadvantages, even the night shift was thought to have some things in its favor: it was judged to provide more spare time and provided greater freedom from supervision while at work.

Wedderburn also discussed problems of performance. The issue of safety and performance seems to be critical when considering the night shift. A phenomenon generally known to night-shift workers is the "3:00 A.M. dip." This is a rather substantial drop in vigilance that occurs about 3–4 hours after the beginning of night shift work (at about 3:00 A.M. if the shift begins at 11:00 P.M.). The solution to this problem depends on whether biological rhythms can be changed to meet the required work rhythms. If biological rhythms can change over time (or "phase shift"), then the dip should gradually disappear on its own; in this case, performance of workers just beginning the night shift would be monitored closely until they have adapted to night work (this might take anywhere from several weeks to several months). If, on the other hand, the worker must be rotated around the three shifts, making adaptation more difficult, it might be better to rearrange the starting and stopping times for the night shift so that workers begin their shift immediately after "dip" period (at about 4:00 A.M.). There are also individual differences in the nature of this dip[3]—it does not occur for the same length of time and at the same time of night for all workers. But in spite of the individual-differences component in

---

[3] An excellent review of research in the area of sleep, shift work, and performance can be found in a book entitled *Aspects of Human Efficiency* edited by W. P. Colquhoun (London: English Universities Press, 1972). In addition, the September, 1978 issue of the journal *Ergonomics* gives careful consideration to many of these issues.

this phenomenon, there is sufficient anecdotal evidence to suggest that the dip occurs and that it is potentially dangerous. In a recent article in a Stockholm, Sweden, newspaper, it was reported that 9 out of 10 freight locomotive operators "blacked out" occasionally at night. One engineer described the experience of passing through a railway station and waking up almost 60 miles further down the track!

Additional Research on Shift Work. Agervold (1976) reviewed much of the research that has been done on shift work in Scandinavia. On the basis of this literature review, he voiced strong opposition to night-shift work. He suggested that if night-shift work was absolutely essential, it would be better to use constant assignment to night shift rather than rotating shifts over time. Once again, the question of adaptation arises. While Agervold may be right with respect to work efficiency or satisfaction, if a phase shift actually *does* occur, this must mean that the worker will be out of phase with respect to some other activity—sleeping, playing golf, doing the laundry, talking with the children. The clear lesson to be learned from much of this research is that whenever one departs from a regular 8:30 to 4:30 schedule, some compromises will have to be made. These compromises will define the relative balance of health, family, work, and leisure in the individual worker's life. We need to know much more about the effects of shift work on workers before we can help them make the best available compromise between working and nonworking hours.

Shift work and Absence. If there is such a great interplay between working hours and nonworking activities, one might expect to see symptoms of stress (both social and physical) in absence data. Nicholson, Jackson, and Howes (1978) studied the absence trends of workers on various shifts. The subjects were 250 male maintenance engineers with a steel corporation in the United Kingdom. The workers were assigned to a 6-on-2-off schedule, as described earlier. The investigators were able to examine the independent effects of shift (day, swing, night), time during the six-day cycle (first two, middle two, last two days) and days of the week (Monday, Tuesday, and so on). All three main effects were significant. Weekend absences were higher and Thursdays (payday) lower; absences were higher in the day and lower in the swing shifts; absences were much higher in the last two days of the six-day cycle than in either the first two or middle two days. In addition, there were complicated interactions among these variables. For example, swing-shift workers were much more likely to be absent toward the end of the six-day cycle when the end of the cycle fell on a weekend. Nicholson et al. concluded that rest days seemed to "infect" the workdays closest to them, and further, that certain shifts increased this effect.

It seems clear from the research described that shift work is a very potent variable in the work environment. It affects satisfaction, performance, safety, family life, physical and psychological well-being, and absences. The results to date suggest that shift work should be considered as a potential stressor on the worker. As was the case with temperature and noise, we need to know much more about the mechanisms by which shifts affect behavior. There are some particular pitfalls in doing cross-sectional research in this area. For example, it might be reasonable to assume that night-shift workers represent a "survivor" population—those who are left after those who cannot or will not adapt to the pressures of night work move to other shifts or other companies. Consequently, it is misleading to compare the responses of cross sections of night-shift workers and other shift workers. In addition, there is evidence that suggests that circadian rhythms may be only part of the problem; mealtime changes and changes in drinking habits may account for variations in physical complaints as well, and the general level of noise around the house may account for sleeping problems. In short, the problem is a very complicated one and will require careful study. Currently a great deal of research is being conducted on the topic of sleep, shift work, stress, cycles, and so on (see, for example, Åkerstedt, Pátkai, & Dahlgren, 1977; Pátkai, Åkerstedt, & Pettersson, 1977). We expect rapid advances in the understanding of the relationship between "hostile" working hours and behavior in the next few years.

Alternative Schedules for Day Work

Work scheduling has also received some attention in traditional 8-to-4 jobs. Two different concepts have been introduced. The first is known as *"flexible working hours"* (FWH) and implies variable start and stop times for job duties. Thus, one individual may begin work at 7:00 A.M. and finish at 3:30 P.M., while a second individual may begin at 9:30 A.M. and finish at 6:00 P.M. The second concept is related to the length of the work week. It has various names, but one common label is the "4–10 plan," which stands for four ten-hour work days instead of five eight-hour work days. In both cases, the worker devotes 40 hours to the job, but in the former case, the individual is free from work for three days instead of the typical two-day break. We will consider these two scheduling systems independently.

Flexible Working Hours. The appeal of FWH is that the worker is given a degree of discretion in arranging her work hours. To a certain extent, she can choose when to arrive at work and when to leave. This should enable the worker to arrange work and nonwork schedules more effectively. A typical FWH arrangement would require the workers to be at work from 10:00 A.M. to 2:30 P.M., but they could arrive any time after 7:00 A.M. and could stay at work until as late as 7:00 P.M. The worker would be expected to accumulate 40 hours of work per week or 160 hours per month, allowing for "balancing" of work hours.

There are both advantages and disadvantages to such a system. Clearly, a flexible time system is totally unsuitable for certain types of work. Bus drivers, police officers, nurses, and schoolteachers would all be poor candidates for such a system, at least as far as the clients of their services are concerned. In addition, any work that requires close coordination and cooperative effort on the part of the workers or groups of workers would be ill suited to such an arrangement. Nevertheless, in situations where it is possible to schedule collective and client-centered activities in a specific block of time during the day, FWH is an interesting possibility. At least on the surface, it would seem to have the potential for allowing individuals to eliminate various stresses placed on them by competing schedules (e.g., the coordination of the working schedules of husbands and wives); additionally, it would seem to provide workers with a greater degree of autonomy in their work environment.

Unfortunately, there has been little substantive research on the results of FWH. An exception is a study conducted by Schein, Maurer, and Novak (1977). They examined the effects of FWH on the productivity of various groups of clerical workers in a large financial institution. In this organization, workers were required to work for 7¾ hours every day but could arrive any time between 7:30 A.M. and 10:00 A.M. and were permitted to leave between 3:15 P.M. and 5:45 P.M. The effects of this schedule were examined after four months. The researchers looked at work volume, work quality, time to completion on various tasks, and other aspects. They were able to compare the work of groups on flexible schedules with other groups on fixed schedules. Their conclusions were cautious. They felt that it could be said with some certainty that FWH did not have any *adverse* effects on productivity, but were unwilling to claim that it increased worker performance. Unfortunately, they did not gather measures of satisfaction, felt stress, motivation, and so on, which might allow us to make inferences about any psychological changes that occurred in the workers. In addition, they did not report how many workers actually took advantage of the opportunity for flexible scheduling. It is entirely possible that all workers continued to come in at 9:00 A.M. and leave at 4:45 P.M.!

The Four-Day Work Week. The opportunity to work for four days rather than five provides a unique opportunity to workers. It allows for more uninterrupted blocks of free time, the possibility of second part-time jobs, expanded familial activities, and so on. But it also implies the possibility that fatigue will affect work quality, work quantity, safety, and worker satisfaction. As was the case with FWH, the four-day work week has received considerably more attention in the popular press and in locker rooms than it has in scientific circles. Nevertheless, the few studies that have been done of the effects of the four-day system have been enlightening.

Nord and Costigan (1973) examined the reactions of workers in a pharmaceutical company that had switched to a 4–10 plan. There was a very favorable reaction among the workers: 81 percent favored the four-day week, and this favorable margin remained even one year after the introduction of the plan; but workers reported that they slept less after the change and there were some negative effects on home life (presumably as a result of longer working hours for the four days).

Goodale and Aagaard (1975) found similar mixed results. They examined the reactions of over 400 clerical and supervisory personnel to a four-day work week. In this organization, the extra day off was a rotating day, so that four-day weekends were not uncommon. In spite of the fact that 86% of the workers were satisfied with the four-day schedule, 62% found the new schedule "more tiring"; in addition, many workers reported that work was more difficult toward the end of the day. There was another interesting difference: younger workers were much more positive about the four-day week than older workers. As a result, they concluded that the four-day schedule may be a problem for the older workers. Several investigators have suggested that an individual on the night shift experiences fatigue similar to that of a worker with diminished physical resources. The work of Goodale and Aagaard leads one to a similar conclusion with respect to the four-day work week. It may be important to consider the nature of the work force prior to making a switch.

Ivancevich investigated the effects of the four-day week on worker satisfaction and performance in a manufacturing organization in two different studies (Ivancevich, 1974; Ivancevich & Lyon, 1977). In the first study, 13 months after the introduction of the new system, he found that workers were generally positive toward the four-day week and that some specific measures of productivity showed some improvements. There were no changes in absenteeism rates or in the workers' perceptions of autonomy or self-actualization. In a follow-up study (1977) he again found positive performance effects after 13 months and no effects on absenteeism, satisfaction, autonomy, or self-actualization. In addition, he found that the differences in performance disappeared after 25 months!

In spite of the fact that there is a need for much more research in this area, some things are clear. First, the glowing reports of the effects of the four-day work week in the popular press seem to be exaggerated. Second, the studies of Goodale and Aagaard (1975) and Nord and Costigan (1973) both suggest that workers may express preferences for schedules that have negative effects on their physical and social well-being. Finally, the work described in Chapter 12 on sociotechnical systems suggests that there may be some rather far-reaching and unanticipated effects of changes in work scheduling.

The Interaction of Working Hours and Pay. With the advent of FWH and the four-day work week, an immediate problem arises: How will we define "overtime"? If overtime is defined as "more than eight hours," there are added costs to the four-day work week. If overtime is defined as "time spent after 5:00 P.M. or before 9:00 A.M., regardless of the number of hours worked," then FWH plans are in trouble. These alternative scheduling schemes may finally force us to consider carefully the nature of human effort. Payment should be at least roughly correlated with the amount of effort required to produce a fixed level of performance (at least within job titles). Thus, if a person is working on the ninth hour of a ten-hour shift, it may very well be that he will have to exert extra energy to yield the same level of performance as a person doing the same task in the sixth hour of an eight-hour shift. It may be that payment schemes will have to be carefully matched to the new demands of alternate-working-hour schedules.

Comment. While the data reported are somewhat scarce, we feel that they do support the contention that alternative methods of scheduling working hours may have a significant effect on the worker, the worker's family and the company. Furthermore, it is likely that some of these effects are short-term and others long-term. It seems to us that this is an excellent opportunity for the behavioral scientist to work closely with other scientists in making a genuine contribution to workers as individuals and to society as a whole.

The discussion of the effects of specific stressors (such as noise) and general stressors (such as working hours) requires one to consider the dangers involved in many working environments. The psychologist often considers danger from the opposite point of view: safe behavior. Stressors are often the concern of the industrial engineer, the plant manager, or the governmental inspectors. But safe behavior is under the control of the individual worker. We will now consider this more general issue of safety.

SAFETY IN THE WORKPLACE

If we were to ask you what was the product of a man-machine system, you would probably suggest an auto body, a bolt, or a computer readout. But another product of a man-machine system is an accident. As we indicated in our earlier discussion of system error, error variance depends on the particular combination of both man and machine error. This combination often results in death or permanent disability for the worker. It has been estimated that more than 12,500 workers die and over 2,200,000 million workers are disabled by industrial accidents (Komaki, Barwick, & Scott, 1978). If you assume that this is only a portion of the workers who engaged in unsafe behavior (the others were "lucky" enough to escape injury), you can see the enormity of the problem.

The issue of safety, more than any other area in I/O psychology, points out the diversity of approaches that might be taken to the same problem. The problem would seem to be relatively simple: reduce accidents. The question is, how shall we begin? There have been three common approaches to the problem. The first has been the engineering approach. This approach has assumed that by modifying the nature of the equipment or process that a worker uses, errors (and subsequently accidents) can be reduced. The second has been the personnel-psychology approach. In this approach, the psychologist attempts to identify particular traits, response patterns, or individual characteristics of workers that seem to be correlated with accident frequency. Subsequently, this correlation is used to select workers with lower probabilities of accident occurrence. Alternatively, training programs are developed to modify those traits, response patterns, or individual characteristics that are correlated with accidents. The third approach is of the industrial/social variety. The assumption is made that accidents are basically motivational problems. While workers may *know* what the safe behavior is, there is no motivation for performing an action in a safe manner. Each of these three different approaches has met with some success. We will present examples of the different strategies for reducing accidents.

The Engineering Approach

If you were courageous enough to take a cab ride in a major city, one thing would become immediately apparent to you: cab driving is different from regular driving. It would seem that local laws require cabs to start and stop quickly, to travel *across* rather than *in* lanes of traffic, and to remove passenger seat belts. It is no wonder that most cabs wear battle scars from their encounters with the world at large. One cab company in San Francisco experimented with a technique for reducing collisions in which the rear of a cab was attacked by the front of another car. They reasoned that part of the problem was that unsuspecting motorists did not have sufficient warning to anticipate cab deceleration. With the help of a psychologist (Voevodsky, 1974), the cab company installed yellow deceleration warning lights on the trunks of 343 experimental cabs. These lights began to blink when the cab began to slow down, and the speed of the blinking was proportional to the rate of deceleration: faster blinking implied more rapid deceleration. As a control, 160 cabs were not fitted with deceleration lights.

If you keep in mind that the company was trying to reduce rear-end collisions, one might interpret the cab and cab driver as the machine and the following motorist as the man in this man-machine system. The company was attempting to reduce errors in the system by changing the nature of the machine—by making it more efficient in terms of the information it provided the man (the unsuspecting motorist).

After 10 months, the rear-end collision statistics for the experimental cabs were compared with those for the control cabs. The results were dramatic. In almost every category, the experimental cabs outperformed the control cabs. The number of rear-end collisions, the costs of repairs necessitated by rear-end collisions, and injuries to cab drivers were all reduced by over 60%. The statistics for the control cabs remained unchanged over the 10-month period. The psychologist concluded that the engineering modification had resulted in accident reduction. But even an introductory psychology student can think of an alternative explanation: those cab drivers with deceleration lights on the rear may have *driven more cautiously* than those without the deceleration lights. Thus, accident reduction might have been the result of training or motivation rather than engineering changes. The psychologist was able to rule out this explanation by examining the statistics for the experimental and control cabs with respect to front-end collisions—collisions in which the cab hit another car from the rear. They found no significant differences between control and experimental cabs

"Now you see why I don't let Roger have any power tools."

Reprinted by permission The Wall Street Journal

with respect to front-end collisions, leading one to conclude that cab drivers did not change their behavior, but motorists behind them did. This study is an interesting example of reducing system error (and accidents) through system design.

The Personnel Approach

"Accident proneness" has been a popular concept in safety research. It is seductively simple. The psychological principle is one of selection: identify the characteristics of individuals likely to have accidents and do not hire individuals who are high on those characteristics. An alternative strategy would be to identify those worker characteristics that are most highly correlated with accidents and attempt to change those characteristics in workers. The latter strategy is a training approach based on the measurement of individual differences.

Since the measurement of individual differences is usually accomplished through testing of one form or another, it is not surprising to find that over the past several decades, clues to the mystery of the accident-prone employee have been sought in the full range of test types: personality, attitude and interest, psychomotor, intellectual, and perceptual. Unfortunately, the concept of accident proneness has not received much empirical support. While it is clear that some individuals have more accidents than others, it is difficult to equate the rate of exposure to accidents. Miners have a higher rate of accidents than people in other occupations, but one suspects that miners are no more accident prone as a group. They simply are exposed to potential accident situations at a higher rate than, say, retail clerks. Furthermore, the fact that some people have more accidents than others is to be expected on the basis of chance. For example, if in a given year there are 1,000 workers in a plant and 500 accidents, it is obvious that at least 500 workers will be accident free. Of those who have accidents, the vast majority will have only one; relatively few will have two; even fewer will have three, and so on. The point is that essentially the same distribution would have occurred had we placed the names of the workers in a hat and drawn from the hat 500 times, replacing each name after it was drawn. That is, we could identify as "lucky" workers those whose names were drawn more than once, but actually, the results could be accounted for by chance alone.

In spite of the fact that it is fruitless to search for individuals who can be stamped "AP" for accident prone, there may be some value in seeking attributes of individuals that are predictive of accident behavior in a specific task or occupational setting. This approach has been taken in several studies. In one study (Barrett & Thornton, 1968) it was discovered that measures of basic perceptual skill were predictive of accidents and near accidents with pedestrians in a simulated driving situation. Subjects were given a test that required them to find a hidden figure in a complicated background. Those who were better at finding the hidden figure also had fewer accidents in the driving simulation.

Mihal & Barrett (1976) examined individual differences in selective attention and perceptual/motor reaction time in addition to capacity to find hidden figures. They administered various perceptual and reaction-time tests to drivers for a utility company and then examined the accident rates of those drivers for the five previous years. Selective attention was the capacity of the individual to select information differentially in making a decision; perceptual/motor reaction time was a complex reaction time requiring both perceptual and motor responses rather than the traditional simple motor reaction-time measures. As in the earlier study, individuals who were able to find the hidden figure had fewer accidents; in addition, those who were able to select certain pieces of information differentially rather than try to process all information available had fewer accidents. There has been some recent research showing that 3-D or stereoscopic perceptual tests are also predictive of accident occurrence (Williams, 1977).

This approach is an interesting one and, as can be seen from the studies described above, a potentially fruitful one. An examination of all the literature that has been published on this approach seems to indicate that traditional trait approaches are not as valuable as "work-sample" or simulation approaches. In addition, recent research and theory in cognitive psychology suggests that the way in which people process information may be a critical individual difference that contributes to safe behavior at the workplace.

The Industrial-Social Approach

A distinctly different hypothesis about the causes of safe behavior and accidents is reflected in the industrial-social approach. This approach proposes that the worker must be *motivated* to behave safely; there must be a *reason*. Common sense would suggest that the protection of life and limb would be sufficient reason for workers to behave safely, but this is clearly not the case, since there are an enormous number of accidents occurring every day. The survival motive is probably not as strong as it could be, since workers engage in unsafe behaviors every day but seldom have accidents. In addition, safe behavior often requires a greater expenditure of energy than careless behavior. Finally, in many work settings, it is considered macho to perform work activities in dangerous ways—at the very least, it is un-macho to use safety goggles, ear protectors, special safety equipment, and so on. Thus, the motivational approach to safety tries to change workers' preferences for and satisfactions with safe behavior.

A good example of this approach is a recent study by Komacki, Barwick, and Scott (1978). They instituted a program of goal setting, positive reinforcement, and feedback in an attempt to stimulate safe job performance by employees in a food manufacturing plant. The subjects were workers from two departments in the plant—the production (makeup) and the wrapping departments. There were 38 employees involved in the study. An analysis of the job led the researchers to conclude that the high accident rate in the plant was a result of a combination of the following forces:

1. Safety was ignored in training and educational programs at the plant.
2. Safe behavior took more time than unsafe behavior.
3. Safe behavior was seldom rewarded by management or co-workers.
4. Unsafe behavior seldom caused actual injuries.

As a result of observation and interviews with workers, the research team was able to identify safe and unsafe behaviors in each of the two departments. Some examples of these behaviors are presented in Figure 14–6.

The behaviors described in Figure 14–6 were made into slides depicting the safe and unsafe ways of going about the same activity. The workers were assembled for discussions of these slides. First, they were shown the unsafe version of the activity and asked to describe what was unsafe about it. After discussion, the workers were shown the slide depicting the safe way of carrying out the task, and the general principle for safe behavior in the particular situation was identified. Workers were then shown graphs that described their own proportion of safe and unsafe behaviors; this was done in confidentiality so that none of the workers was aware of the data for any other worker. The workers were then asked to set a department goal for percentage of safe behaviors. This goal was placed on a conspicuous graph, which was prominently displayed at the work site. The research team continuously observed work behavior and provided frequent feedback

FIGURE 14–6

Sample Items on Observational Codes

Makeup Department

When picking up pans from the conveyor belt, no more than two pans are picked up prior to placing the pans on the pan rack.

Roll pans are stacked no higher than the rear rail of the pan rack.

When lifting or lowering dough trough, hand holds and at no time loses contact with dump chain.

When pulling dough trough away from dough mixer, hands are placed on the front rail of the dough trough and not on the side rails.

Wrapping Department

There are no cardboard spacers (defined as cardboard 30 mm square or larger) on the floor.

When cutting wire bands from stacks of boxes or spacers, employee cuts with one hand and holds the metal strap above the cut with the other hand.

When moving conveyor, at least one person is on each end.

When handling a skid, employee attempts to break its fall in some manner, for example, sliding it off rather than letting it fall flat on the floor.

Both Departments

When mechanical problems arise (e.g., pans jam on conveyor belt, belt breaks), the machine is turned off (the machine is off when the on-off switch is in the off position and machine moving parts have stopped) or maintenance is notified.

Source: Komaki, J., Barwick, K. D., & Scott, L. R. A behavioral approach to occupational safety. *Journal of Applied Psychology*, 1978, *63*, p. 438.

and encouragement with respect to safe behavior. In addition, levels of safe behavior were recorded on the public graph.

The results of the safety program are shown in Figure 14–7. As you can see the results were both immediate and impressive. Shortly after the program was begun the percentage of safe behaviors in the wrapping department increased from 70 percent to 95 percent; in the makeup department, the percentage of safe behaviors increased from 77 percent to 99 percent! After the safe behavior had been clearly established and maintained, the feedback and reinforcement were terminated. As you can see from the figure, safe behavior diminished to levels similar to the preintervention period.

During the course of the experiment, workers became very involved in the safety program. They were aware of increases and decreases in safety percentage and occasionally cheered when the graph showed an increase in safe behavior. In addition, they often put pressure on fellow workers to eliminate unsafe behaviors that were "ruining the graph." In short, the workers reacted favorably to the program. One might conclude that their motivation to behave safely had been increased through the experimen-

FIGURE 14-7

Percentage of Items Performed Safely by Employees in Two Departments of a Food Manu-facturing Plant during a 25-Week Period of Time

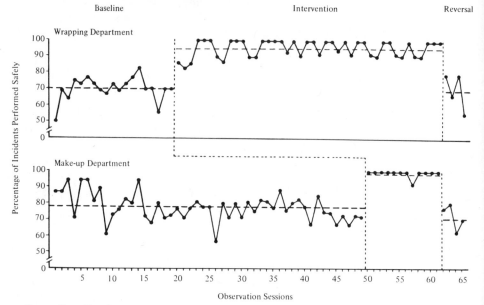

Source: From Komaki, J., Barwick, K. D., & Scott, L. R. A behavioral approach to occupational safety. *Journal of Applied Psychology*, 1978, *63*, p. 439.

tal intervention. While the results are positive and make the point that we originally intended—that accidents may be reduced by addressing motivational issues—there is some disconcerting information in Figure 14–7 as well. The fact that the workers reverted to earlier levels of unsafe behavior *as soon as the motivational program was suspended* (the section labeled "Reversal" in the figure) is a little scary. It implies that safe behavior is very fragile and requires almost constant attention from supervisors.

This last approach was represented by only one of the motivational strategies that might have been used: the reinforcement strategy. It might be possible to adapt other motivational approaches such as the need, the social comparison, or the cognitive approach to motivating safe behavior. Nevertheless, the approach described above is distinctly different from either the engineering or the personnel approach described earlier. Furthermore, it shows a good deal of promise.

Safety Legislation

The federal government has formed an agency to deal with the issue of industrial safety. This agency is called the Occupational Safety and Health Administration (OSHA), and its mission is administering and enforcing the Occupational Safety and Health Act of 1970 (Public Law 91–

596, Dec. 29, 1970). This act has as its stated purpose "to insure so far as possible every working man and woman in the nation safe and healthful working conditions and to preserve our human resources." Everyone agrees with the goals of OSHA, at least in principle. In practice, however, such goals run into economic realities and the conflicting interests of special-interest groups. In addition, the goals often conflict with behavioral patterns of workers. It is common to see workers totally disregarding safeguards placed in their environment to protect their health. Asbestos workers often refuse to wear masks; farm workers often refuse to install roll bars on tractors; riveters often refuse to wear ear protectors. This suggests that while environmental legislation may be the precondition for worker safety, it is a far cry from a guarantee of an accident-free workplace. Safe behavior, like many other behaviors examined by the psychologist, is best considered in a systems context. In that respect, the industrial psychologist would be well advised to consider all three approaches—engineering, personnel, and motivational—when dealing with accident reduction.

Biorhythms and Safety

In our discussion of safety in the workplace, we would be remiss if we did not treat the topic of biorhythm. In the past decade, there has been a growing tendency to blame accidents on the parents of the accident victim for having poorly planned the instant of conception of the person in question. Biorhythm advocates suggest that there are three major cycles that might be used to characterize the human being. These cycles are begun at the moment of birth (although to be exact, they surely must begin at some earlier point—possibly some point between conception and birth) and have different temporal lengths. The *physical* cycle has 23 days, the *emotional* cycle has 28 days, and the *intellectual* cycle has 33 days (except for individuals born in remote sections of northwestern Ohio). Each of these cycles has a high and a low phase. The theory suggests that individuals are particularly susceptible to accidents on days corresponding to the low phases of their cycles. Presumably, the very worst days for accident probability are those days in which all three cycles are at their lowest points.

There have been many accounts in newspapers and magazines about companies that have adopted the strategy of helping employees keep track of their biorhythms in the hope of reducing accidents. If an employee is entering a low phase of one or more cycles, he may be assigned to a relatively harmless operation until the low phase is passed; alternatively, he may be warned to be particularly careful on certain days. Many organizations have claimed that accidents were reduced by the use of the biorhythm system. Unfortunately, there have been few controlled studies of the value of this approach.

From the psychological point of view, the "theory" borders on the ridiculous. Nevertheless, even industrial psychologists are not above the ridiculous if accidents can be reduced. Recently a group of researchers (Wolcott,

McKeeken, Burgin, & Yanowitch, 1977) examined the biorhythms of pilots involved in general aviation accidents to see if the accidents might have been predicted on the basis of low phases in one or more of the pilots' cycles. Biorhythms were calculated for over 4,000 pilots involved in accidents in 1972. Exact dates and times of the accidents were recorded, and they were separated into two groups: those in which the pilot was considered to be at fault and those in which the pilot had no responsibility for the accident.

The results of the analysis clearly showed that there was no relationship between the biorhythm of pilots and aviation accidents. As a matter of fact, if there was any trend in the data, it was that accidents were slightly more probable on "good" days. The lack of a relationship between biorhythms and accidents for pilots is comforting for those of us who worry about the well-being of those who fly the planes we ride in; when a commercial airline pilot has an accident, others often share that accident. The results are also reassuring for scientists who are generally annoyed with mystical techniques. But if we accept the reports of positive results at face value, how can we explain them? Wolcott et al suggest a plausible explanation. If all three cycles are considered independently, critical periods in one or more of those cycles occur approximately six times per month. If the employee is cautioned to be careful for one day before and one day after the critical day (as well as the day itself), the employee is being sensitized to safety for more than 50% of the month! In addition, the introduction of biorhythm systems is like the introduction of many other employee-relations programs—it implies a concern on the part of management for the worker and may have a positive value similar to that of the "Hawthorne effect" described in Chapter 10. The fact that biorhythm can be shown to have effects on accidents only after workers have been made aware of the theory and their own cycles says something about the nature of the approach. A verification of the theory would require that it be able to predict accidents even when the victims were ignorant of the theory and their cycles. In spite of the fact that the theory has no scientific credibility, we have no argument with attempts to increase safety consciousness, no matter how silly they may be. On the other hand, if organizations are going to great lengths to introduce biorhythm principles into work scheduling, with an accompanying increase in overhead and direct production costs, they might be better off spending their money on designing safer machines or procedures. In summary, we find nothing to suggest that biorhythm is anything other than an amusing gimmick. If an organization is truly interested in reducing accidents, we would suggest one or more of the strategies described in the earlier sections.

A CONCLUDING COMMENT

After examining the information we have presented on the effect of environmental variables on worker behavior, you might be tempted to conclude that the field is in a state of chaos. We might be tempted to agree with you. We are a long way from having a comprehensive model or theory of stressors and their effects on behavior. But we are very sure that stressors exist and can be shown to influence work. We are not very sure why. It is our belief that the answer to the puzzle may lie in studying the way in which individuals process information in unusual environmental conditions. At the very least, we need to know which of the components in the processing model described in Chapter 13 are affected by stress. Is the problem one of stimulus identification or response selection? Response selection or response execution?

We will need to know a lot more about which variables in the environment are potential stressors before we can hope to understand their effects. The model of multiple stressors that we presented suggests that unless we are aware of all stressors operating at any moment, we cannot hope to document the effect of any one of them.

Finally, we know less about accidents (or safety) than about any other behavior in the work environment. Nevertheless, it might be a mistake to assume that accidents are primarily responses to stress. Several of the studies that we described dealt with rather normal conditions, not particularly extreme ones. But we can safely conclude that the social, psychological, and physical conditions of work may have an impact on safe behavior.

SUMMARY

It is time to summarize some of the more general and practical results of the research on stressor effects. First, it may be concluded that the more important effects of stressors show up only after considerable time on the job. That is, the effects of stressors seem to accumulate over time and often do not show up until after an hour or so of work. In fact, it appears that some stressor effects do not occur until after the work session and the exposure to stress are over. These aftereffects may not seem so "practical," since they do not affect job performance, yet they should not be ignored, since they may have important consequences for the worker's total well-being. In a sense, these aftereffects may be a sort of barometer of the costs of exposure to the stressor, or the costs of maintaining performance in the presence of it. There are, in addition, some rather immediate effects of *change* in the level of a stressor, as with the onset or offset of noise, or first exposure to a hot room, but these are relatively short-lived. They serve to remind us, however, that people are adaptive, but that adaptation is difficult with changing or intermittent conditions.

Long-range adjustment or acclimatization to environmental conditions reduces their effects on performance, but in some cases the cost may indeed be high. Thus, for example, data on hearing losses indicate that one form of "adjustment" to a noisy work environment may be selective hearing loss. It is not surprising that noise will not affect a deaf worker's performance, but deafness seems a rather high price to pay for adjustment. Adjustment to or familiarity with the job is also associated with reduced stressor effects; quite possibly the task-induced stress is less when the task is more familiar, leaving more tolerance for environmental stressors.

The interactions of environmental stressors and work incentives should be of considerable interest to industrial psychologists. They suggest, for example, that the effectiveness of a work incentive program may well depend on the prevailing level of stress. If this is already too high, for whatever reasons, the addition of an incentive system may "backfire," resulting in a decrease rather than an increase in productive efficiency.

The amount and even the direction of stressor effects often depend on the type of task to be performed. We have suggested that with low-input tasks, arousal tends to be low because there is little task-induced stress. Stimulation from environmental stressors may help to keep arousal from falling too low. When the task is challenging in itself, or because incentives make it so, the added stressor may result in overarousal. There is little evidence that stressors benefit performance on relatively complex tasks. However, just as it is important to know the kind of task, so it is important to know the kind of stressor. The effects of low noise are quite different from the effects of a small change in body temperature, for example.

Little is known about whether qualitative differences in a particular type of stressor are important. We do know that intermittent and high-frequency noise is more apt to interfere with performance than continuous or low-frequency noise, and there is some evidence that music may benefit performance in a vigilance task more than simple noise (Lucaccini, 1969). Incidentally, industrial music has frequently been found to benefit performance on "simple and routine" types of tasks, but there is scant evidence that it has any positive effect on more complex tasks (Fox, 1971). Fox and Embrey (1972) suggest that music is most effective in maintaining performance on routine tasks when it is scheduled for brief periods corresponding to those points when performance normally begins to fall off.

The practical significance of stressor effects also depends on the relative importance of quantity and quality of production. Noise, for example, seldom appears to affect output rate, but may increase errors and the number of very slow reactions. In a job where errors are considered unimportant relative to the number of units produced, noise effects may not be very important. Other stressors, such as sleep loss or perhaps excessive heat, may be much more important for such tasks.

Finally, as we have seen, the effects we can expect from an environmental stress depend on the presence and the nature of other stresses in the worker's physical and psychological environment. Stressor effects may be superadditive, and the effect of a noise-reduction program may be much greater than expected if the effects of noise have been added to the effects of heat or of an incentive system; or they may be counteractive, as with noise and loss of sleep, in which case the results of a noise-reduction program might be surprising—even embarrassing—to its initiators.

It is reasonable to think of certain types of shift work as stressors. Shift work imposes physical, social, and psychological burdens on both the worker and the worker's family. There are certain ways of arranging shifts and shift changes that may minimize these effects. Other variations in work scheduling need considerable study; this would include FWH and the four-day work week.

Accidents and safe behavior are not well understood. There are at least three distinct approaches that might be taken in the reduction of accidents: the engineering approach, the personnel approach, and the social approach. In all likelihood, the best approach would be a combination of the three.

In conclusion, this review of some of the ways human performance is affected by the physical environment should make us even more aware that all the elements in the man-machine-organization-environment system interact. By considering physical factors as stressors, we have placed them in the same general category as task-induced stress, stress arising from job insecurity, interpersonal conflict, and other factors in the mechanical-social environment of the worker. The interaction of these subsystems was hinted at in the beginning of this chapter when the Hawthorne effect was reviewed and again became apparent in the relations of physical factors to work incentives. Further understanding of this complex system may well come from systematic study of the interrelations among variables from all aspects of the system.

REFERENCES

Agervold, M. Shiftwork: A critical review. *Scandinavian Journal of Psychology*, 1976, *17*, 181–188.

Åkerstedt, T., Pátkai, P., & Dahlgren, K. Field Studies of shiftwork: II. Temporal patterns in psychophysiological activation in workers alternating between night and day work. *Ergonomics*, 1977, *20*, 621–631.

Barrett, G. V., & Thornton, C. L. The relationship between perceptual style and driver reaction to an emergency situation. *Journal of Applied Psychology*, 1968, *52*, 169–176.

Broadbent, D. E. Some effects of noise on visual performance. *Quarterly Journal of Experimental Psychology*, 1954, *6*, 1–5.

Broadbent, D. E. Effects of noise on behaviour. In Harris, C. M. (Ed.). *Handbook of noise control*. New York: McGraw-Hill, 1957.

Broadbent, D. E. *Decision and stress*. New York: Academic Press, 1971.

Bursill, A. E. The restriction of peripheral vision during exposure to hot and humid conditions. *Quarterly Journal of Experimental Psychology*, 1958, *10*, 113–129.

Colquhoun, W. P. Effects of hyoscine and meclozine on vigilance and short-term memory. *British Journal of Industrial Medicine*, 1962, *19*, 287–296.

Colquhoun, W. P. (Ed.) *Aspects of human efficiency*. London: English Universities Press, 1972.

Fiedler, F. E., & Fiedler, J. Port noise complaints: Verbal and behavioral reactions to airport-related noise. *Journal of Applied Psychology*, 1975, *60*, 498–506.

Finkelman, J. M., Zeitlin, L. R., Filippi, J. A., & Friend, M. A. Noise and driver performance. *Journal of Applied Psychology*, 1977, *62*, 713–718.

Fox, J. G. Background music and industrial efficiency: A review. *Applied Ergonomics*, 1971, *2.2*, 70–73.

Fox, J. G., & Embrey, E. D. Music—An aid to productivity. *Applied Ergonomics*, 1972, *3.4*, 202–205.

Glass, C. G., & Singer, J. E. Behavioral aftereffects of unpredictable and uncontrollable aversive events. *American Scientist*, 1972, *60*, 457–465.

Goodale, J. G., & Aagaard, A. K. Factors relating to varying reactions to 4-day workweeks. *Journal of Applied Psychology*, 1975, *60*, 33–38.

Hockey, G. R. J. Signal probability and spatial locations as possible bases for increased selectivity in noise. *Quarterly Journal of Experimental Psychology*, 1970b, *22*, 37–42.

Ivancevich, J. M. Effects of the shorter workweek on selected satisfaction and performance measures. *Journal of Applied Psychology*, 1974, *59*, 717–721.

Ivancevich, J. M., & Lyon, H. L. The shortened workweek: A field experiment. *Journal of Applied Psychology*, 1977, *62*, 34–37.

Jerison, H. J. Performance on a simple vigilance task in noise and quiet. *Journal of the Acoustical Society of America*, 1957, *29*, 1163–1165.

Komaki, J., Barwick, K. D., & Scott, L. R. A behavioral approach to occupational safety: Pinpointing and reinforcing safe performance in a food manufacturing plant. *Journal of Applied Psychology*, 1978, *63*, 434–445.

Lockhart, J. M. Effects of body and hand cooling on complex manual performance. *Journal of Applied Psychology*, 1966, *50*, 57–59.

Lucaccini, L. E. Vigilance and irrelevant stimulation: A test of the arousal hypothesis. *Dissertation Abstracts*, 1969, *29* (9-B), 3523–3524.

McCormick, E. J. *Human engineering.* New York: McGraw-Hill, 1957.

Mihal, W. L., & Barrett, G. Individual differences in perceptual information processing and their relation to automobile accident involvement. *Journal of Applied Psychology*, 1976, *61*, 229–233.

Mott, P. E., Mann, F. C., McLoughlin, Q., & Warwick, D. P. *Shift work.* Ann Arbor: University of Michigan Press, 1965.

Näätänen, R. The inverted-U relationship between activation and performance: A critical review. In Kornblum, S. (Ed.) *Attention and performance IV.* New York: Academic Press, 1973.

Nicholson, N., Jackson, P., & Howes, G. Shiftwork and absence: A study of temporal trends. *Journal of Occupational Psychology*, 1978, *51*, 127–137.

Nord, W. R., & Costigan, R. Worker adjustment to the 4-day week: A longitudinal study. *Journal of Applied Psychology*, 1973, *58*, 60–66.

Pátkai, P., Åkerstedt, T., & Pettersson, K. Field studies of shiftwork I: Temporal patterns in physiological activation in permanent night workers. *Ergonomics*, 1977, *20*, 611–619.

Pepler, R. D. Warmth and performance: An investigation in the tropics. *Ergonomics*, 1958, *2*, 63–88.

Poulton, E. C. *Environment and human efficiency.* Springfield, Ill.: Charles C Thomas, Publisher, 1970.

Poulton, E. C., Hitchings, N. B., & Brooke, R. B. Effect of cold and rain upon the vigilance of lookouts. *Ergonomics,* 1965, *8,* 163–168.

Poulton, E. C., & Kerslake, D. McK. Initial stimulating effect of warmth upon perceptual efficiency. *Aerospace Medicine,* 1965, *36,* 29–32.

Schein, V. E., Maurer, E. H., & Novak, J. F. Impact of flexible working hours on productivity. *Journal of Applied Psychology,* 1977, *62,* 463–465.

Teichner, W. H., Arees, E., & Reilly, R. Noise and human performance: A psychophysiological approach. *Ergonomics,* 1963, *6,* 83–97.

Teichner, W. H., & Kobrick, J. L. Effects of prolonged exposure to low temperature on visual-motor performance. *Journal of Experimental Psychology,* 1955, *49,* 122–126.

Voevodsky, J. Evaluation of a deceleration warning light for reducing rear end automobile collisions. *Journal of Applied Psychology,* 1974, *59,* 270–273.

Wedderburn, A. A. I. *Studies of shiftwork in the steel industry.* Edinburgh: Heriot-Watt University, 1975.

Weinstein, N. D. Individual differences in reactions to noise: A longitudinal study in a college dormitory. *Journal of Applied Psychology,* 1978, *63,* 458–466.

Wilkinson, R. T. Interaction of noise with knowledge of results and sleep deprivation. *Journal of Experimental Psychology,* 1963, *66,* 332–337.

Wilkinson, R. T. Some factors influencing the effect of environmental stressors upon performance. *Psychological Bulletin,* 1969, *72,* 260–272.

Wilkinson, R. T., Fox, R. H., Goldsmith, R., Hampton, I. F. G., & Lewis, H. E. Psychological and physiological responses to raised body temperature. *Journal of Applied Physiology,* 1964, *19,* 287–291.

Williams, J. R. Follow-up study of relationships between perceptual style measures and telephone company vehicle accidents. *Journal of Applied Psychology,* 1977, *62,* 751–754.

Wolcott, J., McKeeken, R., Burgin, R., & Yanowitch, R. Correlation of general aviation accidents with biorhythm theory. *Human Factors,* 1977, *19,* 283–294.

Author Index

Subject Index

*This book has been set Videocomp in 10 and 9 point
Avanta, leaded 2 points. Section and chapter numbers
are 14 point Spectra bold with 32 point Spectra bold
numerals; section and chapter titles are 24 point Spectra bold. The size of the type page is 28 x 48 picas.*